SHAKESPEARE SURVEY

74

Shakespeare and Education

SHAKESPEARE SURVEY
ADVISORY BOARD

(1) *Shakespeare and his Stage*
(2) *Shakespearian Production*
(3) *The Man and the Writer*
(4) *Interpretation*
(5) *Textual Criticism*
(6) *The Histories*
(7) *Style and Language*
(8) *The Comedies*
(9) *Hamlet*
(10) *The Roman Plays*
(11) *The Last Plays (with an index to Surveys 1–10)*
(12) *The Elizabethan Theatre*
(13) *King Lear*
(14) *Shakespeare and his Contemporaries*
(15) *The Poems and Music*
(16) *Shakespeare in the Modern World*
(17) *Shakespeare in his Own Age*
(18) *Shakespeare Then Till Now*
(19) *Macbeth*
(20) *Shakespearian and Other Tragedy*
(21) *Othello (with an index to Surveys 11–20)*
(22) *Aspects of Shakespearian Comedy*
(23) *Shakespeare's Language*
(24) *Shakespeare: Theatre Poet*
(25) *Shakespeare's Problem Plays*
(26) *Shakespeare's Jacobean Tragedies*
(27) *Shakespeare's Early Tragedies*
(28) *Shakespeare and the Ideas of his Time*
(29) *Shakespeare's Last Plays*
(30) *Henry IV to Hamlet*
(31) *Shakespeare and the Classical World (with an index to Surveys 21–30)*
(32) *The Middle Comedies*
(33) *King Lear*
(34) *Characterization in Shakespeare*
(35) *Shakespeare in the Nineteenth Century*
(36) *Shakespeare in the Twentieth Century*
(37) *Shakespeare's Earlier Comedies*
(38) *Shakespeare and History*

(39) *Shakespeare on Film and Television*
(40) *Current Approaches to Shakespeare through Language, Text and Theatre*
(41) *Shakespearian Stages and Staging (with an index to Surveys 31–40)*
(42) *Shakespeare and the Elizabethans*
(43) *The Tempest and After*
(44) *Shakespeare and Politics*
(45) *Hamlet and its Afterlife*
(46) *Shakespeare and Sexuality*
(47) *Playing Places for Shakespeare*
(48) *Shakespeare and Cultural Exchange*
(49) *Romeo and Juliet and its Afterlife*
(50) *Shakespeare and Language*
(51) *Shakespeare in the Eighteenth Century (with an index to Surveys 41–50)*
(52) *Shakespeare and the Globe*
(53) *Shakespeare and Narrative*
(54) *Shakespeare and Religions*
(55) *King Lear and its Afterlife*
(56) *Shakespeare and Comedy*
(57) *Macbeth and its Afterlife*
(58) *Writing About Shakespeare*
(59) *Editing Shakespeare*
(60) *Theatres for Shakespeare*
(61) *Shakespeare, Sound and Screen*
(62) *Close Encounters with Shakespeare's Text*
(63) *Shakespeare's English Histories and their Afterlives*
(64) *Shakespeare as Cultural Catalyst*
(65) *A Midsummer Night's Dream*
(66) *Working with Shakespeare*
(67) *Shakespeare's Collaborative Work*
(68) *Shakespeare, Origins and Originality*
(69) *Shakespeare and Rome*
(70) *Creating Shakespeare*
(71) *Re-Creating Shakespeare*
(72) *Shakespeare and War*
(73) *Shakespeare and the City*
(74) *Shakespeare and Education*

Shakespeare Survey: A Sixty-Year Cumulative Index
Aspects of Macbeth
Aspects of Othello
Aspects of Hamlet
Aspects of King Lear
Aspects of Shakespeare's 'Problem Plays'

SHAKESPEARE SURVEY

74

Shakespeare and Education

EDITED BY

EMMA SMITH

CAMBRIDGE
UNIVERSITY PRESS

CAMBRIDGE
UNIVERSITY PRESS

University Printing House, Cambridge CB2 8BS, United Kingdom

One Liberty Plaza, 20th Floor, New York, NY 10006, USA

477 Williamstown Road, Port Melbourne, VIC 3207, Australia

314–321, 3rd Floor, Plot 3, Splendor Forum, Jasola District Centre,
New Delhi – 110025, India

103 Penang Road, #05–06/07, Visioncrest Commercial, Singapore 238467

Cambridge University Press is part of the University of Cambridge.

It furthers the University's mission by disseminating knowledge in the pursuit of
education, learning and research at the highest international levels of excellence.

www.cambridge.org
Information on this title: www.cambridge.org/9781316517123
DOI: 10.1017/9781009036795

First published 2021

Printed in the United Kingdom by TJ Books Limited, Padstow Cornwall

A catalogue record for this publication is available from the British Library.

ISBN 978-1-316-51712-3 Hardback

EDITOR'S NOTE

Shakespeare Survey 74 has as its theme 'Shakespeare and Education'. It was due to have published papers from the International Shakespeare Conference in Stratford-upon-Avon in the summer of 2020. The conference did not, of course, take place, although many of the speakers have submitted their papers to *Survey*. Much of the material published in this volume draws on the extraordinary circumstances of 2020, from challenges to traditional pedagogy in the online environment, to a gap where reviews of an extensive spring and summer performance season ought to be.

Our next volume, 75, is on *Othello* (submissions by 1 September 2021). Volume 76 will take up the theme of the next ISC, 'Shakespeare, the Virtual and the Digital': submissions on this topic are warmly encouraged and should be sent as email attachments to the editor at emma.smith@hertford.ox.ac.uk. The deadline is 1 September 2022. There is also limited space for articles not on the theme, and the Advisory Board is particularly keen to see proposals for small clusters of 3–5 articles on a Shakespearian theme, topic or approach. These can be submitted to the editor at any time in the year. All submissions are read by me and by at least one member of the Advisory Board. We warmly welcome both early-career and more established scholars to consider *Survey* as a venue for their work.

Part of *Survey*'s distinctiveness is its reviews. Review copies, including article offprints, should be addressed to the Editor at Hertford College, Oxford OX1 3BW: our reviewers inevitably have to exercise some selection about what they cover.

EMMA SMITH

CONTRIBUTORS

GINA BLOOM, *University of California–Davis*
EVAN BUSWELL, *Independent scholar*
CHRISTIE CARSON, *Independent scholar*
RUI CARVALHO HOMEM, *Universidade do Porto*
SHEILA T. CAVANAGH, *Emory University*
EMMA DEPLEDGE, *Université de Neuchâtel*
TIMOTHY FRANCISCO, *Youngstown State University*
ALEXA ALICE JOUBIN, *George Washington University*
JANE KINGSLEY SMITH, *University of Roehampton*
GENEVIEVE KIRK, *University of Victoria*
PETER KIRWAN, *University of Nottingham*
PAMELA ROYSTON MACFIE, *The University of the South*
HARRY R. McCARTHY, *Jesus College, Cambridge*
PERRY MILLS, *King Edward VI School, Stratford-upon-Avon*
LUISA MOORE, *Australia National University*
SHARON O'DAIR, *University of Alabama*
SARAH OLIVE, *University of York*
MADDALENA PENNACCHIA, *Roma Tre University*
LOIS POTTER, *University of Delaware*
KEVIN A. QUARMBY, *The College of St Scholastica*
MADHUMITA SAHA, *JD Birla Institute, Kolkata*
ELIZABETH SANDIS, *Institute of English Studies, University of London*
ESTHER B. SCHUPAK, *Bar-Ilan University*
JAMES SHAW, *Bodleian Library Oxford*
JILLIAN SNYDER, *Valparaiso University*
EMILY SOON, *Singapore Management University*
RICHARD STACEY, *University of Glasgow*
LISA S. STARKS, *University of South Florida*
CERI SULLIVAN, *Cardiff University*
NICHOLAS TOOTHMAN, *California State University–Bakersfield*
JEFFREY R. WILSON, *Harvard University*
NIGEL WOOD, *Loughborough University*
LAURA JAYNE WRIGHT, *University College Oxford*
JENNIFER YOUNG, *University of Greenwich*

CONTENTS

vii

CONTENTS

ILLUSTRATIONS

LIST OF ILLUSTRATIONS

WHITHER GOEST THOU, PUBLIC SHAKESPEARIAN?

SHARON O'DAIR AND TIMOTHY FRANCISCO[1]

'You never want a serious crisis to go to waste.' So said Rahm Emanuel, the Chief of Staff for President-elect Obama, in November 2008. But, he continued, 'what I mean ... is that it's an opportunity to do things that you think you could not do before'. Emanuel was hoping to persuade his listeners at the *Wall Street Journal*'s CEO Council that the financial crisis in 2008 presented the country with opportunities to address its serious problems – problems ignored for too long, problems so large solutions might come from either party. That, he said, is 'the silver lining'.[2] Twelve years later, in 2020, the country – and the world, too, as was also true in 2008 – faces another economic crisis, this time instigated by a novel coronavirus, itself a crisis, a pandemic with, as of this writing, no endgame. The long-term problems Emanuel spoke of were not addressed in the wake of the 2008 crisis, which presents us now with greater challenges but perhaps greater political will to address systemic problems – to do ... *something*. Emanuel's words hint at the difficulty, however. If solutions might come from either the Left or the Right, then each knows that you never want a serious crisis to go to waste. Both the Left and the Right can, shall we say, weaponize a serious crisis for their own interests.[3]

Long-term problems have plagued academia, too, including deteriorating economic conditions, the brutal job market for Ph.D.s, deep inequities among the professoriate, and widespread awareness that higher education no longer drives social mobility but, instead, cements social class hierarchies. One response by academia to these material and social problems is the promotion of community engagement, public engagement and renewed attention to pedagogy.[4] In our field, this volume of *Shakespeare Survey* is an important example, as is the prominence recently given to teaching, pedagogy and public engagement by the Shakespeare Association of America, which this year established a Shakespeare Publics Award to be given annually. Such work, in all

[1] The authors thank Jeffrey R. Wilson, who interviewed us for an oral history of Public Shakespeare. Without his interest, we would not have been able to write this article. 'Whither goest thou?' is from 2.4.16 of *The Merchant of Venice*.
[2] Transcription by the authors. See www.youtube.com/watch?v=_mzcbXi1Tkk.
[3] Emanuel reprised the phrase in March of 2020. In an interview on ABC's *This Week*, he said, 'Never allow a crisis to go to waste. Start planning for the future ... We're going to have more pandemics, but this has to be the last economic depression.' The quote was quickly seized by Republicans, who lambasted Emanuel as well as Democrats' attempts to include worker and environmental protections in the stimulus package designed to offset economic losses during the pandemic. Mark Lotter, Director of Strategic Communications for President Trump's re-election campaign, tweeted, 'Democrats are using Rahm Emanuel's playbook of never letting a crisis go to waste. Their demands have NOTHING TO DO with helping the American people combat the China virus.' See Andrew O'Reilly, 'Rahm Emanuel on coronavirus response: "Never allow a crisis to go to waste"', *Fox News*, 23 March 2020: www.foxnews.com/politics/rahm-emanuel-on-coronavirus-response-never-allow-a-crisis-to-go-to-waste.
[4] As will become clear in the course of this article, institutions, organizations and faculty may hold different motivations in promoting such work.

its variety, has coalesced of late as Public Shakespeare, but that coalescence remains undefined, subject to debate. Provisionally, and for our purposes in this article, we define Public Shakespeare as non-peer-reviewed writing on multiple platforms; as pedagogies of social justice; or as local, community work legitimated, inspired or enabled by one's place in the academy. That is, Public Shakespeare consists of expanding audiences for and opportunities to engage in theatrical performance; expanding audiences for our criticism by writing outside scholarly norms; assisting colleagues in the classroom via peer- or non-peer-reviewed work; or promoting and engaging in activism outside the institution. We think all of this work, however, is a form of pedagogy, of teaching, rather than research.

And yet Public Shakespeare is not popular culture; its practitioners hold some form of professional expertise, rooted in the academy. As such, Public Shakespeare offers potential to rethink the prestige economy of Shakespeare studies, in which status and remuneration, at least in the US, are based upon one's distance from the labour of teaching. For, indeed, the relative merits of teaching and research have not always been as they are today: the research culture in literary and cultural study emerged slowly and, shall we say, organically, as John Guillory implies, noting that, in the US, a 'negotiation about what constitutes knowledge in the humanities ... never took place'. Such a negotiation 'of the nature of research, and of the system of rewards in the profession, may have the benefit of applying a braking action on the inflation of research and on the ill effects entailed by that tendency'.[5] Ten years later, in 2010, Tony Judt supported this idea, as he remembered matriculating at King's College in 1966, a time when 'Most of my supervisors ... were obscure, published little, and known only to generations of Kingsmen. Thanks to them I acquired not just a patina of intellectual self-confidence, but abiding respect for teachers who are indifferent to fame (and fortune) and to any consideration outside the supervision armchair'.[6] Even one of us remembers such professors, and if it is true that you never want a serious crisis to go to waste, perhaps now is

a time to renegotiate the meaning of knowledge and the system of rewards within our field.[7]

But will Public Shakespeare do this? Can Public Shakespeare do this? We ask this question of our colleagues: whither goest thou, Public Shakespearian? Again, if it is true that you never want a serious crisis to go to waste, and if it is also true that a serious crisis can be leveraged by the Left and the Right, then in this article we lay out a number of questions for Public Shakespearians and, in doing so, we historicize Public Shakespeare; we do not offer a survey of today's Public Shakespeare. What Gary Taylor suggested in 1989 remains true today: Shakespeare is almost entirely academic. Any account of contemporary work in Shakespeare must consider 'the economics, politics, and social rituals of academic life'.[8] We think placing Public Shakespeare within these rituals remains essential, even though the pandemic of 2020 has – at least temporarily – unhinged academic life from its past. How many colleges and universities – or theatres – will close permanently this year, or next, or in five years? How many tenure-track jobs will be advertised this year, or next, or in five years? Will institutions deliver money for research, whether in the archive or at

---

5 John Guillory, 'The system of graduate education', *PMLA* 115 (2000), 1154–63, pp. 1162, 1162–3. One such ill effect is the off-loading of teaching to a lesser category of professor, the contingent; another is less prestigious institutions' aping of their betters, demanding substantial records of publication from their faculty and new faculty. Today, in order to obtain a position at even a 'teaching institution', a candidate may well need to offer a published book.

6 Tony Judt, 'Meritocrats', *New York Review of Books* 57 (2010): www.nybooks.com/articles/2010/08/19/meritocrats.

7 Jeffrey R. Wilson thinks such a renegotiation is going on within a Public Shakespeare he defines narrowly as 'public writing': 'Once a gated community of tenured white males, Public Shakespeare is undergoing a revolution that prioritizes perspectives from often precarious junior scholars leaning into insights availed by gender, race, class, religion, disability, age, sexual orientation, intersectionalities, and other identities.' See Jeffrey R. Wilson, 'Public Shakespeare': https://wilson.fas.harvard.edu/public-shakespeare.

8 Gary Taylor, *Reinventing Shakespeare: A Cultural History, From the Restoration to the Present* (Oxford, 1989), p. 326.

conferences? How many academic presses will fold? Will professional organizations, and their conferences and journals, survive? We ask colleagues to think about the meanings and development of Public Shakespeare in this moment of extravagant uncertainty about the future of our enterprise. We attempt here to refrain from answering our own questions, although our positionings probably are, or will become, clear. We would rather ask, 'What do you think?' And, more importantly, we would rather ask, 'What are you prepared to do?'

Our questions are these. Will Public Shakespeare reconfigure the status hierarchy of the profession by reinvigorating a teaching culture; or will Public Shakespeare be seen as a top-down effort by the research culture to be relevant and preserve itself in a time of social unrest not seen since the 1960s – social unrest that is significantly anti-elitist? Alternatively, will the elite appropriate Public Shakespeare – that is, the local, community work pioneered by non-elite professors – now that economic conditions for elite institutions have changed; or will Public Shakespeare be a way for elites to acknowledge and recognize the important work non-elites are and have been doing? Does Public Shakespeare resist attempts by institutions to further practices of neoliberal management; or is Public Shakespeare one of those practices? Is it coincidence that Public Shakespeare has blossomed alongside institutions' promotion and marketing of alternative careers for Shakespearians?

If, as we have suggested, the way to consider these questions is to situate Public Shakespeare within the academy, then we offer three placements of Public Shakespeare, moving from the easiest to the most difficult, with the caveat that each crosscuts the others. First is this: a fifty-year effort by literary critics to politicize their work and to democratize it. This effort derives from literary critics' desire for political and ethical meaning in their professional and personal lives, an admirable desire awakened in the late 1960s. Much good has resulted from these efforts to see, or move, outside the ivory tower, and the profession is more diverse and more interesting than it was fifty years ago.

Such gains cannot be gainsaid, although more diversity – in thought and among faculty and students – is necessary and to be welcomed. Nor can one gainsay the sincerity of colleagues' desire for political or ethical meaning in their lives.

This politicization of our work in these ways has been critiqued from the Right and the Left. From the Right, the critique is familiar – the undermining of Western culture will lead to cultural fragmentation, if not decay – and remains with us today, although, as Taylor insisted in 1989, the 'revolution [that critical contras like (Allan) Bloom] deplore[d had already] occurred'.[9] Bloom doubtless was motivated to write *The Closing of the American Mind*, his surprising best-seller, published in 1987, because he knew which way the wind was blowing: that many of his colleagues, and even more students, were questioning the relevance to contemporary society of Shakespeare or Milton or Aristotle or Plato. Of Shakespeare, Bloom observes, the students could see plainly that the plays are 'repositories of the elitist, sexist, nationalist prejudice we are trying to overcome'.[10] Twenty years after Bloom, the aesthete Ron Rosenbaum, who is no friend to theory, pointed out the peculiarity – and, for him, the misguidedness – of critical and theatrical attempts to soften, if not eliminate, the antisemitism of *The Merchant of Venice*.[11] Of *Merchant*, Rosenbaum concludes, 'I don't believe that *Merchant* should be banned or never shown. I'm just not sure of the rationale for showing it rather than reading it. One could study it as a historical artifact. One could study its language and patterns of imagery in relation to their use in other plays. But one cannot airbrush it.'[12] It is a good question: why *do* we continue to perform and write about *Merchant*, *Othello* or *The Taming of the Shrew* if the plays are racist or sexist? In 2020,

---

[9] Taylor, *Reinventing*, p. 322.

[10] Allan Bloom, *The Closing of the American Mind: How Higher Education Has Failed Democracy and Impoverished the Souls of Today's Students* [1987] (New York, 2012), p. 353.

[11] Ron Rosenbaum, *The Shakespeare Wars: Clashing Scholars, Public Fiascoes, Palace Coups* (New York, 2006), pp. 288ff.

[12] Rosenbaum, *Wars*, p. 315.

more than thirty years after Bloom, still more and more of the young, whether students or faculty, see Shakespeare as 'repositories of elitist, sexist, nationalist prejudice'. In a reversal that might amuse the deceased Bloom, one might frame Public Shakespeare as attempting – desperately? heroically? – to answer that question without turning to aesthetics, as Rosenbaum does.[13]

From the Left, our politicization has been critiqued as merely liberal, our moves to democratize and diversify failing to affect patterns of inequality not only in society but also within the profession. Certainly, economic inequality in Western societies has become much, much greater in the fifty years we have pursued political criticism. In the United States, a 'winner take all society' has emerged, with elites taking larger shares of wealth than at any time since the late 1920s.[14] In Europe, more robust redistribution has so far prevented this situation from arising, but, as Thomas Piketty observes, this is less than reassuring, given the fragility of the European social state.[15] Workers have seen their wages stagnate; any gains for the majority of people have come from the creation of a two-income family. Similarly, in higher education, tenured professors are remunerated appropriately for members of the upper middle-class, while many, if not most, of their colleagues not on the tenure-track are remunerated like the working poor. Overall, the profession is being deprofessionalized, with, as of this writing, less than 30 per cent of faculty tenured or on the tenure ladder. Regarding higher education, this is not unfamiliar territory for those who have read John Guillory, Walter Benn Michaels or, more recently, Joseph North.[16]

We will not, therefore, rehearse the argument here, save to note two trenchant comments by John Guillory – one from his magisterial *Cultural Capital: The Problem of Literary Canon Formation*, and the other from 'The system of graduate education'. In the former, Guillory observes that the economics, politics and social rituals of academic life are not 'organized to express the consensus of a community; these social and institutional sites are

complex hierarchies in which the position and privilege of judgment are objects of competitive struggles'. These struggles, like the institutions in which they occur, are not democratic; these

---

[13] High school English teachers in the United States have begun to question the value of teaching Shakespeare to students of colour. See, for example, Christina Torres, 'Why I'm rethinking teaching Shakespeare in my English classroom', *Education Week*, 1 October 2019: www.edweek.org/tm/articles/2019/10/01/why-im-rethinking-teaching-shakespeare-in-my.html. See also Valerie Strauss, 'Teacher: why I don't want to assign Shakespeare anymore (even though he's in the Common Core)', *The Washington Post*, 13 June 2015: www.washingtonpost.com/news/answer-sheet/wp/2015/06/13/teacher-why-i-dont-want-to-assign-shakespeare-anymore-even-though-hes-in-the-common-core. Ayanna Thompson is a key example here of Shakespearians who address such concerns. Torres cites Thompson's interview on National Public Radio, 'All that glisters is not gold', *Code Switch*, 21 August 2019: www.npr.org/transcripts/752850055. See also Thompson's interview with Robin Tricoles, 'The Othello whisperer: an interview with Ayanna Thompson', Arizona State University Knowledge Enterprise, 9 July 2019: https://research.asu.edu/othello-whisperer-qa-ayanna-thompson. See also Ayanna Thompson and Laura Turchi, *Teaching Shakespeare with Purpose: A Student-Centred Approach* (London, 2016). Turchi is a specialist in curriculum development. In the US, eliminating Shakespeare from the secondary school curriculum is arguably serious business for university English departments, since most – if not all –Schools of Education still require prospective teachers to take a course in Shakespeare.

[14] See, for example, Robert Frank and Philip J. Cook, *The Winner-Take-All-Society: Why the Few at the Top Get So Much More than the Rest of Us* (New York, 1996). For academic work on this, see, for example, the work of Thomas Piketty, especially *Capital in the Twenty-First Century*, trans. Arthur Goldhammer (Cambridge, 2014). See also the work of his frequent collaborator, Emmanuel Saez – for example, 'Striking it richer: the evolution of top incomes in the United States (updated with 2018 estimates)', Department of Economics, University of California, Berkeley (February 2020): https://eml.berkeley.edu/~saez/saez-UStopincomes-2018.pdf.

[15] See Piketty, *Capital*, pp. 493ff.

[16] John Guillory, *Cultural Capital: The Problem of Literary Canon Formation* (Chicago, 1993); Walter Benn Michaels, *The Trouble with Diversity: How We Learned to Love Identity and Ignore Inequality* (New York, 2006); and Joseph North, *Literary Criticism: A Concise Political History* (Cambridge, 2017).

institutions are not 'representative' places.[17] In 'The system of graduate education', Guillory amplifies this position. Following French sociologist Alain Touraine, Guillory details 'the relation between democratization and competition for status'. That relation is not intuitive, nor is it progressive, because

democratization does not institute equality in any simple sense. The progress of democratization is accompanied by intensified effects of competition and stratification. As university degrees become more desirable among the populace, the system responds not only by providing an array of bureaucratic economies – ways of delivering degrees for less money – but also by intensifying competition for resources and prestige, the result of which is the highly stratified system we have today.[18]

The competition to secure a place at a prestigious institution, already intensifying in 2000, may have found its apotheosis in 2019, when many wealthy parents were indicted for and convicted of buying admission to elite institutions for their academically mediocre offspring. According to the *New York Times*, the judge who sentenced one of the parents, actor Lori Loughlin, 'expressed astonishment that someone who had what he called "a fairy-tale life" would corrupt the college admissions system out of a desire for even more status and prestige'.[19]

A second placement for Public Shakespeare is within debate about methodology, about what counts as intellectual work. This debate is nuanced but can be described as being between those who favour scholarship and archival research and those who favour criticism, including theoretical or political writing, and even non-peer-reviewed writing such as literary journalism or essays written for literary magazines.[20] One recent example of the latter kind of writing, from the 1990s, was an explosion of academic memoir and personal criticism by the first wave of professors from groups new to the academy – women, working-class people, and people of colour – such as Alice Kaplan's *French Lessons: A Memoir*; Jane Tompkins's *A Life in School: What the Teacher Learned*; Deborah E. McDowell's *Leaving*

Pipe Shop: Memories of Kin; Frank Lentricchia's *The Edge of Night: A Confession*; Henry Louis Gates, Jr's *Colored People: A Memoir*, and Jane Gallop's *Feminist Accused of Sexual Harassment*.[21] Shakespearians, in contrast, were focused on political criticism – the new historicism, cultural materialism and feminist criticism of the 1980s and early 1990s – which was followed by what Hugh Grady called a 'deepening apoliticism' that developed when the 'new' was dropped from historicism and attached to something else – 'the New Boredom', as David Scott Kastan famously put it in 1999.[22] Writing a 'situated overview' of Shakespeare studies in 2005 for the journal *Shakespeare*, Grady concludes that this deepening apoliticism 'has taken the form of a revival of

---

[17] Guillory, *Cultural*, pp. 27, 37.

[18] Guillory, 'System', p. 1155.

[19] Kate Taylor, 'Lori Loughlin and Mossimo Giannulli get prison in college admissions case', *The New York Times*, 21 August 2020: www.nytimes.com/2020/08/21/us/lori-loughlin-mossimo-giannulli-sentencing.html. At the sentencing, Loughlin acknowledged that she had contributed to economic and social inequities in society. She added, 'That realization weighs heavily on me, … and while I wish I could go back and do things differently, I can only take responsibility and move forward.'

[20] North's *History* (2017) documents the long history of this debate in literary study. The tension is clear in Stefan Collini's perhaps biased assessment of the early years of Frank Kermode's career. Collini asks, 'Was he already *that* "Frank Kermode", that effortlessly elegant, perceptive, slyly amusing, wide-ranging critic?' His answer, 'Not really, not to judge by this piece of scholarly flotsam', referring to a bit by Kermode in 'the back pages of the impeccably learned (read: dry as dust) *Review of English Studies* for July 1949': Stefan Collini, 'Early Kermode', *London Review of Books*, 13 August 2020: www.lrb.co.uk /the-paper/v42/n16/stefan-collini/early-kermode.

[21] Alice Kaplan, *French Lessons: A Memoir* (Chicago, 1993); Jane Tompkins, *A Life in School: What the Teacher Learned* (New York, 1997); Deborah E. McDowell, *Leaving Pipe Shop: Memories of Kin* (New York, 1996); Frank Lentricchia, *The Edge of Night: A Confession* (New York, 1994); Henry Louis Gates, Jr., *Colored People: A Memoir* (New York, 1994); and Jane Gallop, *Feminist Accused of Sexual Harassment* (Durham, NC, 1997). These are a sample, only, and do not include essays and articles of this sort published in the same era.

[22] David Scott Kastan, *Shakespeare after Theory* (New York, 1999), p. 18.

positivism (and secondarily, of an apolitical formalism), with a reversion to the older historicist idea that an "objective" factual reproduction of the past is possible'. Worse for Grady than the belief that Shakespeare's work can be known within the conditions of its original production is the thought that 'Kastan's Shakespeare . . . is a Shakespeare who has moved from cultural insurgency to cultural conformity, from an understanding of literary studies as politically engaged to one that attempts to normalize and academicize its practices'.[23]

A couple of years before Grady's overview of the field, Douglas Bruster published *Shakespeare and the Question of Culture*, reinforcing Kastan's position. Bruster mentions a colleague who once told him, privately, that Stephen Greenblatt is 'an extraordinarily talented creative writer'. Although Bruster doesn't say this, one can read envy in the colleague's judgement, but Bruster's point is that Greenblatt's writing – and, we assume, that of his followers – is 'more entertaining' than traditional scholarly writing, which 'begins with a statement of the topic, reviews the critical bibliography on that topic . . . and makes apparent one's differences from existing conclusions about the topic at hand'. Traditional scholarly writing is 'mechanical' and, further, Bruster insists, 'The routine of conventional citation . . . quite literally gets in the way of a good story'.[24] The implication is that the routine *should* get in the way, that creating stories is not what we do. One crucial subtext of this argument, however, is the fate of scholars or critics who are not 'elegant and playful' writers, which well may be most scholars or critics.[25] Indeed, a number of colleagues have pointed out that historicism as a method is exclusionary to those without access to archives or Early English Books Online.[26] And surely this is true, but, in addition, the New Boredom and EEBO enabled the careers of colleagues whose prose plods, allowing the focus to be the 'mechanical' work of digging around in archives, with a 'mechanical' presentation of the results.

What we have, then, is not only a struggle between positivist historicism and engaged political criticism, but also a struggle between mechanical prose and elegant and playful prose.[27] This struggle too has a long history, which continues. In 2013, Michael McKeon responded to Melissa E. Sanchez's '"Use me but as your spaniel": feminism, queer theory, and early modern sexualities', published in 2012 in *PMLA*, in precisely the terms of the former, although the latter emerges, too, in Sanchez's writing, which is a fun read. McKeon is disappointed in 'Use me' because he thought he would read and learn about early modern women's sexualities. Instead, he found 'an account of what we know – and don't know – about early modern women's sexualities as a function of conflicts between feminism and queer theory'. Methodologically, he complains, Sanchez's 'project is dictated by the political encounters in which she frames it, and her implied readership is principally interested in the sex wars of the 1980s and their aftermath'.[28] In words that echo Grady's, Sanchez playfully retorts that 'In contrasting the insubstantial amuse-bouche of theory and politics with the more nourishing fare of true scholarship, McKeon invokes the fantasy of a scholar who is outside politics, an ideological construct frequently used to elevate "real" intellectual work above crude "identity politics"'. But, as we all know – or should, by now – '*all* historical and literary studies do political work, whether these studies conserve or contest dominant values – and whether they own up to their politics or not'.[29]

---

[23] Hugh Grady, 'Shakespeare studies, 2005: a situated overview', *Shakespeare* 1 (2005), 102–20; p. 113.

[24] Douglas Bruster, *Shakespeare and the Question of Culture* (New York, 2003), p. 51.

[25] Bruster, *Culture*, p. 52.

[26] See, for example, Marisa R. Cull, 'Place and privilege in Shakespeare scholarship and pedagogy', in *Shakespeare and the 99%: Literary Studies, the Profession, and the Production of Inequity,* ed. Sharon O'Dair and Timothy Francisco (New York, 2019), pp. 207–24.

[27] The two pairs do not overlap completely. For example, we judge Bruster's writing to be more engaging than Grady's.

[28] Michael McKeon, 'Early modern women's sexuality: two views', *PMLA* 128 (2013), 474–5; p. 474.

[29] Melissa E. Sanchez, 'Early modern women's sexuality: two views', *PMLA* 128 (2013), 476–7; pp. 476, 477.

We would add that valuing traditional scholarship over other sorts of intellectual work and other kinds of writing – including theory, but also *belles lettres* or the essay – results from not only a fantasy of objectivity but also institutional pressures, such as prestige hierarchies within the field and the desire of literary critics to gain the superior status and better remuneration of colleagues in the sciences, including the social sciences. Indeed, looking from below, we might be so bold as to cast differently the debates above – between Kastan and Grady, between Bruster and Greenblatt, between McKeon and Sanchez. What counts as intellectual work is determined by who does it and where they do it. Recall Guillory, cited above: in our profession, 'the position and privilege of judgment are objects of competitive struggles'. Or, as Taylor playfully contended in 1989, 'not every Shakespeare critic on the planet can be fitted onto the program of a four-day conference … Even among the elect, speech is rationed, hierarchically.'[30] Guillory and Taylor imply that in academia one needs visibility, which is difficult to obtain. Visibility is power, and 'invisibility', Taylor pronounces, 'is impotence'.[31] In this light, the most telling bit of McKeon's complaint about 'Use me' is that he promotes his own work to *PMLA*'s readership – a book published in 2005, some seven years prior – as an antidote to Sanchez's essay, which suggests to us that the senior scholar is nervous about visibility, about continuing visibility. McKeon knows that what counts, what gives visibility, is published in *PMLA*, *Shakespeare*, *Shakespeare Quarterly*, *Renaissance Quarterly* or *Shakespeare Survey*.

In thinking about the future for Public Shakespeare within this placement, the trajectory of another critical practice, that of ecocriticism, may be useful. Pioneered by faculty of lesser status – by teachers – ecocriticism became the province of elites, and now counts as serious intellectual work. Ecocritical essays and scholarship are now published in leading journals, such as *PMLA* or *New Literary History*, and by the leading publishers in academia. This was not always the case. In 2005, Lawrence Buell worried about the effects of elite academics like him entering the field, wondering whether ecocriticism would thereby forfeit its original mission –

its local, activist focus and its 'disaffection with business-as-usual literary studies' – to become 'just another niche within the culture of academic professionalism'. Buell thought the additional resources, prestige and critical sophistication brought to ecocriticism by elites – after all, ecocriticism was born 'as an offshoot of an association of second-level prestige whose principal support base lay mostly outside the most prominent American university literature departments' – was worth the risk to ecocriticism's original mission.[32] Fifteen years later, the environmental humanities are another professional niche, and 'business-as-usual literary studies' continues.[33] But also useful in thinking about the future of Public Shakespeare is this: fifteen years has also brought a challenge to Buell's thinking, thinking that assumes resources should be the exclusive province of elites and that elites know best how to use resources. In our field, Kimberly Anne Coles, Kim F. Hall and Ayanna Thompson recently issued a call to action on the problem of race in the profession, and in it the authors offer this rejoinder to thinking like Buell's: 'The twentieth-century model of hoarding expertise at an elite institution or two will not suffice in the twenty-first century when our fields are under attack and vulnerable to collapse.'[34] Outside our field, but almost simultaneously, Matt Brim published *Poor Queer Studies: Confronting Elitism in the University*, in which he too decries such hoarding of resources, whether of expertise or financial, advocating instead a 'queer ferrying' between rich and poor institutions.[35]

---

[30] Taylor, *Reinventing*, p. 338. [31] Taylor, *Reinventing*, p. 371.
[32] Lawrence Buell, *The Future of Environmental Criticism: Environmental Crisis and Literary Imagination* (Malden, 2005), pp. 28, 27, 7.
[33] Nor has the environment improved from those additional resources, prestige and critical sophistication.
[34] Kimberly Anne Coles, Kim F. Hall and Ayanna Thompson, 'BlacKKKShakespearean: a call to action for medieval and early modern studies', *Profession 2020*: https://profession.mla.org/blackkkshakespearean-a-call-to-action-for-medieval-and-early-modern-studies.
[35] Matt Brim, *Poor Queer Studies: Confronting Elitism in the University* (Durham, NC, 2020), pp. 194–202. Disruption to academic practice during the global pandemic has spurred

Such calls lead to our third placement for Public Shakespeare: within deteriorating economic conditions for higher education, including – and especially for our purposes here – the job market for Ph.D.s. This placement complicates the possibility that Public Shakespeare might join theory, *belles lettres*, or the essay in challenging the elite status of archival scholarship in our field. Of course, the deteriorating economic conditions for higher education are likewise familiar territory, and mountains of studies and opinion pieces and data analyses have been produced since 1990 – or 1980 or 1975 – to assess the situation and to apportion blame, appearing in *PMLA*, *Profession*, the *Chronicle of Higher Education*, *Inside Higher Ed* or in sundry magazines or books. And yet, despite the data, the analyses and the opinions, neither the prospects for Ph.D.s nor the working conditions for faculty have improved, whether in the United States or the United Kingdom. These conditions now are leading even professors – not just the contingent – to quit academia, such as early modern historian Malcolm Gaskill, who did so in 2020 at, significantly, the age of 53:

I had dreaded telling colleagues in my field that I was quitting, imagining incredulity and a hushed inference that I was terminally ill or at least having a breakdown. Academia is vocational: people don't usually pack it in or switch careers – although that may become more common. When I finally broke the news, most of the people I told said they would retire early if they could afford it – a few had made calculations about payouts and pensions and most had at least contemplated it in glummer moments. It's just no fun any more, they said. One or two admitted that their self-identity was so bound up with academic life they could never give it up, but even this wasn't a judgment on my decision: they were entirely sympathetic and acknowledged that a wonderful career had lost a lot of its glamour.[36]

For Bill Readings, the situation just described is structural and historical: the university as we knew it – the consolidator of culture – was linked to the nation-state, and the eclipse of the nation-state in a globalized and transnational world reforms the university, enshrining it as a corporation, bureaucratic in nature, focused on matters economic, and obsessed with the notion of excellence.[37] For Guillory, too,

the situation is structural and historical, having to do with the decline of the bourgeoisie as an elite – a group for whom 'literature' was a significant part of cultural capital – and the emergence of a new elite in a technocratic society, the professional-managerial class, an elite that is not 'exclusively white or male' and for whom 'literature' is not a significant part of cultural capital. For the bourgeoisie and its literature, it is 'unquestionably the case that the several recent crises of the literary canon – its "opening" to philosophical works, to works by minorities, and now to popular and mass culture – amounts to a terminal crisis'.[38] Readings and Guillory wrote in the 1990s, but Christopher Newfield, writing in the first decade of this century, looks at this history and sees a concerted attack by nefarious actors – presumably Republicans, capitalists and conservative cultural warriors – to undermine the middle class in the US by undermining the public university. This 'assault', he claims, 'began in earnest just as the American middle class was starting to become multiracial, and as public universities were moving with increasing speed toward meaningful racial integration'.[39] Newfield's implied causality arguably reduces the complexity of higher education's problems, but his assessment exemplifies many such analyses that blame broader forces – 'some other "not us"' – for our plight, such as elitism, capitalism, imperialism, neoliberalism or, shall we say, continuing disaster.[40]

---

such moves, as many conferences, performances, lecture series and pedagogical resources from around the world have moved online, allowing greater access than can be afforded through place-based events.

[36] Malcolm Gaskill, 'Diary: on quitting academia', *London Review of Books*, 24 September 2020, 40–1, p. 41.

[37] See Bill Readings, *The University in Ruins* (Cambridge, 1997).

[38] Guillory, *Cultural*, pp. 38, 265.

[39] Christopher Newfield, *Unmaking the Public University: The Forty-Year Assault on the Middle Class* (Cambridge, 2008), p. 3.

[40] Donna J. Haraway uses the term 'some other "not us"', to describe the way progressive feminists assess the problem of overpopulation. The culprits responsible for overpopulation and its deleterious effects on the planet are familiar – 'Capitalism, Imperialism, Neoliberalism, Modernization' – but they are always 'not us'. This, Haraway insists, must stop.

Arguably, from the perspectives of Readings or Guillory, the blame game misrecognizes, and can only fail to respond appropriately to, the historical processes that have upended the university and literary study. Needed is a sharp slap in the face, such as that provided by Jeffrey R. Di Leo, a professor of English and Philosophy and Executive Director of the Society for Critical Exchange: 'there must be a point where we stop complaining about the conditions of higher ed, and bemoaning a past that is no longer recuperable, and begin to live in the present'. Neoliberalism, student debt and the job crisis are not crises but 'the continuing condition of higher education in America', which is to say: 'the continuing condition of higher education in America is the neoliberal condition'.[41] Until we accept the 'present', accept reality and our own complicity with it, Di Leo urges, we will make little or even no progress in transforming the neoliberal condition of our institutions and our professional lives.

In January 2020, *Inside Higher Ed*'s Colleen Flaherty reported that 'the Modern Language Association is listening' to professors' concerns over the ethics of graduate education. On a panel about admissions, Guillory pushed against the grain to propose, according to Flaherty, 'a thought experiment' that 'the MLA might also help oversee a staggered moratorium on admissions to humanities programs, in which one-third to one-fourth of departments don't admit graduate students every year'. Smaller fixes were also suggested, such as departments' publicizing their Ph.D. placements more transparently, or offering supplementary programmes to their students so that they may find an alternative career to a professorship, whether in or out of academia.[42] Again, this is familiar territory at the MLA and other professional organizations, as well as in journals and books. Yet, as the MLA convention closed and its presenters and attendees made their ways home, whether locally or across the globe, a novel coronavirus, virulent and deadly, was already doing the same, traversing the globe. Within two months, colleges and universities worldwide were closed, and classroom instruction moved online. Conferences, too, were cancelled or moved online, including the Shakespeare Association of America, the International Shakespeare Conference in Stratford-upon-Avon, and the January 2021 MLA convention. As we write, a tiny strand of RNA has begun to accomplish what Guillory suggested in January and what he and many other colleagues have argued for decades. As of early October 2020, eight highly-ranked Ph.D. programmes in English or Comparative Literature have suspended admissions for 2021–2, and twenty-four universities have suspended over 100 Ph.D. programs in other disciplines.[43] At the other end of the graduate student life-cycle, as of early October, the MLA lists three tenure-track positions in Early Modern / Renaissance Literature. But graduate students in early modern studies will have to compete with peers in other fields for these positions. The advertised positions, a cluster hire by the University of British Columbia, require expertise in Critical Race Studies, Studies of Empire and Colonialism, Global English Literatures or Indigenous English Literatures, from 1550 to 1900.

See Donna J. Haraway, 'Making kin in the Chthulucene: reproducing multispecies justice', in *Making Kin Not Population*, ed. Adele E. Clarke and Donna J. Haraway (Chicago, 2018), p. 88. With respect to the economic conditions of higher education, we too would like colleagues to stop blaming some 'not us'. Jeffrey R. Di Leo agrees: 'My own belief is that higher education deteriorated beneath the feet of many of us – and for one reason or another we were powerless to stop it. Using the rhetoric of crisis allows us to assume a level of plausible deniability for the deterioration ... it is always everyone else's fault that the humanities are failing, never our own': Jeffrey R. Di Leo, *Higher Education under Late Capitalism: Identity, Conduct, and the Neoliberal Condition* (Cham, 2017), pp. xiii, xiv.

[41] Di Leo, *Higher*, pp. xv, xiii.

[42] Colleen Flaherty, 'Seeking a culture shift in graduate education', *Inside Higher Ed*, 13 January 2020: www.insidehigh ered.com/news/2020/01/13/mla-discusses-professors-eth ical-responsibilities-training-graduate-students.

[43] Meghan Zahneis, 'More doctoral programs suspend admissions. That could have lasting effects on graduate education', *The Chronicle of Higher Education*, 28 September 2020, updated 2 October 2020: www-chronicle-com.libdata.lib. ua.edu/article/more-doctoral-programs-suspend-admis sions-that-could-have-lasting-effects-on-graduate-educa tion. Of the eight universities in our field, six are private and two public research institutions. This suggests that, in the US, Ph.D. education is expensive for private institutions and much less expensive for public institutions, who must staff many thousands of composition courses.

Early modernists may also compete for a position at Brigham Young University, which advertises four tenure-track positions in American Literature, Folklore or British Literature.

In 2020, almost twenty-five years have passed since Guillory published 'Pre-professionalism: what graduate students want', in which he decried graduate education as 'a kind of pyramid scheme'. What Guillory meant is that graduate students and assistant professors desire to be, or mirror, their mentors – doing research, travelling to conferences worldwide, publishing articles and books, and – especially – teaching graduate students. But 'the number of graduate students would have to increase geometrically for this desire to be gratified for all of us' – hence the pyramid scheme. Because such geometric increase is 'phantasmic', the competition for such jobs intensifies and the result is 'the penetration of graduate education by professional practices formerly confined to later phases of the career, the obvious examples being publication and the delivery of conference papers'.[44] A few years later, Marc Bousquet radicalized Guillory's insight that graduate students 'do everything that their teachers do – teach, deliver conference papers, publish – without the assurance that any of these activities will secure them a job'.[45] Not only are graduate students professionalized too early, as Guillory observed, but, Bousquet insists, 'degree holding increasingly represents a disqualification from practice ... For most graduate employees, the receipt of the Ph.D. signifies the end – and not the beginning – of a long teaching career.'[46] Bousquet does not provide data, and we think he overstates, but data about the careers of Ph.D.s or ABDs ('All But Dissertation's) in English are difficult to come by and difficult for colleagues to trust.[47] Still, whether one agrees with Guillory that we have over-produced Ph.D.s, or with Bousquet that we have under-produced jobs, or with the more recent arguments of Paul Yachnin that none of it matters because the Ph.D., properly reformed, is a degree for multiple careers, one must admit that it is possible – and even likely – for graduate students and early career colleagues to publish and perish.

For young scholars in 1989, like one of us, reading Taylor's 'Present tense' in *Reinventing Shakespeare* was alluring, inspiring and disturbing: alluring and inspiring because of the witty, conversational tone, but mainly for the thrill of imagining how it would be to be someone like Gary Taylor, 'play[ing] the international conference circuit' in 1986 – an average year for him, 'not especially important', but one in which he rolls from London to Berlin to Washington, DC, to Stratford-upon-Avon to Williamstown, landing, finally, in Silver Spring. And it was disturbing because the chapter is, at its core, a bad-boy take-down of exactly the culture Taylor revels in and plays so well – he treats 'academic life as the stuff of satirical fiction' – which even then suggested something like braggadocio or disingenuousness.[48] For us, in 2020, reading 'Present tense' feels like culpable excess – for the planet, for the profession. For young scholars, it must feel like a daydream. The proof is in the pudding and, in this

---

[44] John Guillory, 'Pre-professionalism: what graduate students want', *Profession 1996* (1996), 91–9, pp. 97, 98, 98, 92. In 1999, Maresi Nerad and Joseph Cerny published a study of those who obtained a Ph.D. in English between 1982 and 1985, and noted the following: ten years later, only 2.8 per cent of them were tenured professors at Carnegie Research I institutions. Only 16 per cent of all tenured faculty work at such institutions: Maresi Nerad and Joseph Cerny, 'From rumors to facts: career outcomes of English PhDs', *The Communicator* 32 (1999), 1–12, p. 11.

[45] Guillory, 'Pre-professionalism', p. 92.

[46] Marc Bousquet, 'The waste product of graduate education: toward a dictatorship of the flexible', *Social Text* 70 (2002), 81–104, p. 87.

[47] The Modern Language Association of America frequently analyses data on the status of the profession, much of which arguably obscures rather than clarifies the problem. One sometimes feels pity for David Laurence, MLA's Director of Research, who finds himself reading comments like this by Billiam Pringle: 'It's astonishing that you've seen fit to draw conclusions from these numbers, considering the quality of the data and its statistical non-significance. Borderline dishonest, really – but typical of the MLA. More interested in protecting your reputation than you are in actually serving young scholars': https://mlaresearch.mla.hcommons.org /2015/02/17/where-are-they-now-occupations-of-1996-2011-phd-recipients-in-2013-2/#comments.

[48] Taylor, *Reinventing*, pp. 304, 372.

case, the pudding is, first, the continuing and dramatic decline of positions advertised; second, the continuing slow decline in the percentage of faculty with tenure; and, third, the explosion of interest in departments and professional organizations in the recognition, marketing and selling of 'alt-ac' careers for Ph.D.s, or, perhaps more eerily, in the recognition, marketing and selling of the Ph.D. for 'alt-ac' careers.

Often defined as non-professorial positions within higher education, 'alt-ac' as a term has been in vogue only for a decade.[49] 'Alt-ac' is slippery, however, and sometimes means positions in journalism, non-profit policy organizations and non-profit cultural organizations, such as theatres, museums or heritage sites. But colleagues have been finding fulfilling work both inside and outside the academy since the 1970s, when hiring collapsed, just as they have been doing Public Shakespeare for many, many years.[50] A study published in 1999 of Ph.D.s in English who received degrees between 1982 and 1985 found that, a decade later, 58% were tenured or on the tenure-track, 15% were contingent or working elsewhere in the academy, and 16% were employed in business, government agencies or non-profit organizations – what the authors abbreviated as 'BGN',[51] and what many now call 'alt-ac'. Those numbers have shifted dramatically since. In 2017, in a much smaller study of those who obtained their Ph.D. between 1996 and 2010 – 310 respondents, rather than the 814 of the 1999 study – the MLA reported that 47.9% were tenured or on the tenure-track, 20.3% were contingent, 6% held nonfaculty or 'alt-ac' positions in higher education, and 18.2% worked outside the academy.[52] The earlier study had recommended that if departments continued to train graduate students solely for the professoriate, they should reduce enrolment. Alternatively, if reducing enrolment was not possible or was unpalatable, Ph.D. programmes in English must do a much better job of preparing graduate students for careers outside the professoriate.[53] To say Ph.D. programmes have dithered for twenty years is not understatement, but, as is evidenced by Paul Yachnin's work,[54] as well as initiatives and support by the MLA and the SAA, Ph.D. programmes increasingly edge towards fulfilling the latter recommendation.[55]

Assessing the two studies, however, demonstrates a problem with the argument that solving the problem of graduate admissions only means doing a better job preparing graduate students for careers outside the professoriate. In the 1999 study, Ph.D.s working in BGN sectors made more money than, and expressed satisfaction in their careers on a par with, tenured faculty members. Unsurprisingly, tenured and tenure-track faculty members thought the Ph.D. worth getting (99%), while those with contingent employment and Ph.D.s working in BGN sectors were less likely to think so, at 87% and 89%, respectively. In the 2017 study, all groups reported less certainty about the value of the degree than did their older colleagues: only 95.1% of the tenured, 91.7% of the tenure-track faculty, 65.9% of the contingent, and 69.4% of those working outside the academy

---

[49] Brenda Bethman and C. Shaun Longstreet, 'Defining terms', *Inside Higher Ed*, 22 May 2013: www.insidehighered.com/advice/2013/05/22/essay-defining-alt-ac-new-phd-job-searches.

[50] Notable examples are Curt L. Tofteland's Shakespeare Behind Bars and Hardy M. Cook's Shaksper: The Global Electronic Shakespeare Conference. Both date from the mid-1990s.

[51] Nerad and Cerny, 'Rumors', p. 3.

[52] MLA Office of Research, 'The career paths of modern language PhDs: findings from the 2017 MLA survey of doctoral program graduates', MLA (2018): www.mla.org/content/download/99761/2283567/Survey-of-PhD-Recipients-2017.pdf.

[53] Nerad and Cerny, 'Rumors', p. 11.

[54] See, for example, Paul Yachnin, 'Humanities PhD grads working in non-academic jobs could shake up university culture', The Conversation, 7 January 2020: https://theconversation.com/humanities-phd-grads-working-in-non-academic-jobs-could-shake-up-university-culture-127298.
Note, too, information provided in the links therein to McGill University's TRaCE project.

[55] For an overview, see Maureen Terese McCarthy, 'Summary of prior work in humanities PhD professional development', Council of Graduate Schools, Washington, DC, September 2017. Data in this report indicate that the number of Ph.D.s awarded remains high, increasing again after the Great Recession: https://cgsnet.org/ckfinder/userfiles/files/NEH_NextGen_PriorWork.pdf.

reported thinking the Ph.D. 'advantageous for their careers'. Furthermore, 'Higher percentages of respondents employed outside postsecondary education reported annual incomes at the highest and lowest salary ranges than did respondents employed in postsecondary education.'[56] Although the MLA does not recognize the drops here, since the 1999 study is not mentioned, it seems a safe hypothesis that the lower numbers of tenure, tenure-track and contingent faculty reporting satisfaction with the degree reflect deteriorating working conditions for faculty. As for the drop among those working outside the academy, we hypothesize that the bifurcation in salary among this group largely accounts for it. Those earning at the lowest salary levels, perhaps as self-employed editors or freelance journalists, arguably see less relevance in the degree than do those earning at the highest salary levels, perhaps as management consultants or government employees. And these hypotheses, especially the latter, are crucial for our concluding remarks about our third placement for Public Shakespeare, the deteriorating economic conditions for higher education, including the job market for Ph.D.s.

The most visible work by Public Shakespearians is not pedagogy or community work but non-peer-reviewed writing on multiple platforms. We focus on it here for this reason and because this work relates most clearly to the job prospects for graduate students and early-career Shakespearians. An unscientific and partial assessment of such work reveals two categories:[57] digital sites such as The Conversation, The Rambling or The Sundial, as well as blogs such as those at Oxford University Press or the Folger Shakespeare Library;[58] and traditional journalism, including newspapers or magazines, whether local, national or international, such as the *New Yorker*, *The Economist*, the *Guardian*, the *New York Times* or the *Chronicle of Higher Education*. Obviously, traditional journalism, whether print or digital, reaches laypeople as well as colleagues; it can also provide substantial and well-paid employment to some Ph.D.s, such as Thomas Frank, Rebecca Schuman, Anne Helen Petersen, Sarah Kendzior, or – in a telling instance – to ABDs, such as Lili Loofbourow.[59]

In contrast, the principal readership of venues like The Rambling, The Sundial or the Folger Library's Shakespeare and Beyond is professors and students, who do not rely on publication in them for their principal income. These sites offer academics the opportunity to write outside academic norms and to explore topics outside their fields of expertise, including contemporary culture. The founders of The Rambling explain that they 'love rambling far afield from their academic, um, fields. They started The Rambling in order to give writers a wide space in which they could feel free to ramble, too, and hopefully meet new fellow ramblers along the way.'[60] The Rambling publishes short pieces of 500–1,500 words, The Sundial of 1,000–1,500 words, and neither is peer-reviewed. For their writers, both The Sundial and The Rambling emphasize 'the pitch', and The Sundial offers detailed instructions about the meaning of 'the pitch', underscoring that a pitch is not an academic abstract.[61]

---

[56] MLA Office of Research, 'Career paths'.

[57] For examples of such writing, we used Jeffrey R. Wilson's listing, which numbered 116 at the time of our assessment in September 2020. See https://wilson.fas.harvard.edu/writing-with-shakespeare/public-shakespeare.

[58] These venues for publication supplement a number of peer-reviewed journals established since 2000, including *JEMCS* (2000), *Shakespeare* (2005), *Borrowers and Lenders: The Journal of Shakespeare and Appropriation* (2005), *Early Modern Culture Online* (2010), *The Hare* (2012) and *Upstart* (2013). The previous flowering of peer-reviewed journals in our field occurred in the 1970s.

[59] Thomas Frank received his Ph.D. in History from the University of Chicago in 1994; Rebecca Schuman received her Ph.D. in German from the University of California, Irvine, in 2010; Anne Helen Petersen received her Ph.D. in Media Studies from the University of Texas in 2011; Sarah Kendzior received her Ph.D. in Anthropology from Washington University in 2012. Lili Loofbourow is ABD in English (Early Modern Studies) at the University of California, Berkeley. A staff writer at *Slate*, it is uncertain Loofbourow will complete the degree; her on-line biographies and her personal website do not list her Berkeley affiliation. See www.lililoofbourow.com/?page_id=938.

[60] https://the-rambling.com/about.

[61] https://medium.com/the-sundial-acmrs/welcome-to-the-sundial-2f4fccf3eb42.

These venues are funded differently, and all are subject to financial pressures. The financial pressures journalism faces are well known and we will not belabour the point, save to say that even a venerable magazine such as the *New Yorker*, with its impressive 98.4% subscriber base, must anticipate future trouble, as its subscribers skew heavily towards the elderly; the median age of subscribers is 54, and 48% of subscribers are over 55 years of age. As telling, perhaps, the median household income of the *New Yorker* readership is $129, 631, in the top 15% of household incomes in the United States.[62] The Conversation, in contrast, is funded somewhat like public media in the United States, with a budget between 2 and 3 million dollars,[63] generated from donations, university members and grant-awarding bodies, including the Lumina and Ford Foundations.[64] The Conversation is distributed via the Associated Press and its content lands in venues like the *Washington Post*, *Salon* and *Slate*. As such, member institutions potentially raise their institutional profiles and contributors gain considerable visibility. In yet another model, venues like The Sundial and The Rambling are supported to some degree by universities and offer similar, if smaller, benefits. The Rambling was established by Sarah Tindal Kareem and Crystal B. Lake of the University of California, Los Angeles, and Wright State University, respectively. The two pay the domain and hosting fees out-of-pocket, and fund graduate student editorial and management work through grants from UCLA's College of Arts and Letters, and from Kareem's research budget. The Sundial is a project of The Arizona Center for Medieval and Renaissance Studies, and the digital forum is supported by private donations, grants from foundations, and the University of Arizona System. The Sundial 'is a space for authors to write for broader audiences and gain greater exposure for their work'; the site, it appears, wants to re-imagine pedagogical and publication practices by showcasing in particular the work of non-elite, non-traditional and precarious scholars.

Still uncertain is whether recent ventures like these will create new markets or new publics for Shakespearians or simply democratize existing ones. Also uncertain is whether the visibility afforded to young scholars by these venues will result in tenure-track employment. In 2015, graduate student Lili Loofbourow and Assistant Professor Phillip Maciak introduced a cluster of short essays in *PMLA* under the rubric 'The Changing Profession'. Mostly drawn from a standing-room-only roundtable at the MLA, the essays interrogated the possibilities of what they call 'the semi-public intellectual'. Of special concern to Loofbourow and Maciak, unsurprisingly, is the status of digital, non-peer-reviewed writing in a young scholar's career: does it 'count' in hiring, in promotion?[65] In a nuanced discussion, they urge that this semi-public work not supplant peer-reviewed scholarship but 'be understood as valuable public engagement'.[66] The jury is still out on this, but five years later, Loofbourow, as noted above, is a journalist, and Maciak left his tenure-track position at Louisiana State University and is now an instructor at Washington University. This, along with the emphasis by institutions on training graduate students for alt-ac careers, raises three questions: can this kind of short, accessible and non-peer-reviewed writing lead to secure or tenure-track academic positions and thus join theory, *belles lettres* or the essay in challenging the elite status of archival scholarship in our field? Or does this kind of writing, already promoted as something else − as 'public engagement' − raise an already high bar to securing such positions: newly minted Ph.D.s are expected to publish significantly more than their elders, and will current and future cohorts of Ph.D.s also be expected to have significant work in 'public engagement'? Or, more

---

[62] See MediaMax: https://mediamaxnetwork.com/publica tions/the-new-yorker; and Statista: www.statista.com/statis tics/203183/percentage-distribution-of-household-income -in-the-us.
[63] IRS Form 990, The Conversation US, 2018 ProPublica, Non-Profit Explorer: https://projects.propublica.org/non profits/display_990/460906774/07_2019_prefixes_45-46% 2F460906774_201806_990_2019070516464911.
[64] See The Conversation: https://theconversation.com/us/ partners.
[65] Lili Loofbourow and Phillip Maciak, 'Introduction: the time of the semipublic intellectual', *PMLA* 130 (2015), 439–45.
[66] Loofbourow and Maciak, 'Introduction', p. 444.

ominously, does this kind of work indicate an uneasy acceptance that academic work is becoming a lot like journalism – which is to say, increasingly precarious, increasingly 'gig' work? Writing in the *Columbia Journalism Review*, Atossa Araxia Abrahamian describes her craft in ways that might be applied to the academic precariat, noting that 'journalism can feel less like a job than a vocation masquerading as a profession and compensated like an art'. Increasingly, she writes, it is a 'profession for the young, the hungry, or the independently wealthy'.[67]

What, then, is the future for Public Shakespearians? Will Public Shakespeare reinvigorate a teaching culture? Will Public Shakespeare reconfigure the status hierarchy of the profession by stimulating what Matt Brim has called a 'queer ferrying', a 'cross-class, cross-institutional sharing of opportunity ... [and]

resources'?[68] More radically, will Public Shakespeare undermine the 'hoarding' of expertise, as imagined by Coles, Hall and Thompson? Will Public Shakespeare contest the mechanisms of neoliberal university management? We do not know, but we do know that you never want a serious crisis to go to waste, and that collectively, as a profession, we have power and can affect how Public Shakespeare will develop. And that is why we ask, 'Whither goest thou, Public Shakespearian?'

---

[67] Atossa Araxia Abrahamian, 'The pain and joy of the side hustle', *Columbia Journalism Review* (Spring/Summer 2018): www.cjr.org/special_report/side-hustles.php.
[68] Laura Sell, 'Q&A with Matt Brim', Duke University Press, 4 March 2020: https://dukeupress.wordpress.com/2020/03/04/qa-with-matt-brim.

TEACHING SHAKESPEARE IN A TIME OF HATE

ALEXA ALICE JOUBIN AND LISA S. STARKS

The time of hate in which we live dictates that we answer fully and collaboratively the challenges of all forms of violence, including racism, antisemitism, misogyny, transphobia and other types of bigotry. In a time when the classroom is subject to 'new forms of subterfuge, secret recordings, and professor watch lists',[1] it is all the more important to bring our academic work to build more equitable, sustainable communities, rather than exploiting trendy topics that service academic advancement and not students and community members. One of the core values of the humanities lies in understanding the human condition in different contexts, and Shakespeare's oeuvre as a cluster of complex, transhistorical cultural texts provides fertile ground to build empathy and critical thinking. Developing 'independent facility with complex texts', as Ayanna Thompson and Laura Turchi's research shows, enables 'divergent paths to knowledge', which promotes equity and diversity.[2] Indeed, as Timothy Francisco and Sharon O'Dair point out, the heuristic value of complex texts lies in their ability to expose 'the oppression by a status hierarchy' and encourage the formation of hypotheses and critiques.[3]

In this article, we examine new theories and praxis of listening for silenced voices and of telling compelling stories that make us human. Elucidation of our Levinas-inspired theories of the Other is followed by a discussion of classroom practices for in-person and remote instruction that foster collaborative knowledge building and intersectional pedagogy. The moral agency that comes with the cultivation of ethical treatment of one another can lead to political advocacy. Special attention is given to race, gender and the exigencies of social justice and remote learning in the era of the global pandemic of COVID-19 (2019 novel coronavirus disease). The new normal in higher education, which is emerging at the time of writing, exposes inequities that were previously veiled by on-campus life and resources. Even as they are cause for grief and anxiety, the inequities exposed by COVID-19 can spur change for the better.

LEVINAS'S RADICAL ETHICS AND SHAKESPEARE

Ethics is an essential, but often missed, term in discussions of Shakespeare, even though interpretations and performances lay ethical claims upon the canon. An ethics-first pedagogy promotes awareness of and compassion towards those most vulnerable to oppression and attacks from White supremacists. Ethics refers to mutually accepted guidelines on how human beings should act and

---

[1] Wendy Beth Hyman and Hillary Eklund, 'Introduction: making meaning and doing justice with early modern texts', in *Teaching Social Justice Through Shakespeare: Why Renaissance Literature Matters Now*, ed. Eklund and Hyman (Edinburgh, 2019), pp. 1–26; p. 2.

[2] Ayanna Thompson and Laura Turchi, *Teaching Shakespeare with Purpose* (London, 2016), pp. 1, 7.

[3] Timothy Francisco and Sharon O'Dair, 'Introduction: "Truth in advertising" – Shakespeare and the 99%', in *Shakespeare and the 99%: Literary Studies, the Profession, and the Production of Inequity*, ed. Sharon O'Dair and Timothy Francisco (New York, 2019), pp. 1–19; p. 5.

treat one another, and, in particular, what constitutes a good action. Emmanuel Levinas posits that relations with the Other pre-exist any kind of being, thereby making ethics the most primary philosophy. In Levinas's theory, the human being is constituted in, through, by and for the Other – in the face of the Other – first and foremost. Rather than assuming that the I or ego first exists via its own consciousness and then attempts to interact with others, Levinas argues that it is only *through* the Other that the *I* emerges at all; this interaction occurs pre-consciousness, pre-ego formation, pre- or 'otherwise than' being. For Levinas, then, ethics or moral behaviour is not a supplement or an add-on to an already fully formed subject; conversely, it is the basis upon which the subject is formed, the primary philosophy itself, the foundation of all.

Teaching Shakespeare offers opportunities to help students to cope with these difficult times, to examine their world critically, to learn how to respond respectfully and sensitively to others, and to sharpen their intellect. Drawing on Levinas's philosophy, Alexa Alice Joubin and Elizabeth Rivlin have argued that literary criticism carries strong ethical implications. A crucial, ethical component of interacting with a literary text is one's willingness to listen to and be subjected to the demands of others, creating moments of 'self and mutual recognition'.[4] Seeing the others within oneself is the first step towards seeing oneself in others' eyes. The act of literary criticism is founded upon the premise of one's subjectivity, the subject who speaks, and the other's voice that one is channelling, misrepresenting or appropriating.

Levinas employs Shakespeare's plays as illustrative examples of his philosophical concepts, explaining that the plays render his ideas into a more tangible level or register. Consequently, Levinas sees Shakespeare and other writers such as Dostoyevsky not as conventional moralists who advocate poetic justice and decorous human behaviour but, rather, as writers concerned with ethical imperatives and questions of social justice. Within a framework where ethics are prioritized over knowledge production, students and educators are responsible for the preservation of the alterity of the Other, even as they make the obscure known by plucking it out of the abyss of unknowable otherness. The ethical creation of knowledge works against 'the imperialism of the same', an assertive move of acquisition that forces unfamiliar things to 'conform to what we already know'.[5] Levinas's principle of the Other can help us to hear the voices of the Other by avoiding the tendency to know something merely as our own ideological construct.

For Levinas, Shakespeare may be a means to engage with, rather than only consciously understand, an ethics-first philosophy. His comments concerning Shakespeare's plays and Dostoyevsky's novels indicate his commitment to radical ethics in the literary imagination. In his *Humanism of the Other*, Levinas sees Shakespeare dramatizing his ethics-first philosophy based on one's moral obligation to the other before he himself conceptualized it in philosophical terms centuries later. Levinas uses *King Lear* to illustrate his notion of 'substitution', or 'putting oneself in the other's shoes', as much as is possible, while still maintaining the alterity and respecting the differences of the other.[6] There is profound reciprocity between notions of self and the Other. The subordination of I to You constitutes a subjectivity that recognizes an alterity within. Levinas writes that 'It is through the condition of being hostage that there can be in the world pity, compassion, pardon and proximity – even the little there is, even the simple "After you, sir".'[7] The forcible subjection to the Other is the precondition for ethical action.

[4] Alexa Alice Joubin and Elizabeth Rivlin, 'Introduction', in *Shakespeare and the Ethics of Appropriation*, ed. Joubin and Rivlin (New York, 2014), pp. 1–20; p. 17.
[5] Quoted in Donald R. Davis, 'Three principles for an Asian humanities: care first ... learn from ... connect histories', *Journal of Asian Studies* 74 (2015), 43–67; p. 48.
[6] Emmanuel Levinas, *Humanism of the Other*, trans. Nidra Poller (Urbana, IL, 2003), p. 3; Richard A. Cohen, *Levinasian Meditations: Ethics, Philosophy, and Religion* (Pittsburgh, PA, 2010), p. 166.
[7] Emanuel Levinas, *Otherwise than Being or Beyond Essence*, trans. Alphonso Lingis (Pittsburgh, PA, 1998), p. 117.

A LEVINAS-INSPIRED PEDAGOGY

Levinas's radical ethics thus underscores the importance of teaching the humanities, particularly literature. Levinas's philosophy can inform our approaches to teaching, our methods for engaging students and creating compassionate, ethical, intellectually stimulating learning environments – whether classes are face-to-face, online or in a hybrid format. This approach to teaching includes, in effect, a lesson in ethics, both internal and external to the assigned course materials and course subject matter. A Levinas-based pedagogy considers how instructors treat students and how students treat each other, countering the current trend to bully one's opponent on social media. In today's intensely heated political climate, it is more important than ever to ensure this fundamental, primary ethical principle is in place.

Teaching during the COVID-19 pandemic and multiple protests against injustice around the world, we as instructors have seen this need for care of others – and of the self – foregrounded. Writing pre-pandemic, Ayanna Thompson stresses the need for instructors to take care of themselves when opening up social justice issues, such as anti-racism, in the class discussions, noting the 'emotional labor' such teaching requires.[8] Since that time, this need for self-protection – and for instructors to make sure students show compassion and concern for themselves and each other – is even more pronounced. Although it may be challenging, and at times exhausting, working to ensure that students treat each other with respect and dignity in the classroom and in online discussions, where students and/or instructors may lapse into inconsiderate and/or abusive behaviours, it is crucial to establish and maintain a classroom truly committed to countering hate.

In face-to-face classrooms, we can emphasize collaborative learning and active student participation, focusing on Levinas's operative concept of the saying (*le dire*) in fostering an ethics-first classroom. For Levinas, the importance in communication exists in the saying, or the signifying itself – one's reaching out to the other. It is the *communicating* itself that matters. Levinas's theory of communication – the saying underlying the said (*le dit*) – relies on the self's one-sided obligation to the other, the concept of proximity between people and the face-to-face interpersonal connection between them. The said refers to the semantic content of an utterance and the 'different modalities by which a subject masters the world by assimilating it to the measure of consciousness', such as narratives, history and discourses. The said is an expression of contents. In contrast, the saying is 'expression without content' where the subjectivity emerges as exposition. The saying is an act of signifying that 'I am for the other.'[9] In *Otherwise than Being*, Levinas writes:

> In starting with sensibility interpreted not as a knowing but as proximity, in seeking in language contact and sensibility, behind the circulation of information it becomes, we have endeavored to describe subjectivity as irreducible to consciousness and thematization. Proximity appears as the relationship with the other, who cannot be resolved into 'images' or be exposed in a theme.[10]

'Proximity' rather than 'knowing' allows for 'language contact and sensibility' (or 'saying') – the reaching out to another without attempting to reduce the other into thingness, an objectified 'image' or reductive 'theme' (or the 'said'). Teaching for the 'saying' in the face-to-face classroom can help to create and maintain a compassionate learning environment.

These same principles apply to online teaching, but they should not be implemented in exactly the same way as they are in a face-to-face class. It is important to consider how best to establish a Levinas-inspired classroom that is designed specifically for remote delivery, rather than replicating a face-to-face one. Therefore, as instructors, we

---

[8] Ayanna Thompson, 'An afterword about self/communal care', in *Teaching Social Justice*, ed. Eklund and Hyman, pp. 235–8; p. 237.

[9] Gabriel Riera, '"The possibility of the poetic said" in *Otherwise than Being* (allusion, or Blanchot in Levinas)', *Diacritics* 34 (2004), 14–36; p. 14.

[10] Levinas, *Otherwise than Being*, p. 100.

need to consider how to use technology carefully to enhance rather than impede the goal of a Levinas-inspired pedagogy. To do so, it may be helpful to think through issues concerning Levinas's notions of 'proximity' in light of technology and communication in remote teaching environments.

Although Levinas does not speak directly to matters of online communication, as his work pre-dates the Internet, his ideas lend themselves to matters of technology, mediation and inter-subjective communication, as Lisa S. Starks's research has shown. Levinas's theory provides a way into thinking about teaching online that opens up its transformational potential even while alerting us to its limitations, presenting them as productive challenges rather than obstacles to an ethics-first virtual literature classroom. Useful in mediated communication is Levinas's term 'proximity'. Although, in general usage, the word denotes physical closeness or lack of geographical distance, in Levinas's theory it may suggest something quite different — a figurative rather than literal sense of 'closeness', with a moral imperative. Importantly, as Levinas explains, 'The relationship of proximity cannot be reduced to any modality of distance or geometrical contiguity.'[11] Levinas's notion of proximity has been applied to analyses of mediated communication and online and offline relationships. 'Proximity' entails an ethical obligation beyond remaining geographically close or being present physically. Richard Cohen cautions that 'one can objectify' the 'other's face, "reading" from it symptoms, ideologies', for 'The face can always become a mask.'[12] Objectification and reduction of the Other most certainly can and does occur in online relationships, including in online classroom environments — but the same can also be true for face-to-face relationships and traditional classrooms. Importantly, though, the 'saying' rather than the 'said', Levinas's face-to-face encounter, *may occur* via mediated communication — be it via a letter sent by snail-mail, an email message, a student's discussion post, or a virtual interaction, just as it may — or may not — occur in 'physical' face-to-face interactions.

TEACHING MULTIPLICITY THROUGH RADICAL LISTENING

A number of analogue and digital pedagogical tools could promote radical listening — proactive communication strategies to listen for the roots of stories that allow for 'an egality between teller and listener that gives voice to the tale'.[13] Students learn to listen for motives behind stories, rather than the plot of the narrative. As a cluster of complex texts that sustains both past practices and contemporary interpretive conventions, Shakespeare provides fertile ground for training in radical listening.

Specifically, radical listening draws on the methodology of strategic presentism. Coined by Lynn Fendler, strategic presentism acknowledges the present position of the interpreters of the humanities and empowers them to make a difference by methodically using our contemporary issues to motivate historical studies.[14] By thinking critically 'about the past in the present'[15] — as does the #BlackLivesMatter movement — students analyse performances and dramatic texts with an eye towards changing the present. By foregrounding the linkage between early modern English drama and contemporary ideologies in global contexts, we address 'the ways the past is at work in the exigencies of the present [including] the long arc of ongoing processes of dispossession under capitalism.'[16] In this framework, the past is not an

---

[11] Levinas, *Otherwise than Being*, pp. 100–1.

[12] Richard A. Cohen, 'Ethics and cybernetics: Levinasian reflections', *Ethics and Information Technology* 2 (2000), 27–35; pp. 31–2.

[13] Rita Charon, *Narrative Medicine: Honoring the Stories of Illness* (Oxford, 2006), pp. 66, 77; Portland Helmich, interview with Rita Charon, 'How radical listening can heal division – and why it matters now more than ever', Kripalu, 1 June 2020: https://kripalu.org/resources/how-radical-listening-can-heal-division-and-why-it-matters-now-more-ever.

[14] Lynn Fendler, 'The upside of presentism', *Paedagogica Historica: International Journal of the History of Education* 44 (2008), 677–90; p. 677.

[15] David Sweeney Coombs and Danielle Coriale, 'V21 Forum on Strategic Presentism: introduction', *Victorian Studies* 59 (2016), 87–9; p. 88.

[16] Coombs and Coriale, 'V21 Forum', pp. 87–8.

object of obfuscatory, irrelevant knowledge that is sealed off from our present moment of globalization, but rather one of many complex texts to enable us to rethink the present.

Since strategic presentism decentres the power structures that have historically excluded 'many first-generation students, students of colour, and differently abled students',[17] more students – especially underprivileged ones – are empowered to claim ownership of Shakespeare. The approach has also revealed Shakespeare to be a cluster of texts for critical analysis, rather than simply a 'White' canon with culturally predetermined meanings.

In pedagogical practice, this means fostering connections among seemingly isolated instances of political and artistic expressions. It is paramount, in a time of hate, to cultivate the ability to recognize multiple, potentially conflicting, versions of the same story. Unambiguous, clean and sanitized, singular narratives usually occur during a dark moment of history. Literary ambiguity, as Alexa Alice Joubin argues, 'helps connect minds for global change'. The ambiguity is a welcome gift for the uninhibited mind, for 'it has been an ally of oppressed peoples in the Soviet Union, Tibet, South Africa, and elsewhere. The ambiguity allowed them to express themselves under censorship.'[18] Our Levinas-inspired pedagogy of radical listening takes into account the ambiguities and evolving circumstances that affect interpretations of the texts. A singular, modern edition of Shakespeare's plays is no longer the only object of study. Instead, it is one of multiple nodes that are available for search and re-assembly. Teaching Shakespeare through translated versions and performative possibilities draws attention to dramatic ambiguities and choices that directors must make. In dramaturgical terms, it helps students to discover 'how the same speech can be used to perform ... radically divergent speech acts'.[19] Instead of taking a secondary role by responding to assignment prompts, students examine the evidence as a group, annotate the text and video clips, and ask and share questions that will, at a later stage, converge into thesis statements. Students no longer encounter Shakespeare as a curated, editorialized,

pre-processed narrative, but as a network of interpretive possibilities.

For example, directors filming *King Lear* must carve a path between theatrical elements ('language of drama') and discrete 'cinematic ... codes of communication'.[20] The significance of *King Lear* goes beyond the traditional binary of nihilism and redemption.[21] As students approached the tragedy, some of them invariably became hung up on the question of sympathy. While their interpretations often hinge on their ability to sympathize with Lear,[22] the collaborative exercises revealed that the question of redemption need not and should not be the sole focus of interpretive strategies. Lear can be both sympathetic and unsympathetic, both relatable and not relatable.

Further, it is productive to read Shakespeare in multilingual contexts. Consider, for example, these lines by Macbeth in response to the knocking on his gate shortly after he murders King Duncan: 'This my hand will rather / The multitudinous seas incarnadine, / Making the green one red' (2.2.59–61). The echo of 'incarnadine' and 'red' is serendipitous, but the deliberate alternation between the Anglo-Saxon / Germanic and the Latinate words suggests two pathways to consciousness and two perspectives on the world. As

[17] Danielle Spratt and Bridget Draxler, 'Pride and presentism: on the necessity of the public humanities for literary historians', *Profession* (2019): https://profession.mla.org/pride-and-presentism-on-the-necessity-of-the-public-humanities-for-literary-historians.
[18] Alexa Alice Joubin, 'Global change through Shakespeare', TEDxFulbright talk, the Fulbright Association's 42nd Annual Conference, 26 October 2019: www.youtube.com/watch?v=qvj30Z6a7AY.
[19] Edward L. Rocklin, *Performance Approaches to Teaching Shakespeare* (Urbana, IL, 2005), p. xviii.
[20] Macdonald P. Jackson, 'Screening the tragedies: *King Lear*', in *The Oxford Handbook of Shakespearean Tragedy*, ed. Michael Neill and David Schalkwyk (Oxford: 2016), pp. 607–23; p. 608.
[21] Jonathan Dollimore, '*King Lear* (ca. 1605–1606) and essentialist humanism', in *Radical Tragedy: Religion, Ideology and Power in the Drama of Shakespeare and His Contemporaries*, 3rd edn (Durham, NC, 2004), pp. 189–203.
[22] Jackson, 'Screening', pp. 611, 622.

in the exercises about textual variants, students were called upon to translate into other languages and into modern English such instances of repetitions with a difference.

The inquiry-driven collaboration also turns speakers of other languages into an asset, particularly international students who are not native speakers of English. All too often they are seen as a liability, but their linguistic and cultural repertoire should be tapped to build a sustainable intellectual community. One way to excavate the different layers of meanings within the play and in performances is to compare stage and film versions from different parts of the world. Alexa Alice Joubin has encouraged her students to translate a key passage in a canonical English text into other languages (and to report back in English) to diversify the class's interpretive approaches.[23] Students may be studying a foreign language, or they may speak a language other than English at home. Students are thus able to bring into the classroom new voices and new ways of seeing the world. This collaborative pedagogy reflects the need for racialized globalization to be understood within hybrid cultural and digital spaces. Team projects also encourage students' ethical responsibility to each other as they grow from recipients of knowledge transfer to co-creators of knowledge.

Sharing their linguistic skills, students also looked up historical translations of the plays. Caliban's word, 'language', is translated variously in different languages. For example, Christoph Martin Wieland translates the word in German as *redden*, or 'speech'. In Japanese, it is rendered as 'human language', as opposed to languages of the animal or computer language. Take another word from *The Tempest*, for example. Prospero announces in Act 4, Scene 1, that 'our revels now are ended' (148). The word 'revels' in the Elizabethan context refers to royal festivities and stage entertainments, but it carries different diagnostic significance in translation. Christoph Martin Wieland uses *Spiele* ('plays') and *Schauspieler* ('performer') to refer to Prospero's masque and actors ('Unsre Spiele sind nun zu Ende' in German). Sometimes, translators working in the same language have different interpretations. Liang Shiqiu translated it as 'games' in

Mandarin Chinese in 1964, alluding to the manipulative Prospero's 'games' on the island, but Zhu Shenghao preferred 'carnivals' (1954), highlighting the festive nature of the wedding celebration.

While textual variations and ambiguities can seem irrelevant to students, they are central to our understanding of a play and of our world. For example, is the opening division-of-the-kingdom scene in *King Lear* a psychological game to avoid 'true' love,[24] a contest of expressions of love, a political act or a classic case of a delusional ailing old father? Using open-access tools, such as Perusall.com, that incentivize and support the collaborative annotation of texts and video clips by opening up any PDF text or webpage for annotation, Alexa Alice Joubin establishes a social space where students learn from each other through the creation and circulation of freeform responses to cultural texts. In self-selected groups, some students explore historical meanings of 'cannibal', while others launch a comparative analysis of racialized representations of Caliban in Julie Taymor's 2010 film and Greg Doran's 2016 stage versions of *The Tempest*. There are multiple activation points for knowledge economies. Learning is rhizomatic and nonlinear in nature. As a result, students' experiences in class are enriched by their differentiated, individualized and yet connected explorations.

Perusall and similar computer-mediated scholarly communication platforms have been shown to enhance the quality of collaboration and promote effective learning interactions between students.[25] Annotations are gathered under thematic clusters as distinct 'conversations', as Perusall calls them, for

---

[23] Alexa Alice Joubin, 'Translation as a theme in Shakespeare's plays', *Source* 65 (2015), pp. 24–32.

[24] Stanley Cavell, 'The avoidance of love: a reading of *King Lear*', in *Must We Mean What We Say? A Book of Essays*, 2nd edn (Cambridge, 2015), pp. 246–325.

[25] Kelly Miller, Brian Lukoff, Gary King and Eric Mazur, 'Use of a social annotation platform for pre-class reading assignments in a flipped introductory physics class', *Frontiers in Education* (2018): https://doi.org/10.3389/feduc.2018.00008; J. J. Cadiz, A. Gupta and J. Grudin, 'Using web annotations for asynchronous collaboration around documents', in *Proceedings of CSCW'00: The 2000 ACM Conference on Computer Supported Cooperative Work* (Philadelphia, PA, 2000), pp. 309–18.

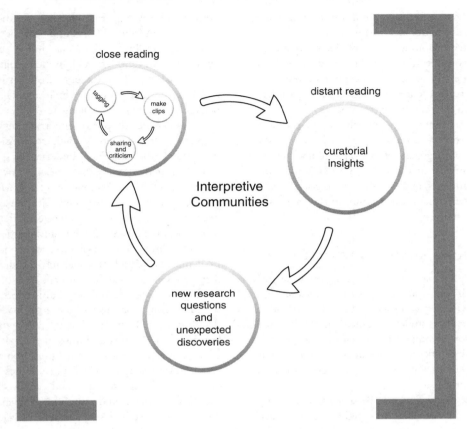

close reading

distant reading

tagging

make clips

sharing and criticism

curatorial insights

Interpretive Communities

new research questions and unexpected discoveries

1 Close and distant reading. Schema by Alexa Alice Joubin.

analysis. For each assigned text, the class would read, annotate and comment on a shared document, engaging in close reading and a critical framework of literary interpretation (see Figure 1). The interactive nature makes reading a more engaging, communal experience, because readers become members of a community.

Writing and circulating rationale for editorial and interpretive choices led to increased awareness of one's own decision-making process, known as 'meta-cognition' in educational psychology.[26] With collaborative close reading, students claim the language, in recognition of the speech act, rather than just the character in the sense of whether a character is 'relatable'. For instance, *King Lear* has opened up new avenues for linking contemporary

cultural life and early modern conceptions of ageing. In one course, Alexa Alice Joubin's students connected what they perceived to be Lear's most eccentric moments (the division-of-the-kingdom scene and the first scene at Goneril's castle) to the generational gap crystallized by the catchphrase 'OK boomer', which went viral after being used as a pejorative retort in 2019 by Chlöe Swarbrick, a member of the New Zealand Parliament, in response to heckling from another member. The goal of the class was not to determine whether

---

[26] Mary Varghese, 'Meta-cognition: a theoretical overview', *International Journal of Advanced Research in Education & Literature* 5 (2019), 1–4.

Lear shares characteristics of entitled 'boomers' but, rather, to use fictional situations to launch cultural criticism with room for both intellectual and emotional responses to the play. The peer-to-peer collaboration excavates layered meanings of key words in a play text that tend to be glossed over by students if they read the text by themselves.

By creating knowledge collaboratively, students and educators lay claim to the ethics and ownership of that knowledge, an act that is particularly urgent and meaningful in the era of COVID-19, when students, more than ever, long to be connected to others, even under quarantine and in a remote learning environment.

TEACHING AGAINST ANTISEMITISM

The same principle of radical listening can be applied to teaching 'one-issue' plays, such as *Othello* (race) and *The Merchant of Venice* (antisemitism). Radical listening activates student engagement, while ensuring that, for example, the antisemitic rhetoric isn't replicated by students in their discussions and assignments, and that Jewish students and faculty are cared for in the process.

Teaching *Merchant* can be a way to raise the awareness necessary to fight antisemitism. Students need to have some basic knowledge about antisemitism, including the Holocaust, to cope with this kind of hate and its current proliferation around the world, and Shakespeare can be one concrete case study for educating students about it. Holocaust awareness is disturbingly low, and Holocaust denial conspiracy theories currently abound. In a recent survey, the Claims Conference found that 63 per cent of adults under 40 in the United States had no idea that 6 million Jewish people were killed in the Holocaust. In a 2019 poll of eighteen European countries, the ADL (Anti-Defamation League) found that around 'one in four Europeans polled harbor pernicious and pervasive attitudes toward Jews';[27] and, overall, antisemitic hate crimes have increased. In 2019, antisemitic offences reached an unprecedented high number in the United States alone.[28] Given the frightening increase in hate crimes that are

buttressed by widespread, global antisemitism that circulates continuously through various kinds of media, especially social media, and is supported by many right- and left-wing political figures, it is crucial that the play be taught from an informed and sensitive perspective, which a Levinas-based pedagogy can help us to navigate.

A Levinas-based approach to teaching *Merchant* emphasizes treating others with compassion, as it strengthens the students' understanding of and active engagement with Shakespeare's play and language. Through the exploration of *The Merchant of Venice*, we can provide students with the awareness necessary to become actively engaged in fighting the proliferation of misinformation, antisemitic rhetoric and propaganda, and working to end the violence in its name. This kind of social justice education is desperately needed, along with anti-racist teaching, in our classrooms. Significantly, this effort to teach the play with social justice as a goal *furthers* rather than *lessens* students' intellectual engagement and learning. As Ayanna Thompson puts it, 'while Shakespeare can be a secret weapon used to get to social justice issues, social justice lenses provide deeper, more sophisticated, and potentially more complex understandings of Shakespeare. Shakespeare needs social justice pedagogies as much as social justice pedagogies benefit from Shakespeare.'[29] Teaching with the goal of social justice strengthens, rather than weakens, students' full engagement with Shakespeare's texts, for, in Hillary Eklund and Wendy Beth Hyman's words, 'we can teach Shakespeare and Renaissance literature in ways that are vital to the pursuit of justice, while also doing literary texts *themselves* justice'.[30] Indeed, teaching with social justice as an aim motivates students to engage even more fully with

27 www.adl.org/news/press-releases/adl-global-survey-of-18-countries-finds-hardcore-anti-semitic-attitudes-remain.
28 www.adl.org/news/press-releases/antisemitic-incidents-hit-all-time-high-in-2019. For select global incidents in 2020, see www.adl.org/resources/fact-sheets/global-antisemitism-select-incidents-in-2020.
29 Thompson, 'Afterword', p. 236.
30 Hyman and Eklund, 'Introduction', p. 11.

Shakespeare's texts, as well as various interpretations of them.

Although students' attitudes vary greatly depending on region and other variables, it is safe to assume that they could benefit from an overview, even if it is a brief one, of the historical contexts of antisemitism, especially in light of the surveys noted above. This overview might consist of collected visual and written texts that introduce students to the medieval treatment of Jews and antisemitic tropes that set the stage for early modern representations like Shakespeare's; modern antisemitism, pogroms and the Holocaust; the resurgence of antisemitic hate today. An overview of the historical background of antisemitism may be coupled with dramatic and theatrical history, such as the development of the Jew on stage, the Jewish moneylender and Jewish father/daughter plots, treatments of Shylock and Jessica on stage and in film. This background gives students the necessary tools to examine antisemitism in Shakespeare's early modern text and provides contexts for assessing how and why later productions on stage and screen interpret the antisemitism in the play in the way they do.

Using a Levinas-based pedagogy, students not only examine the play in both early modern and contemporary contexts, learning to think about it and the issues it raises in new ways, but also think about how to respond to the suffering of the Other with compassion. A pedagogy based in Levinas's ethics underscores the importance of recognizing the Other's alterity while feeling compassion for their pain. For Levinas, the relationship between the self and other is asymmetrical, characterized by alterity, not sameness, which Levinas calls 'non (in) difference'. In other words, the aim is *not* to fuse or become one with the Other – *not* to incorporate, consume, or colonize the Other – but rather to reach out to the Other while acknowledging, respecting and maintaining the Other's difference.[31]

Through this work on *Merchant*, students would learn that, although they feel grief for those who experienced the Holocaust, they should not assume that they can articulate or approximate victims' suffering. The effort of substitution, the attempt to put oneself in the other's shoes, must be mitigated with this awareness of alterity. This concept of non (in)difference may also be factored into analyses of performances on stage and screen, as well as in the students' own performance activities and discussion in class.

Once students have a grounding in the historical and present-day contexts and have examined the play and select adaptations of it, they can engage in a creative activity that sharpens critical skills, increases an awareness of dramaturgy, and gives students a chance to apply what they have learned – to experience the power of Shakespeare adaptations to 'talk back' to hate.

Hatred as a political tool and emotional response to difference emerges at the intersection of wilful ignorance and knowledgeable ignorance – the privileging of one singular ideology over others. The works of Shakespeare, as a canonical author, tend to inspire pursuits for singularity. One way to 'talk back' to hate is to engage with a large number of performance versions. We can raise students' awareness of multiple performative interpretations of the same scenes in *The Merchant of Venice* and encourage students to offer their readings. Students have in their own hands the power to destabilize received interpretations and expand the repertoire of meanings. The outbreak of the global pandemic of COVID-19 in early 2020 closed live theatre events and cinemas worldwide, but the crisis has led to a proliferation of born-digital and digitized archival videos of Shakespeare in Western Europe, Canada, the UK and the US. In her teaching, Alexa Alice Joubin has used one of the self-contained online learning modules (shakespeareproject.mit.edu/ explore) as part of the *MIT Global Shakespeares* (globalshakespeares.mit.edu), which she cofounded with Peter S. Donaldson. Vetted, crowd-sourced film clips with permalinks have been prearranged in clusters of pivotal scenes. While it is feasible to teach in-depth only one or two films of *Merchant* in a given class, instructors can expand students'

---

31 Emmanuel Levinas, *Totality and Infinity: An Essay on Interiority*, trans. Alphonso Lingis (Pittsburgh, PA, 1969), p. 13.

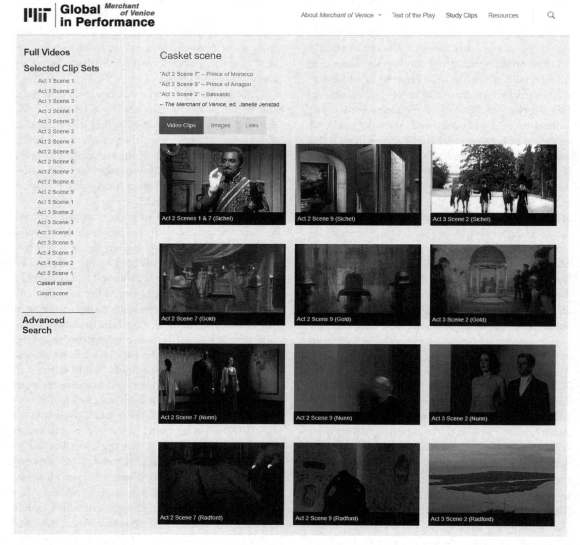

2 Clusters of video clips of pivotal scenes in a learning module, led by Diana Henderson, of the *MIT Global Shakespeares*. Students can launch comparative analyses of contrasting performances of the same scenes in John Sichel's 1973, Jack Gold's 1980, Trevor Nunn's 2001, and Michael Radford's 2004 film versions of *The Merchant of Venice*; studyshax.mit.edu/merchantofvenice.

horizons by guiding them to close-read multiple, competing interpretations of a scene, comparing side by side the portrayals of Shylock in the court scene and of Portia in the casket scene in John Sichel's 1973, Jack Gold's 1980, Trevor Nunn's 2001, and Michael Radford's 2004 film versions in a module edited by Diana Henderson (see Figure 2). While the part cannot stand in for the whole, there are unique advantages to distracted concentration as an intellectual exercise.

In an exercise designed by Lisa S. Starks, students consider how they would rewrite the play with a purpose, how they would adapt it to respond to and counter rising antisemitism today, keeping in mind Levinas's notions of substitution and non (in)difference, as well as the importance of respect for each other during collaborative work. Similarly, Alexa Alice Joubin has encouraged students to work in teams to adapt the play to film, articulating their rationale for such important elements as casting, setting and costumes. Their rewrites must address, grapple with and seek to redress the antisemitism of the play for a contemporary audience. In groups, they would first discuss several questions concerning their adaptations, writing a narrative description of their story arc, aims of the production, role of characters, and so on. There are many options for students to choose, such as the following: what if Shylock does change his mind in the trial scene while he has the chance? Would he be treated fairly, anyway? What if Jessica decides to leave Lorenzo mid-play and return to her father's home? What if Bassanio failed the casket test?

After completing this written portion of the exercise, students would then craft one full scene or trailer for their adaptation, which should include some language from the play as well as their own, submitting their scripts to the instructor for feedback and revision. Once all script revisions have been made, groups of students would perform their scenes – or, if the course is taught remotely, record their scenes to be posted online – accompanied by a cast 'talk back', in which students discuss their scene in light of the full adaptation that they mapped out. In a final reflection piece, students would discuss how and to what extent their adaptations fulfilled the goals of the assignment and what they learned in the process.

TEACHING AGAINST TRANSPHOBIA

In addition to racialized discourses, gender is a key vector in literary and cultural criticism in a time of hate. In particular, we need to be informed about transgender studies and committed to countering transphobia and transmisogyny in our classrooms and communities. Whether we identify as trans ourselves or are trans allies, we can learn how to engage better and more sensitively with students, and model how they need to treat one another, how to respect individual gender identities on and off campus. The field of transgender studies enables us to see gender and its relationship to sex from positive, nonjudgemental points of view, realizing that these differences are, indeed, authentic. It challenges the ways in which the medical field and some religious groups have condemned trans people, either by diagnosing them as pathological or declaring them to be sinful abominations of God's laws. Transgender studies compels instructors and students to pose ethical questions concerning gender and the treatment of others, and to encourage political action to promote social justice and fight against violence perpetrated against trans communities.

Transphobia arises out of anger, fear and outrage that transgendered people disrupt gender norms and destabilize boundaries, and it often results in violent hate crimes. Sadly, this violence has been on the rise in recent years. In the United States under the Trump administration, for instance, there were disproportionately more hostile anti-transgender rhetoric, policy, social media attacks and negative media portrayals, and frequent sexual violence against, and murders of, transgender individuals, in particular transwomen of colour, evidencing the prevalence of transmisogyny, as well as transphobia, in our world today. The Human Rights Campaign (HRC) reports that at least forty transgender and gender-nonconforming people have been murdered in the year ending 9 December 2020. According to the HRC, these numbers surpass any years since it began compiling these figures in 2013.[32] In the United Kingdom, transphobic hate crimes have increased dramatically, quadrupling in the last five years and increasing in the last couple of years by 25 per cent. The BBC reports that many victims of these hate crimes do not feel supported by law enforcement and have nowhere to turn for assistance.[33] These are

---

[32] www.hrc.org/resources/violence-against-the-trans-and-gender-non-conforming-community-in-2020.
[33] www.bbc.co.uk/news/av/uk-54486122.

two among numerous examples globally that indicate the violent effects of transphobia and transmisogyný, and the dire need for activism to educate and fight for the rights and dignity of the trans community. Transfeminism is deeply committed to activism on these fronts.

Over the past decades, prominent films and theatre works have fostered new public conversations about gender politics in Shakespeare around the world. Shakespeare's plays appeal to diverse audiences even though they were initially performed by all-male casts. Many modern adaptations on stage and on screen reimagine those plays as expressions of gender non-conformity. *Stage Beauty* (dir. Richard Eyre, Lions Gate Films, 2004) dramatizes the Restoration-era adult-boy actor Ned Kynaston's trans feminine iden-tities. Specializing in playing female roles such as Desdemona, Kynaston présents as female in his romantic life as well, until he is forced to play Othello. On stage, *Drag King Richard III* (dir. Roz Hopkinson, Edinburgh Fringe, 2004) told the story of a trans masculine character by repurposing Richard's discourse of his deficiency, his status of being 'deformed, unfinished . . . half made up' (1.1.20–21). A film about theatre making, *The King and the Clown* (*Wan-ui namja*, dir. Lee Joon-ik, Eagle Pictures, 2005) chronicles the life of a trans woman in fifteenth-century Korea who shares a trajectory similar to that of Ophelia. Transgender Shakespeare reached a milestone in 2015 when the Transgender Shakespeare Company was founded in London, 'the world's first company run entirely by transgender artists'.[34] When actors embody a role, their own gendered bodies – with perceived or self-claimed identities – enrich the meanings of the performance.

Beyond explicitly trans-inclusive performances, Shakespeare's plays lend themselves to analyses through a trans studies lens. Gender variance is more than just an early modern dramatic device or theatre practice. It is the core of some characters' self-expression and trajectories. Our understanding of the comedies and romance plays would change dramatically if some characters are interpreted as transgender, such as Viola in *Twelfth Night*, Falstaff dressed up as the Witch of Brainford to escape Ford's house in *The Merry Wives of Windsor*,

Rosalind as Ganymede in *As You Like It*, and Imogen disguised as the boy Fidele in *Cymbeline*.

The classroom environment is an ideal place to begin this work against hate because transfeminism calls into question the transphobia and transmisogyny that, unfortunately, often surfaces in our institutions of higher learning in particular, as well as in our culture in general. Susan Stryker and Talia M. Bettcher have defined transfeminism – a term first coined in 1992 by US activists Diana Courvant and Emi Koyama, and further developed by Anne Enke in *Perspectives in and Beyond Transgender and Gender Studies* in 2013 – as a '"third wave" feminist sensibility that focuses on the personal empowerment of women and girls, embraced in an expansive way that includes trans women and girls'.[35] Transfeminism works to save and improve the lives of transwomen and to confront violence against trans communities around the world. Transfeminism intersects product-ively with critical race studies, disability studies and other social justice fields that fight antisemitism, xeno-phobia and other forms of hate and discrimination.

Employing a Levinas-based pedagogy and informed by transfeminism, we encourage students to acknowledge and respect the alterity of each other and the diversity of gender identifications. In an open, compassionate learning environment, students then can discuss the questions, insights and practices of trans studies. This approach can enrich the way we teach literature in general, and Shakespeare or early modern drama in particular. Students examine gender and other intersecting matters that have shaped how the plays have been performed and received in early modern, modern and contemporary contexts. For instance, work in early modern trans studies on the boy actor can help students to navigate the early

---

[34] https://twitter.com/trans_shakes; on trans cinema, see Alexa Alice Joubin, 'Performing reparative transgender identities from stage beauty to the king and the clown', in *Trans Historical: Gender Plurality before the Modern*, ed. Greta LaFleur, Mascha Raskolnikov and Anna M. Klosowska (Ithaca, 2021), pp. 322–49; on the Korean film, see Alexa Alice Joubin, *Shakespeare and East Asia* (Oxford, 2021), pp. 112–20.

[35] Susan Stryker and Talia M. Bettcher, 'Introduction: trans/fem-inisms', *TSQ: Transgender Studies Quarterly* 3 (2016), 5–14; p. 11.

modern territory. In studying Shakespearian performance and adaptation in modern and contemporary contexts, classroom readings and assignments might focus on trans issues to enable students to weigh in on decisions made by artistic directors, production companies, directors and actors, and to decide for themselves what effects these choices have on spectators, as well as their communities.

One exercise might focus on representations of trans people in both popular culture and Shakespearian performances on stage and screen. Television shows, films, documentaries and other media often foreground scenes or photos with news stories that feature trans individuals dressing and undressing, as well as rehearsing their walk, talk and gestures to appear as their 'new' gender, as if they are putting on an artificial gender with their costumes, accessories and mimed behaviour. Julia Serano points out that these scenes attempt to frame transgender people as if they simply portray a gender that they are not in reality. In this sense, media and pop culture portrayals 'reinforce cissexual "realness" and transsexual "fakeness"'.[36] These kinds of scenes are standard in the productions and film adaptations of Shakespeare's comedies, which include cross-dressed characters like Viola and Rosalind, whose trans experiences are often framed as liberatory, in contrast to those of male characters cross-dressed as women, such as Falstaff in *Merry Wives of Windsor*. Rather than liberatory, his – and other instances of transfeminine experience – are often rendered as shameful, typically the brunt of a joke for other characters within the play and sometimes also the audience outside of it, at least in productions in which scenes like Act 5, Scene 5 of *Merry Wives* are staged for laughs.[37] Representations of transwomen in contemporary media and popular culture also foreground these scenes of dressing/undressing, but they amplify them even more, so that transwomen appear as hyperfeminine and hypersexed, presented in images that exaggerate traditional female traits and characteristics to which the transwoman is seen to aspire, and often reduce the transwoman into fetishized body parts.[38]

For the exercise, students would examine popular-culture examples of the representations described above, paired with comparable scenes from Shakespeare film or filmed stage productions. Showing popular-culture examples first can help students to enter into the discussion more freely and openly, without the stress of responding appropriately to the Shakespeare text. When they then view the Shakespeare examples, they can see that many of the same decisions, options and demands exist for these productions as for the others. After the viewings, students could then engage in an active discussion about both, making connections between them and their readings on trans theory and Shakespeare. Following this discussion, they could engage in an activity through which they apply what they have learned by creating their own version of a scene they viewed and compared, or another relevant scene. In this activity, students would have to decide what actors, set, staging or filming choices they would use and why. They would also need to consider how their choices would affect their entire imagined production, and how it would be received by audiences. Sawyer Kemp has argued that teaching Shakespeare's cross-dressed characters as if they are examples of trans people is misguided because of the gaping disparity between the trans experiences of these characters and the lives of and challenges faced by actual trans people in our contemporary moment. To counter this problem, Kemp advocates pairing these texts with readings by and about trans people and assigning students questions that help students to navigate the terrain of these differences; or teaching a character like Hamlet, rather than a cross-dressed one, as exhibiting trans elements.[39] Our exercise offers yet another option.

36 Julia Serano, *Excluded: Making Feminist and Queer Movements More Inclusive* (Berkeley, 2013), p. 116; Julia Serano, 'Skirt chasers: why the media depicts the trans revolution in lipstick and heels', in *The Transgender Studies Reader 2*, ed. Susan Stryker and Aren Aizura (New York and London, 2013), pp. 226–33; p. 116.

37 Simone Chess, Colby Gordon and Will Fisher, 'Introduction: early modern trans studies', *Journal for Early Modern Cultural Studies* 19 (2019), 1–25.

38 Julia Serano, *Whipping Girl: A Transsexual Woman on Sexism and the Scapegoating of Femininity* (Emeryville, CA, 2007), p. 16.

39 Sawyer Kemp, 'Shakespeare in transition: pedagogies of transgender justice and performance', in *Teaching Social Justice*, ed. Eklund and Hyman, pp. 36–45.

Although it does focus on Shakespeare's cross-dressing characters, it requires that students examine how these characters are represented *as* characters, with an eye towards how that representation – as well as those in film, television and other media – shapes cultural perceptions and attitudes towards trans people.

This exercise may be modified for whatever delivery mode is used – face-to-face or online. With a face-to-face format, students could work in small groups and determine collaboratively how they would stage the scene, and then perform it for the class; with an online format, students could write an outline and/or make a short video that summarizes and demonstrates how they would do the scene, and how that scene would fit in the larger imagined production. Whether face-to-face or online, students would be engaged in the decision-making process of production, so they would need to deliberate and consider how their productions might affect spectators and surrounding communities. And, by using a Levinas-based pedagogy, informed by trans theory, we can continue to focus not just on what material is read or digested, but how students learn actively through a compassionate awareness of others within the class and those beyond, improving the lives of trans individuals inside and outside of academe.

CONCLUSION: REPARATIVE PEDAGOGY

The silver lining of teaching in a time of hate is that the social justice turn in the arts has rekindled reparative interpretations of the classics. Since 2009, the Social Justice Film Institute in Seattle has supported activist filmmakers through its Social Justice Film Festivals. The Archbishop Fulton J. Sheen Center for Thought and Culture in New York has sponsored the Justice Film Festivals since 2015 to 'inspire justice seekers by presenting films of unexpected courage and redemption'.[40] Marin Shakespeare Company in San Rafael, California, offers drama therapy and 'Shakespeare for social justice' programmes for inmates and at-risk youths. The group use Shakespeare to 'practice being human together', because Shakespeare offers 'deep thinking about the human condition'.[41]

There is a long tradition of using literature as coping strategy.[42] Works such as *Malcolm X* (dir. Spike Lee, 1992) have played key roles in American civil rights movements and current struggles for racial equality, and Tony Kushner's play *Angels in America* has been an iconic text in the gay movement. Likewise, adaptations of Hans Christian Andersen's 'The Little Mermaid' are a constant point of reference among young trans girls in mainstream media. Renowned for their all-female productions, London's Donmar Warehouse (led by Phyllida Lloyd) aims to 'create a more . . . functional . . . society [and] inspir[e] empathy', because they 'believe that representation matters; diversity of identity, of perspective, of lived experience enriches our work and our lives'. Literature gives language to victims of psychological trauma who lose speech. The popularity of reparative readings of literature lies in the duality of a simultaneously distant and personal relationship to the words.[43]

In closing, we would like to note that diversity in higher education is distinct from advocacy journalism, which means we have to work actively against any ineffectual default to political correctness. When implemented unilaterally as a one-size-fits-all imposition, some gestures of inclusion risk becoming empty rituals. For example, having students self-identify their personal pronouns can be counterproductive; some feel uncomfortable with public confessions, while others may change their pronouns depending on context or over time. Education is only reparative when it is designed from the ground up to be truly inclusive, rather than being a mindless replica of evolving political

---

40 www.sheencenter.org/shows/justice2018.
41 Marin Shakespeare Company Shakespeare for Social Justice Program: www.marinshakespeare.org/shakespeare-for-social-justice.
42 Alexa Alice Joubin, 'Screening social justice: performing reparative Shakespeare against vocal disability', *Adaptation: The Journal of Literature on Screen Studies* (2020), 1–19 10.1093/adaptation/apaa031.
43 Donmar Warehouse official website: www.donmarwarehouse.com/about.

correctness. Independent facility with complex cultural texts enables everyone to pierce the dense, euphemistic cloud of diversity categories that tokenize individuals and fictional characters based on any given identity marker.

We propose that we employ literature for socially reparative purposes to reclaim Shakespeare from ideologies associated with colonial and patriarchal practices. As these narratives connect students to other racialized communities, times and places, the students engage with multiple, sometimes conflicting, versions of the same story. Our Levinas-inspired, intersectional pedagogy serves well a diverse student body with different learning needs.

PLAYFUL PEDAGOGY AND SOCIAL JUSTICE: DIGITAL EMBODIMENT IN THE SHAKESPEARE CLASSROOM

GINA BLOOM, NICHOLAS TOOTHMAN AND EVAN BUSWELL[1]

As elementary and secondary school educators increasingly adopt digital games to teach content in a range of subjects, and as education and game scholars turn their attention to 'serious games',[2] it is worth noting that serious games are nothing new to Shakespeare classrooms. Non-digital games and playful performance practices have long been a standard part of teaching the dramas of Shakespeare.[3] Indeed, the use of physical, play-based methods of teaching Shakespeare – or what we shall call 'playful pedagogy' – has become something of an industry in the world of Shakespeare education. Theatrical games and dramatic playfulness are central to the teacher-training programmes touted by Education departments in many well-established Shakespeare theatres. The Royal Shakespeare Company calls their programme 'rehearsal room pedagogy', Shakespeare's Globe has its 'Globe Strategies', Chicago Shakespeare has its 'drama-based strategies', and there are similar initiatives at other theatres, including the American Shakespeare Center in Virginia and the Folger Shakespeare Library. Education departments of these and other Shakespeare theatres offer specialized workshops that train teachers to use playful pedagogy in their classrooms. Some theatres, such as the Royal Shakespeare Company and Shakespeare's Globe – which face greater hurdles networking with American K-12 schools – have established residency programmes or collaborations with Schools of Education in American universities (The Ohio State University and the University of California, Davis, respectively).

[1] The development of *Play the Knave* has been supported by funding from the Social Science and Humanities Research Council of Canada through the ModLab's affiliation with the Games Institute at the University of Waterloo; and by the University of California, Davis, through an Interdisciplinary Funding for the Humanities and Arts grant. Thanks to Colin Milburn for making this funding available and for his contributions to *Knave*'s development. The *Play the Knave* education programme and research on it have been supported by grants from Margaret Bowles and from UC Davis's Humanities Institute and Senate Committee on Research. Thanks also to Sergio Sanchez for sharing his bibliographical suggestions on drama-based pedagogy; to Seeta Chaganti, Claire Goldstein and Margaret Ronda for comments on an early draft of the article; and to Sara Asnaashari and Amanda Shores for research support. All research on human subjects was approved by the UC Davis Internal Review Board.
[2] James Paul Gee, *Good Video Games + Good Learning: Collected Essays on Video Games, Learning, and Literacy* (New York, 2007); Karen Schrier, *Learning, Education and Games: Curricular and Design Considerations*, vol. I (Pittsburgh, PA, 2014); Karen Schrier, *Learning, Education and Games: Bringing Games into Educational Contexts*, vol. II (Pittsburgh, PA, 2015); Karen Schrier, ed., *Learning, Education and Games: 100 Games to Use in the Classroom and Beyond*, vol. III (Pittsburgh, PA, 2019); Katie Salen Tekinbaş, *The Ecology of Games: Connecting Youth, Games, and Learning*, John D. and Catherine T. MacArthur Foundation Series on Digital Media and Learning (Cambridge, MA, 2008); Constance Steinkuehler, Kurt Squire and Sasha Barab, *Games, Learning, and Society: Learning and Meaning in the Digital Age* (Cambridge, 2012).
[3] Milla Cozart Riggio, ed., *Teaching Shakespeare Through Performance* (New York, 1999); Edward L. Rocklin, *Performance Approaches to Teaching Shakespeare* (Urbana, IL, 2005); Rex Gibson, *Teaching Shakespeare: A Handbook for Teachers*, Cambridge School Shakespeare Series (Cambridge, 1998).

Such an extensive and long-standing investment in playful pedagogy for teaching Shakespeare is not surprising, given that Shakespeare's dramas are, after all, *plays* and thus deeply connected historically and theoretically to ludic culture.[4] But teachers are especially drawn to playful pedagogy because Shakespeare intimidates and/or bores many students – and sometimes their teachers, too.[5] With Shakespeare being the only named author in the US Common Core English Language Arts curriculum and the National Curriculum in the UK, not to mention the national curricula for language arts in most former British colonies across the world, the stakes of student disengagement are high. In workshops for teachers and students, and through published texts of all kinds, scholars associated with major Shakespeare theatres lay out the benefits of playful pedagogy for teaching the bard.[6]

But playful Shakespeare pedagogy has also been criticized by scholars who argue that its experiential, embodied methodology of learning fails to endow students with the capacity for literary, social and cultural critique, while also fostering ahistorical ideas about Shakespeare's characters and themes. Put simply, when used in Shakespeare education, playful pedagogy activities often exist in tension with social justice pedagogy, which emphasizes cultural critique, theoretical reflection and historical awareness.[7] This presumed tension between social justice pedagogy and experiential, embodied learning is surprising, given that many Education scholars have found playful pedagogy to be an ideal way of addressing social justice issues in both primary and secondary schools. Studies on what is variously called 'drama based pedagogy', 'contextual drama', 'narrative theatre' and 'drama in education'[8] have demonstrated that using theatrical techniques to play with ideas and texts – whether dramatic literature or not – spurs students and teachers to recognize and think critically about social inequities relating to embodied differences, including race and gender.[9] So why is it that when these techniques are used to study Shakespeare, social justice concerns are so often diminished or set aside? The short answer may be that ideas about Shakespeare's universalism are well-entrenched in

theatres and in schools, and it takes tremendous critical effort to dislodge learners' and many teachers' assumptions. But we would argue that the reason playful pedagogy ends up usually reinforcing, instead of critically investigating,

---

4 Gina Bloom, *Gaming the Stage: Playable Media and the Rise of English Commercial Theater* (Ann Arbor, 2018).
5 John Haddon, *Teaching Reading Shakespeare* (Abingdon and New York, 2009); Martin Blocksidge, ed., *Shakespeare in Education* (New York and London, 2003); Ralph Alan Cohen, *ShakesFear and How to Cure It: The Complete Handbook for Teaching Shakespeare*, Arden Shakespeare (London, 2018).
6 Joe Winston, *Transforming the Teaching of Shakespeare with the Royal Shakespeare Company* (London, 2015); Fiona Banks, *Creative Shakespeare: The Globe Education Guide to Practical Shakespeare* (London, 2014).
7 For a thorough introduction to Shakespeare and social justice pedagogy, see Hillary Eklund and Wendy Beth Hyman, eds., *Teaching Social Justice Through Shakespeare: Why Renaissance Literature Matters Now* (Oxford and New York, 2019). Notably, the only essay in the collection to deal with playful pedagogy is Ruben Espinosa's, which I discuss further below.
8 Education scholars use a range of terms to describe what we'll call here 'playful pedagogy'. For a good and succinct overview of the history of this approach to teaching by one of its foundational thinkers, see Gavin Bolton, 'Changes in thinking about drama in education', *Theory into Practice* 24 (1985), 151–7.
9 Foram Bhukhanwala and Martha Allexsaht-Snider, 'Diverse student teachers making sense of difference through engaging in Boalian theatre approaches', *Teachers and Teaching* 18 (2012), 675–91: https://doi.org/10.1080/13540602.2012.746502; Kathleen Gallagher and Dominique Rivière, 'When drama praxis rocks the boat: struggles of subjectivity, audience, and performance', *Research in Drama Education: The Journal of Applied Theatre and Performance* 12 (2007), 319–30: https://doi.org/10.1080/13569780701560412; Leigh Anne Howard, 'Speaking theatre / doing pedagogy: re-visiting theatre of the oppressed', *Communication Education* 53 (2004), 217–33: https://doi.org/10.1080/0363452042000265161; Carmen L. Medina and Gerald Campano, 'Drama opens critical spaces within which students access their linguistic resources to negotiate diverse perspectives', *Language Arts* 83 (2006), 10; Dominique Rivière, 'Identities and intersectionalities: performance, power and the possibilities for multicultural education', *Research in Drama Education: The Journal of Applied Theatre and Performance* 10 (2005), 341–54: https://doi.org/10.1080/13569780500276020; Nancy Rankie Shelton and Morna McDermott, 'Using literature and drama to understand social justice', *Teacher Development* 14 (2010), 123–35: https://doi.org/10.1080/13664530036996683.

Shakespeare's universalism is because playful pedagogy typically approaches the bodies of learners as tools for facilitating learning, rather than objects themselves to be critically investigated.

To begin to understand the limitations of playful Shakespeare pedagogy, we can examine a game called 'Words as Weapons', developed by the Globe Shakespeare Education team and described in Fiona Banks's helpful compendium of Globe Teaching Activities, *Creative Shakespeare*.[10] For this activity, students are divided into pairs and engage in a pretend physical battle: each player throws an imaginary weapon at the other; the victim of attack responds physically, altering the response depending on the wounding potential of the weapon. After practising like this for a little while, the teacher introduces the text: a Shakespeare scene involving conflict between two characters, such as Katherina and Petruchio in *Taming of the Shrew*. Students choose a word in the text that hurts the other character. The students then deliver lines from the dialogue, throwing their pretend weapon at the other player when the hurtful word is spoken. Banks and proponents of similar activities have shown that students, particularly those who are visual, auditory and kinesthetic learners, understand Shakespeare better when their bodies are involved in the learning process. This may be true, but the exercise also illustrates how playful pedagogy techniques might easily overlook social inequities relating to race, gender and other kinds of embodied difference. As explicated in Banks's book at least, 'Words as Weapons' does not consider what physical violence might mean for the particular characters involved in the scene, let alone the students performing those characters. The exploration of verbal banter between Katherine and Petruchio through imaginary physical violence is deeply troubling, given the play's dramatization of domestic abuse. Perhaps even more concerning is how the exercise might register for student players enacting these characters. Imagine if the partnership duelling with pretend weapons is comprised of a male student and a female student, a Black student and a White student, a student with a physical disability and an able-bodied student, a queer student and a straight student? A socially responsible form of playful pedagogy clearly needs to be framed by and provoke explicit classroom discussion about identity and embodied difference. The need to marry social justice and playful pedagogies is particularly pressing at this historical moment, when Shakespeare (like other early canonical authors) is so often co-opted to serve White supremacist aims.

But, if playful pedagogy sometimes falls short, the reason is not, we would argue, because these methods are ineffective in twenty-first-century classrooms, as some critics maintain.[11] Rather, as this brief example demonstrates, the problem with traditional playful Shakespeare pedagogy is that play-based techniques often treat the body as a transparent tool of expression. Playful pedagogy tends to dissolve student's self-consciousness about their physical selves, since immersion is presumed to be key to its success; students are encouraged to lose their inhibitions through active, physical, deeply embodied play. Undoubtedly, losing their inhibitions helps students to buy into these techniques and, thus, to learn through them. But when students are encouraged to treat their bodies primarily as tools, students' differences from each other and their historical differences from Shakespeare's characters are more likely also to dissolve and to become invisible. In this situation, it is too easy for students and teachers to fall back on old ways of thinking about Shakespeare's universalism. The key, then, is to find ways to frame the playing body, in all its differences, as an abstract concept open to critical investigation. This does not mean setting aside the body entirely and focusing primarily on difference as an analytic category, as some critics of playful pedagogy suggest. Rather, we need to redefine how the body functions in playful pedagogy in order to enable this technique to serve social justice goals.

---

[10] Banks, *Creative Shakespeare*, ch. 4.

[11] Kate McLuskie, 'Dancing and thinking: teaching "Shakespeare" in the twenty-first century', in *Teaching Shakespeare: Passing It On*, ed. G. B. Shand (Oxford, 2009), pp. 121–41: https://onlinelibrary.wiley.com/doi/book/10.1002/9781444303193; Ayanna Thompson and Laura Turchi, *Teaching Shakespeare with Purpose: A Student-Centred Approach* (London, 2016).

This article argues that one way to bridge the difference between experiential, embodied learning and the kind of social critique and theoretical reflection central to social justice pedagogy is by digitally remediating playful Shakespeare pedagogy. Although, in Shakespeare pedagogy, 'digital' has come to be associated almost entirely with film and video performances – professional and amateur, including student-generated – we are interested here in the promise of mixed-reality interfaces as a way of translating playful pedagogy techniques to the classroom. Our focus will be *Play the Knave*, a mixed-reality digital game we co-developed at the University of California, Davis.[12] Users of *Play the Knave* create virtual theatre productions via avatars on screen by performing physically in real life (RL). Because of the mixed-reality interface, embodied, physical play is mediated by the virtual body of a digital avatar that is and is not fully identified with that of the player. As such, *Play the Knave* underscores a friction between the player's physical and digital bodies. Activating this friction during play encourages learners to think creatively and critically about social and embodied differences within Shakespeare and within the classrooms where his plays are taught.

THE CASE AGAINST PLAYFUL PEDAGOGY

Before exploring the benefits of digitizing playful Shakespeare pedagogy, let us examine more closely the case for and against its current use in Shakespeare classrooms. It is worth noting at the outset that the debate about playful Shakespeare pedagogy is centred largely on its suitability for advanced learners – those in high school and above. There is widespread consensus that playful pedagogy techniques are ideal for engaging and maintaining student interest in and enthusiasm for Shakespeare. However, as Ayanna Thompson and Laura Turchi write, engagement is not a sufficient goal in the case of high school and university students, whose critical thinking and close-reading skills need to be developed. In the words of Kate McLuskie, play-based methods of teaching Shakespeare foreground 'dancing' – by which she

means physical, pleasurable, performance-based engagement – over 'thinking'. She argues that the variety of techniques that I am calling playful pedagogy overlook the complexity of Shakespeare's language in favour of delivering, through 'fun'-based lessons, a universal Shakespeare seemingly more accessible to today's students and teachers.[13] Thompson and Turchi worry, moreover, that one vital area of 'thinking' that gets set aside in playful Shakespeare pedagogy pertains to embodied difference. They note that, too often, these kinds of techniques lead teachers to overlook complex issues of race and gender in Shakespeare's plays and in the contemporary classrooms where the plays are taught.[14] Like McLuskie, Thompson and Turchi accept that playful pedagogy engages otherwise reluctant students in the study of Shakespeare, but maintain that advanced learners would be better served, to borrow McLuskie's words, by 'separating out the analysis from the experience of Shakespeare'.[15]

What is surprising about these critiques is that playful pedagogy has been shown to be highly effective for activating students' critical thinking about social justice issues when the focus is non-Shakespeare content. Education scholars have explored playful pedagogy in the teaching of a range of subjects – including not only English Language Arts,[16] but also Social Studies and even

---

[12] Gina Bloom *et al.*, *Play the Knave* (Davis, CA: ModLab, 2020): http://playtheknave.org.

[13] McLuskie, 'Dancing and thinking'.

[14] Thompson and Turchi, *Teaching*.

[15] McLuskie, 'Dancing and thinking', p. 139.

[16] Alida Anderson, 'The influence of process drama on elementary students' written language', *Urban Education* 47 (2012), 959–82: https://doi.org/10.1177/0042085912446165; Alida Anderson and Sandra M. Loughlin, 'The influence of classroom drama on English learners' academic language use during English Language Arts lessons', *Bilingual Research Journal* 37 (2014), 263–86: https://doi.org/10.1080/15235882 .2014.965360; Audrey Grant, Kirsten Hutchison, David Hornsby and Sarah Brooke, 'Creative pedagogies: "art-full" reading and writing', *English Teaching: Practice & Critique* 7 (2008), 57–72; James S. Chisholm, 'Moving interpretations: using drama-based arts strategies to deepen learning about The Diary of a Young Girl', *English Journal* 105 (2016), 35–41; Teresa Cremin *et al.*, 'Connecting drama and writing: seizing

Math[17] – and have found these techniques to be especially effective in ensuring that learners grapple with racial, ethnic and cultural differences and social inequities. Drawing especially on Augusto Boal's 'theatre of the oppressed' and Paolo Freire's 'critical pedagogy', scholars in Education have found that playful pedagogy fosters in pre-service teachers and in students 'empathy' and 'perspective-taking', reactions that can transform how teachers and students think about those who are different from them. When they take part in workshops and programmes to learn to use theatrical techniques in the literature classroom, teachers discover that 'democracy in society and equity are not "givens" and that power is distributed asymmetrically across certain groups according to race, ethnicity, social class, and gender'.[18] When used in high school classrooms, the techniques have been found to 'productively interrupt conventional notions of "multiculturalism"', leading students to grapple more deeply with gendered and racial subjectivity.[19] Clearly, the problem is not with the techniques themselves but with what often happens to playful pedagogy when these techniques are used to teach Shakespeare.

Some of the challenges of integrating playful and social justice pedagogies in teaching Shakespeare become evident in a recent study of one teacher education programme, a partnership between Globe Education at Shakespeare's Globe in London and the School of Education at the institution where we collaborate, the University of California, Davis. The programme offers pre-service teachers, who are pursuing their post-baccalaureate teaching credential, a chance to receive training in playful Shakespeare pedagogy from artist educators at the Globe. Participating pre-service teachers attend workshops taught by visiting artists; participants who wish to deepen their training after receiving their teaching credential can travel to London to participate in a five-day more intensive workshop at the Globe; and then, as part of an optional Master's degree, programme participants can pursue an inquiry-based MA project to investigate the impact of these teaching techniques in their own classrooms. Notable about the programme is that it is as committed to

equity issues as it is to teaching playful Shakespeare pedagogy – as is evinced by the name of the Center where the programme is housed, the Center for Shakespeare in Diverse Classrooms. Teachers

---

the moment to write', *Research in Drama Education: The Journal of Applied Theatre and Performance* 11 (2006), 273–91: https://doi .org/10.1080/13569780600900636; Brian Edmiston, Pat Enciso and Martha L. King, 'Empowering readers and writers through drama: narrative theatre', *Language Arts* 64 (1987), 219–28; Ann Podlozny, 'Strengthening verbal skills through the use of classroom drama: a clear link', *Journal of Aesthetic Education* 34 (2000), 239–75: https://doi.org/10.2307/3333644; Sharon Fennessey, 'Using theatre games to enhance language arts learning', *Reading Teacher* 59 (2006), 688–91: https://doi.org/10 .1598/RT.59.7.7.

17 There has been wide discussion of how these techniques can be applied across the curriculum. Bridget Kiger Lee, 'Transforming teaching and learning with active and dramatic approaches: engaging students across the curriculum / how drama activates learning: contemporary research and practice', *Research in Drama Education: The Journal of Applied Theatre and Performance* 19 (2014), 216–19: https://doi.org/10.1080 /13569783.2014.895628; Bridget Kiger Lee, Erika A. Patall, Stephanie W. Cawthon and Rebecca R. Steingut, 'The effect of drama-based pedagogy on preK–16 outcomes: a meta-analysis of research from 1985 to 2012', *Review of Educational Research* 85 (2015), 3–49: https://doi.org/10.3102 /0034654314540477. There has been extensive discussion, in particular, of the value of these techniques in teaching second language acquisition. See Julia Rothwell, 'Bodies and language: process drama and intercultural language learning in a beginner language classroom', *Research in Drama Education: The Journal of Applied Theatre and Performance* 16 (2011), 575–94: https://doi.org/10.1080/13569783.2011.617106; Christa Mulker Greenfader and Liane Brouillette, 'Boosting language skills of English learners through dramatization and movement', *Reading Teacher* 67 (2013), 171–80: https://doi .org/10.1002/TRTR.1192; Medina and Campano, 'Drama opens'; Gerd Bräuer, *Body and Language: Intercultural Learning through Drama*, Advances in Foreign and Second Language Pedagogy 3 (Westport, CT, 2002): http://site.ebrary.com /lib/ucdavis/Doc?id=10023342. On the use of these techniques for the math learning, see Yasemin Şengün and Tuba İskenderoğlua, 'A review of creative drama studies in Math education: aim, data collection, data analyses, sample and conclusions of studies', *Procedia – Social and Behavioral Sciences* 9 (2010), 1214–19: https://doi.org/10.1016/j .sbspro.2010.12.309.

18 Shelton and McDermott, 'Using literature', p. 132. For additional references, see note 9 above.

19 Gallagher and Rivière, 'When drama', p. 319.

coming out of this programme will work in public (government) schools in California, which have high numbers of Latinx students in particular, and are generally quite diverse in terms of race, ethnicity and socio-economic status. The Center's Globe teacher education programme is thus an ideal testing ground for assessing how well playful Shakespeare pedagogy and social justice pedagogy align in practice.

Initial research by Steven Z. Athanases and Sergio L. Sanchez on the programme's impact shows mixed results regarding this alignment. On the one hand, researchers found that, despite early exposure to and immersive training in 'Globe Strategies', early career teachers struggled to bridge playful Shakespeare pedagogy with their work in diverse American schools. One of the teachers in the study reported that, although her training helped her to understand how to use drama activities to improve students' comprehension and interpretation of Shakespeare, it did not prepare her to think about 'social justice implications'.[20] To be sure, such challenges are hardly unique to pre-service teachers coming out of this programme. As Todd Butler and Ashley Boyd point out, even the most well-intentioned high school teachers battle to address social justice issues in the classroom, because teacher education programmes tend to focus on content knowledge and on training pre-service teachers to use a range of pedagogy techniques that can address different student learning styles.[21] Boyd and Jeanne Dyches have argued that social justice concerns are by no means peripheral to these latter emphases, provided teacher education programmes use enhanced frameworks.[22] What is concerning about the findings from the UC Davis study is that the participating teachers were coming from a programme that employs such enhanced frameworks, taking educational equity issues as part of its 'core mission'.[23] That is, even pre-service teachers explicitly trained in social justice pedagogy do not naturally make a link between this kind of pedagogy and play-based techniques when they approach their Shakespeare curriculum. This would appear to support the concerns that Thompson and Turchi and others raise about this methodology.

On the other hand, Athanases and Sanchez's research reveals that the challenges teachers faced were not a function of playful Shakespeare pedagogy as a method, but rather of how the pre-service teachers had been exposed to the method. In 2019, the Center added a three-day Summer Institute for teachers who had completed the other stages of the programme and finished their first year teaching in their own classrooms. The Institute explicitly focused on addressing social justice concerns through the Globe's playful pedagogy techniques. Participating teachers discussed how to 'lead difficult conversations about issues including politics and power, LGBTQ rights, forced migration, and the nation's sociopolitical state' and then designed mini-units that utilized the Globe techniques to teach *Julius Caesar*.[24] Research on teacher takeaway from the Summer Institute showed that teachers became quite adept in using drama-based activities to address social justice concerns in their Shakespeare units. Taken alone, the 'Globe Strategies' did not lead to or connect easily with social justice pedagogy, but teachers could be trained to make those connections. These initial findings suggest that the problems Thompson and Turchi cite are not a function of playful pedagogy techniques themselves but of the methods typically used to distribute these techniques and train teachers to use them in their Shakespeare units.

---

[20] Steven Z. Athanases and Sergio L. Sanchez, '"A *Caesar* for our time": toward empathy and perspective-taking in new teachers' drama practices in diverse classrooms', *Research in Drama Education: The Journal of Applied Theatre and Performance* 25 (2020), 247: https://doi.org/10.1080/13569783.2020.1730170.

[21] Todd Butler and Ashley Boyd, 'Cultivating critical content knowledge: early modern literature, pre-service teachers, and new methodologies for social justice', in *Teaching Social Justice*, ed. Eklund and Hyman, pp. 225–34.

[22] Jeanne Dyches and Ashley Boyd, 'Foregrounding equity in teacher education: toward a model of social justice pedagogical and content knowledge', *Journal of Teacher Education* 68 (2017), 476–90.

[23] The Center's mission statement is available at https://education.ucdavis.edu/center-shakespeare-diverse-classrooms.

[24] Athanases and Sanchez, 'A *Caesar*', p. 241.

The question remains about how to ensure that a wide range of teachers can address timely and critical social justice issues when they implement playful pedagogy in their Shakespeare units. Clearly, a programme like the one at UC Davis is the gold standard, but replicating it across America, let alone on a global scale, is next to impossible. A programme so reliant on international travel is unsustainable in the long run due to climate change – with air travel having such a high carbon footprint – and even in the shorter term, as we have seen during the COVID-19 pandemic. As it is, few American universities have the funds to support visiting artists from London, and even fewer can afford to send dozens of pre-service teachers to London for deeper immersion. What's more, even at UC Davis, the teachers who benefitted most from the Globe Academy programme were the small minority who completed the follow-up Summer Institute. Although clearly effective, UC Davis's programme concentrates quite substantial resources on a few privileged participants and, as such, arguably ends up perpetuating inequities in schools. Wide distribution of playful pedagogy techniques is impossible if knowledge of this methodology is delivered only face-to-face and by practitioners affiliated with established Shakespeare theatres. In the next section, we'll suggest that digitizing playful pedagogy techniques not only enables their distribution to many more teachers and classrooms, but also can help to connect these techniques to social justice concerns.

DIGITIZING PLAYFUL SHAKESPEARE PEDAGOGY

The idea of digitizing playful Shakespeare pedagogy will likely strike most advocates of this method as counter-intuitive and possibly sacrilegious. For many practitioners, both within Shakespeare education and in the field of education more generally, playful pedagogy is considered an antidote to the problems of the computer age. As one Education scholar writes, it 'offers participants a focused approach to humanistic learning in a world which is becoming more and more distanced from the real values of humanity, due to an increased dependence upon electronic communication and media'.[25] Teachers participating in the UC Davis Summer Institute discussed above also mentioned using the Globe's playful pedagogy techniques to engage students obsessed with computer games and screens. By getting students up on their feet working collaboratively, drama activities refocus students with short attention spans, which many believe are the result of students' overuse of screens. Suspicion about digital technology is perhaps the most common thread uniting the diverse schools of thought on playful pedagogy. Proponents of these techniques believe very strongly in 'face-to-face social collaboration',[26] and almost all of the activities associated with this pedagogy involve students' physical interactions with each other. Digital technology would seem to undermine the privileged status of the physical body in this pedagogy.

To some extent, this concern about what happens to the physical body when digital tools are incorporated into Shakespeare teaching is well founded. Most of the 'digital theatre' tools currently available for classroom use set aside physical performance by students, inviting them instead to consume and analyse pre-produced, professional digital performances. Indeed, when Shakespeare theatres pursue 'digital' initiatives, these inevitably translate to archives of filmed theatre productions. Although some theatres have engaged in fascinating experiments with using social media platforms for theatrical productions (e.g., the RSC and Mudlark's *Such Tweet Sorrow* on Twitter, and BuzzFeed Original's *Romeo Likes Juliet*), the bulk of digital resources for teaching Shakespeare are 'live' broadcasts available on DVD or online. From the Stratford Festival to the Globe to the RSC, 'digital theatre' has come to mean access – sometimes free, usually paid – to filmed theatre productions.[27] To be sure, these filmed performances have great pedagogical value, particularly as they make global performances of Shakespeare more widely available. And, as Erin Sullivan has argued, broadcast theatre

---

[25] Margaret R. Burke, *Gavin Bolton's Contextual Drama: The Road Less Travelled* (Bristol, 2013), p. 21.
[26] Burke, *Gavin*, p. 21.
[27] As further evidence of how 'digital theatre' has become synonymous with filmed live productions, note that the content of *Digital Theatre Plus* is almost entirely filmed productions.

may even offer spectators certain advantages over traditional live theatre.[28] However, even as filmed productions provide students with access to Shakespeare in performance, they surely are not interchangeable with playful pedagogy, which is valuable because it engages students kinesthetically: instead of consuming a performance created by professional actors, playful pedagogy gets students up on their feet, moving their bodies, engaging with each other and speaking Shakespeare's language, as they create a performance together. It is no wonder that proponents of playful pedagogy are suspicious of the digital realm.

But the mere fact that 'digital theatre' in the classroom has become synonymous with screened productions doesn't mean it should remain so. Over the last decade, there have been several interesting digital Shakespeare projects that engage students more actively in theatrical performance activities, and although most of these have been used for theatre and performance history research, they have potential as classroom resources. For instance, the Simulated Environment for Theatre project developed by Jennifer Roberts-Smith, Shawn DeSouza-Coelho and colleagues offers 3D models of historical and contemporary theatre stages, and allows users to block a production by moving digital actors/avatars, which take the form of geometric shapes, around the virtual stage.[29] Roberts-Smith and DeSouza-Coelho's *Staging Shakespeare* digital game hoped to invite even more playful engagement, as users would create a virtual scene from *Romeo and Juliet* by choosing and combining digital assets that represent props, costumes and other elements of scene design.[30] These kinds of projects widen the definition of 'digital theatre' in ways that can be productive for the theory and practice of playful pedagogy, though, to be sure, they don't replicate digitally what Education scholars have found to be the most effective ingredients for this kind of pedagogy. Indeed, Roberts-Smith and team have themselves drawn attention to the limitations of their digital Shakespeare projects in terms of their ability to simulate the experience of theatrical performance.[31] In our view, this is because, although these projects are more physically interactive than watching a filmed production, they significantly restrict the

kind of kinesthetic movement in which students can engage. As is true with almost all currently available Shakespeare games, the player interacts with the onscreen avatar via a touchscreen, mouse and/or keyboard, instead of through more full-body expression, and there is little to no interaction or collaboration with others using the system.[32]

One way in which teachers have used digital tools to engage students kinesthetically in collaborative Shakespeare performance is by asking them to create video adaptations of Shakespeare, which can then be shared on YouTube.[33] Such assignments can certainly serve social justice pedagogy goals. Ruben Espinosa asked his primarily Chicanx students, who live near the Mexico–America border, to create 5-minute iMovie adaptations of Shakespeare. His students, when given 'absolute creative license', tended to emphasize their cultural and ethnic identities, and the assignment helped them to confront 'apprehensions about pressures of assimilation and the burdens of hybridity and daily bi-national cross-cultural experiences'.[34] But, in the absence of a well-crafted lesson plan that explicitly takes up social

---

28 Erin Sullivan, '"The forms of things unknown": Shakespeare and the rise of the live broadcast', *Shakespeare Bulletin* 35 (2017), 627–62: https://doi.org/10.1353/shb.2017.0047. See also Pascale Aebischer, *Shakespeare, Spectatorship and the Technologies of Performance* (Cambridge, 2020), esp. Part Three: https://doi.org/10.1017/9781108339001.

29 Jennifer Roberts-Smith, Shawn DeSouza-Coelho, Teresa Dobson, *et al.*, 'SET free', *The Shakespearean International Yearbook* 14 (2014), 69–100.

30 A beta version of the game was created but, in the end, not released.

31 Jennifer Roberts-Smith and Shawn DeSouza-Coelho, 'Shakespeare, game, and play in digital pedagogical Shakespeare games', in *Games and Theatre in Shakespeare's England*, ed. Tom Bishop, Gina Bloom and Erika T. Lin, Cultures of Play 1300–1700 (Amsterdam, 2021).

32 Gina Bloom, 'Videogame Shakespeare: enskilling audiences through theater-making games', *Shakespeare Studies* 43 (2015), 114–27.

33 For a useful overview of YouTube in Shakespeare pedagogy, see Christy Desmet, 'Teaching Shakespeare with YouTube', *English Journal* 99 (2009), 65–70.

34 Ruben Epsinosa, 'Chicano Shakespeare: The Bard, the border, and the peripheries of performance', in *Teaching Social Justice*, ed. Eklund and Hyman, pp. 76–82; p. 81.

justice issues, YouTube is hardly a progressive platform for teaching. The compulsion to receive 'likes' when a user takes up the 'broadcast yourself' mantra skews videos towards the lowest common denominators of humour, often perpetuating racial and gender stereotypes.[35] Ayanna Thompson's survey of classroom-inspired YouTube adaptations of Shakespeare produced by Asian-American students found, for instance, that the videos resort to gangster/gangsta stereotypes when representing Black characters in Shakespeare.[36] Student-generated video productions can succumb to the same problems as traditional playful pedagogy: student performers identify uncritically with the characters they impersonate. Arguably, one reason Espinosa's playful pedagogy assignment was effective, whereas the assignments that prompt many YouTube student-generated videos are not, is that Espinosa explicitly directed students to 'find a way to speak to contemporary/regional social issues' through their video performances. His assignment cued and played with the tension between students' embodied personal experiences – as Chicanx living at the borderlands – and the 'white monopoly on Shakespeare on the stage and in film'.[37] Rather than immersing themselves into Shakespeare's predominantly White characters, Espinosa's students were, in effect, being asked to interrogate the differences between those characters and their own ethnic and cultural identities. When student-generated video adaptations work to support social justice pedagogy, it is because students are explicitly asked to think about issues of embodied difference and the tension between their own embodied experiences and those of Shakespeare's characters.

In the remainder of this article, we want to think about the ways in which the digital realm and, particularly, mixed-reality platforms, such as the one we co-designed, are well suited to highlighting the friction between students' embodied identities and Shakespeare's text. Digital tools that can activate this friction are especially important in the Shakespeare classroom, where embodied differences between students can disappear beneath the weight of Shakespeare's complex, historically distant and overly mythologized text. If playful

pedagogy is to be practised by teachers less experienced than Espinosa in social justice pedagogy, and/or in the absence of a well-crafted lesson plan that explicitly draws attention to students' own embodied experiences, then we need platforms that keep the body in play (figuratively and literally) while simultaneously abstracting it. In the analysis that follows, we show how the *Play the Knave* game we designed highlights the body as both performing subject and object of performance. By not only bringing digital bodies into the classroom but also *staging* the relationship between these digital bodies and their physical RL counterparts, *Play the Knave* encourages players to abstract themselves from their embodied performances without forgetting their bodies. As such, the game prompts critical inquiry around embodied difference.

Play the Knave is a Windows-based game played via the Kinect motion-sensing camera, wherein one to four players engage their voices and physical movements to animate avatars in a digital theatre production. Although there are a range of ways the game can be used, it was initially designed for performing scenes from Shakespeare in ways that are akin to traditional playful pedagogy assignments. In this case, however, much of the labour of production is offloaded to the digital system. The platform is preloaded with hundreds of scripts of scenes from Shakespeare's dramas, or players can use an online tool we developed, Mekanimator Scriptmaker, to write and upload a script of their own making.[38] Alternatively, players can skip the script entirely, choosing the 'free play' option. Players then navigate a menu system to design their virtual theatre production by choosing from among a range of costumed avatars, theatre stage

[35] See, for example, Stephen O'Neil, *Shakespeare and YouTube: New Media Forms of the Bard* (London, 2014) esp. ch. 3.

[36] Ayanna Thompson, 'Unmooring the Moor: researching and teaching on YouTube', *Shakespeare Quarterly* 61 (2010), 337–56.

[37] Epsinosa, 'Chicano Shakespeare', pp. 81, 80.

[38] Mekanimator Scriptmaker is available open-access at http://modlab.ucdavis.edu/scriptmaker.

models and background soundtracks. Players then perform with their selected assets. If players choose a script, it will appear in chunks karaoke-style on screen so that players can recite lines aloud as they move their avatars around the virtual stage.[39] Significantly, nothing happens on screen without the player's physical input. To make an avatar speak, the player must voice its lines, reading them from the karaoke interface or improvising as they wish. To make an avatar move, the player must themselves move. As the software processes the movement data from the player, the avatar on screen mirrors the player's movements in what feels like real time. Each player's sound and avatar movement are recorded, resulting in an animated short film that can be viewed, shared or edited. In effect, players create for themselves – and most often for an audience, as well – two performances simultaneously: one virtual on screen, and one in the physical space of real life.[40] *Play the Knave* also includes a suite of mini-games designed by scholar and theatre practitioner Sawyer Kemp, and adapted from well-known theatre improvisation and character-building activities. Through these mini-games, players practise speaking, movement, analytical and/or collaboration tasks, all the while learning to navigate performance via the digital interface. The activities in which players engage through the *Play the Knave* platform are, in effect, very similar to those undertaken in playful pedagogy programmes run by Shakespeare organizations. It is the digital interface that is the primary and crucial difference with *Play the Knave*.

Research thus far has shown that *Play the Knave* engages students in all of the ways in which traditional playful Shakespeare pedagogy does. But the digital platform also helps to support teaching about embodied differences – including, especially, race, gender and size. Although Bloom's current study of *Play the Knave*'s use in secondary schools in the United States and in South Africa is too early in its development to offer overarching conclusions, we have some evidence of *Play the Knave*'s impact gathered from some primary and secondary school classrooms in the United States and from Bloom's extensive use of the game in her own university

teaching. In addition, we will discuss lesson plans Bloom has developed in partnership with secondary school teachers, since these demonstrate the game's potential and imagined uses. Our aim in the analysis that follows is less to argue for and demonstrate the pedagogical effectiveness of *Play the Knave* per se than to use the game as a case study for thinking about how and why social justice concerns can be addressed successfully by digitizing playful pedagogy.

In teaching with *Play the Knave*, and planning lessons centred on the game, Bloom has found that one of the reasons the game is so conducive to conversations about social justice and embodied differences is because the cast of avatars is extremely diverse, including characters that are legible as male, female and non-binary gender, as well as characters representing people of colour and of varying age and size, not to mention species (see Figure 3). Choosing an avatar is a standard part of many videogames, of course, but the significance of this choice is quite particular in the case of a game that is about performing Shakespeare, given that students, like the general public, tend to default to traditional ideas about casting when they think about Shakespeare performance. In his

---

[39] Jennifer Roberts-Smith and Shawn DeSouza-Coelho argue that the digital Shakespeare games produced by academics are too script-centric in their representation of Shakespeare performance, failing to embody ideas about performance that the academics themselves hold ('Shakespeare, game, and play'). They conclude, thus, that videogames are, in general, not a good medium for Shakespeare pedagogy. While I agree that most Shakespeare videogames are overly script-centric – indeed, I offer a similar critique about Shakespeare videogames failing to capture the ethos of theatrical performance in Bloom, 'Videogame Shakespeare' – this critique does not extend to *Play the Knave*. Its modular design actually makes explicit that the script is merely one among many other assets that create a performance. Not only can players choose to move their avatars around on screen without any karaoke lines appearing but, since there is no internal evaluation metric that scores players for their capacity to speak the script, even when the script is there, it does not authorize the performance.

[40] A tour of the user interface and menu system for *Play the Knave*, along with footage of students playing it, is available at www.playtheknave.org/how-it-works.html.

experience of teaching racially progressive and experimental Shakespeare performance adaptations to South African university students, Chris Thurman found that, even in a class that had significant racial, ethnic, and linguistic diversity, students were often suspicious of, or unable to make sense of, non-traditional casting and the cross-cultural settings for the plays that tend to allow for these non-traditional casting options. In Bloom's experience of teaching Shakespeare in American universities, she also has observed that some of her best students are 'stickler[s] for "authenticity"', questioning productions that set Shakespeare in modern times or global locales.[41] In short, students assume that Caesar should be a White man in a toga. And yet, as Thurman also found, when he exposed his students to traditionally cast performances alongside less traditional ones and deconstructed assumptions about 'authentic' Shakespeare, his students, including the most reluctant, could be 'freed from fealty to a false authenticity' and were able to both appreciate and thoughtfully critique filmic adaptations that set Shakespeare plays in Africa.[42]

To be sure, many teachers committed to social justice pedagogy turn to film adaptations, and, thanks to projects such as Thurman's Shakespeare.za, Global Shakespeare at MIT, and Globe to Globe, there are a wealth of resources out there for visualizing and discussing the stakes of diverse bodies in Shakespeare performance.[43] But, as we have begun to suggest above, there is a difference between seeing Shakespeare performed by different kinds of bodies and having learners embody that performance themselves: the core principle at the centre of playful pedagogy. Rather than only analysing the casting decisions made by other directors, student-generated performances put students into the position of making casting decisions themselves. Indeed, choosing an avatar directly engages students in the kind of racial justice work that theatres are reluctant or unable to do.[44] Avoidance around the semiotics of race, as well as other aspects of embodied identity, is far less likely in classrooms where *Play the Knave* is used, however. In typical student-generated productions of scenes, the logic theatres often use to avoid

discussion of the semiotics of race can persist: e.g. a particular student may be chosen for a part because she is the most talented or the only one willing to perform; or one cannot cast Black actors for a part if the class is made up entirely of White students. With *Play the Knave*'s wide range of avatars, none of which is any more talented than the next, availability of particular kinds of bodies is not a factor in casting the virtual production. A teacher need only ask students to explain their choice of avatar in order to lay bare assumptions about casting. Most of the lesson plans that Bloom and collaborators design prompt students to explain their avatar choices in advance or analyse the impact of those decisions afterwards. Both ensure that students think carefully through the semiotics of casting.

Although students' decisions about avatar casting can organically open up conversations about social justice issues, a teacher can push these conversations to the surface by insisting on the use of particular avatars as part of the lesson. For instance, Bloom has collaborated with Cape Town artist and teacher

---

41 Chris Thurman, 'Shakespeare.za: Digital Shakespeares and education in South Africa', *Research in Drama Education: The Journal of Applied Theatre and Performance* 25 (2020), 49–67: https://doi.org/10.1080/13569783.2019.1689111.

42 Thurman, 'Shakespeare.za', p. 59.

43 On teaching social justice issues via MIT's Global Shakespeare archive, see Emily Griffiths Jones, 'Global performance and local reception: Teaching *Hamlet* and more in Singapore', in *Teaching Social Justice*, ed. Eklund and Hyman, pp. 55–63.

44 Ayanna Thompson, *Passing Strange: Shakespeare, Race, and Contemporary America* (Oxford, 2011). Thompson notes that, although non-traditional casting is now the norm in much Shakespeare performance, theatre companies rarely explicitly address and help audiences to understand the semiotics of casting decisions. Thompson argues for the importance of distinguishing not only between colourblind casting (where actors are purportedly selected with no attention to their race) and 'race-conscious' casting (where the production consciously assigns some semiotic meaning to the actor's race), but also between the range of forms of the latter. Noting three significantly different forms of race-conscious casting set out by the Non-traditional Casting Project (societal, conceptual and cross-cultural), she observes that actors and audiences rarely understand which model of non-traditional casting is at work in a production.

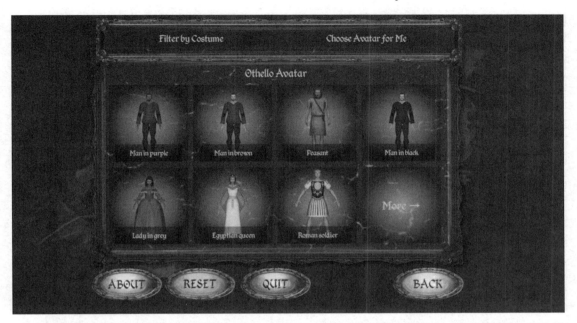

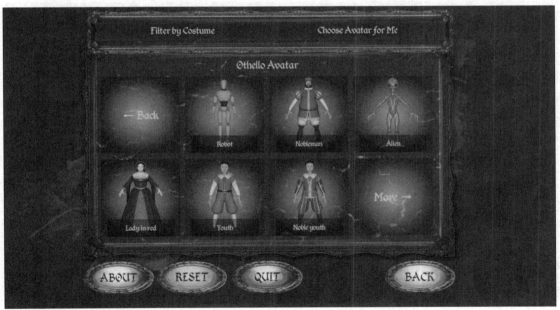

3 Six screenshots of the *Play the Knave* menu, showing avatar choices – in this case, for the character Othello.

Lauren Bates to develop a curriculum of *Play the Knave*-based lessons for South African schools that focus on violence in Shakespeare plays and in South African history and contemporary society. One lesson plan focuses on Act 4, Scene 3, of *Macbeth*, when Macduff learns of the massacre of his family.

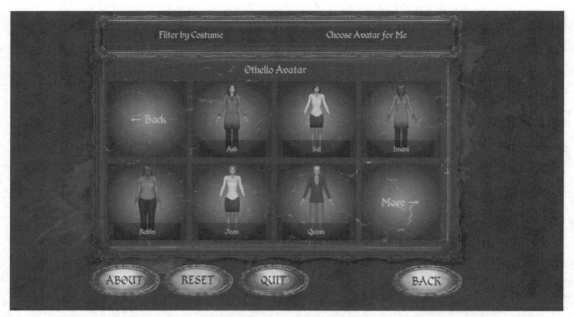

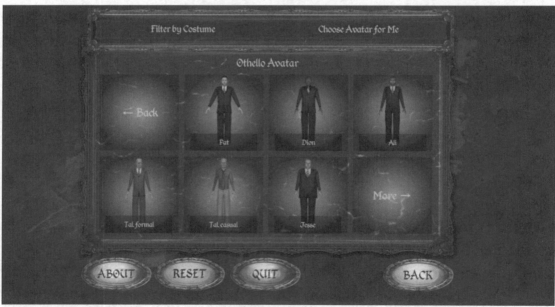

3 (cont.)

The lesson uses well-established playful pedagogy techniques – such as asking students to create statues to represent concepts in the text – to address gender stereotypes around the expression of grief. But the lesson also helps students to think about the violence of civil war in the context of South Africa, and how

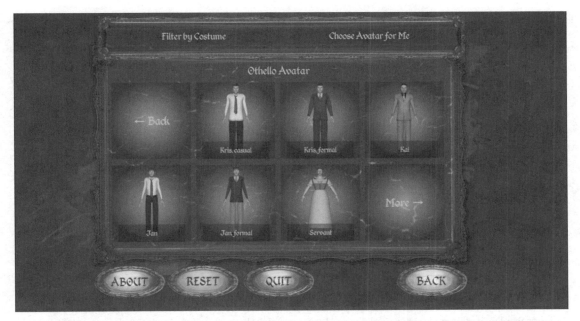

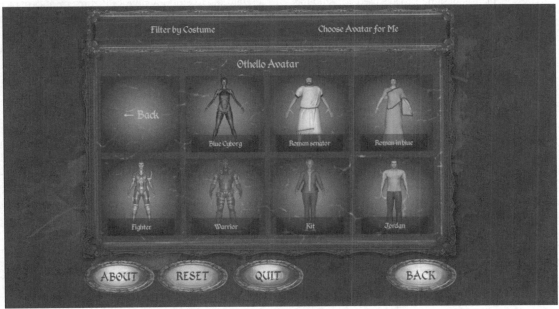

3 (cont.)

that violence impacts Black bodies in particular. To push this contemporary resonance, the lesson plan instructs teachers to choose a Black avatar for Macduff's role, and to imagine that Macduff's massacred family is Black. One of the writing assignments Bloom and Bates developed to accompany this lesson then asks students to recollect the Apartheid police's 1976 massacre of Black school children in Soweto township, a turning point in the fight against Apartheid, to encourage students to think about why, as is the case in *Macbeth*, depictions of massacred children provoke rebellion against tyrannical governments.[45] Macduff's family's blackness, conveyed through the choice of avatar, helps to introduce into study of *Macbeth* a discussion about systemic racism and violence against Black bodies in South Africa's history. Such an assignment could easily be adapted to the American context of Black Lives Matter and similar issues around racial injustice in other countries.

Another lesson plan for South African schools focuses on Othello's murder of Desdemona and uses race-conscious avatar casting to help students to think about the intersection between race and gender in domestic violence – so pervasive in contemporary South Africa that it has been called a second epidemic. The lesson plan is designed to be used for students who have not yet read *Othello* and are being introduced to the play for the first time through a section of the play's climactic final scene. Students use *Play the Knave* to perform four versions of the murder scene (created using Mekanimator Scriptmaker), progressively layering on embodied differences in each version. In the first performance, the parts of Othello and Desdemona are played by science-fiction avatars who lack clear gender markers: 'Warrior', the character speaking Othello's lines, is larger and more imposing than 'Cyborg', who has Desdemona's lines. Students perform the scene and then are asked to think about why 'Warrior' has power over 'Cyborg' and is, thus, in a position to harm the latter physically; the power dynamic between characters is found to be a function largely of their size and presumed strength differences. The second version switches to avatars legible as female and male humans, 'Imani' and 'Dion', both Black and in contemporary dress. Discussion after the performance considers again why Dion has power over Imani, which invites the students to begin thinking about gender differences and male privilege, and how these shape domestic violence. In a third performance, Othello's lines are spoken by 'Kai', a White male avatar, with Imani still in Desdemona's part. This

leads to discussion about racial difference as a factor in domestic violence, the complexities of interracial relationships, and potentially the lasting impact of South Africa's earliest history of sexual violence: the abuse of Black female slaves by White European settlers. Only in the final performance does the lesson set the scene in sixteenth-century Cyprus, with a Black Othello and a White Desdemona, both wearing Elizabethan-style clothing. Having addressed intersections of race, gender and power in contemporary contexts, students are prepared to think about how these variables signify in the historical moment represented by the play.

As these lessons demonstrate, the digital embodiment of Shakespeare characters allows students to experiment, and literally play, with embodied identity (racial, gendered, sized, historical, etc.) in a way that would be difficult in traditional student-generated performances, and impossible if using pre-made film productions of the plays. The game's casting mechanism enables students to visualize concretely and to embody physically the semiotics of race and gender in Shakespeare performance, regardless of the racial and gender composition of the students in the classroom. This is not to say, however, that students' own embodied identities will or can be overlooked. In fact, because of the mixed-reality interface – which insists that a physical body in RL move the virtual avatar – the game encourages teachers and students to think about race, gender and other variables, such as size, not just on screen but in the classroom itself. Even in less nuanced lessons than those we discuss above – such as situations where students choose their own avatars – the choice of avatar tends to open up conversations about embodied identity and its semiotic meaning because the digital avatar and the human actor perform simultaneously. When students have a choice of which avatar to use, do they choose avatars that look like

---

[45] 'Argumentative essay' assignment available at https://drive.goo gle.com/file/d/1uOeJq_7qPDm14giWRDFh_f_7eGeigAXt/ view?usp=sharing<int_u>. The full suite of lesson plans and assignments currently available for the South African curriculum is available at https://drive.google.com/drive/ folders/1vRYQTPk_zv9EKf48QCi527fYu_JzEd4t? usp=sharing<int_u>.

them or that are different from them? These conversations are especially enriched because the game's narrative (you are an actor playing a scene from Shakespeare) intersects in interesting ways with the game's mechanics (the player and the avatar are both – simultaneously – enacting the part of a character in Shakespeare's play). The bodies of digital avatar, physical player and character in the play overlap and become imbricated, though the perceived attributes of identity for each (gender, race, size, etc.) need not correlate.

In their reflections on gameplay, students often revel in this layering of identity and the 'freedom' to perform in different body types. As one of Bloom's university students wrote in response to a *Play the Knave* performance assignment in which student groups could choose their own avatars for scenes from *Henry IV, Part I*: '[*Play the Knave*] allow[s] the player to pick any gender or body type person they desire, with little to no judgement from their audience ... *Play the Knave* affords us a freedom that playing a character onstage and in our bodies does not.'[46] Another writes:

A person playing *Play the Knave* can be any shape and size playing any shape and size character, and the gender and body type of the player and the avatar by no means need to match up.... [I]t is no less plausible for a petite woman to play Falstaff than it is to have a burly man playing the same character, when the script calls for a fat, jolly older man. In other words, because the player is using a virtual avatar to enact the scene, the question of bodies in the space becomes more open-ended.

The avatars allow learners to inhabit a range of kinds of bodies and to play with identity, allowing for a kind of learning that games and education scholars argue videogames facilitate especially well.[47] One could imagine how such identification could work in service of social justice pedagogy, though it is just as easy to see the reverse. A White student who chooses and then identifies with a Black avatar has the opportunity to feel what it is like to be in a Black body, and thus potentially to understand better and empathize with the experiences of people of colour. But, as so much research on the performance tradition of blackface and minstrelsy shows, such

identification bleeds easily into exploitation.[48] Given these dangers, it seems less important to have students identify with their avatars than it is to establish, but then disrupt, that identification. Ultimately, the goal is not to see oneself in the avatar, but to think critically about the process of identification. Education scholars call this 'critical games literacy'[49] but we might also recognize it as Bertold Brecht's *Verfremdungseffekt* ('the alienation effect').[50]

---

46 Due to the terms of Bloom's Internal Review Board approved protocol, we retain the complete anonymity of the students whose work we cite.

47 Gee, *Good Video Games*; James Paul Gee, 'Video games and embodiment', *Games and Culture* 3 (2008), 253–63: https://doi.org/10.1177/1555412008317309; Sherry Turkle, *Simulation and Its Discontents* (Cambridge, MA, 2009): https://doi.org/10.7551/mitpress/8200.001.0001.

48 See, for example, Thompson, *Passing Strange*, esp. ch. 5; Karin H. deGravelles, 'You be Othello: interrogating identification in the classroom', *Pedagogy* 11(2011),153–75: https://doi.org/10.1215/15314200-2010-021; Ian Smith, 'White skin, black masks: racial cross-dressing on the early modern stage', *Renaissance Drama* 32 (2003), 33–67; Robert Hornback, *Racism and Early Blackface Comic Traditions: From the Old World to the New* (Basingstoke, 2018): https://doi.org/10.1007/978-3-319-78048-1.

49 Catherine Beavis, Christopher Walsh, Clare Bradford, Joanne O'Mara, Thomas Apperley and Amanda Gutierrez, '"Turning around" to the affordances of digital games: English curriculum and students' lifeworlds', *English In Australia* 50 (2015), 30–40; Tom Apperley and Catherine Beavis, 'A model for critical games literacy', *E-Learning and Digital Media* 10 (2013), 1–12: https://doi.org/10.2304/elea.2013.10.1.1; Catherine Beavis, Christopher Walsh, Clare Bradford, Joanne O'Mara and Thomas Apperley, 'Literacy in the digital age: learning from computer games', *English in Education* 43 (2009), 162–75: https://doi.org/10.1111/j.1754-8845.2009.01035.x; Thomas Apperley and Catherine Beavis, 'Literacy into action: digital games as action and text in the English and literacy classroom', *Pedagogies: An International Journal: Exploring Pedagogies in Popular Culture and Education Nexus* 6 (2011), 130–43: https://doi.org/10.1080/1554480X.2011.554620.

50 On the link between Brecht's ideas about character and videogames for social justice, see Gonzalo Frasca, 'Videogames of the oppressed: critical thinking, education, tolerance, and other trivial issues', in *First Person: New Media as Story, Performance, and Game*, ed. Noah Wardrip-Fruin and Pat Harrigan (Cambridge, MA, 2004), pp. 85–94.

Play the Knave's mixed-reality interface prompts critical thinking about identification, laying bare the artificiality of performance, because the game stages so explicitly the distinction between the player and the 'mask' of the avatar. Instead of naturalizing gender, race and other aspects of identity, the game's mixed-reality interface constantly asks players to consider where in the body markers of identity reside. This was especially apparent when Bloom used the game to teach the cross-dressing comedies. Bloom arranged students into small groups to perform the wooing scene in *As You Like It*, where Rosaline, cross-dressed as Ganymede, flirts with Orlando. Groups had a choice not only of which avatars to use, but also which students would enact these parts physically. The sex of the student controlling an avatar's movement and voicing its lines could match the sex of Shakespeare's actors historically (male youths), Shakespeare's characters (Rosalind and Orlando), or the fictional characters in the wooing scene (Ganymede and Orlando). More interestingly, these options were also equally available for the avatars selected. The assignment thus offered students a way to grapple in material ways with the intersections between gender and eroticism in the scene. Would performances show Orlando flirting with a male youth Ganymede, or with the female Rosaline, or both?

With very little prompting, students arrived at complex insights about how gender is embodied. One group, which argued for a homoerotic reading of the scene, selected two avatars that, they said, were clearly male. Yet the physical presence of their actors complicated their interpretation: whether by design or by necessity, one of the student actors was cisgender female. To solve this problem for their interpretation, the group decided to have the female student 'affect a male voice during her performance'. This resulted in fascinating conversations about where gender is located in the body and what makes gender legible. Another group tried to recognize the complexities of gender performance by choosing a Rosalind/Ganymede avatar that they argued was clearly male but had 'feminine clothing', making this avatar more

gender ambiguous. They also switched the predicted gender of the actors, having Rosalind/Ganymede played by a cisgender male student and Orlando by a cisgender female student.

What generated some of the most excited conversations and some of the deepest reflections were two groups (hailing from two different sections, thus not aware of the similarities in their production decisions) that chose the 'Robot' avatar to play both Rosalind/Ganymede and Orlando in the scene. Whether they selected the genderless 'Robot' for fun, or whether they did so intentionally to highlight the ambiguity of gender in the play, didn't really matter in the end, because the presence of gendered student bodies playing these avatars shaped subsequent conversations spectating students had about the meaning of the performance. As is evident in the animated films that were produced from their performances, the student groups seemed to believe they needed to contend in some way with the gender coding of the human voice, and they did so in strikingly different ways. One group, which had both characters played by cisgender male students, kept the actors' voices mostly naturalistic, thereby representing the otherwise ungendered robots as two males.[51] The other group, which had switched the predicted genders of the actors (having Rosalind played by a cisgender male student and Orlando played by a cisgender female student) took things one step further by having these students put on falsetto voices. The female student playing Orlando adopted a deep voice, while the male student playing Rosalind used a higher-pitched voice for most of the scene, breaking back into a male voice only in the final lines where Rosalind/Ganymede accepts Orlando's advances and swears to love him.[52]

Play the Knave's mixed-reality platform prompted students to think about the various

---

[51] The gameplay video is available at www.youtube.com/watch?v=mfiLDGohCGQ&feature=youtu.be&ab_channel=ginabloom1.
[52] The gameplay video is available at www.youtube.com/watch?v=SwhsUZR8ahQ&feature=youtu.be&ab_channel=ginabloom1.

places that gender gets located in the body in order to be legible: in the voice, the body shape, the body movement, the clothing worn. If students are tempted to naturalize these aspects of gender identity, the layering of human actor, Shakespeare character and digital avatar kept them thinking and rethinking how they define gender. *Knave*'s mixed-reality platform abstracts gender as a construct by drawing attention to the ways in which gender is mediated. But, crucially, that abstraction is *lived* by the bodies of the students in the room. Student performers have to contend with their own gender expression in order to produce their scenes and to analyse the scenes they and their peers produced. Because of the mixed-reality interface, students cannot ignore or naturalize gender, or other embodied aspects of identity, because embodiment, however abstract it may be, cannot remain abstract during *Play the Knave* performances.

BODIES AS OBJECTS OF CRITICAL ANALYSIS

The layering of identity we have described above is present in any game involving avatars, but is more noticeable in a mixed-reality game such as *Knave* not only because the physical body moving the avatar is so insistently on display during play, but also because the motion-capture technology creates a complex dynamic of identification that foregrounds differences between the digital avatar and the physical body controlling it. This is not simply because of the simultaneous presence of the physical actor and the digital avatar. It is because of the unique nature of live motion-capture performance, particularly the kind of motion-capture performance we use in *Knave*. To understand this point, it helps to know more about how motion capture works as a technical process. Motion-capture technology involves communication between three entities: the player, the motion-sensor camera system, and the computer that processes the captured data. The motion-capture camera system searches for clues about the moving body in the physical, real-life performance space. In the case of the high-end motion-capture systems used in films like *Lord of the Rings* (where the digitized Gollum is animated by an actor) or theatre productions like the Royal Shakespeare Company's 2016 *Tempest* production (where an actor animates an Ariel avatar via live mocap performance), the actor wears a tight-fitting suit covered with hundreds of reflective dots, and cameras use infrared or related technologies to pinpoint the position and location of the dots. Whatever camera system is used, the gathered information gets sent to a computer that quickly processes the data to attempt to decipher and reconstruct where the player/actor's body is, and how that body is moving over time. These data are almost immediately mapped onto the digital avatar, so that the player appears able to control the avatar in real time.

The quality of the motion capture will depend on the quality of all three entities involved. The camera system must be good enough to pick up data from the movement of the player's body, reading the location of the body parts accurately; the computer must be powerful enough to process the data quickly; and the player must move in ways that the technology can understand. When one component of this system is of lower quality, the other components have to compensate. If that compensation is insufficient, the system will seem to malfunction, with the clearest visible symptom being that the avatar looks 'glitchy' – it doesn't move seamlessly and/or doesn't mimic the movement of the player precisely.[53]

One can see this glitchy animation repeatedly in *Play the Knave*, which currently uses a lower-quality motion-capture camera, the Microsoft Kinect v2. The camera is ideal for pedagogical applications of *Knave* because it is cheap: $150–$250, compared to tens, or even hundreds, of thousands of dollars for higher-quality systems. It

---

[53] On the 'glitch' as a perception of viewers rather than a malfunctioning of the system itself, see Michael Bettencourt, *Glitch Art in Theory and Practice: Critical Failures and Post-Digital Aesthetics* (New York, 2017).

is also portable, allowing it to be set up by anyone, anywhere in minutes, instead of taking weeks and a trained construction crew. Finally, it doesn't require the actor to wear any special clothing or need the system to calibrate the actor's body before each performance. This means that, in the course of an hour, multiple groups of players can engage with the technology, and a technologist is not required on site. The downside of using a low-quality motion-capture camera, however, is that it more often fails to read the player's movement data. In effect, the single camera we use, the Kinect v2, sends out infrared pulses that search for the playing body using depth sensors. The software loaded on the computer (Microsoft Software Development Kit) looks for twenty-seven joints on the body that the camera's sensor finds, and tries to match those to a skeleton in its library (see Figures 4, 5 and 6). The animation is, then, only as good as the library, but also only as good as the player. For if a player crosses a hand in front of another hand, the computer cannot tell which joints have moved. Receiving imprecise data, the machine effectively makes its best guess, and the animation usually suffers, sometimes producing hilarious effects.[54]

Bloom has discussed elsewhere how the glitchy presentation of avatars presents opportunities for students to think about their relationship to digital technology, and the ethics around engaging with those that are different from them.[55] For the purposes of this article, however, we want to reflect on the ways the glitchy interface draws attention to the player's body as a performing object, which, as we have suggested, is crucial to the game's pedagogical effectiveness, especially its capacity to shape student thinking about embodied difference. To keep their avatars from looking 'glitchy', players must learn to move in ways that the system can understand. For instance, once they realize that crossing an arm in front of the body makes their avatar's arm contort sideways, players may learn that, if they want to produce a more seamless animation, they must face the camera directly and not cross limbs in front of each other. Players are thus learning

through play that their physical bodies are being objectified by the camera, as it tries to read *them*.

In their comments after they play, students often remark on how the game's mixed-reality mechanics lead to self-consciousness about embodiment. For some, this experience is uncomfortable. One student writes, 'I'll be honest and say that playing the game was pretty awkward and weird. I really don't like playing video games with a lot of body movements because I'm really conscious on how I move.' The student goes on to explain that the game makes players 'think about everything' relating to their bodies. 'You have to think about your tone, your attitude, your body movements, your projections, and even where you move on stage. You can't really just stand there and read the lines because then it comes out really plain and extremely monotone.' For other students, this emphasis on the player's body was a highlight of their engagement with the game. 'One of the unique strengths of *Play the Knave* is that it promotes player awareness of both what is on the screen and how the player fits into the game as an actor rather than simply a gamer.' Another student's comment even more explicitly connects this self-consciousness of the body to the apparent glitchiness of the avatars: 'I was acutely aware of my own body as I watched the avatar flail about on the screen as it tried to correspond to my movements. My stance seemed very unnatural.' The value of this insight was that it helped the student to discover firsthand 'how complex acting could be' and how crucial performance is to the interpretation of Shakespeare's plays, a realization that appears to have had a lasting impact: the student who made this comment went on to get her teacher education credential and to pursue an MA in Education that

[54] See, for example, the gameplay video available at www.youtube.com/watch?v=c33kzAnjBAk&feature=youtu.be&ab_channel=ginabloom1.
[55] Gina Bloom, 'Rough magic: performing Shakespeare with gaming technology' (Shakespeare Birthday Lecture, Folger Shakespeare Library, Washington, DC, 23 April 2019): www.youtube.com/watch?v=l6egGB5EayA.

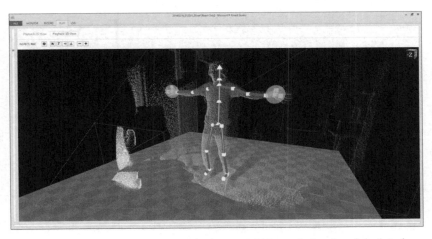

4 Screenshot from Microsoft Kinect Studio, showing Kinect depth sensors picking up the location of a body in the room, and mapping it onto a skeleton from the software library.

```
ThumbRight              Pos: 0.83, 0.53, 1.68        Rot: 0.00, 0.00 0.00 0.00
Frame 1297, SkelID 0
SpineBase               Pos: 0.11, 0.06, 1.77        Rot: 0.00, 1.00 0.05 -0.04
SpineMid                Pos: 0.11, 0.37, 1.79        Rot: 0.00, 1.00 0.03 -0.03
SpineShoulder           Pos: 0.11, 0.59, 1.81        Rot: 0.00, 1.00 0.03 -0.03
Neck                    Pos: 0.11, 0.66, 1.81        Rot: 0.00, 0.00 0.00 0.00
Head                    Pos: 0.12, 0.80, 1.80        Rot: 0.00, 0.00 0.00 0.00
ShoulderLeft            Pos: -0.08, 0.55, 1.84       Rot: -0.14, 0.09 0.76 0.63
ElbowLeft               Pos: -0.33, 0.51, 1.82       Rot: -0.50, 0.44 0.50 0.56
WristLeft               Pos: -0.60, 0.51, 1.79       Rot: -0.44, 0.50 0.48 0.57
HandLeft                Pos: -0.68, 0.52, 1.79       Rot: 0.00, 0.00 0.00 0.00
ShoulderRight           Pos: 0.30, 0.55, 1.81        Rot: 0.26, 0.09 0.77 -0.58
ElbowRight              Pos: 0.50, 0.49, 1.77        Rot: -0.57, -0.38 -0.45 0.57
WristRight              Pos: 0.73, 0.47, 1.70        Rot: -0.51, -0.43 -0.42 0.61
HandRight               Pos: 0.83, 0.48, 1.67        Rot: 0.00, 0.00 0.00 0.00
HipLeft                 Pos: 0.03, 0.06, 1.73        Rot: -0.66, -0.01 0.74 0.12
KneeLeft                Pos: -0.03, -0.33, 1.66      Rot: -0.39, 0.12 0.91 -0.04
AnkleLeft               Pos: -0.04, -0.68, 1.76      Rot: 0.00, 0.00 0.00 0.00
FootLeft                Pos: -0.09, -0.75, 1.72      Rot: 0.00, 0.00 0.00 0.00
HipRight                Pos: 0.18, 0.06, 1.72        Rot: 0.73, 0.01 0.68 -0.10
KneeRight               Pos: 0.23, -0.34, 1.67       Rot: 0.73, 0.10 0.67 0.07
AnkleRight              Pos: 0.25, -0.69, 1.75       Rot: 0.00, 0.00 0.00 0.00
FootRight               Pos: 0.24, -0.71, 1.64       Rot: 0.00, 0.00 0.00 0.00
HandTipLeft             Pos: -0.76, 0.51, 1.79       Rot: 0.00, 0.00 0.00 0.00
ThumbLeft               Pos: -0.66, 0.59, 1.78       Rot: 0.00, 0.00 0.00 0.00
HandTipRight            Pos: 0.89, 0.47, 1.65        Rot: 0.00, 0.00 0.00 0.00
ThumbRight              Pos: 0.83, 0.53, 1.66        Rot: 0.00, 0.00 0.00 0.00
```

5 The computer's calculated data regarding the perceived location of joint positions in the body the Kinect camera is sensing in Figure 4.

focused on playful pedagogy, on which she is now an authority.

Whether or not students take what they have learned about their bodies beyond the classroom, this kind of self-consciousness about embodiment is an ideal stepping-stone towards thinking about issues of bodily difference. The perceived 'glitchi-ness' of *Play the Knave* objectifies the bodies in the room in a way that traditional playful pedagogy does not. The latter treats the body as, and trains the body

6 The avatar 'skin' mapped onto the skeleton for the body shown in Figure 4.

to be, a tool for the actor's expression or for communication of something to an audience. But if our aim in playful pedagogy is not to train actors to produce meaningful performances so much as to use playful activities to encourage critical thinking about Shakespeare and the myriad issues the plays raise, playful pedagogy must do more than teach students to express and communicate with their bodies. It needs to teach them to think about how different bodies signify – how markers of bodily difference carry meaning in and out of the classroom. As *Play the Knave* stages the digital mediation of players' bodies, it prompts students to analyse embodied identity not just in Shakespeare or in digital games, but in the classrooms where the plays are studied.

DIGITAL RESOURCES, TEACHING ONLINE AND EVOLVING INTERNATIONAL PEDAGOGIC PRACTICE

CHRISTIE CARSON

In the summer of 2020, libraries were closed and the universities in the UK were in chaos, in the wake of decisions being made by the government about student results and social distancing. Writing about Shakespeare pedagogy under lockdown conditions sharpens one's focus in terms of the resources that are available, physically, digitally and intellectually. In addition to the loss of access to the libraries in person, having recently given up my position at Royal Holloway University of London, I found myself in digital isolation, in terms of access to resources that were formerly at my fingertips. The cancellation of the 2020 International Shakespeare Conference on Shakespeare and Education in Stratford intensified this isolation in thinking about pedagogic practice in my study, rather than in the classroom or in a conference seminar room. However, what remained available to me was my international network of colleagues, with whom I have been discussing for many years the possibilities that the digital world opens up for supporting the teaching of Shakespeare in performance. In addition, I had the resources of my own library, materials that I have collected in the pursuit of expanding my understanding of the way in which Shakespeare is taught locally, nationally and globally. As a result of this very particular set of circumstances, this article is more personal and relies on fewer sources than might otherwise have been the case. The pandemic lockdown both encouraged and allowed for individual reflection, but collective discussions during this time were largely dominated by the rush to move to online learning in preparation for the autumn term. This concentrated look at my own experience highlights for me the importance of reflecting on the ongoing international debate about pedagogic theory, and hopefully provides for others a context to help with understanding the current shifts in teaching practice.

This article presents an overview of the discussions about the role of digital technology in teaching over a period of enormous change. While the pandemic has accelerated the speed of transition, the movement towards online learning and an international educational market were well under way before the virus hit the world economy. Like many other 'industries', the worldwide market in educational 'products' has been forced into rapid change. My own departure from the academic world is part of that revolution and I would like to take this opportunity to reflect on what it means to remove myself from the institution to which I was attached for nearly a quarter of a century. So, this article has several aims. First, I would like to provide an overview of two parallel processes: the development of digital resources for teaching Shakespeare (particularly in performance), and the evolution of teaching in the digital environment (in real life and online). I want to make a clear distinction between digital resource creation and online learning. While the former has been my aim and area of work since 1996, the latter is relatively new to me and to many colleagues working in Shakespeare studies. Second, I would like to illustrate, through my own experience, the extent to which teaching has become of interest to governments and businesses, as never before. The international 'market' for educational products and the trade in degrees and the 'student experience' have become big business. The online world has helped to support this shift to internationalization and commercialization, but the two processes are not synonymous. And, finally, I would like to look towards a future where the online world can help to facilitate a more collaborative and egalitarian teaching environment. One of the key changes which I will chart is the shift from a Shakespeare world which was predominantly Anglo-American in its focus for the first decade of the twenty-first century to one which is now genuinely global.

The wholesale shift of university teaching to the online environment during the pandemic created a step change which might otherwise have taken a decade or more to achieve. However, the immediate need for an alternative to in-class learning has accelerated change in a way that resulted in many more top-down directives than might otherwise have been the case. Shakespeare teachers have been slowly adopting digital resources in the classroom over the last twenty years, but in the past decade they have been presented with an embarrassment of riches when it comes to online materials, from digital editions to performance recordings to theatrical archive materials, all of which are now widely available. However, the trouble with the speed of change during the pandemic is that many teachers have been thrust into the middle of what has been a slow evolutionary process of development for those of us who have been dedicated to this research field for many years. During the summer of 2020, new methods of teaching were developed under duress, and sometimes with a sense of animosity and frustration. Here, I consider how the developmental process of resource creation has been ignited by the sudden shift to online teaching, but also why this speed may well result in the creation of resources and approaches that favour business models over pedagogic aims. Through a survey of materials published on the topic of teaching Shakespeare over the past two decades, combined with a personal account of the current state of affairs, I hope to demonstrate

that pushing teachers into the marketplace unprepared may result in the dissolution of the degrees that many carefully curated online resources were designed to support. The dangers to the university system are real, but so too are the opportunities. It is important to contemplate both elements of this crucial moment of change. To conclude, I consider potential futures that might result from these changes. In particular, I document a webinar event I set up with Digital Theatre Plus and the Asian Shakespeare Association, which genuinely brought together an international panel of scholars/teachers to talk to a global audience looking for advice and guidance when asked to teach Shakespeare online.

EARLY DIGITAL RESOURCE CREATION: PRESERVING THEATRICAL PRACTICES

The development of online resources for the study of Shakespeare in performance has been my aim for the past twenty-five years, beginning with the first digital edition of a Shakespeare play published by an academic press to focus on performance history. *The Cambridge King Lear CD-ROM: Text and Performance Archive* aimed to create an example of the way in which digital technology could help to illustrate the changing attitude towards editing and performance of Shakespeare's plays over time. The ability to trace trends in performance was also a central aim of the next large project I undertook, 'Designing Shakespeare: An Audio-Visual Archive, 1960–2000', which drew together four databases of material to demonstrate the way the canon had been visualized for audiences in Stratford-upon-Avon and London over a forty-year period. The deep vertical approach of the CD, which looked at one play over 400 years in the English-speaking world, was replaced in this second project with a more horizontal view of the entire canon in two key cities in the UK. In addition to information about over 1,000 productions, this project featured more than 3,000 images of performance, 10 3D models of the stages most used for performance, and 8 interviews with key designers.

As an area of theatre history that had been over-looked, this project used digital technology to focus attention on the work of designers in a key period of performance history when practices were rapidly changing. It also tried to expand the kinds of resources that were freely available at the time. In particular, the 3D models of stages and interviews were relatively new forms for teachers and students to incorporate into teaching and research.

In *Looking at Shakespeare*, Dennis Kennedy articu-lates the issue that the research project *Designing Shakespeare* was created to address: 'the visual history of performance, which has been mostly excluded from Shakespeare studies, rewards extended investi-gation because of its intriguing relationship to the status and uses of Shakespeare, both in the theatre and in the culture at large'.[1] The early stages of the internet allowed for the creation of an audio-visual database that illustrated not just the 'visual history of performance' Kennedy describes but the changing relationship between the plays and their increasingly international audiences over time. Conceived in collaboration with theatre designer Chris Dyer and theatre photographer Donald Cooper, the project was created to fill a gap in the study of Shakespeare in performance for students and scholars working in Shakespeare studies, theatre history and practical stage design. In order to give a rounded experience of the forty-year period that was covered, and to utilize fully the communication properties of the online environment, it was decided that interviews with key designers describing their interaction with directors, the text and the production process were essential. The designer is an often-overlooked linch-pin in productions, and we wanted to illustrate how design could present a valid form of Shakespeare interpretation, alongside the more widely studied practices of acting and directing. In fact, for many audience members, design creates a lasting con-nection with the plays that bypasses the chal-lenges of the Elizabethan text. Theatre design is the link between the past and the present for any audience trying to understand these 400-year-old texts in performance. *Designing Shakespeare* used the newly available properties of the internet to chart the activity of designers from 1960 up until the end of the twentieth century in order both to explain and to preserve it.

The twenty-first century has seen an enormous rise in the availability of digital resources for the study of Shakespeare in performance, and this has resulted in a move in criticism to incorporate more aspects of production, particularly by scholars working outside large urban centres with estab-lished theatre traditions. However, these approaches often fail to acknowledge the rich his-tory of theatrical performance of these plays. *Designing Shakespeare* was created to give users access to several different forms of memories of the performance events of the past to remedy this situation: visual imagery, review extracts, 3D models of theatres that indicate scale and audience relationship in performance, and the memory of the production process by the designers them-selves. A shift from looking at the production in isolation to the process of creation as a social and cultural artefact was key for the creators of this archive. Peter Brook, in *The Empty Space*, articu-lates why this was necessary. He writes:

It is not only the hair-styles, costumes and make-ups that look dated [after five years]. All the different elements of staging – the shorthands of behaviour that stand for certain emotions; gestures, gesticulations and tones of voice – are all fluctuating on an invisible stock exchange all the time. Life is moving, influences are playing on actor and audience, and other plays, other arts, the cin-ema, television, current events, join in the constant rewriting of history and the amending of the daily truth.[2]

Providing access to the thoughts and motivations of key designers from the past, and the social and spatial constraints of the theatres they were work-ing in, was key to highlighting the fact that the plays in performance are not just a form of enter-tainment but are part of an ongoing cultural history that records, and even influences, the way these plays help to form our vision of ourselves. As Kennedy writes, 'the visual signs the performance

---

[1] Dennis Kennedy, *Looking at Shakespeare* (Cambridge, 1993), p. 4.
[2] Peter Brook, *The Empty Space* (New York, 1968), p. 16.

generates are not only the guide to its social and cultural meaning but often constitute the meaning itself'.[3] The increased access to recordings of performance since 2000 has elevated interest in these artefacts, but they are often cut off from their own history, dissociated from the complex ongoing cultural conversation that *Designing Shakespeare* documents. Brook's acknowledgement that history is rewritten (almost daily) is a salient point to highlight in our changing times and one that raises the importance of accurately documenting the recent past.

Increasingly, editions of the plays now routinely include elements of performance history, but they usually miss out any significant analysis of the role of design. Theatre history and English, as disciplines, have increasingly been broken down into segmented studies of the past: Greek, Early Modern, Restoration and contemporary theatre and literature are all studied and analysed separately, often in different departments. This goes against the reality of a continuous post-Restoration Shakespearian performance history and practices that are more akin to the Eastern disciplines, such as Kabuki or Noh Theatre. Design practice has moved, as the result of computer-based design tools, increasingly away from realism towards a focus on spatial design and projection. This shift is wonderfully exciting but often does not acknowledge the lessons learned from the designers of the past. Like so many aspects of the digital world, reinvention and translation to a new medium have been imagined as the creation of things that are entirely new. In order to learn from the rich and complex design history of the past, it seemed essential to give students and researcher access to the experiences of designers working on productions during an important evolutionary moment in the continuous performance history of Shakespeare's plays. The aim of the interviews with designers, in particular, was to capture the working methods of practitioners before they were forgotten, or even erased, by the increasing availability of more recent practices, but also more current productions and reflections. Reintroducing context and cultural history to

contemporary performance was the purpose of the research project 'Designing Shakespeare: An Audio-Visual Archive, 1960–2000'. The photos, reviews, interviews and 3D models captured what things were like before the huge changes of the early twenty-first century took place; they tell the back story to the present moment.

TEACHING SHAKESPEARE IN THE TWENTY-FIRST CENTURY: PHASE I — INNOVATION AND EXPERIMENTATION

A lack of understanding of the history of human society and culture became an increasing problem in the classroom of the early twenty-first century. While access to information had expanded exponentially on the internet, its quick consumption often seemed to take precedence over experience, and the acquisition of facts began to replace an appreciation of accumulated knowledge. The 'expert' opinion was increasingly sought, but then was also increasingly scrutinized as biased. As the hierarchies of knowledge of the past, with their incumbent political and social pressures, have been exposed through shining a light on institutions that had remained closed and protected until now, questions about access to power have rightfully been asked. The exposition of the inequalities and improprieties at the heart of some of the world's largest industries has altered what is considered appropriate, or even possible, to say and do. The power structures of government, the financial world and the entertainment industry were most prominent in the headlines during this decade, but the universities also came under scrutiny.

Looking at my own progress during the first decade of the twenty-first century and mapping it onto work published during this decade, it is possible to chart the slow shift of pedagogic practice which increasingly brought both digital resources and the study of performance into the Shakespeare classroom. In 1999, I began work on *Designing*

---

[3] Kennedy, *Looking*, p. 5.

Shakespeare in the Drama Department at Royal Holloway University of London. In 2003, I moved from the Drama Department, where I was building digital resources, to the English Subject Centre (the national centre for teaching and innovation in this subject), where I was given the opportunity to discuss the use of digital resources in the classroom nationally and to share with colleagues my approach to digital performance history. Working at the English Subject Centre gave me access to colleagues across the country through the events that they organized to discuss pedagogy. I was even given the opportunity to run two national events myself on Teaching Shakespeare (May 2004 and September 2006). The aim of the Centre was to collect, collate and disseminate the work going on in the sector, rather than to evaluate it and determine best practices (as the government had hoped). Preparing teachers working within the system to approach departmental meetings armed with information on national trends was the objective. Evaluation of successful teaching was left to those who came and participated in the conversations about pedagogy. The dialogue was often heated, but always supportive and collegial.

Teaching the plays is not a static business and to illustrate some of the changes that were taking place over the first decade of the twenty-first century I rely on three collections of published material – by Neill Thew, Christie Carson and Farah Karim-Cooper, and G. B. Shand – as well as my own experiences in the English Subject Centre, to highlight the key changes that took place. In 2006, the English Subject Centre produced a report entitled *Teaching Shakespeare: A Survey of the Undergraduate Level in Higher Education* by Neill Thew. The report came out of an Advisory Board Away Day in 2005, as the result of a session entitled 'Shakespeare and the Curriculum' chaired by Ann Thompson. In her foreword to the report, Thompson states:

Every so often, we get a mild media frenzy about the 'dumbing down' of both secondary and tertiary education which, in so far as it relates to English teachers, tends to be accompanied by assertions that students are reading supposedly 'easy' contemporary writers and are not being required to read 'difficult' writers from the past. Most of us who have taught first-year students at university would probably agree that they come to us with quite a narrow range of reading experience and that one of the very few pre-1800 authors they have read is Shakespeare.[4]

The report takes a snapshot of activity in the UK in the academic year of 2005–6 and presents some illuminating results. In *Shakespeare's Globe: A Theatrical Experiment*, Farah Karim-Cooper and I put together a collection of essays that documented the work of the Theatre and Education Departments at the Globe during its first ten years. The unusual practice of turning the theatre over to pedagogic practice for half of the year and employing actors as Globe Education Practitioners provides evidence of the innovative practices of this theatre. The third volume I turn to here is G. B. Shand's edited collection *Teaching Shakespeare: Passing It On*, which brings together thirteen esteemed Shakespeare scholars to discuss their teaching practice. As Shand points out in his introduction: 'It's a curious fact that although teaching and supervision occupy the greater part of any Shakespearean's day-to-day life in the profession, and reach many more people over the course of a career than does the whole of one's scholarly output . . . they are the area of most people's practice that we tend to know least about.'[5] This 2009 collection includes chapters by scholars/teachers in the US and UK who have together accumulated 'something close to five hundred years of experience in the Shakespeare classroom'.[6] These three resources – one statistical and UK-based, the other two reflective and transatlantic – prove the ideal starting point for consideration of the evolution of Shakespeare

---

[4] Ann Thompson, 'Foreword', in Neill Thew, *Teaching Shakespeare: A Survey of the Undergraduate Level in Higher Education*, p. 2: https://issuu.com/englishsubjectcentre/docs/shakespeare.

[5] G. B. Shand, 'Introduction: passing it on', in *Teaching Shakespeare: Passing It On*, ed. G. B. Shand (Oxford, 2009), pp. 1–10; p. 3.

[6] Shand, 'Introduction', p. 2.

pedagogy over the first decade of the twenty-first century. They look at the same question from different angles and help to illustrate the differences, but also the similarities, between the dominant North American and British ways of organizing the teaching of the subject within a larger framework of humanities tuition.

Shand, in his introduction, highlights a key element of my position: 'the Shakespeare experience in the northern hemisphere has frequently been transatlantic'.[7] A number of the contributors in his collection have taught on both sides of the Atlantic Ocean. Richard Dutton, in a chapter entitled 'Divided by a common Bard? Learning and teaching Shakespeare in the UK and USA', illustrates the most notable difference between these two systems when he describes his arrival at Ohio State University after teaching at Lancaster University for many years:

I was, for the first time ever, absolute master of my own classroom. I set my own syllabus, chose my own plays, the order in which to study them, and the perspective from which they would be studied; I chose and set my own assessment – all freedoms which US professors take for granted, but which are still rarities in England.[8]

Shand points out how this difference in university structures manifests itself in the writing of the contributors:

while no one from North America discusses the university or governmental systems (whether of constraint or opportunity) within which their Shakespeare teaching happens, all the British contributors . . . are concerned to place their teaching in its institutional contexts, from the individual department up to the impact of governmental policy and public attitude.[9]

As a Canadian who has worked in the UK for my entire academic career, I certainly fall into the second of these categories, but I was exposed to the North American model as an undergraduate student and have continued to teach North American students through summer programmes. I understand the freedom of the North American system, but must acknowledge it can be open to the possibility of abuse. I am aware of the constraints of the British system, which can hold teachers back

from making bold pedagogic choices, but also recognize the value of collegial discussions of standards of practice. One environment where US and UK pedagogic approaches were combined was at Shakespeare's Globe. Working with the Theatre and Education Departments at the Globe provided an enticing alternative which stood outside the established educational and cultural establishments during this decade.

As a UK academic, I want to highlight here how governmental policy had a direct and positive impact on the work of Shakespeare academics in the UK in the period between 2000 and 2009 through my experience working with a uniquely British entity, a government-funded centre dedicated to teaching innovation in higher education, but also recording the unfunded experimental approaches of Shakespeare's Globe. The English Subject Centre report (2006) provides an overview of what was being taught in the undergraduate programmes across the country. The Executive Summary makes the outcomes clear:

There is a great deal of Shakespeare teaching going on across the sector. Fully 73% of respondents run one or more compulsory courses including significant study of Shakespeare at Level 1. 80% of respondents offer optional courses devoted to Shakespeare at Levels 2+. Many of these courses have very large student enrolments. At Level 1, for example, over half of the respondents are dealing with groups of over 150 students.[10]

The report expresses concern about how well prepared the students arriving at university were for studying Shakespeare, 'with 89% of respondents considering their students at best adequately and often poorly prepared for their studies'.[11] The way in which the courses were structured varied across the country with plays taught chronologically, by genre

---

[7] Shand, 'Introduction', p. 9.

[8] Richard Dutton, 'Divided by a common Bard? Learning and teaching Shakespeare in the UK and USA', in Teaching, ed. Shand, pp. 196–214; pp. 209–10.

[9] Shand, 'Introduction', p. 9. [10] Thew, Teaching, p. 3.

[11] Thew, Teaching, p. 3.

or by theme, but largely by specialists in the field. For the purposes of my argument, two findings are of greatest importance: first, that 'every single Shakespeare text was being taught in full somewhere in the UK'; and second, that 'the majority of respondents use film, electronic/internet resources, and theatre performances as part of their teaching'.[12] The first of these points illustrates the need for a wide range of performance resources to be available, and the second shows the desire to use them in the classrooms nationwide – quite an impressive statistic given the limited number of internet resources available in 2006. But other outcomes of the survey were perhaps less surprising. The way the classes were being taught remained remarkably stable: 'Lectures and seminar remain the most commonly used teaching modes – but newer methods (such as learning through performance) are being introduced.'[13] The final point worth highlighting is the fact that 'There is increasing innovation in assessment, though such innovation is largely concentrated in the post-92 sector.'[14] These statistics reflect my own experience of the sector at this time, both in conversations with colleagues at teaching events and through my own teaching of a large first-year core Shakespeare course in the English Department at Royal Holloway. At the start of the twenty-first century, there was considerable excitement about the use of performance in studying Shakespeare in English Departments, and film and electronic resources were seen as the ideal way to develop innovative teaching approaches. In fact, it was these factors which resulted in my move from the English Subject Centre to the English Department at Royal Holloway in 2004, where I took up the challenge of introducing performance into the curriculum.

In the introduction to *Shakespeare's Globe: A Theatrical Experiment*, Karim-Cooper (a graduate of the English Department at Royal Holloway) and I articulate why we wanted to include an account of the education work as a contributing factor in the success of the enterprise: 'we hope to demonstrate that experiment-led thinking did not confine itself to theatrical practice at the Globe by highlighting the significant interventions that Globe Education has made, not only in Shakespeare studies but in

educational practice nationwide'.[15] In documenting the work of the Education Department with students at all levels, as well as the research work that allowed scholars to come to the theatre to test practical ideas about the plays, the collection illustrates how the Globe provided a significant intervention in the development of practice-led approaches to teaching Shakespeare. The Director of Globe Education, Patrick Spottiswoode, points out the special position of his Department:

The Globe is unique among theatres, in my experience, in its commitment to education. From October to April, Globe Education has exclusive use of the stage so that all workshops and courses can include practical work in the theatre.... We do not educate for the box office. The Artistic Director and the Director of Globe Education are colleagues. We work in support of each other but also on independent projects for our own particular audiences.[16]

In his chapter entitled 'Research and The Globe', Martin White points out the significance of the fact the theatre space was made available to academics who wanted to test specific research questions:

I see the research into past theatre practices as akin to a series of laboratory experiments in which one seeks to identify and test assumptions or discoveries about particular texts and implications for their performance in a way *simply not possible* without the reconstruction. This work is based on the axiomatic link between stage languages (physical and verbal) and the performance space in which those languages are articulated.[17]

The coming together of the theatre and education worlds was very much at the heart of the Globe project from the start, as Spottiswoode points out: 'The dynamic and creative exchanges between our

[12] Thew, *Teaching*, p. 3. [13] Thew, *Teaching*, p. 3.
[14] Thew, *Teaching*, p. 3. 'Post-92 sector' refers to those UK higher education institutions, formerly polytechnics, that were given university status in or after 1992.
[15] Christie Carson and Farah Karim-Cooper, eds., *Shakespeare's Globe: A Theatrical Experiment* (Cambridge, 2008), p. 6.
[16] Patrick Spottiswoode, 'Contextualising Globe Education', in *Globe*, ed. Carson and Karim-Cooper, pp. 134–46; p. 134.
[17] Martin White, 'Research and The Globe', in *Globe*, ed. Carson and Karim-Cooper, pp. 166–74; p. 169.

two worlds enable us to pursue Sam Wanamaker's idea of a maverick theatrical experiment with education at its heart.'[18]

While White and Spottiswoode point out the creative tension of the theatre and education worlds coming together, I highlight, in the same volume, the coming together of North American and British attitudes towards Shakespeare performance and teaching, but also the difficult marriage of commerce and art: 'While the Globe Theatre was initially set up as a scholarly project, it is run as a commercial venture and has succeeded largely because of the broad appeal it has for a range of new and old theatre audiences.'[19] After ten years of trying to reconcile these opposing forces, even the optimistic Spottiswoode expresses some frustration at the developments he was witnessing in 2008:

As Bankside is slowly swallowed up by corporate London and as some of the old 'liberties' are being colonised into an area called 'More London', it is imperative that the Globe retains a maverick spirit, continues to sit happily in the margins of the cultural establishment, challenges rather than comforts ideas about heritage and offers much more than more Shakespeare.[20]

So, during this decade, the commercial world and the government became increasingly involved in capitalizing on London's cultural organizations. It was only a matter of time before these approaches would be transferred into education. In fact, the two worlds, of theatre and education, were being asked to work together by 2005, in service of larger interests than educating a new generation of enquiring young mavericks.

In Shand's collection, Carol Chillington Rutter documents her excitement about being 'the beneficiary of progressive government policy' which allowed her to advance the study of performance in the English Department at Warwick University. She describes the government initiative designed to encourage scholars to become creative in their thinking about teaching by working with cultural organizations:

In 2005, the Higher Education Funding Council for England (HEFCE) launched 74 Centres for Excellence in Teaching and Learning across England. Each of these

CETLs has a specific project and remit, and is funded for five years. The CETL I direct, called the CAPITAL Centre (an acronym: Creativity and Performance in Teaching and Learning), is, as the bid document puts it, a unique venture to forge a partnership between a university and a theatre company.[21]

Rutter goes on to describe what went into the bid document which helped to secure this Centre for Teaching and Learning that brought together Warwick University staff with theatre practitioners from the Royal Shakespeare Company. The outcome, she says, would achieve an 'interdisciplinary approach to teaching and learning by creating a shared space for academics and practitioners – teachers, students, writers, actors – to inform each other's work'.[22] The underlying assumption was that good teaching should use the same approaches as were employed in the rehearsal room. Rutter's excitement about the project is palpable: 'I think of CAPITAL as "a third room": not exactly a rehearsal room; certainly not a classroom; but a space where the practices of actors and students can meet, converse and learn from each other.'[23] The collaborative conversation of the CAPITAL Centre illustrates the emergent thinking about teaching Shakespeare in the UK at the time.

However, despite the enthusiasm of the participants and the extraordinary amount of work that went into developing the programme at the CAPITAL Centre, it never actually did what the government hoped that it might. The aim of the seventy-four Centres of Excellence was to achieve what the Subject Centres refused to undertake, the development of teaching methods that could be given a badge of quality and rolled out across the country. The scheme aimed to develop new methods of approaching all of the subjects of tuition across the university sector using digital

---

[18] Spottiswoode, 'Contextualising', p. 134.
[19] Christie Carson, 'Democratising the audience?' in *Globe*, ed. Carson and Karim-Cooper, pp. 115–26; p. 121.
[20] Spottiswoode, 'Contextualising', p. 145.
[21] Carol Chillington Rutter, 'Playing Hercules or laboring in my vocation', in *Teaching*, ed. Shand, pp. 215–31; p. 226.
[22] Rutter, 'Hercules', p. 227. [23] Rutter, 'Hercules', p. 227.

resources that included industry input as the ideal business model. However, the government formulated the project with the sciences in mind, where often one large laboratory can serve a regional community and there is a discernible industry that might fund research and development. A similar approach, when applied to the teaching of Shakespeare, resulted in some wonderful projects (and some very lucky students) but it did not inspire a wholesale shift in pedagogic practices in the field. The uniqueness of the approach taken by the CAPITAL Centre may also have been somewhat exaggerated. The Royal Shakespeare Company has had a very long-standing relationship with the University of Birmingham through the Shakespeare Institute, so this relationship was not unprecedented. The English Subject Centre Report points out how a movement towards performance was an emergent trend elsewhere in the country in 2005.

In fact, in Shand's 2009 collection, the notion of the classroom as a shared space for exploration dominates. Jean E. Howard, in her chapter entitled 'Teaching Shakespeare: mentoring Shakespeareans', asks the following questions: 'So what is it that we do when we mentor those who will go on to become our professional colleagues and successors? Is it a teachable skill, a highly individual art, or simply a duty? What do we mean by mentoring, anyway?'[24] She describes the teaching of graduate students, rather than undergraduates, as in the English Subject Centre report and Rutter's chapter, but the point remains: is teaching in the humanities about conveying particular knowledge to students, like learning the Periodic Tables, or does it require another model? Shand says about his contributors, 'At the foundation of their teaching activities, all the contributors are consumed with transferring critical and reading skills from themselves to their students, with empowering the "clientele", with making themselves, in Russ McDonald's happy formulation, obsolete.'[25] McDonald, in his chapter, states, 'The teacher's ultimate goal, then, is to instigate a disappearing act in which the talents and capabilities of the instructor are transferred to, adjusted, and extended by the student.'[26] Like a good parent, in

this model, the teacher should create within the student the ability to carry on his or her work without guidance.

There is, of course, a difference between these approaches – Howard's vision of the mentor, Rutter's vision of the rehearsal room, and McDonald's vision of the instructive example – and it manifests itself in the capabilities of the resultant students. What does a student who has completed the courses of these instructors look like? In each case, it seems to be a version of the teacher but one who moves forward with different aims, depending on the instructor. Looking first at Howard's view: 'Consequently, the mentoring relationship can't be all top-down and hierarchical, no matter how much I have skills to impart and experience to transmit. I have to hear as well as talk in order to be able to tease out from students the commitments and intuitions and insights that will be the decisive factors in their projects.'[27] McDonald, by contrast, speaks in defence of the lecture as a means of communicating more than simply information on a topic:

When [the] lecture functions properly, then its receivers are no less intellectually vigorous than the speaker. Ideally students' minds are even more active as the ideas presented interact with their own intellect and experience. The lecturer supplies a model of analysis, constructs and transmits a mode of comprehension, whatever the topic. Having devoted vast intellectual effort to mastering this material, the speaker invites the auditor to assimilate and share it, to master their methodology or that technique for reading so that the student can absorb, reproduce, and eventually surpass the model, ultimately advancing the cause of scholarship further.[28]

I hesitate to point out the gendered language here, of mastery and advancing the cause of scholarship (as if it were a battlefield), but there does seem to be

---

[24] Jean E. Howard, 'Teaching Shakespeare: mentoring Shakespeareans', in *Teaching*, ed. Shand, pp. 11–24; p. 13.

[25] Shand, 'Introduction', pp. 2–3.

[26] Russ McDonald, 'Planned obsolescence or working at the words', in *Teaching*, ed. Shand, pp. 25–42; p. 28.

[27] Howard, 'Teaching', p. 18.

[28] McDonald, 'Obsolescence', p. 34.

a feeling that, for McDonald, the teacher must be on a different level, literally and figuratively. Howard's approach has more to do with a relationship in which teacher and student walk side by side.

Rutter has another approach, which is neither a combative face-to-face exchange nor a mutual ambulatory adventure. Her vision, which uses performance metaphors and examples, is that of the teacher as critical friend – or, perhaps more accurately, the audience:

I'm one who thinks that theatres and universities need each other, that actors and students interpret each other to each other. Shakespeare, it appears, thought so too. In *Love's Labour's Lost*, it takes a pedant and his crew performing that play of the Nine Worthies to deliver the final *coup de grâce* that shows us, the audience, just how foolishly doomed is the antisocial project of those crass, would-be academic recluses who intend to dedicate themselves to books rather than life. And in *Hamlet*, the players, the *play*, need Horatio, the postgrad student from Wittenberg, to witness, to spectate, to make sense of what is being performed.[29]

In my own teaching, I have often used Shakespeare's own dramaturgical techniques to gain the attention and sympathy of my audience/students. The experience of the actors at Shakespeare's Globe has been that playing on that very exposing stage, in full daylight, is an exercise in audience interaction more akin to teaching than to performing to an audience in a darkened space. As the original artistic director Mark Rylance puts it: 'Actors have to learn how to give and take focus, and find new ways of playing the essential situation of the story in this building.'[30] The command of the stage / lecture hall is more about communication than performance, and power must be shared. Rylance writes: 'This architecture does demand much more from an actor. It demands we get over our fear of the audience; that we convince them eye to eye of our reality, that we light our stage with our voices. It gives the audience a different power.'[31] Rylance discusses the Globe audience as one that returned time and again and was influenced by the performances they saw, but also took a hand in creating the theatrical event

each night. Similarly, the ongoing dialogue in the classroom over a term is developmental and iterative. Teachers learn from students, as well as the other way around. In this, I agree with Shand's assessment:

But the wonderful difference between pedagogical obsolescence and that of last year's automobile or cell phone, is that we get to do it all over again, semester after semester, term after term. With a little thoughtfulness and a lot of luck, we even get to do it better. The Shakespeare vocation is organic and ongoing, more like sourdough starter than like a dead computer.[32]

My students, I hope, will run farther and faster than I have been able to, but I hope it will be in generally the same direction. Like Rutter, I have relied on the plays as guides in the practices of tuition and audience interaction, as well as seeing them as the sources of great poetry.

But Shand's collection also includes scholars who look at the way that teaching Shakespeare can give students a sense of agency by awakening in them 'a consciousness about their own positions in a society that has historically traded upon fixed roles and that has often elected to judge on the basis of predetermined affiliations', to quote Ramona Wray.[33] Wray, along with Kate McLuskie, Fran Dolan and Ania Loomba, all address the way teaching the plays can be a first step in challenging the students' existing vision of the world around them.[34] By looking at early modern performance, it is possible to examine what the students see as *their* history. And, as Loomba points out, 'We must

---

[29] Rutter, 'Hercules', p. 229.

[30] Mark Rylance, 'Research, materials, craft: principles of performance at Shakespeare's Globe', in *Globe*, ed. Carson and Karim-Cooper, pp. 103–14; p. 108.

[31] Rylance, 'Research', p. 108.   [32] Shand, 'Introduction', p. 3.

[33] Ramona Wray, 'Communicating differences: gender, feminism, and Queer Studies in the changing Shakespeare curriculum', in *Teaching*, ed. Shand, pp. 142–59; p. 157.

[34] See Kate McLuskie, 'Dancing and thinking: teaching "Shakespeare" in the twenty-first century', in *Teaching*, ed. Shand, pp. 121–41; Fran Dolan, 'Learning to listen: Shakespeare and contexts', in *Teaching*, ed. Shand, pp. 181–95; Ania Loomba, 'Teaching Shakespeare and race in the new Empire', in *Teaching*, ed. Shand, pp. 160–80.

necessarily either challenge these histories, or rehearse them. There is no middle ground.'[35] So, Rutter's idea of an audience is extended here to the vision of the classroom as mirror, as well as window, on the world. Digital resources that feature international performance have a role to play here.

McLuskie adds another level of complexity to the debate, particularly in the UK context. She looks at the way in which teaching Shakespeare has always been associated with particular governmental agendas, in a much more negative way than in the case of the Subject Centres and the Centres of Excellence. She goes back to the Thatcher government to examine the impact of a Conservative government which was determined to force through changes in industrial relations, making way for a new model for commercial relations in the UK. (The strikes by the miners and print journalists were met with strong-arm tactics which aimed to crush organized labour relations.)

An additional aspect of this change in industrial relations involved creating a more vocationally focused and instrumental system, imposed on all levels of education from primary schools to universities. A key factor in those debates was the discussion of the place of 'Shakespeare' in the National Curriculum that was introduced into schools in 1988. Its aim was to ensure that the experience of education should produce clearly identifiable ... 'learning outcomes' for children across the whole state system of education in the UK.[36]

This agenda, to regularize and commodify educational provision, was at the heart of the governmental policies in the UK in the early twenty-first century. My experience of working with initiatives like the English Subject Centre (ESC) and the CAPITAL Centre was that they undertook heroic acts of resistance to the overall aims of the government project to standardize university education across the nation. While resistance was both possible and productive at this time, partly because of the collaborative work undertaken with theatres like the Royal Shakespeare Company and Shakespeare's Globe, the efforts of these initiatives were unsustainable once the funding ended, and are largely unknown to younger scholars who have entered

the teaching profession under a very different regime in the decade that followed. The maverick spirit of experimentation at Shakespeare's Globe was wonderful to experience but difficult to maintain.

TEACHING SHAKESPEARE: PHASE 2 — INDUSTRIALIZATION AND INTERNATIONALIZATION

In 2014, taking inspiration and instruction from the colleagues that Shand draws together in conversation in his collection and combining it with my own experiences of documenting changing cultural and historical trends in performance, I worked with Peter Kirwan from Nottingham University to create an edited volume that would highlight the shifting structures of higher education and changing individual responsibilities for academics in a digital Shakespearian world. The collection we created aimed to point out how the areas of research, teaching, publishing and performance were all altered by digital technology. Through examining the whole spectrum of activities undertaken by academics, it was possible to show how digital methods were shifting educational practices towards commercial models on every level. The involvement of 'industry players', which was encouraged by the early government initiatives, had become part of the fabric of the system by 2014. But it is important to point out that the participants in these industries were far from hard-nosed industrialists – rather, they were increasingly the students who had been trained in the academic system but now were working in publishing, the heritage industry and the performing arts. In order to draw together a range of perspectives to illustrate this complex web of pedagogic influence in the second decade of the twenty-first century, it was essential to extend the focus of examination beyond the classroom. Therefore, the two government initiatives I was involved with (ESC and CAPITAL) in the first

---

[35] Ania Loomba, quoted in Shand, 'Introduction', p. 7.
[36] McLuskie, 'Dancing', p. 128.

decade of the twenty-first century inspired me to include a section on teaching in the collection I co-edited with Peter Kirwan on *Shakespeare and the Digital World*, and guided my hand when I was asked to act as Consulting Editor for the 2020 themed issue of *RiDE* (*Research in Drama Education*) entitled 'Teaching Shakespeare: Digital Processes', edited by Henry Bell and Amy Borsuk.[37] It is the contributors to these two volumes who inform my conclusions about teaching in the second decade of this century, where increased industrialization and internationalization became the norm.

In these two collections of essays, the editors felt it was important to acknowledge the extent to which conferences, publications and performances that formed the focus of analysis in teaching Shakespeare in the Anglo-American world up until this decade were often seen as universal – or at the very least dominant, mainstream. So, while the first collection of essays draws together contributors for the research and teaching case studies that 'include only professional academics currently working with higher education establishments in Britain, Australia and the United States',[38] the second includes writing by educators in Canada, Cyprus, Greece, Mauritius, Singapore, South Africa and Turkey, as well as the UK and the US. Both collections address the world outside the higher education establishment. In *Shakespeare in the Digital World*, the volume has a broad focus:

The second half of the book opens up the theoretical debate to look at the future by discussing publishing, communications and performance in an online world more generally. Given that the world of Shakespeare contains a wide range of participants in the online world we felt it was important to include perspectives coming out of the library, archive, publishing house, theatre company and heritage industry as well as the academy. In this half of the book we include fewer professional academics working in traditional settings and more Shakespeare researchers working in a variety of professional environments.[39]

In the *RiDE* journal, the decision was made to include creators of digital resources outside the realm of those who might consider themselves to be 'Shakespeare researchers' in the theatre and publishing industry. In other words, decision makers, directors, producers and commissioning editors, who work with a range of materials and do not specialize in Shakespeare, coming from Shakespeare's Globe, Digital Theatre Plus, Bloomsbury's Drama Online and Cambridge University Press's Cambridge Core. In both volumes, the specific work of individual teachers in the classroom is set beside the work of professionals operating in large international organizations that deal with Shakespeare in an open, public commercial environment. The role of large commercial distributors of digital resources became increasingly important during this decade as the students trained by the earlier set of initiatives and internet familiarity reached the university ready and eager to study performance. Innovation in the classroom was happening everywhere during this decade, but the extent to which outside forces were impinging on the work of the teacher varied hugely. This is something these collections tried to address.

Being a teacher of Shakespeare in the second decade of the twenty-first century was a much more complex endeavour than it had been in the past. Kirwan and I point out that 'colleagues working in the wider online field of Shakespeare studies tend to have a more self-conscious sense of developing their own identity within a flexible framework, rather than adopting an existing identity and following predetermined intellectual pathways'.[40] We note how 'identity is often hybrid' for those working with Shakespeare (often not exclusively) if they work in publishing or the theatre. The introduction of an impact agenda in the UK encouraged many academics to step into the public arena through

37 Christie Carson and Peter Kirwan, eds., *Shakespeare and the Digital World: Redefining Scholarship and Practice* (Cambridge, 2014); Henry Bell and Amy Borsuk, eds., 'Teaching Shakespeare: Digital Processes', special issue of *Journal for Research in Drama Education (RiDE)* 25 (2020), 1–7: https://doi.org/10.1080/13569783.2019.1704241.

38 Christie Carson and Peter Kirwan, 'Shakespeare and the digital world: introduction', in *Shakespeare*, ed. Carson and Kirwan, pp. 1–8; p. 5.

39 Carson and Kirwan, 'Digital world', p. 5.

40 Carson and Kirwan, 'Digital world', p. 5.

online courses, television and radio programmes and newspaper articles, to comment on current events through a Shakespearian lens. But this extension of the boundaries of the remit of the academic often led to even less time going into thinking about teaching. In his introduction to the section on teaching, Kirwan writes about the way teachers were adopting digital methods in the classroom but without thinking about the pedagogic implications:

In the UK, fee increases and growing concern for the 'student experience' as a Key Performance Indicator for universities inform a climate in which student evaluation of teaching environments, and the student's sense of their value for money, are increasingly important factors in institutional spending. Across the last decade, the number of digital initiatives designed to support teaching – from e-books to virtual learning environments, open-access online courses to tablet devices in the live classroom – has proliferated. Yet the speed at which new technologies are adopted does not always leave time for *pedagogic* reflection on how and why they are being used.[41]

Kirwan goes on to highlight the potential opportunities that a digital pedagogy offers.

Crucially, this book suggests a pedagogy that is at once appropriative of new digital tools (allowing us to improve what we already offered) and generated by those tools (opening up things previously impossible). The modern Shakespeare teacher is required to strike a balance between allowing technology to dictate pedagogy, and utilising effectively those resources that are already part of the student's skills base.[42]

So, like the government initiatives that preceded this period, the market-driven proliferation of digital resources combined with a student population concerned with value for money presented a double-edged sword. The individual teacher in the classroom still held quite a bit of autonomy (although less in the UK than in the US) and students continued to be interested in studying Shakespeare, so there was a fundamental opportunity here. But it was one that was increasingly difficult for teachers to take advantage of because of the pressures placed on them by institutions that were keen to appease and entertain, rather than challenge, their customers/students.

Kirwan points out another paradox in the world of digital teaching of Shakespeare: the pull between the live and the virtual (a challenge that was increased with the requirements of social distancing).

Paradoxically, the shift in tools has led to students coming both closer to and more distant from Shakespeare. Closer, insofar as facsimile editions, performances and live lectures are now accessible via electronic databases, video sites and virtual learning environments. More distant, in that the media can end up standing for the thing itself; why go to an archive when Early English Books Online is a password key away; why go to the theatre when Digital Theatre Plus has recorded it for you?[43]

The sudden availability of recorded performance has made it possible for teachers of Shakespeare who work miles from a professional theatre to make performance part of their curriculum in new ways. The response to the lockdown by theatres, many of which made their recorded performances freely available for a limited time, helped to introduce many teachers to resources that they had not had access to before. The online world became a lifeline for teachers and students during lockdown, and Shakespeare resources filled an important gap in providing content that was seen to be worthwhile for all involved. But, again, this use of Shakespeare resources did not necessary involve any serious thought about the way pedagogic practices were shifting. Kirwan points out the link between the increasingly important position of online learning and the teaching of Shakespeare:

The disjunct between liveness and distance is perhaps best expressed in the expansion of distance-learning courses. Shakespeare has for many years held a major presence in the lifelong learning/correspondence course market, but the twenty-first-century shift in universities towards widening participation and remote learning has placed Shakespeare at the centre of international courses rooted, nonetheless, in named academic institutions.[44]

---

[41] Peter Kirwan, 'Defining current digital scholarship and practice: introduction', in *Shakespeare*, ed. Carson and Kirwan, pp. 58–62; p. 58.

[42] Kirwan, 'Defining', pp. 58–9. [43] Kirwan, 'Defining', p. 59.

[44] Kirwan, 'Defining', pp. 59–60.

Shakespeare's work was called to action in many ways in the digital environment in this decade, but the attention drawn was dissipated through the many channels of delivery which existed. Kirwan concludes, 'the digital classroom now demands a much more imaginative process of students, asking them to step outside of the physical classroom and inscribe their own identity into a globally shared learning discourse'.[45] The shift towards a global digital Shakespeare education economy was enhanced by the celebrations of the Cultural Olympics of 2012, Shakespeare's birth in 2014, and his death in 2016. During this period, the international market seemed to be searching for a commodified educational experience that had global appeal. The work of Shakespeare in performance and adaptation suddenly seemed like the one thing that may be able to unite educators and students, to create a real sense of a global community, yet this arena was largely controlled by commercial players.

The most recent collection of essays I worked on as Consulting Editor carries the subheading 'Digital Processes' and it tries to address this issue head on. As Bell and Borsuk point out in the introduction to the volume, 'teaching Shakespeare with digital technologies is an ongoing *process*, always occurring in the present tense but responding to a rich and varied tradition'.[46] The fact that 'processes are quickly outmoded, updated, disseminated, requiring a constant state of critical reflection' was made evident by the fact that this volume was published in February 2020,[47] just a month before the COVID-19 virus would make the processes it describes critical for scholars of many other topics beyond the realm of literature and the humanities. The *RiDE* collection is genuinely international in its scope, which leads quickly to questions of access to resources; Bell and Borsuk note 'the varying teaching contexts presented highlight the lack of a level playing field in relation to the accessibility and functionality of digital resources'.[48] The inclusion of both teachers who struggle to give access to digital platforms to their students and interviews with the creators of those platforms provides a balanced picture of the current state of affairs.

With the best will in the world, both Robert Delamere of Digital Theatre Plus and Margaret Bartley of Drama Online had to admit to bias in the collections of materials they make available. The editors point out how 'the issue demonstrates the breadth, scope, strengths and pitfalls of global tools like Digital Theatre+, Drama Online and Cambridge University Press, which must balance between casting a wide net and supporting specific institutional, cultural-pedagogical needs'.[49] As with the positions of resistance employed by the educators working in the English Subject Centre, the CAPITAL Centre and Shakespeare's Globe, the teachers of Shakespeare whose work is documented in this volume were able to read digital resources through their own lenses. Bell and Borsuk state:

Digital engagements with Shakespearean text not only serve as a gateway into an interest in digital production and performance but also as an entry point for studying the English language (and culture). Parallel to this, digital Shakespeare resources can serve as a vector for provoking student introspection about their position in their specific cultural and sociopolitical contexts that can challenge authoritative readings and meaning-making processes.[50]

The ability of individual students and teachers to read the resources made available – admittedly often from a White Western perspective – creates a new opportunity for the development of cultural understanding. Loomba's vision of challenging accepted histories is relevant here. The stated goal of the volume is to 'help maintain and create collaborative global networks linked by digital Shakespeare'.[51] My role as Consulting Editor was to introduce the editors to some of the existing collaborative connections which I have been party to, and to open the door for new contributors

[45] Kirwan, 'Defining', pp. 61–2.
[46] Bell and Borsuk, 'Teaching', p. 2.
[47] Bell and Borsuk, 'Teaching', p. 1.
[48] Bell and Borsuk, 'Teaching', p. 4.
[49] Bell and Borsuk, 'Teaching', p. 6.
[50] Bell and Borsuk, 'Teaching', p. 6.
[51] Bell and Borsuk, 'Teaching', p. 6.

to this discussion from across the globe. The resulting volume combines reflective teaching practices with accounts of the aims of digital resource creators.

The work that I have outlined here demonstrates that innovative teaching of Shakespeare using digital resources is not new. Over the past twenty years, there have been a series of important initiatives which have helped to shape the way digital pedagogy has changed the teaching of Shakespeare. It is no longer necessary to travel to the library or the theatre to have access to world-class resources; they all now come directly to the desktop (although economic and institutional barriers to access exist). But having access to materials and creating a productive collaborative conversation in the classroom are not the same thing. This survey of the recent past and the writing on pedagogy that it has inspired is designed to point out that this is a conversation that must not stop. Kirwan and I write about the challenges involved in taking a snapshot of current practice: 'Where we are now is both a practical, physical question and a metaphysical and theoretical issue.'[52] And as Bell and Borsuk point out, it is one that is always pertinent. Answering the question 'Where are we now?' at this moment is particularly difficult. It is impossible to know whether the changes being made to accommodate the current crisis will become permanent practice. To imply that I can see beyond the pandemic is tempting fate. However, by taking a lesson from my own early work, when I helped to record design history through interviews of important designers, I believe it is equally important to capture changing pedagogic practice as it happens.

POSSIBLE FUTURES

The pandemic lockdown has made me realize the extent to which my connections in the Shakespeare world are largely virtual already, with the odd real-life meeting breaking up the more dominant email conversations. As a result of this realization, I decided that my reaction to the pandemic shift to online learning needed to be one which came out of my experiences of the past. The outcome has been two new kinds of collections of viewpoints. The first is a series of Zoom interviews which I have posted to a YouTube channel.[53] Again, the aim here was to bring together colleagues with a range of experiences to discuss their recent encounters with their students and institutions online. This is an ongoing project which will aim to chart the changes of the 2020–1 academic year as it progresses. The second collection of viewpoints I curated was a panel of experts to speak at a webinar on Teaching Shakespeare Online, hosted by Digital Theatre Plus and sponsored by the Asian Shakespeare Association, on 17 September 2020.[54] This webinar brought together pairs of colleagues to create a dialogue that was both practical and international and, not too surprisingly, it involved some of the contributors to the print publications I describe above. The first pair in conversation were Bell and Borsuk, bringing with them the experience of drawing together the case studies in the *RiDE* journal. Next, two colleagues from the Shakespeare Institute (Erin Sullivan and Abigail Rokison-Woodall) discussed their work with distance learners worldwide in the past, present and future. Then, finally, two colleagues from the Singapore National University (Yong Li Lan and Roweena Yip) described their involvement in the multilingual A|S|I|A performance archive, and the course they developed collaboratively with students that employs this resource.[55] These practical discussions about teaching were bookended by the presentation of two key resources: the Shakespeare-in-performance materials available on the Digital Theatre Plus platform, presented by Talia Rodgers;

---

[52] Carson and Kirwan, 'Digital world', p. 5.

[53] Interviews with colleagues are available on the Globe to Globe Again YouTube channel here: www.youtube.com /channel/UCluarRA8d2FRjWwm9i176Jw.

[54] The webinar can be found here: https://education.digi taltheatreplus.com/teaching-shakespeare-online-webinar-0.

[55] *Asian Shakespeare Intercultural Archive* (A|S|I|A), 2nd edn, National University of Singapore: http://a-s-i-a-web.org/en/ splash.php. See also Yong Li Lan and Roweena Yip, 'Teaching with the Asian Shakespeare Intercultural Archive (A|S|I|A)', *Research in Drama Education: The Journal of Applied Theatre and Performance* 25 (2020), 8–25: www.tandfonline.com/doi/full/ 10.1080/13569783.2019.1687291.

and the digitally enhanced texts made available on the LEMDO (Linked Early Modern Drama Online) platform based at the University of Victoria, presented by Janelle Jenstad.[56] The fact that teachers could ask questions during the presentation meant it met part of the aims set out by Bell and Borsuk, to grow international collaborative networks.

The sponsorship of the event by the Asian Shakespeare Association raised a number of questions in terms of creating an international dialogue about pedagogic practice in this area. The first issue was an extremely pragmatic one. A 10 a.m. start in the UK accommodated all of the speakers (but one) and audiences in Europe, India, Australia and New Zealand, as well as in Asia. Asking the North American audience to view the recorded version of the conversation helped to shift attention away from a Western centre of influence. The webinar was designed to challenge several assumptions about teaching Shakespeare. The first was that innovative teaching only happens in the Anglo-American world. The second was to highlight the way in which digital technology enables the study of performance, not only in English. And, third, it tried to show how senior colleagues, who were more familiar with the content of the course curriculum, were working with junior colleagues, who were more familiar with the communication practices and technologies used: an example of Shand's 'Passing it on' in action, but working in two directions. Unfortunately, the rate of change in the pandemic made it very difficult for colleagues to have time to prepare their own classes, let alone have time to help others. This aspect of the crisis may have the greatest impact on the next generation of scholars. Going through the process of trying to accommodate the world as potential audience members meant that we challenged ourselves to think differently about setting up such an event. In 2021, the World Shakespeare Congress will be in Singapore, which helps to highlight how this shift to the East is a general movement, not one that is specific to this event. The key with the webinar was to make certain that a new configuration of expertise was created, but also recorded for future reference.

These two activities, conducting interviews and creating an international webinar which spoke across national boundaries, provided two new models for pedagogic debate and development. Inevitably, others will emerge out of the current crisis. But there is another issue to address: the increasing influence of industry partners, for better or for worse. I chose to work with Digital Theatre Plus on the webinar largely because it stands outside the established academic practices the other resource providers represent. Bloomsbury's Drama Online and Cambridge University Press's Cambridge Core both have digital texts of the plays that are used in teaching, but these are connected with very particular histories of editorial practice through the Arden and Cambridge editions of the plays. The fact that Digital Theatre Plus comes at the question of pedagogy from a performance perspective places this organization on a different trajectory – in a way, it is more akin to Shakespeare's Globe. Shakespeare pedagogy in the Anglo-American academic world has been structured and institutionalized in the past through the work of publishers. Having stepped outside the institution myself, I wanted to work with an organization that was not bound by any particular editorial practices. The inclusion of LEMDO in the debate was designed to show that there are new ways to develop editions that are particular to the internet and independent from traditional publishers. The fact that LEMDO brings together three previous textual endeavours, the Internet Shakespeare Editions, Renaissance Drama and the Queen's Men's plays, means that a new tradition is being developed that places Shakespeare within the larger canon of early modern plays. Again, this is a movement which has been taking place onstage at the Royal Shakespeare Company and Shakespeare's Globe and in the classroom over the past two decades. However, the publication of anthologies of plays that include Shakespeare alongside other authors has not been popular or profitable.

---

[56] See www.digitaltheatreplus.com/education, and LEMDO (Linked Early Modern Drama Online): http://lemdo.uvic.ca.

The online environment allows for this kind of mixing of texts and performances, which opens the door for more innovative course creation in the future.

Therefore, the two projects I decided to undertake in response to the pandemic were designed not only to document the changes taking place – they were also designed to help to facilitate the change that they document. Like the *Designing Shakespeare* project, the resources brought together were designed to create a record and pose questions about the way forward, using new technology as the means of making a challenge into an open-ended question. This article sets out nearly a quarter of a century of posing questions and collecting evidence of the way that performance and pedagogy have developed using online resources. By bringing together colleagues to participate in collegial yet challenging discussions around the topics of design, performance, pedagogy and new forms of publishing, it has been possible to set down new pathways for future debate. The conversations with colleagues about their online teaching were an attempt to hold on to the experiences of this extraordinary time. There may not be time to reflect on this work now, but there will be in the future.

So, the lesson I am taking forward is that capturing changing teaching practices is essential if there is to be a progressive and iterative debate about pedagogy. If the sourdough is to continue to be produced, then we must hang on to the starter – now more than ever. In drawing together these debates about teaching, initially in print but increasingly online through video, I hope to highlight the importance of continuing to discuss what happens in the classroom, as well as on the stage. I want to show what a history of digital pedagogy might look like, and consider how access to past practices may help to inform the future. The printed word, even if it arrives digitally, continues to be an excellent means of drawing together information into a narrative structure with a sustained argument. However, combining this with capturing digital interviews of the past and present will make future reflection possible. The next steps are, therefore, in the same direction but we must move

more quickly to keep up with the speed of change, and involve more international perspectives to gain a sense of what Shakespeare pedagogy can become in the future in a truly global online world.

The pandemic crisis has forced change, but it is change that needs to be managed with full knowledge of the movements that were already in motion before the disease hit. If the pressures of management control and profit outweigh the concerns of pedagogic practice, then the opportunity that this change presents may undermine the work that has gone into getting us to this point. Taking a positive approach to an even more stark situation, the Chief Executive of Oxfam, Danny Sriskandarajah, writes: 'None of us know the full impact coronavirus will have on our world. It's a disaster that will hit a whole generation and perhaps it will only be in the months, even years, to come that we'll get a real sense of how far reaching this crisis has been.'[57] He goes on to document the terrible statistics about the number of people who will face hunger by the end of 2020 (250 million). Rather than dismissing as hypocrisy the notion that 'we're in this together', he suggests that this phrase 'can and should be a lasting global promise to each other'.[58] The pandemic has made the world a smaller place and has also made it clear how interdependent we are as a species. The networks that cut across national boundaries are the ones that have been best able to tackle the scale of this crisis. The existence of a World Health Organization is now recognized and understood worldwide. Charities such as Oxfam, Save the Children, Unicef, etc., which are equipped to work with local communities, are being pushed to the limit, but this is exactly the sort of disaster that they were designed to serve. The universities represent another international network which should be in a position to face the challenge of an uncertain future on a global scale. But national

---

[57] Danny Sriskandarajah, '"We're in this together" can and should be a lasting global promise to each other', *Oxfam News* (2020).

[58] Sriskandarajah, 'Together'.

interests, commercial pressures and rising distrust of the usefulness of the humanities all stand in the way of the international community working together. As Sriskandarajah points out, 'this could be a once in a generation chance to bring about lasting global changes many of us have been pushing for, for decades'.[59] If the same could be said of the move towards digital learning, then this tipping point could be a turning point for education; Shakespeare pedagogy has the potential to lead the charge in this change.

---

[59] Sriskandarajah, 'Together'.

TEACHING SHAKESPEARE WITH PERFORMANCE PEDAGOGY IN AN ONLINE ENVIRONMENT

ESTHER B. SCHUPAK

With the proliferation of online learning, a phenomenon that has been exponentially magnified by the COVID-19 crisis, the physical classroom can no longer be taken for granted as the default Shakespeare learning experience. We are increasingly being asked to transform our teaching in ways that will be compatible with the online environment. At first glance, it may seem that the online environment is more conducive to traditional lecture and discussion-driven pedagogies for teaching dramatic texts because such methods can be transformed into their online counterparts in a relatively straightforward fashion. In contrast, performance and active learning are more complicated to put online, often requiring substantial reimagining to function within an online framework. However, performance brings to the classroom a vital energy and active engagement with drama that is worth the trouble. Focusing on performance and active learning methods, the current article will explore options for engaging with performance pedagogy to teach Shakespeare's dramatic texts in an online setting.

This article is the result of a forced experiment. Because of our geographic location, the COVID-19 emergency situation required us, after teaching one face-to-face lesson, to teach online for a full semester. Like everyone else, we had very little time to prepare for this massive change: two days. I was relatively lucky that I at least had experience teaching online courses in the past, although these courses were always carefully pre-planned over the course of months, not mere days. Even though I usually employ performance methods in my undergraduate Shakespeare courses, when our courses were suddenly thrown online, I switched to more traditional close-reading pedagogy, as it seemed more suitable to the virtual environment and was simpler to implement. I soon realized that this had been a mistake, that the vibrant spirit that usually animated my teaching of Shakespeare was missing when I failed to engage with Renaissance drama as live performance. At the same time, the active-learning exercises that I had used in the classroom in the past were difficult to transmute into something that could be done online, synchronously or asynchronously. While my natural impulse, which I believe many instructors share, was to take my extant performance materials and alter them to suit the exigencies of online instruction, I found that it was actually more productive to start from scratch and reimagine possibilities opened, and simultaneously limited, by this technology – possibilities that I will explore in this article.

A note about the demography of the course: located in an Israeli university with a robust international programme, this course had a markedly diverse student body, in terms of religion, ethnicity and language. With approximately[1] forty students

---

[1] Due to COVID-19, the university bureaucracy was shut down during the add/drop period, so I had contradictory registration numbers from the Learning Management System (LMS) and the university system, in addition to one student who was never able to register officially. Because the university made attendance optional and students experienced various technological and personal challenges, it is difficult to be precise about the numbers, but I was fortunate that most students chose to attend synchronous course sessions.

in the class, the majority were native speakers of either Arabic or English, with a minority of Hebrew or Russian speakers (seven). In order to study in the English Department, pupils need to attain a high level of English language literacy; nevertheless, one might suppose that native speakers of English are at an advantage in the English literature classroom. When it comes to Renaissance literature, however, early modern English levels the playing field as the language is also challenging for English speakers. (Indeed, one of my Arabic-speaking students pointed out that J. K. Rowling's Harry Potter series was actually more difficult for him than Shakespeare, as the strange words in the Harry Potter books cannot be found in the *OED*.) The significance for this article is that my methods and findings are broadly applicable to courses comprised of native speakers of English and/or proficient English language learners.

I will begin the article by providing a brief overview of strategies for performance and active learning in the Shakespeare course as they have been developed for physical classrooms, and I will then offer some suggestions for how these existing modes can be re-imagined for the twenty-first-century online environment, as well as suggesting new possibilities for performance that have no analogue counterpart.

PERFORMANCE PEDAGOGY

Over the course of the last several decades, performance pedagogy and active methods have increasingly dominated the field of Shakespeare pedagogy. Beginning in the 1960s, based on the theories of Austin, Grice, Schechner and Worthen, Homer Swander innovated the earliest performance techniques, as others following in his wake initiated a creative movement that resulted in the 1984 special edition of *Shakespeare Quarterly*, which focused on performance techniques, followed by another such edition in 1990. This method has been cultivated by such diverse organizations as the Folger Shakespeare Library, the National Endowment for the Humanities, the Royal Shakespeare Company and

Shakespeare's Globe. In the last few years alone, several new books have been published on teaching Shakespeare: most of them either entirely focused on performance, or with one or more sections devoted to performance.[2] Similarly, at the National Council of Teachers of English (NCTE) 2015 annual convention, there were a plethora of sessions devoted to teaching Shakespeare, often led by actors and theatre practitioners, all using performance methods. Academic Shakespeare conferences also often feature panels and workshops devoted to performance pedagogy, and although this method has taken longer to filter down to high schools, the publication of special editions devoted to performance methods in *English Journal*, the flagship journal of the NCTE, in 2002 and 2009, suggests that performance pedagogy is also ensconced in the secondary classroom. Thus, this once up-and-coming method seems to have upped and become what Ralph Alan Cohen has called a methodological 'given' and that 'the argument for its benefits has won the field'.[3]

The rationale for using performance pedagogy to teach Shakespeare is beautiful in its simplicity, based upon 'the academic community's discovery that Shakespeare wrote *plays*'.[4] Newlin's tongue-in-cheek observation highlights the fact that, for much of the twentieth century, the traditional methods used to teach the plays were not discernibly different from the methods used to teach novels or poetry, and that the advent of performance as a central concern has brought the function of Shakespeare's dramas as scripts to the fore, in terms of both research and teaching. The ideological core of this approach has somewhat weakened over time, driven by shifts to text-based approaches and those emphasizing book

[2] Fiona Banks, *Creative Shakespeare: The Globe Education Guide to Practical Shakespeare* (London, 2014); Ayanna Thompson and Laura Turchi, *Teaching Shakespeare with Purpose: A Student-Centred Approach* (London, 2016); Joe Winston, *Transforming the Teaching of Shakespeare with the Royal Shakespeare Company* (London, 2015); Mary Ellen Dakin, *Reading Shakespeare with Young Adults* (Urbana, IL, 2009).
[3] Ralph Alan Cohen, 'From the editor', *Shakespeare Quarterly* 41 (1990), iii–v, p. iii.
[4] Louisa Foulke Newlin, 'Shakespeare saved from drowning', *Shakespeare Quarterly* 35 (1984), 597.

history, with a concomitant shift to studying the half-life of Shakespeare's plays as published print phenomena, for example in the work of Lukas Erne,[5] who has found that Shakespeare's plays were bestsellers of his day, or Emma Smith, who has investigated the origins and cultural status of the First Folio;[6] nevertheless, contemporary critical and pedagogical approaches are usually grounded in the assumption that Shakespeare's works were written as playtexts by an actor-writer, to be performed by a specific group of people in a particular context. Indeed, Jonathan Bate has claimed that Shakespeare's playwriting genius largely owes itself to his experience and grounding as an actor,[7] and performance has remained an important locus of critical and pedagogical innovation in the field. Worthen reconciles these disparate approaches by emphasizing the tripartite nature of Shakespeare's work, which simultaneously embodies the multiple discursive realms of theatre, literature and orality:

Shakespeare's plays were written at the intersection of three institutions that continue to exert pressure on drama and performance. First, they were written as saleable commodities in a new mode of cultural and economic production, the emerging professional theatre. Although writing was used very differently in that theatre from how it is today, Shakespearean drama participated in the invention of a recognizably modern institution, in which playscripts are transformed into a different kind of commodity, dramatic performance. Second, Shakespeare's plays also responded directly to a rich oral culture. Our understanding of language and knowledge have been forever altered by the impact of print; yet the Western stage remains an important site for the transformation of writing into the embodied discourses of action, movement, and speech. Finally, Shakespeare's plays were also part of an emerging publishing industry. The fact that Shakespeare's plays were printed not only saved them from oblivion, but also marked the beginning of a fundamental transformation in their status (and in the status of drama), from performance to print commodities.[8]

This balanced attitude towards the multiple realms of Shakespeare study is also a helpful paradigm for conceptualizing pedagogy by offering a balanced curriculum that combines literary and language-based approaches with performance.

But what precisely does performance mean for classroom practice? In my previous work,[9] I have characterized the range of methods that fall under the rubric of performance pedagogy as a spectrum, at one end of which fall activities that entail authentic performance, with a full suite of theatrical paraphernalia, such as costumes and make-up. At the other extreme are 'theatre of the imagination'[10] activities, that are based on a performance sensibility, but involve little to no actual performance in the classroom. In most cases, performance or active pedagogy takes a form lying somewhere in between these extremes, such as informally staging multiple versions/interpretations of a scene, improvisational activities or critiquing film/live performances. These methods usually entail both a performance sensibility and some kind of task that goes beyond merely discussing or writing about the text – instead, involving active engagement with the material.

The importance of active learning, in contrast to more passive modalities for learning, has been well established by numerous studies in the field of education;[11] thus, active engagement with the dramas is a key benefit of such methods. As Edward Rocklin explains:

If the current paradigms in English often define themselves as teaching students to read either *with* or *against*

[5] Lukas Erne, *Shakespeare and the Book Trade* (Cambridge, 2013); Lukas Erne, *Shakespeare as Literary Dramatist*, 2nd edn (Cambridge, 2003).

[6] Emma Smith, *The Making of Shakespeare's First Folio* (Oxford, 2015); Emma Smith, *Shakespeare's First Folio: Four Centuries of an Iconic Book* (Oxford, 2016).

[7] Jonathan Bate, *The Genius of Shakespeare* (Oxford and New York, 2008).

[8] William B. Worthen, *Shakespeare and the Force of Modern Performance* (Cambridge, 2003), p. 3.

[9] Esther B. Schupak, 'Shakespeare and performance pedagogy: overcoming the challenges', *Changing English* 25 (2018), 163–79; p. 169.

[10] Sherman Hawkins, 'Teaching the theatre of imagination: the example of *1 Henry IV*', *Shakespeare Quarterly* 35 (1984), 517–27; p. 519.

[11] E.g., Donald A. Bligh, *What's the Use of Lectures?* 1st edn (San Francisco, 2000); Charles C. Bonwell and James A. Eison, *Active Learning: Creating Excitement in the Classroom*, Ashe-Eric Higher Education Report (Washington, DC, 1991).

the grain of the text, a performance-centered paradigm widens the curriculum by teaching students to read *through* the grain of the text. That is, this model for reading drama engages students in ways that ask them to immerse themselves in the power of the text yet also invite them to develop their own power through rehearsing and shaping that text in performance.[12]

Combining kinesic and textual awareness, such tasks require students to interact with the text and materials, thereby experiencing what Louise Rosenblatt has characterized in a different context as a 'fruitful transaction' between the student and the literary work,[13] as pupils develop a sense of agency and empowerment by participating in the construction of meaning and taking ownership of their learning. As a method for increasing facility with texts, performance pedagogy has been characterized as 'close reading on your feet',[14] while, somewhat less exuberantly, Thompson and Turchi point out that 'many active approaches work because repetition enables students to tease out the subtleties of the text'.[15] Even though the skills-based advantages of such approaches have been established, the literature on the subject makes it clear that the primary benefit of performance / active methods is motivation – such methods help to overcome student resistance to the study of what students sometimes denigrate (and, of course, mischaracterize) as 'ancient English' or 'old English' texts, by bringing the energy and emotion of theatrical engagement to the classroom.[16] Indeed, psychologists have identified three primary factors that create intrinsic motivation: self-determination, competence and interpersonal relatedness,[17] qualities which are often central to performance, entailing that students make their own performative choices (self-determination), master new skills (competence) and work together with their peers to produce various forms of performance (relatedness). Performance thus combines practical, as well as less tangible, motivational benefits.

PERFORMANCE PEDAGOGY INCARNATED ONLINE

In reviewing the extant literature on online teaching, it becomes clear why performance would be a particularly effective modality for this arena. The importance of a learner-centred, empowering pedagogy for the online environment has been established,[18] as well as the importance of providing students with opportunities to collaborate and form learner communities, both online[19] and in multiple environments.[20] Performance activities, which are inherently student-centred and cooperative, are thus well suited to online instruction. The centrality of the social elements to the learning process has been established,[21] and a problematic adjunct to the online teaching environment is that the lack of informal social interactions can cause students to develop a sense of isolation that often pervades the online learning experience, which can

[12] Edward L. Rocklin, *Performance Approaches to Teaching Shakespeare* (Urbana, IL, 2005), p. 82.

[13] Louise M. Rosenblatt, *The Reader, the Text, the Poem: The Transactional Theory of the Literary Work* (Carbondale, IL, 1994).

[14] Michael LoMonico, 'Shakespearean ruminations and innovations', *English Journal* 99 (2009), 21–8; p. 24.

[15] Thompson and Turchi, *Teaching*, p. 126.

[16] Esther B. Schupak, 'Performing Julius Caesar with ultra-orthodox women', *Research in Drama Education* 24 (2019), 155–72.

[17] Edward L. Deci and Richard M. Ryan, *Intrinsic Motivation and Self-Determination in Human Behavior* (New York, 1985); Edward L. Deci and Richard M. Ryan, 'Self-determination theory: a macrotheory of human motivation, development, and health', *Canadian Psychology / Psychologie Canadienne* 49 (2008), 182–5.

[18] Barry Chametzky, 'Andragogy and engagement in online learning: tenets and solutions', *Creative Education* 10 (2014), 813–21.

[19] Margaret Niess and Henry Gillow-Wiles, 'Developing asynchronous online courses: key instructional strategies in a social metacognitive constructivist learning trajectory', *Journal of Distance Education* 27 (2013), 1–23.

[20] John Hattie, *Visible Learning for Teachers: Maximizing Impact on Learning* (Abingdon, 2012); Barbara Means, Yukie Toyama, Robert Murphy, Marianne Bakia and Karla Jones, 'Evaluation of evidence-based practices in online learning: a meta-analysis and review of online learning studies', US Department of Education (2009): www2.ed.gov/rschstat/eval/tech/evidence-based-practices/final report.pdf.

[21] Jean Lave and Etienne Wenger, *Situated Learning: Legitimate Peripheral Participation* (Cambridge, 1991).

easily lead to feelings of alienation.[22] However, especially when conducted in small groups, performance activities can serve to combat this social isolation by ensuring that students have the opportunity to work together and interact informally to create performances.

In *Minds Online: Teaching Effectively with Technology*, Michelle Miller establishes six principles for teaching well, both in person and online:

1. Peer-to-peer interaction
2. Active student engagement in learning
3. Emphasis on practice and student effort
4. Personalization to the individual student
5. Variety
6. Emphasis on higher thought processes.[23]

These elements inhere in and are served by many forms of performance / active pedagogy. Many performance activities entail peer interactions by their nature and are pursued in groups, large or small, which further provides for student interaction. Moreover, in contrast to the passivity fostered by learning via videoconferencing or by viewing recorded lectures, performance methods are inherently active, necessitating student practice and effort. In terms of personalization and empowering students, performance pedagogy is intrinsically learner-centred and, by encouraging students to embody the text, empowers them and gives them agency. In the context of a literature classroom, performance can inject much-needed variety and energy to the range of classroom activities, and, by emphasizing analysis of performances, can demand engaging with higher thought processes. Thus, performance methods can serve in multifarious ways to enrich and develop the online course.

ACTUAL PERFORMANCE

One of the most successful performance activities that we did during the semester was also the simplest and most straightforward: students performed 'live' via videoconferencing. Prior to the performance, the pupils were given time to prepare relatively short scene sections, with costumes optional, and self-selected groups performing for the class. Since they were given a limited number of choices for scenes, we were able to view the same scene as enacted by different groups, and thus to analyse contrasting performance choices and discuss how those choices represented alternative interpretations of the text. While the range of the students' computer cameras limited the possibilities for physical expression and blocking, the closer view of the performers' faces allowed for more expression of emotional nuance, so it did not seem to me that a great deal was lost in terms of the quality of student performance. The one major concession that did need to be made, however, was length. In order to combat the dreaded 'Zoom fatigue', limiting the amount of time spent on teleconferencing is recommended,[24] so the students performed shorter blocks of text than I would have assigned in a physical classroom, and the number of performances was fewer as well. All in all, though, rehearsed performances were a productive and interesting way of approaching the text.

Even more productive were the post-performance discussions and analyses of the scenes. Throughout our examinations of the performances, we focused on the function of performance as interpretation, with G. B. Shand's generative questions serving as a guidepost for exploration:

1. What performative obligations did the text impose upon your group, and on your own role?
2. What important performative options were available to you and/or your group? What choices were made, and why?
3. What was the interpretive result? What readings of character, action, and so on were enabled (or disabled) by your choices?[25]

---

[22] Joanne M. McInnerney and Tim S. Roberts, 'Online learning: social interaction and the creation of a sense of community', *Journal of Educational Technology & Society* 7 (2004), 73–81.

[23] Michelle D. Miller, *Minds Online: Teaching Effectively with Technology* (Cambridge, MA, 2014), pp. 23–4.

[24] Brenda K. Wiederhold, 'Connecting through technology during the Coronavirus disease 2019 pandemic: avoiding "Zoom fatigue"', *Cyberpsychology, Behavior, and Social Networking* 23 (2020), 437–8.

[25] G. B. Shand, 'Reading power: classroom acting as close reading', in *Teaching Shakespeare Through Performance*, ed. Milla Cozart Riggio (New York, 1999), pp. 244–55; p. 247.

Discussing these issues was critical to transforming the 'fun' and engaging performance activity into an opportunity for learning, close reading and analysis. So, for example, one group, which consisted of two hijab-wearing women and two with long, flowing hair, performed a portion of Hamlet's poignant scene with Ophelia that immediately follows his 'to be or not to be' soliloquy. They divided up the parts so that the hijab-wearers performed Hamlet's part and the others performed Ophelia's, a choice that they had not made consciously, but which, when pointed out to them, led to a fruitful discussion of cultural constructions of gender in this drama.

Similarly, but perhaps at the opposite end of the performance pedagogy spectrum, we critiqued Shakespeare film adaptations and videos of live theatrical performances. The online environment is particularly congenial towards video, as clips and links are easily integrated into videoconferencing and online learning platforms. As with our amateur student performances, showing the same scene from different productions opened a space for considering conflicting interpretations of the text, examining which elements are dictated by the text, and contemplating the function of performance as interpretation. This medium also allowed us to consider issues that were limited in the student productions: physical blocking and setting, and how these contribute to constructing an interpretation.

While, with the exception of our discussions of film, I chose to avoid the physical in the online environment, for instructors who prefer to foreground physical movement and stage blocking, as well as gesture and other movement-oriented paradigms, video gaming platforms offer an interesting option. Although I have not yet had the opportunity to try it in the classroom, multiplayer 'first-person shooter' platforms with private maps allow students to move 'characters' around a screen in a way which has the potential to recreate the staging experience. Secondlife is one such nominally free platform that allows players to create characters with body and costume, and one can purchase a private area, which would be necessary for classroom use.[26] For instructors who are willing and able to develop an understanding of video gaming, this technique has interesting possibilities for the Shakespeare course. Of course, the same basic principle could be accomplished in a simpler, less engaging – and more static – format by incorporating stills or clips from filmed productions into the lesson.

IMPROVISATION

Derived from theatre practice, improvisation activities are paradoxical in that they entail working outside the text in order to arrive at a better understanding of the text itself. The idea is to step away from the text in order to delve into character, the situation and other elements, and then to return to the text with a heightened understanding of the subtext. Of course, as Michael Shapiro points out, this type of work has both advantages and disadvantages: 'Such scenes are exhilarating and encourage students to incorporate critical insights about the characters and their relationships gleaned from the true text. But they also deflect attention from Shakespeare's language.'[27] While remaining cognizant of the limitations of methods of teaching Shakespeare that do not incorporate his language, I nevertheless believe there is much to be gained by this type of exercise, when performed in moderation. What improvisation does for the classroom is to combine a deeper intellectual understanding of the characters with a strong emotional component, and the scholarship on teaching and learning has made it clear that including an emotional element in learning increases both the speed of learning and knowledge retention in the classroom.[28] So, while I completely agree with Shapiro about the importance of having students grapple with Shakespeare's language, the value of improvisation is also clear.

[26] Thank you to Mordechai T. Abzug for helping me to explore this option.
[27] Michael Shapiro, 'Improvisational techniques for the literature teacher', in Teaching, ed. Riggio, pp. 184–95; p. 194.
[28] Robert N. Leamnson, Thinking about Teaching and Learning: Developing Habits of Learning with First Year College and University Students (Stoke-on-Trent, 1999); James E. Zull, From Brain to Mind: Using Neuroscience to Guide Change in Education (Sterling, VA, 2011).

In exploring the literature on the topic, it becomes apparent that improvisational techniques usually fall into one of the following categories:

1 **Generalized warm-up improvisational games**

The purpose of such activities is to accustom students to acting and performing in front of their classmates, to being in the moment in a way that is necessary to enact a text. Developing an acting skill that will be needed later in the lesson, such work can also help to alter the particular mood of the class on a given day in order to enhance the planned lesson, perhaps energizing a group that seems tired or disinterested or doing the reverse to a group that seems overexcited.[29] Completely unconnected to the text studied, such activities are usually game-like, invoking the ethos of play that is central to performance pedagogy as well as theatre technique. For instance, the educational practitioners of Shakespeare's Globe recommend an activity called 'triangle, square, circle', where the class together is tasked with – without recourse to talking – creating a shape called out by the group leader. This activity encourages collaboration and prepares the students for the physical embodiment that will constitute the bulk of the lesson.[30]

2 **Enacting a scene in pantomime**

Pantomime, as a theatrical technique, has multiple uses in the Shakespeare classroom. Very practically, it can help students to understand the possibilities for physical movement and the character dynamics of the plays, linking bodily intelligence to interpretation, as well as allowing students to explore the conventions of early modern staging in Shakespeare's Globe. Examples of two such popular activities include playing the assassination of *Julius Caesar* and performing the dumb show in *Hamlet*. Of course, pantomimes can also be immobile as 'live sculptures', whose purpose is to 'depict the relationships among characters in each scene of a drama. Students freeze in place, becoming individual statues in a larger grouping. Through spatial placement, bodily position, gesture, and facial expression, they create a tableau summing up the connections among characters.'[31] The idea of either form of pantomime is to focus on the body and the kinesic intelligence that can help students to understand the interactions between characters and the function of blocking and physical movement on the stage.

3 **Resolving lacunae in the text**

In this sort of exercise, students perform their creative vision for a scene that is left out of the Shakespearian text. For example, in attempting to convince her husband to proceed with the murder of the King, Lady Macbeth asserts: 'I have given suck, and know / How tender 'tis to love the babe that milks me' (1.7.54–5). What happened to that babe, and how can that help us to understand both Lady Macbeth and her husband? In the Fassbender *Macbeth*, the film includes a burial scene, which resolves this gap in the text; students can be encouraged to create their own, suggesting an interpretation of the characters. Michael Shapiro discusses several such exercises for *The Merchant of Venice*, including improvising Portia's visit to the lawyer Bellario, to consult with him about defending Antonio, or creating the missing scene where the disguised Nerissa convinces her husband Gratiano to give her the ring, just as Portia does Bassanio.[32]

4 **Role playing**

In this type of activity, the instructor creates a roughly analogous situation in which the character or situational dynamics parallel the text, enabling the students to explore these dynamics outside the text and then bring that understanding into their reading or performance of the text itself. These exercises in contemporary parallels also render the text more immediate and relevant for students, as do Mary Maloney Toepfer and Kara Haubert Haas when they have their students reimagine Othello in the context of a varsity soccer team, with a player (Iago) who feels that he should have been captain.[33] In my own courses, when I am teaching *Julius Caesar*, students are asked to plead for someone close to them to reveal a secret, in parallel to the scene where Portia pleads with her husband to reveal what is troubling him. The students create as few or as many details as suits their enactment. Then, I ask them to bring that sensibility and their deeper understanding of these interactions into the performance of Shakespeare's words.

5 **Developing the back story**

These types of activities generally address issues of character and setting, building a back story for the characters or filling in context. My favourite example

---

[29] Banks, *Creative*, p. 38. [30] Banks, *Creative*, p. 38.

[31] Charles J. Hakaim, Jr, 'A most rare vision: improvisations on *A Midsummer Night's Dream*', *English Journal* 82 (1993), 67–70; p. 67. See also Lauren Esposito, 'Performing to learn: rethinking theater techniques to interpret, explore, and write about Shakespeare's plays', *CEA Critic* 78 (2016), 183–98.

[32] Shapiro, 'Improvisational'.

[33] Mary Maloney Toepfer and Kara Haubert Haas, 'Imaginative departures with two Shakespearean plays', *English Journal* 92 (2003), 30–4; p. 31.

of such an activity is creating a 'talk show' with titles such as "'Fathers Who Oppose Their Daughter's Marriages," "Arranged Marriages Today," "Men Who Love the Same Woman," ... "Do You Believe in Fairies" ... '.[34] While this exercise emphasizes character, other exercises focus on the historical and/or social environment of the plays – for instance, when teaching *Romeo and Juliet*, having a town meeting to solve the problem of street violence in Verona.[35] Winston explains that such activities utilize 'physicality, sound, voice and role in ways that can draw students emotionally into the world of the play and help them reflect upon it in ways other than through discussion and writing'.[36] These back-story creative improvisations activate learners by having them engage with the classroom concepts through embodiment and, as such, allow instructors to step outside the well-worn grooves of lecture/discussion/writing to explore new pedagogical territory.

So how can these be introduced into the online environment? I will begin by laying out the biggest obstacle that I encountered: the time delay in electronic communication. Whichever teleconferencing platform is being used – Zoom, Skype, Google Hangouts – there is a small lag between speaking and hearing, sometimes a large lag, depending upon platform and bandwidth. Whereas this gap is not terribly problematic in normal conversation, it can kill many improvisational exercises dead, especially warm-up games.

I do not usually use warm-up games myself: the purpose of these games is to build classroom community and encourage students to feel comfortable with performance, and these important goals are already served by other aspects of my pedagogy. However, in the online environment, which tends to generate emotional distance and discourage classroom community,[37] I had hoped that small doses of this sort of 'play' could create positive energy by functioning as community-building tools and icebreakers; unfortunately, these attempts were generally unsuccessful because of the time delay, which impeded the immediacy of responses. While time lag is less of a problem when performing more substantial blocks of text, anything that requires quickly shifting from one actor to another can soon become mired in the bog of time delays.

One exception to this is the well-known Shakespearian insults exercise, which is very helpful in making students feel comfortable acting Shakespeare. Either in small groups or with the class as a whole, students can be asked to perform insults found in, or based upon, Shakespeare; the insult sheet in the Folger Library's *Shakespeare Set Free* is particularly good,[38] but there are also apps and online resources for this topic. The purpose of this activity is twofold: it helps students to become comfortable in the Shakespeare classroom, and it helps students to become comfortable with Shakespeare's language, as they realize they do not have to completely understand an insult to recognize that it is an insult. However, most warm-up activities are not readily translatable to online platforms.

And, of course, warm-up activities that require movement and physical activity were off the table, as well as the other improvisational form that I could not convert to online – pantomime: the physicality of pantomime that allows students to develop a bodily awareness that emphasizes relationships and interactions is unfortunately not accessible in the online environment, unless students record themselves performing in groups, an option not usually available in the online classroom.

However, many other things are accessible, and I was able successfully to incorporate improvisational activities from categories 3, 4, and 5 in my online Shakespeare course. Resolving lacunae in the text, role playing and developing the back story were all eminently doable in the online environment, but they did require adjustment. Normally, I would have asked students to work in small groups, and, upon completion of the task, some or all groups would have performed for the whole class, which would then discuss the implications of

---

[34] Hakaim, 'Most rare', p. 70.
[35] Winston, *Transforming*, p. 49.
[36] Winston, *Transforming*, p. 49.
[37] McInnerney and Roberts, 'Online'.
[38] Peggy O'Brien and Folger Shakespeare Library, *Shakespeare Set Free: Teaching Romeo and Juliet, Macbeth, a Midsummer Night's Dream* (New York, 1993).

the performance. Because everything takes much longer when teleconferencing, while, paradoxically, attention spans are shorter, I had the students work on performance in small groups and then present their 'findings' – that is, what they learned from performing the exercise – orally and/or on a webpage. So the performance actually happened only in small groups, and, in the context of the entire class, we discussed what the students learned from performing. While this is slightly less engaging than performing in front of the class, it does shift the emphasis in the performance classroom away from the active learning process itself to what we *learn* from that process. And, even though I'm not sure whether I would want to do this all the time, that shift in focus is helpful because it keeps the spotlight on pedagogical intentionality, and intentionality is critical to any classroom, but particularly so to the performance / active learning environment, where learning can all too easily become subsumed to the pleasure of theatre and the joy of acting play.[39] The shift to online performance therefore emphasized my role as a 'purposeful facilitator',[40] foregrounding intentionality.

An example of this type of activity is a two-part improvisation-performance that I assigned when teaching *The Merchant of Venice*: for the first part, I asked my students, in small groups, to improvise a scene where someone is trying to borrow money from someone s/he does not like who does not want to lend it, in parallel to the scene where Bassanio and Antonio attempt to borrow money from Shylock. Then, incorporating what they had learned from the improvisation, they were to perform a portion of Shakespeare's playtext (part of 1.3), keeping in mind what we had learned about second-person pronouns in early modern English. This required them to work simultaneously from multiple intelligences:[41] the interpersonal intelligence that they had acquired from the improvisational exercise, their linguistic understanding of the scene, and the rhetorical interplay of status and register that the early modern you/thou pronouns highlighted. While all of this work took place in small groups that I moved between, at the end of the session we discussed the learning

outcomes with the class as a whole, and pupils expressed pleasant surprise at how much they were able to transfer from the improvisation to the performance exercise. Despite the fact that some of the creative energy and excitement that would have come from performing both the improvisations and the text in a classroom full of students was absent, the concomitant focus on understanding the implications of the exercise compensated for the lost energy with increased intellectual understanding.

LANGUAGE PLAY

One of the most important ways in which I integrate performance pedagogy into my physical classroom is through the voice work of Cicely Berry. Berry, the former Voice Director of the Royal Shakespeare Company, developed a series of acting exercises that she published on video, with an accompanying book. These exercises are designed to help actors to find the 'muscularity' of the language,[42] to help actors work *through* Shakespeare's language in order to generate meaning. In order to accomplish this, she created physical exercises that help to bring bodily intelligence to understanding and speaking Shakespeare's texts. What she does in these exercises can be viewed as the opposite of improvisation; rather than bringing external understandings to the text, the actor examines how meaning is intrinsic to these playtexts, contained in multiple aspects of the actual language of Shakespeare, as Berry remarks: 'there is something in the sound of his language that contains its meaning; it is sound that excites us as we listen'.[43]

Instead of highlighting intellectual analysis, these exercises help to generate an embodied, physical

[39] Schupak, 'Shakespeare', p. 172.
[40] Thompson and Turchi, *Teaching*, p. 9.
[41] Howard Gardner, *Frames of Mind: The Theory of Multiple Intelligences* (New York, 2011).
[42] Cicely Berry, *Working Shakespeare: The Workbook* (New York and London, 2004), p. 13.
[43] Berry, *Working*, p. 8.

understanding of the prosody and multi-valanced linguistic complexity of Shakespeare's texts. For example, rather than scanning the verse on a blackboard, she has the actors tap out the iambic pentameter while reading in a chorus. Some other examples of the most helpful exercises include:

1. read the text in a circle, changing the reader at each mark of punctuation or with each reader taking one line
2. read the text while walking about, changing direction at every mark of punctuation
3. read the text and kick an object at the end of each line
4. enact a scene with actors at opposite ends of a room
5. perform a monologue, moving to different places in the room to express different thoughts
6. use a soliloquy as a dialogue, with two people alternately reading lines.

These exercises work beautifully in the conventional classroom, leaving students with a deeper, physical, embodied understanding of the language, but are often defeated by the technicalities of videoconferencing, especially the time lag. In terms of the more action-oriented exercises, even though I tried adjusting some of these – for example, having students tap their desks at the end of each line instead of kicking an object – for the most part, such adjustments left us with attenuated forms of the exercises that were markedly less effective. However, in small groups, the time lag was less marked, so I was able to move some of these activities into Zoom breakout rooms, where we were able to beat out the metre or change readers at each mark of punctuation or the end of the line, helping pupils get a sense of the prosodic and rhetorical elements of the text. Moving from group to group, I helped students to overcome difficulties and focus on the goals of the exercise, which were well served by performing the work in small groups.

The exception to the time lag difficulties was the soliloquy as dialogue activity, which worked remarkably well in a videoconference setting, even with a large group. In general, this exercise functions effectively as a way to articulate inner conflict and is thus particularly useful when

teaching *Hamlet*. When I taught the 'to be or not to be' soliloquy, I was concerned about the way that popular culture has devolved this passage into a cliché, and I wanted to ensure that my students could view it with fresh eyes. I therefore asked for volunteers to perform it as a dialogue, switching off at alternate lines and thereby emphasizing the internal conflict. The class immediately apprehended the purpose of the exercise, which then energized and informed our analysis of the text.

ACTING PREPARATION WORK

In reference to the spectrum of performance activities I mentioned earlier, acting preparation work is closer to the 'theatre of the imagination' end of the spectrum because little actual acting or embodiment is involved – rather, the emphasis is on laying the groundwork for such enactments. In theatrical practice, such work is always a prelude to an actual performance, but in the Shakespeare course, such activities can provide a means to delve into the play without necessarily resulting in an actual performance of the text. Given the limitations and constraints of the online environment, particularly as pertains to time, I turned to acting preparation work as a stand-alone activity. But given sufficient time, such activities can be even more effective as the first stage of the active enactment of a scene.

Since my own education is literary rather than theatrical, I turned to Bruce Miller's *The Actor as Storyteller* in order to generate activities that would encourage students to think like actors. Based on Stanislavski's theories of acting, Miller highlights the importance of actors performing clearly defined objectives. In real life, people may be confused about their goals and desires, but the actors embodying characters on stage must be constantly aware of their characters' objectives so that they can make intelligent acting decisions. These objectives fall into at least one of the following categories:

1. To give information
2. To get information
3. To make someone do something

4. To keep someone from doing something
5. To make someone feel good
6. To make someone feel bad.[44]

Identifying these objectives is not only critical to acting, it is also a useful paradigm for contemplating character and motivation in a particular scene as it helps to avoid the move to hasty generalizations (particularly as they proliferate in internet study guides). Instead of thinking of the character in terms of the arc of the drama, objectives force us to think about a particular dramatic moment, explore its ramifications, and only then contemplate how that moment fits into the overall development of the character. Although Shakespeare preceded Stanislavski by three centuries, Stanislavski's ideas nevertheless provide us with a remarkably robust means to approach these dramas pedagogically.

Asking students to think in terms of objectives translates readily into the online environment and helps learners to structure their thinking about the text. For example, I created an exercise for the first scene of *Julius Caesar*, a scene that foreshadows the political conflicts at the centre of the play, but which can be confusing for those grappling with the unfamiliar historical context. In order to clarify the nature of the action and the underlying dynamics, I divided the students into working groups (using breakout rooms in Zoom) and asked them to identify the objective of each major character in the scene, as well as to create a physical action that would help the character to obtain and personify the objective. Groups were asked to fill out the chart in Table 1.

Table 1

	Cobbler	Marullus	Flavius
Objective			
Physical action			

Each group transcribed this information onto a webpage I created (using Padlet, but this would have worked on other collaboration platforms as well, such as Google Docs). The advantage in allowing students to see each other's online tasks

is that this functions as a kind of discussion and as a source of inspiration and modelling for weaker students; the danger is that, sometimes, the weaker students simply copy the work of their stronger peers – however, because the working groups were heterogeneous, this did not happen. Furthermore, during the activity, I joined each group at least once to provide guidance and to ensure that they understood the task and were appropriately focused. Ideally, when the groups are finished with this sort of task, I like to discuss the highlights and/or troublesome issues with the class, but if the time is insufficient, I instead rely on my written responses to the collaborative document, which is what I did in this case. At the beginning of the next class session, I played the opening scene from the Gregory Doran *Julius Caesar* (RSC, 2012) to the class, and the class compared and contrasted their ideas regarding this scene's objectives and physicality with those of Doran's production.

Conflict, which is so central to acting, is also a useful paradigm for approaching the text pedagogically. Miller discusses the importance of unearthing the latent conflicts in a dramatic work and bringing them to the fore when enacting the piece, and suggests looking at monologues to address the following points:

> Determine who the speaking character is.
> Determine who the character being spoken to is.
> Determine the conflict.
> Determine what the speaker is trying to get from the listener.
> Determine as specifically as possible how the listening character is reacting to the speaking character.
> Determine ... and chart the journey the speaking character makes during the speech. (How is the character different at the end than he or she was at the beginning?)[45]

At the intersection of acting, literary analysis and rhetoric, this list provides a robust focus for analysis,

---

[44] Bruce J. Miller, *The Actor as Storyteller: An Introduction to Acting*, 2nd edn (Milwaukee, WI, 2012), p. 86.
[45] Miller, *The Actor*, p. 78.

particularly for any play that has a preponderance of monologues. I found it especially helpful for teaching *Julius Caesar*, as I emphasize a rhetorical framework in teaching the drama, and this list functions as well rhetorically as it does in performance preparation. Rather than asking all of these questions about all speeches, the questions can be tailored to the specifics of the drama, so, when teaching *Julius Caesar*, I asked students to address the third, fourth and fifth points, and when teaching *Hamlet*, where the focus is less on rhetoric and more on interiority, I asked the students to focus on the sixth. Again, we worked in small groups; they posted their answers on a webpage; and we discussed results with the class as a whole, at the next lesson contrasting the group results with various professional performances.

CONCLUSION

If I were forced to boil down the results of this experiment in bringing performance pedagogy into the online environment, it would be essentialized in this principle: decentre the work. Allow the students to work in pairs and heterogeneous small groups, while guiding them, but still trusting their own learning processes. Of course, the degree to which this will be necessary will depend on the number of students. An instructor who is fortunate enough to teach a class of ten students may be able to do much more with the whole group that someone with a class of forty, fifty or more, but, even in a small group, the more decentred the work, the more power and agency rests in the pupil who is embodying Shakespeare's text. And, at the end of the day, therein lies the power of performance in the classroom: in the one-on-one encounter between the student and the words and work of Shakespeare.

Although I must confess to having felt a certain amount of dismay at the challenges entailed in abruptly changing to online pedagogy, I also found that this was an opportunity to conduct a thorough housecleaning of my methodological toolbox and to rethink what I do by being forced away from my entrenched practices. At the end of the day, this process has made me a stronger and more intentional practitioner, and adversity has provided an opportunity for growth.

PPE FOR SHAKESPEARIANS: PANDEMIC, PERFORMANCE AND EDUCATION

KEVIN A. QUARMBY[1]

CAMILLO: There is a sickness
    Which puts some of us in distemper, but
    I cannot name th' disease, and it is caught
    Of you that yet are well.
                     (*The Winter's Tale*, 1.2.384–7)

The COVID-19 pandemic hit the Shakespeare community hard. Not only were conference meetings cancelled, but also live performances at playhouses and festivals worldwide. Eager to entertain and maintain their loyal fan base, theatre companies with access to a store of pre-recorded productions offered them freely for public home consumption via the internet. At the same time, scholars and teachers scrambled to complete their academic years by converting classroom and lecture hall meetings into virtual educational opportunities. Synchronous and asynchronous teaching models responded to the social distancing needs of twenty-first-century educators and students. If a pandemic could impact the long-dead Shakespeare, then 2020 was the year for it to happen. With video-conferencing the new norm, any classroom, any stage, any 'on your feet' Shakespeare delivery method, along with a host of other in-person activities, seemed stretched to their limits.

Significant in the context of a community of international educators for whom 'Shakespeare and performance' in the classroom remains an intrinsic part of their pedagogy, the impact of the COVID-19 outbreak highlighted certain avoidable inequities associated with the methodology's reliance on personal and professional creativity. As vulnerable populations succumbed to the insidious pandemic – whether through poverty, inequality,

inadequate healthcare or political negligence – and as social and economic disasters unfolded worldwide, many 'Shakespeare in performance' educators found it necessary to reconsider not only their delivery methods, but also the ongoing value of their pedagogical approach given its close interaction with Shakespeare's texts as actionable, breathable and speakable entities. Action, breath and the spoken word, the embodied cultural currencies of Shakespeare in any performance setting, now bore an additional weight – that of infectious disease. Fear of social interaction and proximity, fear of the air we share and breathe, negatively impacted the Shakespeare-consumer value system, turning creatively and spiritually life-enhancing art practices into dangerous sites of communal infection. As this article suggests, however, those most impacted by society's new-found suspicion of close social interaction were the very people on whom Shakespeare and performance pedagogy ultimately relied, and still relies: our nations' actors. Without effective support for actors and other creative personnel, the liveliness of performance, by necessity, could find itself ossified in a cloud-based repository of past artistic endeavour.

Although the virtual ossification of performative expression remains only a conjectural possibility in

[1] My thanks to Ann Thompson for her motivational support when I was writing this article. Also, to Christie Carson for reading an early draft and offering invaluable advice on its development. Finally, to staff members of the Actors' Equity Association and the San Francisco Shakespeare Festival for their generosity in answering my many questions.

any post-pandemic A.C. ('After Corona') world – as the *New York Times* columnist Thomas L. Friedman terms it – personal distancing and state-imposed limits on social gathering had a more immediate existential impact, especially on theatrical production, Shakespearian or otherwise.[2] With theatres registering as dangerous Petri dishes for further infection, creatives who populated this industry – actors, directors, designers, producers, technicians or theatre owners – all found their livelihoods threatened as performance venues and spaces lost their vital revenue streams. The inevitable 'dip in admissions', whereby ticket sales 'disappeared almost overnight', was exacerbated by audiences proving less than willing to return to many B.C. ('Before Corona') communal activities.[3] Already members of a precariously overpopulated profession, actors felt the immediate impact of what arts commentator Valentina Di Liscia described as this 'grim landscape'. Arguably irreplaceable, actors nevertheless remain the most easily replaced constituents of the theatre industry, struggling or otherwise. Sharing in the economic uncertainty that impacted gig-economy workers in the hospitality industries and elsewhere, and often limited to those 'transient, temporary' short-term contractual engagements that director Zelda Fichandler likened to 'piecework', actors found themselves societally inessential, just as supermarket stackers and delivery drivers discovered their essential-worker indispensability.[4] For theatre actors in particular, therefore, fear of unemployment and of infectious disease was compounded by an additional fear: of professional non-survival. The loss of these actors, many of whom had graced our stages and been the subject of our scholarship, threatened the equal loss of a quarter-century of experiential proficiency acquired in the theatrical laboratories Shakespearians often wish they could call home.

While the creative industries suffered fundamental downturns in their economic fortunes, the professionals they employed faced a potentially long, possibly irreversible period of artistic stagnation. As we shall see, however, one Shakespeare venue in the US, the Blackfriars Playhouse of the American Shakespeare Center (ASC), successfully bucked the pandemic trend by employing a select

few creative personnel to stage plays for a paying public, while imposing strict quarantine regulatory practices intended to ameliorate the threat of close-contact infection. The decision to perform live Shakespeare, which the American Actors' Equity theatre union viewed with outrage and dismay, appeared as politicized as it was understandable given the precariousness of such venues, whose duty of care towards their creative and educational employees seemed irrevocably tied to the financial health of their commercial theatre seasons.

Despite the seeming oxymoron, therefore, of teaching Shakespeare and performance at a time when 'performance' of anything had, apart from a few outlying ventures, often been limited to the regurgitation of pre-recorded material, signs of alternative Shakespearian theatrical expressiveness emerging in the virtual sphere offered some cause for cultural relief and muted celebration. Indeed, theatre companies, occasionally tied to the glorified materiality of their facsimile playhouse stages or celebrating their nomadized seasonal existence in local communities, recognized a need to develop new levels of inventiveness if they were to survive the next few years' economic downturn and return to their pre-pandemic edu-performative best. Innovative responses to the loss of live in-person theatre offered, in consequence, an opportunity for Shakespeare educators to consider formulating alternative models for student engagement with a pedagogical methodology that remains an intrinsic part of many a Shakespeare syllabus.

An example of inventive re-envisioning of the theatrical event by a company that considered the

[2] Thomas L. Friedman, 'Our new historical divide: B.C. and A. C. – the world before Corona and the world after', *New York Times*, 17 March 2020: www.nytimes.com/2020/03/17/opinion/coronavirus-trends.html.

[3] Valentina Di Liscia, 'Over 15,000 workers have been laid off or furloughed from 810 NYC cultural organizations', *Hyperallergic Media*, 21 July 2020: https://hyperallergic.com/577706.

[4] Zelda Fichandler, 'Whither (or wither) art?' in *The Art of Governance: Boards in the Performing Arts*, ed. Nancy Roche and Jaan Whitehead (New York, 2005), pp. 19–37; p. 30.

ongoing welfare of its actors as correlative with its continued success as a summer open-air theatre producer is the San Francisco Shakespeare Festival (hereafter SF Shakes, the company's social media identifier). With its 'Free Shakespeare at Home' presentation of *King Lear*, performed and aired on YouTube on Saturdays and Sundays (plus Labor Day Monday) from July to late September 2020, SF Shakes recreated for virtual consumption a wholly 'new' real-time professional production that maintained a social-distancing imperative some other companies chose to ignore.[5] Disseminated to the public through Zoom's virtual platform and using freely available OBS (Open Broadcaster Software) streaming technology, SF Shakes guaranteed its actors, directorial and design creatives, and technicians a salaried rehearsal and performance schedule, complete with Previews and Opening Night, that broke the mould of pre-recorded or firewalled Shakespeare offerings in a significant way. Not presented as a review of the production, but as an example of online performance that closely resembles the Shakespeare classroom, this article's consideration of the SF Shakes *King Lear* is intended as an antidote to the lockdown consumption of pre-recorded or compromised communal performance models, while also as applause for those who recognized the importance of keeping acting careers viable in preparation for the less dangerous years ahead. Before considering the multi-locational live theatre SF Shakes model and how it subtly mirrors the Zoomed classroom experience, as well as the production company's considerable care for the plight of its actors, it is important to discuss the historical significance of Shakespeare and performance pedagogy and its impact on educational practices in the twenty-first century.

SHAKESPEARE AND PERFORMANCE PEDAGOGY: 'AND BY MY BODY'S ACTION TEACH MY MIND'

A noticeable shift in the teaching of Shakespeare over the latter half of the twentieth century is evident in the discipline's near-universal twenty-first-century embrace of broader performance

studies as an adjunct to close literary and historical analysis. Negatively impacted by a coronavirus that prevented the liveliness of theatrical production and audience enjoyment, such performance-oriented educational models faced pedagogical redundancy, however, especially since unfettered use of them in the virtual classroom highlighted a potential for collective learning malaise, closely associated with student reliance on social media gratification and immediacy during forced social distancing and isolation. Shakespeare and performance pedagogies required, it became apparent, a major overhaul if they too were to survive the pandemic. The overarching power of performance in the Shakespearian classroom was the subject of scrutiny, however, even prior to the COVID-19 outbreak, especially by those who questioned the monolithic status of its educational benefits. Concern about the approach's unquestioned reputation is evident, therefore, in Esther B. Schupak's 2018 study of 'Shakespeare and performance pedagogy' (hereafter SPP), in which she explains how this specific educational approach 'has become an – or perhaps "the" – established practice for teaching Shakespeare'.[6] Describing how 'justification' for the practice is traditionally traced to the 'language-games' in Ludwig Wittgenstein's posthumously published *Philosophical Investigations* of 1953, Schupak notes how, by the mid-1980s, the Royal Shakespeare Company's director John Barton was using the approach to demonstrate how 'analysis of the text can drive performance by interpretation of the intentionality of its key elements' (p. 165).[7]

Within a short time, it appears, such language-game rehearsal techniques had transformed into a

5 'Free Shakespeare in the Park', San Francisco Shakespeare Festival (2020): www.sfshakes.org/programs/free-shakespeare-in-the-park.
6 Esther B. Schupak, 'Shakespeare and performance pedagogy: overcoming the challenges', *Changing English* 25 (2018), 163–79; p. 163. Further references appear in the text in parentheses.
7 Ludwig Wittgenstein, *Philosophical Investigations*, 4th edn (Chichester, 2009), p. 15; John Barton, *Playing Shakespeare: An Actor's Guide* (London, 1984).

performance pedagogy that was irreversibly accepted as the educational norm – so much so that, by 1990, the ASC's Ralph Alan Cohen could describe its methodological success in militaristic terms: as having 'won the field' (p. 163).[8] Thereafter, Schupak observes, twenty-first-century scholarly publications, whether 'explicitly performative or active' in their approaches or not, most often provided no 'explicit rationale' for their 'performance methodologies' other than a tacit acknowledgement that this is how Shakespeare should be taught (p. 164). SPP's 'taken-for-granted status' demonstrates, for Schupak, how 'clearly' such an educational practice had 'arrived', without necessarily benefiting from the rigorous scrutiny afforded other pedagogical innovations – rather, a celebratory joy in its inventiveness and warm reception among many (though not necessarily all) students (p. 164).

Of fundamental concern for Schupak is the perpetuation of 'certain underlying assumptions' that are common to a 'wide range of activities, orientations and techniques', and which 'all assume that to perform is to interpret' (p. 170). An exponent of this interpretative hegemony is Michael LoMonico, whose celebration of 'close reading on your feet' describes how performance 'works because it gets students excited about literature', 'because students cannot get enough of it', and helps them to 'truly understand the literature'.[9] Tellingly, however, LoMonico's assertion that the integration of 'performance technologies into the teaching of English' has a 'dramatically positive impact on teachers and students' alike confirms an equal efficacy for the practice in the classroom that veers suspiciously close to an enjoyable and entertaining educational model associated more with student outcomes and cost–value economics than with close reading 'on your feet' effectiveness (p. 116).[10] Indeed, as Schupak argues in her analysis, such statements confirm how SPP has relied too heavily on certain underlying worth assumptions. In consequence, the teaching of students 'to enjoy and to become comfortable' with Shakespeare, albeit 'an important goal', is potentially damaged by the 'hours of classroom time . . . devoted to this kind of "fun" at the expense of literary instruction' (pp. 172–3). Stating

her belief that a 'cost–benefit analysis is in order', Schupak highlights how 'enthusiasm', no matter how beneficial to the classroom experience, must not outweigh consideration of 'issues of time', the 'potential for time-wasting' and the possible drain on 'additional resources' (pp. 173, 176).

Some of the blame for the loss of literary rigour in deference to the 'fun' quest for student 'enthusiasm' stems, as Schupak suggests, from certain 'underlying assumptions' among SPP enthusiasts that 'to perform is to interpret' (p. 171). In consequence, much of the literature about performance pedagogy 'assumes that everyone – or at least everyone who teaches Shakespeare – is a competent actor, director and critic of Shakespearean performances', an 'assumption' that 'logic would lead one to doubt' (p. 176). In reality, and despite the 'fact that performance methods are inherently acting and theatre-based', Schupak observes that most teachers of Shakespeare have 'received a literature-based education', thus making such performance methodologies less effective than as 'depicted' in SPP literature such as LoMonico's (p. 175). Indeed, with performance methods 'in the wrong hands', Schupak fears, the 'potential to squander a great deal of time while accomplishing little' is of real concern, especially since the 'primary purpose of Shakespeare in the English-language arts classroom is not to produce entertainment, but to enhance the learners' language arts skills' (p. 172).

The issue of theatrical entertainment versus classroom analysis is thus symptomatic of the 'qualitative' difference between acting for the professional stage and acting for the performance-based classroom (p. 176). While acting for the theatre represents, in Schupak's opinion, an 'attempt to produce a unified and compelling interpretation of a given script' – which, as every professional actor knows, must remain fresh but identically reproduced for each

---

[8] See Ralph Alan Cohen, 'From the editor', *Shakespeare Quarterly* 41 (1990), iii–v; p. iii.

[9] Michael LoMonico, 'Teaching English in the world: close reading on your feet: performance in the English language arts classroom', *The English Journal* 95 (2005), 116–19; p. 116.

[10] LoMonico, 'On your feet', p. 116.

performance of a specific season – performance in the Shakespeare classroom 'often has a diametrically opposed purpose': 'to explore a *range* of possible interpretations' (p. 176). It is this fundamental difference between the theatre and the classroom – whereby, in 'theatrical performance, the text is a tool for producing the performance, whereas in the literature classroom, performance is a tool for analysing the text' – which should most concern those educators searching for the SPP potential of their post-pandemic lesson plans (p. 176).

Although Schupak's obvious concerns about the efficacy of SPP are based on the theatrical experience (or otherwise) of Shakespeare teachers for whom acting, directing or theatre critiquing are not part of their career résumés, it must not be forgotten how many creative practitioners – bedazzled by the glamour, wealth and bright lights of academe – have brought their performance skills to the classroom. The transition from onstage actor to in-class instructor has, for some, seemed relatively seamless. Past expertise in mass communication in a theatre translates well to academic environments where the new 'audience' consists mainly of fee-paying students. If the theatre was the matrix for practitioners to hone certain communication skills that made their journey into academe that much easier, then it is not hard to appreciate the significance of theatre-based material culture on performance methodologies, whose development accompanied the approach's burgeoning success.

INTUBATING THE PANDEMIC PLAYHOUSE: 'SICKNESS IS CATCHING; O, WERE FAVOUR SO'

With nearly a quarter-century of investment in the historical and material functions of early modern performance, combined with an educational imperative that borders on the evangelical, it is unsurprising that early modern playhouse structures such as Shakespeare's Globe Theatre (1997) and the Sam Wanamaker Playhouse (2014) in London, or the ASC's Blackfriars Playhouse (2001) in Staunton, Virginia, should gain in

pedagogical popularity and near cult status. SPP might represent a significant and invaluable educational tool on college and university campuses, especially in the Anglophone world, but its value owes much to the venues that employ educators and creatives, both to analyse and teach, and to perform and entertain. Without the liveliness of theatrical inventiveness presented in tandem with the education departments of these facsimile playhouses, SPP techniques would undoubtedly be sown on less fertile academic ground.

The facsimile playhouse enterprises so vital for SPP's ongoing success in the academy inevitably struggled through the pandemic to maintain their economic stability and statuses as repositories for everything Shakespeare, whether Zoomed, YouTubed or Facebook Lived. The financial viability of these theatrical ventures, encapsulated in the 'myth of growth' that, as theatre director Carey Perloff suggests, was 'inherited and zealously adopted from the corporate sector and prioritized above all else', is primarily reliant on live-performance ticket sales and audience attendance funds.[11] In addition, Shakespeare theatre finances remain closely predicated on what Christie Carson calls the 'increasing importance and prominence' of in-house 'education departments', whose creation was 'largely the result of the movement towards an interactive engagement with audiences that [an] online world demands', while promoting proximity to the actorly process.[12] Proximity and education seemed incompatible bedfellows, however, in the midst of COVID-19, when audiences were banned from gathering or self-selectively absented themselves from exposure.

Viewed by some as unsustainable in the unprecedented closure crisis, and exacerbated by the social distancing lockdowns that forced theatres

---

[11] Carey Perloff, 'Artists first? Charting a future for the American theater', The Clyde Fitch Report, 10 June 2020: www.clyde fitchreport.com/2020/06/artists-theater-acting-company.
[12] Christie Carson, 'eShakespeare and performance', *Shakespeare* 4 (2008), 254–70; p. 258.

worldwide to 'go dark' – the theatrical term for the temporary mothballing of performance spaces, some never to reopen – the 'rescue package' model advocated by campaigners such as the director Sam Mendes seemed an unsatisfactory option.[13] In the UK, for example, government loans 'issued on generous terms' to venues such as Shakespeare's Globe, still, as Tosin Thompson notes, ignored the 'real "crown jewels" of the arts', the freelance actors who necessarily populate theatre stages.[14] Likewise, as Perloff argues, such bailouts only perpetuate the notion that 'artists are endlessly disposable and replaceable'. Accordingly, Perloff adds, production houses that focused 'less on the work that animated [their] stages' and more on the 'buildings and infrastructures' that accommodated their art were now experiencing a downturn that rendered publicly financed bailouts all but essential.[15]

Shakespeare theatres worldwide were (and are) undoubtedly suffering from a pandemic that fundamentally impacted their ability to function, either as educational or as creative resources. Government loans and subsidies, support from philanthropic institutions and private individuals, and the determination of supporters to keep the furloughed or inactive actively engaged might have offered short-term relief. Nonetheless, the crisis continued to impact the delivery of Shakespeare and performance in the classroom, not least with respect to teachers' increased reliance on pre-filmed or YouTube accessible content. Although recorded performances have for many years proved suitable supplemental resources for close textual analysis, while also reminding students of Shakespeare's dramatic intensity, these same recordings are not without certain limitations, especially if considering the plight of those upon whose creative skills these visual teaching aids rely.

PRE-FILMED SHAKESPEARE: 'THE LIVING RECORD OF YOUR MEMORY'

In the wake of COVID-19, difficulties that impacted in-person group performance workshopping were

highlighted, exacerbated further by some teachers and students finding themselves unable or unwilling to return to college classrooms that *New York Times* columnist Frank Bruni described as 'ideal theaters of contagion'.[16] The development of hybrid or 'concurrent classroom' blended learning models, with some in-class student attendees regularly swapping places with online Zoom participants and vice versa, while all practising as safe a social distancing and cleansing regime as practicable, did little to restore faith in the short-term feasibility of a return to classroom normality.[17] Live group modelling intended to excite student interest in Shakespeare needed rethinking – and rethinking fast. When disseminated via a computer screen and the ubiquitous Zoom videoconferencing platform, with its individuated and isolated two-dimensional access window experience, Shakespeare as a performance construct was getting lost in screen-share translation. A collective need to reinvent the SPP experience, at least until freed from further pandemic constraints, seemed therefore self-evident, not least because of the ease with which we now access past Shakespeare productions for presentation in our classes. Too heavy a reliance on pre-recorded, pre-filmed material proved unsatisfactory, however, especially for students used to accessing movies or binge-watching

---

[13] Sam Mendes, 'How we can save our theatres', *Financial Times*, 5 June 2020: www-ft-com.eur.idm.oclc.org/content/643b7228-a3ef-11ea-92e2-cbd9b7e28ee6.

[14] Will Gompertz, 'Coronavirus: emergency money for culture "won't save every job"', *BBC News*, 7 July 2020: www.bbc.com/news/entertainment-arts-53302415; Tosin Thompson, 'The real "crown jewels" of the arts? An unprotected freelance workforce', *The Guardian*, 22 July 2020: www.theguardian.com/stage/2020/jul/22/the-real-crown-jewels-of-the-arts-an-unprotected-freelance-workforce.

[15] Perloff, 'Artists'.

[16] Frank Bruni, 'The end of college as we knew it?' *The New York Times*, 4 June 2020: www.nytimes.com/2020/06/04/opinion/coronavirus-college-humanities.html.

[17] Ted Ladd, 'Optimizing concurrent classrooms: teaching students in the room and online simultaneously', *Forbes*, 19 June 2020: www.forbes.com/sites/tedladd/2020/06/19/optimizing-concurrent-classrooms-teaching-students-in-the-room-and-online-simultaneously/?sh=3c05cc8e3451.

series from media platforms such as Netflix or YouTube. Digital pedagogy needed to develop alongside the Generation Z ease with technology and information retrieval.

Although, as we know, the digital delivery of pedagogy has travelled vast distances and at such speed over the preceding decades, the same cannot be said for the pre-recorded Shakespeare we traditionally rely on to supplement our 'on your feet' activities. As far back as 1974, for instance, the educator John Gerlach was espousing the use of Shakespeare on film as an 'attempt to visualize the implications of the printed word' for college-level students, in his case using Laurence Olivier's 1944 film version of *Henry V*.[18] When choosing Olivier's film for his classroom activities, however, Gerlach's principal concern was its artistic and (in his opinion, limited) literary merit, despite the fact that, with the movie distributor Walter Reade 'offering the film for approximately $1500' to any interested educational clients, one might now consider the astonishing cost of greater significance.[19] Although hard to imagine an age before VHS, DVD or the internet, it is salutary to remember the enormous outlay required to show filmed reproductions in the classroom prior to these everyday technologies entering our lives.

Less expensive recordings of Shakespeare performance now flood the educational marketplace, freely available via YouTube or the *MIT Global Shakespeares* international archive, or firewalled by Digital Theatre+ or Drama Online, whose collections offer a range of material from prestigious companies in the US and UK.[20] Depending on an academic institution's willingness or ability to pay the costs of access, an obvious variability in content is evident whichever platform an educator chooses, with subscription-based sites offering the most sophisticated product. Whether filmed using static long-range single cameras or benefiting from multi-angle televisual or filmic post-production investment, these recordings sometimes display inconsistent sound quality or directorially selective close-up editing that often mediate in strangely voyeuristic non-theatrical ways. As Pascale Aebischer and Susanne Greenhalgh note when

discussing the difference between 'live' theatre broadcasts ('live-mixed' during capture and simultaneously distributed), 'theatre broadcasts' (captured with 'multi-camera setup' over several live performances and post-produced for retrospective dissemination) and 'recorded theatre' or 'edited theatrical film' (for later release on DVD or streaming/downloading), the 'boundaries' between these different 'modes of production and distribution' are as permeable as they are consistent in their desire to capture not only onstage action, but also live audience reaction.[21]

Excellent as the better-produced Shakespeare recordings are, for the socially distanced pandemic classroom such products still emerge as remediated 'distracted viewing' consumer goods that demand little by way of personal involvement.[22] While agreeing with Aebischer and Greenhalgh's desire to 'confront the arguments about the ontology of performance and its dependence on presence and liveness' when addressing the 'co-presence in a single time and space of performer and spectator' of a captured Shakespeare event, and their consequent desire to redirect 'attention towards the devices of inclusion, immersion and interaction deployed within the performance captures' they discuss, I find such redirection less convincing in the pandemic's aftermath.[23] Indeed, Aebischer and Greenhalgh's shift of focus to the 'broadcast

---

[18] John Gerlach, 'Teaching the Shakespearean Film: Olivier's Henry V', *Annual Meeting of the National Council of Teachers of English* (1974), pp. 1–12, accessible at *ERIC: Institution of Education Sciences*: https://files.eric.ed.gov/fulltext/ED103907.pdf.

[19] Gerlach, 'Teaching', p. 12.

[20] Peter S. Donaldson and Alexa Alice Joubin, *The MIT Global Shakespeares Project* (2020): https://globalshakespeares.mit.edu; Digital Theatre+, Digital Theatre (2020): www.digitaltheatreplus.com/education; Drama Online, Bloomsbury (2020): www.dramaonlinelibrary.com/home.

[21] Pascale Aebischer and Susanne Greenhalgh, 'Introduction: Shakespeare and the 'live' theatre broadcast experience', in *Shakespeare and the 'Live' Theatre Broadcast Experience*, ed. Pascale Aebischer, Susanne Greenhalgh and Laurie Osborne (London, 2018), pp. 1–16; p. 4.

[22] Aebischer and Greenhalgh, 'Introduction', p. 12.

[23] Aebischer and Greenhalgh, 'Introduction', p. 12.

spectators' *experience* and *practices of presence and participation*' seems, in its audience-centricity, to downplay the agency of the very creatives that make such broadcasts possible because their participation is now petrified in a historicized performance 'past'.[24] The same creative personnel who have provided the backbone of Shakespeare in performance studies since the 1990s, and whose enactments can be reproduced, paused, fast-forwarded or endlessly rewound in any classroom setting, now faced a threat to their livelihoods as great and as lifechanging as the disease that loomed invisible and silent over their collective heads.

Understandable and commendable as the short-term fix of technologically disseminated performance events were, whether pre-recorded and regurgitated or created anew, the forced transition by several theatre companies to offering free access to their firewalled products did little to attract new Shakespeare consumers, but seemed instead intentionally focused on maintaining their existing audience interest-base. In addition, such activities did not address a far more pressing problem for the Shakespeare theatre industry, and one correlative to the very debate between 'literary versus performance' methodologies in the academy: the long-term care for its actors and creatives. As the arts commentator Nicholas Berger observes, '[s]imply relocating existing structures of theatrical art production online' does little to 'solve the problems that existed in those structures'.[25] While none of the theatrical venues associated with Shakespeare and education would consider themselves anything other than caring and dutiful towards their acting personnel, the inability of so many of these 'artists, natural-born hustlers, empaths, and problem-solvers' to survive in the virtual environments they found themselves in is specifically related to their 'defining quality': their 'liveness'. Perhaps, as Berger suggests, the cult-like status of some 'glamorous' venues might 'wane as we come to realize that theatre exists in the artists that make it, not the buildings that house it'.[26]

Such comments accord with opinions expressed by Perloff, whose clarion-call that 'the artist must always be at the center' of all theatrical decision-making recognizes the hardships that

performers were experiencing (and continue to experience) in a world in which traditional demands of the 'commercial marketplace' no longer seemed to apply. Asking whether, at a time 'when the entire future' of theatrical expression was 'up for grabs', producers would be 'strong enough to imagine an industry that is more artist-centric', Perloff seeks fundamentally to 'reassign value' to the acting profession.[27] A reassigning of value would be of little benefit, however, for actors facing the incredible quandary of being offered work in whatever form at a time of continued collective danger. Should actors, directors or designers really be placed in the position of considering whether any job offer is a health risk worth taking – or, because of financial pressures, cannot be ignored? The very concept of Shakespeare being presented as a live performance, in the socially distanced climate of COVID-19, seemed as fraught with potential dangers for its acting personnel as playhouse stagings during the plague closure years of the late sixteenth and early seventeenth centuries.

Actors continued, however, to be asked to perform together, in the sure knowledge many would find the temptation and the need irresistible. Such temptation is evidenced, perhaps, by the American Shakespeare Center's Summer 2020 'SafeStart' programming, with its 'carefully developed series of mitigation protocols designed to keep actors, staff, and audiences safe'.[28] As an ASC 'SafeStart' rehearsal video demonstrates, actors were allowed to rehearse safely in masks, but it is hard to equate how the company's 'Universal Masking' policy 'for all audiences and *non-performing* staff and volunteers' (italics

[24] Aebischer and Greenhalgh, 'Introduction', p. 12.
[25] Nicholas Berger, 'The forgotten art of assembly: or, why theatre makers should stop making', *Medium: Culture*, 3 April 2020: https://medium.com/@nicholasberger/the-forgotten-art-of-assembly-a94e164edf0f.
[26] Berger, 'Forgotten art'. [27] Perloff, 'Artists'.
[28] 'American Shakespeare Center announces Summer 2020', American Shakespeare Center press release, 12 June 2020. https://americanshakespearecenter.com/2020/06/safestart-summer-2020-news.

mine) was any less contentious than Disney World Florida's public spat with the US Actors' Equity Association over the threat to its members who 'cannot practice social distancing' when interacting on stage.[29] Indeed, in their own online appeal to keep 'theater workers and audiences safe', the Actors' Equity union highlighted its care for its members in demanding 'fair compensation and safer theaters for everyone', while listing the ASC as one of only five companies nationwide that '[s]hamefully' had 'decided to abandon their commitment' to their union employees.[30] Intent, Actors' Equity claimed, 'on moving forward on timelines that make collaborating to ensure a safe workplace impossible', the ASC was accused of having 'water[ed] down their health and safety standards' so drastically as to ensure their loss of status as Equity-approved theatre producers.[31]

While some US producers 'met or exceeded the safe and sanitary conditions necessary for presenting live theater during the COVID-19 pandemic', and were hailed by the Actors' Equity union as 'conscientious artists for their attention to the health and safety of theater workers and audiences', others seemed less concerned for their onstage creative colleagues.[32] Should Shakespeare producers imperil their most valuable living assets in the quest to maintain their 'glamorous' theatrical spaces, as Berger terms them? The health and welfare of theatre professionals, especially those potentially compromised in any non-masked performance setting, should be of principal concern at times of pandemic threat – or any other time. Without the Shakespeare actor, there would be no Shakespeare theatre, and no need for an educational department at its performative core. One company that did, however, consider the financial, mental and safety needs of its actors, and in the process created a unique and unforgettable online performance experience that offers a potential model for in-class group activities in the Zoom-distanced virtual classroom, is SF Shakes with its summer 2020 production of *King Lear*. Responding to the COVID-19 pandemic, SF Shakes embraced Zoom technology, while promoting company wellbeing, job security and

creative innovation, all of which resulted in a culturally significant production worthy of closer consideration.

SAN FRANCISCO SHAKESPEARE FESTIVAL: 'SWEET PRACTICER, THY PHYSIC I WILL TRY'

In the 'wake' of the pandemic 'tragedy', Berger observes how theatres and their practitioners responded with 'immediate, ad hoc, digital projects', often disseminated via Zoom, that 'highlight not a resiliency, but a deep fear' of 'being alone'. With artists 'addicted to creation', and a 'whole world [that] has moved online', the 'crowded' field of creativity led inevitably to questions of whether a 'demand' for such projects exists 'outside' the theatre community. The realization that theatre workers 'have been deemed non-essential in this moment' and the 'refusal to acknowledge' this uncomfortable fact by those required 'to exit the stage, not give an encore', had resulted, in Berger's opinion, in 'disposable digital work that dismantles the very intimacy [theatre] demands'. Unfortunately, Berger maintains, the 'migration of [the theatrical] art form to a digital medium seems to deny theatre that durability, not increase it'. With barely disguised irony, Berger offers 'a reason theatremakers weren't staging readings of plays over Zoom two-months ago': 'The singular transcendence of human congregation is irreplaceable. So why are we trying so hard to make theatre without it?'[33]

---

[29] 'We are back: Summer 2020 SafeStart season', American Shakespeare Center video, 10 July 2020: https://americanshakespearecenter.com/2020/07/we-are-back-summer-2020-safestart-season; ASC Press Release, 12 June 2020; Ashley Carter, 'Disney World, Actors' Union rift keeps shows in the dark', *Spectrum Bay News 9*, 29 July 2020: www.baynews9.com/fl/tampa/attractions/2020/07/29/actors-equity-association-disney-world-dispute.

[30] Actors' Equity Association, 'Keep theater workers and audiences safe', Safety Spotlight, Actors' Equity Association (2020): https://actorsequity.org/safetyspotlight.

[31] Actors' Equity, 'Keep'. [32] Actors' Equity, 'Keep'.

[33] Berger, 'Forgotten'.

One US West Coast theatre company, SF Shakes, did succeed in creating an intimate 'human congregation' experience, however, with their summer 2020 production of *King Lear*. Directed by Elizabeth Carter, herself an actor turned director and teacher, the SF Shakes *King Lear* required a major re-envisioning by its traditionally open-air production team following the advent of the COVID-19 lockdowns. No longer deeming it safe to rehearse and perform for a community audience, SF Shakes management decided to move from their Cupertino, Redwood City and San Francisco parkland touring venues to the home computer screens of their followers. Broadcast live to its audience via Zoom and YouTube, the SF Shakes 'Free Shakespeare in the Park' became 'Free Shakespeare at Home'. The lessons learned from this bold experiment, which most closely resembles Aebischer and Greenhalgh's 'live-mixed' theatre broadcast model with its simultaneous distribution, are significant in offering a possible alternative for educators to explore 'on your feet' SPP methodologies in their distanced classrooms.

As an example of the 'rapidly evolving technologies' that Pascale Aebischer discusses in her analysis of *Shakespeare, Spectatorship and the Technologies of Performance*, the SF Shakes *King Lear* appears particularly innovative.[34] 'Technological innovation', as Emma Rice's directorial tenure at Shakespeare's Globe Theatre London confirmed, has nonetheless led to accusations of technological contamination in the context of twenty-first-century Shakespeare spectatorship and material culture.[35] Proposing instead a 'historicised theoretical approach to digital and analogue performance technologies' that effectively counters the criticism directed at innovators such as Rice, Aebischer argues for an alternative critical model that consciously 'complicates the focus on interactivity and immersion as the be-all and end-all of postdramatic performance in the digital age'. In doing so, Aebischer addresses how technologies 'contribute to the distancing of spectators from an illusionist spectacle and offer them a sense of control without responsibility', the result leading to 'enhanced, intensified and accelerated

ways of experiencing the shared response-ability /responsibility of performers and spectators as they confront the ethical predicaments and political problems' in the present, and in earlier ages.[36]

Although the pandemic threatened communal 'sharing' on so many levels, with Berger's 'non-essential' actor-addicts experiencing real and emotional redundancy as social gatherings were banned, Aebischer's argument for 'enhanced, intensified and accelerated' social and political shared responsibility seems particularly apposite when applied to a Zoom production that employed digital technologies and imagery to inform the topical immediacy of its narrative (10). As the company's press release explained, the 'pervading state of distress' in *King Lear* 'resonates with the dis-ease engendered by modern pandemics and current crises', such inflection represented throughout the production by TV 'Storm Watch' warnings and 'Black Lives Matter' protest news broadcasts, announced via social media sound and haptic nudges on actors' omnipresent smartphones.[37]

The topical nuance of any production that situates its *Lear* opening scenes outside and within the White House Oval Office, complete with wall-mounted US map divided longitudinally into three equal regions, might reasonably stand accused of clichéd modernization. What made the SF Shakes production truly different, however, was the fact that, even though the audience screen was populated by multiple actors performing in the same virtual, perspectively photographic scenic environment – whether Atlantan 'MacMansion', trash-strewn garbage dump, storm-wracked prairie or tented military encampment – the actors were

---

[34] Pascale Aebischer, *Shakespeare, Spectatorship and the Technologies of Performance* (Cambridge, 2020), p. 3.

[35] Kevin A. Quarmby, 'OP PC or PAR RIP', *Shakespeare Bulletin* 36 (2018), 567–98; pp. 572–3.

[36] Aebischer, *Shakespeare*, pp. 2–3, 10.

[37] 'SF Shakes announces cast & schedule for Free Shakespeare @ Home', BroadwayWorld.com, 6 July 2020: www.broadwayworld.com/san-francisco/article/SF-Shakes-Announces-Cast-Schedule-For-Free-Shakespeare-Home-20200706.

not in the same location as anyone else, and could not see each other in real time. Each actor was filming themselves in front of a basic home-mounted green screen, while relying on Zoom's Virtual Background facility to isolate their active bodies and, in close-up, faces. Thirteen actors presented the play as a three-hour live performance event (including fifteen-minute thunder and lightning Intermission), broadcast via the SF Shakes YouTube channel, with the product 'live-mixed' by the technical director and scenic/graphic designer, Neal Ormond. Hugh Bailey's Open Broadcaster Software (OBS Studio), a free 'open source software for video recording and live streaming' that can be downloaded and activated for Windows, Mac or Linux computing platforms by anyone willing to experiment with it, was chosen as the most effective method, its technical use explained in great detail (including sound, camera positioning and lighting information) on the SF Shakes blog site.[38] Ormond mixed the thirteen actors' Zoom screens to achieve a unified though safely distanced production that pushed the boundaries of videoconference interactivity to create a theatrical product of great intensity.[39]

Asked in a private telephone conversation why the decision was taken to embrace this new technology, the SF Shakes artistic director Rebecca Ennals, who also adapted and edited the script, discussed the reasoning behind the company's radical move and the impact it had on the actors and creatives. Explaining how the choice of *King Lear* was made at a 'resident artists' retreat' in 2019, with the company deciding that, in a time of 'mental dysfunction and environmental chaos', 2020 could not be considered 'a comedy year', Ennals confirmed that the expectation was always to perform the traditional open-air Shakespeare season.[40] All proceeded accordingly, with Carter accepting her directorial contract in time for casting in December 2019, and Ormond fulfilling his regular creative role of designing, and preparing to workshop-build, a traditional wood and steel touring set suitable for the play's open-air locations. Carter even described her 'original concept' plan for the touring set, envisioning a 'cathedral of trees that

collapsed and deconstructed' in front of the audience, as 'nature [began] taking over' Lear's crumbling nation.[41] By January, as Ennals explained, costume and lighting designers were readied and a new production manager hired to begin preparations for the upcoming season's 'cathedral of trees' production. Sensing the irony, Ennals noted how the creatives and 'cast all came into the project thinking it was going to be a regular in-person free Shakespeare in the Park production'.

As we all know, however, unexpected world events were to change the SF Shakes plans in fundamental ways. Ennals well remembers the first day of rehearsals when things, in her words, went 'crazy'. The COVID-19 virus already was impacting San Francisco, which caused 'an additional layer of stress', though people were at that point still freely travelling on public transit. The first day of an 'in-person two-week' rehearsal period was called for Wednesday 11 March 2020, with cast and crew 'gathered round the table' in a space that was 'doused' in 'cleaners and in disinfectant' to try and make the first read-through 'as sanitary as possible'. Two actors could not be present in person, however, so, knowing 'about this new videoconferencing software called Zoom' – which Ennals had experienced at an earlier conference but that few actors had at this stage even heard of – the decision was made 'to try it out'. Despite Carter's understandable insistence that it was 'so important' that the company 'be in person' – 'we really have to be in person', Ennals recalled the play's director stressing – the decision was made for the absentees to Zoom into the rehearsal room. In consequence, Jessica Powell and Diana Lauren

---

38 See https://obsproject.com; Arin Roberson and Eliana Lewis-Eme, 'A peak behind the (virtual) curtain of *King Lear*', Shake It Up: The Blog for San Francisco Shakespeare Festival, 15 July 2020: https://sfshakes.wordpress.com/2020/07/15/a-peek-behind-the-virtual-curtain-of-king-lear.

39 Hugh Bailey ['Jim'], 'OBS Studio', OBS: Open Broadcaster Software website (2020): https://obsproject.com.

40 Rebecca Ennals, private telephone conversation, 17 July 2020.

41 Elizabeth Carter, private telephone conversation, 27 October 2020.

Jones, who played King Lear and Cordelia/Fool respectively, became the first of the company to begin the SF Shakes season via Zoom, never to meet their fellow artists 'in person' again.

Experiencing discomfort at meeting with fifty-plus people over the course of that first day because of the threat she might pose to others if actually contagious, Ennals decided to make the second day's 'script workshop' a Zoom-only event. Thankful that the play's director was 'immensely flexible', while heeding Carter's caveat that this was acceptable only 'for one day', Ennals ensured that this supposed one-off Zoom event was as productive as possible. As the first rehearsal day ended and news about health concerns continued to 'get more dire', the Zoom experiment was extended to include Thursday 12 March. Only two days into rehearsals, that same Thursday night saw everything change, with San Francisco's mayor, London N. Breed, issuing the Bay Area's stay-at-home order, effective Friday 13 March onward. Poignantly acknowledging that SF Shakes was 'a couple of days ahead of the whole thing' by employing Zoom so promptly, Ennals admitted to adopting a 'multi-scenario approach' to forward planning, with an absolute cut-off date of 15 July (only three days before the first scheduled Preview performance) chosen for a final decision whether or not an in-person season was possible. Four months after rehearsals first began, and aware that the situation just could not improve, the company decided to resist any further 'maybe-maybe zone' dithering and committed to an entirely online production conceived from the virtual ground up.

Fortunately for SF Shakes, Ormond had begun exploring all possible outcomes back in early March when the stay-at-home order was activated. His prior experience in graphic design meant he considered 'virtual reality and augmented reality' as possible performance modalities, especially since the traditional Zoom multi-square talking heads delivery – reminiscent of those 'immediate, ad hoc, digital projects' scathingly referenced by Berger – was discounted as a performative option early on. As if agreeing with Berger's negative appraisal of the 'migration' of Shakespeare performance using standard Zoom technology,

Ennals explained the reasoning behind Ormond's decision, and how many of the 'Zoom readings' that other theatre companies and actors were offering to the public could not escape feeling uncomfortably 'like a Zoom meeting'. Rather than an exciting new medium to showcase Shakespeare performance, such ventures highlighted a malaise that soon infected many of their viewers: 'Zoom fatigue'. Because of the 'mistaken idea for a lot of theatre companies that production online would be less work', and the accompanying non-creative use of a talking-heads videoconferencing functionality that failed to recognize many 'Zoom fatigue' job or job-hunt burnouts, such 'disposable digital work' was inevitably doomed to fail.

Eventually deciding upon OBS, with its functionality of combining multiple Zoom images, Ormond created what Ennals called a 'backstage area' of actors, each performing in their individual homes with 'nothing fancy' by way of technology, just the tiny cameras from a 'typical laptop'. Thirteen separate home Zoom camera feeds were then combined on Ormond's central computer, with him 'orchestrating images' by effectively layering the actors on his screen as they entered and exited scenes. The multi-layered, remotely and individually acted, and simultaneously remixed live-action performance was finally 'sent out to YouTube for everyone to watch'. Able to pass behind and in front of each other and thus appear 'in perspective', the actors created a 'mind-blowing' world for their YouTube audience – one in which, as Ennals celebrated, it was easy to 'forget' that no actor could see the other. Indeed, the fact that the production was not pre-recorded, but performed live in individual locations, only became evident at the end-of-play Curtain Call when all the actors danced and gyrated against green backdrops, each isolated and entrapped in their individual Zoom 'Gallery View' windows, but projected simultaneously onscreen. The technical wizardry of OBS/Zoom for facilitating socially distanced group performances was fully appreciable at this point.

Despite the obvious distances involved, actors even seemed able to 'touch each other', as well as exchange stage properties like letters and messages or circle and fight at close quarters with daggers, such simulated tactility achieved through pre-directed 'calibrated movements' (and occasional sleight of hand) that required both memorizing, and adjusting to, their fellow performers' virtual positions in any scene. 'It's an enormous test of the skills of each actor', Ennals acknowledged when describing the innate 'kinaes-thetic sense' the process relied on. Only by 'transfer-ring that kinaesthetic knowledge into imagining the space' and reacting to 'other bodies' invisibly moving around them could the isolated actors create the illu-sion of ensemble connectivity in the micro-theatrical universes of their homes. Admitting that 'for some people' it was 'magic', and for others 'more technical', Ennals still expressed astonishment at the ultimate effect of 'this new medium'. Moments of moving intensity were 'all felt' by the management and tech-nical crew when first they watched the actors, united by technology, perform powerfully emotional scenes on their respective computer screens.

Explaining the emotive power of this digital experiment and its ability to touch its audience on a personal, visceral level, Ennals mused how 'there's a lot of talk about the collective breath and how you can't have this collective breath in digital theatre, but I don't know if that's really true': 'I think the jury's out because this is all so new. Maybe we are having a collective breath – we may not know it – but we are all having a collective emotional experience even though we're not physically together.' Of course, Ennals admitted, the company would all have pre-ferred in-person connectivity, but the OBS platform noticeably elevated one specific aspect of their per-formances: the clarity with which Shakespeare's lan-guage was communicated. Without the 'distractions in open-air theatres', where 'sometimes the language is lost', the OBS format heightened textual appreci-ation for Shakespearian dialogue that was heard 'reigning supreme', its dramatic intent expressed 'clearly and intimately', especially when actors offered their soliloquies and asides full face and dir-ectly into camera.

Awareness of the audience's heightened engage-ment with the text came via YouTube's 'live elec-tronic chat' function, described in an SF Shakes

blog as 'a great tool that allows the audience to express their reactions to the performance as well as engage with their fellow audience members'.[42] YouTube's 'Chat' function also allowed immedi-ate communication with the audience by the SF Shakes college student 'literary interns', who sup-plied pre-researched textual and background com-mentary, intermixed with immediate responses to audience queries about the play. The chat allowed, for example, 'Fun Fact' informational snippets, such as Carter's choice 'very deliberately [to] cast the more senior characters with white actors, while the younger generation [were] played by mostly actors of color', thus ensuring a White female King Lear was surrounded by daughters purposely chosen, as Ennals confirmed, as a 'metaphor' for the racial diversity and 'generational shift' in her nation.[43] In addition, information could be shared as and when questions arose in real time, such as the production's 'blood budget' of '$685 for 5 gallons of blood and 34 ounces of Blood Jam', or how '26 computers in total' were used 'to run the show', with Ormond alone employing two computers, four screens, and an iPad to create the final per-formance product.[44] Evident from this live com-bination of visual performance and associated electronic messaging was the pedagogical potential of providing a group with real-time supplemental information about the nuances of a play (in effect, offering textual apparatus in an immediately con-sumable form), while simultaneously inviting active opinions, feelings and reflections in return.

If the SF Shakes *King Lear* broadcast offers a positive alternative model for Shakespeare and per-formance pedagogy, its affirmative impact on those

[42] Arin Roberson and Eliana Lewis-Eme, 'O, for a Zoom of fire: reimagining Free Shakespeare in the Park', Shake It Up Blog, 27 May 2020: https://sfshakes.wordpress.com/2020/05/27/o-for-a-zoom-of-fire-reimagining-free-shakespeare-in-the-park.

[43] Arin Roberson (@SFShakes), '"Fun Fact" for *King Lear* live broadcast: Preview night', YouTube Chat transcript, 19 July 2020.

[44] Arin Roberson (@SFShakes), '*King Lear* live broadcast opening night', YouTube Chat transcript, 25 July 2020.

actively involved likewise cannot be ignored, especially since the company's actors most closely equate to the students in our classrooms whose engagement with Shakespeare's texts we aim to inspire. As if responding to Berger's crowded field of creativity comments, Ennals acknowledged that, because 'actors want to work – they want to create', she was heartened to receive personal messages from *Lear* company members expressing not only their gratitude, but also how the 'very comforting space' was emotionally 'keeping [them] going'. Emotional comfort aside, and with the welfare of actors very much in mind, SF Shakes also ensured that they were not exploiting their performers by saying 'We'll run a video of a show', but instead working closely with the Actors' Equity union to guarantee as normal an employment experience as possible. With an Equity contract deemed 'essential from the beginning from all levels of the production', and the company determined to fulfil its professional and personal obligations, Ennals explained the process that led to their non-exploitative YouTube event.

As the pandemic took hold along with the realization that an online venture was likely, Equity's 'Theatre Authority' (TA) contract was initially considered an option.[45] Described by the SF Shakes executive director, Toby Leavitt, as a 'less expensive alternative', traditionally associated with charity benefits or telethons and limited to two broadcast events, the TA contract was immediately discounted since the company was 'looking for a more fully-produced experience'.[46] Alongside the TA option, Ennals confirmed the company 'briefly toyed' with moving over to a SAG (Screen Actors' Guild) contract, which covers 'the work of media professionals in front of a camera or behind a microphone'.[47] Such a contract might have suited the filmed 'radio theatre' style of the SF Shakes *King Lear*, but that agreement was likewise discounted, Ennals noted, since US actors would have found it 'difficult' to qualify for all-important healthcare. Although unrelated to the company's final decision, it is noteworthy that this discrepancy between workers' rights and benefits led to extended contractual 'conflict' between these two powerful acting unions,

with SAG-AFTRA entering a 'jurisdictional dispute' with its theatre union counterpart over the 'streaming of live events'.[48]

The contractual shortfalls of such agreements highlight the long-standing 'discriminatory position in terms of performers' rights' that 'audio-visual' artists suffer, in the US, the UK and worldwide, a circumstance challenged by the Switzerland-based World Intellectual Property Organization's 2012 Beijing Treaty on Audiovisual Performances, which came into full effect on 28 April 2020.[49] With its stated 'overall aim' to 'improve earning conditions for actors and other audio-visual performers' made more urgent by the 'devastating impact on cultural production' from COVID-19, the Beijing Treaty was intended to ease the plight of those who 'live from job to job in precarious economic circumstances' by expanding the 'audio-visual workers' performance-related rights', especially with regard to 'increased payments from retransmission'.[50] The 'retransmission' or 'rebroadcasting' of pre-recorded material, so evident during the pandemic lockdown and so financially unrewarding for those Shakespeare creatives most in need, was paramount in this international treaty's remit.[51]

Since Equity's TA agreement was unsuitable and the SAG contract considered a less equitable option,

[45] 'Theatre Authority', Actors' Equity Association website (2020): https://actorsequity.org/resources/theatre-authority.

[46] Toby Leavitt, private email, 7 July 2020.

[47] 'Contracts & industry resources', SAG-AFTRA (2020); www.sagaftra.org/contracts-industry-resources.

[48] Dave McNary, 'SAG-AFTRA taking jurisdictional dispute with Actors' Equity to AFL-CIO', *Variety*, 17 October 2020: https://variety.com/2020/legit/news/sag-aftra-jurisdictional-dispute-actors-equity-1234808609.

[49] Sarah Phipps, 'Help us make your voices heard – Beijing Treaty', British Equity Collecting Society Ltd (BECS), 15 July 2020: https://becs.org.uk/help-us-make-your-voices-heard-beijing-treaty.

[50] 'Beijing Treaty on Audiovisual Performances (BTAP)', British Equity Collecting Society Ltd (BECS) (2020): https://becs.org.uk/campaigns.

[51] 'Main provisions and benefits of the Beijing Treaty on Audiovisual Performances (2012)', World Intellectual Property Organization (WIPO) (2016), pp. 1–8; p. 3: www.wipo.int/edocs/pubdocs/en/wipo_pub_beijing_flyer.pdf.

and with only a week before rehearsals finished and Preview performances began, a Los Angeles Actors' Equity branch representative, Christa Jackson (herself subsequently a casualty of staff 'furloughs/layoffs'), negotiated an Equity union contract for SF Shakes based on a 'live' performance, non-recorded theatrical model.[52] *King Lear*'s six acting and one stage-managing Equity members benefitted from what Ennals described as her company's commitment to 'get people employed and to keep them employed'. Additionally, the SF Shakes non-union employees were eligible for Equity Membership Candidate Program (EMC) status as trainees who could credit their theatrical work towards eventual union membership, while also earning their full health insurance benefit weeks.[53] The 'liveness' of the venture, which, as Ennals noted, 'wasn't recorded to make a good-looking video', but instead engaged fully with the company's 'mission' to 'make community theatre . . . free and live and available', guaranteed the welfare of the creative energies involved and their status within their artistic and union communities, in line with changes demanded by our digital era. The spirit of the Beijing Treaty – with its recognition of performers as 'both artists and cultural workers', whose rights 'against the unauthorized use of their [endeavours] in audiovisual media' need 'safeguarding', and whose work acts 'as a carrier and multiplier of other creative expressions' that are 'extremely relevant to furthering cultural diversity', is evident in the SF Shakes *King Lear*.[54] An example of best practices in support of live digital creativity, equitable artistic expression, diversity and inclusion, and the free availability of localized community theatre on a mutually supportive scale, these San Francisco-based 'Shakespeare at Home' performances also demonstrate how technological innovation can offer alternative models for safe student engagement, thus encouraging educators, likewise, to experiment in their virtual classrooms.

CONCLUSION: 'HEALTH SHALL LIVE FREE, AND SICKNESS FREELY DIE'

The after-effects of the global pandemic are set to impact international theatre creativity for some time to come. With a vaccine, the threat of further social, political and economic disruption will, hopefully, recede. In COVID-19's wake, however, many Shakespeare educators found themselves reconsidering their pedagogical roles, not least with regard to the physical, mental and intellectual welfare of students who experienced isolated distance learning, or size-rationed hybrid or blended classroom delivery methods, both of which relied, and continue to rely, heavily on technology to unite in-person and/or virtual constituent learning. For many, Zoom remains the most practical tool for such interactivity, the near-universal adoption of this platform by institutions demonstrating how swiftly teachers could and would embrace technological innovations when necessitated by extreme circumstances, and how reliant we now are on evolving technologies to provide safe and effective education in the 'new normal' teaching environments we find ourselves in. As observed in the early months of 2020, however, technology is only as good as the means we have to access it. To food insecurity, health inequity and job uncertainty can be added, therefore, technology insecurity. Education, for the foreseeable future, will remain dependent on ready access to personal devices and hardware, as well as constant and consistent internet connectivity. Without the meeting of these fundamental technological needs, students will be deprived of their basic educational rights.

For those whose teaching practices have long prioritized Shakespeare and performance pedagogy, their very approach to the subject, by necessity, had to change to accommodate the technology restrictions imposed upon them. Gone – hopefully only in the short term – was the opportunity for in-person group 'on your feet' activities, with the breath and life of Shakespeare's language shared in a communal

[52] Albert Geana-Bastare (AEA Business Representative), private email, 23 July 2020.
[53] 'The EMC Program', Actors' Equity Association (2020): https://actorsequity.org/join/emc.
[54] 'Beijing Treaty', pp. 5–7.

setting. In its place, the individuated Zoom square, with its remote, often secluded and strangely voyeuristic opportunities for observational study. If the live audience's 'collective breath' was lost in the Zoomosphere, then the 'collective breath' of student exploration and experimentation seemed equally compromised by Zoom's stacking-box screen delivery format. Heavily reliant on pre-recorded materials or engaged with swiftly generated digital theatrical experiments that attempted to restore to practitioners some semblance of creative validation, Shakespeare and performance classrooms steered dangerously close to their film studies counterparts. We do not expect film studies students to engage kinesthetically with the movies they analyse, because the filmic entity is the final product, ossified in its artistic entirety. How, then, could we expect our Shakespeare and performance students to experiment with performative textual analysis if only offered 'final product' examples for comparison?

In addition to the shortfalls of media-dependent observational Shakespeare studies becoming the norm in the socially distanced near future, the regurgitation of pre-recorded material or the expectation of live performances by actors desperate to maintain their careers became, likewise, fraught with ethical, economic and health dangers. Veering uncomfortably close to exploitation during these troubling times, the repeated use of pre-recorded material, the attempts to forge an alliance of online performance experiences, and the individual efforts of artists to justify their creative existences through either digital enterprises of variable quality or occasional attempts at group theatre normalcy, all confirmed the need to find alternative methods of Shakespeare delivery that did not follow traditional corporate economic models of theatrical production and dissemination. Artists – whether actors, directors, designers or producers – would need certain protections, over and above those associated with health, if they were to survive the economic downturn that seemed inevitable in the 'After Corona' years to come. In addition, the theatre spaces that traditionally employed these creative talents had to reconsider their trading practices, especially if their all-important educational departments, which remain so vital to Shakespeare and performance pedagogy, were also to be restored to their 'Before Corona' best. Global directives like the Beijing Treaty might aim to protect those for whom the unfettered reuse of pre-recorded material threatens their very cultural and economic existence, but such voluntary measures alone cannot heal the wounds already inflicted on a creative world where YouTube offers the easiest and cheapest means to share Shakespeare as a performed dramatic construct.

As we have seen, however, one theatrical company did recreate its regular Shakespeare season in a socially distanced digital space without compromising the welfare and health of its employees, or of the public. San Francisco Shakespeare Festival's 2020 'Shakespeare at Home' production of *King Lear*, fully and professionally rehearsed and presented in real time via Zoom, OSB and YouTube technology, offered a tantalizing glimpse of what could be achieved in a Shakespeare and performance classroom if educators stepped out of their literary comfort zones and embraced the technological opportunities made newly available to them. With their realization that, in order to create, actors, like their audiences, needed and deserved to feel safe, and with the ethical imperative of guaranteeing meaningful, contractually rewarded and union-recognized work for its employees, SF Shakes set a standard for artistic welfare through innovative technologies that is worthy of emulation. Translated to a Shakespeare classroom, the SF Shakes performance model points to the possibility of creating a pedagogical experience that would allow students, safely distanced and isolated in their individual virtual Zoom spaces, to come together as a community of learners, to experiment with the text, and virtually to 'stage' interactive presentations that engage fully with their intellectual faculties.

The COVID-19 pandemic forced Shakespeare educators along an educational path strewn with professional doubt and unease. That same path highlighted the need for pedagogical responsiveness and openness when experimenting with new and potentially alien practices, all to ensure the passion for performed Shakespeare translated across a digital divide imposed on teachers and students by a virus that stubbornly refused to be defeated. If PPE for any Shakespearian meant an acknowledgement that pandemic restrictions had not made performance and education incompatible, but had instead led to discovery of innovative ways to stimulate student intellectual development, then the active liveliness so many of us admire about Shakespeare and performance pedagogy might, if we are lucky, avoid the need for future intubation in the ICUs of our academic successors – provided, that is, we express continued willingness to experiment with new technologies as and when they present themselves

'IN INDIA': SHAKESPEARE AND PRISON IN KOLKATA AND MYSORE

SHEILA T. CAVANAGH

Shakespeare claims a significant place in pedagogical and performative environments of many kinds, including an increasing number of correctional facilities. As the increasing number of book and articles focused on Shakespeare in Prison describe, textual and performative engagement with this drama offers thematic resonances, while supporting physical, emotional and intellectual development; and opportunities to engage in communal activities for people who have often experienced more trauma than success in their previous lives. Thanks to the virtual Shakespeare in Prison Network and the biennial Shakespeare in Prison conference,[1] many international prison practitioners, current programme participants and alumni are forging strong ties that help individual groups to create programming, share strategies and gain the confidence built through common pursuits. These bonds have been particularly important during the COVID-19 pandemic, when many face-to-face meetings were cancelled, particularly in correctional spaces, since these environments often breed widespread infection.[2] Virtual associations, therefore, have provided valuable opportunities to geographically distanced Shakespeare in Prison practitioners, eager for community during challenging times. Connections between far-flung Shakespeare and Prison programmes have only recently begun to encompass India, however. In 2017, Shakespeare Behind Bars's Founder, Curt Tofteland, spoke at Heritage College in Kolkata, where he met well-known classical dancer and prison practitioner Alokananda 'Mamma' Roy, whom he later invited to the 2018 Shakespeare in Prison conference held at the Old Globe Theatre in San Diego.[3] At 2020's virtual Shakespeare in Prison

conference, hosted by Shakespeare at Notre Dame and the Folger Shakespeare Institute, I electronically interviewed Roy, and Hulugappa Kattimani from Sankalpa prison theatre company in Mysore, Southern India. This gradual expansion of the Shakespeare in Prison Network to include India promises to highlight a number of important practices that make these programmes vibrant contributors to the group of educational and theatrical practitioners bringing Shakespeare into correctional facilities.

Supported by funding from Emory University,[4] I was able to visit both prison practitioners and meet many of their currently and formerly incarcerated actors and designers in January 2020.[5] This

---

[1] Shakespeare in Prison Network, www.facebook.com/groups/609718715846164; Shakespeare in Prison conference, https://shakespeare.nd.edu/about/news/2020-shakespeare-in-prisons-conference-information.

[2] Some practitioners, including Rowan Mackenzie (www.birmingham.ac.uk/schools/edacs/departments/shakespeare/news/2020/rowan-mackenzie-prisons.aspx) and Frannie Shepherd-Bates (hwww.detroitpublictheatre.org/sip-photos-1?fbclid=IwAR0u1uouawtxsiaLUJoowNaS6mCTeCAP5fqqxfn5lOvop-lSMVS5JEFf2PI) developed materials to be sent to prisoners during the pandemic.

[3] www.facebook.com/TheHeritageSchoolKolkata/posts/1557152641045488.

[4] I am grateful to Emory and to the many people in India who made this trip enjoyable and productive, particularly Alokananda Roy, the Kattimani/Bengre family and the Shakespeare Society of Eastern India.

[5] Many American prison practitioners refer to their released Shakespearians as 'returned citizens', but it remains unclear how widely used and recognized this vocabulary is more broadly.

opportunity was revelatory, only partially because 2020 soon became inhospitable to travel and interaction with others. Roy and Kattimani oversee programmes with long records of successful productions, exemplary artistry and life-changing engagements. Rightly renowned for their dedication and for the achievements of their company members, these inspiring leaders (who, to my knowledge, do not know each other) have earned the acclaim they frequently receive. Their practices do not focus exclusively on Shakespeare, although those plays often appear in their repertoire. Shakespeare provides avenues to explore many of the deep emotional issues – such as anger, jealousy, vengeance and domestic turmoil – that have contributed to these learners' traumatic experiences. The practitioners also expand the material presented to include a range of artistic, cultural, movement, mindfulness and breath-related practices. The work they model and enact incorporates innumerable tools that facilitate their participants' artistic, physical, emotional and spiritual growth, in a context that draws from Shakespeare as well as Indian literary traditions, but which also includes yoga, martial arts, music, painting, sculpture, folk dance and community building. One of the news articles describing Sankalpa's workshops, for instance, focuses on the many artistic activities enjoyed by both inmates and guards:

The participants were also trained in painting wheir [sic] their imagination was recorded on the canvas. Their real life itself was a model for them. Their paintings have depicted tribal life. The prisoners are also taught statue making. Red soil was brought in from outside and they were given training in preparing models. The impact of the workshop was such that even the guards who were on duty have also started showing keen interest in the workshop and joined in.[6]

Roy's performers also engage in a number of physical and artistic pursuits, including the creation of complicated sets and costumes. The holistic practices followed by these talented leaders accord philosophically with the approaches undertaken by many Shakespeare in Prison and Shakespeare for Veterans programmes, while offering new

perspectives on the ways in which diverse cultures can address individual and communal social needs.[7]

Kattimani and Roy have each been involved in these activities for many years and have received considerable local and some international publicity for their accomplishments. Actor Felicity Kendal, for instance, included Kattimani's programme in the 2012 documentary *Shakespeare, India, and Me*. Kendal appeared in the 1965 Merchant Ivory film, *Shakespeare Wallah*, which was loosely based on her family's experiences during her childhood in India. In the documentary, she returns to many of the places her family visited as a travelling Shakespeare troupe, seeking to find past and present Shakespearian resonances across the country. Kendal remains well known in India and her visit to the Mysore correctional facility brought welcome attention to the programme.[8]

Roy's endeavours also attract public notice, initially because she is an acclaimed cultural figure. A skilled classical dancer, she was named Miss Calcutta in 1969; later that year, she was the first runner-up for Miss India.[9] In my numerous talks on Shakespeare in Prison programmes to undergraduates in eastern and southern India, the students and their instructors invariably nodded knowingly and smiled when Roy's name was mentioned, even though they had no previous familiarity with prison education or arts programmes. Roy's work as an artist is widely recognized, however, which has undoubtedly contributed to her success as a social activist and prison educator.

Roy's and Kattimani's programmes differ, but they share several key elements. Their syncretic approaches incorporate significant recognition of their performers' experience of history and of home, for example. As prominent human geographer Yi-Fu Tuan notes, 'Human groups nearly

---

[6] 'Bringing about a dramatic change in jail inmates', *Express News*, n.d.: Kattimani archive.
[7] There are many programmes using Shakespeare with veterans, including Feast of Crispian (www.feastofcrispian.org) and DeCruit (www.decruit.org).
[8] *Shakespeare, India, and Me* (dir. Patrick McGrady, Wavelength Films, 2012).
[9] https://alokanandaroy.com/year-1960-1969.

everywhere tend to regard their own homeland as the center of the world.'[10] Tim Cresswell makes a similar point, remarking that 'people, things, and practices [are] often strongly linked to particular places'.[11] Rooting these performances in local traditions thus helps to engage the performers, while keeping them in touch with the outside world. In addition to linking their Shakespearian performances with vernacular languages and cultural practices, these leaders also introduce their participants to diverse physical regimens, encouraging mindfulness and the healing of trauma through the development of a range of movement, social and artistic skills. Furthermore, they both interact closely with their participants (and their families) while they are incarcerated and after they are released. Roy has advocated successfully for schools to be opened in local correctional facilities and helps to address the many issues with spouses, children and other family members that emerge when someone is incarcerated.[12] Notably, as sociologist Nayanee Basu reports, the performances presented by Roy's practitioners:

generate income, a part of which is channelled into the Prisoners' Welfare Fund. Close to 20 lakhs [more than 2 million US dollars] have been generated during the last three years, which are spent on the education of prisoners themselves, the disbursement of scholarships to their children, financial assistance to prisoners for their daughters' weddings, their own rehabilitation upon their release, and various other welfare programmes.[13]

Such efforts create long-lasting ties between leaders and performers in both regions. In Mysore, several alumni of Kattimani's programme spent the day with me at their former jail, and another one joined me that evening at the Kattimani home. While not all correctional facilities will allow prior residents to return, prison environments in India sometimes have unexpectedly fungible boundaries. Roy explains, for instance, that those who have been brought into custody and charged with crimes are not allowed to leave the premises until they are tried.[14] After conviction, however, they are potentially eligible for programmes such as these performance groups,

whose participants often offer their creations, under supervision, in public spaces, as this newspaper article about Sankalpa indicates:

The packed audience at the Chowdiah Memorial Hall witnessed the staging of a unique cultural event lately, the staging of Jundi Sheshanayaka, a Kannada adaptation of Julius Caesar by the inhabitants of the Bangalore Central jail. The spectacular production was the outcome of a 45 day workshop directed by Hulugappa Kattimani of Rangalayana, Mysore.

Changing the unpronounceable Roman names to Indian ones was perhaps the only concession their director had allowed these novices.[15]

Public prison performances appear to be comparatively common in India, unlike in the US, as Roy notes: 'For the past 11 years, my group has travelled to many states and cities including Mumbai, Delhi, Pune, Bangalore, and Bhubaneshwar.'[16] In my own meetings with these two programmes, I encountered far less paperwork than I have experienced in visits to correctional facilities in the US or the UK. Security guards accompany the performers when they are making public appearances, but, as Basu relates, B. D. Sharma, the former Inspector General of the West Bengal Correctional Services, 'instituted the practice of "reward parole" by which each performing inmate is given five days of parole to visit his or her family without police protection'.[17] Kattimani further indicates that performing prisoners always hope

---

[10] Yi-Fu Tuan, *Space and Place: The Perspective of Experience* (Minneapolis, 1977), p. 149.

[11] Tim Cresswell, *Place: An Introduction*, 2nd edn (Chichester, 2015), p. 42.

[12] https://economictimes.indiatimes.com/news/politics-and-nation/jails-in-bengal-to-have-schools-soon-for-children-of-inmates/articleshow/47158235.cms?from=mdr.

[13] Nayanee Basu, 'Improvising freedom in prison', *Critical Studies in Improvisation* 8 (2012), p. 10.

[14] Private conversation, 7 January 2020.

[15] Laxmi Chandrashekar, '"Breaking free to face the world"', no publication info., Kattimanni archive.

[16] Sharmistha Ghosal, 'Alokananda Roy plans a dance-drama starring prison inmates from the US and Kolkata', *Indian Express, Indulge* (2018), p. 3.

[17] Basu, 'Improvising', p. 10.

for longer-term paroles on Indian Independence Day (15 August).[18]

Such intersections between public and carceral spaces also became clear after my visit with Kattimani's troupe, when two programme alumni took me to Mysore Palace, a significant local tourist site, with strong connections to Kattimani's practice. As we approached the entrance gate, there was much joyful commotion. The police officer checking visitors outside the Palace had also worked at Mysore Central Jail and recognized my escorts immediately. In general, it seems that, like most correctional facilities, the prisons in India contain innumerable security measures to keep those inside safely ensconced. At the same time, there are sometimes moments of remarkable freedom, which outsiders often query. As one article reports, interviewers focusing on Sankalpa frequently wonder why the inmates don't escape. The performers remain devoted to their artistic practice, however: 'Something that prisoners themselves have borne out, one particular performance, upon being asked why he didn't just run away when the lights went off, a prisoner answered: "Then who will play my role?"'[19] Roy told Basu a similar story about her performers' disinclination to bolt:

You know, we have been performing in Rabindra Sadan; about ten or twelve times we have been there. Now, officers keep changing . . . now it's just a formality. They even don't look at that side. Sometimes my boys, if there is a new officer, . . . they will tell them – 'Sir there's the gate there also, so guard it.' [Laughs] [. . . Where will they run away? They say, 'Ma, from what? Will we ever be able to survive if we try to escape? We won't. We will still be on the run all the time. But here we are getting so much love and respect.'[20]

Basu additionally remarks that none of those granted short-term family visits attempted to escape either.[21] It may be impossible to determine definitively why these inmates do not seek opportunities to flee, but noted trauma expert Bessel van der Kolk indicates that theatrical pursuits can bring significant benefits to individuals dealing with traumatic circumstances: '[I was] treating three veterans with PTSD whom I'd met at the VA, and when they showed a sudden improvement in their vitality, optimism, and family relationships, I attributed it to my growing therapeutic skills. Then I discovered that all three were involved in a theatrical production.'[22] The programmes

discussed here display similar results to those noted by van der Kolk.

MYSORE

Typical news reports in India, for instance, invariably make positive comments about Kattimani's endeavours (although they often refer to the performers as 'jailbirds'), as these accounts indicate. Aarushi Agrawal reports, for instance:

Through Hulugappa Kattimani and his wife Pramila Bengre's Sankalpa Kala Sangha, who work with Central Jail Mysore, inmates are able to focus intently on the universal themes Shakespeare appeals to. Among others, the husband–wife duo uses Shakespeare plays, including *Macbeth*, *Julius Caesar* and *King Lear*, for the themes of guilt and redemption to which their actors can relate. While the plot and themes remain the same, the character names and settings are Indianised, turning, for instance, Macbeth into Marnayaka.[23]

Kattimani's ensemble members typically offer congruent testimonials, as this news piece suggests:

Sitting in a corner of the festival venue and memorizing his part, Mahesh Bagoli, 28, appeared far away from the hustle and bustle around him. Sentenced to life imprisonment in 2003 on charges of murder along with his mother Rajamma, Bagoli is serving his jail term in Mysore prison.

I can't wait to go back to the jail to share my experiences with my mother. She will be waiting for me to hear about the outside world and the theatre festival, he said.

It is the dream of every convict to come out of the stone walls of the jail, said Amburag, another convict. Jailed for supporting forest brigand Veerappan in 1998,

---

[18] Private conversation, 17 January 2020.

[19] Jaideep VG, 'Gandhi class', timeoutbengaluru.net, 19 September – 2 October 2008, p. 68.

[20] Basu, 'Improvising', pp. 10–11.

[21] Basu, 'Improvising', p. 10.

[22] Bessel van der Kolk, *The Body Keeps the Score: Brain, Mind, and Body in the Healing of Trauma* (New York, 2015), p. 333.

[23] Aarushi Agrawal, 'World Book Day 2019: Shakespeare's influence on Indian theatre is as diverse as the country's culture', 24 April 2019: www.firstpost.com/living/world-book-day-2019-shakespeares-influence-on-indian-theatre-is-as-diverse-as-the-countrys-culture-6495691.html.

he gets a chance to come out of the prison once in a year to perform in drama festivals organized by Mysore based Sankalpa theatre repertoire: 'I was extremely depressed for years, but ever since I started participating in dramas, I am at peace with myself.'[24]

While I was in Mysore, I had telephone conversations with regional prison officials who provided corroborating narratives. There seems to be widespread agreement that Sankalpa's strategies work well.

Part of Sankalpa's success appears to result from its interconnected efforts to build a number of what Benjamin Bloom's taxonomy labels cognitive, affective and psychomotor skill sets.[25] The participants are often illiterate and generally lack any prior experience with the activities they encounter here, as their leader introduces a number of practices designed to develop communication, trust, creativity, mindfulness and thoughtful physical movement. The programme draws, for instance, from the rich tradition of yoga in Mysore,[26] where, according to N. E. Sjoman, much current yoga practice emerged: 'The yoga tradition that evolved through the participation of the Wodeyar royal family, rājās of the kingdom of Mysore, has today supplanted or affected a majority of the yoga teaching traditions, primarily through the teaching of B.K.S. Iyengar and his students.'[27] In the context of Sankalpa's practice, the story of the Wodeyar family at Mysore Palace is particularly relevant, as Sjoman describes:

Mummani Krishnaraja Wodeyar was the greatest patron of the arts in Mysore. The artisans and scholars of the Vijayanagara kingdom had fled to Mysore and Tanjavur with the collapse of that empire. During the reign of Mummani Krishnaraja Wodeyar there was a renaissance in Mysore of painting, music, literary productions and architecture. Over sixty literary productions, many of them artistically illustrated, were attributed to the Maharaja alone.[28]

In fact, the programme's name emanates from yoga. In yogic terms, 'Sankalpa' is:

a Sanskrit term in yogic philosophy that refers to a heartfelt desire, a solemn vow, an intention, or a resolve to do something. It is similar to the English concept of a resolution, except that it comes from even deeper within and tends to be an affirmation.

This term comes from the Sanskrit roots *san*, meaning 'a connection with the highest truth', and *kalpa,* meaning 'vow'. Thus, it translates to denote an affirming resolve to do something or achieve something spiritual.[29]

Individuals fashion sankalpas in order to help them to achieve specific, challenging goals:

1. Possibly to reform a habit
2. To improve the quality of life/living
3. To create changes in our personality
4. To realize what you want to achieve in life
5. The sankalpa can also be visualized[30]

By calling this acting company Sankalpa and incorporating yoga into the training, Kattimani emphasizes the personal and communal transformative goals of this multi-faceted endeavour. As Sjoman notes, noticing and reorganizing many kinds of habits also lies at the heart of yoga developed at Mysore Palace: 'the prime determinant of movement pattern is habit; habit is primarily the effect or consequence of all past influences on the body/mind and matures as unconscious'.[31] This jail in Mysore, therefore, fosters healing with a practice closely linked to this region, even as it expands participants' awareness of Shakespearian drama.

When Kattimani introduces his ensemble to the breathing and movement techniques associated with yoga, he begins at an elementary level. Combined with artistic endeavours, these new skills help the participants with their personal evolution as well as

---

[24] On Veerappan, see www.britannica.com/biography/Veerappan;*Times City*, no publication info., Kattamanni archive.
[25] Benjamin S. Bloom, *Taxonomy of Educational Objectives: The Classification of Educational Goals* (New York, 1956).
[26] Scott Jackson, Mary Irene Ryan Family Executive Director of Shakespeare at Notre Dame, engages with a different yoga tradition, but I appreciate his insights into the intersection between yoga practices and applied Shakespeare for prison populations and other trauma survivors.
[27] N. E. Sjoman, *The Yoga Tradition of the Mysore Palace* (New Delhi, 1999), p. 35.
[28] Sjoman, *Yoga*, p. 41.
[29] www.yogapedia.com/definition/5751/sankalpa.
[30] https://bahiayoga.com/5-tips-on-how-to-choose-a-sankalpa.
[31] Sjoman, *Yoga*, p. 45.

with their creation of drama. Notably, these practices align with those described by Rishi Eric Infanti, a former Marine turned yoga teacher, who travelled to Mysore for additional study in yoga in order to strengthen his ability to work successfully with veterans and others:

We ease them into it, we give them baby steps to get their internal wiring to reset, to start to learn what is normal again, and to simply begin a process of unraveling the deeply engrained, learned ways of being, the mental framework in how they now see the world and the psychological landscape that they hold so dear.[32]

Infanti further discusses why yoga works well with those suffering from trauma or associated disturbances:

The gross physical movement of a Yoga class is the hook to get veterans and anyone dealing with anxiousness, bouts of anxiety, depression, both under control and to step towards relaxation. It's from relaxation, which I believe firmly that we need to learn and re-learn as a skill set, so that we can step gradually into the calmer, more meditative aspects of our practice.[33]

Similarly, when members of Sankalpa engage with art, yoga and acting, changes in habits and perceptions are often at the forefront of their minds. They may be enacting Shakespeare, but their performances only represent part of the outcomes they create, as this description of the workshops preceding rehearsals indicates:

The workshop starts with a pranayama and meditation. In the initial stage they were unable to bend their bodies but with continuous hearing of music and devotional songs they are in a better position to perform yoga.

The unique feature of the event is that the participant is allowed to speak in his mother tongue. A person who can fluently speak Telagu and not knowing Kannada is allowed to render his dialogue in Telagu. 'Language is not important, but participation is', according to Kattimani.

Adds Kattimani: It is not a drama staging for the public but a 'therapy through theatre'.[34]

Van der Kolk suggests why adding yoga into these Shakespearian endeavours may inculcate the 'therapy' Kattimani locates in these practices:

cultivating sensory awareness is such a critical aspect of trauma recovery. Most traditional therapies downplay or ignore the moment-to-moment shifts in our inner sensory world. But these shifts carry the essence of the organism's responses: the emotional states that are imprinted in the body's chemical profile, in the viscera, in the contraction of the striated muscles of the face, throat, trunk, and limbs. Traumatized people need to learn that they can tolerate their sensations, befriend their inner experiences, and cultivate new action patterns.[35]

As van der Kolk also notes: 'In yoga, you focus your attention on your breathing and on your sensations moment to moment. You begin to notice the connection between your emotions and your body.'[36] Many applied Shakespeare practitioners understandably resist making therapeutic claims for their work, but yoga and theatre both appear to create beneficial results in many venues. Van der Kolk and others explain how this combination of cognitive, affective and physical engagement can produce these advances. Distinguished Harvard educator Doris Sommer, for instance, suggests why interweaving Shakespeare, art, theatre, yoga, breathing and social connection might be beneficial. In her terms, 'Necessarily hybrid, conscientious cultural agency requires the collaboration of various skill sets to hitch stale and unproductive social patterns to the motor of unconventional interventions.'[37] The successes of Roy's and Kattimani's performers appear to illustrate Sommer's hypothesis.

Kattimani and van der Kolk also help to answer the common, but often elusive, question of: why Shakespeare? While Kattimani incorporates other narratives into his practice, reporters note that he:

picked plays by Shakespeare, consistently, over the next few years. His newly minted actors screamed as Duncan,

---

[32] Rishi Eric Infanti, *Marine on the Mat: Patanjali's Eight Limbs of Yoga from Parris Island to Mysore India* (New York, 2016), p. 202.

[33] Infanti, *Marine*, p. 202.

[34] Express News Service, no publication info., Kattimani archive.

[35] Van der Kolk, *Body*, p. 275. [36] Van der Kolk, *Body*, p. 275.

[37] Doris Sommer, *The Work of Art in the World: Civic Agency and Public Humanities* (Durham, NC, 2014), p. 7.

sparred as Horatio and railed as Antony in the theatrical Kannada. 'I chose Shakespeare because guilt plays such a strong part in his plays,' Kattimani said. 'I mean, look at Duncan for instance, or Lady Macbeth, they are wrought with guilt. This is something every prisoner I've encountered experiences.'[38]

Shakespeare also facilitates opportunities for the actors to grapple with emotions, and for audiences to perceive the performers from a new perspective, as Kattimani explains to Geeta Ramanujam: 'I chose Shakespeare because he deals with human emotions such as compassion, mercy, love, violence and hatred which would give a chance to prisoners to feel, think and redeem. It also provides spectators to view the prisoners differently, says Kattimani.'[39]

The population of this prison (and of the Presidential Correctional Home in Kolkata) includes many people whom societies and families have often ignored. Shakespeare and drama presented in this context help to address these challenges, however: 'Housed in that prison were criminals who had murdered their wives, who had severed heads and limbs of fellow humans. [These] heinous crimes were committed in a moment of weakness, were followed by a feeling of remorse. This was also the theme of the play selected for enactment.'[40] While this largely illiterate troupe has not encountered Shakespeare previously, Kattimani indicates that Shakespeare as a writer appeals to him and to his performers: 'For Kattimani, Shakespeare is not just a playwright; he's a "haunting person, cheerful person, a happy man and a very crooked man". After comparing Shakespeare to one of the *navaratnas*, Kattimani adds with a laugh, "I like Shakespeare. Our actors like Shakespeare too, very much."'[41] The affinity between Shakespeare and this population may seem unusual. Nevertheless, van der Kolk further points out why Shakespeare fits well within the prison environment and within the physical framework Kattimani crafts, by explaining the allure of this drama for young men in a detention setting:

With no words to express the effects of their capricious upbringing, these adolescents act out their emotions with violence. Shakespeare calls for sword fight, which,

like other martial arts, gives them an opportunity to practice contained aggression and expressions of physical power. The emphasis is on keeping everyone safe. The kids love swordplay, but to keep one another safe they have to negotiate and use language.[42]

Shakespeare is not the only avenue towards healing the traumas associated with incarceration, but this combination of physicality, emotion, breath and creativity regularly leads to positive outcomes.

Professionals studying art therapy in the context of trauma recovery make points resembling those associated with yoga, which may indicate why the range of artistic practices associated with these ensembles appears to create additional healing. As Lukasz M. Konopka notes, for instance, 'Spatial summation indicates that cellular learning occurs most efficiently with converging multisensory input, which, from the standpoint of human behavior, can be used to understand memory establishment.'[43] When Sankalpa participants begin, they approach clay and paints much as children would.[44] They become acquainted with the colour, smell and texture of these artistic materials, then begin to manipulate them and create rudimentary, and later more sophisticated, pieces. Now that the programme has been in place for over twenty years, the group has assembled an extensive collection of paintings and sculptures that they proudly display to visitors and share with those

---

[38] VG, 'Gandhi', p. 68.

[39] Geeta Ramanujam, 'He spots versatile theatre artistes among prisoners', *The Hindu*, 24 July 2000, n.p., Kattimani archive.

[40] Gudihalla Nagaraja, 'Artistic flight for jailbirds', *Deccan Herald*, n.d., Kattimani archive.

[41] www.firstpost.com/living/world-book-day-2019-shakespeares-influence-on-indian-theatre-is-as-diverse-as-the-countrys-culture-6495691.html. 'Navaratnas (Sanskrit dvigu nava-ratna- or "nine gems") or Nauratan was a term applied to a group of nine extraordinary people in an emperor's court in India': www.definitions.net/definition/navaratnas.

[42] Van der Kolk, *Body*, p. 344.

[43] Lukasz M. Konopka, 'Neuroscience concepts in clinical practice', in *Art Therapy, Trauma and Neuroscience: Theoretical and Practical Perspectives*, ed. Juliet L. King (London, 2016), pp. 11–41; p. 12.

[44] Private conversation, 17 January 2020.

who are newly incarcerated and just joining this enterprise.[45] Only a few of them develop professional-level skills but, as an ensemble, they provide the music and craft the sets and costumes used in their productions. Laxmi Chandrashekar comments, for example: 'The harmony of their movement heightened the beauty of group composition. Costumes, woven by the prisoners themselves had a neutrality about them and did not pin the story down to any specific period or culture. Their pleasing colours and artistic design added much to the beauty of the production.'[46] While some of those incarcerated at this facility spend time creating materials for sale with looms and woodworking equipment, few of them have previously achieved the level of artistic creativity that Sankalpa provides. This combination of crafting art in conjunction with learning lines, emotional expression and physical communication appears to produce memorable productions of Shakespeare and other texts at the same time that these pursuits improve the lives of those involved.

Art therapy research indicates that the different materials used in these artistic endeavours may contribute to the benefits Sankalpa offers by incorporating these pursuits into their theatrical creations and performances, as Vija B. Lusebrink and Lisa D. Hinz suggest:

Media choices can influence processing channels to promote or contain brain functioning. Fluid media such as watercolors and chalk pastels are likely to evoke and allow for emotional expression. Sensory engaging materials such as finger paint and wet clay quickly will bring a client in touch with trauma memories ... Resistive media such as hard clay or crayon on rough paper are likely to require rigorous work to manipulate and thus engage the Kinesthetic component.[47]

Art may also help with the prisoners' pathway away from trauma. According to Tally Tripp, for example: 'Expression through art can facilitate a shift of traumatic material from implicit to explicit memory. Ultimately, the creation of a coherent pictorial narrative of the trauma may be required for symbolic processing and trauma resolution to occur.'[48] As many writers from diffuse fields

associated with trauma suggest, the interconnection of these various interventions creates an environment within which personal change and growth can flourish.

Another key component in developing the sense of community that leads to these groups' creative expression often startles those unfamiliar with common practices in this carceral realm. Typically, incarcerated individuals in these spaces are not known to each other by name. Instead, they are called by their case number or by their offenses.[49] Accordingly, one of the men who brought me to Mysore Palace is addressed outside Kattimani's theatrical community as 'Three Murders'. Normally, those incarcerated here do not share personal stories or really get to know each other, apart from participating in close proximity during daily prison activities. Kattimani rejects these common habits, however. His groups use each other's actual names and exchange narratives about their lives and histories, including the incidents that brought them into custody. Kattimani builds a strong community among his theatrical troupe, which significantly offsets the challenging circumstances generally created in this environment:

In the ten years that I have done this, I have realised one thing – prisoners might know why someone else is in jail (they have intimate knowledge of the section the inmate was booked under and the amount of time he will be spending in incarceration), but they don't really know each other, Kattimani said. So I paired them and asked them to first talk about each of their lives.[50]

Once again, these broad introductions to physicality, community-building and the creation of art

[45] 'An exhibition of handicrafts and sculptures made by prisoners was also held at the venue', DH News Service, Kattimani archive.

[46] Chandrashekar, 'Breaking free'.

[47] Vija B. Lusebrink and Lisa D. Hinz, 'The expressive therapies continuum as a framework in the treatment of trauma', in *Art Therapy*, ed. King, pp. 42–66; p. 50.

[48] Tally Tripp, 'A body-based bilateral art protocol for reprocessing trauma', in *Art Therapy*, ed. King, pp. 173–92; p. 174.

[49] Private conversation, 17 January 2020. [50] VG, 'Gandhi'.

help to shape an environment conducive to theatricality, while simultaneously encouraging personal growth. Positive performative and personal outcomes result. Kattimani encourages these actors to immerse themselves in their parts. In one memorable incident, the man playing Lear during the storm scene was not sufficiently engaged, so the director abruptly emptied a bucket of water over his head to encourage a deeper connection with the former King's despair on the heath.[51]

KOLKATA

The performers in Kolkata engage with dance rather than the staged drama undertaken by Sankalpa, but the two programmes share many elements. Roy, for instance, also incorporates familiar local cultural practices into her prison-based productions, reflecting Cresswell's belief that 'Place is also a way of seeing, knowing, and understanding the world. When we look at the world as a world of places, we see different things. We see attachments and connections between people and place. We see worlds of meaning and experience.'[52] Her production of *Othello*, for example, which is currently in development, will draw heavily from Chhau dancing traditions from Purulia, West Bengal,[53] a region where many of Roy's incarcerated performers grew up.[54] In this piece, Iago will be presented as a trio of Chhau dancers when this character works to undermine Othello's belief in Desdemona. Roy often includes Chhau in her productions because of its physicality and its deep roots in the tribal backgrounds of many of her participants. Chhau is a distinctive art form that is widely known in this region of West Bengal, partly because the local economy is supported significantly by the creation of the elaborate masks, costumes and instruments needed for these performances.[55] Traditional Chhau narratives come from well-known mythological tales that correlate readily with the emotional strength and powerful characterizations often found in Shakespearian drama. The dancers are strikingly athletic and undertake complicated gymnastic movements, even while wearing the large, highly decorated masks that are closely associated with Chhau. This folk tradition differs significantly from the yoga practice fostered in Mysore, but there are resonances between the two activities that Shovana Narayan's description of Chhau emphasizes:

Physical exercises concentrated on each part of the body, facilitating easy movement, totally making its structure perfect and well built. Exercise training like 'sama-suchi' or stretching of legs to both sides is an 'asana' of 'yoga'. Such 'asanas' such as the technique of jumping, turning, smashing, and finally sitting on the floor with crossed legs or crouching on the floor for further strategic movements, facilitate quick body movements and preserve sound health.[56]

Narayan also details the way in which Chhau transformed from a martial art into a ritualistic, cultural phenomenon:

Chhau originated as martial exercises for self-defence as well as for the mental and spiritual development of men, responsible for the well being of the tribe, in the eastern part of India. It slowly became part of ritual and religious celebrations. Developing in an area that abounded with

[51] Conversation with Kattamanni's ensemble, 17 January 2020.

[52] Cresswell, *Place*, p. 18.

[53] The etymology of Chhau is uncertain. There are many competing spellings for its name, but I am using 'Chhau'. For further information about Chhau, see Rahul Mahata, *The Journey of Purulia Chhau Dance: From Vague to Vogue* (Munich, 2017).

[54] I am grateful to the Shakespeare Society of Eastern India, particularly Professor Amitava Roy, Professor Subir Dhar, and Dr Tapu Biswas, for introducing me to Purulia and Chhau many years ago. On numerous visits to Purulia, I have been warmly received and greeted with Chhau performances and visits to the villages where the masks are made. Principal Indrani Deb of Nistarini College, Dr Chhandam Deb of J. K. College and Dr Aparajita Hazra of Sidho-Kanha-Birsha University in Purulia have been cordial, knowledgeable hosts and guides to this martial art and folkdance tradition. It was a delightful surprise to see Chhau highlighted in Roy's work.

[55] In 2010, UNESCO designated Chhau as an intangible cultural heritage: https://ich.unesco.org/en/RL/chhau-dance -00337.

[56] Shovana Narayan, *Folk Dance Traditions of India* (New Delhi, 2014), p. 46.

tigers and other wild animals, their movements were athletic and reflected sinuos [sic] animal-like positions (especially that of a tiger) such as crouching, extended leg positions, sudden leaps and circular motions that allowed for free flowing positions which helped in permitting instant changes in the axis of rotation.[57]

As these descriptions make clear, Chhau requires considerable strength and physical dexterity, and plays a vital role in its geographical environment.

Chhau productions are massive, social affairs. Performed in the evening and often lasting throughout the night, at grassy, outdoor venues, the loud and distinctive music associated with Chhau immediately draws a crowd when it is heard. Spectators form a circle around the performance space. The stories, largely drawn from well-known Indian narratives, such as the *Ramayana* and the *Mahabharata*, incorporate figures and episodes familiar to the local audiences, and the flips, jumps and complicated choreography provide lively entertainment and help to keep regional artistic traditions alive.[58] There are signs that these practices are suffering from economic and cultural shifts, but Chhau dancing remains prominent in these tribal regions currently, and Vice Chancellor Dr Dipak Kumar Kar of Purulia's Sidho Kahno Bursha University assures me that he is committed to the preservation and study of these arts,[59] a goal he also announces on the university website: 'We have a big role at our shoulder to conserve, preserve and restore its age-old tradition, various ethnic composition and distinctive cultural facets relevant in present socio-economic milieu. We have adopted a series of activities in this regard. Introduction of courses on traditional knowledge and culture like Lac, Chhau … '.[60] Chhau holds a significant place in Purulia's cultural heritage.[61]

Like much of India, Purulia is developing rapidly, but, for many years, it has predominantly been known as an agricultural, tribal community, officially often called a 'backward region'.[62] Historically, the town attracted attention when it became the location of a prominent Lutheran Leper Hospital in the nineteenth century.[63] More recently, the district has often been under siege by Maoist rebels,[64] and one of its claims to fame in the twentieth century involved Russian guns pouring

down from the sky.[65] There is a direct, though frequently tardy, train line between Purulia and Kolkata, but service is often disrupted due to terrorist activity. A few years ago, the Shakespeare Society of Eastern India was assigned to a train compartment filled with armed guards who were there to protect a group of retired judges heading into the surrounding countryside in order to inform the impoverished population of their civil rights. Without regular access to legal information, the inhabitants of this area remain prey to violent threats against their lives and livelihoods from money lenders and other predators.[66] The availability of education and other resources is expanding around Purulia, but many of Roy's performers grew up in this region when opportunities were scarce. Drawn to Kolkata in search of economic advancement, these Purulian natives instead ended up on pathways leading to incarceration.

Since Chhau retains a prominent role in this community, Roy can productively include these movement traditions in performances involving

---

[57] Narayan, *Folk*, p. 48.
[58] This is not Roy's work, but it includes a Chhau version of *Macbeth*: https://shakespeareinbengal.in/dakini-mangal-a-chhau-adaptation-of-macbeth.
[59] Private conversation, 8 January 2020.
[60] https://skbu.ac.in/index/pagedata/gg4fof1fhl8fjj1f1fof8fkj7l6fok9f6kalbg.
[61] Chhau can be seen 'in action' in the documentary *Surviving Chhau* (dir. and written by Mainak Bhuamik, Black Coffee Productions, Watertown, MA: Documentary Educational Resources, 2005).
[62] Notably, the pandemic has slowed Purulia's economic growth significantly: https://thewire.in/rights/west-bengal-purulia-jangalmahal-lockdown-hunger.
[63] www.leprosymission.in/what-we-do/institutions-and-projects/hospitals/tlm-purulia-hospital.
[64] www.newindianexpress.com/specials/2018/aug/05/maoists-rear-heads-in-bengal-after-6-year-lull-1853496.html.
[65] See Chandan Nandy, *The Night It Rained Guns: Unravelling the Purulia Arms Drop Conspiracy* (New Delhi, 2015). For a broader explication of the social and economic challenges facing Purulia, see Binoda Kumar Mishra, *Politics of Indebtedness of Indigenous People: Study of Purulia District* (Kolkata, 2012).
[66] www.newindianexpress.com/nation/2020/apr/11/purulia-villagers-get-back-ration-cards-2128620.html.

her imprisoned students. In fact, martial arts practices like Chhau indirectly helped to spark her initial engagement with this incarcerated community of performers. When Sharma invited Roy to an International Women's Day event at the Presidential Correctional Home in Kolkata, he asked whether she might be interested in working with female prisoners.[67] She immediately agreed, but surprised her host by expressing a desire to work with imprisoned men also.[68] When Sharma asked whether she was courageous enough for that population, Roy responded: 'Of course I have the courage.'[69] Both officials and inmates initially raised questions, however, about perceptions that dance is 'female'. Roy promptly reminded them of the martial arts origins of many dance traditions, including Kalaripayatu (a martial art form originating in Kerala) and Thangta (a Manipuri martial art form).[70] These movement practices include intensive athleticism, and performers need to be physically strong and agile. The truth of these assertions is undeniable to anyone who has attended such performances, and Roy was able to captivate these men's interest in participating in these athletic, artistic endeavours. When her work began in earnest, the Purulian background of many of her incarcerated performers made Chhau an obvious choice for this ensemble. Since Shakespeare contains the kinds of stories conventionally presented through this dance, it also fits well within this new context.

The performance I saw in Kolkata included a number of segments incorporating Chhau. The performers were, understandably, not as adept as dancers who spend their entire lives training in this art, but they offered impressive, visually striking interludes in their presentation of a story about redemption and forgiveness. Incarcerated artists provide the music and costuming. Roy insists that hosting sites or organizations provide buses, so that the performers do not travel in prison vehicles.[71] A number of guards accompany the actors, dancers and musicians, but the groups are not sequestered away from the rest of the people present. Like Kattimani's ensemble, Roy's group remains quite busy, with public and privately booked productions.

Many, such as Tripp, who work at the intersection of art therapy and neuroscience, indicate that 'Art therapy utilizes both hemispheres of the brain, pairing the emotional right-brain sensations with rational, verbal left-brain processes.'[72] From this perspective, it makes sense that Roy also includes considerable visual arts work in her largely physical practice. Chhau dancers, for instance, are noteworthy for their masks, as Roma Chatterji describes:

The dancers wear masks that portray the dominant moods of the characters they are supposed to represent. The masks of the gods (dévas) are painted in pastel shades and have features that are delicately modelled showing expressions that are serene or benign. The masks of the demons (asuras) have bulging eyes and snarling lips and are painted in colours that are darker than those representing the gods. The hand gestures used by the dancers are natural though exaggerated. They do not express the moods (bhāva) of the characters. This is done in terms of the styles of movement displayed through the torso, the legs, and the arms.[73]

Julia Hollander further remarks on the 'coding' associated with these masks: 'The masks are stylized, dreamy human faces, the designs for specific roles instantly recognizable for an audience tutored in the Chhau conventions.'[74]

The masks require substantial artistry to create, which means that Roy's artisans need to develop impressive construction skills. Balwant Gargi explains how the traditional masks are crafted, a process that would be familiar to prison performers from Purulia:

The Chhau mask is made of a dark clay found on the bank of the Kharkai River. This clay is pounded, strained, dissolved in water, and made into a thick

---

[67] Basu, 'Improvising', p. 4.
[68] Roy also brings her performance workshops to victims of acid attacks: www.youtube.com/watch?v=3pkW3Bv3e9I.
[69] Basu, 'Improvising', p. 4. [70] Basu, 'Improvising', p. 9.
[71] Private conversation, 7 January 2020.
[72] Tripp, 'Body-based', p 174.
[73] Roma Chatterji, Writing Identities: Folklore and Performative Arts of Purulia, Bengal (New Delhi, 2009), p. 4.
[74] Julia Hollander, Indian Folk Theatres (New York, 2007), p. 28.

paste. The clay model of the character is fixed on a small wooden plank and cooled for two or three days to harden it. A muslin gauze is pasted on it, and over the gauze 'two or three layers of paper; then again muslin, again paper, and over it a thick coating of the clay. The nose and eyes are fashioned by a sharp steel instrument (*karni*). After the mold is dry, the clay is scooped out from the hollow of the mask by the *karni* and the mask is scrubbed, polished, and painted.[75]

While Roy's craftsmen are unlikely to be skilled in the art of creating these masks when they join her ensemble, those from Purulia will be well aware of the intricacy of the task before them.

***

As noted, Roy and Kattimani have each devised regimens that address several of the learning styles described in Bloom's taxonomy. Their approaches to prison education and performance interweave elements from a number of relevant physical and theoretical models. Applied theatre, trauma recovery methodologies, art therapy, Shakespeare, community building and foci on concepts of place join modalities such as martial arts and yoga that incorporate cognitive, affective, physical and spiritual dimensions. These practices take enormous effort and coordination, but they have a significant influence upon those involved. As Shakespeare in Prison becomes more prominent in critical discourse, the question 'why Shakespeare?' often re-emerges. Rob Pensalfini, among others, offers an answer corresponding with the practices discussed here: 'Prison Shakespeare is inherently reflective, and usually embodied, making it one of the few programmes in prisons to simultaneously engage body, intellect, voice, and emotion.'[76]

These Indian programmes suggest that the themes and characterizations found in Shakespeare's plays are often compelling material for these prison ensembles, but their success owes significant credit to their syncretic approaches.

Like many creative practitioners, including those focusing prominently upon trauma, Kattimani and Roy recognize that many components contribute to the productive integration of dramatic education into carceral environments. Van der Kolk, for instance, emphasizes the importance of acknowledging and furthering correlations between mind

and body: 'One of the clearest lessons from contemporary neuroscience is that our sense of ourself is anchored in a vital connection with our bodies. We do not truly know ourselves unless we can feel and interpret our physical sensations. We need to register and act on these sensations to navigate safely through life.'[77] Acting teachers and theorists such as Michael Lugering and Dick McCaw make similar observations about the value of strong ties between mind and body. As Lugering comments: 'Moving, breathing, sounding, and speaking – all the components that make human expression possible – are not so much *nouns* or *things*, but rather, a series of *integrated actions* occurring simultaneously in the body.'[78] This concept of integration appears to be key in the practice Lugering promotes, as well as in the programmes initiated by Kattimani and Roy:

It is important to remember that the *well-coordinated body* and the *well-conditioned mind* go hand in hand. The prerequisite technical skills required for successful mental and emotional expression and successful physical and vocal expression are one and the same. When a sophisticated level of integration is achieved, physical flexibility and dexterity is linked directly to emotional and mental flexibility and dexterity.[79]

McCaw further posits the importance in these undertakings of 'a kind of anthropological sociology that has taken an interest in the physical learning and adaptation of the human body in a social environment'.[80] These talented Indian practitioners have created programmes that incorporate these elements. The prisoners' homes, families and personal identities are honoured; their ability to develop new artistic skills, whether on stage or with textiles or tempura, is nurtured; their breath and their bodies are

75 Balwant Gargi, *Folk Theater of India* (Seattle, 1966), p. 173.
76 Rob Pensalfini, *Prison Shakespeare: For These Deep Shames and Great Indignities* (London, 2016), p. 228.
77 Van der Kolk, *Body*, p. 274.
78 Michael Lugering, *The Expressive Actor: Integrated Voice, Movement and Acting Training* (London, 2013), p. 4.
79 Lugering, *Expressive*, p. 9.
80 Dick McCaw, *Rethinking the Actor's Body: Dialogues with Neuroscience* (London, 2020), p. 9.

supported in order to increase their mindfulness and reduce the residual effects of previous traumas. As Ramanujam indicates, these practitioners offer 'the entire package': 'The rehearsals [for *Julius Caesar*] end and a group of prisoners began to discuss and compare the Government today with that of the Roman Empire. They get up early to do yoga, then do painting and clay-modelling after which the rehearsals begin. Kattimani and the jailors have designed the entire package.'[81] For many years now, educators in more conventional pedagogical environments have used performance and art to bring vibrancy to their classroom explorations of Shakespeare. The structures created to support the incarcerated performers in Kolkata and Mysore offer valuable models for further enhancements to dramatic education in innumerable spaces. As Sommer notes: 'Whether or not a work of art intends to change behaviors, its effect is provocative. Art reframes relationships and releases raw feelings that rub against convention.'[82] Historian William H. McNeill, moreover, in his intriguing study of the power of unified movements, whether in dance or the military, indicates that 'Dance, music, and song are the most reliable way to generate inspiration; they also cement solidarity among participants.'[83] The prisoners performing with the ensembles created by Roy and Kattimani demonstrate the power of these integrated approaches. As the Shakespeare in Prison Network continues to expand and to strengthen its interconnectivity, programmes such as these bring welcome pedagogical strategies and examples to us all.

---

[81] Ramanujam, 'He spots'. [82] Sommer, *Work of Art*, p. 50.
[83] William H. McNeill, *Keeping Together in Time: Dance and Drill in Human History* (New York, 1995), p. 66.

SHAKESPEARE FOR COPS

JEFFREY R. WILSON

Tim Smith was born on 24 April 1955, his birthday falling, in his words, 'the day after Shakespeare's – probably'.[1] His father, an evangelical minister, surrounded his son with Bible stories, like the father of the protagonist, Luke Jones, in the novel series Smith later wrote about a Shakespeare-loving cop: 'I was raised in a land of absolutes. I'm not comfortable living in a land of absolutes. My dad's a fundamentalist preacher. He's a good man, but he can form a stronger opinion in less time, on less information, than anyone I've ever met.'[2] Like Luke Jones, the young Tim Smith's exposure to the King James Bible gave him a cultural baseline and good footing on language when he later came to study Shakespeare. It was the language, especially Shakespeare's poetry, that attracted Smith. He saw his first live production at the Oregon Shakespeare Festival when a sophomore in high school: *As You Like It* featuring Powers Boothe, Jean Smart and James Avery. He took his first Shakespeare class the following year, then went back for more in his senior year, disregarding the school counsellor's attempt to turn him away because he 'wasn't intellectually equipped to take an advanced class'.[3] Shakespeare then brought Smith to a remarkable English teacher who changed his life, named Ben Limoli. Some thirty-five years later, Smith dedicated his first novel in the Luke Jones series to him – 'the teacher that mattered' – as well as Smith's daughter, Miranda.

Smith attended Mesa Community College in San Diego for two years – as did I, which we bonded over when we first met. I felt I was speaking with an alternate version of myself: I could just

as easily have become a cop, and he a Shakespeare scholar. By his own account, Smith was 'a thoroughly crappy student until upper division', when he transferred over to San Diego State University to study literature and creative writing – as did I some thirty years later. He took courses in Shakespeare, drama and mythologies of the world. Today, he boasts of having seen all of Shakespeare's plays live, 'including *Two Noble Kinsmen*'. But upon graduation from college, he took a sharp turn: 'I got into police work to have something to write about. At a young age, I knew I was a writer, but I also knew I had nothing to say.'[4]

Smith joined the San Diego Police Department (SDPD) in 1978 only a short time after Mayor Pete Wilson branded San Diego 'America's Finest City'. It was an aspirational declaration: the city was moving from the traditional crime-fighting approach to policing – arrest the bad guys – to emerging philosophies of community-oriented policing (replacing

---

[1] T. B. Smith, 'Q&A interview for LA Times feature article', *Copworld*, 6 June 2011: https://copworld.wordpress.com /2011/06/06/qa-interview-for-la-times-feature-article. Smith's 'probably' suggests a more than casual knowledge of Shakespeare. We think – but aren't certain – that Shakespeare was born on 23 April.

[2] T. B. Smith, *The Sticking Place* (Ashland, OR, 2011), pp. 146–7. Further references appear in the text in parentheses.

[3] T. B. Smith, interview with the author (11 January 2018). Unless otherwise noted, quotations from Smith come from this interview.

[4] T. B. Smith, quoted from Vickie Aldous, 'The tales cops could tell', *Mail Tribune*, 10 April 2017: www.mailtribune.com/news/ 20170410/tales-cops-could-tell.

antagonism between the public and the police with partnerships for maintaining order) and problem-solving policing (bringing more thoughtfulness to the distribution of police resources by encouraging rigorous interpretation of the problems at hand). 'In the '70s,' Smith later wrote, 'incorporating this kind of utopian philosophical change into the daily oper-ations of an inherently conservative organization proved impossible.'[5]

Shortly after Smith joined the SDPD, the British novelist James McClure accompanied officers on some ride-alongs in preparation for his non-fiction book *Cop World: Inside an American Police Force*, pub-lished in 1984.[6] McClure used real names for the upper ranks, pseudonyms for beat officers, sergeants and lieutenants. Smith was dubbed 'Luke Jones', the name later given to his own protagonist: 'The Shakespeare thing made him really stand out in the police crowd. He could quote the Bard faster than they could read a suspect his Miranda rights. He knew the sonnets better than they knew the California Penal Code and loved skewering them with an on-the-nose quote from *Hamlet* or an obscure tidbit from *Coriolanus* or *Titus Andronicus*' (*Sticking Place*, p. 3).

Luke Jones climbing onto a table in a cop bar to recite Shakespeare is more memoir than fiction: 'The usual response was a barrage of apple cores or wadded napkins', Smith said.[7] The barbs in the novel are sharper: 'What are you, some kind of faggot or something?' one officer asks Luke (*Sticking Place*, p. 38). Smith says peers thought he was a weird duck, at least until he established his street cred. Future San Diego Mayor Jerry Sanders, himself an English major from San Diego State and a sergeant in 1978 when Smith joined the SDPD, had frequently to remind Smith to cool it with the flashy writing. 'I could tell he wanted to be a novelist', Sanders said. 'That's not necessarily what you want on a police report.'[8]

Smith rose through the ranks: patrol, adminis-tration, in-service training, field operations man-agement, community relations, special projects, long-range planning. In the early 1990s, he took a couple of years off to try freelance writing – including essays for *Police* magazine on the Rodney King case[9] – but that went nowhere.

'Starting over with the school district's police department gave me a chance to enjoy working with educators', Smith recalled.[10] In 1998, police work and higher education further blended as Smith attended the Delinquency Control Institute at the University of Southern California, where he was voted class president and an honour graduate:

As class president, I delivered a speech entitled 'Lessons from Lear.' The audience was comprised of class attendees, their families and friends, numerous police executives from across the country, and quite a few administrators from USC. During my preparation for the speech, the person responsible for running the day-to-day operations of the institute asked about the topic for my talk. He almost cringed when I told him what it was and strongly recom-mended that I go in a different direction. A suggestion which I ignored. The good news is that the speech was greeted by a long and loud standing ovation.

An off-duty traffic accident in 2003 led to back surgery and Smith's retirement. He moved back to Oregon to be near his daughter, and the Oregon Shakespeare Festival. He started writing again, attending the Southern California Writers' Conference in 2009 and meeting Wes Albers, a fellow author from the SDPD whom Smith credits for launching his writing career.[11] The

---

[5] T. B. Smith, 'Introduction to Cop World II', *Copworld*, 10 February 2010: https://copworld.wordpress.com/2010/02/10/introduction-to-cop-world-ii.

[6] See James McClure, *Cop World: Inside an American Police Force* (New York, 1984).

[7] T. B. Smith, quoted from Tony Perry, 'Dealing with the police Bard', *LA Times*, 1 June 2011: http://articles.latimes.com/2011/jun/01/entertainment/la-et-sdcop-book-20110601.

[8] Jerry Sanders, in Perry, 'Police Bard'.

[9] See Tim Smith, 'In the Rodney King case, police have taken a beating, too', *San Diego Union Tribune*, April 1991; 'Meltdown', *Police: The Law Officer's Magazine* 16 (June 1991); 'The accountability factor', *Police: The Law Officer's Magazine* 16 (1992), 46–8.

[10] Smith, 'Q&A interview'.

[11] See Tim Smith, 'A link to Signonsandiego's Q&A interview with feature writer John Wilkens', *Copworld*, 14 March 2011: https://copworld.wordpress.com/2011/03/14/a-link-to-signonsandiegos-qa-interview-with-feature-writer-john-wilkens.

next year, he started a blog, calling it 'Copworld' after McClure's 1984 book. He also started a sequel to McClure's book, titled *Cop World II*, which sought to update the history of the SDPD by narrating the fall of community- and problem-oriented policing in favour of more aggressive tactics. Years later, Smith partnered with Harley Patrick of Hellgate Press to create an imprint called CopWorld Press that (almost) exclusively publishes law enforcement authors.

The first post on Smith's blog included the opening chapter of what would become his first novel, *The Sticking Place*, published in 2011.[12] It's a page-turner – reads quickly, enjoyable. It is clearly written by a cop, with an emphasis on paperwork and radio codes, not the kicking down doors shown in film and TV. 'Smith does what so many other police writers don't', notes Bonnie Dumanis on the back cover: 'He gets the little things right.' For cops, the value of the book comes in the realism of both the police response to day-to-day incidents, and the endless repetition of those incidents with ever-shifting particulars and dangers. The cops in the book are human beings who have personal lives which – like those of plumbers, teachers and accountants – can spill over into their jobs. There is excellent character differentiation to keep clear the large cast of both cops and citizens: the Shakespeare-quoting rookie cop, the well-intentioned but inept classmate from the academy, the jaded senior officer, the gambling addict, the neurosurgeon cruising for sex. The city of San Diego is one of the central characters. Amidst the brisk narrative – *just the facts, ma'am* – Smith's literary flourishes often land gracefully, as at the cop bar in Chapter 10: 'Every tale represented a sermon without a moral and the One-Five-Three Club was the church of the non-sequitur' (p. 42).

The book defies plot summary. When the first chapter starts with the suicide of an aircraft engineer named Phillip McGrath, it feels like this is the intrigue that will keep the reader in suspense as the affair is investigated, *à la* John Grisham. But that incident is dealt with and falls away after only three short chapters. As the book weaves through a series of three- or four-chapter episodes, it becomes clear that *The Sticking Place* is not detective fiction. There's no grand mystery our hero will solve. There's no discovery of clues. If detective fiction invokes the story of epic conflict between powerful forces, and adversity overcome through the exercise of individual talent, strength and will, *The Sticking Place* reads more like an episodic romance where our hero bounces aimlessly from one story to another. It's more Philip Sidney's *Arcadia* than Shakespeare's *Macbeth*, the structure of *The Sticking Place* mimicking the cyclical repetition of the beat cop. There's no more of a beginning, middle and end to the book than there is to an eight-hour shift. The end of one call is just the beginning of another.

But the police procedural façade of the book is a cover for what it's really about: the place of humanistic thought in the gritty day-to-day of law enforcement, a tension between mind and body or, in Prince Hamlet's terms, 'thought' and 'action' (*Hamlet*, 3.1.87–90). Smith confronts the challenges of policing in a self-critical way often heard from arm-chair commentators, but rarely from cops themselves. There's a gripping tension between the older cops who represent older and more aggressive approaches to fighting crime and the younger cops who represent community-oriented policing, which is aligned with Shakespeare.

For Shakespearians and other general readers, the value of the book comes in the only thing that remotely resembles an over-arching plot: a young man with fairly conventional American attitudes about the value of kindness, decency, fairness, freedom and justice comes face to face with the challenge of implementing those ideals in on-the-ground policing situations leading law enforcement officers (most of whom are a mixture of good intentions, jaded cynicism and various strengths and weaknesses) to resort to sometimes imperfect, sometimes clearly illegal, means of protecting and serving their communities. In this book, as in life, the challenge of police work is

---

[12] At book signings, Smith was joined by members of the San Diego Shakespeare Society, who did guest readings.

finding the balance between the safe and secure city that everyone wants and the rough justice tactics sometimes employed to achieve it. That's where Shakespeare comes in, according to Smith:

I use Shakespeare in my novels to illustrate the difficulties confronted by young officers as they try to gain acceptance by their older peers. In the case of Luke Jones, he feels compelled to confront hypocrisy and some of the bullying that goes on during the training and acculturating phases of a young cop's development. I also use Shakespeare to illustrate the difficulties attendant when enforcing laws that are really designed to control the disenfranchised in our society. Most importantly, I use Luke's love of Shakespeare to heighten the emotional impact that the job of modern policing has on young officers. Employed as a strategy, I use specific quotes the way my dad used specific passages in the Bible to illustrate his sermons. He'd decide on a theme, then use scripture to help make that point.[13]

At the novel's start, when Luke comes upon Phillip McGrath's body, his mind flashes to the 'hell-broth' of the Weird Sisters (p. 7). When Luke contemplates McGrath's suicide, it's Lady Macbeth he hears – 'What's done cannot be undone' (p. 9) – and later Richard II – 'Of comfort let no man speak' (p. 44). Chapter 10, set in the cop bar, has the aura of the Boar's Head Tavern in *1 Henry IV*, complete with denigrations of a hated sergeant as Falstaff and a base-minded training officer as Bardolph (p. 38). Later, while talking a suicidal man off a bridge, an officer becomes suddenly belligerent, sending Luke's thoughts to Coleridge's reading of the 'motiveless malignancy' in Shakespeare's villains: 'Francie's animosity was positively Shakespearean. There was just no rational explanation for how angry he was, just as there was no rational explanation for the hatred of Edmund in *King Lear*, Don John in *Much Ado About Nothing* or Iago in *Othello*' (p. 62). When the jumper comes down safely, Luke responds to his claim to be helpless against fortune with this from *Julius Caesar*: 'Of your philosophy you make no use, if you give place to accidental evils' (p. 69). At the end of his shift, Luke goes back to *Caesar*. 'O that a man might know, / The end of his day's business ere it come' (p. 82). It's *Pericles* when a senior officer tries to lure his trainee into a crooked scheme: 'Here's a fish hangs in

the net' – later elaborating, 'I marvel how the fish live in the sea . . . As men do a-land; the great ones eat up the little ones' (pp. 96–7). A Luke feeling trapped by his job and a UCLA English professor about to go to jail quote Richard II together: 'I have been studying how I may compare the prison where I live unto the world' (p. 105).[14]

A later conversation between Luke and the Professor is the conceptual climax of the novel. The Professor voices a more philosophical critique of justice than any given by the cops themselves, including a weary Luke who is just doing his job. Describing *King Lear* as a play about a powerful man who doesn't know how to be a human being and only learns by losing everything, even his clothes, and seeing others who are naked and hungry because of him, the Professor quotes Lear crying, 'O, I have taken too little care of this' (p. 157). Echoing Smith's earlier 'Lessons from Lear' lecture, this need for self-reflection is his central warning to a criminal justice system that does not reflect in a philosophical way upon its role in society. In the Professor's gloss, 'Protecting and serving doesn't mean supporting the power structures of society; it means using individual might to help people in need' (p. 156). The lecture smacks Luke in the face. In Smith's words to me, 'It very clearly illustrates that Luke's love for and knowledge of Shakespeare makes it more difficult to survive the ravages of his job, not easier.'

If Shakespeare challenges Luke's police work, the job also challenges Luke's education, which becomes clear when we try to make sense of the title and epigraph of the book: 'But screw your courage to the sticking point, and we'll not fail' (which Smith annotates for readers as 'Lady Macbeth exhorting her husband to murder the

---

[13] Beyond Shakespeare, Luke's library in *The Sticking Place* includes *Oedipus Rex*, Coleridge's 'Kubla Khan', Dostoyevsky's *The Gambler*, Nietzsche's *Human, All Too Human* and Jack London.
[14] While the Shakespeare material generally plays well, the set-ups can be a bit contrived: '"That sort of reminds me of a quotation," Luke said. "Aw, Jesus, of course it does," Harrison said. Luke let fly' (p. 82).

King of Scotland'). Lady Macbeth's line is not about having the courage to persevere in the face of adversity. It's about the deplorable actions some are willing to perform when all they care about is their end-goal, not the means employed to achieve it. That idea could be applied to an approach to policing which only cares about achieving social order without any concern for the closed-fisted strategies employed to secure it. Lady Macbeth's line could also be a gloss on Luke's final episode in the book, where he shoots and kills a citizen he likes to save a cop he doesn't. Despite all that episodic cycling, the book ends in tragedy. It is Luke's innocence that dies. He wanted to be a cop, but didn't fully appreciate what he'd have to do to achieve that goal. Lady Macbeth knew she and her husband would have to commit murder for him to be king; Luke Jones realizes he may have to take someone's life if he wants to be a cop. In this reading, the 'sticking place' in the book's title is the profession of policing that leads one to perform harrowing acts most humans would never do, like taking another's life.[15] For Luke Jones to screw his courage to the sticking place is for him to abandon those core principles of human being – refined through his study of the humanities – as he climbs the social ladder to success. In a compelling twist, the job of policing challenges the values of the humanities just as much as those values challenge the police. Thus, in true Shakespearian fashion, the novel concludes with a question: 'How could he "Protect and Serve" to please the Professor and live to tell about it?' (p. 226).

***

In America, policing is viewed – wrongly – as a profession of action and the use of force. The vast majority of police work involves interpretation and the use of thought. While officers receive constant in-service training for physical and technical skills, they get next to nothing for intellectual and ethical skills. Intelligence and ethics are not thought of as skills, but as nebulous personality traits that one either has or doesn't.

I learned this firsthand when, shortly after completing my English Ph.D., having just finished a dissertation on Shakespeare, I was hired to teach writing classes in the Department of Criminal Justice at Cal State, Long Beach. The chair of the department, a proponent of the value of the liberal arts in criminal justice education, wanted to emphasize writing in the department's curriculum because criminal justice employers in the area were telling him they needed their workers to be better writers.[16] In the courses I taught, we focused on subject–verb agreement and APA style, but also made our foundation the idea that good writing is inseparable from good thinking. I encountered a few cowboy cops yearning for Bruce-Willis-style rough justice. Mostly, however, students were simply uninterested in thinking deeply about the theoretical and ethical challenges of criminal justice. Many who wanted to wrestle with those challenges were unprepared, having been systematically underserved by the LA Unified School District.

Halfway through my first year, after a student declared in class that revenge is perfect justice, we threw our syllabus out the window and read *Hamlet*. If you can understand how crime and justice work in *Hamlet*, understanding them out on the street is easy. That was the beginning of an ongoing research project called 'Shakespeare and Criminology'. Published pieces include readings of terrorism as revenge tragedy; the insanity defence in *Hamlet*; broken-windows policing in *Measure for Measure*; masculinity, madness and murder in *Macbeth*; and

---

[15] This reading is encouraged by the opening of the second book in the series, *A Fellow of Infinite Jest*, which parallels Luke with Lady Macbeth when she goes mad. *A Fellow of Infinite Jest* works largely the same as *The Sticking Place*. Like Lady Macbeth, Luke can't sleep. He begins brooding, Hamlet-like. He goes to therapy. He starts a journal, where we see his innermost thoughts, much like a Shakespearian soliloquy. He writes poetry of his own, starts dating women. There's less Shakespearian quotation, especially in the second half of the novel. Smith is currently at work on the third entry in the series, titled *The Winter of Our Discontent*.

[16] For the chair's view of criminal justice in light of the liberal arts, see Stephen S. Owen, Henry F. Fradella, Tod W. Burke and Jerry W. Joplin, eds., *Foundations of Criminal Justice*, 2nd edn (Oxford, 2014).

desistance from crime in *1 Henry IV*.[17] The over-arching argument is that modern criminology can help us to understand Shakespeare, and Shakespeare can help us to understand crime and justice in the modern world. I argue Shakespeare was himself a criminologist: the practice of developing abstract theories of why crime happens – as Shakespearian tragedy does – is much older than the emergence of the word and the discipline of 'criminology' late in the nineteenth century.

But recently I have been haunted by a new problem. What are the practical consequences of the encounter between Shakespeare and criminology? Does this research have what social scientists call 'policy implications'? Does it suggest a programme of action, rather than merely a kernel of knowledge? At a time when the United States is asking whether it should reform, defund or abolish the police, how can humanities scholars offer expertise and service?

My answer has been to envision a programme called 'Shakespeare for Cops'. The point is not flowery personal enrichment. My thesis is that you can do better police work if you study Shakespeare and other literature. This idea draws upon the social value of the humanities as argued in books like Martha Nussbaum's *Poetic Justice: The Literary Imagination and Public Life* (1995), but diverges from standard arguments in the field.[18] Shakespeare for Cops is not for undergraduates or even law students or lawyers, the main focus of law-and-literature scholarship and teaching, as in *Shakespeare and the Law: A Conversation Among Disciplines and Professions* (2013) and *Teaching Law and Literature* (2011).[19] Shakespeare for Cops is for officers on the job. It grows from Julia Reinhard Lupton's recent calls for 'thinking with Shakespeare' and, more to the point, 'working with Shakespeare' – 'a concerted mindfulness with respect to the capacities and virtues developed in the reading of literature and their possible uses in various employment settings'.[20] The programme jettisons old ideas about humanistic education – where expertise flows in one direction, and scholars have all the knowledge that the world needs – to embrace a more expansive pedagogy allowing for a mutually beneficial exchange of knowledge and development of skills. That orientation, hopefully,

extracts this enterprise from the fraught history of using Shakespeare as a 'civilizing' tool, a bludgeon for colonial enlightenment.[21] 'One can make an argument for Shakespeare's value even if that argument is not couched in claims of universality', as Ayanna Thompson and Laura Turchi write in *Teaching Shakespeare with Purpose: A Student-Centred Approach*.[22] Shakespeare for Cops is, like Hillary Eklund and Wendy Beth Hyman's collection *Teaching Social Justice through Shakespeare*, 'about praxis': 'the implementation, through teaching early modern texts, of a set of hopeful ideas about the potential of education, with the aim of making those ideas both better understood and materially significant'.[23]

[17] See Jeffrey R. Wilson, 'Shakespeare and criminology', *Crime, Media, Culture* 10 (2014), 97–114; 'Violent crime as revenge tragedy; or, how Christopher Dorner led criminologists at CSU Long Beach to Shakespeare', This Rough Magic, June 2016: www.thisroughmagic.org/wilson%20article.html; '"When evil deeds have their permissive pass": broken windows in William Shakespeare's *Measure for Measure*', Law and the Humanities 11 (2017), 160–83; 'Macbeth and criminology', *College Literature* 46 (2019), 453–85; '"Redeeming time": the dramatization of desistance in *1 Henry IV*', in *Shakespeare On Stage and Off*, ed. Kenneth Graham and Alysia Kolentsis (Montreal, 2019), pp. 139–55; (with Henry F. Fradella), 'The Hamlet Syndrome', *Law, Culture, and the Humanities* 16 (2020), 82–102.
[18] Martha Nussbaum, *Poetic Justice: The Literary Imagination and Public Life* (Boston, 1995).
[19] Bradin Cormack, Martha Nussbaum and Richard Strier, eds., *Shakespeare and the Law: A Conversation Among Disciplines and Professions* (Chicago, 2013); Austin Sarat, Cathrine O. Frank and Matthew Anderson, eds., *Teaching Law and Literature* (New York, 2011).
[20] Julia Reinhard Lupton, *Thinking with Shakespeare: Essays on Politics and Life* (Chicago, 2011); Julia Reinhard Lupton, 'Working with Shakespeare: introduction', in *Shakespeare On Stage and Off*, ed. Graham and Kolentsis, p. 93.
[21] See Jyotsna Singh, 'Shakespeare and the "civilizing mission"', in *Colonial Narratives/Cultural Dialogues: 'Discoveries' of India in the Language of Colonialism* (London, 1996), pp. 120–52.
[22] Ayanna Thompson and Laura Turchi, *Teaching Shakespeare with Purpose: A Student-Centred Approach* (London, 2016), p. 7.
[23] Hillary Eklund and Wendy Beth Hyman, 'Introduction: making meaning and doing justice with early modern texts', in *Teaching Social Justice through Shakespeare: Why Renaissance Literature Matters Now*, ed. Eklund and Hyman (Edinburgh, 2019), p. 9.

As discussed more fully at the end of this article, there are two possible manifestations of this programme. One would be as part of in-service training for officers through the police academy. The other would be more of a public event where cops and Shakespearians provide perspectives on the issues of crime and justice that arise in his plays, staged as a conversation for a general audience, who are invited to join in. In either case, I will insist, Shakespeare for Cops should be funded not by humanities agencies – where resources are scarce – but from the flush pockets of police department budgets. At this moment in American history, the humanities and the police both have what the other needs – the humanities have the knowledge and skills lacking in current police practices, and the police have the funding lacking in current humanities institutions. Despite a tradition of mutual suspicion, the humanities and the police are well positioned to help each other, and to bring about better forms of both enterprises – a more thoughtful approach to public safety, and a more powerful activation of academia.

Studying Shakespeare won't magically fix the police. Only laws, policy and funding decisions will create systematic change. But I also want to live in a world where the humanities scholars who know the most about the history of crime, abuse of authority, and tragic violence are closer to the powers making policy. A programme like Shakespeare for Cops can be part of a larger cultural effort to reimagine public safety more humanely and more humanistically. Shakespeare doesn't have the answers, but does have a demonstrated history of serving as a venue for institutions to create conversations about how older traditions of humanistic thought and art relate to emerging social problems, as in the many Prison Shakespeare programmes.[24] Shakespeare can be a contact zone for conversations between isolated groups that otherwise wouldn't come together, a rendezvous in which police officers and early modern scholars meet to ask: 'What can I learn from you?'

***

I recently saw two cops having lunch at a sandwich shop. I asked what percentage of police work involves physical skills (such as the use of force), what percentage involves technical skills (such as specialized strategies or equipment), and what percentage involves mental skills (such as reading a situation). '10 – 20 – 70', said one of the officers. 'Can't say', said the other. 'You can't do the physical or technical without the mental.'

Better-educated officers are stronger officers – not in some nebulous feel-good way, but because they are demonstrably more effective at the job. The higher an officer's education, the fewer the complaints logged against them;[25] the less they use physical force, including deadly force;[26] the less they abuse authority;[27] the more they will succeed in a community-policing setting;[28] and the higher their salary will be.[29]

---

[24] See Amy Scott-Douglass, *Shakespeare Inside: The Bard Behind Bars* (London, 2007); Laura Bates, *Shakespeare Saved My Life: Ten Years in Solitary with the Bard* (Naperville, 2013); Niels Herold, *Prison Shakespeare and the Purpose of Performance: Repentance Rituals and the Early Modern* (New York, 2014); Rob Pensalfini, *Prison Shakespeare: For These Deep Shames and Great Indignities* (New York, 2016); Sophie Ward and Roy Connolly, 'The play is a prison: the discourse of Prison Shakespeare', *Studies in Theatre and Performance* 40 (2020), 128–44.

[25] See Kim Michelle Lersch and Linda L. Kunzman, 'Misconduct allegations and higher education in a Southern Sheriff's Department', *American Journal of Criminal Justice* 25 (2001), 161–72; Jennifer Manis, Carol A. Archbold and Kimberly D. Hassell, 'Exploring the impact of police officer education level on allegations of police misconduct', *International Journal of Police Science & Management* 10 (2008), 509–23.

[26] See Eugene A. Paoline, III and William Terrill, 'Police education, experience, and the use of force', *Criminal Justice and Behavior* 34 (2007), 179–96; James P. Mcelvain and Augustine J. Kposowa, 'Police officer characteristics and the likelihood of using deadly force', *Criminal Justice and Behavior*, 35 (2008), 505–21; Jason Rydberg and William Terrill, 'The effect of higher education on police behavior', *Police Quarterly* 13 (2010), 92120.

[27] See Cody W. Telep, 'The impact of higher education on police officer attitudes toward abuse of authority', *Journal of Criminal Justice Education* 22 (2011), 392–419.

[28] Allison T. Chappell, 'Police academy training: comparing across curricula', *Policing: An International Journal* 31 (2008), 36–56.

[29] Christie Gardiner, 'College cops: a study of education and policing in California', *Policing: An International Journal* 38 (2015), 648–63.

If the mind is a police officer's greatest asset, how should they be educated? In a classroom, or out on the street? At the police academy, or at a college? Vocational training, or the liberal arts? Should the minimum be a high school diploma, an associate's degree, or a bachelor's? Is continuing education best done through in-service training at the academy, or through coursework at a college or university?

These questions have been asked at least since the days of August Vollmer, the first chief of police of Berkeley, CA, the first US chief to require college degrees in his officers, and the man who got the University of California to start teaching classes in criminal justice.[30] In 1968, the establishment of the Law Enforcement Educational Program (LEEP) provided financial aid for cops to attend college, boosting programmes in political science and criminal justice.[31] Since then, the number of criminal justice bachelor's degrees awarded has boomed from 2,045 in 1972 to 60,269 in 2013, nearly a 3,000 per cent increase (in contrast to the 119 per cent increase of degrees overall).[32] Criminal justice is now 1 of the 10 most awarded undergraduate degrees in the country.[33] While only 1 per cent of police departments require a 4-year degree, roughly 45 per cent of cops hold bachelor's degrees or higher.[34]

Whether or not one has a degree, the process of becoming a cop starts with an initial screening involving a background investigation and mental and physical fitness tests.[35] Cadets then spend an average of 3 months and 750 classroom hours at a local police academy learning state laws, police procedures and skills needed for the job (compare that with some European countries where police attend a national academy for 3 years).[36] Supervised field training usually lasts around 300 hours, cadets gaining experience to supplement the theory of the academy. Then follows a probationary period, usually between 12 and 18 months, where officers perform independently and are evaluated. Cops continue to receive in-service training throughout their careers, usually around 40 hours a year spent refreshing the skills and knowledge of veteran officers, updating them on laws and procedures,

educating them on emergent kinds of crime, and honing skills of ethics, stress management and the use of force, among other things. If officers pursue management training, that's usually an 8–13 week course held at a regional site.

Over the past 50 years, the central question has been: 'Should we be training guardians or warriors?' The guardian image of the cop led to the rise of community policing – the friendly neighbourhood officer on foot patrol, protecting and serving the public. The warrior image led to militarization – riot gear and armoured cars giving the impression of a law-enforcement battalion at war with the forces of evil in our nation. Recently, the sickening string of police officers killing unarmed Black people – Eric Garner, Michael Brown, Tamir Rice, John Crawford, Walter Scott, Freddie Gray, Sandra Bland, Philando Castile, Breonna Taylor, George Floyd, Jacob Blake – has led to the #BlackLivesMatter movement, protests, public scrutiny and pressure on lawmakers, thundering down urgency on police efforts to examine and strengthen their approach to training. And now the police have a problem. It

---

[30] See G. E. Carte and E. H. Carte, *Police Reform in the United States: The Era of August Vollmer, 1905–1932* (Berkeley, 1975).

[31] See Eugene A. Paoline, III, William Terrill and Michael T. Rossler, 'Higher education, college degree major, and police occupational attitudes', *Journal of Criminal Justice Education* 26 (2015), 49–73.

[32] See John J. Sloan, III and Jonathan W. Buchwalter, 'The state of criminal justice bachelor's degree programs in the United States: institutional, departmental, and curricula features', *Journal of Criminal Justice Education* 28 (2017), 307–34.

[33] Sloan and Buchwalter, 'Criminal justice'.

[34] Paoline, Terrill and Rossler, 'Higher education'.

[35] This overview of police training is distilled from John S. Dempsey and Linda S. Forst, 'Becoming a police officer', in *An Introduction to Policing* (Clifton Park, NY, 2012), pp. 115–29.

[36] See Sara Miller Llana, 'Why police don't pull guns in many countries', *The Christian Science Monitor*, 28 June 2015: www.csmonitor.com/World/2015/0628/Why-police-don-t-pull-guns-in-many-countries; Paul Hirschfield, 'Why do American cops kill so many compared to European cops?' *The Conversation*, 25 November 2015: https://theconversation.com/why-do-american-cops-kill-so-many-compared-to-european-cops-49696.

won't be solved with more good will. It will only be solved with better strategies.

***

Humanities scholarship helps us see that the problems in American policing date back to the slave patrols of colonial days and the frontier logic of White settlers viewing indigenous people as dangerous and savage – embarrassing origin stories often left out of criminal justice textbooks.[37] The institution of slavery was abolished, but its legacy lived on in anti-Black racism ranging from the White supremacist violence and terrorism of groups such as the Ku Klux Klan to structural social inequality perpetuated through redlining and incarceration.[38] Policing Black America brought centuries of routine emotional and symbolic violence, low-income communities of colour excluded from the comforts of law enforcement.[39] Black culture and blue culture developed with mutual distrust. But the police had government funding, which started increasing dramatically in the 1970s on the backdrop of closing libraries and stalled teacher's salaries.[40] Beginning in the 1980s, police increasingly spent resources on militarizing the force.[41] That means 911 emergency calls can lead, for example, to armed and angry police officers responding to mental health situations they are not well trained for. Dicey situations can easily lead to abuses of force, including cops murdering citizens.[42] There are payouts for police misconduct. There are also union contracts that purge misconduct from officers' records. Lax federal oversight leads to systemic corruption. But only recently has the 'morbidly expanding roll call of the racialized poor killed by police and vigilante violence' and the waves of public protest in support of Black Lives Matter revealed the reality of police racism to White America.[43]

While much American literature, film and television romanticizes the police, Black culture – from hip hop to Afropessimism – has mounted a sustained critique of policing. Black Lives Matter is not possible without NWA and Frank B. Wilderson, III, who would be equally annoyed to find themselves cited in an argument aimed at building bridges with law enforcement.[44] I'm

risking their ire – and that of both humanities scholars sceptical of progress, and police officers resentful of critique – on the prospect that we might build a better system for our grandchildren.

First there were calls to reform the police.[45] Make them wear body cameras. Train them in de-escalation and implicit bias. Prohibit chokeholds. Give officers a duty to intervene in abuses of force. Make efforts to build trust between the police and

---

[37] See Sally E. Hadden, *Slave Patrols: Law and Violence in Virginia and the Carolinas* (Cambridge, 2001); K. B. Turner, David Giacopassi and Margaret Vandiver, 'Ignoring the past: coverage of slavery and slave patrols in criminal justice texts', *Journal of Criminal Justice Education* 17 (2006), 181–95; Nikhil Pal Singh, 'The whiteness of police', *American Quarterly* 66 (2014), 1091–9; Chris Cunneen and Juan Tauri, *Indigenous Criminology* (Bristol, 2016); Kevin F. Steinmetz, Brian P. Schaefer and Howard Henderson, 'Wicked overseers: American policing and colonialism', *Sociology of Race and Ethnicity* 3 (2017), 68–81; Sanna King, 'Colonial criminology: a survey of what it means and why it is important', *Sociology Compass* 11 (2017), e12447; Robyn Maynard, *Policing Black Lives: State Violence in Canada from Slavery to the Present* (Halifax, 2017).

[38] See Ibram X. Kendi, *Stamped from the Beginning: The Definitive History of Racist Ideas in America* (New York, 2016); Michelle Alexander, *The New Jim Crow: Mass Incarceration in the Age of Colorblindness* (New York, 2010).

[39] See Monica C. Bell, 'Police reform and the dismantling of legal estrangement', *The Yale Law Journal* 126 (2017), 2054–2150; Laurence Ralph, *The Torture Letters: Reckoning with Police Violence* (Chicago, 2020).

[40] See, for example, Clarence Taylor, *Fight the Power: African Americans and the Long History of Police Brutality in New York City* (New York, 2018); Ryan Lugalia-Hollon and Daniel Cooper, *The War on Neighborhoods: Policing, Prison, and Punishment in a Divided City* (Boston, 2018).

[41] See Daryl Meeks, 'Police militarization in urban areas: the obscure war against the underclass', *The Black Scholar* 35 (2006), 33–41; Radlet Balko, *Rise of the Warrior Cop: The Militarization of America's Police Forces* (New York, 2013).

[42] See Franklin E. Zimring, *When Police Kill* (Cambridge, 2017).

[43] Christina Heatherton and Jordan Camp, eds., *Policing the Planet: Why the Policing Crisis Led to Black Lives Matter* (London, 2016), p. 1.

[44] See NWA, 'Fuck the police', Straight Outta Compton (Ruthless, 1988); Frank B. Wilderson, III, *Afropessimism* (New York, 2020).

[45] See Samuel E. Walker and Carol A. Archbold, *The New World of Police Accountability*, 3rd edn (Thousand Oaks, 2019).

Black communities. But there's a strong tension between outside forces advocating for a more ethical approach to policing and the inside traditions socializing cops to maintain the status quo. In 2005, Norman Conti and James Nolan wrote that 'the cultivation of a "truly" ethical police force is improbable within the system as it currently stands'.[46] The repeated and documented failures of reform have led to arguments that the police are beyond reform.[47] Calls for reform have become calls to defund the police. Or abolish the police.

Since the 1970s, Black women activist scholars such as Angela Y. Davis, Mariame Kaba and Ruth Wilson Gilmore have advocated for the abolition of prisons and the police.[48] Through organizations like Say Her Name – honouring the lives of women such as Eleanor Bumpurs, Sandra Bland and Breonna Taylor – they have drawn attention to police brutality against Black women, women of colour, and people from queer communities who receive less media attention than Black men.[49] Abolitionists seek reparative justice and reparations.[50] The goal of the abolitionist cause is to achieve public safety; to do so, it argues, America must disentangle public safety from policing.[51] You can't change the police without changing the social structure that empowers them and disempowers Black Americans.[52] Seeking alternate systems of safety means shifting public funding priorities. Reform efforts just pump more money into the policing industry. Money spent on military-grade police weapons can go instead to Black community organizations.

Critics say the abolition of the police is unrealistic. They think it could never gain popular support. While pundits on the Right declare that 'Blue Lives Matter', debates on the Left ensue about what is achievable, politically, and the best rhetoric to use: *reform, defund, abolish*.[53] But if you say, 'We could never abolish the police', ask yourself whether you also would have said, 'We could never abolish slavery.'

***

A gussied-up status quo seems to be the most likely outcome. One feels hopeless, helpless. But now, thanks to these movements, when asked what

makes a good cop, police departments are less likely to emphasize raw strength, fearlessness in the face of danger, and obedience to authority. They are more likely to emphasize integrity, an orientation towards community service, good communication skills, good problem-solving skills, stability, maturity and emotional intelligence (an ability to understand and manage one's own and others' feelings). Thus, in *The Final Report of the President's Task Force on 21st Century Policing* (2015), the first of six 'pillars' is 'Building Trust and Legitimacy': 'Law enforcement agencies should adopt procedural justice as the guiding principle.'[54] Pillar 4 calls for

46 Norman Conti and James J. Nolan, III, 'Policing the Platonic cave: ethics and efficacy in police training', *Policing and Society* 15 (2005), 166–86; p. 184.
47 See Alex S. Vitale, *The End of Policing* (London, 2018).
48 See Angela Y. Davis, 'The truth telling project: violence in America', in *Freedom Is a Constant Struggle: Ferguson, Palestine, and the Foundations of a Movement* (Chicago, 2016); Mariame Kaba, 'Yes, we mean literally abolish police', *New York Times*, 12 June 2020; and Ruth Wilson Gilmore, *Change Everything: Racial Capitalism and the Case for Abolition* (Chicago, 2021).
49 See Kimberlé Crenshaw and Andrea J. Ritchie, *Say Her Name: Resisting Police Brutality Against Black Women* (New York, 2015); Andrea J. Ritchie, *Invisible No More: Police Violence Against Black Women and Women of Color* (Boston, 2017); and Emma K. Russell, *Queer Histories and the Politics of Policing* (London, 2019).
50 See Ta-Nehisi Coates, 'The case for reparations', *The Atlantic*, June 2014; Keeanga-Yamahtta Taylor, *From #BlackLivesMatter to Black Liberation* (Chicago, 2016).
51 See Glenn Cartman Loury, 'Relations before transactions: forty years of thinking about persisting racial inequality in the United States', in *Difference without Domination*, ed. Danielle Allen and Rohini Somanathan (Chicago, 2020), pp. 171–86.
52 See Marc Lamont Hill, *Nobody: Casualties of America's War on the Vulnerable, from Ferguson to Flint and Beyond* (New York, 2016).
53 See Mark P. Thomas and Steven Tufts, 'Blue solidarity: police unions, race and authoritarian populism in North America', *Work, Employment and Society* 34 (2020), 126–44; Taimi Castle, '"Cops and the Klan": police disavowal of risk and minimization of threat from the Far-Right', *Critical Criminology* (2020): https://ezproxy-prd.bodleian.ox.ac.uk:2102/10.1007/s10612-020-09493-6.
54 President's Task Force on 21st Century Policing, *The Final Report of the President's Task Force on 21st Century Policing* (Washington, DC, 2015), p. 1.

'community policing as a guiding philosophy', in the hopes of seeing law enforcement agencies 'working with neighborhood residents to co-produce public safety'. Pillar 5 is about training and education, including the suggestion that 'law enforcement agencies should engage community members, particularly those with special expertise, in the training process and provide leadership training to all personnel throughout their careers'.[55]

Accordingly, the Mobile, AL police academy's curriculum was recently 'revised to emphasize delivery of fair and equal law enforcement while helping citizens in need. All Mobile police officers are taught to "see" the situations of the people they protect.'[56] One of the four core curriculum areas for the Missouri police academy is now 'Interpersonal Perspectives', meaning 'communication skills such as cultural diversity training, ethics, conflict management, victim sensitivity and stress management'.[57] In 2016, the Portland, OR police academy introduced a new course called 'Strengthening Our Foundation', designed to 'increase comfort in talking about race; increase knowledge of institutional racisms; identify institutional racism in policy, practice, and procedures; increase understanding of implicit bias; and explore strategies to address institutional racism in the workplace'.[58] There is a theme here: the kind of education police officers are looking for right now is to be found in the humanities.

If the United States ever commits to systematic change in its approach to public safety, let it be remembered that, often, humanities scholars specialize in the knowledge and skills lacking in US policing. Instrumentally, the humanities offer skills of judgement, critique, historicization, ethical reasoning, empathy, discernment, reflection, justification, communication and performance. Substantively, they offer knowledge of racism, White supremacy, structural inequality, US history, human rights and human psychology. Supporting the leadership of the Black Lives Matter heroes protesting, humanities scholars can be leaders in the movement to create a more intelligent and ethical approach to public safety in America.

***

What are the humanities? *Better living through interpretation.* Institutionally speaking, the humanities is an umbrella term that refers to a set of academic disciplines usually including Classics, History, Philosophy, Religion, Literature, Linguistics, the Visual Arts (such as Painting, Photography and Film) and the Performing Arts (such as Music, Theatre and Dance). Basically, the humanities study the things humans have made, from art and literature to language and culture. (The sciences study naturally occurring phenomena, the things that humans didn't invent: rocks, stars, molecules, animals, gravity, chemical reactions, the circulation of blood, and so forth.) The humanities help us to understand the experience of being human by asking the big questions that individuals and societies face day after day, year after year, generation after generation, and century after century: *What is true? Why do we do what we do? How should we lead our lives?* The humanities try to get to the bottom of things when the best way to understand something is unclear, asking and answering questions that aren't easily accounted for with common sense. They usually treat answers as provisional and open to revision. Thus, we come to reckon with the relationship between the past and the present. The humanities identify historical objects, events and traditions that deserve to be known and thought about today, raising questions about how we exercise judgement and how we determine value. Forcing us to articulate what we think is true and good, and why, the humanities train our mental capabilities: our ability to interpret and our ability to explain. Thus, we develop the skills needed to think about and talk about why we do what we

[55] Task Force, *Final Report*, p. 3.

[56] Mobile Police Department, 'New academy and in-service training': www.mobilepd.org/enforcement/newacademytraining.

[57] Missouri Department of Public Safety, 'Continuing law enforcement education requirements': https://dps.mo.gov/dir/programs/post/edrequirements.php.

[58] The City of Portland Oregon, Police Bureau, '2016 sworn member in-service training plan': www.portlandoregon.gov/police/article/620802.

do. A premium is placed on both reflection (bringing about the possibility of changing one's own mind) and justification (bringing about the possibility of changing someone else's mind). For instance, older Eurocentric understandings of the humanities were firmly rooted in ancient Greek literature and philosophy; newer understandings are more global, more accountable to humanity in all its diversity. The humanities provide neither rules for living (as the church does), nor training for a certain job (as vocational schools do). Instead, they provide the skills that equip people with the ability to do other things better. That's why it's equally mistaken to believe: (1) that the humanities are a self-contained end in themselves that can remain cosily insulated in academia; and (2) that people don't need the humanities if they're going to pursue a vocation outside academia.

For example, in *Policing and the Poetics of Everyday Life*, the self-described 'philosopher-cop' Jonathan Wender brought his Ph.D. training to bear on his fifteen years of police work, identifying what he called the 'bureaucratic paradox' of policing: 'though it is their official role as bureaucratic agents that first brings them into the presence of their fellow human beings, that role is precisely what often must be transcended in order truly to ameliorate the given predicaments at hand'.[59] A number of police departments have hired Project Humanities, an initiative out of Arizona State University, to conduct its Humanity 101 in the Workplace workshop, which 'addresses the intersections of various systems of privilege and the hidden biases that inform our personal decisions and professional behaviors'.[60]

That's a cultural studies seminar. There's also history. More than 80,000 officers have done training sessions at Law Enforcement and Society: Lessons of the Holocaust, a four-hour programme created in 1999 by the US Holocaust Museum in partnership with the Anti-Defamation League.[61] Officers tour the museum, discuss the role of police in the Nazi state, and consider the questions relevant to American policing today. 'The question – then and now – is still the same', said Charles H. Ramsey, chief of Metropolitan Police in

Washington, DC, and one of the originators of the programme: 'Where were the police?'[62] He continued:

Where were the police when libraries were being looted and books burned? When Jewish businesses were being illegally targeted? When people were being classified and publicly harassed, and ultimately imprisoned and slaughtered? Where were the police? And where was the rest of the community – the local politicians, other government officials, civic leaders and everyday citizens, most of whom stood by silently and watched it all happen?

Fast forwarding several decades, where were the police when crack cocaine and other drugs invaded our communities? When gangs, armed with powerful automatic and semi-automatic weapons, took control of many of our streets? When shootings and homicides became everyday occurrences in far too many of our communities? Where were the police? And, once again, where was the rest of the community when crime was gaining its strangle-hold on many of our communities?

Rather than dwell upon the tragedies possible in police complicity, Ramsey saw the 'Lessons of the Holocaust' as a call to positive action: 'When basic human and civil rights are threatened or denied, it is the police who need to be the first, the very first, to stand up in protest.'[63]

There's also literature and philosophy, which detective Ed Gillespie teaches to cops in the Baltimore Police Department, as related in David Dagan's essay for *The Atlantic*, 'The Baltimore cops

---

[59] Jonathan Wender, *Policing and the Poetics of Everyday Life* (Urbana, IL, 2008), p. 4.

[60] Project Humanities, 'Humanity 101 in the Workplace': https://projecthumanities.asu.edu/content/humanity-101-workplace.

[61] See the United States Holocaust Memorial Museum, 'Resources for professionals and student leaders: law enforcement': www.ushmm.org/professionals-and-student-leaders/law-enforcement.

[62] Charles H. Ramsey, 'Learning the Lessons of the Holocaust to Train Better Police Officers for Today and Tomorrow', keynote address at the 'Law Enforcement and Society: Lessons of the Holocaust' symposium, 12 April 2000: https://mpdc.dc.gov/release/learning-lessons-holocaust-train-better-police-officers-today-and-tomorrow.

[63] Ramsey, 'Learning the Lessons'.

studying Plato and James Baldwin'.[64] Gillespie is a 48-year-old detective in Baltimore who leads traditional in-service training courses in terrorism response, extremism and gangs, as well as an ethics course asking officers to think about policing from the perspective of the humanities. As a complement to the more traditional physical and technical skills of in-service training, Gillespie's humanities-based course presents literature as 'a safe way to look at circumstances and ask yourself, "What does this tell us about us? . . . What does this tell me about myself? What does this tell me about the human condition?" . . . "What does this tell you, officer, about policing?"' To Gillespie, studying literature and philosophy connects cops to the history of justice that they are a part of. 'Tradition is a big thing for officers, and we are in the tradition of the western world', Gillespie said. 'We're kind of government on the ground. I mean, we have to represent democratic values. We have to represent those Enlightenment values in a very immediate way.'[65]

And there's art history. The New York Police Department, the US Secret Service and the Department of Homeland Security have all sent agents to The Art of Perception, a programme at the Metropolitan Museum of Art run by art historian Amy Herman.[66] She originally offered the programme to medical students, then realized it could be tailored to any group that could benefit from enhanced observation skills. Now, law enforcement agents learn to observe and describe in detail what they see in pieces at the Met – often finding the line between observation and interpretation tricky to hold – leading to better police reports and better communication. 'Instead of telling my people that the guy who keeps looking into one parked car after another is dressed in black,' one participant noted, 'I might say he's wearing a black wool hat, a black leather coat with black fur trim, a black hoodie sweatshirt and Timberlands.'[67] Some cops say they hate art; some say they don't get it; and some don't care. It doesn't matter, Herman says. She isn't teaching art appreciation; she's developing skills officers use on the job.

In 2017, when President Donald Trump proposed eliminating the National Endowment for the Humanities and the National Endowment for the Arts, University of California, San Diego history professor Frank Biess took to the pages of the *San Diego Union–Tribune* with an op-ed about one of his Ph.D. students, David Livingstone, who had just become the new police chief of Simi Valley. Narrating Livingstone's criticism of militarized policing, his intolerance towards police abuse and his use of a historian's skills to research and reveal a young man's wrongful imprisonment, Biess concluded that 'David's case shows that the humanities can actually save lives.'[68]

***

Clearly, there has been a rise of – as the cop-teaching art historian Amy Herman said to me in an interview – 'programs that seek to enhance the "softer skills" – empathy, communication, observation, temperament. In reality,' she continued, 'these soft skills are not so soft; they are critical for law enforcement professionals in myriad scenarios.'[69]

How can the humanities help the police? It's not with the physical and technical skills of the job. 'Cops must be able to fight, drive, shoot, and make

[64] David Dagan, 'The Baltimore cops studying Plato and James Baldwin', *The Atlantic*, 25 November 2017: www.theatlantic.com/politics/archive/2017/11/the-baltimore-cops-studying-plato-and-james-baldwin/546485.

[65] Dagan, 'Baltimore cops'.

[66] See Amy Herman, The Art of Perception, www.artfulperception.com/about-course.html, as well as her book *Visual Intelligence: Sharpen Your Perception, Change Your Life* (Boston, MA, 2016).

[67] Quoted from Neal Hirschfeld, 'Teaching cops to see', *Smithsonian Magazine* (October 2009): www.smithsonianmag.com/arts-culture/teaching-cops-to-see-138500635. See also Sarah Lyall, 'Off the beat and into a museum: art helps police officers learn to look', *New York Times*, 26 April 2016: www.nytimes.com/2016/04/27/arts/design/art-helps-police-officers-learn-to-look.html.

[68] See Frank Biess, 'Why the humanities save lives', *San Diego Union–Tribune*, 28 April 2017: www.sandiegouniontribune.com/opinion/commentary/sd-humanities-save-lives-20170428-story.html.

[69] Amy Herman, interview with the author, 7 February 2018.

use of the law', as Ed Gillespie, the humanities-teaching cop in Baltimore, told me. 'Those brass-tacks things are handled generally well.'[70] The humanities help with the mental skills needed to do the job, Gillespie said, but that idea is controversial:

There has been a touch-and-go relationship with the intangible concepts of things like cultural awareness, history, philosophy, etc. Often the pivotal question of the 'why' of policing is not coupled with the method-ology of the 'how' of policing. When those things are introduced, there is considerable pushback. In many cases, this is because many officers feel that they are being distracted or softened by political-special-interest pap. Be this as it may, police agencies, and the Baltimore PD in particular, must stay the course and continue to emphasize and reemphasize the importance of the humanist element. We need to say outright that we are servants and champions of a Western democratic tradition.[71]

I also asked David Dagan, author of the piece on Gillespie in *The Atlantic*, what the humanities have to offer a vocation such as policing. What might aca-demics be able to see about crime and justice that cops usually don't?

That cops' frustrations are normal and can have an outlet; that the police occupy a vital place in a democracy and need to embrace it; that the people they encounter all have stories of their own; that de-escalation is just as heroic as shooting someone; that you can embrace these ideas with-out turning yourself into a 'social worker'; that we've always asked them to do our dirty work and they should push back by demanding we actually integrate the margin-alized communities we ask them to keep under control.[72]

At a time when police are looking to increase the empathy, thoughtfulness and cultural awareness in officers, these are precisely the skills offered by the humanities. Shakespeare's plays wrestle fiercely with crime and justice, refusing to give easy answers, requiring and training a mind capable of complex analysis and ethics. It's one thing to tell officers, 'Be ethical.' It's another thing entirely to give them the experience of being lost in interpret-ation, not knowing which way is up, and asking them to identify the abstract concepts in play. That's why thinkers such as Lynn Hunt, Steven

Pinker and Elaine Scarry have argued that there is an 'ethics of reading': increased literacy in the seventeenth and eighteenth centuries led to an increased number of books published, which led to an increased capacity for empathy (seeing the world through someone else's eyes) and deliber-ation (debating the meanings and values of things), which led to legal reforms, which led to decreased violence towards others (ranging from the end of burning witches to the abolition of slavery).[73]

Herman observed that much police work 'depends on initial critical inquiry to lay a foundation for further examination'. By enhancing officers' skills in writing, speaking and thinking, she said, the humanities can 'help them daily with the work that they do' and 'help them be more effective practi-tioners and better leaders'.[74] It is important to empha-size that Shakespeare for Cops is job training, not personal enrichment. That's why I like terms such as 'emotional intelligence' and – in Herman's book – 'visual intelligence'. These are skills and talents that can be learned and deployed, not personality traits or aery flights of fancy. The promise of Shakespeare for Cops is not that you will become a better human being; it's that you will become a better cop because you will better understand why crime occurs and what justice is. Here's how Gillespie put it to me:

Stories and representations of the human condition get cops to explore the 'why' of the human animal. They fortify the capacity for empathy, and they get the officer to ponder experiences beyond the immediacy of 'what is in front of me right now'. In a very practical sense, it gets the officer thinking about whether her or his approach to a problem might be impactful in light of the factors that led to it.[75]

***

[70] Ed Gillespie, interview with the author, 10 February 2018.
[71] Gillespie, interview.
[72] David Dagan, interview with the author, 25 January 2018.
[73] See Lynn Hunt, *Inventing Human Rights: A History* (New York, 2007); Steven Pinker, *The Better Angels of Our Nature: Why Violence Has Declined* (New York, 2011); and Elaine Scarry, 'Poetry, injury, and the ethics of reading', in *The Humanities and Public Life*, ed. Peter Brooks (New York, 2014), pp. 41–8.
[74] Herman, interview. [75] Gillespie, interview.

Lots of literature addresses crime and justice – from the Epic of Gilgamesh to the Book of Genesis, from Sophocles' *Antigone* to Augustine's *Confessions*, from *The Thousand and One Nights* to *The Canterbury Tales*, from Dickens and Poe to Conan Doyle and Dostoyevsky, on down to Susan Glaspell, Franz Kafka, Agatha Christie, Langston Hughes, Gwendolyn Brooks, Shirley Jackson, Flannery O'Connor, Truman Capote, Harper Lee, Toni Morrison, Elmore Leonard, S. E. Hinton, Margaret Atwood, Spike Lee and Quentin Tarantino, among many others.[76] Film has become particularly popular in criminal justice pedagogy.[77] That makes sense. Film is easy to access and of the moment. Shakespeare is the opposite. But Shakespeare is a special site where his obsession with tragedy, usually involving issues of crime and justice, comes together with both his deep conditioning by the classical tradition – connecting us back up with ancient ethics and philosophy – and his continued popularity today, bridging the texts to urgent social issues. 'Shakespeare's works can speak to a wide range of issues related to justice', as Eklund and Hyman write, 'because he thematizes justice so often in his plays.'[78]

Shakespeare for Cops has three main objectives:

1. to enhance analytical and ethical skills in police officers by training them in humanistic ways of thinking about crime and justice
2. to build legitimacy for the police by disseminating knowledge about crime and justice derived from on-the-job experience to academic and public audiences
3. to create a new community partnership between cops and academics, fostering trust between two groups traditionally suspicious of each other.

The second and third objectives are added benefits; the first is the focus of the programme. How can Shakespeare help people to be better cops? Because interpreting Shakespeare provides analytical training: learning to better understand and prevent crime by discerning the social and individual factors that bring it about. And it provides ethical training: learning to recognize and negotiate the moral dilemmas associated with police work.

76 See Paul E. Dow, *Criminology in Literature* (New York, 1980); J. David Hirschel and John R. McNair, 'Integrating the study of criminal justice and literature', *American Journal of Criminal Justice* 7 (1982), 75–98; Daniel J. Kornstein, 'Literature and crime', in *Encyclopedia of Crime and Justice*, ed. Sanford H. Kadish: www.encyclopedia.com/law/legal-and-political-magazines/literature-and-crime; Beverly A. Smith, 'Literature in criminal justice education', *Journal of Criminal Justice* 15 (1987), 137–44; Biko Agozino, 'Radical criminology in African literature', *International Sociology* 10 (1995), 315–29; Steven T. Engel, 'Teaching literature in the criminal justice curriculum', *Journal of Criminal Justice Education* 14 (2003), 345–54; Vincenzo Ruggiero, *Crime in Literature: Sociology of Deviance and Fiction* (London, 2003); Blythe Alison Bowman, 'Classical literature for the criminal justice classroom', *Journal of Criminal Justice Education* 20 (2009), 95–109; Jayme Anne Powell, 'Criminal justice in literature: a teaching curriculum' (MA thesis, California State University, Sacramento, 2010): http://hdl.handle.net/10211.9/854; Elizabeth Burney, 'Crime and criminology in the eye of the novelist: trends in nineteenth-century literature', *Howard Journal of Criminal Justice* 51 (2012), 160–72; Afra Saleh Alshiban, 'Exploring criminology in literary texts: Robert Browning – an example', *Journal of Literature and Art Studies* 2 (2012), 454–63; Michael Hviid Jacobsen, ed., *The Poetics of Crime: Understanding and Researching Crime and Deviance Through Creative Sources* (New York, 2014); and Lawrence Karson, Claudia Slate and Rebecca Saulsbury, eds., *Crime, Justice and Literature: A Reader* (Dubuque, IA, 2017).
77 See Nicole Hahn Rafter, *Shots in the Mirror: Crime Films and Society* (Oxford, 2006); Jon Frauley, *Criminology, Deviance, and the Silver Screen: The Fictional Reality and the Criminological Imagination* (New York, 2010); and Nicole Rafter and Michelle Brown, *Criminology Goes to the Movies: Crime Theory and Popular Culture* (New York, 2011).
78 Eklund and Hyman, 'Introduction', p. 8. See, for example, K. R. Srinivasa Iyengar, 'Crime and punishment in Shakespeare', *Journal of the Annamalal University* 22 (1960), 1–66; C. J. Sisson, *Shakespeare's Tragic Justice* (London, 1962); Robert B. Heilman, 'The criminal as tragic hero: dramatic methods', *Shakespeare Survey* 19 (Cambridge, 1966), 12–24; John Lewin, 'The victim in Shakespeare', in *Victims and Society*, ed. Emilio Viano (Washington, DC, 1978), pp. 451–64; Robert Rentoul Reed, Jr, *Crime and God's Judgment in Shakespeare* (Lexington, KY, 1984); E. A. J. Honigmann, 'Crime, punishment, and judgement in Shakespeare', in *L'Europe de la renaissance: cultures et civilisations: mélanges offerts à Marie-Thérèse Jones-Davies*, ed. J. C. Margolin and M. M. Martinet (Paris, 1989), pp. 285–93; Richard Wilson, 'The quality of mercy: discipline and punishment in Shakespearean comedy', *The Seventeenth Century* 5 (1990), 1–42; Frank Kermode, 'Justice and mercy in Shakespeare',

Working to accomplish these objectives, there are five points of emphasis in the Shakespeare for Cops curriculum:

1. *Close Reading*: Often, events have a surface understanding that is obvious to most people, but a deeper explanation that only becomes apparent upon further thought or with specialized knowledge.
2. *Sympathetic Imagination*: Not 'sympathetic' in the sense of 'feeling sorry for', but the act of seeing a situation from someone else's perspective (a talent Shakespeare famously possessed).
3. *Identity Criminology*: Like Shakespeare's plays, police work involves many connections between identity (who someone is) and actions (what someone does), including issues of stereotyping.
4. *The Exercise of Power*: Police officers have more power than average citizens; thus, the police have a greater responsibility to wield that power properly. While Shakespeare's kings and modern police officers are obviously exercising power on different orders of magnitude, the same questions about virtue, prerogative and discretion arise.
5. *The Performance of Policing*: As recent media coverage shows, policing is not just about doing a good job. Whether we like it or not, it's also about appearing to do a good job. Shakespearian drama can help cops to increase their awareness of their audiences and make the theatricality of policing work for them.

The programme covers these topics through a series of excerpts from Shakespeare's plays – some shorter, some longer. After acknowledging the different historical contexts – the laws, values and cultural norms in Elizabethan England versus the contemporary United States – the instructor frames each excerpt with some plot summary to orient the audience to the scenes under consideration. It is also helpful to provide some preparatory questions to indicate the direction of the discussion. I recommend using film clips with subtitles to present the scenes in question. Students also benefit from having a printed copy of the text in front of them, allowing them to underline key passages and make notes for discussion. Those texts also include editorial notes glossing difficult vocabulary words and tricky sentences.

For example, the first discussion looks at a scene from one of Shakespeare's most accessible texts, *The*

Tempest, where the mighty magician Prospero polices the enslaved savage Caliban. Banished from his home in Italy, where he was a duke, and sent out to sea, Prospero and his daughter Miranda washed ashore on Caliban's island. Everyone got along at first. Prospero even invited Caliban to live with them in their home, but then Caliban tried to rape Miranda, and Prospero became an agent of criminal justice. The first thing I ask is how this crime will affect Miranda. How will it change her life? What would you do if you were a first-responder on Shakespeare's magical island? The second is why Caliban tried to rape her. Answers might span from raging hormones to an effort to assert dominance to resentment and revenge for the invasion of his homeland. Shakespeare's text doesn't affirm any of these answers any more than the world explains to us why rape happens in real life. But did Caliban commit a crime? There were no laws against rape on the

---

Houston Law Review 33 (1996), 1155–74; R. S. White, *Innocent Victims: Poetic Injustice in Shakespearean Tragedy*, 2nd edn (London, 1988); Theodore Meron, 'Crimes and accountability in Shakespeare', *The American Journal of International Law* 92 (1998), 1–40; Victoria M. Time, *Shakespeare's Criminals: Criminology, Fiction, and Drama* (Westport, CT, 1999); Bryan Reynolds, *Becoming Criminal: Transversal Performance and Cultural Dissidence in Early Modern England* (Baltimore, MD, 2002); Victoria M. Time, 'Shakespeare's female victims: criminology and fiction', *Women and Criminal Justice* 14 (2003), 81–105; Jon D. Orten, '"That perilous stuff": crime in Shakespeare's tragedies', in *Modi operandi: Perspektiver på kriminallitteratur*, ed. Elin Nesje Vestli, Eva Lambertsson Björk and Karen Patrick Knutsen (Halden, 2003), pp. 75–90; Daniel Kornstein, *Kill All the Lawyers? Shakespeare's Legal Appeal* (Lincoln, NE, 2005); William M. Hawley, *Shakespearean Tragedy and the Common Law: The Art of Punishment* (New York, 1998); Kenji Yoshino, *A Thousand Times More Fair: What Shakespeare's Plays Teach Us About Justice* (New York, 2011); Derek Dunne, *Shakespeare, Revenge Tragedy and Early Modern Law: Vindictive Justice* (New York, 2016); Paul Griffiths, 'Criminal London: fear and danger in Shakespeare's city', in *The Oxford Handbook of the Age of Shakespeare*, ed. Malcolm Smuts (Oxford, 2016), pp. 580–95; Regina Schwartz, *Loving Justice, Living Shakespeare* (Oxford, 2016); Paul Raffield, *The Art of Law in Shakespeare* (Oxford, 2017); and Tzachi Zamir, 'Justice: some reflections on *Measure for Measure*', in *The Routledge Companion to Shakespeare and Philosophy*, ed. Craig Bourne and Emily Caddick Bourne (London, 2019), pp. 279–87.

island, out in the state of nature. So I ask officers how they respond to acts that might not be explicitly illegal but are clearly harmful. Then I ask them how, if Prospero can be seen as an agent of criminal justice, we should evaluate his response to the incident. Confinement and community service seem like wise decisions, but the verbal and physical abuse that Prospero heaps on Caliban is more problematic. Degrading and torturing a prisoner isn't taught at the police academy, even for someone who sexually abuses children. In fact, it seems to be Caliban's experience with an overly aggressive criminal justice system that transforms him from a sexual deviant into a political revolutionary who conspires to overthrow Prospero.

Our discussion of *Macbeth*, in which a Scottish war hero conspires with his wife to assassinate the king and claim the throne for himself, starts with a simple question: why did Macbeth kill King Duncan? Interpretations might invoke ethical, psychological and sociological theories of criminology, leading to a series of follow-up questions that seek to bridge fiction with reality: (1) Why is Macbeth ambitious? What's wrong with ambition? What connections between ambition and crime have you experienced on the job? (2) How might Macbeth's wartime service affect his criminality? What do you see as the relationship between veterans and crime out on the street? (3) How does the pull of masculinity affect Macbeth's criminality? Where do you see the pull of masculinity out on the street?

In a quick discussion of *Much Ado About Nothing*, which includes the clownish constable Dogberry, who gets all his words wrong and has no clue how to conduct an investigation, we ask where the 'dumb cop' stereotype comes from. What's the best way to dispel the stereotype? What's the best way to dispel any stereotype? And how can cops leverage their experience with the 'dumb cop' stereotype to understand how others experience stereotypes?

Perhaps the most resonant Shakespearian text for our current moment, *Measure for Measure* depicts an effort to reform the police in Vienna. For years, the city hasn't enforced its laws, leading to widespread crime and disorder. The Duke of Vienna deputizes a strict lawman named Angelo to crack down on crime by instituting a zero-tolerance policy. But soon we see Angelo wielding his power in horrible ways. He sentences a man to death for a petty crime that hadn't been enforced for years. Then, consumed by a perverse desire for the criminal's sister, who is about to become a nun, Angelo offers to release the man if she will sleep with him. The Duke of Vienna's response to Angelo's abuse of power is equally despicable: the Duke arranges to have Angelo raped. Tracking the minor lapses that built up to a major scandal, our conversation seeks to identify how police reform went haywire in Shakespeare's Vienna. Resonances with the challenge of police reform in America today quickly come into focus.

Our final text is *The Merchant of Venice*, which depicts the racial animosity between a Christian and a Jew spiraling out of control into hate crimes, attempted murder and a legal system which must decide what to do when enforcing the laws of the land just doesn't seem fair or right. How should we deal with racism and revenge against it from a criminal justice perspective? What should law enforcement officers do when they don't have the authority to stop harmful actions from taking place? What's more important: enforcing the law or doing what you think is right?

The course segues into an independent writing session asking officers to think about the course's five points of emphasis as they arise out on the street. Students are asked to bring with them to the class a report from a particularly memorable incident they were involved in. Working off that report, officers respond in writing to a series of questions. On the topic of Identity Criminology, they are asked:

1. What were the identities involved in this incident – whether of the offenders, of the bystanders, or your own?
2. What was the relationship between the identities involved and the actions taken in this incident?

On Sympathetic Imagination, they are asked:

3. Beyond identity, what were the factors contributing to the perpetrator's actions?

On The Exercise of Power, they are asked:

4. What power did you hold in this situation?
5. What were the ethical questions that arose?

On The Performance of Policing, they are asked:

6. Who or what was your audience for this incident, either in the moment (perps, bystanders) or later (supervisors, media)?
7. What did you do – or, as you look back, what could you have done – to perform the role of the good cop?

Building off these responses, officers are asked to imagine they are Shakespeare writing out this incident in a scene. The details of the scene have all been written: they are in the report. You just need to write two soliloquies. Don't worry about iambic pentameter or flowery imagery, but ask yourself how you can articulate the hidden factors, motives, thoughts and goals at work behind the actions taken. To explain is not to excuse, of course. So, first, write a soliloquy from the perpetrator's perspective, articulating why they are doing what they are doing. Give us a glimpse into the criminal's mind. Second, write a soliloquy from your own perspective, articulating why you're doing what you're doing. To be clear, the point of this activity is not to suggest that you may have done something wrong. The point is that you may understand better than anyone else what happened and why, and these steps can help you to articulate it and communicate your knowledge. The hope here is that, in writing out these soliloquies, officers will come to make explicit the forces that motivate both crime and justice, opening up discussion. Cops love to tell stories. And they love to debate.

Studying Shakespeare can be intellectually and ethically beneficial, not because he was a model human being or wise moral leader. He was neither, often showing a complete disregard for how to lead a good life. Instead, he was obsessed with the causes and effects of injustice: tragedy. Making sense of his plays requires discernment. That's what cops need too. Studying Shakespeare doesn't make you a better person, but it does render you better able

to explain the causes, structures and meanings of harmful social behaviour. That includes the harmful things Shakespeare did to characters – the smiley depiction of domestic abuse in *The Taming of the Shrew*, the breezy use of rape as a plot point in *Titus Andronicus*, the happy endings for the perpetrators of hate crimes in *The Merchant of Venice* and *The Tempest* – as well as the harmful things done in Shakespeare's name. Bardolatry figures cultural greatness as old, White and male. Shakespeare's centrality excludes other writers, including women and people of colour. And there are limits to how far Shakespeare can take us in a modern criminal justice setting. What about female and LGTBQ+ voices on crime and justice? What about African American, indigenous and immigrant perspectives? What about when Shakespeare's language, which presents difficulties for even the most talented English majors, becomes too big a barrier?

That's why the Shakespeare for Cops curriculum concludes by moving to adaptations that update Shakespeare's plays to modern criminal justice settings. These include allusions to golden-age crime fiction as well as recent detective television.[79] *West Side Story* (1961) frames *Romeo and Juliet* as rival ethnic gangs singing songs about criminology to Officer Krupke. In Geoffrey Sax's *Othello* (2001), officer John Othello must navigate Ben Jago's racism in the modern London police force. Margaret Atwood's novel *Hag-Seed* (2018) resets *The Tempest* in a Canadian correctional facility. The final season of *Oz* (2003), *Shakespeare Behind Bars* (2006), *Mickey B* (2007) and *Caesar Must Die* (2012) all stage Shakespeare in prison. And there are recognizably modern police officers and scenes of criminal justice in Baz Luhrmann's *Romeo + Juliet* (1996), William Morrissette's *Scotland PA* (2001), Joss Whedon's *Much Ado About Nothing* (2011) and Michael Almereyda's *Cymbeline* (2014).

Then we end by hearing from some people who have spoken back to Shakespeare. That includes

---

[79] Lisa Hopkins, *Shakespearean Allusion in Crime Fiction: DCI Shakespeare* (New York, 2016).

prominent twentieth-century writers such as Virginia Woolf ('What would have happened had Shakespeare had a wonderfully gifted sister?') and James Baldwin ('I condemned him as one of the authors and architects of my oppression').[80] There are also recent statements from thinkers like Ayanna Thompson ('he's writing from the vantage point of the sixteenth and seventeenth-century, and I hope we've moved on'), Marcos Gonsalez ('the language of Shakespeare is the language of whiteness') and Ruben Espinosa ('racist complicity abound[s]').[81] These voices provide cops with models for one of the most challenging aspects of police work: recognizing cases of systemic inequality even when it is deeply codified in culture and comes from a person in a place of authority. Shakespeare himself is not removed from the power dynamics critiqued in Shakespeare for Cops. Understanding the identity politics of bardolatry could be a step towards doing the same with American policing.

***

Insofar as the primary goal of this programme is police education, the ideal setting would be in-service training, management training or a continuing education course. We couldn't do an undergraduate course or recruit training because the project asks cops to use their on-the-ground experience to inform their in-the-classroom reflection, with the hope that the inverse will then happen as well. Venues could include in-service training at local police academies, the Institute for Law Enforcement Administration's Contemporary Issues and Ethics Conference or the International Association of Police Chiefs' Annual Conference. I think it would be a mistake to bring in Shakespeare scholars to teach these classes, inevitably creating the atmosphere of some ivory-tower outsider trying to tell cops how to do their jobs. As David Dagan noted, 'It can take insiders to make new ideas seem legitimate, like something *real cops* talk about.'[82] The programme should be led by criminal justice professionals who are enthusiastic about the value of the humanities; perhaps literature professors could be brought in as co-teachers

providing classroom support when questions arise, and to help facilitate discussion.

At the same time, I selfishly want to advocate for the secondary goal of the programme, the transmission of experiential knowledge from the police to academics. I can think of nothing more fascinating and beneficial to me as a Shakespeare scholar than a room full of people who are involved with the work of justice on a day-to-day basis talking about the way crime and justice work in Shakespeare's plays. Cops have as much to teach academics as academics have to teach cops. As Gillespie told me, 'Cops can take the neat-and-tidy ideas of academics and put them up against the real-world tests that they run daily', and then he turned the tables on me: 'Have you seen a person truly prove that they do or don't have free will? Have you ever seen someone go full-Hamlet on his enemies?'[83] Even as academics have the time, skills and inclination to think deeply about the challenges of crime and justice, cops have the experiential evidence needed to test the quality of academic ideas. David Dagan also noted that 'cops might be better anthropologists than academics. They understand slang, implicit norms, and interpersonal power dynamics that academics might not immediately see.'[84] Amy Herman thinks 'police officers could readily demonstrate to academics in the humanities how to speak less rhetorically and communicate more directly. Exigent circumstances mandate precise and concise communication.'[85] Even as Shakespearians work

---

[80] Virginia Woolf, *A Room of One's Own* (London, 1929), p. 48; James Baldwin, 'Why I stopped hating Shakespeare', *The Observer*, 19 April 1964, p. 21.

[81] Ayanna Thompson, interviewed by Gene Demby, 'All that glisters is not gold', *Code Switch*, NPR, 21 August 2019: www.npr.org/transcripts/752850055; Marcos Gonsalez, 'Caliban never belonged to Shakespeare', Literary Hub, 26 July 2019: https://lithub.com/caliban-never-belonged-to-shakespeare; Ruben Espinosa, 'Shakespeare and your mountainish inhumanity', The Sundial, 16 August 2019; https://medium.com/the-sundial-acmrs/shakespeare-and-your-mountainish-inhumanity-d255474027de.

[82] Dagan, 'Baltimore cops'. [83] Gillespie, interview.

[84] Dagan, interview. [85] Herman, interview.

up from the evidence of his plays to abstract ideas about crime and justice, cops can work those ideas back down to human experience, evaluating both their truth and their implications for policy.

And conversations between cops and Shakespearians could be revelatory for everyday citizens. Thus, I want to keep alive the possibility of a version of 'Shakespeare for Cops' that operates as a public event through some sort of Shakespearian community outreach programme such as the Public Shakespeare Initiative, the Folger Shakespeare Library, the American Shakespeare Center or the Oregon Shakespeare Festival. Beyond achieving the educational objectives of Shakespeare for Cops, such an event would do the important work of creating community partnerships among academics, cops and citizens, all working together towards justice.

YOUNGER GENERATIONS AND EMPATHIC COMMUNICATION: LEARNING TO FEEL IN ANOTHER LANGUAGE WITH SHAKESPEARE AT THE SILVANO TOTI GLOBE THEATRE IN ROME

MADDALENA PENNACCHIA

In a speech delivered in 1943 at the British–Norwegian Institute in London at the British Council's request, T. S. Eliot asked his audience what relevance poetry had in the society of that period; of course, he could not articulate more explicitly the question that was clear to all those attending the conference: that is, what is the use of poetry when society is being devastated by a global war? The conflict was raging throughout Europe, and when it finally ended, Eliot repeated the same speech and asked the same question in a recently liberated Paris, in May 1945. According to T. S. Eliot in 'The social function of poetry' – the title under which his address was finally published in *The Adelphi* in July 1945 – it is undeniable that poetical language must in the first place 'give pleasure';[1] however, the author is also persuaded that poetry is not only pleasure-giving but useful, in that it is able to convey 'some new experience, or some fresh understanding of the familiar, or the expression of something we have experienced but have no words for, which enlarges our consciousness or refines our sensibility'.[2] To put it differently, poetry possesses a unique power to endow all people, even those 'who do not enjoy poetry',[3] with words for what they experience but would not know how to say otherwise. *Ergo*, it *does* have a relevance in any society and at any time in history. And this is true for all poetic languages, I argue, including dramatic poetry, and Shakespeare's above all.

Interestingly, while addressing a non-English audience in both London and Paris, T. S. Eliot slowly turned the crucial topic of his conference – what does poetry do for us? – into a further, and perhaps deeper, philosophical interrogation: why should getting acquainted with poetry in a 'foreign language'[4] be of any importance in a world of 'national' cultures, especially when these cultures have been traumatized by wars and other kinds of international conflicts and social tensions? More than ever this question is of great relevance today, in particular in the field of modern languages learning; we could reword it as follows: is it still useful, when learning a modern language, to get acquainted with its poetry? Is it still important to try and comprehend the literary culture of a specific language? Can the four language skills be developed through literature? I seriously wonder what the answer to these questions would be among teachers of English as L2 (second or other-than-native language) in Italian secondary schools today. T. S. Eliot, however, is markedly clear and assertive on the matter: 'The *spiritual* communication between people and people cannot be carried on without the individuals who take the trouble to learn at least one

---

[1] T. S. Eliot, 'The social function of poetry', in *On Poetry and Poets* (London, 1957), pp. 15–25; p. 18.
[2] Eliot, 'Social function', p. 18.
[3] Eliot, 'Social function', p. 18.
[4] Eliot, 'Social function', p. 19.

foreign language as well as one can learn any language but one's own, and who consequently are able, to a greater or less degree, to *feel* in another language as well as in their own.'[5] These reflections have long been at the core of a study carried out at the Department of Foreign Languages, Literatures and Cultures at Roma Tre University, which aims to explore the field of teaching English as L2 by using Shakespeare's poetry for the theatre, while also investigating the power of Shakespeare's dramatic poetry to create empathic relations among young people.[6] I am here referring to those whom Marc Prensky, a writer and game designer in the field of education, famously defined as 'digital natives' – that is, natural-born users of digital technologies who are endowed with 'thinking patterns' that, according to him, have changed from those of 'digital immigrants' who, instead, learnt how to use digital media as a 'second language'.[7] Prensky, therefore, not only gave a name to a new group of people, but also brought to the fore the fact that those who happen to be in charge of the transmission of knowledge, as well as of training the skills or moulding the attitudes of 'digital natives' via educational institutions (schools and universities), are 'digital immigrants'. Being a 'digital immigrant' myself, I feel challenged and fascinated by the learning processes of teenagers and the way they communicate their thoughts and feelings. As a recent book wonders, I have asked myself whether there is a crisis of connection among young people,[8] and, if so, how we should face it as their teachers. Considering that an interdisciplinary approach is needed to deal with such a complex phenomenon, the scientific literature on empathy and emotional contagion that can be found in seminal works such as *The Social Neuroscience of Empathy* has been particularly inspiring.[9]

In this article, I will sketch the theoretical framework and methodology of an educational programme, 'The Potentialities of Shakespeare's Theatre for L2 Learning', which (as the linchpin of the above-mentioned research) is targeted at a group of Italian high school students in their fourth or fifth year (16 to 18 years of age); I will also report the main practical results. To Eliot's inspirational post-war approach to poetical language, a passionate belief in the power of Shakespeare's theatre to affect

multilingual audiences has been added. This project is in line with 'on your feet' educational projects for younger generations created by leading theatrical institutions with strong educational departments, such as Shakespeare's Globe and the Royal Shakespeare Company.[10] The following pages report how, in Rome, those inspirational models have been adapted for Italy's latest generations of digital natives through a collaboration between the Department of Foreign Languages, Literatures and Cultures of Roma Tre University and the Silvano Toti Globe Theatre, the Italian replica of an Elizabethan theatre in Villa Borghese in Rome.

***

The Silvano Toti Globe Theatre stands in the green heart of Villa Borghese like a sort of spellbinding performance space. The idea of building a Globe replica in Italy's capital city was first conceived by Gigi Proietti, a celebrated Roman actor, director and writer who has long appealed to a vast, transgenerational and steady audience of fans and followers on diverse media, from theatre to cinema and television. At the celebration of the park's centennial as a public garden in 2003, Proietti suggested to Walter

---

[5] Eliot, 'Social function', p. 23.

[6] Maddalena Pennacchia, 'Intermedial products for digital natives: British theatre-cinema on Italian screens', *Intermédialité* 30–1 (2017): https://doi.org/10.7202/1049952ar.

[7] Marc Prensky, 'Digital natives, digital immigrants, part I', *On the Horizon* 9 (2001), 1–6; pp. 1–2. Since that pioneering article, a number of studies have been published on the topic, but I would like at least to mention Alexiei Dingli and Dylan Seychell, *The New Digital Natives: Cutting the Chord* (Berlin, 2015). Dingli and Seychell focus on what they call 2DN (the second-generation Digital Natives) – that is, those who were born when wireless and mobile technologies had already been invented (pp. 20–2).

[8] Niobe Way, Alisha Ali, Carol Gilligan and Pedro Noguera, eds., *The Crisis of Connection: Roots, Consequences, and Solutions* (New York, 2018).

[9] Jean Decety and William Ickes, eds., *The Social Neuroscience of Empathy* (Cambridge, MA, 2009).

[10] Fiona Banks, *Creative Shakespeare: The Globe Education Guide to Practical Shakespeare* (New York and London, 2014); Joe Winston, *Transforming the Teaching of Shakespeare with the Royal Shakespeare Company* (London and New York, 2015).

Veltroni, Rome's mayor at the time, that an Elizabethan theatre would be a welcome 'gift' to the city; no sooner said than done (in less than three months): the playhouse was built by the Fondazione Silvano Toti, a charity founded by the Toti family, owners of an important construction firm, and donated to the municipality of Rome. The first play to be performed in the new playhouse, in September 2003, was *Romeo e Giulietta* directed by Gigi Proietti, who has been artistic director of the theatre since then; the theatre aroused the immediate curiosity of a wide audience that was initially attracted by the fame of its artistic director; since then, however, its long summer season (from June to October) of Shakespeare performed in Italian has gradually grown into a well-established festivalized Roman event, particularly appreciated by young spectators.[11]

In 2018, thanks to a formal agreement between the Silvano Toti Globe Theatre and Roma Tre University, a digital archive has been created with the aim of collecting all the materials related to the Silvano Toti Globe Theatre's productions from 2003 to date: recorded performances, pictures, translations, scripts, costume and scenography sketches, statistical data, press releases.[12]

A collaboration between academics and practitioners was consequently set up and explored in the following year, 2019, through the research and teaching programme under consideration:[13] 'The Potentialities of Shakespeare's Theatre for L2 Learning', which is now in its second edition.[14] This is an intensive extracurricular course for Italian high school students that has been designed with careful attention to the 'Key Competences for Lifelong Learning – a European Reference Framework' (22 May 2018). More specifically, the programme's objectives are calibrated on 'knowledge', 'skills' and 'attitudes' related to 'multilingual competence' and 'cultural awareness and expression competence'.[15] The teaching method has accordingly been devised around five goals: (1) prompting the acquisition of a basic *knowledge* of the historical and cultural context in which Shakespeare's plays were produced, with a special focus on the double nature of the playtext as

[11] Lisanna Calvi and Maddalena Pennacchia, 'Festivalising Shakespeare in Italy: Verona and Rome', in *Shakespeare on European Festival Stages*, ed. N. Cinpoes, F. March and P. Prescott (London, in press).

[12] The Archive has been created thanks to a formal agreement signed on 18 May 2018 between Gigi Proietti's Politeama S.r.l., entrusted with the exclusive artistic management of the Silvano Toti Globe Theatre, and the Department of Foreign Languages, Literatures and Cultures of Roma Tre University. The Archive is hosted at the Multimedia Centre of the Department and is open to consultation for all visitors who ask for it; however, documents can only be consulted on site, for copyright reasons. This ongoing scientific project is directed by Maddalena Pennacchia, together with the Advisory Board composed of Masolino d'Amico (Roma Tre University), Maria Del Sapio Garbero (Roma Tre University), Keir Elam (Bologna University), Viola Papetti (Roma Tre University) and Gilberto Sacerdoti (Roma Tre University). See https://bacheca .uniroma3.it/archivio-globe/chi-siamo.

[13] The teaching staff of the project includes, from Roma Tre University, Maddalena Pennacchia (project designer and coordinator), Michela Compagnoni, Chiara Degano and Sabrina Vellucci; and from the Silvano Toti Globe Theatre, Loredana Scaramella (stage director and acting coach), Carlotta Proietti (producer and actress) and Susanna Proietti (producer and costume designer). In 2019, Márta Minier (University of South Wales) was guest teacher in residence, while in 2020 Lara Phillips (Oxford MA, Head of Drama, Dame Allan's School, Newcastle-Upon-Tyne) distance-taught via Zoom.

[14] The first edition has been filmed for documentary reasons and is kept in the Archive; see the dedicated page via the website: https://bacheca.uniroma3.it/archivio-globe. See also the short filmed documentary produced by Politeama S.r.l., to be found on the Silvano Toti Globe Theatre's website: www.globetheatreroma.com/notizia/bf84b63b-75d4-46c9-9c70-51a9fb2d959b.

[15] https://eur-lex.europa.eu/legal-content/EN/TXT/PDF/? uri=CELEX:32018H0604(01)&from=EN. As stated in the document, 'Key competences' are those 'which all individuals need for personal fulfilment and development, employability, social inclusion, sustainable lifestyle, successful life in peaceful societies, health-conscious life management and active citizenship', and they are 'a combination of knowledge, skills and attitude' – more specifically: 'knowledge is composed of the facts and figures, concepts, ideas and theories which are already established and support the understanding of a certain area or subject ... skills are defined as the ability and capacity to carry out processes and use the existing knowledge to achieve results, ... attitudes describe the disposition and mind-sets to act or react to ideas, persons or situations' (pp. 7–8 and 11–12).

belonging with both literature and theatre; (2) training the ability (*skill*) to close-read the playtext in English, with a stress on the dramatic language as a privileged vehicle for human interaction and communication; (3) training the ability (*skill*) to express and manage emotions and to feel empathy through performance in the original language; (4) training the ability (*skill*) to engage in creative processes with a 'what Shakespeare means to me' approach; (5) facilitating the development of an open and accepting *attitude* towards cultural diversity via the understanding of Shakespeare's theatre as both the product of a specific linguistic and cultural heritage and a world-wide legacy, i.e. a privileged fertile ground for exploring the universality of human values while putting them to the test within local cultures. Importantly, the student-centred pedagogy developed in the programme, which is language-focused with a stress on the processes of translation and adaptation, is carried out in two different places which *both* come to be finally related to each other as spaces of creative learning: the classroom, at Roma Tre University, and the stage, at the Silvano Toti Globe Theatre.

The choice of the plays to be investigated during the course depends each year on the theatrical season of the Globe in Villa Borghese, since attending and discussing one or more productions on the bill is a mandatory part of the programme, which also aims to develop new theatre audiences. In 2019, when we worked with more than seventy students from six schools, three plays were selected: *Giulio Cesare* (*Julius Caesar*), *Sogno di una notte di mezz'estate* (*A Midsummer Night's Dream*) and *Romeo and Juliet* (in English). In 2020, we decided instead to work on a single play, *La dodicesima notte* (*Twelfth Night*), that was newly (and courageously) produced by Politeama S.r.l. (the company entrusted with the artistic direction), when they obtained permission to open the theatre following a very strict COVID-19-related health protocol, to be applied on stage and off stage. The play was directed by Loredana Scaramella with a company of twelve actors, who were on stage for the whole duration of the performance, without ever touching each other

and constantly sanitizing their hands, in a sort of choreographed gesture. Accordingly, only twelve students were selected among those who presented their application for the 2020 programme – the same number as the actors since that was the maximum amount of people who were allowed to move on stage while keeping a safe distance between them. In order to explore and illustrate the kind of activities devised and results gained during the project, I will focus, for space reasons, only on one of the three modules into which the programme was divided – that is, 'Words, Music and Emotions', the other two being 'Shakespeare and the Entertainment Industry' and 'Languages of Love'.

As is well known, *Twelfth Night* is considered to be one of the most musical of Shakespeare's comedies; it is not by chance that the word 'music' stands out as the first noun of the play, for the quantity of music that can be made and listened to in productions might be very relevant. In fact, as Keir Elam contends in his edition of the play: 'the comedy's principal artistic paradigm ... becomes the interaction or co-operation between words and music, best exemplified in the song or ballad'.[16] Loredana Scaramella's effective translation, adaptation and direction of *La dodicesima notte* (on from 11 September to 18 October 2020) exploited to the full the musical potential of the comedy with a strongly emotional use of live music. The William Kemp Quartet (Adriano Dragotta – violin, Daniele Ercoli – double bass, Daniele De Seta – guitars, Alessandro Luccioli – drums and percussions) provided both live incidental music and the music for the songs, whose pop-rock original scores are by Mimosa Campironi. The talented Carlotta Proietti (Olivia) and Carlo Ragone (Feste) were the captivating leading singers, but all actors – who were arranged in a circle and moved as if following the rules of a game of 'musical chairs' – joined their singing as if they

---

[16] Keir Elam, 'Appendix 3: music', in William Shakespeare, *Twelfth Night*, Arden Bloomsbury Shakespeare (London, 2008), pp. 383–94; p. 383.

were a 'comic' – instead of a tragic – chorus.[17] This Shakespeare with a rock twist – the drums and electric guitar being particularly impressive within the general soundscape – was enthusiastically received by Roman audiences, especially by young ones. Students participating in the programme saw the show and, as witnessed by their comments on the 'viewing chart' they had to fill in as one of their assignments, were enthralled and fascinated by the music as well as by the dancing and comic exuberance of the production, which, in the course of Scaramella's exploration of Shakespeare's comedies over the years, have become key features of her directorial style.[18]

That said, it is fair to clarify that young audiences in Italy are usually very unfamiliar with *Twelfth Night*; when secondary school students in their third year (15/16 years old) start reading anthologized short texts from English literature to integrate their linguistic competence, their textbooks usually present them with extracts from *Romeo and Juliet* or, alternatively, *Hamlet* and *Macbeth*, and they are very seldom introduced to any of the comedies, which include plenty of songs, as well as references to instrumental music and dance.

We started the module 'Words, Music and Emotions' at the university, in the classroom, illustrating the importance of music in Elizabethan theatre.[19] David Lindley's authoritative book on *Shakespeare and Music* was referred to in order to introduce high school students to the kind of academic research which has been led on the topic, with a particular focus on popular songs and ballads.[20] Participants were pleasingly surprised to realize that 'pop' music was among the most widespread forms of entertainment in the Elizabethan age. They were, then, guided through the close reading of twenty-five lines of the second act (*Twelfth Night*, 2.3.29–54) that include one of the seven songs in the play, that is 'O mistress mine'. The contents of the song were discussed, and students had to try to figure out the reactions of the two listeners on stage, Sir Toby and Sir Andrew. For, as David Lindley rightly remarks: 'The song performed to an audience on stage invites us to attend not only to the music in and for itself, but

to register its effect upon those to whom it is directly addressed within the world of the play.'[21]

Focusing on the reactions of the characters 'within the world of the play' is also a productive way to explore reactions in the world outside the play – that is, our own emotional response as spectators. Prompted by the lively discussion on the contents of the song – namely, love as a fleeting moment of joy and pleasure that has to be caught when one is young and is finally remembered with melancholy longing in old age – one of the students, Francesca D., connected Shakespeare's 'O mistress mine' to Lorenzo de Medici's well-known 'Song of Bacchus' ('Quant'è bella giovinezza che si fugge tuttavia'), perhaps the poem that any person who studied in an Italian school would acknowledge as the quintessence of the Renaissance. This spontaneous intercultural and intertextual observation was of extreme interest to those of us who were there not only as teachers but also as scholars, for it invited us to explore further the comparison between Italian and English Renaissance popular songs as another output of the fruitful creative climate of the programme.[22]

---

[17] The circle of chairs where the actors sat with their heads covered in black veils, crying and lamenting at the sound of music when Olivia's mourning theme is introduced by Sir Toby (*Twelfth Night*, 1.3.1), seemed to me like a visual play on the idea of the classical tragic chorus, and this was confirmed by Scaramella in a conversation to be published.

[18] Maddalena Pennacchia, '"But not love [...]": an interview with Loredana Scaramella about her translation, adaptation and direction of *La bisbetica domata* (*The Taming of the Shrew*) at the Silvano Toti Globe Theatre in Rome (2018)', *Journal of Adaptation in Film & Performance* 12 (2018), 91–106.

[19] All the activities of the 2020 programme have been filmed by RAI Scuola (the educational department of the Italian broadcast company RAI – Radiotelevisione italiana); the filmed documents have been turned into a short series in four episodes entitled *Learning English with Shakespeare*.

[20] David Lindley, ed., *Shakespeare and Music* (London, 2006), pp. 142–68.

[21] Lindley, *Shakespeare*, p. 142.

[22] See, for instance, the essay on Renaissance music for *Il Magnifico*'s carnival songs that can be interestingly connected with Lindsey's research on Elizabethan music: Walter H. Rubsamen, 'The music for "Quant'è bella giovinezza" and other carnival songs by Lorenzo de Medici', in *Art,*

We then asked students to learn by heart the tune of the song, providing them with the recorded version on the CD annexed to Ross Duffin's *Shakespeare's Songbook*.[23] They were informed about the controversy among Shakespearian scholars over the fact that this may be the actual tune sung by the actor, probably Robert Armin, who played Feste in Shakespeare's company at the time, the Lord Chamberlain's Men. As Peter Seng explains in *The Vocal Songs in the Plays of Shakespeare: A Critical History*:

Music for a sixteenth-century tune called 'O Mistress mine' survives in three early versions. The earliest is Thomas Morley's *The First Book of Consort Lessons* (1599, 1611), an instrumental arrangement for treble lute, pandora, cittern, bass viol, flute, and treble viol ... Whether Shakespeare's song was originally sung to this basic tune is a matter of considerable controversy, and it appears that the controversy will not be settled to the satisfaction of all the musical and literary scholars who have engaged themselves in it until new evidence is discovered.[24]

In order to entice students into singing, the William Kemp Quartet was invited to participate in one of the sessions at the Silvano Toti Globe Theatre; Adriano Dragotta, who is also an ethnomusicologist, studied Thomas Morley's notation as reported in Duffin's book[25] and conducted the quartet accordingly. On stage, Loredana Scaramella, in the role of acting coach in the programme, had students perform a series of warm-up exercises, and then arranged them in a circle to sing with the accompaniment of live music. While singers and musicians were performing together, those who were observing the activity (teachers and scholars) could distinctly perceive a change in the general mood: a growing feeling of communion was spreading among us at an unpredicted speed, confirming the views of those theorists of the evolution of music in its relation to language and dance, such as Ian Cross, who, through their complex interdisciplinary studies, contend that music is 'foundationally interactive and social' – i.e. it plays a crucial role in building communities.[26]

In order to make sense of what happened after that, we need to get back to Eliot's essay on 'The social function of poetry' with which this article started. The power of poetry to expand people's grasp of human reality as it is shaped by language also affects, in Eliot's opinion, those who are not perfectly acquainted with the language in which poetry is composed; communication beyond understanding is almost a 'magic' quality of the poetical language per se, as he observes from his own experience: 'I have also found sometimes that a piece of poetry, which I could not translate, containing many words unfamiliar to me, and sentences which I could not construe, conveyed something immediate and vivid, which was unique, different from anything in English – something which I could not put into words and yet felt I understood.'[27] When the understanding fails to get the exact meaning in terms of semantics and syntax, the 'natural' inclination of human beings for poetry helps us, according to Eliot, to catch the uniqueness and immediacy of any piece of poetical language. This happens because 'poetry has to do with the expression of feeling and emotion; and ... feeling and emotion are particular whereas thought is general'.[28] Eliot is not contradicting his belief in the impersonality of the poet, for he is referring to feeling and emotion in a broader, anthropological sense, with words that very much recall Giambattista Vico's views in the *Nuova scienza* (1744):[29] 'The impulse towards the literary use of the languages of the peoples began with poetry ...

Science and History in the Renaissance, ed. C. S. Singleton (Baltimore, MD, 1967), pp. 163–84.

[23] Ross W. Duffin, *Shakespeare's Songbook* (New York and London, 2004).

[24] Peter J. Seng, *The Vocal Songs in the Plays of Shakespeare: A Critical History* (Cambridge, MA, 1967), p. 96.

[25] Duffin, *Songbook*, p. 286.

[26] Ian Cross, 'The nature of music and its evolution', in *The Oxford Handbook of Music Psychology*, ed. Susan Hallam, Ian Cross and Michael Thaut (Oxford, 2016) pp. 3–17.

[27] Eliot, 'Social function', p. 24.

[28] Eliot, 'Social function', p. 19.

[29] This is not surprising, considering that in 1944 Max Harold Fisch had just published his American translation of the *Autobiography* of the Neapolitan philosopher, who was being rediscovered in those years by critics and repositioned within the general picture of pre-Romantic and Romantic culture.

Therefore no art is more stubbornly national than poetry',[30] for it constantly reminds us 'of all the things that can only be said in one language, and are untranslatable'.[31] If poetry, even when it is composed in a language we do not perfectly know, is capable of communicating feelings and emotions which belong to the culture of that language, how does it achieve such a goal? It perhaps does so through its most sensuous component: the sound. When we think of Shakespearian dramatic poetry as a 'foreign' language – both for L2 learners and for native English speakers, for whom early modern English often sounds like a foreign language too – what can be felt and emotionally experienced as unique is its 'untranslatable' rhythm, its distinctive music which can only be grasped in English. This is a truism that cannot be taken for granted in Italy, where audiences can very seldom listen to Shakespeare's plays in English, given that Italy prides itself on a long and prestigious tradition of translating Shakespeare.[32]

These ideas prompted us into training the students' ears to perceive the sound of the iambic pentameter, as opposed to prose. In the classroom and, later, on stage, teachers, who are all NNES (Non-Native English Speakers), read, with exaggerated emphasis, the lines of the four scenes that had been selected for the modules.[33] This listening exercise, which is often practised in British high schools, was thoroughly new for Italian students. They were amazed by how the rhythm of the verse helped them to understand its content: in stressing specific words, the beats of the iambic pentameter helped them to catch the gist of the sentence, somehow clearing it from linguistic elements that were not strictly necessary to a 'quick' comprehension of what was going on in the text.

After having been introduced, in the classroom, to such phenomena as 'Rap Shakespeare',[34] students were then nudged into comparing the use of rhythm in the iambic pentameter and in Italian hip-hop music. Rap and trap music being currently the most popular genres among Italian teenagers, teachers pointed out that it is often not easy for adults to understand the meaning of the songs belonging to these genres, as if they were actually sung in a 'foreign' language, also confessing that

they often only get bits and scraps when the stress falls on certain words. In his pioneer study on 'the use of indigenous languages other than English in rap music', Tony Mitchell defined the languages used in such a hybridized genre as 'resistance vernaculars', also highlighting how they 're-territorialize not only major Anglophone rules of intelligibility but also those of other "standard" languages such as French and Italian'.[35] This discussion rebalanced the teachers/learners relation, and Italian students felt empowered and more confident with their treatment of Shakespearian language, which they initially thought to be just a product of high culture, and this also facilitated grass-roots suggestions.

On the stage of the Silvano Toti Globe Theatre, students were invited to try to think of a way to rap Shakespeare's words: after creating a climate of reciprocal trust and sharing via singing 'O mistress mine' to Morley's tune, musicians were asked to change the rhythm and play to a rap beat; while the music went on, Scaramella started to describe the festive and even riotous mood that characterizes Sir

---

[30] Eliot, 'Social function', p. 19.

[31] Eliot, 'Social function', p. 23.

[32] Enza De Francisci and Chris Stamatakis, eds., *Shakespeare, Italy and Transnational Exchange: Early Modern to Present* (New York and London, 2017). See also Maddalena Pennacchia, 'William Shakespeare, Mme de Staël and the politics of translation', *Folio. Shakespeare-Genootschap van Nederland en Vlaanderen* 13 (2006), 9–20.

[33] The selected scenes were: 1.5.220–318, Viola/Cesario meets Olivia for the first time and woos her on Orsino's behalf (module on the 'Languages of Love'); 2.3.31–57, Sir Andrew and Sir Toby ask Feste for a love song and he sings 'O mistress mine' (module: 'Words, Music and Emotions'); 2.4.48–137, Orsino and Viola/Cesario listen to Feste singing 'Come away, come away death' and Viola/Cesario tells the story of 'his sister' who died of love concealment (module on the 'Languages of Love'); and, finally, 2.5.83–211, Malvolio is tricked by Maria's false love letter (module on 'Shakespeare and the Entertainment Industry').

[34] Douglas Lanier, *Shakespeare and Modern Popular Culture* (Oxford, 2002), pp. 73–80.

[35] Tony Mitchell, 'Doin' damage in my native language: the use of "resistance vernaculars" in hip hop in France, Italy, and Aotearoa/New Zealand', *Popular Music & Society* 24 (2000), 41–54.

Toby and Sir Andrew's revels. Empathizing with the two characters' presumed feelings, students started to dance, keeping a safe distance but each aware of the movements of the others; they were visibly engaged in a 'process of entrainment', which is 'the coordination in time of one participant's behaviours with those of another . . . around temporal regularities that are inferred (generally non-consciously) from musical sounds and actions in the form of a pulse or a periodic beat that is sensed by all participants'.[36] What, most of all, struck those off stage who were observing what was happening on stage was, I believe, the power of language, music and dance to connect the necessarily distanced bodies of these young people through entrainment. The level of connection was very high when, suddenly, one of the girls who is an amateur rap singer, Martina N., automatically began to read out loud from her hand-out the lines she had studied in the classroom and rapped them, instinctively following the natural rhythm of the blank verse. When Scaramella took the sheet from her hand, Martina, inviting the others to clap their hands at the sound of the beat, started a free-style rap in Italian, with words that told of taking the risk of expressing one's emotions and communicating to others what one feels. It was an intense moment, when those who were off stage had the distinct perception that the twelve young people on stage were experimenting with their 'emotional intelligence', what Keith Oatley sees as 'a distinctive faculty of understanding that enables us to recognize our own emotions and those of others so that we can manage our lives and relationships'.[37]

There and then, Shakespeare had really found 'a local habitation and a name' among the Italian teenagers who took part in our educational programme; their comprehension of his poetical language and of what it can really do for people of diverse cultures was literally resonating all over, and surrounding those who were present as if amplified by the wonderful soundbox of the Globe Theatre in Villa Borghese.

---

[36] Cross, 'Nature of music', p. 7.
[37] Keith Oatley, 'Emotional intelligence', in *Emotions: A Brief History* (Malden, MA, and Oxford, 2004), pp. 134–55; p. 135.

SHAKESPEARE IN NINETEENTH-CENTURY BENGAL: AN IMPERATIVE OF 'NEW LEARNING'

MADHUMITA SAHA

Wherever English language, literature and culture have travelled in this world, it has been Shakespeare who received the greatest adulation. Bengali literature too was not divorced from such an activity. It was quite natural that Bengali literature adopted the subject, content and style of Shakespeare as evidenced in the schema of world literature. However, in the context of Bengal, the assimilation was not restricted to aspects of dramatic forms only, and mediated beyond literary imagination to engage into a deeper level of political and cultural discourse. While nineteenth-century Bengal evidenced widespread changes in intellectual temperament leading to a heightened intellectual ferment and creativity, it also resulted in a restructuring and reshaping of imported ideas, thereby evolving a new indigenous culture, which gave Bengal a distinctive identity. The inclination for an education in the English language among the middle classes eager to take advantage of knowing the language and acquiring the culture of the colonial rulers, along with a rapidly growing print culture, led to a growing demand for Shakespeare's works, which at least initially, captured the imagination of Bengalis as a repository of Western culture. With the institutionalization of English education in Hindu College in 1817 and later the establishment of the Calcutta University in 1857, Shakespeare came to occupy an important position in the curriculum, instilling rationalistic and humanistic values among young aspirants, thereby encouraging ideas of freedom and free thinking.

This article seeks to interrogate how Shakespeare's position in the curriculum altered the dynamics of the nineteenth-century intellectual and political history of Bengal, and how Shakespeare's introduction in the curriculum also stimulated a growing appetite for the ideas of humanism and rationality in a rapidly changing milieu of the nineteenth century. It further seeks to argue Shakespeare's role in the very definition of humanistic enquiry in the context of nineteenth-century Bengal. Some of the larger issues this article tries to explore are: what was the role of Shakespeare in shaping modernity in the context of nineteenth-century Bengal? How did Western modernity represent itself in Shakespeare?

The article begins with a discussion of Shakespeare teaching in schools and colleges, followed by the Anglicist and Orientalist debates, which then leads towards a closer observation of missionary initiatives as another defining character in the discourse of Shakespeare studies in Bengal. Thereafter, the unique position of Hindu College and the role of Shakespeare in the curriculum in missionary and government institutions provide a fascinating account of how Shakespeare came to define the tenets of a secular form of enquiry, which in turn challenged the established religious, political and social conventions of the society. This then brings us to the wider question of the role of Shakespeare studies as an aspect of 'new learning' in the context of the resurgence in Bengal, variously debated as the Bengal Renaissance.[1]

---

[1] The term 'renaissance' was ideated in nineteenth-century Calcutta by Rammohan Roy, who noted that the contemporary developments in Bengal were comparable to the European Renaissance and Reformation. Bankimchandra Chattopadhyay also repeatedly took up the word 'renaissance' either to refer to a revival of Bengali literature or to denote the

CRITICAL PEDAGOGY AND
SHAKESPEARE

It is imperative to view the formation of this ideology through the tenets of critical pedagogy, connecting the role of Shakespeare in curricula during the long nineteenth century and the dissemination of knowledge through the pedagogic apparatus. Critical pedagogy developed from the applied concepts of critical theory and related traditions to the field of education and the study of culture. Advocates of critical pedagogy view teaching as an inherently political act, rejecting the neutrality of knowledge and insisting that issues of social justice and democracy itself are not distinct from acts of teaching and learning.[2] True to its spirit, the enthusiasm of the young students was a result of the active contribution of pedagogy in heralding a defining moment in the history of modern India. In Richard Shaull's summary of Paolo Freire's view: 'Education either functions as an instrument which is used to facilitate integration of the younger generation into the logic of the present system and bring about conformity or it becomes the practice of freedom, the means by which men and women deal critically and creatively with reality and discover how to participate in the transformation of their world.'[3]

In this case, the 'pedagogical imperative' was a means through which the study of Shakespeare became a vehicle of empowering the youth to be seekers and contribute towards an active regeneration of their society.

A pedagogy focused on critical literacy would reveal 'Shakespeare' as a body of knowledge shaped and constructed by critical and pedagogical apparatuses, rather than a distinct and substantial subject which exists independently of our work as scholars, teachers and students. As Gerald Graff has observed in *Beyond the Culture Wars* (1992), familiar subjects and methodologies of our curricula are themselves products of historical conflicts which have been systematically forgotten.[4] What the teacher can do, in this situation, is to acknowledge his or her implication in the institutional assumptions and conceptual frames which produce our particular constructions of 'knowledge'. This acknowledgement in turn calls

for a questioning of those intellectual boundaries and opens up the possibility for alternative knowledge produced in other cultural sites to contest the social values implicit in the institutionally supported curriculum. Any 'knowledge' (even an aesthetic appreciation of Shakespeare as 'knowledge') which is not self-conscious about its enabling assumptions and conceptual frames can only reproduce itself, can only adduce new data and win new converts to support what it already knows. Such teaching is inherently limited to the passive transmission of known information as 'knowledge' and can only stumble upon new ways of understanding by accident, when the system breaks down, when someone misunderstands and others happen to recognize the misunderstanding as a viable alternative. Much is to be gained, therefore, from a pedagogy which systematically focuses on misunderstanding. The 'indoctrination' model of literary study – similar to what Paolo Freire has called the 'banking' model of education – assumes that students come into the university as blank slates waiting to be stamped with a set of values. In fact, of course, students enter our classrooms as subjects situated within complex networks of sociopolitical power. Students are always already indoc-

---

modern reinterpretation of the Hindu tradition. Perhaps the noted Brahmo intellectual Shibnath Shastri, in his celebrated work *Ramtanu Lahiri O Tatkalin BangaSamaj* (1904), first used the term 'renaissance' in the context of Bengal's transition to modernity. The English translation of the original text written in Bengali appeared in 1907 with the title *Ramtanu Lahiri, Brahman and Reformer: History of the Renaissance in Bengal* (1907).

[2] The goal of critical pedagogy is emancipation from oppression through an awakening of the critical consciousness. When achieved, critical consciousness encourages individuals to effect change in their world through social critique and political action. This is a pedagogy which must be forged with, not for, the oppressed in the incessant struggle to regain their humanity. This pedagogy makes oppression and its causes objects of reflection by the oppressed, and from that will come their necessary engagement in the struggle for their liberation.

[3] Richard Shaull, 'Foreword', in Paolo Freire, *Pedagogy of the Oppressed* (London, 1972), pp. 9–14; pp. 13–14.

[4] See Gerald Graff, *Beyond the Culture Wars: How Teaching the Conflicts Can Revitalize American Education* (New York, 1992).

trinated; they are 'organic intellectuals' – according to Graff, in the Gramscian sense – who already have a stake in the political struggles that shape our society. Literary study presents itself to the progressive intellectual as one of several important sites of ideology production available for political struggle. In the course of this article, we will try to figure how the classrooms became a veritable site of negotiation in the context of early nineteenth-century Bengal, and to what extent Shakespeare studies was a guiding factor.

SCHOOLS, COLLEGES AND THE STUDY OF SHAKESPEARE

In the early nineteenth century, when English education was organized only by European and Anglo-Indian enterprises, Shakespeare's dramas formed a part of the curriculum at David Drummond's Academy at Dhurumtolla, Sherbourne's school at Chitpur, David Hare's school at Gol Dighi (College Square of today), Reverend Duff's institute at Hedua, and Gour Mohun Adhya's Oriental Seminary at Chitpur – all centres of new education in Calcutta.[5] When, afterwards, English education ceased to be an affair mainly of the English-speaking minority and was taken up on a wide national basis, Shakespeare inevitably entered schools in three ways. First, easy prose extracts or songs from the plays were included in the courses of reading; second, students were offered an acquaintance with the dramatist's works through simple prose narratives; and third, passages from the plays were selected for recitation by the boys.

Some of the songs included in the textbooks were Ariel's songs; in the Third and Fourth classes (corresponding to today's seventh- and eighth-standard classes), the students were initiated into the works of Shakespeare through the famous *Tales of Shakespeare* by Charles and Mary Lamb, first published in 1807. The Lambs' *Tales* (as the book is commonly called) used to be universally read in schools and outside, and continued to be part of the curriculum for the eighth standard at a prestigious school for girls in Calcutta till 2012!

Perhaps it was Drummond who first taught Indian schoolboys in Calcutta to recite Shakespeare. He encouraged his boys to display their histrionic abilities before guests at school functions, at which some extracts from Shakespeare would invariably figure. In 1822, Derozio, then a boy of 13, was a student at Drummond's Dhurumtolla Academy. A local newspaper, *The India Gazette*, wrote on 31 December 1822: 'The English recitations from different authors were extremely meritorious and reflect great credit upon scholars and teachers. A boy named Derozio gave a good conception of Shylock.'[6] It is also interesting to note that, two years later, on another occasion at this school, on 20 January 1824, Derozio recited a poem of his own which included the following lines:

> No Mighty KEMBLE here stalks o'er the stage –
> No mighty SIDDONS all your feelings to engage,
> But a small band of young aspiring boys
> In faintest miniature the hour employs.[7]

---

[5] The first schools to impart English education among natives in Bengal were under missionary guidance, dating back to 1747 (a detailed account follows in a later section). A progressive increase in student numbers gradually led to the establishment of the Calcutta School Book Society in 1789, which emerged in itself as a successful and profitable enterprise. Soon, there were individuals trying to make a fortune in the business of education, and by the turn of the century there were private institutions set up in Calcutta by Archer, Fresco, Pidrus, Sherbourne, Farell, Drummond, Halifax, Draper and others. There were also three women's schools organized by Mrs Pete, Reverend Lawson and Mrs Darrell. The profitability of these undertakings can be gauged from an advertisement by a gentleman named George Furly, for the monthly fees of his school: first standard, Rs 30, second standard Rs 40, and third standard Rs 64. Other than Drummond's Dhurumtolla Academy and Sherbourne's School, not much is known about the curriculum taught at the other schools, which were perhaps confined to introduction to basic alphabet and numericals.

[6] 'A sketch of the origin, rise, and progress of the Hindoo College', reprinted in *The Calcutta Christian Observer* (June–Dec. 1832), in *Derozio Remembered: Birth Bicentenary Celebration Commemoration Volume*, ed. Sakti Sadhan Mukhopadhyay (Calcutta, 2008), vol. I, p. 44.

[7] Abirlal Mukhopadhyay, Amar Dutta, Adhir Kumar and Sakti Sadhan Mukhopadhyay, eds., *Song of the Stormy Petrel: Complete Works of Henry Louis Vivian Derozio* (Calcutta, 2001), p. 269.

Thus, it appears that as early as 1824, schoolboys were aware of John Philip Kemble and Sarah Siddons. A few years later, Derozio wrote a couple of sonnets on Shakespearian subjects (on *Romeo and Juliet* and on Yorick's Skull) and read the plays with his students at Hindu College, becoming a teacher there in 1826. On 12 January 1828, the trial scene from *The Merchant of Venice* was enacted by Hindu College boys. A contemporary comment on the performance was 'Surely then this may be called a remarkable epoch in the history of India, seeing as we do, the native youth of Bengal cultivating the dramatic literature of the west, and even encountering the difficulties of theatrical presentations.'[8] There is a reference to the talents of a boy at Drummond's Academy: 'I have now to remark the singular phenomenon of a Hindu lad, Kissen Chunder Dutt ... only fourteen years of age ... his correct pronunciation and action in the character of Shylock ... drew forth the most enthusiastic admiration of the whole audience.'[9] Krishna Chandra Lahiri mentions in his essay 'Shakespeare in the Calcutta University' that:

From Drummond's School the practice spread to other institutions. There could hardly pass any ceremonial occasion at which something from Shakespeare would not be included; among the favourite passages were: Portia's homage to Mercy; Mark Antony's oration at Caesar's funeral; Shylock's outburst against persecuting Christians; and Hamlet's soliloquy on death. At these functions, the special prize awarded to the best oration would invariably be a de-luxe volume of the complete works of Shakespeare, bound in morocco-leather.[10]

As in European schools, so in colleges run by Europeans, Shakespeare found an easy access. Shakespeare was formally adopted in Bengal's educational curriculum with the establishment of Hindu College, on 20 January 1817, as a centre of higher education in Western literature and science. Krishna Mohan Banerjee, Rasik Krishna Mallik, Ram Gopal Ghosh, Tara Chand Chakravarti, Shiv Chandra Dey, Peary Chand Mitra and Ramtanu Lahiri were among the earliest batch of students who passed out from Hindu College. As Shibnath Shastri says, 'From this group Kalidasa retired and

Shakespeare was enthroned in his place.'[11] In their day Madhusudan Dutt and Rajnarayan Basu had to study in the first form (1843) as many as four plays of Shakespeare: *Macbeth*, *King Lear*, *Othello* and *Hamlet*. It may be observed from the publications in contemporary newspapers that the annual prize-giving ceremonies of Hindu College from 1825 to 1838 regularly featured recitations from Shakespeare's plays. Here is one such report from a Bengali newspaper: 'In the Prize Distribution function of the Hindu College some young students recited from memory, with excellent pronunciation, several parts from the poems of an English poet named Shakespeare.'[12] At one such function, Madhusudan Dutt appeared in the role of the Duke of Gloucester in a scene from *Henry VI, Part I*.[13]

Calcutta University not only played a key role in promoting Shakespeare studies in Bengal, but extended its influence to the far reaches of the subcontinent. Throughout the wide administrative purview of the university across diverse linguistic and cultural backgrounds, Shakespeare was disseminated by teachers, and consequently this dispersal must have impacted and influenced the literatures of those regions as well. Though Calcutta University was exclusively an affiliating and examining body during the early years of its inception from 1857, it becomes quite evident that, by the middle of the nineteenth century, Shakespeare studies had gathered a momentum and was institutionalized in the academic curriculum of an Indian university long before Shakespeare was actually institutionalized in a British university. English literature was instituted formally in London and

---

8   *The Calcutta Gazette*, 7 January 1828.
9   Reena Ghosh, *Shakespeare Anubad Ebong Anubad Samasya* (Calcutta, 1975).
10 Krishna Chandra Lahiri, 'Shakespeare in the Calcutta University', in *Calcutta Essays on Shakespeare*, ed. Amalendu Bose (Calcutta, 1966), pp. 173–91; p. 174: https://archive.org/stream/in.ernet.dli.2015.460338/2015.460338.Calcutta-Essays_djvu.txt).
11 Shibnath Shastri, *Ramtanu Lahiri O Tatkalin BangaSamaj* [1904] (Calcutta, 2009), p. 154.
12 *Samachar Darpan*, 20 February 1830.
13 Lahiri, 'Shakespeare', p. 175.

Oxford as a discipline only after the Indian Civil Service began to include a 1,500-mark paper on it in 1855, as it was assumed that knowledge of English literature was essential for those who would be administering British interests.[14]

From this brief discussion of the early nineteenth-century engagement with Shakespeare at the school, college and university levels, it is clear that a section of Bengali youth had already taken an interest in the study of Shakespeare quite independent of any official colonial enterprise.[15] What started off as an educational practice for children of the company's writers, soon spread and received admiration from a section of Bengali youth. The study of Shakespeare, an apparently uncomplicated, simple and straightforward academic pursuit, gradually acquired vital and serious political dimensions, which not only affected the intellectual environment, but also went further to pose as a defining characteristic in the socio-political and cultural history of nineteenth-century Bengal.

However, the initiation of Shakespeare in Hindu College as part of the curriculum was born out of a complex intellectual scenario in the early nineteenth century that featured, on the one hand, the influence of Western ideas of rationalism and humanism from Francis Bacon and Thomas Paine, and, on the other, a renewal of the ancient Hindu thought by the British Orientalists. The matter was further complicated by the Christian missionary enterprise, which aimed at another dimension of educational and intellectual activity based on proselytization. Therefore, I will argue that the distinctive position accorded to Shakespeare may be credited neither to the colonizers nor to the colonized, but was the product of relentless effort by a section of the intelligentsia, with members from both European and Indian communities, who favoured humanistic education.

The humanism that arrived in Bengal in the nineteenth century came to be filtered through the ideas of the Renaissance and the Reformation as well as the Enlightenment. This version of humanism divested from any religious association was also reflected in the Shakespeare teaching in Hindu College, based on the philosophical models of Matthew Arnold. The teachers of Hindu College were liberal humanists who believed in the universality of literature and considered it to be an important means for educating the sensibility of the young.

ORIENTAL AND WESTERN ENQUIRY

The body of scholarship produced by the Orientalists, such as Charles Wilkins, Nathaniel Brassey Halhed and William Jones, has been interpreted in a fresh insight by Rosinka Chaudhuri, who has pointed out that 'While acknowledging, always, the complicity of colonial rule in the creation of knowledge about the colonies, it is important to see the particularities of Orientalist studies (its idiom, its ideology, its rhetoric) *also* as regenerative material.'[16] It is imperative to point out here that a system of British enquiry into Indian antiquity also spearheaded a parallel development, a keen interest in the study of Western learning by the Indians, elaborately theorized by several scholars, including Ketaki Kushari Dyson who attempts to examine this cultural encounter and its impact on the Indian intelligentsia:

There was the European discovery of India's cultural heritage, with the emergence of Oriental scholarship, the reconstruction of the history of ancient India, the discovery of the Indo-European family of languages, etc., leading to the growth of modern disciplines such as comparative philology, comparative mythology, and comparative religious studies; starting with the response of the Bengali intelligentsia to Western education, there was the Indian discovery of Western learning and

---

[14] Reports from Commissioners: Vol. XV Appendix No. 2 – 'Prospects on Courses of Study adapted for the India Civil Service and for the Royal Military Academy at Woolwich, 1958', p. 55.

[15] For more on adaptation of Shakespeare's plays as a basis of critical exploration of identity formation in India, see Sharmishtha Panja and Babli Moitra Saraf, eds., *Performing Shakespeare in India: Exploring Indianness, Literatures and Cultures* (New Delhi, 2016).

[16] Rosinka Chaudhuri, *Gentlemen Poets of Colonial Bengal: Emergent Nationalism and the Orientalist Project* (Calcutta, 2002), p. 8.

thought; finally as a result of these two events working together, there was an Indian cultural revival, beginning in Bengal, and in early stages specifically referred to by historians as the Bengal Renaissance.[17]

During the nineteenth century, there was also a growing interest in the ideas of Bentham, Malthus, Ricardo and Mill, referred to as Utilitarianism. James Mill, follower of Jeremy Bentham, disagreed with the Orientalists. Along with his son John Stuart Mill, James Mill discouraged any form of Oriental enquiry and articulated in favour of the introduction of English education among the natives in India. According to the Utilitarians, a knowledge of the English language would facilitate the study of modern science and serve as an instrument of 'useful' education. Meanwhile, Rammohan Roy approached Lord Amherst in his famous letter of 1823 asking for the discontinuation of Sanskrit and introduction of the sciences.[18] The government did not pay heed to Roy and established the Sanskrit college in 1824, but the dispatch of 18 February 1824 from the headquarters of the East India Company in London indicates support for the Utilitarians: 'The great end should not have been to teach Hindu learning but useful learning.'[19] By 1828, Bentinck, a staunch supporter of the Utilitarians, was appointed as Governor General. In 1833, Horace Hayman Wilson, a prominent Orientalist advocate, went back to England, and in the same year the Charter of 1833 brought T. B. Macaulay as Law Member on the council of the Governor General. So, the tide had turned in favour of an education that was based more on an aspect of usefulness, irrespective of diverging opinions within the government. English education came to be viewed by the natives as a prospective language of instruction not only to secure jobs, but also as a medium through which the youth could access the 'new learning' of the West. They were also exposed, outside of the curriculum, to the influential writings of Tom Paine, who ignited the young minds with the ideas of equality and liberty, and also awakened a spirit of individuality, urging men not to be judged by their religion or race. Paine's role in the American revolution became a model for Bengali youth, as they sought to replicate a similar model that

led to a nationalistic consciousness. Therefore, 'new learning' became synonymous with the new ideas of liberty and equality, of nation and state. It was time to change from religious learning in favour of a secular and scientific knowledge based on reason. The pioneering role of Hindu College in imparting a secular education became the first instance of education completely divested from any religious affiliation that led to an awareness of a changing modern world. This article will show in subsequent sections how the study of Shakespeare became a decisive factor in determining a secular curriculum in Bengal.

THE MISSIONARY ENTERPRISE

Gauri Viswanathan has elaborately theorized on the relation between missionary and English literary education in India. She has argued that the entry of the missionaries into India led to a new role for English literary study, where the literary text was viewed as a form of secular knowledge. She has also argued that the dissociation of English literature from religion is a form of reactionary response by a cautious British administration, which was keen on avoiding any charge of interfering in native religions. Viswanathan argues that:

---

[17] Ketaki Kushari Dyson, *A Various Universe: A Study of the Journals and Memoirs of British Men and Women in the Indian Subcontinent 1765–1856* (New Delhi, 1978), p. 2.

[18] In a letter addressed to Lord Amherst, the Governor General of Bengal, on 11 December 1823, Rammohan writes: 'The Sangscrit [sic] system of education would be the best calculated to keep this country in darkness, if such had been the policy of the British Legislature. But as the improvement of the native population is the object of the Government, it will consequently promote a more liberal and enlightened system of instruction, embracing mathematics, natural philosophy, chemistry and anatomy, with other useful sciences which may be accomplished with the sum proposed by employing a few gentleman of talents and learning educated in Europe, and providing a college furnished with the necessary books, instruments and other apparatus': Henry Sharp, ed., *Selections from Educational Records, Part I (1781–1839)* [Calcutta, 1920] (reprint Delhi, 1965), pp. 98–101.

[19] A. N. Basu, 'Introduction', in *Indian Education in Parliamentary Papers* (Bombay, 1952), p. xi.

Literature's relation to Christianity undoubtedly stemmed from an awareness of the operational value of English literature's double stance in reinforcing the validity of the knowledge to be imparted and, by extension, of the authority of those imparting it. Further, literature's doubleness enabled the validation of Christian belief by the disciplinary techniques of European learning while at the same time deflecting attention from its self-referential, self-confirming aspects. Its power rested on the idea that European disciplines, being products of human reason, were independent of systems of belief based on pure faith.[20]

Viswanathan points out that initially, English literature was invested with a dual role of providing English literary education as well as disseminating Christian values. She argues that Alexander Duff had dismissed any comparison of the study of Indian literature with the study of Western literature on the grounds that classical literature was read in Europe as literary production and not as divine authority. This then brings us to a wider analysis of viewing literature as a subsidiary of religion, on the one hand, and as completely disavowed of religious significance, on the other. Therefore, it entails an endorsement of a classical as well as secular approach to literary studies, establishing language, rather than belief and faith, as a source of culture and value. The study of English literature then achieves equivalence with classical studies, as a mode of secular knowledge production. She mentions: 'The discriminations between English and Indian literature in their relation to Christianity and Hinduism respectively yielded a pure and almost severe understanding of English literature as intellectual and linguistic production. As a parallel process to the survival of English studies, secularization reintroduced a classical emphasis in English studies.'[21]

While Viswanathan's views endorse a classical-humanist approach to English studies, as a consequence of British appropriation by the education system in India, she has magnified only one side of the picture and has completely obliterated the other. Alexander Duff's position has been mentioned as a point of reference to show that Indian systems of knowledge have been relegated to the background on account of their religious affiliation, but there is complete silence on the role of Hindu College in ushering in a secular and humanistic education. Duff's institute and Hindu College offered two opposing poles of colonial pedagogy in Bengal in the early nineteenth century. As Rosinka Chaudhuri has shown in her discussion of Viswanathan, it is important to view the role of Hindu College as a counterpoint to Duff, and as a significant contributor to the production of a body of knowledge based on reason – and not race or religion – that went on to shape the character of Indian modernity. Additionally, the seminal role of David Hare in the foundation and functioning of Hindu College is strategically eliminated by Viswanathan.[22] I will argue that it was due to the sustained effort of David Hare and Raja Ram Mohan Roy that a curriculum based on rational enquiry in European science and English literary studies was instituted in Hindu College. Shakespeare was introduced as a part of English literary studies as a vehicle to articulate the same standards of secular and humanistic enquiry that the college came to define.

THE POSITION OF HINDU COLLEGE

Rammohan Roy (1772–1833) and David Hare (1775–1842), among others to a greater or lesser degree, fostered ideas of freethinking and a fresh outlook through the teaching of literature, and remained unequivocal in their support of rationality, always opposing the bigotry of both Hindus and Christians in the Calcutta public sphere. Rammohan Roy was a firm believer in the virtues of Western education. Being proficient in the richness of Sanskrit literature and himself an eminent scholar of Hindu philosophy, he found ancient learning inadequate to the cause of awakening the masses from the grip of superstition and ignorance. His profound knowledge of both Indian and Western intellectual traditions

---

[20] Gauri Viswanathan, *Masks of Conquest: Literary Study and British Rule in India* (New York, 2014), pp. 108–9.

[21] Viswanathan, *Masks*, p. 117.

[22] This idea was first articulated by Chaudhuri in *Gentlemen Poets*.

urged him to create an alternative educational apparatus modelled on the West and based on reason and freethinking. Hailed by Max Muller as 'a truly great man ... [as] one of the greatest benefactors of mankind',[23] Roy worked relentlessly in the face of severe criticism and stern condemnation from a section of his own countrymen, headed by Radhakanta Deb, who favoured modern education within the ambit of Dharma Shastras and not through Western education.[24] Determined in his purpose and unflinching in his commitment to expose his countrymen to the liberal ideas of the West, Roy collaborated with men of similar intellectual temperament, irrespective of race and religion. Roy was 'admirably suited, not only to lead the advanced sections of Indians but also to act as the intermediary between them and those Europeans who were solicitors [sic] of the wellbeing of Indians'.[25]

When Hindu College officially came into existence in 1817, and English literary studies was instituted as a part of the curriculum, it was not just for the first time in the history of the British empire, but also long before any formal department for similar enquiry was instituted in Britain.

Established as a rival to English education imparted in the institutions managed by the missionaries in Calcutta which attempted to promote the religion and culture of the imperial authority, Hindu College aimed at keeping its education in English literature and European science free from the influence of all religions, including Hinduism, emphasizing promotion of a secular and humanistic outlook on life.

Michael Madhusudan Dutt's expulsion from Hindu College has been discussed by postcolonial critics such as Gauri Viswanathan, who theorized elaborately about this possible space of collusion between the imperial agenda and the missionaries' will to Christianize. Contrary to this belief, I would like to argue that Christian proselytization was not the singular attribute of colonial educational policy, and that academic engagements were also strategized as per the demands of the intelligentsia, who clearly laid out a distinction between humanistic and other forms of religious study. In disagreement

with Viswanathan's single-faceted and highly angular view of the situation, I would like to point out that recent critical studies by Rosinka Chaudhuri in *Gentlemen Poets of Colonial Bengal* have put forward a more rational and precise version of the historiography, which views the seminal role of Hindu College as an epicentre of intellectual activity offering an altered set of dynamics instead. The following excerpt, cited by her from Jogindranath Basu, biographer of Madhusudan Dutt, disproves Viswanathan and clearly establishes that Hindu College had a distinctive position strategized by Hare (and also Rammohan Roy), unrelated to Christianity (or any religion for that matter):

It is true that the efforts of the Christian missionaries such as Alexander Duff saw the conversion of one or two students in their colleges; but there was absolutely no possibility of their influence spreading in the Hindu College ... both David Hare and D. L. Richardson were firm unbelievers in the Christian religion ... thinking that on the top of this [the controversy over the anglicized behaviour of Derozio's students] if any of the college students embraced Christianity, it would be especially harmful for Hindu College, as the path of English education in this country would be obstructed, the great soul Hare always kept ... a sharp eye on his students. Although Richardson did not have an eye as Hare, nevertheless he never hesitated to declare to his students his inner convictions concerning his lack of confidence in the Christian religion.[26]

The intellectuals who held the reins of power in Hindu College understood that any kind of religious affiliation would become an impediment towards fulfilling their larger objective of providing a secular and humanistic education to the students of the institution. The following comment by

---

[23] P. Rajeswar Rao, *The Great Indian Patriots*, vol. 2 (New Delhi, 1991), p. 10.

[24] *Journal of the Royal Asiatic Society of Great Britain and Ireland* 17.6 (1829).

[25] M. K. Haldar, *Renaissance and Reaction in Nineteenth Century Bengal* (Calcutta, 1977), pp. 10–12.

[26] Jogindranath Basu, quoted in Chaudhuri, *Gentlemen Poets*, p. 96.

Kishorilal Mitra further illustrates the temperament of the students during these years:

The youthful band of reformers who had been educated at the Hindu College, like the top of the Kanchenjunga [the highest peak in the Himalayas], were the first to catch and reflect the dawn ... When had an opposition to popular prejudices been dissociated with difficulty and trouble? ... To excommunication and its concomitant evils, our friends were subjected ... Conformity to the idolatrous practices and customs evinces a weak desertion of principle. Non-conformity to them on the other hand is a moral obligation which we owe to our conscience.[27]

SHAKESPEARE IN CURRICULA

Established as a rival to English education imparted in the institutions managed by the missionaries of Calcutta, whose evangelical interests were held in preference over literary scholarship, Hindu College kept its education in European science and English literature free from any kind of religious influence, whether Hindu or Christian. A brief analysis of the English curriculum of Hindu College shows that Shakespeare was placed alongside Bacon, Newton, Johnson, Addison and Milton. An account of the syllabus at Hindu college is as follows: 'The books prescribed for the senior class in 1828 showed a strong bias towards English history and literature ... The reading list included Goldsmith's *History of Greece, Rome and England*, Russel's *Modern Europe*, Robertson's *Charles the Fifth*, Gay's *Fables*, Pope's [translation of the *Iliad and Odyssey* of] Homer, Dryden's *Vergil*, Milton's *Paradise Lost* and one of Shakespeare's tragedies.'[28]

The missionary curriculum, on the other hand, prescribed the Bible; a poetical reader; Cowper's poems; Milton's *Paradise Lost*; Pollock's *Courses of Time*; selections from Southey, Montgomery, Campbell and Wordsworth; Macaulay's *Lays of Ancient Rome*; Bacon's *Moral and Civil Essays*; and Hallam's *Literary History of the Fifteenth, Sixteenth and Seventeenth Centuries* – to mention a few.[29]

While literary texts are preponderant in this list as well, the absence of Shakespeare is conspicuous in the missionary curriculum as its predominant aim was to preach Christianity through literature, and Shakespeare was perceived as a serious threat to its crucial evangelical interests. However, the intellectual and political scenario in Bengal was complicated by the fact that the East India Company strictly followed a policy of religious neutrality in anticipation of any hostility among the natives. As Jyotsna Singh mentions in *Colonial Narratives/ Cultural Discourse*, 'While the missionaries questioned whether it [the literary text] could replace the Bible, they could not do much to alter the governments' restrictions on an explicitly religious education.'[30] The missionaries had to settle in Serampore and had restricted access to Calcutta in the early years of the nineteenth century. It was only when the British were more secure in their territorial administrative capacities after 1835 that the missionaries were granted access to Calcutta. The missionary enterprise was funded by the Danish Baptist Mission, which aimed at proselytizing and spreading a Protestant version of the gospel produced in Bengali under the initiative of William Carrey in 1793 and 1801. It was only later that, in Calcutta, the General Assembly's institution, which was under the auspices of the General Assembly of the Church of Scotland and established by Alexander Duff on 13 July 1830, carefully crafted a quintessentially religious curriculum, offering a counterpoint to Hindu College, which offered a secular curriculum based on a Western

---

[27] Kishorilal Mitra, quoted in M. K. Haldar, *Renaissance*, p. 56.

[28] A chapter from John Berwick's Ph.D. thesis titled 'From Vidyalaya to Presidency College' submitted at the University of Sydney (Australia) traces the genesis and evolution of the Presidency College prior to 1922, and has been reproduced in *Nostalgia: An Illustrated History of Hindu-Presidency College (1817–1992)*, ed. Koustubh Panda (Calcutta, 1993), pp. 23–36; p. 23.

[29] Mavra Farooq, 'The aims and objectives of missionary education in the colonial era in India': http://pu.edu.pk/images/journal/studies/PDF-FILES/Artical-7_v15_no1.pdf.

[30] Jyotsna Singh, 'Shakespeare and the "civilizing Mission"', in *Colonial Narratives/Cultural Dialogues: 'Discoveries' of India in the Language of Colonialism* (London, 1996), p. 108.

rationalistic enquiry and strictly excluded any religious influence.

In addition, in the secular curriculum, Shakespeare's texts were placed alongside Pope's translated edition of Homer's *Iliad* and *Odyssey*, which were essentially conforming to a pagan ideology and were anti-Catholic in temperament. Besides, Shakespeare's works at all times emphasized the relation of 'man' with his 'Maker', with 'Nature' and with 'himself' more than the affirmation of an omniscient divinity presiding over human conditions. The works of Shakespeare abound in human frailties, follies and flaws, exploring human weaknesses which account for the imminent destinies of his protagonists. Critical scholarship since 1985 has debated, and produced a body of literature trying to identify, the true nature of Shakespeare's religious beliefs. While some critics have tried to validate a Catholic element in Shakespeare, others, including Harold Bloom, find the whole question of Shakespeare's religious commitments laughably irrelevant. Bloom argues that 'Shakespeare seems to be too wise to believe anything' political or religious. He goes on to add, 'I am baffled when critics argue as to whether Shakespeare was a Protestant or Catholic, since the plays are neither.'[31] Stephen Greenblatt also attempted to explore a complex religious question in *Hamlet in Purgatory* (2002), where he sought to demystify Catholic elements in Shakespeare.[32] The general consensus among academic scholarship, therefore, is focused on a secular approach to the works of Shakespeare. Elucidating the same idea in *Infirm Glory: Renaissance Image of Man*, Sukanta Chaudhuri mentions: 'Man is placed at the centre of an inexhaustible play of forces. He may command this by an effort and discipline that is basically moral in nature, though intellectual in its sphere of operation.'[33] Therefore, Shakespeare's works came to highlight the high Renaissance ideology of 'Man' as the centre of the universe, displacing a medieval concept of 'God' as the epicentre.

From the accounts published in contemporary newspapers depicting annual prize-giving ceremonies at Hindu College from 1825 to 1838, there is regular reference to the participation of students in recitation contests in which they primarily chose excerpts from Shakespeare's plays. In one such report, on the recommendation of the General Committee of Public Instruction, the government instituted forty-two senior English scholarships, which were attached to Hindu College and some other colleges in Bengal. The reports go on to mention that a majority of these scholarships were won by the students at Hindu College. Interestingly, according to the records, the missionary institutions did not compete for these scholarships. Giving more weight to Shakespeare than any other individual writer in the question paper for the scholarship examination came to be a disadvantage for the students at the missionary institutions, which strictly followed an exclusionist policy for Shakespeare.

The missionary institutions opted out because of their dislike of teaching Shakespeare and other dramatists. Hema Dahiya, in her recent treatise on Shakespeare teachers in Bengal in the early nineteenth century, has pointed out: 'Despite the great disadvantage to the students of Missionary Institutions in the race for scholarships, Shakespeare remained excluded in their curriculum of English studies. Decidedly, their religious bias determined their choice of writers.'[34] Interestingly, her treatise points to the gap in literary scholarship which has not viewed the cause and effects of Shakespeare's absence from the missionary curriculum. The missionaries not only eliminated Shakespeare from their curriculum, but also held the study of Shakespeare in deepest contempt. Reverend Lal Behari Dey reminiscences about one such missionary teacher, John Macdonald, in his memoirs:

I still remember his asking me once what book I had been reading. I told him a play of Shakespeare.

---

[31] www.crisismagazine.com/2002/how-catholic-was-shakespeare.

[32] See Stephen Greenblatt, *Hamlet in Purgatory* (Princeton, NJ, 2002).

[33] Sukanta Chaudhuri, *Infirm Glory: Renaissance Image of Man* (New Delhi, 2006), p. 82.

[34] Hema Dahiya, 'The Hindu College (1817–1912)', in *Shakespeare Studies in Colonial Bengal: The Early Phase* (London, 2013), pp. 63–90; p. 80.

'Shakespeare!' he repeated. He then told me that he, when a young man, had a copy of Shakespeare's works in his library, and that instead of burning it he foolishly exchanged it in shops for another book – foolishly, because another might have bought the book and injured his soul.[35]

Such an attitude is different from that observed in the words of Revd William Keane, who, as a faithful advocate of missionary pursuits, provides the following description of the proselytizing powers of English literature in a testimony before officials:

Shakespeare, though by no means a good standard, is full of religion; it is full of the common sense principles which none but Christian men can recognize. Sound Protestant Bible principles, though not actually told in words, are set out to advantage, and the opposite often condemned. So with Goldsmith ... and many other books which are taught in the schools ... [which] have undoubtedly sometimes a favourable effect in actually bringing them to us missionaries.[36]

While Revd Keane is of the opinion that Shakespeare's works are replete in Christian religious values, on other occasions there were serious disagreements among missionaries as to whether Shakespeare's language depicted a pagan rather than a Protestant morality. There is evidence confirming the missionary 'uncertainty' in the *Bengal Magazine* in 1876, in a lively exchange between a devout Indian Christian and the editor of the newspaper, the former establishing a moral distinction between 'Shakespearians' and 'Christians', arguing: 'Shakespeare is of the earth ... but the Bible is of the heaven heavenly. The one says – Be ye like the heroes of the world who never pocketed an insult and never forgave an enemy! The other says – Be like your Father in heaven who causeth His sun to rise both on the just and the unjust.'[37]

The government curriculum, on the other hand, placed its emphasis on the classical-humanist tradition. This spirit was reflected in the construction of the syllabi of the College, where, in contrast to missionary institutions, D. L. Richardson taught the Hindu College boys *Hamlet*, *Othello*, *Macbeth*, *King Lear* and two parts of *Henry IV*. Richard

Helgerson, who has reviewed the London literary scene between 1570 and 1580 in his book *The Elizabethan Prodigals*, makes a comparison between humanistic and romantic literature: 'I see humanism and romance as opposed members of a single consciousness, as the superego and id of Elizabethan literature, competitors in a struggle to control and define the self. Humanism represented paternal expectation and romance, rebellious desire.'[38] The traditional 'humanistic' attributes associated with literature are paternalistic (and masculine), related to the shaping of character, development of an aesthetic sense or the principles of ethical thinking, etc., while the romantic was viewed as effeminate. Postcolonial critics Ania Loomba and Jyotsna Singh have treated this humanistic function associated with English literature as an instrument of imperialist strategy, whereby Shakespeare's works came to be identified by the attributes of 'humanism', 'morality' and 'wisdom', and viewed as essential tools of the processes of imperial control. However, the definition of humanism changed with the times. In the age of Enlightenment, it was characterized by such keywords as 'autonomy', 'reason' and 'progress', and it may usually be distinguished from Renaissance humanism because of its more secular nature. While Renaissance humanism had an amount of religious affiliation (which influenced the Protestant Reformation), Enlightenment humanism marked a radical departure from religion. It reduced religion to those essentials which could only be rationally defended, i.e. certain basic moral principles and a few universally held beliefs about God. Taken to one logical extreme, the Enlightenment even resulted in atheism. The study of the classics and Shakespeare was perceived to have amounted to outrageous social behaviour by young students, who were perhaps imbued with the altered

---

35 Revd Lal Behari Day, *Recollections of Alexander Duff, D.D., L.L.D., and of the Mission College which He Founded* (London, 1879), p. 195.

36 Quoted in Viswanathan, *Masks*, p. 80.

37 Anonymous, *Bengal Magazine* (1876), p. 232.

38 Richard Helgerson, *The Elizabethan Prodigals* (Berkeley, 1976), p. 41.

form of humanism as a spirit of liberation not only from traditions of religion, but also as a vehicle to articulate their desire to bring about a cataclysmic change in society. The study of Shakespeare assumed even greater significance by becoming an inseparable aspect of an emergent humanism observed in the literary, cultural and social sphere of nineteenth-century Bengal.

It is also imperative at this point to distinguish the humanism which emerged in Bengal from a study of Western classics in the early nineteenth century, which was not identical to what was formed in Europe in the late sixteenth century or its later manifestations, and which had arrived in Bengal on the back of conquest and commerce. Bengali intellectuals of the early 1800s were experiencing a state of flux, not only due to the dynamics of the interaction between British and Bengali cultures, but also because they were made aware of a newly discovered historical dimension. While the Orientalists evoked the glory of an Indian golden age, the Serampore missionaries transmitted a Protestant concept of the European medieval period as a dark age. The psychological uncertainty of the Bengali intelligentsia was heightened by the social consequences of this newly formed relationship with the European. The humanism that emerged as a result of this 'new learning' in Bengal was a conflicted and contradictory discourse that was beginning to show the marks of a 'battle for cultural parity' and gradually urged the Bengali intellectuals to renew and rejuvenate their own literature and culture. So, the cultural and political coordinates from which Shakespeare was resisted or appropriated in the curriculum of nineteenth-century Bengal show that the situation clearly evolved as a form of response to justify the claims of differing ideological positions operational in the intellectual environment of early nineteenth-century Calcutta.

In summary, this article has tried to interrogate how the study of Shakespeare obtained a distinctive position in the curriculum, whereby the 'presence' and also 'absence' of Shakespeare in curricula has opened up a fresh insight into the historiography of English education in nineteenth-century Bengal. It has tried to explore the intellectual and historical dimensions related to the 'absence' of Shakespeare from the missionary curriculum, which has remained uncharted by scholarship. It has been an integral part of this study to locate the fundamental causes which led to the establishment of Shakespeare studies in Bengal as a form of humanistic and secular enquiry, and it has attempted a comparative study of the government and missionary curricula. In this, the position of Hindu College shows that the Bengali Hindus themselves desired an education in English literature, and the roles of David Hare, Rammohan Roy and H. H. Wilson were to augment a growing trend among the Indians. What began as the study of a desirable language to secure profits or jobs soon began to witness an increasing popularity among a section of Bengalis who then viewed English language as the chosen medium through which they could access the scientific and intellectual knowledge of the West. This spirit of enquiry also applied to the interest in the study of Shakespeare, which arrived in India with all its colonial baggage but soon struck a chord with the youth, who found a liberating and empowering spirit in his works, and this study subsequently went on to alter the dynamics of the intellectual, political and social fabric of nineteenth-century Bengal.

FORGING A REPUBLIC OF LETTERS: SHAKESPEARE, POLITICS AND A NEW UNIVERSITY IN EARLY TWENTIETH-CENTURY PORTUGAL

RUI CARVALHO HOMEM[1]

This article addresses the role played by Shakespeare in a short-lived but influential educational endeavour 100 years ago. In 1919, a new school of humanities – or, literally, 'faculty of letters' – was set up in the recently founded University of Porto (1911–), aiming to respond to the formative aspirations of the republican regime created in 1910 through the revolution that had put an end to Portugal's constitutional monarchy. Education was ideologically central to the Republic's secularizing project of creating a free and self-aware citizenry, and these ideals were explicitly invoked in pleas for the reshaping of Portuguese higher education voiced in Parliament, the press and other public fora.[2]

Creating a school of humanities in Porto became a matter of civic and republican pride, but the Faculty of Letters was to operate for little more than a decade: a decision to close it was made (ostensibly for economic reasons) in 1928, two years after the coup that ended what is now known as Portugal's 'First Republic' and laid the grounds for the 'Estado Novo', the right-wing dictatorship that was to prevail for nearly half a century. This 'first Faculty of Letters' was effectively closed in 1931, after completing the training of its final cohort of students. Nonetheless, in a mere twelve years it had managed, despite severe financial constraints, to create a decent up-to-date library and generate intellectual capital of some consequence, especially through a series of publications.

English studies, with Shakespeare firmly at its centre, was one of the disciplines on offer, within the broader framework of 'Germanic Philology', and its presence in the curriculum obtained both academic and public attention through the activity of Luís Cardim (1879–1958) – philologist, Shakespeare scholar and translator.

The pages below will move towards a discussion of Cardim's trajectory, landmarked as it was by Shakespearian contributions. This will be preceded, however, by an overview of the contexts and texts – including the perplexed narratives of Anglo-Portuguese relations – that allow for Shakespeare to become a gauge of the conditions that shaped an intriguing chapter in cultural and educational history.

THE REPUBLIC AND THE UNIVERSITIES: A 'PROGRESSIVE' ASPIRATION

After 1910, the government's decisions to create new universities provoked great controversy, both for their general political underpinnings and the local and institutional rivalries that they set off. These concerned especially the 'monopoly' until then enjoyed by Coimbra as the only university in the country (Lisbon and Porto had only a few schools or institutes of higher education, awarding degrees that were

[1] Research for this article was supported by Fundação para a Ciência e a Tecnologia (Portugal) through CETAPS (Ref. UIDP/04097/2020).
[2] See Jorge Fernandes Alves, *A Universidade na República, a República na Universidade: a UP e a I República (1910–1926)* (Porto, 2012), esp. pp. 15–16, 79–80.

officially of a lower order). Before and after the revolution, Coimbra was often denounced, by proponents of a 'scientistic' and 'positive' approach to knowledge, as a 'reactionary' academic body, 'Tridentine' in its abidance by the values, protocols and ideological control of the Catholic Church.[3] This was somehow epitomized in the fact that the teaching of humanities in Coimbra had been embedded in a Faculty of Theology, which was converted into a faculty of letters only in 1911 as part of the republican drive to secularize and modernize higher education.[4]

Porto, which still today takes civic pride in heading the country's northern industrial and commercial powerhouse, had, since the middle of the nineteenth century, been the seat of medical and technical/engineering schools. These offered training in applied skills to a new professional elite that proved more easily open to notions of change, and to knowledge imported from industrialized countries.[5] The ideological affinities of such training were apparent in the combined scientific and revolutionary mindset that prevailed in local academia in the early years of the century — and this against a broader civic context that included a sizeable presence of republicans and freemasons among the city's intelligentsia.[6]

The circumstances that framed the 1919 decision to create a faculty of letters in Porto were likewise ideologically marked, as made evident by records of heated parliamentary discussions that included academics who were also prominent politicians, one of whom (Leonardo Coimbra) was to become the Dean of the new school.[7] As well as pitting the proponents of a 'republican' education against perceived traditionalists, the decision was further complicated by its costs, at a moment in the country's political history that was not only turbulent and violent, but also persistently haunted by the prospect of bankruptcy, made worse by the consequences of Portugal's participation in World War I. In such a context, it is indicative of the seriousness with which education was viewed by the republican authorities that parliamentary pleas for adequate funding for the new Faculty of Letters — with a well-supplied library[8] — were at least partially accepted.

The controversies that enveloped that decision in 1919 were also of a more strictly academic, and professional, nature. Partly reflecting the perceived need to counter a reactionary staff and further the republican agenda, positions at the new Faculty were largely filled by appointment, rather than 'concurso' (a public application and selection process). This involved co-opting independent scholars or secondary school teachers who had already distinguished themselves as public lecturers, through a track record of publications, and by periods of study or research abroad — as was indeed the case with Luís Cardim.[9] Several of these 'appointed' academics were to prove distinguished scholars and public intellectuals, and yet the new school often found itself under a cloud of suspicion regarding its academic standing.[10]

In this light, there is a case to be made for seeing Cardim's ultimate decision to focus his scholarly endeavours on Shakespeare (rather than on didactics and the philological scholarship that attracted his earlier efforts) as part of a concern with academic legitimation, duly served by the canonical centrality of the English bard.

OF ANGLOPHILES, ANGLOPHOBES, BARDS AND ANTHEMS: A CONTEXT FOR (RE)PRESENTING SHAKESPEARE

The relative visibility of English studies within the disciplinary range of the new Faculty, set up as part of a republican programme, was inevitably affected

[3] Alves, *A Universidade na República*, pp. 17, 66–7, 74–7, 84.

[4] Manuel Augusto Rodrigues, 'Da Faculdade de Teologia para a Faculdade de Letras da Universidade de Coimbra', *Revista de História das Ideias* 11 (1989), 517–42.

[5] Alves, *A Universidade na República*, p. 23; Cândido dos Santos, *História da Universidade do Porto* (Porto, 2011), pp. 27–8, 67–72, 91–3, 99–100.

[6] Paulo Almeida, *A Maçonaria no Porto durante a 1a República* (Lisbon, 2015).

[7] Alves, *A Universidade na República*, pp. 250ff., 331.

[8] Alves, *A Universidade na República*, pp. 350, 358.

[9] Manuel Gomes da Torre, 'Dr. Luís Cardim: Dos liceus para a antiga Faculdade de Letras do Porto', *Revista da Faculdade de Letras do Porto – Línguas e Literaturas* 2.4 (1987), 279–300.

[10] Alves, *A Universidade na República*, pp. 345, 368; Torre, 'Dr. Luís Cardim', pp. 279–80.

by the manner in which English culture, and the British as a people, were considered in Portugal in and around the 1910 proclamation of the Republic.

The final decades of the monarchy had been marked by national and international crises, involving financial strains and colonial rivalries, that included humiliating episodes in Portugal's relationship with Britain, nominally Portugal's oldest ally (since the 1386 Treaty of Windsor). Some of the key developments in this crisis occurred in the reign of King Luís I, a constitutional monarch who was also a man of letters and patron of the arts. Signally, the King's literary achievements included translating four of Shakespeare's plays (between 1877 and 1885), and this active interest in Shakespeare was seen by some as part of an Anglophilia for which he was regularly attacked.[11]

An instance of this can be seen in a cartoon published in 1889, the very year King Luís died, by Manuel Gustavo Bordallo Pinheiro (see Figure 7).[12] The cartoon features the national bards of both countries – Luís de Camões (the sixteenth-century author of the Portuguese national epic, *The Lusiads*) and Shakespeare – in dialogue over the figure of John Bull, lying drunk on the ground. The caption reads:

SHAKESPEARE – My dear Luís [de Camões], please pay no attention to this drunkard, he is a shame to me.
CAMÕES – Thank you for your concern, dear William, but you needn't worry. I know well that this John Bull is none other than your own John Falstaff, that *centaur of man and pig*, in the words of our young confrère Victor Hugo.
SHAKESPEARE – Quite so.[13]

This exchange belongs within a context of increasing anti-British feeling over conflicting colonial claims, following the redefinition by the Conference of Berlin (1884–5) of colonial possession as legitimized by actual territorial occupation, rather than by historical rights of discovery. Portuguese efforts to occupy the African territories between Angola and Mozambique collided with Cecil Rhodes's plans for a central African British dominion extending from Cairo to Cape Town, and led to the British Ultimatum of January 1890, which forced the

Portuguese authorities to withdraw from the contested territories.[14] This atmosphere of political and international acrimony had intensified over the previous decade, with Portugal's humiliation enhanced by the fact that the culprit was none other than its partner in the longest-standing political alliance in Europe.

This environment had generated a spate of (often satirical) denunciations in the press in which supposed national traits acted as synecdoches for the perceptions generated by political resentment or indignation. Raphael Bordallo Pinheiro depicted Queen Victoria on a donkey replacing the equestrian statue of King Joseph I on the Terreiro do Paço ('Palace Square', the epicentre of power) in Lisbon; and another of his cartoons, featuring a famous stereotype of the Portuguese common man whom he called *Zé Povinho* (Joe Littlefolk), shows Zé on all fours, saddled by his many burdens, humbly facing King Luís and John Bull, who are jointly sitting in state.[15] Fialho de Almeida, a prominent novelist and polemicist, also construed the King's Shakespeare translations (which he decried, rather unjustly, as inept) as an epitome of the perceived decline of the Portuguese constitutional monarchy.[16]

---

[11] For a more extensive discussion of the King's translations, see Rui Carvalho Homem, 'Of negroes, Jews and kings: on a nineteenth-century royal translator', *The Translator* 7 (2001), 19–42; and also Helena M. Agarez Medeiros, 'O rei tradutor e os traduzidores empreiteiros: contributo para a história da tradução de drama em Portugal nos séculos XVIII e XIX' (unpublished dissertation, University of Lisbon, 2002).

[12] An illustrator, he was a son of the better-known visual satirist and all-round artist Raphael Bordallo Pinheiro.

[13] Manuel Gustavo Bordallo Pinheiro, *Na Mansão dos Poetas Immortaes* [lithograph], *Pontos nos ii* 5 (18 July 1889), 232. The English version of the caption is mine – as with all translations of Portuguese sources throughout this article.

[14] Amadeu Carvalho Homem, 'O avanço do republicanismo e a crise da monarquia constitucional', in *História de Portugal*, ed. José Mattoso, vol. 5 (n.p., 1993), pp. 131–45; pp. 142–4; Maria Manuela Lucas, 'Organização do Império', in *História de Portugal*, ed. Mattoso, vol. 5, pp. 285–311; pp. 310–11.

[15] Reproduced in João Medina, ed., *História Contemporânea de Portugal* (Lisboa, n.d.), vol. 1, tome 1, p. 148; vol. 1, tome 2, p. 85.

[16] Fialho de Almeida, *Os gatos: publicação mensal d'inquerito á vida portugueza* (Porto, 1889–94), p. 109.

7 Manuel Gustavo Bordallo Pinheiro, 'Na Mansão dos Poetas Immortaes' ('In the Mansion of Immortal Poets') [lithograph], *Pontos nos ii* 5 (18 July 1889), 232. Reproduced from a copy at the Porto Municipal Library, courtesy of Câmara Municipal do Porto.

However, it is the first of the cartoons mentioned above that is most relevant here, by signifying national dignity and emotions through an imagined living pantheon of poets sharing a loftier view of political matters and an exemplary mutual respect. The international dimension of such an imagined rapport is emphasized by the involvement not only of the English and Portuguese national poets, but also of a French counterpart, a *tertium* that validates the cumulative wisdom of the two interlocutors: Victor Hugo is attributed with a quip that had apparently become current for execrating Britain through its national stereotype, since it also occurs in Fernando Leal's *Palmadas na pança de John Bull*

('Slaps on John Bull's paunch'), an anti-British pasquinade published in Porto in 1884.[17] As in Bordallo Pinheiro's cartoon Shakespeare was to express his shame over John Bull's behaviour, Leal's *Palmadas* exempted Shakespeare from its indictment of Britain and the British: 'the courtroom of posterity, in which England will stand accused by History on behalf of the world's peoples, will only accept, for the countless and monstrous crimes of that odious nation, one single extenuating circumstance: Shakespeare!'[18]

Such statements reflected the growing political malaise of the mid- to late 1880s, but tensions in Anglo-Portuguese relations had already become charged with literary allusions since the 1880 commemorations of the tricentenary of the death of Luís de Camões, planned as a great occasion for national-(ist) feeling.[19] Strongly imbued with republican values, the initiative was explicitly positivistic in tone, as repeatedly stressed by Teófilo Braga – influential academic and man of letters, but also prominent politician. According to Braga, 'one owes the idea of commemorating Camões's centenary in 1880 to the introduction of positive philosophy in Portugal';[20] 'each people chooses the genius that synthesizes its national character'.[21] These pronouncements reflected the positivist belief in the social and civic virtues of commemorative designs, such as centenaries. Indeed, celebrating great men became a prominent way for free thinkers to inscribe the calendar with admired figures that could replace the Christian saints in a progressively inflected popular imagination.[22]

Homologies and comparisons involving writers as representative figures regularly feature, therefore, in texts from the period, as in a lecture on national authors given at the Royal Academy of Sciences:

Dante is immortal, but his poem is inspired by mysticism and revenge. Also immortal is Tasso, but his epic is the chivalrous novella, which folds and unfolds around the sacred walls of Jerusalem. Immortal is Shakespeare, but his muse, which probes and uncovers the remotest fibres of the human heart, is cosmopolitan rather than framed to embrace and proclaim the glory of Britons. Immortal is Cervantes, but the half-sublime, half-comic figure of his hero is more than the symbol of Spain, he is the personification of humankind.... Immortal is Camões, but he is so both to his own people and to strangers.[23]

In this comparative paean, Shakespeare is ascribed a quality which arguably becomes an impairment in this context: the subtleties with which he 'probes and uncovers the remotest fibres of the human heart' (a commonplace for Shakespeare's universal humanity that the speaker derives from Romantic criticism) are matched (he suggests) by a lack of vocation for the more epic task of 'proclaim[ing] the glory of Britons'.

As noted above, the 1890 British Ultimatum was to stimulate a collective need to proclaim Portuguese national glory in a manner that was not just relational and compensatory, but indeed conflictual – and this was retained and extended in civic memory by a major development: the country's future national anthem was a direct response to that Anglo-Portuguese crisis. Written by Alfredo Keil, a Portuguese composer of German descent, with lyrics by Henrique Lopes de Mendonça, *A Portuguesa* consciously echoed *La Marseillaise* in its title and some of its strains. However, its greatest relational significance lay in the evocation of past glories and the rallying cry 'To arms! To arms!', prompted by the perceived

---

[17] 'John Bull is the modern, trafficking avatar of John Falstaff – that centaur of a pig, in Victor Hugo's saying': Fernando Leal, *Palmadas na pança de John Bull* (Porto, 1884), p. 15. The phrase comes from Victor Hugo, *William Shakespeare* (Paris, 1864), p. 263.

[18] Leal, *Palmadas na pança de John Bull*, pp. 71–2.

[19] Homem, 'O avanço do republicanismo', pp. 138–40; Lucas, 'Organização do Império', pp. 308ff.; José M. Tengarrinha, '1870–1890: Charneira entre o velho e o novo Portugal', in *História contemporânea*, ed. Medina, vol. 1, 177–96; pp. 186–7.

[20] Teófilo Braga, 'O centenario de Camões no Brazil', *O Positivismo* 2 (1880), 513–20; p. 513.

[21] Teófilo Braga, 'O centenario de Camões em 1880', *O Positivismo* 2 (1880), 1–9; p. 2.

[22] Mário Vilela, 'Recepção de Camões nos jornais de 1880', *Revista da Universidade de Coimbra* 33 (1985), 403–18; pp. 404–7.

[23] Latino Coelho, cited in Figueiredo Magalhães, *Camões e os portuguezes no Brasil; reparos críticos* (Rio de Janeiro, 1880), pp. 118–19.

betrayal by the British. Hugely popular over the following decades, often played by brass bands and sung by crowds, marched to by the revolutionaries of 1910, it was adopted officially in 1911 (and is still today the national anthem).[24] Its adoption by the Republic as a positive celebration of a progressive ethos did not occlude a perception of its confrontational origins. The tale that the words 'against cannons' in the anthem's refrain originally read 'against Britons' may be apocryphal, but it was persistent enough for the French press to note 'with surprise and indignation' in 1916 – when Portugal pointedly entered World War I on the side of the Allies to stress its continued friendship with the British[25] – that the Portuguese Expeditionary Corps were 'preparing to march to the trenches to the tune of an anthem composed by a German against Britain'.[26]

BOOKS AND THE TALES THEY TELL: READING SHAKESPEARE IN PORTO 100 YEARS AGO

Rather than mere curiosities, the Anglo–Portuguese perplexities outlined above were an integral part of the cultural perceptions that shaped the environment in which the new Faculty of Letters was set up in 1919, energized by the Republic's civic and political commitment to education. Its disciplinary range included history, philosophy, geography and philology – both Romance and Germanic. The latter comprised English and German studies, materially organized into courses focusing on language, literature and some historical and geographic information.[27]

The activities of the new school were supported by a library that was put together under the severe material constraints that persistently ailed the Republic – and in just a few years (the fact that few titles in the collection bear publication dates later than 1925 may indicate little investment after the coup that put an end to the Republic in 1926, let alone after 1928, when the decision was made by the new regime to close the Faculty). Once these contingencies are taken into account, the 'Fundo Primitivo' ('original holdings'), embedded in the current

Faculty's library as a special collection, may be meagre, but hardly an embarrassment. Amounting to a few thousand volumes, of which roughly 500 were in English (mostly bought to support English studies, and supplemented by a few more representing French and German scholarship in the field), it would have made up a small but up-to-date library for the humanities. Among the English-language books (unsurprisingly, given the history of English as a discipline, and the Republic's interest in great authors as 'secular saints'), Shakespeare occupied a prominent position.

More than merely embodying such prominence, that small but academically adequate item of Shakespeariana proves representative of the disciplinary tendencies that attended on the rise of English over the period, especially regarding the 'battle' between 'the respectably "scientific" regime of philologists, mostly trained in German universities, who ensured that [priority was given] to the classification of historical and linguistic facts' and 'those who championed the study of literature "as literature" rather than as linguistic data', wresting it from its reputation as 'a lightweight matter of private opinion and chatter beyond the scope of serious scholarship'.[28] In the 'Fundo Primitivo', the former approach, justified by the emphasis on teaching the language that a non-Anglophone context required, and by the philological training of the staff themselves, was duly sustained by several German tomes on the history of the language and 'Englische Philologie'; while its application specifically to the study of Shakespeare was represented by volumes such as Edwin A. Abbott's *A Shakespearian Grammar: An Attempt to Illustrate Some of the Differences between*

---

[24] For a full account of its origins, contexts and fortunes, see Rui Ramos, *O Cidadão Keil: Alfredo Keil, A Portuguesa e a cultura do patriotismo cívico em Portugal* (Lisbon, 2010).
[25] See Rui Ramos, 'A segunda fundação (1890–1926)', in *História de Portugal*, gen. ed. José Mattoso, vol. 6 (n.p., 1994), pp. 495–500.
[26] Ramos, *O Cidadão Keil*, p. 14.
[27] The full curriculum is transcribed in Torre, 'Dr. Luís Cardim', pp. 280–1.
[28] Chris Baldick, *Criticism and Literary Theory: 1890 to the Present* (London and New York, 1996), p. 24.

Elizabethan and Modern English (originally published in 1869, the reprint in Porto dating from 1909). But the collection also provides evidence of the Faculty's attention to those approaches to literature and drama that in 1914 Arthur Quiller-Couch (from his Chair of English Literature at Cambridge) had reportedly championed, while scoffing at the views of literary history represented by 'Teutonic and Teutonising professors'.[29]

At its most traditional, the abundant non-philological strand in these holdings is represented by studies of texts set against general historical contexts, such as a large tome originating in the 1916 Shakespeare commemorations, *Shakespeare's England: An Account of the Life & Manners of His Age* (Oxford, 1917); this compiled contributions from such luminaries of academia and the world of letters as Walter Raleigh, Professor of English at Oxford, and the Poet Laureate, Robert Bridges, with his 'Ode on the tercentenary commemoration of Shakespeare'. The library also included historical overviews ranging from erudite to popular, as suggested by the coexistence on the shelves of George Saintsbury's *A History of Elizabethan Literature* (London, 1918) and G. B. Harrison's *The Story of Elizabethan Drama* (Cambridge, 1924). The immediate needs of an educational context were duly catered for by the inclusion of manuals such as Tucker Brooke's *Shakespeare of Stratford: A Handbook for Students* (New Haven, 1926). And, in an age that celebrated the exceptionality of great authors, it featured biographies, such as *A Life of William Shakespeare* (Boston, 1923) by the American scholar Joseph Quincy Adams, later to become director of the Folger Shakespeare Library.

The age's interest in individuality, rather evidently developed from Romantic criticism, indeed looms large in the Shakespeariana at the 'Fundo Primitivo', where it is also represented by Raleigh's *Shakespeare* (1907), his often cited contribution to the 'English Men of Letters' series, with its resonant plea for a uniqueness that saw Shakespeare 'separated from his fellows'.[30] Even less surprising, given its commitment to exploring human singularity, is one of the collection's most well-thumbed

specimens, A. C. Bradley's *Shakespearean Tragedy* (London, 1904) – only in this case the exploration famously targets not the playwright himself but his major tragic characters, as representations of human profiles. Bradley was arguably the most influential critic in the history of Shakespeare in education over the past century,[31] and the evidence of his ample use by scholars and students in Porto in the 1920s suggests that this community, despite all the sociopolitical contingencies and the Faculty's brief life, was indeed connected through its small library to what was then the most current scholarship in the field.

However, biographical and/or psychologizing approaches should not be seen as a programmatic or dominant trait in the collection (and hence in the training and scholarship that was to emerge from the Faculty): on the contrary, they are put in perspective by the sheer diversity of the holdings. A no less prominent strand – balanced against the literary processing of Shakespeare the poet, encountered and enjoyed on the page – involves views from the stage. The library includes several studies from the first quarter of the century in which Shakespeare, the playwright, is read against contexts provided by precursors and contemporaries, and also crucially by data from the history of drama and theatre that (through a sense of tradition and continuity) mitigate the discourse of authorial salience. This angle is represented in the collection both by what one might call traditional and by (for the time) new scholarship, ranging therefore from

---

[29] Cited in Baldick, *Criticism*, p. 32.

[30] Walter Raleigh, *Shakespeare* (London, 1907), p. 2.

[31] As noted by Tiffany Stern nearly two decades ago, when pondering her own formative experience, 'the Edwardian Shakespeare who came straight out of A. C. Bradley's *Shakespearean Tragedy* of 1904 ... was still, bizarrely, flourishing in the universities of the 1970s ... [his] psychological criticism ... continues to live on in the schoolroom – my own education was strictly Bradleian – so that much classroom teaching of Shakespeare is now 100 years behind current criticism': Tiffany Stern, 'Teaching Shakespeare in higher education', in *Shakespeare in Education*, ed. Martin Blocksidge (New York and London, 2003), pp. 120–40; pp. 131–2.

Tucker Brooke's *The Tudor Drama: A History of English National Drama to the Retirement of Shakespeare* (Boston, 1911) to the four volumes of E. K. Chambers's *The Elizabethan Stage* (Oxford, 1923) – its consequence easily gauged by Chambers being, by far, the authority that Cardim tends to cite most often (as noted below).

This brief overview of the contents and perceived significance of the Shakespeariana at this library would be incomplete without stressing – again – that it was put together in a non-Anglophone context, for the study of a foreign language, culture and literature, and in a host context that was starkly aware of its politico-historical contingencies. As noted by Balz Engler:

This difference of perspective between doing English in an English-speaking country and doing English elsewhere is crucial. In English-speaking countries it may be taught without much reference to other literatures, languages, and cultures. Elsewhere English will always be viewed against other languages. But the two perspectives, mother-tongue and foreign language, cannot simply be put beside each other either. The foreign perspective will always include the English perspective as well, if only because much of the secondary material used is written from an English-speaking perspective, and because the scholarly community is dominated by Anglo-American voices.[32]

The paragraphs above will have made clear that 'Anglo-American voices' indeed prevailed in the collection in question, which sampled all of the major scholarly approaches of the age in the English-speaking world. To this, however, the 'Fundo Primitivo' added a few volumes of continental European scholarship, especially French and German contributions to Shakespeare studies. French titles included Victor Hugo's extensive and idiosyncratic *William Shakespeare* (Paris, 1864), which combined biography, critical opinion and an assessment of posthumous fortune with an overview of the world's major literary geniuses; and a recent reprint of a French edition of writings on Shakespeare by the German dramatist and man of letters Otto Ludwig (1813–65), posthumously published in 1891.[33] The German titles in the collection amounted to a more substantial and

complex presence, including a few studies of life and work – both Helene Richter's *Shakespeare der Mensch* (Leipzig, 1923) and Friedrich Gundolf's *Shakespeare, Sein Wesen und Werk* (Berlin, 1928) – but also volumes published in English under German imprints, in some cases on the initiative of the German Shakespeare Association, and ranging from source studies and textual history to the history of drama.[34]

Material evidence (the wear and tear on the books) indicates that the collection was intensely used, but its consequence can also be gauged by the regularity with which the books in the holdings were quoted in the academic output of the most prominent of the English staff in the 'first Faculty of Letters', Luís Cardim – whose record of publications is a salient section in this brief chapter of educational history.

TEACHING SHAKESPEARE IN INTERESTING TIMES: LUÍS CARDIM – SCHOLARSHIP, CRITICISM, TRANSLATION

In 1919, Luís Cardim, until then a schoolteacher of English and German in the Lisbon area, became a university lecturer in Porto, under conditions that many would have seen as unpromising, considering the highly politicized – and hence controversial – decision to create a faculty of letters in the north of the country and appoint its staff on the

[32] Balz Engler, 'Writing the European history of English', in *European English Studies: Contributions towards the History of a Discipline*, ed. Balz Engler and Renate Haas (Leicester, 2000), pp. 1–12; p. 7.
[33] Léon Mis, ed., *Les études sur Shakespeare d'Otto Ludwig exposées dans un ordre méthodique et précédées d'une introduction littéraire* (Lille, 1922).
[34] Examples include H. R. D. Anders, *Shakespeare's Books: A Dissertation on Shakespeare's Reading and the Immediate Sources of His Works* (Berlin, 1904); Wilfrid Perrett, *The Story of King Lear from Geoffrey of Monmouth to Shakespeare* (Berlin, 1904) (a published lecture); and Charles William Wallace, *The Evolution of the English Drama up to Shakespeare* (Berlin, 1912) – included in the series Schriften der Deutschen Shakespeare-Gesellschaft.

basis of a government mandate, rather than conventional academic protocols.[35] Key elements in his professional trajectory, however, were consistent with what our age would see as proper to an academic researcher (though limited by the time constraints imposed by a full-time job in secondary education). Roughly twelve years earlier (still in the final years of the monarchy), Cardim's reputation as a young teacher had justified a ministerial decision to award him funded periods of advanced training-cum-research in Britain and Germany, where he focused on psychology (for teaching), phonetics, English literature, and methodologies for language teaching.[36] These opportunities, combined with teaching experience, resulted in the publication, in the years preceding his move to Porto, of a manual and a couple of articles on educational matters.[37]

Beyond this, his formative experience had yielded a 'wealth of capital' (as phrased decades later, in a posthumous tribute lecture, by his colleague and major figure in Portuguese letters Hernâni Cidade) that 'could no longer be contained within the classroom', and spilled over into public lectures – some on literary topics.[38] These lectures were given at civil society institutions such as the Academia de Estudos Livres ('Academy for Free Study'), a 'popular university' that had been founded by freemasons in 1899 to help to 'foster a taste for study and science'.[39] This dimension of his work confirms Cardim's commitment to teaching in disciplinary areas and frameworks other than those of the secondary schools where he worked until the age of forty, while also signalling his broad position on the developments that transformed Portugal in his lifetime. More specifically, it suggests affinities with projects for extending knowledge socially – either through the 'popular instruction' provided by the Academia de Estudos Livres, or indeed through the Faculty in which he was to serve, a school geared from the outset towards training future teachers in a manner that would suit the Republic's aspirations for socio-political change.[40] Although he did not achieve widespread public fame, let alone material rewards,

Cardim could then count on audiences that would not doubt 'the public value of the humanities', nor indeed the relevance of public intellectuals – to cite concepts that in more recent years have been intensely questioned.[41]

Cardim's publications from the period when he served as a university lecturer confirm an interest in combining new research (sometimes on rather arcane topics) with efforts to write both for his studentship – one of his contemporaries notes the much-needed 'syntheses' that he provided[42] – and for broader audiences outside academia. This balance, as also the breadth of his interests, is in evidence in his *Estudos de literatura e de lingüística* ('Studies in literature and linguistics'), a volume of essays in Portuguese and English published in 1929 under the university's own imprint. His philological training yields long essays under titles such as 'Portuguese–English grammarians and the history of English sounds' and 'Caracteres rúnicos e caracteres ibéricos' (which ponders possible affinities between runes and 'Iberian script') – but also an overview (one of those syntheses for students?) on

35 Torre, 'Dr. Luís Cardim', pp. 279–80.
36 Hernâni Cidade, 'Luís Cardim, no convívio, na aula e na obra de investigador e poeta', *O Tripeiro* 5th ser., 15.8 (1959), 240–4; p. 240; see also the institutional bionote at https://sigarra.up.pt /up/pt/WEB_BASE.GERA_PAGINA?P_pagina=1004199.
37 Luís Cardim, *Iniciação ao estudo do inglez* (Lisbon, 1911); 'Sobre o ensino do inglês nos liceus', *Revista de Educação Geral e Técnica* ser. 3, 4 (1915), 351–7; 'One of Portugal's debts to England', *Portugal – A Monthly Review of the Country, its Colonies, Commerce, History, Literature and Art* 3 (1915), 79–80.
38 Cidade, 'Luís Cardim', p. 240.
39 Joaquim Pintassilgo, 'As Universidades Populares nas primeiras décadas do século XX: o exemplo da Academia de Estudos Livres', in *Modelos culturais, saberes pedagógicos, instituições educacionais*, ed. Marta Maria Chagas de Carvalho and Joaquim Pintassilgo (São Paulo, 2011), Repositório da Universidade de Lisboa: http://hdl.handle.net/10451/8354.
40 On the new Faculty's mandate to train future secondary school teachers, see Torre, 'Dr. Luís Cardim', p. 280.
41 See, for example, Jonathan Bate, ed., *The Public Value of the Humanities* (London and New York, 2011); Helen Small, ed., *The Public Intellectual* (Oxford, 2002); Jeffrey R. Di Leo and Peter Hitchcock, eds., *The New Public Intellectual: Politics, Theory, and the Public Sphere* (Houndmills, 2016).
42 Cidade, 'Luís Cardim', p. 243.

the history of language teaching. Research-wise, the intercultural perspective prevails on both the linguistic and literary sides of his interests, involving a focus on the perceived relevance of aspects of 'Germanic' languages and cultures for Portuguese audiences. This understanding of the scholar as cultural mediator is evident in his opening essay on 'Syr Torrent of Portyngale' (a medieval romance known from a fifteenth-century manuscript), and also in a bibliographic discussion of a sixteenth-century edition of *The Canterbury Tales* found at the Porto Municipal Library. But the volume also collects critical contributions of a more general reach, including a discussion of Shakespearian stage practice – a piece in English on 'the killing of Julius Caesar'.[43]

This article, Cardim's only Shakespearian contribution in that 1929 collection, is a relatively short text on the implications of a stage direction and lines of dialogue for an understanding of original practices. It is described in a footnote as the development of annotations included in his translation of *Julius Cesar*, published four years earlier. But its relevance lies in the way it brings out Cardim's interest in Shakespeare as stage- rather than just page-bound (when the latter could easily appear more congenial to Cardim's scholarly profile), and the connections it has with his other major Shakespearian publication from those years: a book on Shakespeare and English drama, published in the closing year of the Faculty of Letters.[44]

Knowledgeable and densely referenced, the slim volume (totalling 175 pages) is competent, and even occasionally sophisticated, in its management of the most current scholarship – but also consciously derivative: as acknowledged in the preface, 'we evidently do not claim originality'.[45] Indeed, the book offered a historically arranged compilation of received information and opinion that allowed Cardim to consolidate his credentials as a public educator. Construing his task almost like that of the curator of heritage that has to be adequately framed and explicated, since 'preparation' proves key both to acquisition of knowledge and aesthetic enjoyment, Cardim describes his monograph as 'a book for preparing to read Shakespeare' (p. 8) – a phrase that, in context,

sees its ostensible modesty mitigated by a pervasive sense of a mission.[46]

Of all Cardim's output, *Shakespeare e o drama inglês* is also the work that best illustrates the productiveness of a cohesive but broad-ranging body of publications – the Shakespeariana that he had surely helped to select for the Faculty's library. This corpus was here put to good use in outlining both the historic course of English drama (from late medieval conditions to a Shakespearian aftermath) and the scholarship and criticism that it had generated. Cardim is unusually candid and open about his debts, since his list of sources, rather than featuring at the end of the volume, is brought to the front (after a short preface, the book opens with a five-page list of 'recommended authorities' featuring most of the specimens mentioned above, with their relevance for the various chapters specified in the endnotes). For the book's historical backbone in theatre scholarship, E. K. Chambers was by far Cardim's topmost source, with close to thirty citations from *The Medieval Stage* (1903) and *The Elizabethan Stage* (1923). But the book is also keen to acquaint its readership with current criticism, especially in its closing chapters. Cardim proves aware of a critical shift towards context, contingency and performance, and he navigates his way through insights afforded by both 'Romantic' legacies and 'realistic' alternatives – a critical front on which Bradley's 'penetrating examination of the four major tragedies' enjoys particular favour.[47]

Cardim's embraced role of educator and mediator can therefore be found to fashion his work on Shakespeare through the 1920s, when he was preparing his brief monograph as well as another substantial engagement with Shakespeare, his annotated translation of *Julius Caesar*. Despite the more limited esteem that translations traditionally enjoyed in the academic context, this venture

---

[43] Luís Cardim, 'The killing of Julius Caesar in Shakespeare's tragedy', in *Estudos de literatura e de lingüística* (Porto, 1929), pp. 73–87.
[44] Luís Cardim, *Shakespeare e o drama inglês* (Porto, 1931).
[45] Cardim, *Shakespeare*, p. 8. [46] Cardim, *Shakespeare*, p. 8.
[47] Cardim, *Shakespeare*, p. 151.

significantly deepens the argument for the relevance of Shakespeare in the interesting times of the First Republic in Portugal.

'OMENS / OF SOME MONSTROUS NEW STATE': *JULIUS CAESAR* AND PORTUGAL IN THE MID-1920S

Published in 1925, Cardim's version of *Julius Caesar* was the first book-length publication to emerge from his term as university lecturer (preceding by a few years both the collection of essays and the short Shakespeare monograph mentioned above). Judging from its material presentation – a cheaply produced paperback, its cover featuring a drawing rather poorly based on the Droeshout portrait – the volume was clearly aimed at a broad, non-specialized readership. However, there was nothing casual or facile about the text or its surrounding apparatus. Shakespeare's blank verse was rendered by Cardim into impeccably regular Portuguese decasyllables, reflecting both a scholarly understanding of the text and the prosodic ease proper to 'the practitioner'[48] (Cardim was a published poet in his own right). As for the volume's critical apparatus, it included a 23-page chapter positioned *after* the translated text but fully matching what one would expect from a critical introduction (with remarks on textual history, the Elizabethan stage, characterization, the structure of the play, the use of verse and prose, and the translator's strategies), as well as 76 pages of detailed endnotes.

Unlike later volumes, Cardim's *Julius Caesar* was not published under the university's own imprint but by 'Renascença Portuguesa' – literally, 'Portuguese Renaissance' (or 'Revival'), a Porto-based movement bent on retrieving the country from a perceived cultural decline.[49] Cardim was an active participant in this venture, which brought together the efforts of a fair number of Portuguese intellectuals in this period. All over Europe, publishing distinguished versions of canonical texts from other literary traditions had been a regular strategy, since the Romantic era, on the part of cultural nationalists

keen to revive and extend the imaginative franchise of their cultures[50] – so the movement's decision to publish a Shakespeare play, translated by one of their own, was hardly surprising. What is intriguing, however, is that Cardim should have chosen a play that had *twice* been published in Portuguese translation over the previous decade – in both cases in Porto, and in one of these also by Renascença Portuguesa.[51] If most of Cardim's other Shakespearian ventures reflected a perceived need to fill gaps, as regards the access of either students or a general readership to the riches of foreign cultures, his option for *Julius Caesar* followed a distinct rationale.

A full century before the political readings that have shaped criticism in our time, Cardim, lecturing at an openly republican institution, may or may not have anticipated the perception that 'Shakespeare's work emerged out of a culture that was saturated with republican images and arguments'; or that '*Julius Caesar* . . . depicts a dying and perverted republican Rome that has lost the ability to inspire

---

[48] Eliot's famous phrase for the poet (when also considered in a parallel capacity as scholar or critic): T. S. Eliot, 'Milton II' [1947], in *On Poetry and Poets* (London, 1957), pp. 146–61; p. 146.

[49] For Jaime Cortesão, a key member of the Portuguese intelligentsia, acknowledged by some as original mentor of the movement, the project aimed to 'create an association of Portuguese artists and intellectuals whose main goal should be . . . social action, providing guidance and education in an environment . . . that lacked big ideas . . ., fostering a more highly conscious and cultivated public': Jaime Cortesão in a letter to Raul Proença, 26 July 1911, cited in Alfredo Ribeiro dos Santos, *A Renascença Portuguesa: um movimento cultural portuense* (Porto, 1990), p. 78.

[50] For a set of seminal studies on the topic, see Dirk Delabastita and Lieven D'hulst, eds., *European Shakespeares: Translating Shakespeare in the Romantic Age* (Amsterdam and Philadelphia, 1993).

[51] As noted in João Almeida Flor, 'Shakespeare in the Bay of Portugal: a tribute to Luís Cardim (1879–1958)', in *Translating Shakespeare for the Twenty-First Century*, ed. Rui Carvalho Homem and Ton Hoenselaars (Amsterdam and New York, 2004), pp. 243–54; p. 253. The two translations were: Domingos Ramos, trans., *William Shakespeare – Júlio César* (Porto, 1913), and A. J. Anselmo, trans., *William Shakespeare – Julio César* (Porto, 1916) – the latter under the Renascença Portuguesa imprint.

its citizens to behave virtuously'.[52] Again, he may have known or sensed that, within the Shakespeare canon, *Julius Caesar* is one of the plays that more promptly lend themselves to appropriation, as a textual and dramatic space that has proved fit for historical and political ventriloquizing in a variety of contexts.[53] But he certainly realized that key issues verbally dramatized by Shakespeare (after Plutarch) around the killing of Caesar – the perceived risks of tyranny; the prospect of a republic sliding into a monarchical regime; the sense that free citizens could disenfranchise themselves by yielding to the seductiveness of an ostensibly magnanimous, but effectively overbearing strongman – could hardly be politically more congenial to the concerns of Portugal's intelligentsia in the 1920s.

Indeed, when Cardim was translating *Julius Caesar*, little more than a decade had passed since the country had discarded a long-standing monarchy. The Republic, however, brought with it all the new challenges posed by a full-blown elective democracy. These included the constant factious quarrels of political parties and ambitious individual agents, causing permanent instability in government (with ministers and prime ministers sometimes lasting just a few days on the job, and a constant risk of military or civilian coups). Such circumstances led many, in politics and the country at large, to feel the allure of strong, 'law and order' leaders – which helped to justify the short episodes of dictatorship that punctuated the mere sixteen years that the First Republic lasted.[54] As if to make this context even more apt for refraction through the concerns over polity (as much as plot) in *Julius Caesar*, political assassination, carried out in the public eye, had inscribed itself in the country's recent political memory, especially through two landmark moments separated by a decade: the regicide of 1908 and the assassination of President Sidónio Pais in 1918.

In 1908, republican conspirators had fatally shot King Carlos I and the Crown Prince on the Terreiro do Paço, when the royal family were returning home in an open carriage. News of this was received with shock, and yet, considering the country's pious and deferential ethos, the response of the population was relatively subdued – as noted by a British observer in a letter to Luís Cardim.[55]

This mitigated sympathy for the victims reflected the general erosion of popularity of the monarchy in its final decades, but especially the reputation for 'tyranny' that King Carlos, an otherwise bonhomous constitutional monarch, had obtained when he sponsored a dictatorial episode.[56] Its murderous onus quickly attenuated, the regicide came to be seen, in Portugal's prevalent historical narrative, as inevitable, and as a dress rehearsal for the triumph of the Republic two years later.

The 1918 assassination occurred in a different context, and involved different political emotions. In December 1917, Sidónio Pais (an army officer but also an academic, freemason, diplomat and proactive politician) had led a coup in the name of law and order, inaugurating a period of dictatorship. Enjoying huge popularity, he sought validation through the ballot by getting himself elected president (directly, and hence extra-constitutionally) in April 1918. Sidónio (usually evoked by his first name) fashioned for himself a unique and heroic figure, but became politically isolated. In December 1918 he was shot, at a central railway station in Lisbon, by a disgruntled republican and democrat ostensibly acting alone, but believed by many to have been mandated by conspirators who felt Sidónio, with his charismatic personal rule, had betrayed the Republic.[57] His death was followed by outpourings of public emotion – but it allowed the

---

[52] Andrew Hadfield, *Shakespeare and Republicanism* (Cambridge, 2005), pp. 1, 167–8.

[53] For a few examples, see Michael Anderegg, 'Orson Welles and after: *Julius Caesar* and twentieth century totalitarianism', in *Julius Caesar: New Critical Essays*, ed. Horst Zander (New York and London, 2005), pp. 295–305; Mariangela Tempera, 'Political Caesar: *Julius Caesar* on the Italian stage', in *Caesar*, ed. Zander, pp. 333–43.

[54] See Ramos, *A segunda fundação*, pp. 267–97, 616–18.

[55] William A. Bentley, letter to Luís Cardim, dated 5 February 1908, included in a documental database relating to Cardim created by José Manuel Martins Ferreira: https://luiscardim.wordpress.com/2018/11/11/05-02-1908-carta-para-luis-cardim.

[56] Ramos, *A segunda fundação*, pp. 267ff.

[57] Maria João Neto, ed., *Sidónio Pais: o retrato do país no tempo da Grande Guerra* (Casal de Cambra, 2018); Armando Malheiro da Silva, 'Sidónio Pais e sidonismo: uma síntese no

constitutional order of the Republic to be resumed (although the following years were regularly to witness murderous violence on the public scene).[58] Sidónio's continued presence on the nation's imaginative landscape was to become inseparable from the stanzas in which the modernist poet Fernando Pessoa was to eulogize him as 'President-King', a much cited integrative epithet for a figure that Pessoa mourned as a lost messianic figure.[59]

In a variety of ways – mostly discreet, but hardly missable – Luís Cardim grounded his version of *Julius Caesar* in this turbulent context.[60] The book's first topical implication is explicit, but paratextual: the volume is pointedly dedicated to Ginestal Machado, a well-respected republican moderate, one of the few prominent figures of the Republic whose reputation emerged mostly unscathed from the factiousness of those years. And then there are the translator's options, in the form of turns of phrase and lexical choices which, while mostly remaining rhetorically and semantically close to the source, resonate strikingly in the target context – precisely because Shakespeare's text itself seems, uncannily, to comment on its defining tensions. Such is the case with passages from Act 1, Scene 2 on the conspirators' fears that Caesar may want to become a monarch: 'What means this shouting? I do fear the people / Choose Caesar for their king' (1.2.81–2); and 'There was a Brutus once that would have brooked / Th'eternal devil to keep his state in Rome / As easily as a king' (1.2.160–2). Both of these were rendered by Cardim in the most literal manner, and yet, to a Portuguese readership, they could not but come across as seductively topical just a few years after the consulate (and assassination) of Sidónio, the populist 'President-King' – with the slightly more distant memory of the 1908 regicide in the background.

With a few other passages, however, Cardim proved a more refractive and less invisible translator.[61] In Act 3, right after the assassination, Cassius predicts a future when 'So often shall the knot of us be called / The men that gave their country liberty' (3.1.118–19); this Cardim translates as 'seremos proclamados a facção / que deu ao seu

país a Liberdade!'[62] – resorting to a lexical choice, 'facção' ('faction'), which, in Portuguese, carries a negative charge, inevitably enhanced by the divisiveness that had blighted the country's political scene following the 1910 republican revolution and its promise of 'Liberty' (a word that Cardim, almost ironically, capitalizes). A little further on, when Brutus notes that Antony will 'receive the benefit of [Caesar's] dying: a place in the commonwealth' (3.2.42–3), Cardim translates the latter phrase as 'uma posição na República'[63] – literally (once rendered back into English), 'a position in the Republic', again capitalized; in the target context this was bound to suggest, rather than the place every citizen can call theirs in the *res publica*, those 'positions' that political arrivistes arguably scrambled for under the post-1910 conditions (as, indeed, in most regimes).

Sometimes the topicality in Cardim's version involves uplifting imagery, a case in point occurring when he renders 'the east' (the daybreak that the conspirators glimpse at 2.1.100) as 'oriente'. Though a synonym of 'leste' (the immediate cognate in Portuguese), this lexical option enjoyed a particular currency in Cardim's environment because of its use in the names of masonic lodges (as in the 'Grande

---

centenário da sua morte', *Brotéria: Cristianismo e Cultura* 188 (2019), 93–104.

58 Armando Malheiro da Silva, 'As "misteriosas" noites sangrentas da República', in *Sidónio Pais*, ed. Neto, pp. 53–69.

59 Fernando Pessoa, 'À memória do Presidente-Rei Sidónio Pais', in *Obra poética*, vol. I (n.p., 1986), pp. 143–51.

60 As previously noted by Flor, 'Shakespeare in the Bay', pp. 253–4.

61 On 'refraction' as 'the adaptation of a work of literature to a different audience, with the intention of influencing the way in which that audience reads the work', see André Lefevere, 'Mother Courage's cucumbers: text, system and refraction in a theory of literature' [1982], in *The Translation Studies Reader*, 3rd edn, ed. Lawrence Venuti (London, 2004), pp. 203–19; p. 205. On the notion that translators become 'invisible' when they produce versions which readers will not recognize as translations, see Lawrence Venuti, *The Translator's Invisibility: A History of Translation* (London, 1995).

62 William Shakespeare, *A tragédia de Júlio César*, translated into verse and prose, according to the original, and annotated by Luís Cardim (Porto, 1925), p. 93.

63 Shakespeare, *Júlio César*, trans. Cardim, p. 105.

Oriente Lusitano'),[64] with their iconography of the rising sun. But some of those passages in his translation that were bound to come across as hauntingly topical involved violence and intimations of disaster. In Act 1, Scene 3, remarking on the prodigies that marked the stormy night, Cassius construes them as 'instruments of fear and warning / Unto some monstrous state' (1.3.70–1), which is rendered by Cardim as 'meio de prenúncio / de qualquer novo estado monstruoso'[65] (literally, 'omens / of some monstrous new state'). It is the political sense of the word that prevails when 'state' is calqued as 'estado', but its combination with 'novo' ('new'), an adjective that the translator did not derive from the source text, grants it an additional resonance in the immediate context: Sidónio had called his populist, caudillista regime 'Nova República' (the 'New Republic'); and the dictatorship that was to emerge from the 1926 coup that ended the Republic, a year after Cardim's Júlio César came out, was to style itself as the 'Estado Novo' (the 'New State'). That future development, however, Cardim could never have guessed.

AFTERMATHS: A LIFE, A MOVIE

The dictatorship that prevailed in Portugal after 1926, for most of its duration under the leadership of former Coimbra professor António de Oliveira Salazar, was to determine the closure of the still young Faculty of Letters in Porto – and, when its final intake of students graduated in 1931, Luís Cardim and his colleagues saw their academic positions terminated. Some found positions elsewhere, but Cardim, after unsuccessfully applying for a state pension, opted out of teaching and settled into a rather obscure clerical job as secretary of the Portuguese League for Social Prophylaxis,[66] a charity founded in 1924 by medical doctors concerned with the welfare of the poor.

Despite such unpromising, even poignant circumstances, Cardim went on writing and publishing – as a poet, occasional translator and all-round scholar. In 1940, he brought out a book on the Portuguese national poet, Camões, and his 'impact on English letters',[67] a book ostensibly

intended to occupy a symmetrical position to his work on Shakespeare. Cardim's circumstances outside academia saw him, however, increasingly writing for non-specialized audiences. This included preparing a biography of Shakespeare, again showing great familiarity with a vast array of historical and critical sources – and, again, declaredly derivative.[68] It offered a late positivistic celebration of a 'great man', and became one of the means through which Cardim managed to extend his calling as educator in the direction of 'popular instruction', a goal of scholars from his generation and background that was also in line with the philanthropic rationale of his employers at the 'Liga'.

This vocation arguably found a more stimulating and revealing outlet, also because of its circumstantial nature, in Cardim's final book-length Shakespearian publication, a short volume (125 pages), from 1949, containing a series of reflections on the challenges of staging Hamlet – prompted, however, not by stage productions, but rather by Laurence Olivier's film, premiered the previous year.[69] It began as a series of articles for Seara Nova, a journal that for decades was a persistent force of ideological opposition to Salazar's dictatorship.[70]

Cardim provides detailed contextual information: Olivier's film had been repeatedly screened, for weeks, in both Lisbon and Porto, and had generated so much interest that all English-language copies of Hamlet had sold out in the bookshops and second-hand booksellers, with Portuguese translations also

---

[64] See www.gremiolusitano.pt.
[65] Shakespeare, Júlio César, trans. Cardim, p. 47.
[66] This literal version is the League's official title in English. See www.lpps.pt/index.php/en.
[67] Luís Cardim, Projecção de Camões nas letras inglesas (Lisbon, 1940).
[68] Luís Cardim, A vida de Shakespeare: factos, lendas e problemas (Lisbon, 1943).
[69] Luís Cardim, Os problemas do Hamlet e as suas dificuldades cénicas: a propósito do filme de Sir Laurence Olivier (Lisbon, 1949).
[70] All of the journal's issues are now online at http://ric.slhi.pt /Seara_Nova/o_monumento_democratico?lang=en.

in great demand.[71] This is, in itself, culturally relevant – when one bears in mind that the Portuguese intelligentsia then tended to have French, rather than English, as its main 'language of culture'; and that Salazar's Portugal was somewhat isolated from the major centres of intellectual and artistic debate. No less revealingly, it shows that, for a series of articles on Shakespeare tailored for a cultivated (but non-specialized) readership, Cardim was still seen as the expert and educator to approach – a full eighteen years after his academic occupation had ceased. And yet, rather poignantly, that former affiliation still defined and validated him, since the cover of the book described him as 'Formerly a professor at the Faculdade de Letras do Porto'; and Cardim also opted to evoke his truncated career by dedicating the volume to his 'former students, now my friends'.

This sense that his academic authority was anchored in a past circumstance does not, however, appear to constrain Cardim in his ability to pass critical judgement. Indeed, he makes it clear that his remit in those articles is not simply to heap praise on Shakespeare or Olivier, and that he has retained a practice of critical reflection, engaging with the most current scholarly and critical sources, as much as with items from mass culture.[72] Cardim's discussion not just of Olivier's film, but also of *Hamlet* in general and its overwhelming imaginative consequence, thus allows him to signal that he is not merely a former scholar, made redundant by political vagaries. He ponders and categorizes the history of discussions on the perplexities posed by Hamlet the character, browsing a great variety of authors – British, American, German; some already present in that Faculty library in the 1920s, others more recent.[73] He describes his moment in critical history as one of eclecticism (including a certain sceptical mitigation of bardolatry), navigating a territory that he sees as stretching between the critical polarities of Romantic-psychological and realist-historical approaches, and sometimes pouring some irony on his major references – with Bradley dubbed 'high priest of psycho-aesthetic criticism'.[74]

Prior to commenting directly on Olivier's *Hamlet*, Cardim scrupulously hedges his competence by stressing that he is not a film critic, but rather a scholar with a specialized interest in the play, and hence in the manner in which it is processed and translated into the medium of film.[75] This is combined, throughout the book, with reminders that Shakespeare wrote primarily for the stage[76] – again, an emphasis to be noted, since Cardim was primarily a literary scholar (and a poet himself). While admiring Olivier's film, he admits from the outset to some misgivings, gradually clarified into a critical argument: he praises Olivier's decision to opt out of a naturalistic set-up to favour, instead, the projection of inner landscapes, a certain lyricism in the treatment of character and circumstance, psychological complexities insinuated through an uncanny ambience; but he finds the actor-director ultimately unable to sustain such options consistently, yielding to an excessive concern with the 'naturalness' of acting styles, and with making the plot as clear-cut as possible.[77]

The rhetoric of the series has a certain oral quality, including asides and snatches of imagined dialogue with Cardim's addressees: this is the voice of the Shakespeare scholar and educator who, before operating in a university classroom, had lectured occasionally at a 'popular university' – and, many years on, even when addressing an audience on the page, enlivens his prose with the echoes of the public lecture room. This quasi-theatrical manner becomes apparent in the opening piece, with a little performative gesture that is also curiously topical: Cardim reveals to his readers that he is holding in his hands a copy of a new journal, which he has just received – none other than 'the

---

[71] Cardim, *Os problemas*, pp. 11, 91.

[72] As when he cites the film magazine *Sight and Sound*: Cardim, *Os problemas*, pp. 86–7.

[73] Cardim, *Os problemas*, pp. 57–70. For access to more recent books in English, Cardim often depended – as he acknowledges in a note of thanks – on the good offices of the British Council (then effectively an instrument of cultural diplomacy) (p. 115).

[74] Cardim, *Os problemas*, p. 58.

[75] Cardim, *Os problemas*, p. 12.

[76] Cardim, *Os problemas*, pp. 20, 56.

[77] Cardim, *Os problemas*, esp. pp. 10–11, 85–95.

first volume of a new and valuable publication, *Shakespeare Survey*, ... edited by the noted critic and drama historian, Prof. Allardyce Nicoll'.[78] The inaugural issue of the *Survey* (1948) focused on 'Shakespeare and his Stage', and Cardim uses it to cite a reticent stage review of Olivier's *Lear* as a mock cue for his own reticent assessment of Olivier's screen *Hamlet*.[79] More than for its actual content, the passage is striking for the lightness with which Cardim wears his learning to retain contact with a broad readership. It is almost as if, decades before the sense of instant communication afforded by digital social media, the lifelong educator could not keep himself from sharing with his readers, as if in 'real time', the exciting hereness of the new Shakespeare journal that had just landed on his table.

BRIEFLY, BY WAY OF CONCLUSION

The pages above have delineated the role played by Shakespeare in a fraught educational and cultural context: the short-lived operation of a new school of humanities, prompted by exalted hopes for 'progress' and human betterment, and its politically sombre but revealing aftermaths. This rise-and-fall pattern finds a protagonist in an accidental academic, a scholar conscripted from a solid schooteaching job (with occasional forays into public lecturing) into the headier but contested territory of the new 'Faculty of Letters' in Porto, only to see his career cut short by the political termination of that School and find himself relegated to an obscure professional afterlife, with some solace in opportunities for publication.

This trajectory, however, is not just a personal – and local – narrative of the fortunes of a lectureship in English (and Shakespeare), but boasts a broader intercultural context, framed by the tense historical bonds between a small country on a European periphery, with an inflated sense of its past greatness, and its oldest ally and occasional nemesis that is just emerging from its heyday of global power. The tensions that shaped Anglo-Portuguese relations in the decades that preceded and enveloped

Portugal's First Republic will have made, at best, reluctant Anglophiles of even those who, like Luís Cardim, had English for their academic remit – and, one suspects, cultural passion. The perception of a historically determined inevitability (combined with a sense of political necessity) prompted Portuguese statesmen to go on courting Britain intensely after both the regicide of 1908 and the republican revolution of 1910, and ensured that in 1916 Portugal (in spite of local adversities) sent an Expeditionary Corps, to a battlefront distant from its own territory, to join the Allies in World War I. It is tempting to postulate that a correlative sense of cultural affinity and necessity helped to secure the relatively prominent presence (from 1919 into the 1920s) of English studies in the curriculum of the new Faculty of Letters in Porto, and of a small but distinguished cohort of English books in the foundational holdings of its library.

At the centre of that library and its academic consequence, of the morality play that is the story of Luís Cardim – indeed, of this whole historical chapter in all its perplexities – we find Shakespeare. As argued in a recent study, if his plays continue to matter to us, it will have to be, crucially, because 'Shakespeare means freedom', in the complex latitude of the word's range of meanings.[80] The scholarly outcomes fostered by the Shakespeariana in the 'Fundo Primitivo' narrate a story of release – a release into enhanced intellectual consequence, with personal and communal benefit, epitomized in Cardim's trajectory. In him, indeed, we read the tale of a scholar who found in Shakespeare not just an instrument for formal education and 'popular instruction' – the great ideal of a Republic of Letters – but also a cultural and imaginative force that liberated him from inconsequence and oblivion, the worst adversities for those who commit to the life of the imagination.

---

[78] Cardim, *Os problemas*, p. 10.

[79] The review in question was included in Charles Landstone, 'Four Lears', *Shakespeare Survey* (Cambridge, 1948), 98–102.

[80] Ewan Fernie, *Shakespeare for Freedom: Why the Plays Matter* (Cambridge, 2017), p. 1.

CULTURAL INCLUSIVITY AND STUDENT SHAKESPEARE PERFORMANCES IN LATE-COLONIAL SINGAPORE, 1950–1959

EMILY SOON[1]

An important part of the ongoing quest to make literary education more inclusive has involved recognizing the individuals who have enriched Shakespeare studies over the years. This includes acknowledging the students and teachers operating within that most unlikely of places: the colonial school. While Gauri Viswanathan argued that, in British India, 'the Eurocentric literary curriculum of the nineteenth century' was 'a vital, active instrument of Western hegemony',[2] a growing number of critics have drawn attention to the ways in which the students and teachers within the colonial English literature classroom refused to accept imperial diktat, and instead re-interpreted Shakespeare on their own terms. Writing about Shakespeare performances in colonial Malaysian and Filipino schools, Judy Ick notes that performing Shakespeare gave students 'the power to subject colonial culture to critical evaluation';[3] Nurul Farhana Low bt. Abdullah has discerned suggestive nationalist undertones within the Malay Shakespeare productions staged by the students of Sultan Idris Training College in 1930s Malaysia;[4] and Harish Trivedi has contended that some English-educated Indians considered it their 'patriotic duty ... to disparage and debunk' Shakespeare's legacy.[5] Analysing the contributions made by Irish, South African and Burmese representatives to *A Book of Homage to Shakespeare*, published to commemorate the 1916 Shakespeare tercentenary, Coppélia Kahn similarly observes that these educated colonial subjects consistently presented their national heritage as being as deserving of recognition as Shakespeare was.[6] Cumulatively, this scholarship has enriched our understanding of how students and teachers across the colonial world productively placed Shakespeare's legacy into conversation with their own traditions, thereby making literary studies a more diverse discipline.

However, not all outposts of empire possessed a shared indigenous culture that could be meaningfully compared with Shakespeare. To return to Bill Ashcroft, Gareth Griffiths and Helen Tiffin's foundational observation, the 'post-colonial experience' – which the authors define as beginning 'from the moment of colonization' – is a 'syncretic and hybridized' one.[7] This is particularly true of colonial cities from Philadelphia to Penang, where the native population could be outnumbered – often substantially – by

---

[1] I thank the National Museum of Singapore for the Research Fellowship that enabled this study. I am similarly grateful to the National Archives of Singapore, the National Library Board and the National University of Singapore for granting me archival access, and to the anonymous *Shakespeare Survey* reviewer for the helpful feedback.

[2] Gauri Viswanathan, *Masks of Conquest: Literary Study and British Rule in India* (New York, 2014), pp. 166–7.

[3] Judy Celine Ick, 'Performing Shakespeare in colonial Southeast Asia', *Asian Scholar* 3 (n.d.), unpaginated.

[4] Nurul Farhana Low bt. Abdullah, 'The politics of Shakespeare translation and publication in Malaya', *Tradução em Revista* 12 (2012), 39–60.

[5] Harish Trivedi, *Colonial Transactions: English Literature and India* (Manchester, 1995), p. 14.

[6] Coppélia Kahn, 'Remembering Shakespeare imperially: the 1916 tercentenary', *Shakespeare Quarterly* 14 (2001), 456–78.

[7] Bill Ashcroft, Gareth Griffiths and Helen Tiffin, *The Empire Writes Back: Theory and Practice in Post-Colonial Literatures* (London, 2002), pp. 40, 2, 40.

167

an eclectic mix of migrant workers. Therefore, rather than continue the current critical investigation into Shakespeare education's capacity to elicit a renewed commitment to an existing native heritage, this article explores instead the potential for students and teachers to use Shakespeare as a platform to create a new cultural identity for both the school and the nascent state by drawing together the varied migrant groups and cultures within the colonial city. To apply Douglas Lanier's useful characterization of the 'vast web of adaptations, allusions and (re)productions that comprises the ever-changing cultural phenomenon we call "Shakespeare"' as a 'rhizome',[8] this article focuses on the intersections between the 'Shakespearean rhizome' and the broader cultural systems within society, tracing how student Shakespeare performances helped to forge links between previously disconnected parts of the community, thereby augmenting both the Shakespearian and societal networks.

This article concentrates on a former British colony whose early engagement with Shakespeare education has received scant attention: Singapore, an island located south of the Malaysian peninsula. Sir Stamford Raffles established a British colonial presence in Singapore in 1819; the port-city gained self-governance in 1959, and, after briefly merging with the Federation of Malaysia in 1963, became fully independent in 1965. Singapore is a nation shaped by immigration. A 1957 population census noted that the 'most striking fact' about the city-state was 'its cosmopolitan nature', a result of people coming from 'most parts of the world' to 'trade and settle' in this entrepôt hub.[9] In the mid twentieth century, migrants from China made up the largest proportion of the population (75.4%), with the indigenous Malays comprising 13.6%, Indians and Pakistanis 8.6%, and the remaining 2.4% consisting of smaller groups such as the Eurasians, Europeans, 'Ceylonese' (Sri Lankans), Arabs, Nepalese, Jews, Filipinos, Thais, Japanese and Burmese.[10] Singapore-based theatre practitioners and scholars have made significant contributions to the field of Asian Shakespeare in recent decades. Singaporean director Ong Keng Sen's Shakespearian adaptations

(LEAR (1997), Desdemona (2000) and Search: Hamlet (2002)) have received international attention,[11] and the Asian Shakespeare Intercultural Archive, led by Yong Li Lan, continues to advance scholarship and teaching in the field.[12] However, Singapore's connections with Shakespeare in the early to mid twentieth century remain largely overlooked,[13] with this critical neglect perhaps perpetuated by twentieth-century Singapore's unflattering reputation as a 'cultural desert'.[14]

Yet Shakespeare formed a core part of the educational experience for students in twentieth-century Singapore's English-medium schools. During the 1950s, the decade when Singapore's nationalists fought for, and won, self-governance, the English education system expanded rapidly, and with it the vogue for Shakespeare performances by secondary and pre-university students. As this article will argue, through creating space for Singapore's migrant communities and their cultures within their Shakespeare productions, the students and teachers of 1950s Singapore helped to make the English

---

8 Douglas Lanier, 'Shakespearean rhizomatics: adaptation, ethics, value', in Shakespeare and the Ethics of Appropriation, ed. Alexa Alice Joubin and Elizabeth Rivlin (New York, 2014), pp. 21–40; p. 29.
9 Chua Seng Chew, Report on the Census of Population 1957 (Singapore, 1964), p. 68.
10 Chua, Report, pp. 68, 71.
11 See, for instance, Yong Li Lan, 'Ong Keng Sen's "Desdemona", ugliness, and the intercultural performative', Theatre Journal 56.2 (2004), 251–73. In this article, Chinese names are given surname first followed by given name(s).
12 Asian Shakespeare Intercultural Archive (A|S|I|A): http://a-s-i-a-web.org.
13 For a concise history of Shakespeare in Singapore, see Yong Li Lan, 'Singapore', in The Oxford Companion to Shakespeare, 2nd edn, ed. Michael Dobson, Stanley Wells, Will Sharpe and Erin Sullivan (Oxford, 2015), p. 503. On Chicken Rice War (2000), a Singaporean film adaptation of Romeo and Juliet, see Yong Li Lan, 'Romeos and Juliets, local/global', in Shakespeare's Local Habitations, ed. Krystyna Kujawinska Courtney and R. S. White (Łódź, 2007), pp. 135–54, and Mark Thornton Burnett, Shakespeare and World Cinema (Cambridge, 2012), pp. 126–59.
14 C. J. Wan-ling Wee, The Asian Modern: Culture, Capitalist Development, Singapore (Hong Kong, 2007), p. 12.

school system – and, by extension, Singapore society itself – more inclusive. Colonial Shakespeare education, this article suggests, thus functions as an unexpected catalyst for the creation of a new national culture. This article begins with an overview of the factors that enabled Shakespeare to play this transformative role in Singapore, before exploring a series of school performances. I look first at a 1950 production of *Twelfth Night*, staged at a point when English schools were considered a vital platform for building social cohesion and combating communism. Next, I interrogate the fashion for students to participate in Shakespeare performances that utilized Chinese opera costumes and performance styles, and which sometimes rendered the dialogue in Singlish, the colloquial form of English spoken in Singapore.

These school Shakespeare performances extend and complicate our existing understanding of the connections between colonial Shakespeare education and the development of Asian nationalism. Dennis Kennedy and Yong Li Lan have proposed three broad 'explanations' for Asian Shakespeare productions – namely, 'colonial instigation', where an imperial overlord mandates the performances; 'nationalist appropriation', in which Shakespeare is staged by local groups keen to reform society; and 'intercultural revision', where Asian cultural forms are used to dramatize Shakespeare in a 'self-consciously aesthetic' manner.[15] Yong and Kennedy observe that the three categories are 'not mutually exclusive';[16] the school Shakespeare productions discussed in this article amply testify to the complex connections between the trio. Despite being organized to comply with the curriculum first designed by the colonial authorities, the intercultural dimension within many of these performances can be said to serve the ongoing nationalist bid to forge a new identity for this emergent state, testifying to the considerable creative independence exhibited by students and teachers in 1950s Singapore, and to the broader capacity for Shakespeare education to facilitate cultural change in classrooms across the world.

***

Two interlinked factors enabled school Shakespeare performances to foster social cohesion in late-colonial Singapore. The first was the strong desire among people in Singapore – particularly young people – to create a new, syncretic culture that the island's disparate ethnic groups could identify with. As a group of undergraduates at the University of Malaya in Singapore discerned in 1950, 'the way to nationhood is through the way to culture',[17] a statement that prefigures Benedict Anderson's conception of the nation as an 'imagined community' held together by a sense of 'deep, horizontal comradeship' and 'fraternity'.[18] Since Singapore's heterogeneous society was divided by race and language, the island-city had no shared heritage with which to create this sense of belonging. Rather than allow 'any of the main cultural streams' present in Singapore to gain 'predominance' over the others, the undergraduates argued that a new 'common culture' was needed, which was to be created from 'a synthesis between' the 'conflicting currents' generated by the island's diverse communities.[19] Singapore's undergraduates perceived that they had a personal part to play in creating this pioneering identity, with an association of medical students writing elsewhere that they 'hope[d]' their literary efforts would help to create 'Malayan thought' (since nationalists in 1950s Singapore envisioned that the island would permanently unite with present-day Malaysia to create an independent state, the undergraduates used the term 'Malayan' rather than 'Singaporean' to describe this cultural ideal).[20] These medical students were not alone in their conviction that they, as youths, were instrumental in this nation-building endeavour:

[15] Dennis Kennedy and Yong Li Lan, 'Introduction: why Shakespeare?' in *Shakespeare in Asia: Contemporary Performance*, ed. Dennis Kennedy and Yong Li Lan (Cambridge, 2010), pp. 1–23; pp. 7–11.
[16] Kennedy and Yong, 'Introduction', p. 7.
[17] 'The way to nationhood', *New Cauldron* (Hilary Term 1949–50), 6.
[18] Benedict Anderson, *Imagined Communities: Reflections on the Origin and Spread of Nationalism* (London, 2006), pp. 24, 7.
[19] 'The way', p. 6.
[20] 'Editorial', *Cauldron* 3.1 (March 1949), 1.

articles in 1950s school magazines repeatedly remind students that it is they who would shape Singapore's future.[21]

Secondly, the dominant place Shakespeare occupied in Singapore's English school system, and the rapid pace at which the system expanded in the 1950s allowed Shakespeare's plays to serve as a ready platform for young people in Singapore to experiment with creating this new national culture. This is somewhat ironic, given that Singapore's colonial schools, which were run either by the government or by private, often faith-based, organizations, had used Shakespeare to rally support for the British empire earlier in the century. For the prize-giving ceremony at St Joseph's Institution in 1900, for instance, the school stage had been decorated with what the press described as 'a monster Union Jack'. A 'portrait of Shakespeare ... was suspended directly underneath' the flag, creating a visual statement fusing these symbols of British nationalism.[22] The Victoria Day celebrations at Raffles Girls' School in 1904 similarly used Shakespeare to foster a sense of loyalty towards the British crown. Victoria Day (later renamed Empire Day) was an annual celebration of the late Queen Victoria and her empire. That year, some of the girls 'recited' *Richard II* as part of their school concert.[23] Including this performance, which may have been twentieth-century Singapore's first school Shakespeare production,[24] within the propagandistic Victoria Day celebrations further strengthened the playwright's imperial associations. For Philip Holden, Suzanne Choo and Adeline Koh, the broader English language and literature curriculum used in 1930s Singapore was likewise geared towards maintaining colonialism.[25] That said, Shakespeare was not solely taught in order to strengthen the empire: studying the playwright's works was also believed to 'greatly improve' students' English, as the principal of St Joseph's Institution declared in 1902.[26]

By the 1950s, the political situation had changed. India had gained independence in 1947, and the British were willing to acknowledge publicly that Singapore would also 'eventually ... manage its own affairs', even if the nature and timing of the island's political emancipation remained disputed.[27] Nonetheless, Shakespeare remained a central part of the Singapore school syllabus. At the School Certificate examination, taken by all students in Singapore and much of the British Commonwealth upon completion of their secondary school education, the post-war English Literature paper featured a compulsory Shakespeare question.[28] Traces of the pre-war push to use Shakespeare to inculcate allegiance to the British empire remained. In 1951, the privately run Mercantile Institution taught students using *The Pupils' Class-Book of English History*. The exercises within this textbook repeatedly asked students to 'Learn ... verses' from Shakespeare's plays that portrayed Britain in a triumphant light, such as John of Gaunt's speech in *Richard II* where England is exalted as 'This royal throne of kings, this sceptered isle, ... / This blessed plot, this earth, this realm, this England' (2.1.40–50).[29] However, the bulk of the other extant Shakespeare teaching aids used in post-war Singapore are largely free from such jingoism. W. A. Illsley's *Shakespeare Manual for Malayan Schools*

---

[21] See, for instance, John Young, 'Foreword', and Velauthar Ambiavagar, 'Farewell message', *Rafflesian*, 29.1 (May 1955), pp. ii–iii; and Alexander Oppenheim, 'Foreword', *Rafflesian*, 31 no. 2 (November 1957), p. vii.

[22] 'St. Joseph's Institution', *Singapore Free Press and Mercantile Advertiser*, 22 January 1900, 3.

[23] 'Victoria Day', *Straits Times*, 25 May 1904, 1.

[24] On nineteenth-century student Shakespeare performances in Singapore, see the *Singapore Free Press and Mercantile Advertiser*, 31 December 1894, 8.

[25] Philip Holden, 'On the nation's margins: the social place of literature in Singapore', *Sojourn: Journal of Social Issues in Southeast Asia* 15 (2000), 30–51; Suzanne Choo, 'Globalizing literature education in Singapore: reviewing developments and re-envisioning possibilities for the future', in *Literature Education in the Asia-Pacific: Policies, Practices and Perspectives in Global Times*, ed. Loh Chin Ee, Suzanne Choo and Catherine Beavis (New York, 2018), pp. 224–37; Adeline Koh, 'Educating Malayan gentlemen: establishing an anglicized elite in twentieth-century colonial Malaya', *BiblioAsia* 3 (2007), 10–15.

[26] 'St Joseph's Institution Prize Distribution', *Straits Times*, 24 December 1902, 5.

[27] A. W. Frisby, in *Education Week* (Singapore, 1950), unpaginated.

[28] University of Cambridge Local Examinations Syndicate, *Subject Syllabus EL(O)* (Cambridge, 1974), p. 5.

[29] E. J. S. Lay, *The Pupils' Class-Book of English History. Book II: The Tudors* (London, 1950), p. 102.

(1957), for instance, concentrates on the requirements of the School Certificate examination, not the bygone glories of the British empire.[30]

During the post-war years, an ever-growing number of young people in Singapore enrolled in English schools. The wartime Japanese Occupation of Singapore (1942–5) had wreaked havoc on the education system: the Japanese had closed all English schools, repurposed many of their buildings and destroyed their textbooks.[31] Educational reconstruction hence ranked highly on the government's list of post-war priorities. In January 1950, the British announced the Five Year Supplementary Plan, which aimed to build enough schools to allow 'nearly 200,000' additional children to receive a primary-level English education, a policy that naturally resulted in an increasing number of secondary-level students over time.[32] As Sai Siew-Min has argued, this policy was prompted by the government's fear that Singapore would fall sway to the rising tide of communism that was sweeping across Asia, as was evident from Mao Zedong's October 1949 establishment of the People's Republic of China, as well as the ongoing guerrilla war waged in Singapore by the Malayan Communist Party since 1948, which aimed to turn the island into a communist state.[33] The communists in Singapore and Malaysia were reliant on the Chinese community for support, with the Chinese supplying the jungle-based fighters with food, and Chinese-medium schools in Singapore serving as hotbeds of communist activity.[34] Consequently, the British believed that it was imperative to reduce the political influence wielded by Chinese-medium schools by swiftly increasing the enrolment within their English-medium counterparts, which the government felt could help to inculcate a sense of 'civic-mindedness' and mould Singapore's young people into 'a loyal citizenry'.[35]

The Singaporean leaders who increasingly took over the reins of government from the British as the island prepared for self-governance in 1959 continued to support the expansion of English schools, albeit for different reasons. Although English was then spoken only by a minority of the city-state's residents, Singapore's first prime minister, Lee Kuan Yew, chose the language to be the island's lingua franca, because it provided Singapore's diverse racial groups with a relatively neutral language to communicate with. In contrast, choosing to make one of the vernacular languages (such as Mandarin, Malay or Tamil) Singapore's language of government and business would have exacerbated ethnic divides and fostered resentment among the diverse groups. English could also give the fledgling state an economic edge by enabling Singaporeans to participate in global commercial networks.[36] Parents were well aware that an English education could provide their offspring with good employment prospects, and, correspondingly, there was a robust demand for places in English schools.[37]

Unlikely as it may sound, studying English Literature at School Certificate level – a task that necessarily involved studying Shakespeare – was perceived to prepare students for the brave new post-war world, and the subject was therefore popular. Educators remained convinced that increased exposure to literary works could enhance students' mastery of English. Writing to the Ministry of Education in 1957, Velauthar Ambiavagar, then principal of Raffles Institution, a leading boys' school, emphasized that it was 'well known that the chief way to teach or learn

---

30 See, further, W. A. Illsley, *Shakespeare Manual for Malayan Schools* (Cambridge, 1957), p. 52 onwards.

31 H. E. Wilson, 'The implications of Japanese educational policy in Singapore', in *Social Engineering in Singapore: Educational Policies and Social Change, 1819–1972* (Singapore, 1978), pp. 85–113.

32 Frisby in *Education Week*.

33 Sai Siew-Min, 'Educating multicultural citizens: colonial nationalism, imperial citizenship and education in late colonial Singapore', *Journal of Southeast Asian Studies*, 44 (2013), 49–73; pp. 65–7.

34 Wilson, *Social Engineering*, pp. 166–7.

35 Sai, 'Educating', p. 66.

36 Lionel Wee, *The Singlish Controversy: Language, Culture and Identity in a Globalizing World* (Cambridge, 2018), pp. 22–4.

37 Department of Education, *Annual Report of the Department of Education for the Year 1952* (Singapore, 1952), p. 15.

a language is through more intensive study of Literature'.[38] Moreover, a School Certificate pass in English Literature was required for numerous university, scholarship and job applications. This applied even for positions that had little intrinsic connection to the subject: right into the 1960s, scholarships for occupational therapy,[39] courses on radiology[40] and jobs in sales required applicants to have mastered English literature.[41] Consequently, the subject was well subscribed, and most of the School Certificate cohorts at Raffles Institution appear to have sat for the English Literature examination during the 1950s.[42]

A popular way of preparing School Certificate pupils for their Shakespeare paper was to get students to stage the plays. Educators in Singapore had been encouraged to incorporate drama within their Shakespeare curriculum for decades. The syllabus, or Education Code, used in Singapore just before the war recommended that local students should 'act a scene from the play', and that teachers should refer to The Teaching of Shakespeare in Schools, a pamphlet first published by the English Association in London in 1908, for more guidance.[43] This pamphlet had recommended that students perform Shakespeare, because 'The living voice will often give a clue to the meaning, and reading aloud is the only way of ensuring knowledge of the metre.'[44] Illsley's Shakespeare Manual further highlighted the merits of 'taking parts' and 'reading the play aloud ... in class'.[45] Performing Shakespeare was an especially valuable experience for students in mid-twentieth-century Singapore because at that point the island did not have any professional English theatre companies. Students could sometimes watch Shakespeare productions by amateur theatrical groups, such as the Teachers' Repertory and the Stage Club, or attend professional productions by touring companies.[46] However, local students were not always permitted to attend these productions: in 1945, a mere twenty local undergraduates were admitted to Sir John Gielgud's visiting performance of Hamlet, and this only on the condition that they served as ushers.[47] Under such circumstances, the most effective way to ensure that students could

watch a live Shakespeare performance was for schools to produce one themselves.

This is precisely what students in Singapore did. Before World War II, these performances were often held as part of a larger school event, such as the annual concert or Victoria or Empire Day celebrations. These pre-war shows typically featured costumes and stage-sets that 'attempt[ed] to recapture the conditions' in which the plays had been 'originally presented' in Elizabethan times, as St Andrew's School did in 1937.[48] When the English education system re-started after the war, these pre-war productions

---

[38] Letter from Velauthar Ambiavagar to Chief Examinations Officer, Ministry of Education, 10 December 1957, 1107/53, National Archives of Singapore (NAS).

[39] 'Public appointments', Straits Times, 27 April 1963, 17.

[40] Ken Hammonds, 'If you don't like to be a nurse, choose radiology', Straits Times, 31 December 1961, 3.

[41] 'Are you a well educated lady with a strong, friendly personality?' Straits Times, 1 February 1963, 15; 'Books books books', Straits Times, 1 February 1963, 15.

[42] For instance, in 1954, 171 students sat for English Literature, out of the total cohort of 201 students who sat for English Language. 'Cambridge School Certificate results', Rafflesian 29.1 (May 1955), 45. In 1958, 199 students sat for English Literature, the same number that sat for English Language: 'Cambridge School Certificate results', Rafflesian 33.1 (July 1959), 60.

[43] Education Department, Education Code Part III (Straits Settlements and Federated Malay States) (Singapore, 1936), p. 10.

[44] Cited in Tracy Irish, Teaching Shakespeare: A History of the Teaching of Shakespeare in England (Stratford-on-Avon, 2008), p. 2.

[45] Illsley, Shakespeare, p. 52.

[46] On the Teachers' Repertory, see 'S'pore schools plan Macbeth', Straits Times, 11 April 1948, 3. Students performed alongside teachers in Repertory productions. On student attendance at Stage Club Shakespeare productions, see, for instance, the National Museum of Singapore's copy of the poster for the Stage Club's 1964 Twelfth Night (Accession No. 2015–02145). On students attending touring Shakespeare performances, see, for instance, Loh Chee Harn, 'Sybil Thorndike and Lewis Casson recital', RGS Magazine (1955), 20–1.

[47] Lloyd Fernando, 'Theatre', Write, no. 1 (December 1957), p. 8; 'Famous Artistes Here for ENSA Shows', Malaya Tribune, 13 December 1945, p. 4.

[48] 'Elizabethan atmosphere for schoolboys "Julius Caesar"', Straits Times, 15 November 1937, 13.

appear to have faded from collective memory: in May 1950, the press asserted that Victoria School's new production of *Twelfth Night* was 'the first attempt by [the] schoolboys of Singapore to stage a complete Shakespearean play', and that previously 'students have only produced isolated scenes'.[49] Given that there are multiple accounts of students dramatizing Shakespearian plays (as opposed to scenes) before the war, this claim is probably mistaken, but it is nonetheless indicative of the extent to which schools of the 1950s perceived their Shakespeare productions to be pioneering. Victoria School's *Twelfth Night*, which I will look at in more detail in the next section, was swiftly followed by a plethora of others, igniting a fashion for school Shakespeare performances that would last for the next quarter-century. For instance, from 1953 onwards, the Raffles Players, the joint dramatic society of Raffles Institution and Raffles Girls' School, regularly staged Shakespeare.[50] When Singapore's Ministry of Education organized Shakespeare Week in August 1959, seven schools pitched in to stage six different plays.[51] Overwhelmingly, schools dramatized the texts set for the School Certificate examination each year, and either did so in the school hall or at external venues such as the Cultural Centre or Victoria Theatre, inviting students from other schools to watch.[52]

Records of these 1950s performances are sketchy, but surviving newspaper articles, school magazines and oral history interviews indicate that schools worked hard to make their productions as elaborate as possible. The Raffles Players' 1958 production of *Henry V*, for instance, had a cast of 'sixty girls and boys', of whom thirty were clad in home-made suits of aluminium armour. Aided by the school Art Club, the Players also produced 'a considerable number of stage sets' and 'gorgeous costumes'. The production ran for six nights at the Cultural Centre and was watched by 'Over 2,100 people'.[53] On occasion, schools would stage plays by other dramatists, such as George Bernard Shaw or James Bridie,[54] but Shakespeare was easily the playwright whose works were most frequently acted by local students, making the school Shakespeare production the most common platform for the island's young people to express

themselves dramatically. In contrast to the pre-war productions, many of the 1950s productions exercised a considerable degree of innovation in terms of performance location, costume, style and dialogue, as the next two sections will discuss.

***

In 1950, 8–13 May was designated Education Week in Singapore. During this week, 'all Singapore school-children . . . participate[d] in a series of exhibitions, mass rallies' and other activities designed 'to show the progress, expansion and future plans of the Singapore education department'.[55] In the words of Singapore's governor, Franklin Gimson, this Week served as 'propaganda for democracy and consequently against practising Communism'.[56] Given Shakespeare's central role in the English school system, a performance of one of his plays was naturally included within the programme.[57] The young men of Victoria School staged their production of *Twelfth Night* in the Alkaff Gardens, a public recreational site established by the Arab businessman Syed Shaik Alkaff that featured large trees, sloping lawns and a lake.[58] While the *Singapore Free Press*'s assertion that the production was Singapore's first complete school Shakespeare performance is likely mistaken, Victoria School can probably justly claim to have

49 Ruth Langdon, 'Enter three Cupids – with scenery', *Singapore Free Press and Mercantile Advertiser*, 12 May 1950, 5.

50 'A brief history of the Raffles Players', *Rafflesian* 46.1 (1975–6), 79–80.

51 'Shakespeare Week in schools was so busy', *Singapore Free Press*, 24 August 1959, 7.

52 Marie Ethel Bong, interview by Jesley Chua Chee Huan, NAS Oral History Centre, Accession Number 001390, Reel 62.

53 Velauthar Ambiavagar, 'The Principal's review', *Rafflesian* 32.2 (November 1958), 5; 'Raffles Players', *Rafflesian* 32.2 (November 1958), 78.

54 'A brief history of the Raffles Players', 79.

55 '"Education Week" to open soon', *Straits Times*, 2 May 1950, 4.

56 Franklin Gimson, cited in Sai, 'Educating', p. 66.

57 *Education Week*.

58 Gary Maurice Dwor-Frecaut, 'Alkaff Lake Gardens', *Singapore Infopedia* (Singapore, 2010): https://eresources.nlb.gov.sg/infopedia/articles/SIP_604_2005-01-24.html.

mounted the first such post-war show. More importantly, Victoria School's *Twelfth Night* is groundbreaking in that it publicly enacted a vision of the new, cohesive society the British government hoped to create within the expanded English school system, and, by extension, Singapore as a whole.

The composition of the cast was central to staging this societal ideal. The press noted that the 'young actors' came from 'five different communities' and were 'Chinese, Ceylonese, Indian, Malay, [and] Arab', with the boys taking on female parts as per Elizabethan tradition.[59] The multiracial cast may not immediately appear noteworthy, for it seems logical to assume that young people growing up in Singapore would have been used to interacting with members of different races. This was not necessarily so: since establishing a colonial presence on the island in 1819, the British had broadly pursued a divide-and-rule ethnic policy, and Singapore's different racial groups largely lived in separate enclaves.[60] English schools had provided a rare platform for the 'gathering of children of many races',[61] but until the 1950s, only a select few were able to attend such institutions,[62] and the young people who enrolled in the vernacular Chinese-, Malay- or Tamil-medium schools were likely to mix mainly with members of their own ethnic group. The expansion of the English school system from 1950 onwards was therefore instrumental in facilitating 'inter-racial mingling'.[63] Victoria School's *Twelfth Night* served as a high-profile platform to publicize this new societal development, with the manner in which the production featured indigenous Malay youths performing alongside migrants from East and South Asia, as well as the Middle East, emphasizing the extent of ethnic integration within English schools.

The choice of performance location likewise contributed to this utopic vision. The school made good use of the available environs, 'mov[ing] up and down' the 'grassy banks' with ease.[64] At one point, a 'dripping sailor emerged' from the lake, presumably accompanying the shipwrecked Viola as she arrives on the coast of Illyria in Act 1, Scene 2.[65] In Britain, Shakespeare had been performed in the open since the late nineteenth century at

least,[66] and the Singapore press had duly reported on such Western productions,[67] with at least one Singapore-based school catering to European children staging Shakespearian scenes outdoors.[68] Yet Victoria School's decision to mount their production in the open was far from a straightforward case of a colonial institution replicating a Western trend. Staging a performance in which the multicultural cast gambol across the gardens and blend in with their natural surroundings perfectly exemplifies the government's vision that English schools would help Singapore's migrant communities to integrate into Southeast Asia. Furthermore, at a time when the Malayan Communist Party had made the jungle their stronghold, using it as a base for their armed resistance movement, the performance reclaimed this green space on behalf of the English-speaking authorities who funded the school, allowing all who saw or read about the event to draw their own distinctions between the activities of the jungle-based communist fighters and the wholesome, cultured entertainment provided when English schools took over Singapore's landscape. For members of the public attuned to cultural developments in China, it would have also been noteworthy that this Shakespearian performance was staged in English. Because Karl Marx and

[59] Derek Drabble, 'Midsummer madness at Alkaff Gardens', *Singapore Free Press*, 19 May 1950, 5.

[60] Brenda S. A. Yeoh, *Contesting Space in Colonial Singapore: Power Relations and the Urban Built Environment* (Singapore, 2003), pp. 40–8.

[61] 'Raffles Girls' School Prize Day', *Eastern Daily Mail and Straits Morning Advertiser*, 23 December 1905, 3.

[62] H. E. Wilson, 'Educational policy prior to the Pacific War', in *Social*, pp. 29–84.

[63] Sai, 'Educating', p. 66. [64] Drabble, 'Midsummer', p. 5.

[65] Clarissa Oon, *Theatre Life! A History of English-Language Theatre in Singapore through the 'Straits Times' (1958–2000)* (Singapore, 2001), p. 36.

[66] Michael Dobson, *Shakespeare and Amateur Performance: A Cultural History* (Cambridge, 2013), pp. 164–5.

[67] See, for instance, Mary Heathcott, 'A woman's diary', *Singapore Free Press and Mercantile Advertiser*, 27 September 1940, 5.

[68] 'Natural setting for "A Midsummer Night's Dream"', *Morning Tribune*, 14 September 1940, 4.

Friedrich Engels 'approv[ed]' of Shakespeare, the communist leaders of the People's Republic of China prioritized the Chinese translation and performance of Shakespeare's works across the 1950s, thereby appropriating Shakespeare for their communist state.[69] In contrast, Victoria School's *Twelfth Night* was in English, underscoring that in Singapore, Shakespeare and the young people who studied him were allies of Western democracy, not East Asian communism.

Apart from being all-male, Victoria School's *Twelfth Night* epitomized the type of cohesive, multicultural Asian society the British government hoped English schools could help to create. However, the production is perhaps best viewed as enacting a relatively limited vision for Singapore's future – one in which the colonial authorities maintained their influence over the city-state. The student actors were directed by their British teacher, Shamus Frazer, and were dressed in the European-style 'cloaks, doublets and hose' he designed.[70] Tellingly, when 'one young boy' who had been tasked to produce his own costume 'turned up with a *sarong* and *kebaya*', two distinctively Malay items of clothing, Frazer said he had the student's clothes altered so that 'it looks less now as if he were going to visit the Sultan Mosque and more like *Twelfth Night*'.[71] The decision to use Western-style costumes could have been a purely pedagogical one, made to help students in tropical Singapore better visualize the play's original socio-cultural context. Nonetheless, dressing students in doublets and hose still had the effect of immersing students in Western culture. Victoria School's *Twelfth Night* is therefore perhaps most accurately described as exemplifying the type of controlled cultural independence that the British were keen to see take root in Singapore, one in which the island's diverse members allowed their varied native cultures to be refashioned, like the student's *kebaya*, into a pattern derived from, and approved by, the colonial authorities.

***

Where many of the student Shakespeare productions that came after the 1950 *Twelfth Night* followed Victoria School's lead in utilizing Renaissance-style

costumes, a considerable number did not. Instead, schools looked to Asia for inspiration when deciding how their student actors should dress, move and speak. In so doing, Singapore schools can perhaps be considered to have staged early experiments in intercultural theatre, in which Shakespeare's text is dramatized using Asian performance traditions.[72] Where intercultural theatre is often 'self-consciously aesthetic',[73] in late-colonial Singapore, the incorporation of Asian cultural elements within student drama made a 'symbolic' statement that helped to redress existing cultural inequalities, as an anonymous contributor to the Raffles Institution school magazine observed.[74] British colonialism had perpetuated the belief that Western culture was superior to its Asian counterpart, as captured in the Victorian imperialist Thomas Babington Macaulay's 1835 assertion that 'a single shelf of a good European library was worth the whole native literature of India and Arabia'.[75] To the extent that the literature curriculum in colonial Singapore's English schools chiefly focused on Western rather than Eastern classics, these institutions can be said to have shared Macaulay's Eurocentric bias and to have functioned as centres for imperial culture within Asia. By incorporating Eastern elements within their Shakespeare productions, the students and teachers in these institutions counter this misplaced assumption. To employ Salman Rushdie's phrase, the students and teachers 'writ[e] back' to the colonial 'centre', asserting that the previously marginalized cultures that flourished within Singapore's migrant society were as worthy of being celebrated on the English stage as the works of Shakespeare himself.[76]

[69] Li Ruru, *Shashibiya: Staging Shakespeare in China* (Hong Kong, 2003), pp. 44–50.

[70] Drabble, 'Midsummer', p. 5. [71] Langdon, 'Enter', p. 5.

[72] See, further, Catherine Diamond, *Communities of Imagination: Contemporary Southeast Asian Theatre* (Honolulu, 2012), p. 17.

[73] Kennedy and Yong, 'Introduction', p. 10.

[74] 'Rafflesian notebook', *Rafflesian* 28.1 (April 1954), 32.

[75] Thomas Babington Macaulay, 'Minute on education', in *Literature and Nation: Britain and India 1800–1990*, ed. Richard Allen and Harish Trivedi (London, 2000), pp. 198–205; p. 199.

[76] Salman Rushdie, cited in Ashcroft et al., *Empire*, p. 32.

The most popular way students and teachers incorporated Asian culture within their Shakespeare performances was via costumes and performance styles taken from the Chinese opera, or *wayang*, to adopt the Malay term used locally to refer to the art form.[77] In 1952, Mr Seah Yun Chong, who taught English to the Singapore Police Force, directed a production of *As You Like It* in which a mixed cast of students, educators and other enthusiasts from a range of institutions performed in the 'long, flowing, multi-coloured Chinese costumes' 'borrow[ed] ... from a Chinese "*wayang*"', accompanied by specially written 'music with an Eastern air'.[78] Professor Koh Tai Ann likewise recollects collaborating with her schoolmates at Crescent Girls' School to 'd[o] both *Macbeth* and *A Midsummer Night's Dream* dressed in Chinese opera-style costumes',[79] with the latter production taking place in 1958.[80] Mrs Rosie Lim, a teacher and RADA-trained amateur actress similarly recalls working with her students at Bartley School to produce an adaptation of the tale of Pyramus and Thisbe, the play staged by Bottom and his compatriots in *A Midsummer Night's Dream*.[81] Lim's daughter Stella Kon, author of the iconic Singaporean play *Emily of Emerald Hill*, remembers watching this performance as a child in the 1950s.[82] Kon recollects that it was 'a very localized version' staged in the '*wayang* style', noting that watching the Bartley performance inspired her youthful self to write an adaptation of *Romeo and Juliet* in rhyming couplets, which her classmates then staged – also in the 'Chinese *wayang* style' – for a school concert at Raffles Girls' Primary School. To help bridge the cultural divide between the play's European origins and the world of Chinese opera, Kon appears to have Sinicized the names of Shakespeare's lovers. As Kon recalls, in her adaptation, 'Romeo' was pronounced as 'Lo Me Oh', and 'Juliet' as 'Zhu Li Et', with the alteration of 'R' to 'L' and 'J' to 'Zh' replicating the way native Chinese-speakers tended to articulate these English consonants.[83]

Staging Shakespeare using Chinese opera costumes and performance styles in the 1950s is not itself pioneering, for actors in China had been performing *xiqu* or Chinese opera versions of Shakespeare 'since the early twentieth century'.[84]

Doing so in Singapore's English schools, however, was. Where the idea of Chinese opera may today conjure up images of an elite, courtly art form, the variety of *xiqu* that was most visible in twentieth-century Singapore was the street opera, or *jiexi*. Performed on makeshift outdoor stages by the roadside or within Chinese temples, and paid for by religious, community or business organizations, the *jiexi* provided the casual crowds who drifted by with free, popular entertainment, usually in the audience's native Hokkien, Teochew or Cantonese dialects.[85] Although Chinese-speakers easily formed Singapore's largest community, they remained on the city's economic and political margins, for these recent migrants lacked the English language skills required for the well-paid, influential positions open to Asians in government and business.[86] This created a marked societal divide and a 'mutual wariness, or even animosity' between the English- and Chinese-educated Chinese.[87] The former were 'despise[d] ... for

[77] Arnold Perris, 'Chinese *wayang*: the survival of Chinese opera in the streets of Singapore', *Ethnomusicology* 22.2 (1978), 297–306; p. 297.

[78] S. C. Lim, 'As Shakespeare would have liked it – in Chinese dress', *Straits Times*, 5 October 1952, 14.

[79] Cited in Teng Siao See, Chan Cheow Thia and Lee Huay Leng, eds., *Education at Large: Student Life and Activities in Singapore 1945–65* (Singapore, 2013), p. 35.

[80] 'Music and drama report', *Crescent Girls' School Magazine* (1958), 52–3.

[81] Rosie Guat Kheng Lim, interview by Tan Beng Luan, NAS Oral History Centre, Accession Number 001386, Reel 8.

[82] *Emily of Emerald Hill* was first staged in 1984 and continues to be performed in the twenty-first century.

[83] Stella Kon, interview by Michelle Low, NAS Oral History Centre, Accession Number 002996, Reels 1, 2 and 3.

[84] Alexa Huang [Joubin], *Chinese Shakespeares: Two Centuries of Cultural Exchange* (New York, 2009), p. 13. See also Hao Liu, 'The dual tradition of bardolatry in China', *Shakespeare Survey* 71 (Cambridge, 2018), 39–45; p. 41.

[85] See, further, Lee Tong Soon, *Chinese street opera in Singapore* (Urbana, IL, 2009), pp. 5–6; Perris, 'Chinese', p. 298.

[86] See, further, 'English: its use in future by the New Malayans', *Straits Times*, 17 August 1959, 1.

[87] Karen M. Teoh, *Schooling Diaspora: Women, Education and the Overseas Chinese in British Malaya and Singapore, 1850s–1960s* (Oxford, 2018), p. 60.

their supposedly slavish adoration of all things British', while the latter were disliked for their 'alleged clannish traditionalism', 'Chinese chauvinism' and political activities.[88]

For English-medium schools to feature the *wayang*, traditionally the preserve of the Chinese-speaking community, shows that, far from having lost contact with their cultural roots, at least some individuals in the English education system actively created opportunities for ethnically Chinese students in English schools to reconnect with their cultural heritage, and for their non-Chinese classmates to learn more about this art form too. The fact that the students and other cast members in Seah Yun Chong's 1952 *As You Like It* wore costumes borrowed from a local *wayang* group further suggests that this Shakespeare production helped to forge ties between the English- and Chinese-speaking communities. It is particularly notable that Rosie Lim and Stella Kon were involved in *wayang*-themed performances, for they came from a Straits Chinese family. The Straits Chinese (also known as the Peranakans or Babas) had lived in Southeast Asia for generations and inter-married with the local Malay community, developing their own hybrid Malay–Chinese culture.[89] Many Straits Chinese had little direct knowledge of East Asian languages or cultures: speaking of her childhood, Kon recollects that she was not 'taken to watch Chinese opera on the street … because nobody in our circle could have understood the lingo'.[90] When Rosie Lim and Stella Kon organized *wayang*-style Shakespeare performances, they were thus establishing connections with a part of their Chinese heritage that their family had lost touch with ages ago, making their productions especially culturally pioneering.

The adaptation Rosie Lim's students put on at Bartley School was also 'a breakthrough', as Kon noted, because the dialogue was 'in Singlish'.[91] Singlish is an informal version of English spoken in Singapore that includes vocabulary and syntactical elements from Malay, Mandarin and Tamil, as well as Chinese dialects such as Hokkien and Cantonese.[92] This variety of English developed organically over time as Singapore's ethnically diverse population – most of whom were not native English speakers – sought to communicate with one another in English. Singapore has long had a complex relationship with this local patois: though championed by some twenty-first-century Singaporeans as part of the city-state's unique multiracial composition, its usage remains controversial. For much of the twentieth century, detractors condemned this 'broken' and 'ungrammatical' form of English and the government tried hard to encourage Singaporeans to speak and write standard English instead.[93] Within the education system, students who were unable to move beyond Singlish to standard English found themselves academically disadvantaged. Lim's students were likely all too aware of this, for Lim recalls that her students attended Bartley 'as a last choice' after being 'reject[ed]' from more established institutions.[94] It is probable that their limited knowledge of the English language had contributed to their lack of educational success: Kon recollects that her mother's students came from 'homes where they probably didn't even speak English regularly' and suggests that they may have been 'incapable of speaking regular English'.[95] In all likelihood, the students would have been both aware and ashamed of their weak English skills, and felt ill at ease within the English school system.

Inviting these students to perform Shakespeare in Singlish, rather than drilling them in how to declaim Shakespeare's language in standard English, the way most Singapore schools did, helped to reassure the students that they, and the variety of English they spoke, were a welcome and valued part of the English school system. Asking the students to reinterpret the scenes in their own words was effectively an exercise in translation, which required them first to understand Shakespeare's original text.

[88] Teoh, *Schooling*, pp. 59–61.
[89] Felix Chia, *The Babas* (Singapore, 2015).
[90] Kon, interview, Reel 3. [91] Kon, interview, Reel 1.
[92] 'Many tongues, one vernacular', *Passion365* (January–March 2020), 2–3.
[93] See, further, Lionel Wee, 'Introduction', in *Singlish*.
[94] Lim, interview, Reel 8. [95] Kon, interview, Reel 1.

Successfully re-writing Shakespeare's scenes would have proved to the students that, despite their academic track record, they too could master the playwright's complex lines and meet the intellectual rigours of the English school. Performing Shakespeare in Singlish would also have helped to reassure the students that there was a place for the type of English they spoke among themselves within the English-speaking world. To the extent that this performance was well received – and Kon, for one, remembers that the show 'so impressed' her and was 'very influential' on her own 'development as a - playwright'[96] – the Bartley production further showed that Singlish could be as dramatically effective a method of communication as Shakespeare's language itself. Given that it remained taboo to use Singlish within Singapore's emergent television, radio and theatre industries for much of the twentieth century, Lim's decision to allow her students to perform in Singlish was also well ahead of broader societal developments. Where the use of *wayang* costume or performance styles indicates the schools' receptiveness to a traditional cultural form that Singapore's Chinese-speaking migrants had brought with them from East Asia, the use of Singlish within the Bartley Shakespeare production suggests a willingness to accept a more recent – and much more controversial – product of Singapore's immigrant culture.

Singapore's schools are by no means the only colonial educational institutions to incorporate Asian culture within their productions of Shakespeare: Ick notes that the students in peninsular Malaysia did so on occasion too, with the students of Malay College Kuala Kangsar performing *Julius Caesar* wearing Malay dress in 1921, and most of the cast in the 1949 Victoria Institution production of the *Merchant of Venice* in Kuala Lumpur doing likewise.[97] However, there is an important difference between the Singaporean and Malaysian performances. As Malays are native to peninsula Malaysia, by staging Shakespeare in Malay dress, the Malaysian students can reasonably be said to use the productions to re-invigorate the indigenous heritage that colonialism had suppressed. The same cannot be said of Singaporean

productions discussed here, for the island's residents had no shared native traditions to draw upon. Instead, the Singapore performances function as cultural experiments in which members of the city's English-speaking community made space for, and accepted, elements of this island's migrant cultures that they had previously felt little affinity towards. In the process, the productions helped to create a new, syncretic Asian cultural identity for this island-city.

That said, it should be noted that Shakespeare was not the only playwright whose works were used to help students in Singapore connect with their Asian roots. For instance, in the late 1930s, Percival Frank Aroozoo, a Eurasian teacher at Outram School, wrote a play about the founding of Beijing for his primary-level students to perform. Titled *The Probation of Yen Wang*, the play was staged in 'the style of the Chinese opera', with the student actors dressed in 'Chinese opera costumes' 'borrowed' or 'hired' from a *wayang* company. Aroozoo directed a school production of Hsiung Shih-I's *Lady Precious Stream*, a play set in Tang-dynasty China as well.[98] In the late 1950s, Crescent Girls' School and Pasir Panjang Boys' Secondary School also collaborated to produce Hsiung's play,[99] which the Ministry of Education placed on its recommended school text list in 1960.[100] It should further be acknowledged that these school Shakespeare productions were not perfect models of cultural inclusiveness. Singlish may have been spoken across Singapore's diverse ethnic groups, but the *wayang*, despite its local Malay name, was associated specifically with the Chinese.[101] Students from non-Chinese backgrounds may have wondered why this East Asian art form was repeatedly featured within 1950s school Shakespeare productions, as opposed to Malay, Indian or Eurasian performance traditions.

[96] Kon, interview, Reel 1. [97] Ick, 'Performing'.
[98] Bong, interview, Reel 7.
[99] Teng *et al.*, eds., *Education*, p. 35.
[100] 'List of recommended books for secondary schools – for English schools only', Ministry of Education, 175/60, NAS.
[101] Lee, *Chinese*, pp. 4–5.

It is also unclear how authentic the *wayang* versions of Shakespeare were, given that Kon concedes that she had not attended a Chinese opera performance herself and that her knowledge of the art form was 'totally imitative' and derived from what she refers to as 'pastiche' operas.[102] Moreover, Bartley School's decision to present a Singlish version of the tale of Pyramus and Thisbe, the skit acted by the play's 'rude mechanicals' (*Dream*, 3.2.9), may have inadvertently reinforced the perception that Singlish is a type of English spoken by those of low socio-economic status. Nonetheless, these 1950s Shakespeare productions should still be credited with being among the earliest – if not *the* earliest – intercultural performances staged in Singapore. Despite their imperfections, these early theatrical experiments contributed to the ongoing quest to knit Singapore's disparate ethnic groups into a cohesive whole. In however small a way, the students and teachers involved in these productions thus helped to make Shakespeare education, the English school system and Singapore itself more culturally inclusive and creatively independent.

---

[102] Kon, interview, Reel 3.

USING PERFORMANCE TO STRENGTHEN THE HIGHER EDUCATION SECTOR: SHAKESPEARE IN TWENTY-FIRST-CENTURY VIETNAM

SARAH OLIVE[1]

[1] This article could not have been written without the unstinting support provided by the following: the British Academy small grant scheme; Trực Quang Lê, Trực Dương, Ân Thiên Phạm and students at Ho Chi Minh City (HCMC) Open University; their consultants from the world of Vietnamese professional theatre, Khánh Hoàng and Huỳnh Tấn; staff and students of the English Department at Vietnam National University Hanoi, especially Lê Thanh Dung; Le Duong, Pham Hong and Danny Whiting at the British Council in HCMC; Anthony R. Haigh, Professor of Theatre, Centre College, Danville, Kentucky; Tracy Irish, for her advice on the wikiShakespeare entries that she headed up while working with the RSC; and research leave and grant administration from the Department of Education, University of York.

Textual note: Where I have identified individuals or organizations, the information given about them is publicly available, with the exception of Trực, about whom additional details were gained in conversation while he kindly hosted me at his university. I shared this article with him so he could approve and/or amend my representation of him. In writing the names of individuals in this article, I have used each individual's way of writing their name (their use, or not, of diacritical marks and word order) in their communications with me to determine the format. Where I have not communicated with them in writing, I have used the rendering of their name given in the publications, websites or theatre programmes through which I encountered them. I use 'Ho Chi Minh City' (HCMC) throughout, as this name for the city appears in the name of the university which was the focus for my research in the south of the country. It is also the name for the city used by the British Council, whose 2016 Shakespeare Lives project features heavily in this article. However, in everyday conversation in English, there is much slippage between HCMC and 'Saigon' (Sài Gòn). I follow the widespread anglicization in Anglophone publishing of Hà Nội as Hanoi and Việt Nam as Vietnam: partly in the hope of ensuring that this article is returned in Anglophone searches (my experience in researching this article is that Google copes well with divergent transliterations and diacritical marks, while Word does not).

SHAKESPEARE IN TWENTY-FIRST-CENTURY VIETNAMESE HIGHER EDUCATION

Writing from a Western, Anglophone context, Andrew Hartley argues that 'university production ... is a crucial index of what Shakespeare has become', since productions manifest and shape the 'ideas about Shakespeare which the audience, cast, and crew subsequently t[ake] out into the world'.[2] This article uses Ho Chi Minh City (HCMC) Open University's production of Shakespeare, and its context within the wider Vietnamese Shakespearian scene, to explore 'what Shakespeare is' in twenty-first-century Vietnam, from the creative industries to higher education. In doing so, it redresses two gaps in the existing literature. Firstly, Shakespeare studies scholars have 'mainly ignored the Shakespeare going on right under our noses' – that is, university productions.[3] Secondly, Judy Celine Ick writes that Southeast Asia is overwhelmingly absent from the construct 'Asian Shakespeare'.[4] It is, in any case, a construct that often assumes and reinforces 'essentializing notions of Asian collective identity' – Asian homogeneity – as Yong Li Lan has shown.[5] The focus within the burgeoning field of Asian Shakespeare studies, including considerations of Shakespeare in the region's education sectors, has been on Shakespeare in India, Japan and China. This neglect of Southeast Asia is evident in theatre studies more widely: Vietnam is one of several countries whose entry in the phenomenally wide-ranging *The World Encyclopedia of Contemporary Theatre*, volume 5: *Asia/Pacific* is styled as an overview article, compared to the fuller accounts given of the Asian

[2] Andrew Hartley, ed., *Shakespeare on the University Stage* (Cambridge, 2014), pp. 1–2.
[3] Paul Menzer, 'The laws of Athens: Shakespeare and the campus economy', in *University Stage*, ed. Hartley, pp. 201–15; p. 203.

'powerhouse' nations listed above.[6] To fulfil its two-fold aims, the first part of this article gives an overview of the existing literature and resources in English, as well as performance events in both Vietnamese and English, concerning Shakespeare in early twenty-first-century Vietnam. The second part of this paper explores a performance of the balcony scene from *Romeo and Juliet* by undergraduate students from HCMC Open University – led by Trực Quang Lê, their lecturer and the director of an in-class and extramural activity called 'Theater in Education'. It closes with a consideration of the potentially fruitful intersections between weaknesses in the current Vietnamese higher education system and the perceived benefits of university students performing Shakespearian and other texts.

VIETNAMESE SHAKESPEARE IN LITERATURE AND DIGITAL RESOURCES

Productions of Vietnamese Shakespeare are not well represented in English-language Shakespeare scholarship and resources. Yong analyses accounts of a production of *A Midsummer Night's Dream* written by David Booth, its director, and Mike Ingham, who acted in the production and is an academic at Lingnan University.[7] The show was produced in Hong Kong, where it played in 1992, before touring to Hanoi in 1993. Furthermore, much literature by non-Vietnamese academics and educators invokes Vietnam in writing about Shakespeare only in relation to military conflict. Vietnam features fleetingly in Bi-qi Lei's chapter on Taiwan's early Shakespeare in her discussion of the Vietnamese war's impact on US and Taiwanese cultural relations in the 1960s.[8] Scholarship on Roman Polanski's *Macbeth* and Kenneth Branagh's *Henry V* films analyses the way in which they contributed to public debate about the war or are informed by cinematic conventions from the Vietnam war genre.[9] John O'Toole writes of using a direct analogy between the Final War of the Roman Republic and the Vietnam war when teaching *Antony and Cleopatra* to his students in Australia.[10] In this way, much scholarship has,

however inadvertently, constructed a very limited role for Vietnam in Shakespeare studies, informed by outsider (non-Vietnamese, Western) perspectives on the war.[11]

In terms of online resources, the international Reviewing Shakespeare blog, which grew out of the World Shakespeare Festival in 2016, has received no contributions from or about Vietnam in its history. The Asian Shakespeare Intercultural Archive (A|S|I|A) features over sixty productions from across Asia on its website, of which one is Vietnamese: a 2002 Vietnam Youth Theatre production of *Macbeth*. It features in Yong Li Lan's article on A|S|I|A's work in the *Oxford Handbook of Shakespeare and Performance*.[12] MIT's Global Shakespeare website,

---

[4] Judy Celine Ick, 'Shakespeare, (Southeast) Asia, and the question of origins', in *Shakespeare in Culture*, ed. Bi-qi Beatrice Lei and Ching-Hsi Perng (Taipei, 2012), pp. 205–30; p. 206.

[5] Yong Li Lan, 'Ong Keng Sen's "Desdemona", ugliness, and the intercultural performative', *Theatre Journal* 56.2 (2004), 251–73; p. 251.

[6] Katherine Brisbane, Ravi Chaturvedi, Ramendu Majumadar, Chua Soo Pong, Don Rubin and Minoru Tanokura, eds., *The World Encyclopedia of Contemporary Theatre: Asia/Pacific* (London, 1998).

[7] Yong Li Lan, 'Shakespeare and the fiction of the intercultural', in *A Companion to Shakespeare and Performance*, ed. Barbara Hodgdon and W. B. Worthen (London, 2008), pp. 527–49.

[8] Bi-Qi Beatrice Lei, '"I may be straight, though they themselves be bevel": Taiwan's early Shakespeare', in *Shakespeare's Asian Journeys: Critical Encounters, Cultural Geographies, and the Politics of Travel*, ed. Bi-Qi Beatrice Lei, Judy Celine Ick and Poonam Trivedi (New York, 2016), pp. 89–108.

[9] Peter Drexler and Lawrence Guntner, eds., *Negotiations with Hal: Multi-Media Perceptions of (Shakespeare's) 'Henry the Fifth'* (Braunschweig, 1995); Sarah Hatchuel and Pierre Berthomieu, '"I could a tale unfold, I could a tale enlighten": Kenneth Branagh ou l'art de la clarté', *Actes des congrès de la Société française Shakespeare* 16 (1998), 131–40; Bryan Reynolds, *Performing Transversally: Reimagining Shakespeare and the Critical Future* (New York, 2003).

[10] John O'Toole, 'Teaching Shakespeare: why Shakespeare still matters in school', *Teacher*, October 2007, 46–9; p. 48.

[11] Kevin Wetmore, Siyuan Liu and Erin Mee, *Modern Asian Theatre and Performance, 1900–2000* (London, 1999), p. 249.

[12] Yong Li Lan, 'Translating performance: the Asian Shakespeare Intercultural Archive', in *The Oxford Handbook of Shakespeare and Performance*, ed. James C. Bulman (Oxford, 2017), pp. 619–40; p. 628.

which details over 270 productions, lists *A Dream in Hanoi*. This 2002 documentary film in the 'making of' mode about a collaborative US/Vietnamese production of *A Midsummer Night's Dream* has received the most (if somewhat fragmented) attention of all Shakespeare productions in Vietnam, among those written in English. The self-proclaimed 'first American documentary about American/ Vietnamese relations that does not focus on the war or its legacy of human suffering' features in work by Sukanta Chaudhuri and Chee Seng Lim, Terri Bourus, and Richard Burt.[13] Its publicity claims that it captured the first Vietnamese production of the play, without problematizing this label in terms of the US co-production aspect. Meanwhile, the 1993 *Dream* production purported to be the first full-length Shakespeare play staged in the city, something Yong does not question, despite the director Pham Thi Thanh having directed full-length productions of *Romeo and Juliet* (1982) and *Othello* (1988) at the Youth Theatre, which she helped to establish.[14] The urge of these productions to claim a 'first' is understandable in terms of marketing originality, but such claims arguably hold back Shakespeare in Vietnam from receiving the recognition it deserves by underrepresenting the volume of activity. It is wrong to suggest that the paucity of scholarship and resources on Shakespeare productions in Vietnam is a reflection of there being nothing to consider. Admittedly using a broad definition of 'performance events' to include public film screenings framed by live activity (sonnet readings, a quiz, a pre-show talk), and 'Shakespeare in Vietnam' to include international, touring productions, I have identified eighteen instances in the first seventeen years of the twenty-first century (see Table 2). The scale is relatively small, heavily skewed towards the two main cities and by the British Council's Shakespeare Lives programme of events to celebrate the 400th anniversary of Shakespeare's death, in 2016. There are also notable absences, such as film versions of Shakespeare from Vietnam besides *A Dream in Hanoi*. This is perhaps explained by the relative scarcity of Vietnamese translations of the work, in comparison to Japan, China and Thailand. Van Nhan Luong argues that unlike these neighbouring countries, Vietnam has focused

on producing adaptations rather than translations.[15] Nonetheless, Shakespeare does have a larger existence in Vietnam than is currently acknowledged.

Despite evidence of Shakespearian activity in Vietnam, it is worth bearing in mind some subdued impressions of the scene gathered from Vietnamese residents during research mobility visits to Hanoi in 2016 and HCMC in 2017, where I visited theatres producing Shakespeare to meet with directors and observe rehearsals (working with a Vietnamese translator), taught classes to Vietnamese undergraduates, met with colleagues teaching Shakespeare in higher education, participated in a continuing professional development event for high school teachers and attended the launch of an exhibition on 'Shakespeare Lives' by the British Council in Hanoi as part of the Shakespeare Lives programme, for which I had curated some quotations. Although many of the students I spoke to, in Hanoi and HCMC, first recalled hearing of Shakespeare on television, film or stage as teenagers, for Le Quang Minh (a young professional who majored in Chinese at university), Shakespeare is associated with middleaged audiences whom he perceived as having leisure time, enjoying complementary activities such as visiting bookstores, and using Shakespearian theatre as a way to maintain their mental agility. In both Hanoi and HCMC, there was a perception that the popularity of film and television, including that imported from Korea and the US as well as Korean–Vietnamese co-productions, has had

[13] Bullfrog Films, *A Dream in Hanoi*, dir. Tom Weidlinger (2002): www.bullfrogfilms.com/catalog/adih.html; Sukanta Chaudhuri and Chee Seng Lim, *Shakespeare Without English: The Reception of Shakespeare in Non-Anglophone Countries* (Delhi, 2006); Terri Bourus, *A Midsummer Night's Dream* (Naperville, 2006); Richard Burt, 'Mobilizing foreign Shakespeares in media', in *Shakespeare in Hollywood, Asia and Cyberspace*, ed. Alexander Huang (West Lafayette, 2009), pp. 231–8.
[14] Yong, 'Fiction', p. 528. Catherine Diamond, 'The supermuses of stage and screen: Vietnam's female dramatists', *Asian Theatre Journal* 16.2 (1999), 268–84; p. 277.
[15] Van Nhan Luong, 'Drama translation in Vietnam: a review of Shakespeare's plays', *International Journal of English Language & Translation Studies* 4 (2016), 14–29.

Table 2 Some twenty-first-century Shakespeare performance events

Year	Production	Company/event	Language	City
2016–17	*Hamlet* film screening (2015)	British Council. Shakespeare Lives in Film	English	HCMC Hanoi
2016	*Romeo & Juliet* film screening (1968)	British Council. Shakespeare Lives in Film	English	HCMC Hanoi
2016	*Much Ado About Nothing* film screening (1993)	British Council. Shakespeare Lives in Film	English	HCMC Hanoi
2016	*Richard III* film screening (1995)	British Council. Shakespeare Lives in Film	English	HCMC Hanoi
2016	*Romeo & Juliet*	Open University of HCMC British Council. Shakespeare Lives in Words	English	HCMC
2016	Shakespeare hip hop dance	British Council. Shakespeare Lives in Photography	None	HCMC
2016	Readings of Shakespearian sonnets	British Council. Shakespeare Lives in Sonnets award ceremonies	English Vietnamese	HCMC Hanoi
2015–16	*Hamlet*	Vietnam National Drama Theatre British Council. Shakespeare Lives	Vietnamese	Hanoi
2015	*Hamlet*	The Hamlet Project	None	HCMC
2012	*King Lear*	TNT (The New Theatre) American Drama Group Europe Vietnam Performing Arts Centre (Department of Performing Arts)	English (Vietnamese scene titles)	HCMC Hanoi Danang
2011	*Macbeth*	TNT Vietnam Performing Arts Centre	English	HCMC Hanoi Danang
2010	*Othello*	Wellington College (UK public school) Viet Nam – Britain Friendship Association HCMC City Ballet Symphony Orchestra and Opera	English	HCMC Beijing Hong Kong Singapore
2009	*Romeo & Juliet*	TNT American Drama Group Europe	English	HCMC Hanoi
2009	*Another Midsummer Night's Dream*	North-East-South-West (NEWS)‡	Vietnamese	HCMC
2002–3	*Midsummer Night's Dream (A Dream in Hanoi)*	Central Dramatic Company of Vietnam Artists Repertory Theater in Portland, Oregon National Theater of Music and Dance The Cheo Theater of Hanoi (Bullfrog Films)	Both (film with English subtitles)	Hanoi

(continued)

Table 2 (cont.)

Year	Production	Company/event	Language	City
2002[*]	*(Tragedy of) Macbeth*	Vietnamese Youth Theatre	Vietnamese	HCMC Hanoi Beijing Ningbo
2001[*]	*The Healing Arts* *(Othello / Tale of Kieu* adaptation)*	Le Duy Hahn Shaun MacLaughlin Bristol Old Vic Theatre School	Both	HCMC Hanoi
2001[†]	*Romeo & Juliet*	Nguyễn Đình Thi Nguyễn Thị Minh Ngọc Robert Chamberlain	?	HCMC Hanoi?

N.B. TNT productions tour internationally, only Vietnam performances are included here.
[*] These productions were both Vietnamese contributions to international theatre festivals.
[‡] An excellent source of information on the intercultural group's foundation is co-founder Nguyễn Khải Thư's Another Midsummer Night's Dream in Ho Chi Minh City', *Asian Theatre Journal* 28.1 (2011), 199–221.
[†] This production is cited by Nguyen who had a telephone conversation with one of the directors, Nguyễn Thị Minh Ngọc, about it. The language of the performance is not given.

a deleterious effect on audience numbers at the theatre (an impact also mentioned by Wetmore *et al.*).[16] Shakespearian cinema was sometimes perceived to be easier to understand than Shakespearian theatre, while celebrity film actors were acknowledged to be a drawcard. A particular hurdle spoken of in relation to Shakespearian theatre was that English culture and news does not attract the same following in Vietnam as their American counterparts – with the possible exception of Premier League football – and Shakespeare remains inextricably affiliated with English national identity in the minds of those with whom I spoke. Nguyễn Khải Thư argues more bluntly that neither traditional Vietnamese theatre forms nor Shakespeare 'have the attention of the Vietnamese contemporary audience'.[17] Additionally, Minh noted that in recent decades there has been a flurry of interest in and activity around Chinese language and culture in Vietnam, due to its rising global power and buoyant economy. He felt this might have distributed efforts and attention away from Anglophone literature to the language and culture of Vietnam's neighbour. While China is always going to be a major influence on Vietnam for historical and geographical reasons, Minh's perception in

2016 was that this spike of interest has waned somewhat due to reporting of an economic slowdown for China, as well as political tensions between Vietnam and China over the national boundaries in the East, or South China, Sea.

The paucity of internationally known literature and resources on Shakespeare in Vietnam by Vietnamese scholars might reflect a lack of interest, as described by Minh, but it might also reflect the prioritization of teaching over research, and the widespread segregation of teaching from research in Vietnamese universities, with the latter largely occurring in separate research institutes, along a Soviet model.[18] There is also a marked lack of parity between British and

[16] Wetmore *et al.*, *Modern Asian Theatre*.
[17] Nguyễn, 'Another', p. 205.
[18] Nick Clark, 'Higher education in Vietnam: student growth, faculty shortages and international partnerships', *World Education News & Reviews* (2010): https://wenr.wes.org/2010/08/wenr-julyaugust-2010-practical-information; *ICEF Monitor*, 'Challenges in Vietnamese higher education contributing to demand for study abroad', *ICEF Monitor* (2015): https://monitor.icef.com/2015/09/challenges-in-vietnamese-higher-education-contributing-to-demand-for-study-abroad.

Vietnamese higher education institutions in terms of the emphasis on, and resourcing of, research by academics – at least in Shakespeare studies. This contributes to the continuing under-representation of Vietnamese scholars in the English-language literature. In comparison to the handfuls of monographs or edited collections on Shakespeare in China, India and Japan published in English, comparable publications on Vietnamese Shakespeare are sparse. Vu Kim Chi published a chapter in a German Shakespeare collection on issues relating to Vietnamese translations of Shakespeare sonnets, around the use of kinship terms, rhyming and lack of relative stress.[19] Luong's monograph *Translation and Shakespeare in Vietnam* has a strong focus on *Romeo and Juliet* – the play Vietnamese students are most likely to encounter in school, excerpted and translated into Vietnamese, during their study of world literature.[20] Nguyễn Khải Thư's article '*Another Midsummer Night's Dream* in Ho Chi Minh City' further details which plays Vietnamese school students are most likely to encounter (*Romeo and Juliet*, maybe *Hamlet*) and discusses the perceived deficiencies of actor training for performing Shakespeare in Vietnamese drama schools.[21] In relation to the possibility that Vietnamese scholars are hampered from writing and publishing on Shakespeare in Vietnam by material differences in support, funding and resources available, note that Nguyễn describes herself as an American film-maker based in San Francisco Bay with a Ph.D. from University of California, Berkeley; while Luong is Vietnamese- and UK-educated, employed within the British higher education system (University of Huddersfield). I mention this not to debate these scholars' national identities, but to demonstrate that their scholarly work has been enabled largely outside Vietnam. This is suggestive of a drain of Shakespearian expertise away from Vietnam to the West, which is perhaps indicative of and contributing to the wider 'crisis' in the Vietnamese higher education sector that I consider in the conclusion. In the intervening sections, I contribute to redressing the imbalance of attention to Vietnam in Asian Shakespeare, and campus Shakespeare in Shakespeare studies, by exploring a performance of the balcony scene from *Romeo and Juliet* by undergraduate students from HCMC Open

University, in the context of an activity called 'Theater in Education'.

'THEATER IN EDUCATION' AT HO CHI MINH CITY OPEN UNIVERSITY

Many Vietnamese university students in foreign language departments have encountered Shakespeare at school through excerpted passages in textbooks, and only occasionally involving active methods.[22] This does not deter Trực from staging Western authors, including Shakespeare, with his students. Trực studied for a Master's degree in TESOL education at the University of Sydney, having previously worked as a teacher of Vietnamese literature in schools and then English language in universities, including teaching American, Japanese and Chinese students. He attributes his ability to use drama methods with the students to explore, adapt and perform publicly literary texts, to observing guest professional theatre practitioners working with a few of his students. He then began to try out their techniques himself in rehearsals with larger student groups. Trực calls this activity, ongoing within his English literature classes, 'Theater in Education' – a title not to be confused with the post-war British movement that saw theatre practitioners going into schools, using drama activities across the curriculum to teach social and environmental issues. He has facilitated students in performing Shakespeare and other UK or US classical and contemporary texts as part of his classes since 2009.

Students work with texts of their own choosing – the 'literary works they love', explained Trực in an email to me in 2017. These have included *Brokeback Mountain*, *Little Women* and *The Great Gatsby*, alongside Shakespearian drama such as

[19] Vu Kim Chi, 'Shakespeare's sonnets in Vietnamese', in *Unser Shakespeare*, ed. Frank Günther (Munich, 2014), pp. 51–64.

[20] Van Nhan Luong, *Translation and Shakespeare in Vietnam* (Saarbrucken, 2016). See also Sarah Olive, 'Perceptions of and visions for Shakespeare in early twenty-first century Vietnamese schools', *Use of English* 1.69 (2018), 75–85.

[21] Nguyễn, '*Another*', p. 207.   [22] Olive, 'Perceptions'.

Twelfth Night. Many of them are novels or short stories originally, so their adaptation for the stage involves some cutting and re-scripting. Students build up to an initial performance for peers through a rehearsal process in class, with each group also attending to design issues such as costume and music. The most successful productions are subsequently performed at a public event. These events are publicized on social media sites, such as Facebook, to which many students subscribe. Beyond students, friends and family, and people otherwise affiliated with the university, audiences consist of intellectuals and English language learners. Staging his students' productions, up to twenty-five in one month alone (nineteen in December 2016, for example), has seen Trực working significantly more hours than are strictly required of an academic at his institution: activities such as supervising contractors setting up the stage have seen him busy until midnight, having already started teaching much earlier than UK colleagues, at 7 or 8 a.m., and – although he never mentions this – within a higher education system that has been criticized for its low pay of staff.[23] However, Trực describes deriving a strong sense of purpose and worth from passing on his passion for English literature and dramatic methods to his students.

The leap to regular performance events transpired in the following way. In November 2012, with the support of the manager of the Drama Theatre of Ho Chi Minh City, Khánh Hoàng, Trực gained professional directorial input and the use of the theatre for 'Oscar Wilde's Night', his students' performances of *The Nightingale and the Rose* and *The Happy Prince*, selected from the best work produced by his classes that year. In June 2016, his 'Theater in Education' activity reached a milestone when, with the support of his university, he was 'allowed to take the students of two English Literature classes ... to the Theater of Ho Chi Minh City to stage three literary works [over two nights]: *The Nightingale and the Rose* by Oscar Wilde, *Vanity Fair* by William Thackeray, and *Atonement* by Ian McEwan'.[24] The involvement of theatre professionals in the activity resonates with descriptions of the way in which 'campus productions might inhabit a middle ground between the world of the theatre and that of academia' and marry 'fledgling talent with skilled oversight'.[25] The local theatre professionals, who had helped to rehearse and attended the event – and therefore should have some favourable bias – acclaimed the performances.[26] The event – attended by Ian Gibbons, the British Consul General in Ho Chi Minh City, and some members of staff from the local British Council offices – was well received in 'a burst of news reports and articles on television, magazines, and newspapers', including the *Saigon Times Daily*.[27] External support and acclamation led to the embrace of the event, and its recurrence, within the higher education institution.

Trực declares himself unconcerned with what or how much previous experience students have of drama, and does not see that as determining the success of a group's work. Rather, the students' personalities, attitudes to the activity, and the group dynamic are seen to determine whether they will have a good learning experience. One of Trực's foremost aims with the productions is to encourage his students to speak English clearly: these productions are a tool for their study of and attainment in English as an Additional Language (EAL), something that has been identified as a necessary area for improvement by commentators on Vietnamese higher education.[28] Indeed, as

[23] My Phuong Thanh Ho and Dennis Berg, 'Educational Leadership Challenges: Vietnam's System of Higher Education', paper presented to the Asia Leadership Roundtable, Hong Kong Institute of Education (2010), p. 4.
[24] Truc, 'Romeo and Juliet kiss on Book Street in Ho Chi Minh City', *Teaching Shakespeare* 18 (2020), 6–8.
[25] Hartley, ed., *University Stage*, p. 4; W. B. Worthen, 'The Shakespeare performance campus', in *University Stage*, ed. Hartley, pp. 264–87; p. 268.
[26] Truc, 'Romeo'. [27] Truc, 'Romeo'.
[28] Le Huong, 'Vietnamese higher education in the context of globalization: qualitative or quantitative targets?' *The International Education Journal: Comparative Perspectives* 13 (2014), 18–29; p. 17; Thomas Vallely and Ben Wilkinson, 'Vietnamese higher education: crisis and response', Higher Education Task Force, Harvard Kennedy School: Ash Institute for Democratic Governance and Innovation (2008), 2: https://pdfhall.com/vietnamese-higher-education-harvard-university_5b0b3b298ea doe4e2d8b4581.html.

I spoke with clusters of students in the classroom, he periodically encouraged them to be confident and speak more loudly. He is familiar with research into the benefits of drama activities for EAL students in terms of improved pronunciation and intonation, speaking, writing, reading, vocabulary and grammar.[29]

He views using drama methods in English literature as a way 'to innovate literature learning at the Faculty of Foreign Languages of Ho Chi Minh City Open University' and 'to keep up with educational practices promoting creativity in developed countries'.[30] He also perceives the potential to benefit individual students' imaginative and creative capacities, citing existing research on this.[31] Ideally, he would like to have the means to take the student productions to Anglophone countries for knowledge exchange with Anglophone students and academics engaged in similar activities. These objectives tally with observations that embracing Shakespearian performance, or drama methods at least, is (increasingly) a feature of English departments and courses in both Anglophone countries and countries where Shakespeare is encountered as part of English as an Additional Language studies – not just the preserve of theatre departments or schools – and respond to criticism of the lack of pedagogical innovation in Vietnamese higher education.[32] More unusual is Trực's objective 'to inspire the English language-learning community', reaching beyond the students, for example, to the wider public of Ho Chi Minh City who are among the audience members.[33] This outreach objective resonates with much of the university Shakespeare in Hartley's book, but especially Jonathan Heron's project, in which staging 'Shakespeare was used to generate specific opportunities for humanities students to engage with local communities'.[34]

A final objective for 'Theater in Education' is to foster inclusivity and 'to convey [meaningful] messages of [shared] humanity about members not belonging to the majority in society'; these include the LGBT community, transgender community and people with disabilities.[35] Hartley notes that university is a 'formative time when one's identity develops radically' and that participating in theatrical performance is one way in which university students are able to explore their identity, and diverse, other identities.[36] In 2016–17, several of Trực's student groups were engaging with representations of sexual and gender diversity – staging gay, lesbian and heterosexual desire and transgender characters, including within their productions of *Twelfth Night*, *Brokeback Mountain* and *The Danish Girl*. They were also interested in how to draw attention to the socially constructed and performative nature of gender through their productions. One group performed *Forrest Gump*, best known to audiences through the Oscar-winning film about the eponymous character, who had physical disabilities as a child and whom many interpret as having learning disabilities. Trực explained that *Brokeback Mountain*, *The Danish Girl* and *Forrest Gump* productions 'are about individuals who do not belong to the majority of the population and who are likely to face serious stigma or to be ostracized in society with discrimination, insults, intimidation, and even beatings. I am proud

[29] Le, 'Vietnamese', p. 19; Filippo Fonio and Geneviève Genicot, 'The compatibility of drama language teaching and CEFR objectives – observations on a rationale for an artistic approach to foreign language teaching at an academic level', *Scenario* 5 (2011), 75–89; Stefanie Giebert, 'Drama and theater in teaching foreign languages for professional purposes', *Recherche et Pratiques Pédagogiques en Langues de Spécialité*, 33 (2014), 138–50; Charlyn Wessels, *Drama* (Oxford, 1987).

[30] Trực, private correspondence, 2017.

[31] Le, 'Vietnamese'; Colleen Ryan-Scheutz and L. Colangelo, 'Full-scale theater production and foreign language learning', *Foreign Language Annals* 37 (2004), 374–89.

[32] Le, 'Vietnamese', 23; Worthen, 'Shakespeare', 268; Mark Pilkinton, 'Performance, religion, and Shakespeare: staging ideology at Notre Dame', in *University Stage*, ed. Hartley, pp. 27–42; p. 27. My and Berg, 'Educational'; Duong Minh-Quang, 'The changing needs for higher education organizations structure in Vietnam: evidence from Japanese, Taiwanese and Thai universities', *Journal of Education and Learning* 7.1 (2013), 21–8; p. 21.

[33] Trực, private correspondence, 2017.

[34] Jonathan Heron, 'Shakespearean laboratories and performance-as-research', in *University Stage*, ed. Hartley, pp. 232–49; p. 233.

[35] Trực, private correspondence, 2017.

[36] Hartley, ed., *University Stage*, p. 6.

of my students' mature thinking, bravery in choosing such stories to perform.'[37]

He is familiar with, and inspired by, a range of existing publications on the use of drama with EAL students to promote social competences, social life, psychological wellbeing and individuality.[38] Staging Shakespeare's plays not only in order to develop the students' and audiences' English language skills, but also to tackle pressing social issues such as equality, diversity and inclusion quite explicitly, is not unheard of in campus drama. Several participating teams in the Chinese Universities Shakespeare Festival, for instance, staged productions that included political commentary, ranging from critiquing corruption in Taiwan's political elite to celebrating endangered minority ethnic Chinese culture.[39] In an American context, Chad Allen Thomas has written about student productions queering Shakespeare in the South.[40] Nonetheless, a concern with social justice is a prominent, consistent and distinctive aspect of Trực's 'Theater in Education' activity. Even where it is not apparent in the choice of text, it is manifest in the inclusive attitudes and behaviours expected of staff and students involved.

ROMEO AND JULIET BY HO CHI MINH CITY OPEN UNIVERSITY

In this section, I use HCMC Open University's performance of the balcony scene from *Romeo and Juliet* in November 2016 to consider its constructions of Shakespeare by Vietnamese staff and students for a predominantly Vietnamese audience. The production came out of Trực's 'Theater in Education' programme in that the British Council – having witnessed his work, and that of his students – invited him to create a fifteen-minute performance to help celebrate the launch of their Shakespeare Lives exhibition. This featured quotations in English from Shakespeare's works in colourful wall displays and word sculptures, accompanied by some context from the plays they belonged to as well as their Vietnamese translations; other components of the launch included a sonnet reading by a Western staff member from the British Council and a reading of a Vietnamese translation by the winner of a 2016 sonnet translation competition. However, the *Romeo and Juliet* performance differed somewhat from the usual 'Theater in Education' programme in that students did not have free choice of texts, nor was a whole class involved. Trực chose 'the classic' *Romeo and Juliet* and, due to the constraints placed on the length of the performance by the British Council, he opted to perform just one scene: the balcony scene. He argues that it is 'the highlight' and 'widely considered the most romantic of the play'.[41] This matters because the 'love' aspect of *Romeo and Juliet* is foregrounded in Vietnamese school Shakespeare, the most widespread encounter with Shakespeare the Vietnamese public will have had.[42] His cast and crew were formed from his selection of a handful of students who had participated in the 'Theater in Education' performances that year: Juliet and Nurse were played by two female students,

---

[37] Trực, private correspondence, 2017.

[38] Le, 'Vietnamese'; Ryan-Scheutz and Colangelo, 'Full-scale'; Giebert, 'Drama'; Lorna Carson, 'The role of drama in task-based learning: agency, identity and autonomy', *Scenario* 6 (2012), 47–60; Evelyn Gualdron and Edna Castillo, 'Theater for language teaching and learning: the E-theater, a holistic methodology', *Profile: Issues in Teachers' Professional Development* 20 (2018), 211–27; Chris Boudreault, 'The benefits of using drama in the ESL/EFL classroom', *The Internet TESOL Journal* 16 (2010): http://iteslj.org/Articles/Boudreault-Drama.html; Ana Marjanovic-Shane, 'Play and theater in education', *Journal of Russian & East European Psychology* 35 (1997), 3–9; Astrid Ronke, 'Wozu all das Theater? Drama and theater as a method for foreign language teaching and learning in higher education in the United States' (unpublished doctoral dissertation, Technischen Universität Berlin, 2005); Wessels, *Drama*; Lenka Šmardová, 'Performance projects: an alternative to English language teaching' (unpublished dissertation, Masaryk University, 2008); Mariko Yoshida, 'Playbuilding in a Japanese college EFL classroom: its advantages and disadvantages', *Caribbean Quarterly* (2007), 231–40; Sarah Olive, 'Outside interference or Hong Kong embracing its unique identity? The Chinese Universities Shakespeare Festival', *Palgrave Communications* (2019).

[39] Olive, 'Outside'.

[40] Chad Allen Thomas, 'Queering Shakespeare in the American South', in *University Stage*, ed. Hartley, pp. 216–31.

[41] Trực, 'Romeo', p. 6.   [42] Olive, 'Perceptions'.

Romeo and Narrator by two male students, and two additional male students selected music for the soundtrack and played it during the performance. He calls them 'volunteers', which emphasizes that this performance was not part of their formal studies (unlike his usual 'Theatre in Education' activities). Trực was aided in the direction of the scene by Huỳnh Tấn (a professional actor who had also helped to direct the plays in the 'Theater in Education' 2016 performances) and Khánh Hoàng, a retired director of the HCMC Drama Theater and Huỳnh Tấn's private teacher. Khánh Hoàng's participation was noted in media coverage of the event, suggesting his involvement bestowed a certain amount of kudos onto the performance. Both Trực's programme and the Chinese Universities Shakespeare Festival drew heavily on expert advice and gate-keeping around what constitutes a good performance of Shakespeare. A noticeable difference is that the former was dominated by White Anglophone experts, the latter by Vietnamese experts.[43] The cast and crew's mission, as Trực articulates it, was 'to get an excerpt from a worldwide-known literary work by Shakespeare introduced to the public in Ho Chi Minh City'.[44] The age and student status of the actors constructed Shakespeare as something done by young people from a formal educational setting – if not necessarily as a mandatory part of their degree programme, as an extra-curricular activity.

Perhaps influenced by their own experiences of encountering Shakespeare's texts in education in Vietnamese, the team 'agreed not to speak the characters' lines in the original text written in Elizabethan-era language in case it was too challenging for the target audience' of the Vietnamese general public. 'Rather, we chose the version from *No Sweat Shakespeare*, translated into modern English.'[45] In this, for example, Juliet's lines,

> O swear not by the moon, th'inconstant moon
> That monthly changes in her circled orb,
> Lest that thy love prove likewise variable.
> . . .
> Or if thou wilt, swear by thy gracious self,
> Which is the god of my idolatry,
> And I'll believe thee.
>
> (2.1.151–3, 155–7)

become 'Oh, don't swear by the moon! The moon's too changeable . . . But if you must, swear by your self. You're the god I worship. Swear by your self and I'll believe you' (*No Sweat Shakespeare* exists as a prose story with dialogue).[46] His embrace of a modernized English text was constructed as a practical decision, representing one solution to the tension several writers on 'Campus Shakespeare' note between the company's aspirations and the audience's assumed abilities.[47] The choice of a modern-English resource, that started out as a kind of study-guide Shakespeare, does render the production markedly different from those with an emphasis on Shakespeare as a 'model of great writing in the English language', which inspires much other student performance in English in and beyond the Anglophone world.[48] It also contrasts with translations of Shakespeare into Asian languages using historic or high-culture linguistic forms. Furthermore, the use of *No Sweat Shakespeare* is interesting given that the aegis for the performance was, at least in part, the British Council's desire to promote its Shakespeare Lives exhibition, focused on Shakespeare's words. A huge poster for the exhibition, in English and Vietnamese, formed the backdrop for the performance. Both the performance and the exhibition contributed to a broad, glocalized, construction of Shakespearian texts, or of 'Shakespeare's words', as those spoken, heard, written and read around and about – not just 'by' – him. 'Glocalized' is a contested term. I use it here primarily to describe 'how the global flow of Shakespeare may be filtered through local environments', i.e. how the choice of textual source for the script met a local need for a particular kind of English discerned by Trực. Critics of *No Sweat Shakespeare* and the

---

43 Olive, 'Outside'.   44 Trực, 'Romeo', p. 7.
45 Trực, 'Romeo', pp. 7–8.   46 Trực, 'Romeo', pp. 7–8.
47 Peter Holland, 'Campus Shakespeare: fragments of a history, fragments of a concept', in *University Stage*, ed. Hartley, pp. 10–26; p. 25. Christa Jansohn, 'Shakespeare isn't just for the professionals', in *University Stage*, ed. Hartley, pp. 126–52; p. 132.
48 Pilkinton, 'Performance', p. 27; Olive, 'Outside'.

British Council, however, may prefer Mark Houlahan's description of it as 'the multinational and the corporate, blandly disseminating sameness throughout the world'.[49]

Starting at 9.30 a.m. – an unusual time to see theatre, but a time when downtown HCMC is already bustling, since its busy markets begin to open from 5 a.m. – it was a free event, in a very open and public, on-street location: a temporary stage at 37 Đường Nguyễn Văn Bình, HCMC's Book Street (a cluster of book shops and cafés popular with locals and tourists alike). Audience members could move reasonably freely in and out of spectating. In addition to local passers-by, the audience was made up of British Council dignitaries in the front row (one of whom gave a welcome speech and thanked the sponsors – Nhã Nam publishing house and Book Street – in English, with parallel Vietnamese translation, before the performance), event/press photographers and a few tourists, some of whom may have been native English speakers. The performance's timing and pop-up location contribute to the construction of Shakespeare as part of a special occasion: celebrating his anniversary, the larger programme of Shakespeare-related events in 2016, and the linguistic and cultural work of the British Council in Vietnam.

The stage was a temporary, outdoor one, on the same level as, and demarcated by, the three-sided seating. It was somewhat buffeted on the day by a strong breeze. The audience's plastic bucket chairs fanned out, four rows deep, from the front of the stage. The set comprised a curtained window topped with a fanlight, an ivy-covered balcony accessed by symmetrical flights of steps at either end, and a stone-effect balustrade. It vaguely suggested historical European architecture, elements of which can be seen in Vietnam's French colonial buildings. The costumes approximated medieval Italy, with a touch of the eighteenth and nineteenth centuries and Disney princes: Romeo (Thiên Tư) had a mandarin-collar, frill-fronted white shirt, black trousers and belt, and wore his hair in a floppy, jaw-grazing style; Juliet (Nguyễn Bình) sported a plain, wide-sleeved, fit 'n' flare white dress, with the top section of her dyed-

auburn, straight hair braided; the Nurse (Phương Nghi) donned a similar grey dress with white Puritan collar and a white Bo-Peep bonnet; the narrator (Nguyễn Đức) was resplendent in a black and gold doublet, black trousers and a jewelled crown. He carried a reddish-brown, hard-backed book that he only pretended to read from (the pages being devoid of the playtext). Although it used historical Western dress, this was not a 'white-face' production, such as those described in professional and student Chinese theatre in not-too-distant decades, which use curly, blonde wigs, prosthetic noses and white face-paint to give a Caucasian appearance.[50]

The actors wore discreet headset microphones in this location full of ambient noise. The music, chosen by Nguyễn Long and Vũ Hiếu, was drawn from globally popular Western film and popular culture. It included excerpts from Nino Rota's score for the Zeffirelli Romeo and Juliet film (which all the cast had watched as part of the rehearsal process) and acoustic, indie tracks for the couple kissing; rousing synthesized music of the sort used for the soundtrack of a blockbuster war film or the videogame Civilization as the narrator descended the steps to downstage centre; rockabilly blaring out for the curtain call. It was culturally diverse in the sense of drawing on Italian, British and American musical traditions, which have travelled but are not traditionally Vietnamese – what Marvin Carlson terms the 'culturally foreign', rather than the 'culturally familiar'.[51] The sounds and mise-en-scène suggested to Vietnamese audiences that Shakespeare may take

[49] Anston Bosman, 'Shakespeare and globalization', in *The New Cambridge Companion to Shakespeare*, 2nd edn, ed. Margreta Grazia and Stanley Wells (Cambridge, 2010), pp. 285–302; p. 290. Mark Houlahan, 'Hekepia? The *Mana* of the Maori *Merchant*', in *World-Wide Shakespeares: Local Appropriation in Film and Performance*, ed. Sonia Massai (London, 2005), pp. 141–8; p. 141.

[50] Lee Chee Keng and Yong Li Lan, 'Ideology in student performances in China', in *University Stage*, ed. Hartley, pp. 90–109.

[51] Marvin Carlson, 'Brook and Mnouchkine: passages to India?' in *The Intercultural Performance Reader*, ed. Patrice Pavis (London, 1996), pp. 72–92.

place in tongues, times and locations that are distant, even foreign, but that Shakespeare can be performed by Vietnamese actors, as Vietnamese actors.

The narrator, Nguyễn Đức gave a bite-sized, tantalizing overview of the scene in modern English that synthesized parts of the prologue and cut others. His speech flagged up the feud between the Montagues and Capulets, Romeo and Juliet's love-at-first-sight encounter preceding the balcony scene, and their 'romantic speech … under the shining moon', compressing the highs and lows of the first two scenes into a minute's preview that echoed the focus of the play as taught in Vietnamese schools. His overview constructed Shakespeare as accessible (with the help of this team), entertaining, emotionally dramatic and fast-paced. The bulk of the scene was occupied with Romeo and Juliet telling the audience about their love for each other, with Juliet at first oblivious to Romeo's presence; then their passionate declarations to each other, punctuated with occasional interruptions through the open window from the shrill and rather nonplussed nurse, forcing them to spring apart and Romeo to hide, creating some comic relief. The performance highlighted the aspect of 'boy meets girl' first and foremost, with the element of teenaged, forbidden love also evident. There was a discernible stage chemistry and intimacy between actors playing Romeo and Juliet. The couple kissed copiously and genuinely (as opposed to using lip-dodging, fake-kissing techniques), held each other's hands, touched each other's face, hair and shoulders, embraced each other face to face and with Romeo standing behind Juliet. Compared to student workshops and performances experienced in Japan where there may be requests for sexual content to be 'toned down', some reluctance to stage sexual intimacy by many mainland teams at the Chinese Universities Shakespeare Festival, and assertion by the makers of *A Dream in Hanoi* that 'full-mouth kissing on stage [is] an intimacy that's taboo in traditional Vietnamese theater', there was a considerable emphasis on their sensuality and sexuality in this performance.[52] This seems to have been influenced by the theatre practitioners involved in the project,

rather than initiated by the students, since Thiên Tư (Romeo) told me in class that his movements across the stage and in terms of gesticulation had been determined by Tấn and Hoàng and that he had memorized them along with his lines. The acting style was emotionally realist, energetically physical and grand, evidence of the 'formal presentational acting' described by Nguyễn.[53]

The narrator brought on each member of the cast for their curtain call, addressed the audience and thanked them for their attendance, apologized for not delivering the whole play on this occasion, and bid them farewell with 'goodbye and have a - good day'. His apology for presenting only an excerpt firmly constructed the whole play as a superior experience. While this sentiment is familiar to anyone who has worked with the English National Curriculum in the twenty-first century, it is perhaps surprising in this context, given that excerpts or cut-down versions are the norm in 'Theater in Education', the Chinese Universities Shakespeare Festival and the Shakespeare Schools Festival internationally.[54] Yet it implicitly invited the audience to find ways of accessing more Shakespeare, should they discover they have a thirst for it that needs slaking, perhaps through the remaining Shakespeare Lives events, so there may have been a pragmatic reason for drawing the audience's attention towards its partialness. The DVD of the event shows the cast and crew chatting to diverse members of the audience after the production, perhaps furthering the sense of Shakespeare (or, at least, those who 'do' Shakespeare) as accessible to and interesting for the wider public. It also depicts them posing in front of the Shakespeare Lives display, for press and audience photographs, complete with

---

[52] 'Dream synopsis', *A Dream in Hanoi*: www.adreaminhanoi. com/story/synop.html; Saeko Machi, 'Beyond the language barrier', *Teaching Shakespeare* 7 (Spring 2015), 12–13; Ayami Oki-Siekierczak, 'The treatment of bawdy in Japanese classrooms', *Teaching Shakespeare* 6 (Autumn 2014), 9.
[53] Nguyễn, '*Another*'. Similarly, Young, 'Translating', p. 628.
[54] Olive, 'Outside'; Sarah Olive, *Shakespeare Valued* (Bristol, 2015).

waves at the camera and peace-sign fingers. They also took selfies as a group and with friends and family. These behaviours echo those seen globally at entertainment events: for example, Ellen DeGeneres's 2014 Oscars selfie as host. Along with the 'fancy costumes [which] signify Shakespeare's cultural status' previously mentioned, the selfies suggest that staging Shakespeare is fun, somewhat glamorous, and bestows a kind of 'star quality' or celebrity status onto those involved.[55]

Overall, the performance focused on the play as a universal love story, as plot and character represented through clear-speaking of modern English. It constructed Shakespeare as 'classical' in appearance and acting style, making a claim to belong to a long-standing, historical, Western, dramatic tradition and standard of high art: much of the media coverage explicitly referred to this. Yet the performance was also radical in its use of a modernized English text, something rarely seen in professional or amateur productions, since Shakespearian English and translations/adaptations into languages other than English dominate Shakespeare productions globally: something not picked up in media coverage, which instead focused on the novelty and achievement of the Vietnamese students performing in English.[56]

Trực describes the performance as 'successful in its mission to draw greater attention from the public' to the exhibition and, perhaps, the British Council's Shakespeare Lives programme in HCMC that year more generally. It featured in an English-language report, titled 'Ho Chi Minh City students perform *Romeo and Juliet* at Book Street', and three articles in Vietnamese translated as 'Romeo and Juliet kissed each other on the Book Street', 'Bringing English drama to the Book Street', and 'Staging Shakespearian drama on the Book Street'.[57] These headlines suggest that the media took away from the production a strong sense that Shakespeare (foreign, 'English drama') could be done by local students on a local street and, again, that Shakespeare is romantic ('Romeo and Juliet kissed each other') in a way that is universally meaningful and affective (it conveys their love as well on Book Street as it does in English theatres). The time lag between the event and my

visit to HCMC, a change in British Council staffing, as well as the limitations on my research of not speaking Vietnamese, mean that I have not been able to find out other audience members' perspectives on the performance. Some of the actors had moved on from HCMC Open University by the time I visited, but one was continuing to perform in English-language student productions, mentoring other casts and crews, and was pursuing the idea of postgraduate study in English. Nonetheless, the influence of the event seemed to have rippled out among the HCMC Open University students I spoke to in class about their visions for the future of Shakespeare in Vietnam – most noticeably, their advocacy of performance.[58] While these students' sense of attraction to performance is not unique, it has unusual aspects in that it is used in class, in assessment, and not just as an extra-curricular activity. Elsewhere, such features tend to be embraced by students on theatre and drama courses, while literature students at university who are asked to undertake performance may resist and express dissatisfaction.[59] Additionally, champions of active-methods Shakespeare in schools have advocated using drama activities, interspersed with other approaches, to explore the play in English classes, rather than to stage a production.[60] This is predicated on the assumption that the performance experience is daunting, demotivating and exclusive for teachers and students, or does not align well with curriculum and assessment (specifically those in the UK). This contrasts sharply with the benefits of performance articulated by students in and

---

[55] Lee and Yong, 'Ideology', p. 91.

[56] Angelie Multani, 'Appropriating Shakespeare on campus: an Indian perspective', in *University Stage*, ed. Hartley, pp. 75–89; Olive, 'Outside'; Sarah Olive, 'The west and the resistance: perceptions of teaching Shakespeare for and against westernisation in Japanese higher education', in Sarah Olive, Kohei Uchimaru, Adele Lee and Rosalind Fielding, *Shakespeare in East Asian Education* (London, in press).

[57] Trực, 'Romeo', p. 8.   [58] Olive, 'Perceptions'.

[59] G. B. Shand, *Teaching Shakespeare: Passing It On* (Chichester, 2009).

[60] Rex Gibson, *Teaching Shakespeare* (Cambridge, 1998).

organizers of the Chinese Universities Shakespeare Festival (from a gamut of disciplines) and the Indian students in Multani's chapter – most of whom have in common not just their location in Asia but also English as a foreign, or additional, language.[61] The red-carpet, performance orientation of drama methods in the (non-drama/theatre) higher education classroom highlights a pronounced difference between Asian and Anglo approaches to teaching Shakespeare.

SHAKESPEARE, PERFORMANCE AND VIETNAMESE HIGHER EDUCATION

To summarize, HCMC Open University's performance of the balcony scene from *Romeo and Juliet* portrayed Shakespeare in Vietnam, by Vietnamese students, for the Vietnamese public, as beneficial for improving English language skills – though early modern English was noted to be challenging for the performers and the audience alike. The performance was constructed as conveying a story from a distant, foreign place but eminently able to be done by local, Vietnamese actors; better in its entirety, but more realistically done as an excerpt or 'taster'; romantic and glamorous, an extraordinary 'event', for both those staging and those attending. Such 'eventness' constitutes value added, or an extra hook, for participants and audiences.[62] The performance happened within the context of formal education, though this particular staging was undertaken as an extra-curricular activity reaching out to the wider community, disseminating Shakespearian performance as part of an internationally celebrated Shakespeare anniversary. The performance resonates with existing research demonstrating the important roles universities in Asia have played in the introduction of, and developments to, modern theatre in the region. According to Wetmore et al., universities in Asia have played this significant role over three centuries: not only training the next generation of theatre artists and the next generation of audiences, but also as an archive of historic theatre materials and as publishers of theatre magazines and journals: 'Universities have been the cradles,

incubators, shelters and spiritual and literal homes of the modern theatres of Asia.'[63] Hartley has acknowledged both the importance of universities internationally in hosting Shakespeare productions and the benefit this has for students in terms of access: 'For many students, their theatrical encounters with Shakespeare in college – whether as company members or audiences – will be especially formative, particularly if they live in one of the many parts of the world where the professional staging of Shakespeare is rare or prohibitively expensive. Campus productions may be the only Shakespeare those people ever see live.'[64] In the Vietnamese context, censorship (and beyond) of the theatre, as well as the practicalities of applying for and obtaining a permit, can mean that educational institutions and spaces are the most viable venues for small, experimental or internationally collaborative theatre. In addition to the perceived advantages to students discussed above, embracing performance of Shakespeare gives universities, such as HCMC Open University, the opportunity to model their identity and values – such as facility in English, as well as knowledge of world/Western literature and culture – for a wider Vietnamese audience, including prospective students.[65]

Paul Menzer argues that 'what those [university] performances teach us . . . should be among the most urgent concerns of anyone professing Shakespeare in the early 21st century'.[66] I argue that using rehearsal and performance techniques in the classroom – including, but also going beyond, the teaching of Shakespeare, as Trực's 'Theater in Education' does – could provide a lesson about pedagogic benefits for Vietnamese higher education. In terms

---

[61] Olive, 'Outside'; Multani, 'Appropriating'.

[62] Emily Linnemann, 'The cultural value of Shakespeare in twenty-first-century publicly-funded theatre in England' (unpublished doctoral dissertation, University of Birmingham, 2011).

[63] Wetmore et al., *Modern Asian Theatre*, pp. 267–8, 128, 145.

[64] Hartley, ed., *University Stage*, p. 2.

[65] Menzer, 'Laws', p. 203; Pilkinton, 'Performance', p. 42; Thomas, 'Queering', p. 216.

[66] Menzer, 'Laws', p. 203.

of higher education policy, the Vietnamese government has previously indicated a focus on expanding science and technology and continues to have centralized control of much education at all levels, despite the Đổi Mới economic reforms of the late 1980s onwards in other sectors. These were intended to move Vietnam from a centralized economy to a socialist-oriented market one. The Vietnamese government has been criticized by foreign and domestic commentators for producing a 'crisis' in the sector through poor governance. Admittedly, this criticism tends to use yardsticks, such as institutional league tables, attended to and courted by senior management in Western, neoliberal, higher education, but whose transfer onto the Vietnamese context may be seen as overwriting it with 'inappropriate practices and beliefs drawn from a quite different society'.[67] However, if the Vietnamese government does adopt these yardsticks, which seems somewhat inevitable given their dominance in globalized higher education, critics say it will need to make progress on the following: modernization, innovation and creativity; meaningful international connections; 'key' or 'essential' skills demanded by graduate employers and postgraduate education providers, especially international ones, by improving proficiency in English, promoting coursework that prizes critical enquiry over that 'laden with indoctrination', and accountability.[68] Some of these shortfalls of Vietnamese higher education, described in the last decade, may be countered by the performance work undertaken by Trực with his EAL students: demonstrating creativity by staging plays on a shoe-string budget; promoting international connections by observing and critiquing international theatre practitioners on stage or screen, in seminars or workshopping with them, and participating in international theatre festivals (a cherished hope for the future of Trực's 'Theater in Education', though funding remains a sticking point); hosting events and performing in English; as well as expecting students to explain critically their artistic choices. Advocates for the benefit of EAL students performing literary texts such as Shakespeare (here in English, but elsewhere in translation), within Vietnamese higher education and seeking to influence policy-makers, can additionally draw on strong regional precedents from countries with world-ranking higher education sectors, such as Hong Kong, China and India.[69] If their advocacy is successful, there will be yet more need for Shakespeare studies to redress the gaps in its attention to Shakespeare in Vietnam and Southeast Asia.

---

[67] Dan Rebellato, *Theatre & Globalization* (Houndmills, 2009), p. 55.

[68] Le, 'Vietnamese', pp. 23, 17; Clark, 'Higher Education'; Vallely and Wilkinson, 'Vietnamese higher education', pp. 2, 4, 5; Duong, 'Changing', p. 21; My and Berg, 'Educational'.

[69] Olive, 'Outside' and 'West'; Lee and Yong, 'Ideology'; Multani, 'Appropriating'.

COUNTERPUBLIC SHAKESPEARES
IN THE AMERICAN EDUCATION
MARKETPLACE

JILLIAN SNYDER

Imagine this scene: an American high school student picks up an edition of *Macbeth*. The edition, however, differs from those read by her peers. It omits, for example, the moment Lady Macbeth describes dashing out an infant's brains while nursing. It excludes the Porter's drunken soliloquy as he pretends to stand watch at the gates of hell. It forgoes Malcolm's fraudulent disclosure of his insatiable lust to Macduff. And when the student reaches the moment when the somnambulating Lady Macbeth scrubs Duncan's blood from her hands, the line reads, 'Out, foul spot!'[1] Other readers, of course, know it as 'Out, damned spot', but the text contains no indication of the change. One might wonder whether this student had unwittingly acquired Thomas Bowdler's nineteenth-century *Family Shakespeare*, but no. This student is reading an edition of Shakespeare published in 2004 by A Beka Book out of Pensacola, Florida. A Beka, along with a cottage industry of other publishers, create editions of *Macbeth* for private and home-schooled students across America. This specific edition of *Macbeth* is marketed towards fundamentalist Protestants, who, editors believe, may find such material objectionable. Such editions do more than bowdlerize lines and scenes, they insert these plays – and Shakespeare himself – into a larger polemic against American mainstream education. Moreover, they circulate within what Michael Warner calls a 'counterpublic', a group subordinate to a dominant public which nevertheless performs their subordination through discord and dissent.

Within their editions, these groups construct a variety of counterpublic Shakespeares, whose culture, faith, and drama legitimate the groups' hostility towards a regime of public education steeped in secular humanism.

This article investigates the cultural work performed by counterpublic Shakespeares in American education. It will analyse the counter temporalities and counter rhetoric imbued in the paratext of *Macbeth* produced by two religious publishing houses, one Protestant and one Catholic. The article will first consider how dominant publics construe the Shakespearian curriculum, by analysing editions from a popular publisher of Shakespeare for American classrooms, the Folger Shakespeare Library in Washington DC. Perhaps due to the Folger's predominance in American education, few, if any, studies have considered its critical premises. This article, however, examines how the Folger's 'modern' interpretations of Shakespeare imagine and create a reading public. This analysis provokes a broader question around the interpretative demands governing a specific public – that is, what are the prerequisites for 'right' interpretation? As the article argues, editions from the Folger – as much as those from religious publishers – organize this answer around the interplay between historiography, character study and hermeneutic priors. While the Folger uses cultural criticism to problematize the moral certainty of traditional critics, those

---

[1] *Macbeth by William Shakespeare*, ed. Catherine Pendley (Pensacola, FL, 2004), p. 110.

from religious counterpublics engage in an interpretative chiasmus, contending that moral readings expose the falsehood of secular humanism.

The article then turns to those counterpublics to explore the historical and confessional motivations that have promoted the development of their editions. It first examines an edition from one of A Beka's fundamentalist Protestant counterparts, Bob Jones University Press (BJU), in Greenville, South Carolina. The article examines BJU's edition through the institution's adherence to presuppositionalism, a school of Christian apologetics which avers that the Bible provides the only basis for all other truth claims. Starting from this hermeneutic framework, the article analyses how BJU's historiography bolsters its portrayal of Tudor England as the apex of biblical thought and culture. BJU thus esteems *Macbeth* – and, by extension, Shakespeare – as a paragon of the great art that can emerge from a culture grounded in fundamentalist interpretations of the Bible. In so doing, it rearticulates its resistance to secular education.

Resistance also characterizes the edition of *Macbeth* published by Ignatius Press out of San Francisco, California. Edited by Joseph Pearce, who has written two books alleging Shakespeare's Catholicism, the editions posit the same goal as those from BJU – to offer a religiously oriented alternative to mainstream editions – but with a completely counter-confessional historiography. In this rendition, Shakespeare's secret Catholicism – tacitly manifested in his plays – helped to resist the secularizing forces of the Tudor and Stuart regimes, both of which aimed to eradicate traditional faith in England. The editions thus present a suffering and stigmatized Shakespeare as a model for dissent from states – past and present – that are hostile to the faithful. And in the same way that biblical presuppositionalism uses an exclusivist hermeneutic lens by which to read Shakespeare's plays, so too does this confessional reading, which the edition argues can only reveal itself to those already sympathetic to it.

Analysing these counterpublic editions of Shakespeare broadens a prevailing narrative around Shakespeare's role in American education, which has emphasized Shakespeare as a dominant, normative force. This narrative appears in Jonathan Burton's work, which outlines how Shakespearian orations in the nineteenth-century McGuffey readers underlay efforts to transform a populace 'variegated with diverse constituencies' into a 'collective citizenry'.[2] It also manifests in Lawrence Levine's contention that Shakespeare's growing cultural capital gradually elevated him to a figure associated with high-brow tastes.[3] And it appears in Denise Albanese's study, which links Shakespeare's cultural capital to the standardization of mass education in the twentieth century, embedding Shakespeare within what she calls an American 'national imaginary'.[4] Studies such as these have led scholars to contend that Shakespearian education offered 'a *lingua franca*' for different American communities over the centuries.[5] Inasmuch as the claims these counterpublics make to Shakespeare draw upon his cultural capital to legitimate their resistance, they confirm that continued dominance. At the same time, the divergent historiographies and hermeneutics governing both publics and counterpublics highlight a deepening fracture within American education, undergirded by an increasing perception of it as a consumer-driven marketplace. Here, claims to the 'true meaning of Shakespeare' – as well as to the 'true Shakespeare' – are contingent upon radically different epistemological frameworks, all of which demand a set of a-priori commitments that then confirm the validity of their claims. If, as James Shapiro argues, 'the history of Shakespeare in America is also a history of America

[2] Jonathan Burton, 'Lay on McGuffey: excerpting Shakespeare in nineteenth-century schoolbooks', in *Shakespearean Educations: Power, Citizenship, and Performance*, ed. Coppélia Kahn, Heather S. Nathans and Mimi Godfrey (Newark, 2011), pp. 95–111; p. 96.

[3] Lawrence Levine, *Highbrow/Lowbrow: The Emergence of Cultural Hierarchy in America* (Cambridge, MA, Harvard University Press, 1986), pp. 35ff.

[4] Denise Albanese, *Extramural Shakespeare* (New York, 2012), p. 70.

[5] Coppélia Kahn, Heather S. Nathans and Mimi Godfrey, 'Introduction', in *Shakespearean Educations*, ed. Kahn *et al.*, 13–29; p. 15.

itself, not the straightforward narrative found in textbooks, but rather one that runs parallel to the conventional story of the nation', this cacophony of editions parallels a broader shift in American culture in which tribalization has produced increasingly conflicted bases of knowledge.[6]

'MODERN' SHAKESPEARE: THE FOLGER EDITIONS

As one of the predominant editions of *Macbeth* in the American educational landscape, those published by the Folger Shakespeare Library establish the discourse to which other editions respond. The Folger editions were first published in 1957, and they continue to be among the most popular used in public schools today. The Folger's authoritative position means the editions exemplify some of the major shifts occurring in mainstream education. Indeed, while the McGuffey readers would proffer Shakespearian oration as a means to moral citizenship, they were influenced by a broadly Calvinist system of values.[7] By the twentieth century, these values had shifted as university and secondary school curricula reoriented their focus from the 'moral questions' raised by the plays to 'social questions'.[8] This shift appears in the Folger, which boasts of providing a 'fresh assessment of [a] play in the light of today's interests and concerns'.[9] Its introduction to *Macbeth*, for example, notes that '[i]n earlier centuries', readers primarily interpreted Macbeth as a 'heroic individual who commits an evil act and pays an enormous price as his conscience – and the natural forces of good in the universe – destroy him'.[10] But it then observes that 'interpretations of the plays have been undergoing significant change'.[11] The Folger's essay for discussion at the rear of the text elucidates these changes. The essay, written by Susan Snyder, opens with a quote from Coleridge, who argued the play lacks the 'reasonings of equivocal morality' found in other characters such as Brutus and Othello.[12] The essay initially affirms Coleridge's certainty, acknowledging that the play contains a 'stark black-and-white moral opposition' in the

portrayal of the saintly Duncan and scheming Lady Macbeth.[13] But it proceeds to undercut this confidence, proclaiming that 'the moral universe of Macbeth is not as uncomplicated as some critics have imagined'.[14] The essay thus probes the 'old certainties' of Duncan's 'saintly status' and Lady Macbeth's machinations before concluding, when 'viewed through various lenses … the black and white of *Macbeth* may fade toward shades of gray'.[15]

The Folger predicates its interpretive shift from moral understandings to social ones on the cultural and scholarly consensus around the imbalances created by social hierarchies. Speaking of Duncan's reaction to the execution of Macdonald, the essay remarks, 'we see Duncan exulting not only in the victory but in the bloodshed, equating honor with wounds', which evinces 'his society's warrior ethic'.[16] It continues, 'But isn't this what we condemn in Lady Macbeth?'[17] Indeed, to read Lady Macbeth's action against this 'warrior ethic' demonstrates how she appears 'restless in a social role that … offers no choice of independent action and heroic achievement', in contrast to readings from 'traditional critics' who find her actions 'unnatural'.[18] The essay comments

---

[6] James Shapiro, ed., *Shakespeare in America* (New York, 2013), p. xxii.

[7] See John H. Westerhoff, *McGuffey and his Readers: Piety, Morality, and Education in Nineteenth-Century America* (Nashville, 1978).

[8] Alden T. Vaughan and Virginia Mason Vaughan, *Shakespeare in America* (Oxford, 2014), p. 2; see also Karen Cunningham, 'Shakespeare, the public, and public education', *Shakespeare Quarterly* 49 (1998), 293–8.

[9] Barbara A. Mowat and Paul Werstine, 'Preface', in *William Shakespeare's Macbeth*, ed. Mowat and Werstine (New York, 2012), p. ix.

[10] Barbara A. Mowat and Paul Werstine, 'Introduction', in *William Shakespeare's Macbeth*, ed. Mowat and Werstine, p. xv.

[11] Mowat and Werstine, 'Introduction', p. ix.

[12] Coleridge as qtd in Susan Snyder, '*Macbeth: a modern perspective*', in *William Shakespeare's Macbeth*, ed. Mowat and Werstine, p. 201.

[13] Snyder, '*Macbeth*', pp. 201, 204.

[14] Snyder, '*Macbeth*', p. 206. [15] Snyder, '*Macbeth*', p. 211.

[16] Snyder, '*Macbeth*', p. 208. [17] Snyder, '*Macbeth*', p. 208.

[18] Snyder, '*Macbeth*', pp. 208, 209.

that such observations only become apparent in light of 'cultural analysis'.[19] Key then to understanding *Macbeth* is careful reading, juxtaposed with a postulation concerning forms of oppression embedded within Christian and Aristotelian hierarchies. Right interpretation, as modelled by the essay, dredges up the seabed of certainty to see what constitutes it. A close reading premised on ambiguity is thus what the editors mean when they speak of 'modern' readings. Opening with Coleridge's assessment of *Macbeth*'s indisputable evil implies that moral certainty belongs to the past. Even the term 'traditional critics' connotes a past historical epoch since it describes those who accept without critique the world as presented in the text, implying that they themselves remain part of that world. The Folger's paratext thus demonstrates that to speak with a 'new voice', as the editors hope to do, one must discard scholarship unable to wash its hands of the hierarchies presented within the text.[20]

The Folger's emphasis on cultural relevance exemplifies a common concern of editors whose field's success is dependent on reaching new readers; nevertheless, this emphasis also underlines how editions transmit values, which, in this case, one can locate in the Folger's pedagogical telos. Observing a meeting between Folger editor Barbara Mowat and American high school teachers, David Bevington reports that teachers remain uninterested in 'introductory essays that lay out any sort of dogmatic interpretation'.[21] But they 'welcome an essay or so in the back of the book by a recent critic who can raise issues for classroom discussion'.[22] But what does it mean to be 'dogmatic'? While the critical ground-clearing of the discussion essay may be familiar to scholars, the move may appear confusing or startling to readers uninitiated into broader critical discourse. The essay's rhetorical turn, of course, might spark discussion, especially for students who find traditional readings convincing or helpful to the play. Nevertheless, to supply an essay that associates traditionalism with an outdated view of culture embodies the etymology of 'dogma', which means 'teaching' or, in the Greek, to 'seem

good'.[23] To be sure, the essay's tone is not doctrinaire; nonetheless, when it explains to students that 'relevant' readings are ones informed by contemporary criticism, the essay inculcates students into a sphere of concerns and values.

This inculcative framework tallies with Michael Warner's notion of a public. Publics use argument and polemic to speak to a group of strangers, who organize themselves not geographically but according to 'identity and belief'.[24] The essay in the Folger, meant to 'raise issues for classroom discussion', offers an argument suited for a dominant public. It instills in students the values of mainstream American education – which itself connotes the values of mainstream American culture; moreover, its insistence on the 'modern', the 'contemporary', the 'today' follows the temporal dictates of public speech, which are, according to Warner, positioned towards futurity.[25] Matters of intellectual and cultural capital also prove germane to this public: the Folger operates as a symbolic locus of Shakespeare in America. As Michael Bristol explains, the Folger's physical location near the Supreme Court and the Library of Congress, two dominant spaces of American judicial and intellectual power, 'helps to explicate the claim that Folger's Shakespeare's collection promotes the nation's interest'.[26] The language of scholarly expertise thus merges with institutional heft, the foundations upon which public dominance are established.

---

[19] Snyder, '*Macbeth*', p. 208.
[20] Mowat and Werstine, 'Introduction', p. xv.
[21] David Bevington, 'The New Folger Library Shakespeare', *Archiv für das Studium neueren Sprachen und Literaturen* 230 (1993), 378–84; p. 379.
[22] Bevington, 'New Folger', p. 380.
[23] 'dogma, n.', etymology, *OED Online*, June 2019: www.oed-com.proxy.library.nd.edu/view/Entry/56479?redirectedFrom=dogma.
[24] Michael Warner, *Publics and Counter Publics* (New York, 2005), pp. 75, 91.
[25] Warner, *Counter Publics*, p. 94.
[26] Michael D. Bristol, *Shakespeare's America, America's Shakespeare* (New York, 1990), p. 76.

Given the cultural authority of publishers like the Folger Shakespeare Library, it should be no surprise when a series appears that describes themselves as follows:

The Ignatius Critical Editions represent a tradition-oriented alternative to popular textbook series such as the Norton Critical Editions or Oxford World Classics, and are designed to concentrate on traditional readings of the Classics of world literature. While many modern critical editions have succumbed to the fads of modernism and postmodernism, this series will concentrate on tradition-oriented criticism of these great works.[27]

The Ignatius Critical Editions explicitly position themselves as a cultural counterweight to editions such as the Folger: they offer 'alternatives' focused on 'tradition-oriented criticism', which highlight the critical orientations of mainstream texts only to dismiss them as 'fads'. The derisiveness of the term 'fad' suggests that Ignatius finds the 'futurity' of mainstream editions to be superficial, even sophistic. In contrast, their editions 'represent a genuine extension of consumer choice, enabling educators, students, and lovers of good literature to buy editions of classic literary works without having to "buy into" the ideologies of secular fundamentalism'.[28] If, as Denise Albanese observes, an 'economy of mass production' is 'conjuncturally related' to mass education, Ignatius's invocation of 'consumer choice' accords with burgeoning support for educational choice in the United States in which goods and services are specifically tailored to diverse consumer bases.[29] Further, by listing 'educators, students, and lovers of good literature' as potential readers, the edition imagines an audience sympathetic to its polemic, an educational counterpublic.

Ignatius's posture of dissent exemplifies the discourse of the many counterpublics in the American educational landscape. For Warner, counterpublics describe 'a dominated group [that] aspires to re-create itself as a public and, in doing so, finds itself in conflict not only with the dominant social group, but also with the norms that constitute the dominant culture as a public'.[30] Such groups, Warner argues, use discord to maintain their

consciousness of subordination to that public.[31] The tactic by which counterpublics perform their subordination is discourse. Jonathan J. Edwards thus characterizes counterpublicity as 'a rhetorical process by which social movements continually rearticulate the boundaries of marginalization and resistance through discursive constructions of public exclusion and oppression'.[32] Edwards explores this resistance in the discourse of fundamentalist Protestantism, but it also appears in conservative Catholicism, as demonstrated in the Ignatius Critical Editions. These groups deploy their editions of *Macbeth* not only to challenge the discursive and temporal frameworks of mainstream education but also to establish their legitimacy as publics, a legitimacy built upon Shakespeare's cultural capital.

LEGITIMACY AND PURITY: BOB JONES UNIVERSITY PRESS

Let us first turn to an edition of *Macbeth* published by Bob Jones University Press. The publishing house remains inseparable from the university, which, since its establishment in 1927, has provided a bulwark defending fundamentalists in their protracted campaign against modernity. BJU's identity as 'fundamentalist' connotes both the resistance and marginalization common to counterpublics. For George Marsden, Protestant fundamentalism today echoes refrains present at its founding, which include a mandate to evangelize, to engage in personal piety, and to resist ardently both 'liberal theology and secularizing culture'.[33] Much fundamentalist resistance has focused on schooling. As the German research

---

27 'About the series', Ignatius Critical Editions: www.ignatius.com/promotions/ignatiuscriticaleditions/about.htm.

28 'About the series'.

29 Albanese, *Extramural Shakespeare*, p. 70.

30 Warner, *Counter Publics*, p. 112.

31 Warner, *Counter Publics*, pp. 118–19.

32 Jonathan J. Edwards, *Superchurch: The Rhetoric and Politics of American Fundamentalism* (East Lansing, 2015), p. 9.

33 George Marsden, *Fundamentalism and American Culture* (New York, 2006), p. 231.

model influenced American universities in the late nineteenth and early twentieth centuries, Protestant ministers and seminarians found themselves increasingly excluded from biblical scholarship.[34] They were also placed on the defensive following the Scopes Monkey Trial of 1925, which concerned whether the theory of evolution should be taught in state-funded Tennessee schools.[35] While the trial ended in victory for anti-evolutionists, they were often caricatured as uneducated and parochial – what satirist H. L. Mencken would call 'the simian faithful of Appalachia'.[36] Out of this cultural strife, institutions such as BJU emerged as godly alternatives to mainstream universities.

But even as these institutions openly positioned themselves as outside the landscape of mainstream education, they sought cultural legitimacy. BJU's founder, Bob Jones, Sr, believed evangelism and education went hand-in-hand with cultural refinement. Jones encouraged civility, contending that 'Jesus was a gentleman everywhere He went.'[37] The vision of the cultured fundamentalist extended to the fine arts. Within a year of the university's opening, BJU formed a troupe of actors called the 'Classic Players' who performed Shakespeare.[38] But, as Adam Laats avers, institutions like BJU 'always had to balance their absolute need for academic legitimacy with their equally non-negotiable need to maintain their reputations for religious purity'.[39] For BJU, the performances resulted in internecine strife: first, from fundamentalist leaders and institutions who claimed that 'drama eroded the spiritual sensitivity or receptivity of the American people', and second, from faculty members opposed to the performances, one of whom 'organized prayer meetings for the sole purpose of praying against Shakespearean plays'.[40] Bob Jones Sr, however, insisted on the performances, referring to Shakespeare as 'the most moral of playwrights'.[41] BJU's inclusion of Shakespeare provided a clear cultural signal: that it could cultivate the arts in a way contemporaneous with elite institutions such as Yale – which had recently formed a drama department; moreover, it justified that inclusion on moral grounds.[42] Such an approach also informs BJU's high school curriculum.

BJU expanded into the curriculum market in the 1970s with a series of textbooks aimed at Christian day schools and homeschooling families. According to Milton Gaither, the institution sought 'to create an authentically Christian curriculum from the ground up', but while BJU was interested in maintaining ideological purity, it needed to incorporate mainstream content, particularly at a time when home education had little legislative backing.[43] This tension between public legitimacy and counterpublic purity manifests in BJU's pedagogy. In *Christian Education: Its Mandate and Mission*, BJU English professor and *Macbeth* editor Ronald Horton models how fundamentalists justify texts found in mainstream education while still appealing to their counterpublic. Considering whether Christian teachers should censor texts, Horton turns to the Bible. Maintaining that the 'Bible is in reality completely self-consistent and purposeful in its presentation of evil', Horton argues that any literature would be permitted as long as it 'treats evil in the same way that it is treated in the Scriptures'.[44] His case study is *King Lear*'s blinding of Gloucester. Horton

---

[34] See B. M. Piestch, *Dispensational Modernism* (New York, 2015), p. 52.

[35] For an overview of the Scopes Trial and its impact on conservative education, see Adam Laats, *The Other School Reformers: Conservative Activism in American Education* (Cambridge, MA, 2015), pp. 25–72.

[36] As qtd in Molly Worthen, *Apostles of Reason: The Crisis of Authority in American Evangelicalism* (New York, 2014), p. 69.

[37] As qtd in Daniel Turner, *Standing without Apology: The History of Bob Jones University* (Greenville, SC, 1997), p. 80.

[38] Turner, *Standing*, p. 89.

[39] Adam Laats, *Fundamentalist U: Keeping the Faith in American Higher Education* (New York, 2018), p. 4.

[40] Turner, *Standing*, p. 64, 92.

[41] As qtd in Turner, *Standing*, p. 92.

[42] On the creation of American university playing troupes, see Mark Pilkinton, 'Performance, religion, and Shakespeare: staging ideology at Notre Dame', in *Shakespeare on the University Stage*, ed. Andrew James Hartley (New York, 2015), pp. 27–42; p. 28.

[43] Milton Gaither, *Homeschool: An American History* (New York, 2007), p. 153.

[44] Ronald Horton, *Christian Education: Its Mandate and Mission* (Greenville, SC, 1992), p. 55.

juxtaposes Gloucester's loss of sight against several biblical passages. He insists: 'Like Samson's blinding, Gloucester's is not gratuitous, nor is it, in relation to what Shakespeare means to emphasize, overtly explicit. It is a part of a scheme of moral consequences, and the moral tone is clear.'[45] The 'moral consequence' Horton describes is lechery, which he supports by citing Matthew 5.29: 'if your right eye causes you to sin, tear it out and throw it away'.[46] Such connections suggest how *Lear* presents a fitting image of evil conducive for moral and spiritual growth.

Benchmarking literature against the Bible illustrates a central tenet of fundamentalist thinking: presuppositionalism. A school of Protestant apologetics with parallels in postmodern epistemology, presuppositionalism argues that truth can only be revealed based on one's primary assumptions and that no knowledge arrives without those assumptions. For presuppositionalists – who include the softer cousin of fundamentalists, evangelicals – the Bible offers the only foundation for truth claims since it is divine revelation.[47] As Molly Worthen explains, presuppositionalists reject 'the Enlightenment ideal of pure, objective fact, insisting instead that no assumptions are neutral, and that the human mind can comprehend reality only by proceeding from the truth of biblical revelation'.[48] As the philosophical basis for fundamentalist counterdiscourse, presuppositionalism offers a standard by which all other perspectives are measured. BJU's *British Literature for Christian Schools*, for example, informs teachers that studying British literature can 'strengthen the student against the ungodly influences of the modern world'.[49] A reader can only achieve this aim, however, by first acknowledging the Bible to be the touchstone for all other texts.

BJU argues that *Macbeth* illustrates the virtues of moral perspicuity and individual responsibility, fitting its standard for godly literature. It situates *Macbeth* at the conclusion of a subunit on Tudor literature, which celebrates the 'Renaissance belief in the moral influence of poetic example' and touts the drama as a paragon of the 'Christian heroic worldview'.[50] The phrase implies that *Macbeth* contains a perspicuous moral in which good

ultimately triumphs over evil. Like the earlier appearance of evil in *King Lear*, evil in *Macbeth* is intentional. The appearance of witches, for instance, is not necessarily 'unedifying and spiritually subversive'; rather, the issue is whether evil manifests 'in the same way and to the same purpose and effect as it appears in the Scriptures', which it does, being a 'satanic deception' and a 'snare for the soul'.[51] At the same time, BJU finds at least one unedifying element in the play since it bowdlerizes portions of the Porter's speech without indication. This expurgation is not as significant as A Beka's, but it nevertheless signals where BJU finds the text unsuitable for fundamentalist readers.

BJU encompasses its Student Edition of *Macbeth* in a paratext that includes glosses, discussion questions and commentary notes, while its Teacher's Edition features supplemental instruction tips. The paratext emphasizes interpretative perspicuity, arguing that Shakespeare's audience would have viewed the play as a primarily didactic work. Learning objectives, for example, explain that students will be able to 'See . . . the compatibility of the didactic and artistic functions of literature'.[52] BJU enforces this didacticism in Teaching Notes, which clarify how student opinion should fall on specific discussion questions. For example, a question concluding Act 1 asks, 'Why does [Macbeth] say in lines 130–31 of Scene iii that "This supernatural soliciting / Cannot be ill, cannot be good"? Do you agree with his conclusion?'[53] According to the answer key, 'He says that the witches' prophecies cannot be ill because they have told him an initial truth; they

[45] Horton, *Christian Education*, p. 58.
[46] Matthew 5.29, *The Harper-Collins Study Bible* (New York, 2006).
[47] See Julie Ingersoll, *Building God's Kingdom: Inside the World of Christian Reconstruction* (New York, 2015), pp. 19–23.
[48] Worthen, *Apostles of Reason*, p. 30.
[49] Ronald Horton, *British Literature for Christian Schools*, 2nd edn (Greenville, SC, 2011), p. i.
[50] Horton, *British Literature*, pp. 119, 283.
[51] Horton, *British Literature*, pp. 201, 202.
[52] Horton, *British Literature*, p. 199.
[53] Horton, *British Literature*, p. 218.

cannot be good because his thoughts of murder greatly disturb his conscience. *Students should disagree with Macbeth's confusion of good and evil.*'[54] This emphasis also leads BJU to disavow readings of the play that veer from didacticism. The introduction in the Teacher's Edition repudiates presentist readings that come from 'directors and critics of this generation [who] tend to read into Shakespeare's plays their own meanings'.[55] 'This generation', it warns, is a 'modern skeptical generation with humanistic values and goals'.[56] The phrase 'this generation' is a biblical trope common to fundamentalists, who use it to condemn unbelieving outsiders in the same way that Christ did to condemn unbelieving Jews.[57] The claim characterizes the polemic common to counterpublics, heading them off from any interpretation belonging to the dominant public; moreover, it follows the counter temporal suspicion of futurity. Right interpretation, for BJU, is located in the past.

BJU also encourages character study as a means of demonstrating the play's didactic function and highlighting its relation to biblical exemplars. In this case, they focus almost exclusively on Macbeth's spiritual downfall. Calling Macbeth 'the most fearsome picture of spiritual desolation in literature', the Overview remarks, 'What can be more momentous, more dramatic, than the conflict within the soul concerning its eternal destiny?'[58] The Teaching Notes contain subtitles such as 'The cause and consequence of sin', 'The temptation of Macbeth', 'The progressive degeneration of Macbeth' and 'The ironic culmination of evil' and chart a trajectory of spiritual decay that educators can highlight for students. The emphasis on Macbeth eclipses the play's other characters, as evinced by the bland, singular subtitle, 'The character of Lady Macbeth'. The edition genders Lady Macbeth's ambition by linking her to biblical temptresses: Eve and Jezebel. A commentary note to Lady Macbeth's lines, 'Hie thee hither, / That I may pour my spirits in thine ear', explains, 'the line suggests evil spirits: a communication of supernatural inspiration from Satan to woman to man, repeating the process of the fall'.[59] Teaching Notes further link the force of her appeal to physical

allurement, arguing that her temptations are far more powerful than the Weird Sisters 'because of the contrast between her fair appearance and their ugliness'.[60] While commentary notes across editions identify biblical allusions, BJU's interest transcends historical and literary contextualization. Rather, these allusions attempt to ground characters' actions in broader biblical principles. They thus act as moral guideposts for readers assumedly familiar with the biblical text, and they reinforce the edition's presuppositionalist framework. In this way, BJU's emphasis on moral interpretation simultaneously teaches students the vocabulary of counterpublic discourse.

The moral certitude of BJU's *Macbeth* reflects a broader historiographical argument central to the textbook: that the height of British literary achievement coincided with a period that embraced a biblical worldview. This proposition appears in the Introduction, which lauds England's missionization and trade efforts before lamenting, 'The blessing of God rested richly upon England, though she proved far from worthy and eventually let it slip from her grasp. As England turned from God, she lost the spiritual leadership of the world. Her history and legacy are a faded glory and a - warning.'[61] The 'warning' speaks to the textbook's thesis, that 'literature from an early tradition was written, by and large, from a Biblical framework' before being corrupted by secular humanism.[62]

BJU carefully unyokes this secularism from the Protestant Reformation itself, arguing that Renaissance 'strengthened rather than weakened the Christian world view'.[63] The explicit target here is the Burckhardtian argument based in

---

[54] Horton, *British Literature*, p. 218 (emphasis mine).
[55] Horton, *British Literature*, p. 193.
[56] Horton, *British Literature*, p. 193.
[57] See Matthew 12.41–2; Luke 11.29–32.
[58] Horton, *British Literature*, p. 200.
[59] Horton, *British Literature*, p. 211.
[60] Horton, *British Literature*, p. 211.
[61] Horton, *British Literature*, p. iii.
[62] Horton, *British Literature*, p. 116.
[63] Horton, *British Literature*, p. 112.

progressivist historiography. In a note to teachers, BJU acknowledges that, while 'Burckhardt saw the Italian Renaissance as the beginning of the modern secularist world view and as the origin of modern individualism', contemporary historians 'have tended to stress the continuity of the Renaissance with the Middle Ages'.[64] Indeed, the perspective of most people 'was largely medieval', altered only by the 'new spiritual illumination from Protestantism'.[65] For this reason, fundamentalists should 'challenge the secularist view of the Renaissance', especially since, during this age, 'thought and literary expression came closer to a Biblical standard than they ever had before or have since'.[66] At stake for BJU is not the clarification of historical fact – indeed, the textbook maintains a fairly low opinion of medieval Christianity for its ties to Rome – but the legitimacy of a confessional identity predicated upon opposition to secularism.

These questions of confessional identity extend to the way BJU links literary accomplishment to presuppositionalism. For BJU, writers such as Edmund Spenser, John Foxe and William Shakespeare, those who specifically evoked the 'Christian heroic worldview', could only emerge from an era in which the Bible formed the foundation for thought and culture. According to the editor, this worldview remains unique to the Elizabethan Age. By the Stuart period, theatre's moral capacity had greatly diminished, with 'comedy tending toward sentimentality and tragedy toward sensationalism'.[67] BJU thus celebrates the moral perspicuity of an age that produces a work like *Macbeth*, an age that no longer resembles the present but one to which its reading public can aspire. Indeed, quoting Jonson's prefatory poem to the First Folio, the editor remarks, 'Shakespeare is "for all time" not only because great artistry is universally admired and retains its interest but also, and especially, because his writings communicate universal truths, permanently valid and basic to human happiness. These truths are Biblical principles.'[68] This logic illustrates what George Marsden views as the fundamentalists' relationship between 'right doctrine or right reason and right morality'.[69] One can add to that list right literature.

MARGINALIZATION AND DISSENT: IGNATIUS PRESS

When David Scott Kastan appraised the growth of theories surrounding Shakespeare's personal faith, he remarked, 'No document survives to satisfy our desire, but the absence has done little to quench the yearning for it.'[70] Kastan conjectures that the expanding scholarship around Shakespeare-as-recusant exposes a lacuna in prevailing accounts that tend to ignore or dismiss questions of belief. 'A dissident Shakespeare', he observes, 'is for us more appealing, perhaps more useful, than the Shakespeare who for so long has been co-opted to articulate and guarantee the norms of a dominant structure.'[71] In Kastan's view, Catholic versions of Shakespeare are proxy for the shortcomings of a historiography still grappling with a Shakespeare who, perhaps unwittingly, retains the residue of Whig history. But Kastan also gestures towards a broader failure, the demurral from the secular telos of Enlightenment thinking, one also taken up by counterpublics who find in this non-dominant narrative a Shakespeare whose faith – and consequent persecution for that faith – becomes paradigmatic of their own subordination.

This polemic characterizes the editions published by Ignatius Press. Founded in 1979 by Joseph Fessio, SJ, the Press forms part of the St Ignatius Institute, an independent undergraduate programme housed at the Jesuit-run University of San Francisco. The Institute and Press both emerged in response to theological and cultural

---

64 Horton, *British Literature*, p. 116.
65 Horton, *British Literature*, p. 116.
66 Horton, *British Literature*, p. 117.
67 Horton, *British Literature*, p. 283.
68 Horton, *British Literature*, p. 193.
69 Marsden, *Fundamentalism*, pp. 26–7.
70 David Scott Kastan, *A Will to Believe: Shakespeare and Religion* (New York, 2014), p. 18.
71 Kastan, *Shakespeare and Religion*, p. 17.

shifts occurring in the mid twentieth century. Fessio, whose Ph.D. supervisor was Joseph Ratzinger (Pope Benedict XVI), helped to organize the Fellowship of Catholic Scholars, a group of scholars whose intent was to resist 'radical' interpretations of the Second Vatican Council.[72] After leaving the St Ignatius Institute, Fessio became the provost and then theologian-in-residence of Ave Maria University, an institution founded by Domino's Pizza tycoon Tom Monaghan in 1998 and devoted to the teaching of the Catholic magisterium. Fessio thus established one part of a network of conservative institutions, organizations and presses, a network that forged counterpublics in ways similar to fundamentalist Protestant groups.

Conservative Catholics share much of the same counterdiscourse found in their fundamentalist peers, but, as R. Scott Appleby contends, they focus on 'preserving or defending Roman Catholic orthodoxy ("right belief")', a defence often couched in the language of 'tradition'.[73] The term speaks to the cultural orientation of conservative Catholicism which, in its current incarnation, surfaced in the theological wake of the Second Vatican Council and *Humanae vitae* (the Catholic teaching on birth control), as well as the cultural upheaval around reproductive rights and the Equal Rights Amendment. These movements led to a belief, according to James Hitchcock, that 'under liberal administrations, government power was being used to promote an objectional social agenda'.[74] 'Tradition' then, which literally signifies the handing-down of received teaching, suggests not only adherence to the dictates of established Catholic doctrine but also resistance to social or cultural challenges to those doctrines.

These questions around tradition and their relationship to counterpublicity permeate the Ignatius Critical Editions. Marketed towards Catholic educational institutions and homeschooling families, the Ignatius editions are standalone texts whose paratext features an introductory essay along with supplemental essays written by scholars who are not necessarily Catholic but sympathetic to the series methodology. Separate study guides are also available for purchase. An introduction to the study guides explains that the editions provide readers with a 'tradition-oriented perspective', which means those 'seeking deconstruction, "queer theory", feminism, postcolonialism, and other manifestations of the latest academic fads and fashions will be disappointed'.[75] These editions thus hope to inoculate students against the 'post-modernist context of radical skepticism', leading them instead to 'highlight what is true and great ... and expose and defang what is false'.[76] In this respect, the Ignatius editions share with BJU an intent to deploy literature as a means of ideological boundary marking, an action performed within the paratext.

The editor of the Ignatius editions, Joseph Pearce, is a former writer-in-residence at Ave Maria University. Pearce follows Richard Wilson's thesis that Shakespeare's furtive Catholicism influenced his plays, but, while Wilson takes aim at the cultural underpinnings informing scholarly bias, Pearce's target is broader, being the scholarly community writ large. In *The Quest for Shakespeare: The Bard of Avon and the Church of Rome*, also published by Ignatius Press, Pearce proclaims that 'Shakespeare was a Catholic, at a time when Catholics were subject to a great deal of ruthless persecution.'[77] Pearce's insistence on highlighting the persecution of Shakespeare's faith community as much as the faith itself is indicative of a larger anxiety around cultural marginality. For him, the oppression of English Catholics resembles contemporary efforts

---

[72] James Hitchcock, 'The Fellowship of Catholic Scholars', in *Being Right: Conservative Catholics in America*, ed. Mary Jo Weaver and R. Scott Appleby (Bloomington, IN, 1995), p. 189.

[73] R. Scott Appleby, 'The triumph of Americanism: common ground for U.S. Catholics in the twentieth century', in *Being Right*, ed. Weaver and Appleby, p. 37.

[74] Hitchcock, 'Fellowship', p. 188.

[75] Eleanor Bourg Nicholson and Joseph Pearce, eds., *Study Guide for Macbeth by William Shakespeare* (San Francisco, 2010), p. 12.

[76] Nicholson and Pearce, eds., *Study Guide*, p. 8.

[77] Joseph Pearce, *The Quest for Shakespeare: The Bard of Avon and the Church of Rome* (San Francisco, 2008), p. 9.

to marginalize religious conservatives. In his discussion of *King Lear*, Pearce argues that Shakespeare created a 'dialectic against secularism and the secular state', manifested in the contrast between Goneril and Regan's flattery and Cordelia's honesty.[78] For him, the scene recalls the anguish following Henry VIII's Act of Supremacy in which Catholics 'were forced to choose between conforming to his wishes and incurring his wrath', leaving 'only the most courageous [to choose] conscience before concupiscence'.[79] The analogy extends to the present. In an article for the *National Catholic Register*, Pearce outlines how the persecution of recusants resembles the disenfranchisement felt by conservative Catholics: 'Henry VIII was not a Protestant but a tyrant. In declaring himself the head of the Church in England he was making religion a servile subject of the secular power. He was demanding that the things of God be rendered unto Caesar. Parallels with the secularism of our own time and its war on religious liberty are palpable.'[80] Pearce's counterdiscourse contains several parallels: the first between the ruthless secularism of the Tudor/Stuart regimes and the present state; the second between persecuted recusants and marginalized counterpublics. This persecutory leitmotif not only permeates Pearce's writings on Shakespeare's life, it also informs the Ignatius edition of *Macbeth*.

Unlike BJU's historiography, which celebrates Shakespeare's work as emerging from the Golden Age of biblical thought, the Ignatius editions imagine his plays as responding to the intense persecution of English Catholics. The introductory essay, written by Pearce, focuses on the 'equivocator' described by the Porter in Act 2, a term commonly associated with conspirator Robert Catesby's defence following the Gunpowder Plot. For Pearce, the allusion to Catesby symbolizes the initial disappointment and subsequent fear expressed by James I's Catholic subjects, who longed for toleration following the King's ascension but faced increased suspicion after the Gunpowder Plot. The essay also links the plot to the Stuart court through the 'Machiavellian

machinations of Sir Robert Cecil', who knew about the plot 'well in advance' and wanted James to 'increase the persecution of England's "papists"' – a claim also advanced in an accompanying critical essay.[81] The ensuing persecution, according to the Introduction, was the impetus for a tragedy in which Shakespeare offers his audience two separate visions of kingship: one built on the 'Christian virtue' of Duncan and Edward the Confessor, and a second rooted in the Machiavellian scheming of Macbeth.[82] Pearce connects this latter image of kingship to James through 'an intriguing metadramatic subplot', the Gowrie Conspiracy, in which James was believed to have murdered the Earl of Gowrie and confiscated his estate.[83] After the court banned an earlier play based on the event, Shakespeare found in *Macbeth* a means of taking subtler aim at James. The play thus condemns a 'Machiavellian monarch', such as James, who invents 'conspiracies in order to profit thereby', and issues a call to return to the noble image of kingship found in the Catholic monarchs of ages past.[84]

The confessional historiography presented in the introduction also appears in the edition's critical essays. One argues that *Macbeth* contrasts the 'new Renaissance secularism' – apparent in Lady Macbeth's wiles and Macbeth's treacherous hospitality – with the 'traditional understanding of man' found in the 'living tradition of pre-Reformation Christianity'.[85] Another essay, which examines how Shakespeare adapted *Macbeth* from Holinshed's *Chronicles*, contends that parallels

---

[78] Pearce, *Quest*, p. 184. [79] Pearce, *Quest*, p. 184.
[80] Joseph Pearce, 'Recusants and martyrs who resisted England's Tudor terror', *National Catholic Register*, 8 July 2019: www.ncregister.com/blog/josephpearce/recusants-and-martyrs-who-resisted-englands-tudor-terror.
[81] Joseph Pearce, 'Introduction', in *William Shakespeare's Macbeth*, ed. Pearce (San Francisco, 2010), pp. ix–xxx; p. ix.
[82] Pearce, 'Introduction', p. xiii.
[83] Pearce, 'Introduction', p. xiii.
[84] Pearce, 'Introduction', p. xxiv.
[85] Robert Carballo, '"Fair is foul, and foul is fair"', in *William Shakespeare's Macbeth*, ed. Pearce, pp. 147–60; pp. 148, 156, 158.

between the bloody Makbeth of Holinshed and bloody monarchs like Henry VIII could 'hardly be overlooked' in light of Shakespeare's Catholicism.[86] Other essays remain more discreet on the nature of Shakespeare's faith, observing that it 'requires a depth of nuance', but nevertheless maintain that belief remains central to Shakespeare's artistry, arguing that 'real assent to quasi-religious convictions – such as the existence of the soul, the existence of a natural order, and the existence of evil – is not only necessary for the imaginative work of Shakespearean drama but is the actual sign of its artistic origins'.[87] Such claims echo one of BJU's primary assertions – that what makes Shakespeare 'for all time' is his adherence to orthodoxy, which, for Ignatius, is inseparable from his desire to create powerful drama that tacitly resisted the state.

Inasmuch as the paratext of *Macbeth* offers a confessional historiography amenable to its counterpublic, amalgamating and interpreting history to celebrate the ingenuity and perseverance of England's Catholics, it also must broach the peripherality of its contentions. To justify its claims, the introductory essay invokes an epistemological scaffolding also found in BJU and the Folger, suggesting that right belief can produce right readings. The essay contends that 'Shakespeare's commentary on the issues of his own time can be fathomed only by diligent detective work on the part of later generations, and when such detective work is deficient or defective, the contemporary meaning of the plays is lost'.[88] That the Introduction focuses on 'the contemporary meaning' of the plays suggests a link between Shakespeare's time and the present. This claim also appears in Pearce's *The Quest for Shakespeare*. Likening the quest for Shakespeare's faith to that of the Holy Grail, Pearce remarks:

there are those critics who join the quest for Grail but discover that it was not, in fact, holy; it was a mere cup, like any other, or, at any rate, a cup remarkably like the graven image of the critics themselves. For these critics, Shakespeare emerges, in spite of the abundance of evidence for his Catholicism, as a progenitor of modern secularism, as a man who, ahead of his time, turned his back on the faith of his fathers and embraced the agnosticism of his time.[89]

The passage's pilgrimage metaphor, along with the problem of misrecognition, imply that Shakespeare's true faith can only be discovered by the truly faithful. This refrain should sound familiar by now since it follows the same rhetorical strains apparent in not only BJU's retort against 'this generation', but also the Folger's dismissal of 'traditional critics'. Such interpretative boundary-marking draws readers into publics by characterizing naysayers as misguided or misinformed. In this way, all three of these publishers appear to share strands of BJU's presuppositionalism, in which a person must begin from a standpoint of right belief to discover a text's correct interpretation. One, however, plays the dominant role, while the others perform their subordination through acts of resistance.

CONCLUSION: COUNTERPUBLICS, CONSUMER CHOICE AND FRACTURED REALITIES

As movements constituted of discord and dissent, counterpublics craft a vision of Shakespeare that legitimates their resistance to mainstream education. Within a market-driven economy, however, that resistance manifests through consumer choice as much as through political or social action. Parents may remove their children from public schooling as an act of dissent, but they may also purchase curricula that accord with the realities, narratives and assumptions that govern their counterpublic identity. But Shakespeare retains a central role in these curricula. For BJU, his works highlight Protestantism's contribution to the great classics of literature. This elevation does not hold even for other authors who explicitly

---

[86] Hildegard Hammerschmidt-Hummel, 'The Tragedy of Macbeth: A History Play with a Message for Shakespeare's Contemporaries?' in *William Shakespeare's Macbeth*, ed. Pearce, pp. 161–80; p. 169.

[87] Lee Oser, 'The vision of evil in Macbeth', in *William Shakespeare's Macbeth*, ed. Pearce, pp. 189–204; p. 194.

[88] Pearce, 'Introduction', p. xvi. [89] Pearce, *Quest*, p. 18.

cite the Scriptures. The works of Gerard Manley Hopkins are only 'religious' rather than 'Christian' since his Catholicism implies that 'he did not profess the saving faith of the Scriptures'.[90] Shakespeare's works are unique, being rooted in a culture that fundamentalists believe elevated the Bible as the source of all truth. For conservative Catholics, the case is similar. Under the editorial hand of Ignatius Press, Shakespeare's alleged Catholicism has expanded from a coterie of sympathizers to Catholic school students across the nation. For these readers, Shakespeare's plays offer the possibility of not only viewing the world as he did but also living as he did, striving to retain the virtue of tradition amidst the hostility of secularism – past and present. As with BJU, no other author receives the attention that Shakespeare does in the Ignatius editions. While critical editions exist for authors such as Charles Dickens

and Jane Austen, Shakespeare's plays far outnumber the works of other authors. Shakespeare's predominance within these curricula illustrates his continuing role as a source of cultural capital as well as a symbol of being 'educated'. At the same time, the fractious and fractured interpretations of Shakespeare's plays – and Shakespeare himself – found in these curricula demonstrate how, even as Shakespeare may contribute to the 'lingua franca' of American education – and, by extension, American culture – the language itself is increasingly devolving into a series of mutually unintelligible dialects, all vying for power. Indeed, these disparate images of Shakespeare exemplify an America struggling to articulate not only who should share its common tongue, but also what it should say.

---

[90] Horton, *Christian Education*, p. 103.

TAKING LOVE'S LABOUR'S LOST SERIOUSLY

NIGEL WOOD

One of Jack Cade's more utopian demands in *King Henry VI, Part II* is to dispense with books altogether, arraigning the Lord Say not only for being complicit in the loss of Normandy but also for the corruption of 'the youth of the realm in erecting a grammar school' whereby books were the new currency issuing forth from his own paper-mill, 'contrary to the King his crown and dignity' (4.7.31, 34–5). This is no simple parody of the fall-guy conspirator, however, for there – unexpectedly – is some force in his objections to civility. The act of appointing Justices of the Peace who could try poor men who knew not how to answer so as to claim benefit of clergy (4.7.38–43) has its own cogency, even if it is bundled up with the same mob mentality that also cares not to enquire about personalities when Cinna the Poet in *Julius Caesar* is in the wrong place and at the wrong time (3.3). Say compounds his errors by quoting Latin (even if it had become proverbial by the 1590s),[1] and then confirming his humanist credentials by objecting to the fact that 'ignorance is the curse of God / Knowledge the wing wherewith we fly to heaven. / Unless you be possessed with devilish spirits' (4.7.72–4). The passage is shot through with a deeper level of irony, for Cade's case against Say illustrates that it was attempted with an accurate recall of correct legal formulae, whereby imputed crimes 'contrary to the King his crown and dignity' were worth detailed investigation, and Cade foretells a time when no wife is safe once he is regarded as '*in capite*', enjoying status and power in direct line of command from the crown (4.7.121). He is more learned than he would like his men to discover.

The deliberate anachronism Shakespeare introduces directs an audience to a contemporary context. Caxton's introduction of printing into England is dated 1476, whereas Say's death occurred in 1450. Paper mills were first established in 1495. There is some distinction between the aired learning of a Cade and of a Say, and some of the allusions at play in this scene had become proverbial. Say's proxy leadership – short of battlefield involvement – is underpinned by an Ovidian allusion that 'Great men have reaching hands' (4.7.79),[2] which was probably generally known,[3] but Say's eulogy on behalf of Kent derives from Julius Caesar's *De bello gallico* (4.7.53),[4] a particularly recondite item of knowledge. Shakespeare's allusive reach, however, comprehends both the popular and the learned.

Holinshed himself might have given Shakespeare the germ of this idea, for his depiction of the anti-intellectual climate reigning during Wat Tyler's rebellion brings home the basis for a swingeing revolution in the removal of all past records and

---

[1] See Morris P. Tilley, *A Dictionary of the Proverbs in England in the Sixteenth and Seventeenth Centuries* (Ann Arbor, 1950), E146.

[2] *Heroides*, XVII.166, in *Ovid: Heroides, Amores*, trans. Grant Showerman, rev. G. P. Goold (Cambridge, MA, 1977), p. 237.

[3] See Tilley, *Proverbs*, K87: 'Kings have long arms.'

[4] Julius Caesar, *De bello gallico*, 5.14, in Caesar, *The Gallic War*, trans. H. J. Edwards (Cambridge, MA, 1917), p. 252. In Golding's translation (1564), this is rendered as 'Of all the inhabitants of this isle the civillest are the Kentish folke.' Quoted in *King Henry VI, Part 2*, ed. Ronald Knowles (London, 1999), n. to 4.7.55–6.

those – in law – who might support the status quo with their records. Tyler's group recognized the taint of corruption in grammar schools:

What wickedness was it to compel teachers of children in grammar schools to swear never to instruct any their art? ... For it was dangerous among them to be known for one that was learned, and more dangerous if any man were found with a penner and inkhorn at his side; for such seldom or never escaped from them with life.[5]

It is worth dwelling on the complexities that emerge in the debate (of long standing) that surrounds Shakespeare's learning and how it might extend into matters of interpretation. The verdict on his natural genius is always to be placed in the cultural context of the judge, be it Milton's discovery of 'fancy's child', apt to 'Warble his native wood-notes wild' (*L'Allegro*, ll. 133–4),[6] or Jonson's celebration of his gift, wherein his 'small Latin, and less Greek' had little part in celebrating the Bard in her/his own terms – and to confirm the deployment of decorative uses of classical allusion.[7]

Andrew Gurr opens up a carefully nuanced approach to where the debate about Shakespeare's own individual talent might lead us and how it may be indebted to tradition by focusing on a Jonsonian term, 'application' – that is, the encouragement for an audience to use any allusive source text as a lens through which to trace thematic significance, either locally in a particular passage or, holistically, across the whole action. Jonson's concern about this opportunity for latitude in understanding is best exemplified in the 'Epistle' to *Volpone*:

Application is now grown a trade with many; and there are that profess to have a key for the deciphering of every thing: but let wise and noble persons take heed how they be too credulous, or give leave to these invading interpreters to be over-familiar with their fames, who cunningly, and often, utter their own virulent malice, under other men's simplest meanings.[8]

Some editorial annotation might unearth echoes that record merely an appreciation of felicitous phrasing brought to mind out of one's own commonplace book, and this may not direct us further than to a conclusion that they were signs of a well-stocked and well-educated memory. As Gurr puts it, 'what needs to be sought out is evidence that the playwrights themselves, and even better their audiences, did have an interest in and capacity to seize on the applications we now find in the plays'.[9] Jonson exhibits a preoccupation with misapplication, the appropriation of any original meaning that is misapplied with some malice. This poses the question as to how to take further Gurr's judicially chosen words, 'seize on', in relation to how the original target audience (or at least the sufficiently literate portion) might have regarded these learned items: as simply well-expressed, or as carrying deeper meanings, or both. The 'trade' of application covers a range of interpretation that is more willed by the spectator than could possibly have been intended by the author. His Virgil in *Poetaster* (1602) helps Jonson take aim against the invectives and in-fighting that surrounded 'applications':

'Tis not the wholesome sharp morality,
Or modest anger of a satiric spirit
That hurts, or wounds the body of a state;
But the sinister application
Of the malicious, ignorant, and base
Interpreter: who will distort, and strain
The general scope and purpose of an author
To his particular, and private spleen.[10]

---

[5] Raphael Holinshed, *The Chronicles of England, Scotland and Ireland*, 2nd edn (1587), 6 vols. (reprinted 1808), vol. 2, p. 737.

[6] The Milton text consulted is *Milton: The Shorter Poems*, ed. John Carey (London, 1968).

[7] 'To the Memory of My Beloved, The Author Mr William Shakespeare: And What He Hath Left Us', l. 31, in *Ben Jonson: The Complete Poems*, ed. George Parfitt (Harmondsworth, 1975), p. 264.

[8] Ben Jonson, *Volpone*, 2nd edn, ed. Robert N. Watson (London, 2003), p. 167.

[9] Andrew Gurr, *Shakespeare's Workplace* (Cambridge, 2017), p. 186.

[10] Poetaster, or His Arraignment, V.iii.118–25, in *The Complete Plays of Ben Jonson*, 6 vols., ed. G. A. Wilkes (Oxford, 1981), vol. 2, p. 208. See also his ambiguous verdict on truth-telling:

For he knows, poet never credit gained
By writing truths, but things like truths well feigned.
If any yet will, with particular sleight
Of application, wrest what he doth write,

Jonson presumes that this malice is prevalent on account of spectators who are ill disposed but it is supposed that, aside from the vulgar who simply demand spectacle, there may be over-interpretation either due to their learning (which leads to an excess of ingenuity) or their imagining that they are in the know about contemporary affairs. One might bring to mind the fatuous Sir Politic Would-Be who construes a meeting with Volpone in disguise as an Italian mountebank as an encounter with one of the 'only knowing men of Europe!', largely as they are the best 'languaged men of all the world!'[11]

How might the authentic artist escape the temptation that a facility with words presents? In theatrical terms, it is largely a matter of knowing how much learning carries the footlights so that the audience might be able to 'seize on' presented learning, including allusions and any trading off known narratives. Indeed, the need to amplify an argument was embedded in any humanist education via Erasmus's preference for *copia verborum*, wherein, far from enlisting a method of self-display, one established the foundation for any premise by quoting precedent from one's reading and also a store of allusions that converted any Latin formulae into the vernacular through application.[12] Less well documented is the possibility that – far from simply adopting an honoured check-list to show one's learning – practice might actually alter the source evidence in the resort to contemporary application. Peter Mack's concluding remarks highlight not only the educational ubiquity in Elizabethan syllabi of memorizing classical sentences to enable graceful exposition, but also how they could be used to exploit tradition as well as develop it, involving how 'moral sentences' led to a classification of events, wherein they could be used as 'starting points for arguments about policy and legislation', even as they could also be methods for evasion.[13] Whilst the wording or trope might remain constant, its significance does not. This does not prevent Shakespeare offering up copiousness as absurd redundancy; one might remember in *Love's Labour's Lost* Holofernes's pedantry in trying to impress Nathaniel and discountenance Dull at 4.2, with what one might call failed copiousness and

impractical classical allusion. The deer in question is not part of a political proposition and the over-arching sky requires no necessary embellishment; it is rhetorical trickery and perhaps a test of Holofernes's Latin, where 'synonomy' is clumsily interspersed with the vernacular (4.2.3–21).[14]

This could add to our recognition of a dichotomy in early modern drama wherein its original qualities (a striving for selfhood and the attainment of a persuasive and resonant linguistic register) might arise from a standardized rhetorical education. Shortcuts towards both intelligibility and significance lay in the centrality of imitation as a classroom practice. Roger Ascham in his *The Scholemaster* (1570) was not alone in advancing the claims of imitation in a well-balanced education, and this is often understood as an evaluative scale based merely on the need to polish the language so that truths may be rendered evident to all without the quirks of modishness. His pedagogy was based on an alliance of apt words that brought into view nature and basic human responses: '*Imitation*, is a facultie to expresse liuelie and perfitelie that example: which ye go about to folow. And of it selfe, it is large and wide: for all the workes of nature, in a maner be examples for arte to folow.'[15]

And that he meant or him or her will say,
They make a libel which he made a play.
　　　　('Another [Prologue], Occasioned by some
　　　　person's impertinent exception', ll. 9–14,
　　　　in *Epicoene or The Silent Woman*, ed
　　　　R. V. Holdsworth (London, 1979),
　　　　pp. 9–10)

[11] *Volpone*, ed. Watson, p. 46, II.ii.9–13.

[12] See a fuller account in Peter Mack, *Elizabethan Rhetoric: Theory and Practice* (Cambridge, 2002), pp. 31–2, 76–84, 293–7.

[13] Mack, *Elizabethan Rhetoric*, p. 298. Erasmus's demonstration of how *copia* might amplify and lend resonance to any statement can be found in his *De copia*, ed. B. Knott, in the *Opera omnia*, 10 vols., vol. 1-6 (Amsterdam, 1988), pp. 202–15.

[14] See H. R. Woudhuysen's notes to ll. 3–4, and 5, in William Shakespeare, *Love's Labour's Lost*, ed. H. R. Woudhuysen (Walton-on Thames, 1998), pp. 186–9.

[15] Roger Ascham, *The scholemaster or plaine and perfite way of teachyng children, to vnderstand, write, and speake, the Latin tong but specially purposed for the priuate bryngyng vp of youth in ientlemen and noble mens houses, and commodious also for all such, as haue forgot the Latin tonge* ... (London, 1570), p. 45.

A rhetorical education served as a tool for comprehending how the 'example' one chose might be made visible; indeed, it served as a means by which one came to know oneself: 'For as ye vse to heare, so ye learne to speake; if ye heare no other, ye speake not your selfe',[16] in that you were condemned to parrot the linguistic registers that were merely convenient. Ascham's aim, the provision of a model fitted for a 'priuate brynging vp of youth in ientlemen and noble mens houses', according to the title page, did not directly apply to grammar schools, even if its preferences bore upon such education. There is the temptation to follow the most obvious motives for such pedagogy and conclude that linguistic propriety could promote semantics as if the signifier encompassed the signified in this regard. This is to simplify – to a fault.

Ascham's objective to marry a rhetorical training with ethics is in line with the humanist aspiration to instil choice above obedience and reason above tradition, even if such qualities were initially moulded by inherited models of expression:

Ye know not, what hurt ye do to learning, that care not for wordes, but for matter, and so make a deuorse betwixt the tong and the hart. For marke all aiges: looke vpon the whole course of both the Gréeke and Latin tonge, and ye shall surelie finde, that, whan apte and good wordes began to be neglected, and properties of those two tonges to be confounded, than also began, ill deedes to spring.[17]

This could lead in at least two subtly alternative directions: towards a focus on smoothness of style that would promote, and in some cases actually provide, a coherence in judgement and ethical decision-making; and, alternatively, an avoidance of the eccentric and ossified repetitiveness of mere rote learning. For George Puttenham, imitation was inescapable if one wished to escape the 'naturall', for it only through 'study & discipline or exercise' that one could learn how to see the external world: 'better to see with spectacles then not to see at all'.[18]

What is therefore at stake in the use of rhetorical tropes is not just euphony or clarification. When Nathaniel castigates Dull for his slowness, it is because he has 'never fed of the dainties that are bred in a book', and not ever eaten 'paper' or 'drunk ink' (4.2.24–6). It would be a test case for audience response as to whether in performance Dull is actually diminished by this charge. His identification of Holofernes and Nathaniel as 'bookmen' (4.2.34) simply confirms their own status as pedants, where their (fallacious) belief in words as a means to manage and/or define reality is of similar comic potential.

In the case of *Love's Labour's Lost*, its verbal gymnastics and its playing with roles and status is a well-worn topic. Indeed, these features have bedevilled its stage history – little action and sometimes excessive and now impenetrable allusions have seen its significance limited to contemporary satire or an attention to issues now irrelevant. What has generated a more recent recuperation of the play's attractiveness is its metatheatrical sport and the attendant holiday from high seriousness, all leading up to that abrupt entrance of Mercadé that puts a stop to frivolity and recreation. One might conclude that most audiences are kept waiting over-long for the ironic counterpoint to arrive, the deliverance from wordplay and diversion to cease and an outer reality to intrude. Indeed, in more than one production, the King's desperate attempt to halt Costard's interjections with 'No words!' (1.1.225) has been known to meet with ripples of laughter. Any audience reaction to this display of rhetoric is difficult to ascertain, then as now. Harold Bloom's appreciation of its linguistic exuberance is a fond and unashamedly subjective verdict, illustrating how its 'fireworks' prove that 'Shakespeare seems to seek the limits of his verbal resources, and discovers that there are none.' This makes it almost a predestined failure on the stage, as any production he had seen had not performed 'to its vocal magnificence'.[19] There is a critical

---

[16] Ascham, *Scholemaster*, p. 46.
[17] Ascham, *Scholemaster*, p. 46.
[18] George Puttenham, *The Arte of English Poesie Contriued into Three Bookes: the first of poets and poesie, the second of proportion, the third of ornament* (London, 1589), pp. 255–6.
[19] Harold Bloom, *Shakespeare: The Invention of the Human* (London, 1999), p. 121.

heritage feeding into this judgement, most memorably from Samuel Johnson, who, in the Preface to his edition (1765), depicted his Shakespeare as addicted to the pun or witty diversion – a 'quibble' – that resembled the 'luminous vapours' that beset the traveller, apt to 'engulf him in the mire', or as the 'fatal Cleopatra for whom he lost the world, and was content to lose it'.[20] For Johnson and his contemporaries, Shakespeare slipped the noose of education or correctness to reveal a mind naturally fertile and a talent that is an instinctive rebuke to art.[21]

In theatrical terms, the recent re-discovery of the play's merits has taken two routes: a delving into yesteryear escapism; or a more persistent and embedded distrust of the rhetoric, leading to the aperçu that the 'honest plain words' of harsh reality that Berowne comes to discern (5.2.745) have been waiting in the wings throughout. On the one hand, the action is sustained by glitter and song, as in Kenneth Branagh's film of 2000 or the locker-room japes of Alex Timbers's adaptation (Delacorte Theater, Shakespeare in the Park, 2013). On the other, minus the interpolated musical numbers redolent of the golden age of film or prom night, there is a vespertinal desperation underlying the role-play, an almost Chekhovian melancholy that is apt to anticipate Mercadé's entrance. This mood, which leads ironically to a concluding coming of age for the male characters, was most influential from Peter Brook's RSC production of 1946, where there was a whistling to keep the post-war spirits up yet, simultaneously, a trope of *et in Arcadia ego* derived indirectly from the Watteau-inspired set.[22] This has survived in an occasional re-location of the action in the fragile pre-war calm before the storm of world conflict, most recently (and in a return to ourselves) captured in Christopher Luscombe's RSC version (2014), where the four 'academicians' change into battle dress for the last scene, and march off, leaving the rest of the cast in a fixed pose of deep reflection.

We either immerse ourselves in the verbal texture or gradually come to distrust it. When, in *The Merchant of Venice*, Lorenzo loses patience with

Gobbo's own brand of quibbling, his exasperation resembles the King's in the search for plainness: 'How every fool can play upon the word! I think the best grace of wit will shortly turn into silence, and discourse grow commendable in none only but parrots' (3.5.41–3). This fear that one might be reliant on some hand-me-down lexicon, feasting off – as Costard notes to Moth about Armado – an 'alms-basket of words' (5.1.38–9) is one of the threads throughout the play. With Jonson's fear of 'application' in mind, one might turn to his image of the 'vita humana' in his *Timber: or Discoveries* (written c. 1635; pub. 1640):

I have considered, our whole life is like a play: wherein every man, forgetful of himself, is in travail with expression of another. Nay, we so insist in imitating others, as we cannot (when it is necessary) return to ourselves: like children, that imitate the vices of stammerers so long, till at last they become such; and make the habit to another nature, as it is never forgotten.[23]

This loss of self is one consequence of an over-reliance on education, as is the attainment of a 'correct' one. 'Another nature' is dual in its significance for Jonson and others, and it adds a width of significance to his oft-quoted dictum: 'Language most shows a man: speak that I may see thee . . . No glass renders a man's form, or likeness, so true as his

---

[20] *Samuel Johnson*, ed. Donald Greene, Oxford Authors (Oxford, 1984), p. 429.

[21] This debate might be best exemplified by the first-wave commentators on Shakespeare's text in the mid eighteenth century. In Richard Farmer's *An essay on the learning of Shakespeare: addressed to Joseph Cradock, Esq; By Richard Farmer, M.A. Fellow of Emmanuel-College, Cambridge, and of the Society of Antiquaries, London* (Cambridge, 1767): 'It is indeed strange that any *real* Friends of our immortal POET should be still willing to force him into a situation which is not tenable: treat him as a *learned* Man, and what shall excuse the most gross violations of History, Chronology, and Geography?' (quoted in *Shakespeare: The Critical Heritage*, ed. Brian Vickers, 6 vols. (London and Cambridge, MA, 1974–81), vol. 5, p. 260.

[22] For a fuller account, see Miriam Gilbert's *Shakespeare in Performance: Love's Labour's Lost* (Manchester, 1993), pp. 45–51.

[23] *Ben Jonson*, ed. Parfitt, p. 407.

speech.'[24] To approach *Love's Labour's Lost* as an exercise in epistemology is not to ignore its preoccupation with language as this stems from a variety of humanist educational projects.

It is notable that it is difficult to locate source material for the play. It is entirely possible that it has local roots in satire or recondite allusions to contemporary events. Richard Wilson has recently constructed a detailed case for its 'worldly' status, tying in its penitential terms of charity – to 'move wild laughter in the throat of death' whilst tending to the 'speechless sick' and 'groaning wretches' (5.2.837–41) – to news that Henri, King of Navarre, at Easter 1594, had undertaken several acts of charity, namely tending to the dying at the Hôtel-Dieu, washing the feet of beggars and touching the suppurating sores of some 660 sufferers of the king's evil, as well as extending clemency to several prisoners. This is the same figure that underwent a religious volte-face in converting to Catholicism, culminating in a glittering Mass at the abbey of Saint-Denis on the outskirts of Paris on 25 July 1593.[25] That such echoes are thematic and are to be regarded as contributing to a path through the self-deluding display of erudition is less easy to decipher. As several have discovered, the sudden sobriety that the academicians embrace as a closing gesture in the play may just as easily result from one of the possible models for the action, Thomas Bowes's translation (1586) of Pierre de La Primaudaye's *L'Académie française* (1577). There, the thwarting of a romantic ending is due to 'sudden and sorrowful newes of the last frantike returne of France into civill war', not the death of a king.[26] It also carries the narrative past the ensuing peace, whereupon they resume a sort of contemplative life, love interest not worth a mention. Indeed, the educative goal here is ethically commendable, and the more worldly distractions of love not in question. The 'doctrine of good living' is the aim of this almost monastic programme, whereby they focus on the 'knowledge of things past from the first ages' to educe 'profit and utilitie', ultimately to grasp 'the glorie of the divine majestie'.[27] For Shakespeare, the striving for a clear-sighted view of the eternal verities and the self-knowledge that love brings is a significant substitution.

In comic vein, however, the high seriousness of the Primaudaye narrative was never going to survive intact. The basic question revolves around why a victory of the secular over the celestial good was called for. Was it merely to satisfy the needs of comedy, or was it a necessary contextualizing of the learned pursuit of words for words' sake? In order to investigate the dramatic capital of the play, one has to estimate just how the 'application' of an audience might have been enlisted. One of the metacritical factors dredged from the work's early history is Shakespeare's quoted reaction to William Jaggard's *The Passionate Pilgrim* (1599), an octavo volume of twenty poems, attributed on the title page to 'W. Shakespeare'. Jaggard's collection was opportunistic; it soldered together two of Shakespeare's sonnets (139 and 144) – the first two items in the volume – with the sonnets performed in 4.3 by Longaville (the third item), and Dumaine (item 16) plus Berowne's own contribution in the intercepted letter from 4.2 (item 5). The rest were not Shakespeare's – but some could have been, to the untutored eye, if one remembered the themes and six-line stanzaic form of *Venus and Adonis*. Such awareness – catching hold of the vogue for poetic collections – might have been welcomed (Dumaine's sonnet was indeed reprinted in *England's Helicon* [1600] as 'The passionate Sheepheards Song'), but apparently it was not.[28] Thomas Heywood, in a prefatory letter to his *Apology for Actors* (1612), reported that Jaggard was guilty of 'dishonesties' in passing off some of his own verses as Shakespeare's and remembered the 'Author' being 'much offended' in that the collection 'presumed to make so bold with his

---

[24] *Ben Jonson*, ed. Parfitt, p. 435.

[25] Richard Wilson, *Worldly Shakespeare: The Theatre of Our Good Will* (Edinburgh, 2016), pp. 53–8.

[26] Geoffrey Bullough, ed., *Narrative and Dramatic Sources of Shakespeare*, 8 vols. (London and New York, 1957–75), vol. I, p. 435.

[27] Bullough, ed., *Sources*, vol. I, pp. 434–5.

[28] See the copious evidence in Lukas Erne and Tamsin Badcoe, 'Shakespeare and the popularity of poetry books in print, 1583–1622', *The Review of English Studies* 65 (2014), 33–57.

name'.[29] There is another factor in Shakespeare's displeasure and it is to do with a matter of dramatic meaning.

The respective media of a poem and a play and their processes of consumption are crucial in discovering why both Heywood and Shakespeare objected to what we would now term Jaggard's 'piracy'. To do so, we have to lay aside the prevalent suggestion that Shakespeare was merely a force of nature, preferring to display a profusion of his own invention rather than any other's. Poetry had a far greater potential for securing a writer's reputation for posterity than drama.[30] It could not – or should not – have been confused with the *oratio obliqua* of dramatic discourse. In a literary context, the attempt at drawing a line between a character's expressiveness and an author's was not observed by Jaggard. As Lukas Erne has observed, the objection to the collection 'presents us with a picture of an unfamiliar Shakespeare: keenly aware of what is and what is not his literary property, concerned about his reputation, proud of his name and unwilling to have it associated with lines that did not flow from his pen'.[31] It illustrated not only an interest in his own literary personality, but also his stake in the dramatic craft: Shakespeare wrote for Berowne, Dumaine and Longaville as *dramatis personae*; his sonnets he wrote *in propria persona*. Thus, it is dramatically apposite for Dumaine's trochaic rhythms to help to illustrate a breathless passion, but also to have it littered with particularly derivative tropes such as love's association with May, the figuring of the lover as 'heavens' breath', a result of some 'wanton air' that could 'passage find' to his mistress, and the instance of Jove becoming mortal for love's sake (4.3.99–118). Similarly, Longaville's contribution fleshes out a proverbial address to a celestial figure, possessing a 'heavenly rhetoric' in her eyes that causes the lover to break sublunary vows, venial due to the special grace afforded by an addressee that is more than a mortal woman. The 'vapour-vow' is part of a train of figures wherein 'breath' is but wind, and as insubstantial, leading to the adoption of proverbial tropes – 'words are but wind' – and wherein fools become wise by winning a paradise by losing an oath (4.3.59–72).[32]

Berowne's own contribution helps to construct his character just as his companions' poetry does theirs, and the less startling effusions of Dumaine and Longaville confirm them as followers rather than leaders. One can trace a preoccupation with the making and breaking of vows in all three poems, and indeed one could regard them as securely within the dramatic context of the play as a whole: the fragility of any vow once changed circumstances prove a challenge. In Berowne's case, the connection with the fabric of the action is more marked. What can prove constant if what we once thought of as promises as sturdy as oaks prove to be as pliable as osiers? The faith one instinctively feels supplants an abstract one, made in a hypothetical situation, but then how durable could this new impulse be, where 'thine eyes' wean one off one's books, and new knowledge – of the

<hr/>

[29] Thomas Heywood, *Apology for Actors* (1612), sig. G4r–v. The issues surrounding early pre-copyright definitions of plagiarism certainly lie behind Heywood's concerns, in that he probably wished to separate his own name from any corruption of text in the collection and the lack of acknowledgement due his patron (the collection carried no dedication). See Max W. Thomas, 'Eschewing credit: Heywood, Shakespeare, and plagiarism before copyright', *New Literary History* 31 (2000), 277–93.

[30] Although, as Erne has argued, as early as the 1590s, the legitimation of printed playbooks was under way; one authorial eye might have been on the requirements of theatrical shock and comic reach, but the other was probably on securing his text through print. This latter project was as much a booksellers' priority as any author's. Creating an audience for playtexts was to open up wider commercial potential. See Lukas Erne, *Shakespeare as Literary Dramatist*, 2nd edn (Cambridge, 2013), pp. 55–79.

[31] Erne, *Literary Dramatist*, p. 27. Douglas Bruster has claimed that it was specifically in the 1590s that the availability of a print identity became a possession to be exploited and protected; see his 'The structural transformation of print', in *Print, Manuscript, Performance: The Changing Relations of the Media in Early Modern England*, ed. Arthur F. Marotti and Michael D. Bristol (Columbus, 2000), pp. 49–89. On the other hand, the process of transferring performance text to print, from 'foul papers' to Quarto, still involved several intermediaries; see Tiffany Stern, *Making Shakespeare: From Stage to Page* (Abingdon and New York, 2004), pp. 137–58.

[32] cf. 'Winds are but wind' (Tilley, *Proverbs*, W833) and 'to bring one into a fool's paradise' (Tilley, *Proverbs*, F523).

beloved – seems more authentic than any study that lacks 'wonder'. At its most basic, this is merely a dramatic conceit, yet one can trace its serious exploitation throughout the play (4.2.106–19). There is a return to Berowne's own concerns as early as 1.1.72–93, where there is the duality of intellectual and physical vision: the temptation to

> pore upon a book
> To seek the light of truth, while truth the while
> Doth falsely blind the eyesight of his look.
>
> (1.1.74–6)

This doubt regarding where or how knowledge might be found and on what it might be based reaches out beyond the academic confines of the play's setting. In the lines only to be found in Q and F (and not in Q1), after 4.3.292, this is more insistent:

> Learning is but an adjunct to ourself,
> And where we are, our learning likewise is.
> Then when ourselves we see in ladies' eyes,
> With ourselves.[33]

This oblique attempt at encapsulating how books might intercede in – and may falsify – a form of more authentic education is a preoccupation in the play but also throughout humanist educational theory. Jane Donawerth's valuable study of early modern linguistic theory dwells upon two main issues with special reference to *Love's Labour's Lost*: both an interrogation of the assumption that language is 'an ordered system of rational symbols through which speakers generate meaning'; and one's fascination with this form of epistemology as ordered yet also heterocosmic in its resistance to external interference – forces that might embrace change and individuation.[34]

There is always the view to be considered that the play was never intended to be anything other than pastime entertainment, and that to treat it as possessing a subtextual gravity is to come near to crushing a butterfly upon a wheel. The critical challenge to the image of the oral poet whose drama was primarily calculated to address contingencies of audience reception has some consequences for how we might approach *Love's*

Labour's Lost. The recent investigation into the possible content of Shakespeare's education at the King's New School at Stratford-upon-Avon has guided interpretation of the play in two distinct directions: towards its festive qualities, exhibiting a verbal exuberance that would have delighted an audience; or, on the other hand, towards the rather more serious contemplation that sheer wit and the *copia* of language are some variety of defence mechanism against the *copia* of life outside an academy. The former has been traced and illustrated rather more often than the latter. As Keir Elam has noted, there were available for Shakespeare not only the curricular demands of imitation and learned allusion (which put into practice the supposed virtues of *copia*) but also a gathering weight of opinion that the sign might not be directly deduced from existence and, indeed, might not be able to structure it reliably.[35] The magic of words, providing a sacramental status, had often been questioned in antiquity, but there was a prominent contemporary revival of nominalism, a freeing of the word from denotation that at the same time eroded its capacity to capture and control the mess of life. William Perkins, the Cambridge Reformed theologian, in his *A Discourse of Witchcraft*, attempted to dismantle the power of curses by observing that they were 'but sounds but framed by the tongue, of the breath that commeth from the lungs'. Words therefore 'have no virtue ... to cause a reall worke, much lesse to produce a wonder'. They might affect the mind by 'their sweetnes' but there is no power in them to promote 'the procuring of good' or any

---

33 To be found in Appendix 2.1 of *Love's Labour's Lost*, ed. Woudhuysen, p. 340.

34 Jane Donawerth, *Shakespeare and the Sixteenth-Century Study of Language* (Urbana and Chicago, 1984), pp. 142–3. Donawerth investigates the variety of ways in which the wits attempt to frame the world within the confines of a grammar book (see pp. 146–8), and concludes that the full effect of this representation is more dramatic than thematic; they grow into maturity once they see and sense a dislocation between a rational system and the demands of a sentimental education.

35 Keir Elam, *Shakespeare's Universe of Discourse: Language-Games in the Comedies* (Cambridge, 1984), pp. 114–76.

'inflicting of hurts and harmes'.[36] This emphasis on human agency – language as instrumental – contributes to a distrust of *verba* preceding *res*, but it need not stem from religious motives. For Francis Bacon, the study of 'words, and not matter' constituted the 'first distemper of learning', for words were but the 'Images of matter, and except they haue life of reason and inuention', the regard for them is idolatrous.[37] One of Elam's reflections on this contest as to the status of language is pertinent here: linguistic conventions may or may not be grounded in a reality deduced from their longevity. If one did regard their persistence as a guide to the 'real', then 'language may be studied, empirically and independently of what it represents, as an autonomous system of rules'.[38] The question remains: rules of what?

Given that the comic world celebrates a temporary suspension of the regular or ordained, this question might indeed get us to one of the foundations of rhetorical mirth. There is a delight in wit, the unlikely yoking together of ignored or unlikely items by dint of verbal dexterity, but there could be a more generic and consonant significance that is promoted thereby. The grammatical 'rules' regulate more than just linguistic correctness, a contribution to a cultural capital that trains the self for professional service and/or class acceptability. The space occupied by most drama in the early modern period escaped such 'rules' or posed alternatives. Deducing from Peter Mack's study of Elizabethan rhetorical training, it is clear that, whilst there was a consistency in most forms of educational practice, especially in grammar schools, it did not follow that – as with a national curriculum at the present moment – practice led to uniformity. The amassing of a variety of moral sentences gave the debater a decided advantage: 'moral sentences were used to interpret actions as instances which illustrate continuing norms of ethical, military or political behaviour . . . The proverb or moral axiom was easier for an audience to understand and harder for an opponent to argue against.'[39] Wit, however, owed its power to subversion and an initial location of discord that lay beyond accepted rules.

The most prevalent comic tactic in Shakespeare's early comedies was to provide a context for any display of wit that had the potential both to supply admiration at its learning and, at the same time, to interrogate its exercise as apparently pointless – in every sense. Viola attempts to come to terms with Feste's foolery by claiming that 'they who dally nicely with words' tend to make them 'wanton' in unfixing them from any settled sense (*Twelfth Night*, 3.1.14–15). It is, after all, Portia's tactic in *The Merchant of Venice*'s trial scene (4.1) to outflank Shylock's reliance on the apparently forensic wording of a legal bond by relying on a yet more literal sense of a 'pound of flesh'. Feste may 'dally' with words in a festive or a too exact way, in a celebratory gesture as well as drawing on an unexpected – yet still admissible – denotation. Feste holds that a 'good wit' is apt to destroy sense, whereby any sentence 'is but a chev'rel glove' that s/he could 'quickly' turn the 'wrong side . . . outward' (3.1.11–13), by demonstrating its polysemy. For Viola, the dawdling in the grove of words is to render them too elastic. Indeed, Feste is apt to agree, for there is a prevalence of oath-breaking, wherein 'bonds' were so often rendered worthless by the appropriation of sense, and 'reason' by no means evident – or even *present* – because words had grown so 'false' (3.1.20–3), and thereby his foolery had resulted in assuming a role as a 'corrupter of words' (3.1.35). Dramatic dialogue is a strange form of 'corruption' for it is licensed on account of its entertainment value: would we want a stage fool to obey linguistic convention?

To take this reflection on stagecraft a stage further, Viola regards the dalliance with verbal expression as possessing a 'niceness' that combines a reliance on exactitude with a foppish fastidiousness (see the available senses of 'niceness' ranging from *OED*.1.a, 'foolish, simple, ignorant', or 2.a,

---

36 William Perkins, *A discourse of the damned art of witchcraft* (Cambridge, 1610), pp. 134–5.
37 *The Two Books of Francis Bacon. The Proficiencie and Advancement of Learning, Divine and Humane* (London, 1605), pp. 17–18 (page numbers duplicated).
38 Elam, *Universe of Discourse*, p. 167.
39 Mack, *Elizabethan Rhetoric*, p. 298.

'encouraging wantonness', shading into 2.d, 'finely dressed', and tipping over into an area near to its opposite: *OED*, 3a, 'precise or particular in matters of reputation'; 3b, 'Fastidious, fussy'; 7b, 'Not obvious'; or 10a, 'That enters minutely into details'). This dual reference is pivotal in the comedies especially, and, in *Love's Labour's Lost*, it supplies a particularly persistent thread based on a thematic and fruitful ambiguity. For Moth, the 'nice wenches' that could be betrayed by the compliments and/or humours manifested by the stereotype of the courting male might (3.1.21) indeed, on the one hand, be 'coy' as noted by William C. Carroll, or 'fastidious' as noted by John Kerrigan, yet for H. R. Woudhuysen and G. R. Hibbard they are more likely to be 'wanton'.[40] In 5.2, there is repetition of this ambiguity with interest. The byplay between the King and Rosaline (passing off as the Princess) on the need to be 'nice' (coy or shy or punctilious) exploits a subtle distinction between pardonable (even commendable) reticence and a pedantic concession to social convention, where, before the 'Muscovites', the Princess exhibits a measure of courtesy alongside wariness: 'We'll not be nice. Take hands. We will not dance', answered by the King's punning on 'measure' (stricture/care) with reference to the polite taking of hands and the finale to the music – 'More measure of this measure. Be not nice' (5.2.218, 222). By both 5.2.232 and 5.2.325, Berowne's perspective stresses the possession of niceties as beside the point in any lived experience. The threefold repetition of qualities – 'Metheglin, wort, and malmsey', for example – is part of a formulaic stress – with no advance in knowledge – that is really more an adherence to the conventions of the linguistic world than any attempt at mimesis. Indeed, his acerbic verdict on Boyet sees him as 'the ape of form, Mounsieur the Nice', principally composed of merely courtly gestures.

This attempt at reaching beyond formal constraints is a persistent trait in the Shakespearian outputs of the 1590s. Can words accomplish that? Extending the figurative trail to, say, Prospero's final gesture to return to Milan at the end of *The Tempest*, wherein his contract with himself is to rely on his own strength (Epilogue, 2), is to throw himself on an audience's charity, the immediate world of the theatre. Indeed, Caliban's advice to Stephano and Trinculo to seize Prospero's books (3.2.93–6) is in a direct line of descent from the leap away from inherited rules that signifies the least reassuring, yet thrilling, aspects of the early comedies. As Alan C. Dessen has noted, both *Love's Labour's Lost* and *The Tempest* share one significant feature: the repetition of word-patterns around a 'study/studying' cluster and associated semes, such as 'books'. Word-searches of any electronic text indicate possible thematic patterns that elude traditional narrative analysis, yet in the oral context, repetition becomes rather more insistent: *Love's Labour's Lost* 'contains more than a third of Shakespeare's dialogue usages of study and its varying forms (with most examples coming in 1.1 and 4.3, both of which scenes are centered upon book and writings)'.[41] One could simply conclude that this follows from the contours of plot. There would be a common-sense expectation that any action set in the King's 'little academe' (1.1.13) would prompt some reference to book-learning as scene-setting, yet the repetition might also alert us to its thematic *as well as* its dramatic force.

One way to regard the fascination with the dramatic appearance of books in plays of the period is that – separated as props or references of central concern in a debate – they are figures that gesture towards the ingredients of selfhood and how learning might not deliver the mature individual. Indeed, the arbitrary link between a word and a precise meaning contributes both to the comedy where clowns as well as wits put too much trust in a reality contoured by language, on the one hand, and, more seriously, the tantalizing inefficacy of words to express feeling. As Elam observes – in

---

[40] All recent editions of the play: ed. William C. Carroll (Cambridge, 2009), p. 94; ed. John Kerrigan (Harmondsworth, 1982), pp. 177; ed. Woudhuysen; and ed. G. R. Hibbard (Oxford, 1990), p. 133.

[41] Alan C. Dessen, *Recovering Shakespeare's Theatrical Vocabulary* (Cambridge, 1995), p. 164.

a perceptive and yet passing comment – 'speech is no longer *mentis character*, sign of the mind, but *character mensio*, measure of personality as a whole'.[42] A most assiduous student can pose as intelligent because they are obedient; an individual achieves that status by iconoclasm.

In the contrived debates in John Lyly's plays, there is a hidden distrust of the rhetoric so obviously on display. Certainly, Euphues's sage advice to 'a young gentleman of Naples', Alcius, is that it was more 'seemly' to have 'thy study full of books than thy purse full of money', yet the main way to preserve one's inheritance is by one's 'own wit'. The pursuit of virtue earns you more approbation than riches – or learning.[43] Epiton, the resourceful servant to the clueless Sir Topas in *Endymion*, outflanks his master with his native wit, claiming – in a travesty of the medieval model of the microcosm, Man – that he was 'an absolute microcosmus, a petty world of myself' and that his 'library [was] his head' possessing 'no other books but [his] brains'.[44] One might remember Faustus's embrace of error through reading, the laying aside of Scripture to fill the mind with, according to the Evil Angel, 'all nature's treasury'. On the other hand – to go some way towards negating the thrill of the forbidden fruit of natural treasure – it is Envy, in the parade of the Seven Deadly Sins, who 'cannot read, and therefore wish all books were burnt', and well may Faustus, at the last, wish he had burnt his books.[45]

The book as a stage prop is, indeed, doubled in significance once it is situated in a study. Of the numerous instances of books in the inventory compiled by Alan C. Dessen and Leslie Thomson of stage directions in the drama of 1580–1642, there are, as one might expect, some that are ciphers and scenic details, but there are many that are figures of thematic significance.[46] Reading is sometimes a measure of melancholy (in the more positive early modern sense) and the act of perusing a book is rarely an act in itself. However, there is no dramatic capital in portraying books on a stage, an essentially static detail unless it is involved in the analysis of how book-learning rarely captures the complete individual or, what is more, the selfhood

that stems extensively from such a foundation – and thereby is not measured reliably by a bibliographic yardstick, a bookish inheritance that accrues from learning. In Webster's hands, it can display guilt and an attempt at repentance, a contemplation of one's fate. This is surely the predicament of the Cardinal in *The Duchess of Malfi*, who, entering V. V. with a book, is much affected by a fixation on the 'one material fire' that 'may not burn all men alike' and the search for how he might face death from a theological perspective (V.V.0–3). Flamineo accosts Vittoria, '*with a book in her hand*' in *The White Devil* to disturb her prayers with 'worldly business' (V.VI.0, 2).[47] There is in this trope a requirement to look beyond the page in front of one, as Yves Bonnefoy has recently urged. In 'lifting one's eyes from the page' one is going further than analysis can ever accomplish: 'for what a poet hopes for from words is that they might open to that plenitude that descriptions and formulations cannot reach', a lesson that the wits – in their own terms – are eventually forced to realize. This

[42] Elam, *Universe of Discourse*, p. 214.

[43] 'Euphues to a young gentleman in Naples named Alcius, who, leaving his study, followed all lightness and lived both shamefully and sinfully, to the grief of his friends and discredit of the university', in John Lyly, *Euphues, the Anatomy of Wit*, ed. Leah Scragg (Manchester, 2003), p. 146.

[44] John Lyly, *Endymion*, IV.II.40–2, ed. David Bevington (Manchester, 1996), p. 147. A fuller context for Lyly's staged dialectics concerning bookishness can be found in Joel B. Altman's *The Tudor Play of Mind: Rhetorical Enquiry and the Development of Elizabethan Drama* (Berkeley, 1978), pp. 196–228.

[45] Christopher Marlowe, *Dr Faustus: A- and B-Texts (1604, 1616)*, ed. David Bevington and Eric Rasmussen (Manchester, 1993), 'A' text: I.I.77, II.III.133–4, V.II.123. Mephistopheles uses a volume to seduce Faustus with a promise of gold ('A' text: II.ii.162–8); and consider the capture of Faustus's spell book by Robin the ostler, who, though illiterate, believes in its talismanic power of conjuring derived from the 'brimstone devil' ('A' text: II.III.1–22).

[46] *A Dictionary of Stage Directions in English Drama, 1580–1642* (Cambridge, 1999), pp. 34–5.

[47] John Webster, *The Duchess of Malfi*, 3rd edn, ed. Elizabeth M. Brennan (London and New York, 1993), p. 127; and *The White Devil*, 3rd edn, ed. Christina Luckyj (London and New York, 2008), p. 150.

manoeuvre is not always a deliberate ignoring of detail, for, whilst one needs to 'leave the text', it is as a consequence of having 'gone into and crossed through [the work] as well'.[48] Some characters never manage that in *Love's Labour's Lost*, but some do.

The result of taking the play seriously is not that one discounts its festive qualities. It might, though, summon us to dwell on how the festive might be a complex comic ingredient. For Elam, the *metalinguistic* factors that result from placing any verbal expression in a dramatic frame lends a force to comedy, especially in its 'exploiting language as activity and as object'.[49] How we might decipher the goal of the linguistic fireworks is a less recognized critical question, and it supplements an approach that stresses their technical qualities *tout court*. For example, there is a strain in New Historicist readings of Shakespearian comedy that utilizes linguistic copiousness as an exercise in polysemy, catching at its deconstructive potential and the place of diversion in an early modern context. Louis A. Montrose's quest for a 'politics of play' is, however, a venture outside the 'text' that has been deservedly influential.[50] Navarre is thus a playground, 'a special place marked off from the pressures of social reality and the unpleasant implications of a world of fallen nature', but one that also results in a steady grid for analysis, where action distracts less to allow space for self-disclosure.[51] *In toto*, the imaginative world wished into existence by the *personae* of the narrative is not commensurate with how the play as a whole affects an audience. Montrose perceives – and analyses – the provisional qualities of the ending, where we are confronted by an 'open form' of relationships as well as plotting. When, for example, secure within his perch in 4.3, Berowne looks down on the courtly poetry of Longaville and the King, he casts himself as one of those demi-gods from 'an old infant play' (4.3.75) who observes all, yet by line 186, when his own poetry is introduced to the others by Jacquenetta and Costard, this parallel no longer holds good; there is no fixed point of hierarchy. Ultimately, he concludes that the 'wooing doth not end like an old play', as it is tied up with the metatheatrical comment that the year's hiatus of

mourning in France is 'too long for a play' (5.2.860, 864). The narrative exceeds the traditional scope of theatre.

The *Figurenposition* of Morality plays that Robert Weimann tries to discern in this scene is mobile, and an audience is expected to be sufficiently agile to keep pace with the series of comic displacements, in which the King and then Longaville and then Dumaine in turn become observers, unaware that they themselves are observed. For Weimann, the search for 'a fundamental link with the audience' is alternated, or at least divided, if not defeated.[52] In Bonnefoy's terms, this is an invitation to sense wider issues on top of a series of comic inversions, a perception that allows us to assess where enlightenment might be found. The 'right Promethean fire' that Berowne regards as deriving from beauty is also a route to self-knowledge; any retreat from irregularity, including an escape from imitation or traditional form, is where the book or an oath leads us: 'we lose ourselves to keep our oaths' (4.3.327, 337). The question remains – as it does for any leap into the void – where might that leave us, and who might we be – in ourselves?

This is not to claim that the play attempts to answer that question in full. Q and F, at 5.2.812, have Rosaline far sterner in requiring a sea-change in Berowne's character, expecting him to be 'purged', whereby his 'sins' might be 'rack'd' and his limbo of tending to the sick for a year is an atonement for his being 'attaint with faults and perjury'.[53] There was a perfectly tenable version,

---

[48] Yves Bonnefoy, 'Lifting our eyes from the page', trans. J. Naughton, *Critical Inquiry* 16 (1990), 794–806 pp. 800, 802–3.

[49] Elam, *Universe of Discourse*, p. 21.

[50] Louis A. Montrose, '"Sport by sport o'erthrown": *Love's Labour's Lost* and the politics of play', *Texas Studies in Language and Literature* 18 (1976–7), 528–52.

[51] Montrose, 'Sport', p. 529.

[52] Robert Weimann, *Shakespeare and the Popular Tradition in the Theater: Studies in the Social Dimension*, ed. Robert Schwartz (Baltimore, MD, 1978), p. 229.

[53] *Love's Labour's Lost*, ed. Woudhuysen, p. 340. These lines were included in both of John Barton's RSC productions (1965 and 1978).

therefore, that expected a deep repentance from the wits, or Berowne at least. If retained in any performance, the segue to the songs of Hiems and Ver is more powerfully anticipated; the hopes of spring experienced by the fearful husband give way to something approximating to a degree zero of winter's mundane realism, where, repeatedly, 'greasy Joan doth keel the pot' (5.2.904, 912). Instead of communion, there is dislocation. Whoever utters the closing phrase, 'you that way, we this way' (5.2.914), and to whom, the gesture leads to a rupture of illusion, at one with the harshness of Mercury's words that replace the 'songs of Apollo' (5.2.913–14).[54]

The contrast between the world now inspired by Mercury and the recent inspiration derived from Apollo is a sort of unsentimental education. The audience as well as the Navarre Academicians and the visitors from France have – if the verbal magic has been effective – been transported, yet no green world was ever called into being to last. Berowne at 4.3.320 figured love's potency as Promethean – a reaching above the foreseen and repeated action – where there is subtlety in melodies 'as sweet and musical / As bright Apollo's lute strung with his hair' (4.3.318–19). That is now at an end. The time for music and poetry is also not to last beyond the play-world. Rhetoric and vows have proved a protection, but we are left with their dissolution. The world of Mercury calls to mind Mercadé's harsh message, but that may not be all (5.2.913–14). Of the various attributes called to mind by this representative of the future, there is a cluster of loose associations: a god of commerce, communication (as a messenger of Jove) and travel on the one hand, but, on the other, that very mutability leading to a rare ability to pass into the underworld and also thievery and trickery. The most persistent association that Shakespeare uses is that of the winged bearer of news,[55] but at the same time there is a connotation of lightness, even unreliability – perhaps stepping onto shifting sands.

A competition between Apollo and Mercury takes place in Ovid's *Metamorphosis XI*, where both couple with Chione;[56] their offspring are markedly different from each other. On the one

hand, there is Apollo's son, Philammon, 'famous for song and zither',[57] and, on the other, there is Autolycus, who, 'littered under Mercury, was likewise a snapper-up of unconsidered trifles' (*The Winter's Tale*, 4.3.25–6), a possible sign of harshness and inconstancy outside the certainties of the academy, which awaits us all.

The same distinction was more recently drawn by Henry Petowe's *The Second Part of* Hero and Leander, *Containing their Further Fortunes* (1598), a continuation of Marlowe's account (completed by George Chapman) but mainly a decorous lament for the poet, where he appears as Apollo, a conduit of 'heaven's sacred beauty', and possessor of a 'honey-flowing vein'. With his death, much has left the earth, and what remains resembles the reign of 'harsh Mercury', amenable more to prose than to poetic inspiration:[58]

> Apollo's lute bereaved of silver string,
> Fond Mercury doth harshly gin to sing,
> A counterfeit unto his honey note;
> But I do fear he'll chatter it by rote.[59]

To put the objection another way: there is inspiration by Apollo's lute and then there is obedience to the rote learning and standardization

---

[54] Succinct accounts of the textual variations and their associations can be found in Carroll's edition, p. 180, and Hibbard's, pp. 41–2.

[55] E.g. *King John*, 4.2.174 (the King sending the Bastard to seek out the Lords Bigot and Salisbury, setting 'feathers to [his] heels'); *1 Henry IV*, 4.1.105–6 (Vernon describing Hal's vault into the saddle 'like feathered Mercury'); *Henry V*, 2.0.7 (the youth of England gathering to the cause 'With winged heels, as English Mercuries'); and *Antony and Cleopatra*, 4.16.36 (Cleopatra wishing she had the power of 'strong-winged Mercury' to heave Antony up to the top of her Monument).

[56] See *Ovid: Metamorphoses Books IX–XV*, 2nd edn, trans. Frank Justus Miller, rev. G. P. Goold (Cambridge, MA, 1984), pp. 141–3, XI.301–20.

[57] *Ovid: Metamorphoses*, p. 143, XI.317.

[58] *Christopher Marlowe: The Complete Poems and Translations*, ed. Stephen Orgel (London and New York, 2007), pp. 80–81, ll. 1, 59, 109.

[59] Marlowe, ed. Orgel, pp. 82–3, ll. 91–4. Marlowe/Chapman had regarded Mercury as 'cunning' and 'deceitful' (*Sestiad*, 1.417, 446; pp. 16, 17).

encouraged by a reliance on bare imitation and a cautiousness derived from books alone.

One cannot rescue *Love's Labour's Lost* from its detractors simply by relying on its escapist potential. Taking the play seriously does not entail a negation of the delight in excessive wordplay. In Jonson's sense of 'application', how an audience is permitted to search for more than this is also embedded in the narrative: how we might note a world where books are not the prime reservoir of learning, and what emerges once we look beyond the word and its defence mechanisms. The answer is not reassuring. Berowne embraces a world of light and self-knowledge, away from those who are 'continual plodders' whose authority is simply 'base' and won from 'others' books' (1.1.86–7). What we see enacted is an invitation not to take at face value Rosaline's commendation of Berowne as 'conceit's expositor', and as master of 'apt and gracious words', the world of 'becoming mirth' (2.1.72–3, 67). The

journey to her last words involves a gazing into an abyss where comedy itself cannot offer comfort, and that necessitates a removal of wit's 'wormwood from [a] fruitful brain' in order that a deeper and more urgent succour is brought into play in the face of mortality: a mirth that is less self-regarding, and thereby is a sign of 'reformation' (5.2.833, 855). The dawning of this darker perspective brings, however, a problem to the fore, where scepticism reigns and the materiality of repetition involving the mundane tasks of 'greasy Joan' (5.2.904) obscures a world of vision and imagination. For Primaudaye's French academy, the interruption is one of civil war, an opportunity to grow through combat and to manufacture peace and personal heroism – and where there is a cheerful return; for the wits, there promises to be no resurgence of such norms in the immediate future, for the setting of their trial is a charity to the terminally sick, not the practice of chivalry.

THE THYESTEAN LANGUAGE OF ENGLISH REVENGE TRAGEDY ON THE UNIVERSITY AND POPULAR STAGES

ELIZABETH SANDIS

I

In the London playhouses, the sound of Latin was a regular feature of the auditory experience, albeit in bitesize bursts. At the same time, although Latin was firmly entrenched at the universities as the language of academic drama, Oxford and Cambridge students did, on occasion, write plays in English. Running counter to what many early modern writers liked to claim, therefore, neither side had exclusive use of the language with which their production centre was associated: professional dramatists did not stick to English, and amateur dramatists at the universities did not stick to Latin. To understand English revenge tragedy, we should keep Latin in the picture and be open to the idea of multiple streams of influence running between the different production centres of Oxford, Cambridge and London. To this end, in this article I present a new way of viewing English revenge tragedy that allows us to embrace the corpus in all its variety. I show how, in the world of early modern drama in England, there exists a common language which transcends the choice of Latin or English: the Thyestean language, steeped in a tradition of ambition and one-upmanship. This language is used by the dramatists to compete with one another and offers something of a level playing field: the cultural significance of the Thyestean challenge holds good whichever city a dramatist is writing for and whichever language he is writing in.

A great deal has been written about the Elizabethan and Jacobean fascination with Seneca and the taste for revenge tragedy on the London stage, and yet the centres for drama which powered the growth of

Senecanism from outside of the capital have largely been forgotten. The colleges of Oxford and Cambridge were key production centres for revenge tragedy and self-consciously adopted Seneca's language and style. The tradition of Latin as the dominant language of university drama presented scholars with challenges – but also opportunities – to create a special kind of self-conscious wordplay using Seneca's own words, fragmented and re-scripted into neo-Senecan ('new-Senecan') monologues and dialogues. This Latin-based tradition at Oxford and Cambridge is less familiar to us than the English-based tradition we find at court, at the London playhouses and at the Inns of Court, but it is equally influential in the development of English drama, not least because many of the London-based playwrights were scholars who trained at the universities.

As we might expect from an author who permeated the grammar school curriculum, Seneca's influence does not crop up haphazardly at one or two Oxford or Cambridge colleges in isolation; neo-Senecanism, the appropriation of his language and style, is a phenomenon which we see right across the board in university drama. From biblical tragicomedies such as Nicholas Grimald's *Christus Redivivus* ('Christ Reborn'), in which the resurrection of Jesus is given a Senecan treatment, to history plays set in Seneca's own time, such as Nathaniel Lee's *Nero, Emperor of Rome*, the Roman tragedian makes his mark on the university dramatists of early modern England. Nicholas Grimald attended several different university colleges, but *Christus Redivivus* was performed at

Brasenose College, Oxford, during Grimald's time there as a student in the 1540s, and he dedicated the play to the college head, Matthew Smyth. In contrast to Grimald, writing in pre-Reformation England, Nathaniel Lee's work is grounded in his experience of post-Restoration England, over 120 years later. Yet Seneca is still central to his works.[1] In many ways, this is no surprise, for he had been fed on a diet of the same canonical texts, during his time at Westminster School and then Trinity College, Cambridge. Lee then transported the culture of the early modern university to the public stage: after receiving his BA degree from Trinity College in 1668, he left Cambridge for London and his *Nero* was acted at Drury Lane in 1675. University-trained playwrights continued to feed the playhouses of the capital with works steeped in the Senecan tradition.

The study of university drama is in its infancy. The two book-length studies available to the reader thus far are separated by a hundred-year gap: F. S. Boas's *University Drama in the Tudor Age* (Oxford, 1914) and Christopher Marlow's *Performing Masculinity in English University Drama, 1598–1636* (Farnham, 2013). Boas's achievement has never been matched: his study concluded with the death of Elizabeth I, and comparable studies of the Jacobean and Caroline eras, despite the obvious continuity in dramatic terms between all three of these periods, do not exist. Boas's work, though hugely valuable, is not accessible by modern standards; he does not, for example, offer translations for the many Latin quotations he employs in his argument. Marlow's monograph, a century on from Boas, represents a much-needed re-opening of the field. However, as the author himself admits in his introduction, his analysis is significantly restricted by his decision only to engage with English-language sources, leaving out the dominant force in early modern university drama: Latin literature and culture. *Early Modern Academic Drama* (Farnham, 2008), a collection of essays, still appears fresh and has much to offer, though it was published over a decade ago. Its editors, J. Walker and P. D. Streufert, succeeded in bringing together a ground-breaking range of types of educational

institution, and the volume demonstrates the success of allowing multilingual evidence to speak for itself: English, Latin and Greek texts all take their natural places in the narrative, and, in contrast to Boas's study, translations into English are always provided. I have followed this principle in my own work, with the aim of opening up the multilingual corpus of university drama to a wider readership and integrating it into the mainstream of English Renaissance drama criticism. All translations are my own.

More recently, in 2016, Oxford University Press issued two articles by D. F. Sutton in their series of Oxford Handbooks Online. These two studies, entitled 'Oxford drama in the late Tudor and early Stuart periods' and 'Cambridge drama in the late Tudor and early Stuart periods', are accessible and informative, drawing on Sutton's unparalleled knowledge of the field.[2] The Philological Museum, Sutton's magnum opus, is an extraordinary resource, which has been making editions of neo-Latin texts and English translations available at the click of a button for over two decades.[3] Despite ever-increasing access to online translations, we are still playing catch-up when it comes to English university drama; the huge advances made in the field of English-language professional drama in early modern England contrast with the slow, piecemeal progress so far made in contemporary neo-Latin drama.

---

[1] As discussed by Helen Slaney in 'Restoration Seneca and Nathaniel Lee', *Canadian Review of Comparative Literature* 40 (2013), 52–70.

[2] D. F. Sutton, 'Oxford drama in the late Tudor and early Stuart periods', ed. Colin Burrow, Oxford Handbooks Online: www.oxfordhandbooks.com/view/10.1093/oxfordhb/9780199935338.001.0001/oxfordhb-9780199935338-e-99?rskey=lUECRe&result=1921; D. F. Sutton, 'Cambridge drama in the late Tudor and early Stuart periods', ed. Colin Burrow, Oxford Handbooks Online: www.oxfordhandbooks.com/view/10.1093/oxfordhb/9780199935338.001.0001/oxfordhb-9780199935338-e-20.

[3] The Philological Museum is available at www.philological.bham.ac.uk. The flip side to having such an accessible and widely used resource is that any play, poem or treatise *not* covered by the project has fallen into a new kind of obscurity.

In the modern era, our own ideological objections to Latin, as a symbol and tool of class-based and education-based discrimination, have elevated the examples of English-language plays to greater heights and made it difficult to see the relationship between the revenge tragedy traditions of Oxford, Cambridge and London. University plays written in English – such as *Caesar's Revenge* (author unknown) from Trinity College, Oxford, and Thomas Goffe's *The Tragedy of Orestes* from Christ Church, Oxford – have received a disproportionate amount of critical attention.[4] In the case of *Caesar's Revenge*, we have the dual temptations of a play in English and a play with obvious potential as a Shakespearian source: generations of scholars have returned to ask this question, and critique each other's answers to this question, decade after decade.[5] Goffe has given us rare insights into performance practices, thanks to the preservation of four actors' parts in Harvard MS Thr. 10.1, two of which appear to be in his hand.[6] This enticing cache of evidence led Palfrey and Stern to conclude that university members have noticeably different requirements from their professional counterparts when taking to the stage.[7]

Orestes from Christ Church, Oxford, like *Caesar's Revenge* from Trinity College, tends to be analysed solely in relation to English-language examples from the London stage, without bringing Latin-language examples from the same production centres into the discussion. English-language *comparanda* may seem more straightforwardly relevant to the London stage, but this is a reductive approach which does not do justice to either the complexity of the London stage or the university stages. I suggest, instead, that we let the evidence of a bilingual culture guide us as we study early modern playwrights' interest in Seneca and the revenge tragedy tradition, letting their English and Latin responses do the talking.

II

Seneca's *Thyestes* is not just a play but a challenge, and one which particularly resonated with the communities of academic writers in early modern England. Having grown up on a diet of Seneca's works at school, students who went on to

[4] These English-language plays have been allowed to dominate studies billed as offering overviews or wider coverage of the corpus as a whole. Recently, for example, the promisingly entitled 'Rehabilitating academic drama' offered an opportunity for moving the field onto new ground, but confined much of its fifteen pages to a study of one theme, friendship, in one particular play, Goffe's *Orestes*: Stephanie Allen, Elisabeth Dutton and James McBain, 'Rehabilitating academic drama', in *The Routledge Research Companion to Early Drama and Performance*, ed. Pamela King (London, 2016), pp. 221–36. The essay represents a gentle way in to one of the more immediately accessible plays and builds on Marlow's in-depth study of friendship in his monograph of 2013. However, unlike Marlow's study, 'Rehabilitating academic drama' introduces errors which lead us astray at crucial moments. For example, when discussing the child-killing scene, a climactic moment in the play, Orestes' victim is twice misidentified as 'the son of Clytemnestra and Agamemnon'; if this were true, the boy would be a full brother to Orestes, removing a key tenet of the tragic plot. The child is the son of Clytemnestra and her lover *Aegystheus*, not Agamemnon, and it is this parentage which makes the boy the target for Orestes' revenge. (Orestes performs the murder in order to avenge his father, Agamemnon, stabbing the little boy up close to Aegystheus' face to ensure that the father is sprayed with his son's blood.)

[5] See Ernest Schanzer, 'A neglected source of *Julius Caesar*', *Notes and Queries* 199 (1954), 196–7; Jacqueline Pearson, 'Shakespeare and *Caesar's Revenge*', *Shakespeare Quarterly* 32 (1981), 101–4; René Weis, '*Caesar's Revenge*: a neglected Elizabethan source of *Antony and Cleopatra*', *Shakespeare Jahrbuch* (1983), 178–86; William Poole, '*Julius Caesar* and *Caesars Revenge* again', *Notes and Queries* 49 (2002), 227–8; George Mandel, '*Julius Caesar* and *Caesar's Revenge*, yet again', *Notes and Queries* 59 (2012), 534–6.

[6] David Carnegie's analysis of the handwriting reveals Thomas Goffe as the scribe of two of the four parts in Harvard MS Thr. 10.1, and he argues that there is significant cross-over between Goffe's roles of author, scribe and also actor of these pieces: David Carnegie, 'The identification of the hand of Thomas Goffe, academic dramatist and actor', *The Library* 26 (1971), 161–5.

[7] Comparison of the four actors' parts preserved in Harvard MS Thr. 10.1 (which come from four different early seventeenth-century plays performed at Christ Church, Oxford) with what has survived of professional scripts from the commercial stage reveals that the level of instruction given to the amateur players at university through the medium of cued scripts is much greater: full stage directions are regularly provided, cues are significantly longer, and strategies to prevent mistakes are embedded in the text, such as instructions to prevent premature speaking or 'over-speaking': Simon Palfrey and Tiffany Stern, *Shakespeare in Parts* (Oxford, 2007), pp. 24–9; p. 26.

university found themselves in a highly competitive environment, tasked with demonstrating their rhetorical abilities to their tutors and their peers. These literary 'brothers' in the academic communities of the Oxford and Cambridge colleges saw plays as a competitive enterprise, knowing that their work would be judged by fellow scholars in the same way other intellectual exercises would be judged. High-quality Latin composition was something each student was required to master, and the ability to give an impressive rhetorical performance was crucial to any debate or disputation. Writing and/or performing in plays in Latin, therefore, was not just about entertainment but about displaying important skills — the same kinds of skills being assessed during and at the end of a university degree. Responses to Seneca, therefore, were deeply rooted in a culture of competition and display, with the genre of revenge tragedy providing an important vehicle for writers and performers to showcase their skill and express their ambition.

'I must dare some fierce, bloody outrage, such as my brother would wish his own.'[8] So declares Atreus, when he first appears in Seneca's *Thyestes*. We meet him as he is gearing himself up for an act of revenge, in retaliation for the nefarious actions of his brother, the eponymous Thyestes. His brother had an affair with Atreus' wife Aerope and, temporarily, managed to steal Atreus' throne, but now Atreus is back as the King of Argos and ready to settle the score. It is clear from Atreus' speech, with its self-conscious and cold-blooded, calculated approach, that the idea of committing an 'outrage' (*nefas*) is not just a matter of inflicting pain, but a method of Atreus re-asserting himself and displaying his superiority over Thyestes. This is about winning personal power in a battle of wits: Atreus sees himself as in competition with his brother, and hopes to design a plot and carry it out with such crafty power and ingenuity that Thyestes will 'wish it had been his own idea' ('suum esse mallet').

The phrase *frater meus* ('my brother') is, on the face of it, a straightforward reference to the character in the play who will be Atreus' victim. However, since this plot is not just about hurting his brother but also winning his admiration for clever thinking, what Atreus is really expressing is his need for an audience to witness and appreciate the horror of his crime. This is the self-conscious way in which Seneca's protagonist introduces himself to the audience in his first appearance in the play, presenting the idea of plotting revenge as an intellectual challenge and inviting his brothers to judge it.

One of the key figures in developing this personal, competition-led tradition in the mid sixteenth century was Jasper Heywood, the Oxford scholar who wins the glory for being the first person on record to translate Seneca's *Thyestes* into English, in 1560. Heywood gained this reputation partly because he was the first to get his translation published (doubtless many before him had done the work, but kept the results for their own use) and partly because he took pains to set himself apart from and above others in a clever act of self-fashioning: he promoted the story that he had been singled out and specially chosen for the task, by none other than Seneca himself. Heywood dramatizes the moment with great aplomb. Entering his rooms at Oxford, the Ghost of Seneca announces that he is looking for an author, and one in particular: 'here I come to seek someone that might renew my name' (Preface to Heywood's *Thyestes*, l. 42).[9] His target is a certain 'young man' who lives 'in th'isle of Brittany' (45) and has already translated one of his plays, the *Troas*. The year before, Heywood had published a translation of

---

8
aliquod audendum est nefas
atrox, cruentum, tale quod frater meus
suum esse mallet

(Seneca, *Thyestes*, 193–5)

All quotations from Seneca's plays are taken from the Oxford Classical Texts edition: Otto Zwierlein, ed., *L. Annaei Senecae tragoediae* (Oxford, 1986).

9 All quotations are taken from the following edition, which contains Jasper Heywood's *Troas* and *Thyestes* together with John Studley's *Agamemnon*: James Ker and Jessica Winston, eds., *Elizabethan Seneca: Three Tragedies* (London, 2012).

Seneca's *Troas*, and so he knows exactly whom Seneca is looking for: 'I blushed and said, "The same you seek, lo here I stand you by"' (50).

As the chosen man, Heywood is given privileged access to that Holy Grail of books, Seneca's own copy of his tragedies. With a taste for the dramatic, Heywood describes himself gawking at the book, handling it with wonder while the great man stands by. In stately tone, the ghost of the Roman playwright confirms what we have all been wondering: '"These are", quoth he, "the Tragedies indeed of Seneca"' (207). By chance, the page falls open at one tragedy in particular: 'Even at Thyestes chancèd first the leaves abroad to fall' (294), and Heywood's challenge has been set.

This is all, of course, a dream which Heywood is recounting, but the setting for it – Heywood describes falling asleep with his head upon his book – ensures that the world of the dream grows out of, and reflects, the real world of Heywood's life as a scholar. He had been sent up to Oxford very young, aged 12, and he studied at Merton College before being elected a Fellow of All Souls. Heywood dedicates his translation of Seneca's *Thyestes* to John Mason, a diplomat who had himself been Fellow at All Souls College and was now on his second stint as the Chancellor of the University of Oxford. The title page to the work proclaims Heywood's scholarly credentials as a 'Fellow of All Souls College in Oxford', whilst the preface reflects his personal connections to the Inns of Court. In a show of apparent modesty, Heywood worries that he is too young to undertake Seneca's challenge and recommends, instead, that he try at the Inns, where the 'finest wits' are to be found: 'In Lincoln's Inn and Temples twain, Gray's Inn and other mo, / Thou shalt them find whose painful pen thy verse shall flourish so' (85–6). This was, indeed, a time of great literary flourishing at the Inns of Court, and Heywood, who himself moved to Gray's Inn in 1561, reels off an impressive list of names.[10] Seneca, however, will not be dissuaded from choosing his Oxford man, Jasper Heywood.

Continuing with the personal drama he has created, Heywood describes, at length, the agony of

waking from his dream and losing the figure of Seneca from his side. After much grieving and crying of tears, described with great rhetorical alacrity, Heywood makes an appeal to Megaera, one of the Furies of the Underworld. The Fury responds straightaway, by setting his breast on fire: 'I felt the Fury's force enflame me more and more, / And ten times more now chafed I was than ever yet before' (337–8). With this passion in his heart, the Oxford scholar takes up the Thyestean challenge and begins turning Seneca's Latin into Heywood's English: 'And down I sat with pen in hand and thus my verse begun' (342).[11] Heywood's presentation of the process of translation emphasizes the creative spirit required and the poetic inspiration which graces his endeavour.

Heywood's *Thyestes* is not just a translation of a play; it is a play set inside the author's own drama, self-consciously privileging the figure of Heywood as the true protagonist. The preface functions as an induction scene, in which Heywood shows he can lay claim to the *Thyestes* as his own personal territory. Closing the frame, he ends the play with another additional scene of his own making: Thyestes, the title role, has the last word, given a new speech by Heywood. After Atreus has spoken Seneca's final lines, the traditional ending to the play, Thyestes is left alone on stage to deliver Heywood's soliloquy. He invites the monsters of Hell to come and look upon something *worse* than themselves ('Come see a meetest match for thee,

---

[10] Jessica Winston analyses Heywood's list and sets it in context in '"Minerva's Men" – the Inns of Court in the 1560s', in *Lawyers at Play: Literature, Law, and Politics at the Early Modern Inns of Court, 1558–1581* (Oxford, 2016), pp. 46–73.

[11] As Evelyn Mary Spearing has pointed out, Heywood's approach to translation changes over time: the first play he tackles, *Troas*, he encapsulates more freely, whilst in his third play, *Hercules Furens*, his use of English becomes somewhat stilted and unnatural under the strain of reproducing the Latin so closely (he largely retains the Latin word order and attempts to offer one line of English for every line of Latin). See Evelyn Mary Spearing, *The Elizabethan Translations of Seneca's Tragedies* (Cambridge, 1912), pp. 16–19. His version of *Thyestes*, tackled second in the series of three, represents a compromise between these two approaches.

a more than monstrous womb', Act 5, Scene 4.19) – the womb being his stomach, now full of his sons' flesh. Thyestes declares that, however bad his ancestors have been, he has been worse ('your guilts be small in sight / Of mine', Act 5, Scene 4.25–6). Heywood's addition of Thyestes' closing soliloquy brings us back to the figure of the author, Heywood himself, and shows us that the Thyestean challenge is rooted in the idea of comparative judgement. That is, the value of a character's act of revenge is determined by its relationship to previous examples, and the value of an author's contribution to the revenge tragedy tradition is judged on whether he has succeeded in going further than his predecessors in some way. This is the challenge which Seneca has set his followers, and which Heywood passes on to generations of writers, composing in English or in Latin, or both.

III

Heywood's approach to his translation does not separate Senecan Latin from Senecan English, quite the opposite: he portrays the 1560 *Thyestes* as the achievement of a Classically trained Oxford academic working with the most intimate, detailed knowledge of Seneca's Latin, so that his work, Seneca's play 'faithfully Englished' (as it says on the title page), is seen permanently rooted in, not shooting off from, the Latin tradition. Heywood's challenge to his fellow Englishmen paved the way for generations of innovative responses. The earliest of these, Thomas Kyd's *The Spanish Tragedy* and Shakespeare's *Titus Andronicus*, have received much critical attention, and Shakespeare's engagement with Seneca's *Thyestes* is particularly conspicuous. For Titus' method of revenge is that of Atreus in Seneca's play: he cuts up and cooks the bodies of Tamora's sons, Demetrius and Chiron, in a grisly repeat of Atreus' dinner for his brother Thyestes. In each case, the parent unwittingly eats the sons' flesh whilst the revenger watches.

It is significant that both *The Spanish Tragedy* and *Titus Andronicus*, regarded as fundamental building blocks in the English-language revenge tragedy tradition, are stocked with Latin phrases. Kyd and Shakespeare use Senecan soundbites as intensifiers,

evoking the atmosphere and intensity of Roman tragedy through the sound of the Latin language and allowing a character to vent their feelings with a grander sense of display. At 4.1.80ff. of *Titus Andronicus*, for example, Shakespeare has his protagonist switch from English into Latin at the moment of a horrifying discovery: it is Tamora's sons that have raped his daughter. How can Titus respond? How is he to express the inexpressible? A soundbite from Seneca's *Phaedra* is the answer: Titus slips into Latin, performing the opening lines of a speech in which Seneca has distilled the young man Hippolytus' feelings of outrage on making his own alarming discovery. Lines 671–2 of the *Phaedra* begin Hippolytus' angry response to the confession he has just heard from his stepmother – that her love for him is more than maternal. In *Titus Andronicus*, the sound of Seneca rings out, marking out Titus' reaction as its own special moment, a moment of heightened drama: '*Magni dominator poli, / Tam lentus audis scelera, tam lentus vides?*' (4.1.80–1, 'Ruler of the wide heavens, are you so slow to hear of crimes and so slow to see them?'). The scenarios in the two plays are aligned in terms of atmosphere and emotion; they do not need to be exactly in parallel for the lyrical quality of the Latin to do its work. It is instructive to compare Titus' thundering lines with the spluttering reaction of Uncle Marcus: 'What, what? The lustful sons of Tamora / Performers of this heinous, bloody deed?' Marcus' response is functional: his words articulate that the rapists have been identified. This leaves the rhetorical fireworks to his brother, who is free to vent with the passionate language of a Senecan hero.

The passionate lyricism of a Medea or an Atreus lends itself well to a moment of crisis, or confused indecision, or even a kind of madness. Hieronimo experiences a mixture of all three when, in Act 3, Scene 13 of *The Spanish Tragedy*, he emerges on stage with a book in his hand and declares '*Vindicta mihi*' (3.13.1).[12] Audience members with

---

[12] All quotations are taken from the following edition: Thomas Kyd, *The Spanish Tragedy*, ed. Clara Calvo and Jesús Tronch (London, 2013).

a knowledge of Latin might understand him as saying 'revenge is mine', or might recognize the phrase as a quotation from the New Testament, Romans 12.19 ('Vengeance is mine; I will repay, saith the Lord'); others might simply note the sense of triumph in his voice as he says these words. Hieronimo then replies to himself in English: 'Ay, heaven will be revenged of every ill / Nor will they suffer murder unrepaid' (3.13.2–3). For all those listening, regardless of background, interests or experience, it should now be clear that the hero has announced his commitment to carrying out an act of revenge. This is where the clarity ends, however, for Hieronimo's speech then meanders curiously for another forty lines, peppered with Senecan quotations which do not make his meaning clearer. If anything, they complicate his meaning still further, the Latin verses seemingly being thrown out at random. Scott McMillin argues that the incongruence of the quotations and their context is not a result of carelessness or of Kyd misunderstanding his Senecan sources: 'To pass the matter off as an accident – some combination of errors in the printer's shop and bad training in Latin at the Merchant Taylors' school is required – would be a type of critical negligence.'[13] McMillin explores the literary contexts where these quotations come from, Seneca's *Agamemnon*, his *Troades* and his *Oedipus*, and finds ingenious ways to explain how, in fact, Hieronimo's choice of words is far from random. However, this argument seems motivated by the need to find pattern or reason in every moment of a text, even when a character is clearly in the grip of passionate emotion, the very antidote to reason. Furthermore, our desire to determine what an author means or intends by his choice of words presumes that the author is in control of the meaning. In reality, the meaning of any utterance or moment in a play is up to its audience, since auditors and spectators play an active, not a passive, role when they watch and listen in the theatre.[14] Therefore, it is up to the audience what their individual listening experiences might be: sound-bites from Seneca might go unrecognized, might be deliberately ignored, or might be enjoyed purely for their sound, adding a curious mystery and lyrical beauty to the actors' performances.

John Marston's eponymous protagonist in *Antonio's Revenge* goes one further than Kyd's Hieronimo, in performing not just a minor sprinkling of Senecan fragments but a full-blown rhetorical deluge, declaiming eight lines (lightly reworked) from the opening scene to the *Thyestes* (lines 13–15, 75–9, 80–1). In Seneca's play, these lines are spoken by the Ghost of Tantalus in dialogue with an unnamed Fury; in Marston's hands, they become a tool for self-advertisement, as he proclaims that it is *his* arch-revenger whose name shall be remembered: 'the voice of Tantalus' ('Tantali uocem': *Thyestes*, 80) becomes 'the voice of Antonio' ('*Antonii vocem*': *Antonio's Revenge*, 3.2.21).[15] Once again, each member of the audience listening to the speech unfold would bring their own level of interest and experience to bear: for some, Antonio's Latin tour de force would be dramatic and atmospheric; for others, the sound might be clearly identified as Seneca, pointedly reworked by Marston to signal his own dramatic ambitions.

Marston shows skill in being able to play to multiple sections of the audience at one and the same time. Antonio's speech is followed by the response of his mother, who reacts in troubled wonder, assuming his sudden shift into the

---

[13] Scott McMillin, '*The Book of Seneca in The Spanish Tragedy*', *SEL* 14 (1974), 201–8; p. 201.

[14] Here I intersect with the work of Matteo Pangallo, whose analysis of the role of the early modern audience is informative and well argued. In '"Mayn't a spectator write a comedy?" The early modern idea of playgoers as playmakers', Pangallo explores different attitudes to the playgoing public and expectations of their role in the drama – from intruders whose engagement with the play needed to be closely managed by professionals to autonomous, creative authorities possessing the ultimate productive power in the playhouse. See Matteo Pangallo, '"Mayn't a spectator write a comedy?" The early modern idea of playgoers as playmakers', in *Playwriting Playgoers in Shakespeare's Theater* (Philadelphia, 2017), pp. 31–73.

[15] All quotations from Marston's play are taken from John Marston, *Antonio's Revenge*, ed. W. Reavley Gair (Manchester, 1978).

Roman tongue is some kind of madness: 'Alas, my son's distraught' (III.II.23). Coming after such a grand speech, this short phrase is comic, and does not rely on the audience having caught the gist of the Latin preceding it. Marston then ensures that the audience are all on the same page as to the plot by scripting an English-language version of the same speech, so that everyone is focused on this moment as a key turning point for Antonio: 'Ulciscar' ('I shall take revenge') in line 22 becomes 'I'll be revenged!' in line 28.

In the next scene, Marston draws on the *Thyestes* again and morphs Seneca's words into another display of his authorial control. Antonio is on the point of drawing his dagger to stab Julio, son of Duke Piero, but first converses with the boy in a macabre moment of tenderness. Little Julio nonchalantly declares ''Truth, I love you better than my father, 'deed' (III.III.5), a fateful use of the word 'father' which makes Antonio chuckle; as the son of Piero, the man who had Antonio's own father murdered, Julio's innocent compliment is dangerously on point. Antonio toys with his victim's ignorance in his response:

> Thy father? Gracious, O bounteous heaven!
> I do adore thy justice: *venit in nostras manus*
> *Tandem vindicta, venit et tota quidem.*
>
> (3.3.6–8)

For those in the know, the Latin quotation reveals the truth about whom Antonio loves best (his father, Duke Andrugio) and signals to the audience that the vengeful figure is about to close in on his target. The line, which we can translate as 'at last vengeance has come into my hands, it has come – yes, in its entirety', is an almost verbatim quotation from Seneca, *Thyestes*, 494–5, with the exception of one word: Marston has removed 'Thyestes' (which would give the game away) and substituted the word 'revenge' (*vindicta*), adjusting *totus* ('whole') to *tota*, in agreement with its feminine noun. Antonio's outburst is the more passionately expressed for being couched in Seneca's grave tones, and it also emphasizes the contrast between his powerful position of knowledge and the vulnerable Julio's position of ignorance. The boy will soon be speared by Antonio's dagger and served up to his father, Piero, at a grotesque Thyestean banquet.

Writing at the turn of the century, Marston's competitive spirit was channelled through his engagement with Seneca and the revenge tragedy form. This was a way of challenging the dramatists of his own era, taking them on by producing, as Atreus would say, 'some fierce, bloody outrage, such as my brother would wish his own'. Whilst the *Thyestes* is not the only tragedy to offer a fiercely competitive revenge figure, it does have the advantage of such memorable soundbites as these, to which later writers could directly respond. We see, for example, Ben Jonson throw his hat into the ring in scripting a soliloquy for Sejanus, the protagonist of his revenge play, who announces to the audience:

> Adultery? It is the lightest ill
> I will commit. A race of wicked acts
> Shall flow out of my anger, and o'erspread
> The world's wide face, which no posterity
> Shall e'er approve, nor yet keep silent: things
> That for their cunning, close and cruel mark,
> Thy father would wish his
>
> (*Sejanus*, Actus Secundus, 150–6)[16]

These lines form a close reworking of Atreus' declaration at *Thyestes* 192ff., creatively re-imagined for a new scenario, in which Sejanus, the ambitious advisor to Emperor Tiberius, is seeking revenge against the Emperor's son, Drusus. Drusus is his rival for power and has humiliated Sejanus by striking him in public; it is time for a revenge plot which will begin with the seduction of Drusus' wife, Livilla. That is just for starters: 'Adultery? It is the lightest ill / I will commit.' He will engineer a whole series of crimes, 'A race of wicked acts', so bad that they will become known the world over; the phrase 'o'erspread / The world's wide face' neatly evokes the shocked expressions which Jonson hopes will spread across the faces of his audience as they watch his grim revenge plot

---

[16] All quotations from *Sejanus* are taken from Ben Jonson, *Sejanus His Fall*, ed. Philip J. Ayers (Manchester, 1990).

unfold. For Sejanus' crimes are to be both terrible and memorable, so that he, and Jonson through him, will be remembered for all time: 'wicked acts ... which no posterity / Shall e'er approve, nor yet keep silent'. Not only has Jonson echoed Atreus' line about wreaking a revenge so brilliant that others will wish it had been theirs, he has also worked in here another memorable soundbite from the same speech in the *Thyestes*: 'Age, anime, fac quod nulla posteritas probet, / sed nulla taceat' (*Thyestes*, 192–3). Literally translated, the Latin means 'Come, my soul, do what no posterity will approve of, but none will be silent on.' Jonson's version shows an author eager to engage closely with his model, not for the sake of intertextual allusion alone, but to announce his take up of the Thyestean challenge.

Jonson and Marston were both grammar-schooled and therefore both well versed in Latin. Jonson had had the advantage of a Westminster education under William Camden, whilst Marston went on to study at Brasenose College, Oxford, and thereafter at the Middle Temple (where his father had chambers). Both playwrights were ambitious for themselves and driven by the desire to outdo their rivals; Senecan revenge tragedy provided an excellent vehicle for these ambitions, with its in-built theme of one-upmanship. In the powerful language of their protagonists' we hear something of the authors' own passion and determination, to outstrip their competitors in the field:

Thou lost thyself, child Drusus, when thou thoughtst
Thou couldst outskip my vengeance, or outstand
The power I had to crush thee into air

(*Sejanus*, Actus Secundus, 143–5)

Each author sought a way to show his audience he had gone further than his predecessors, in whichever way his imagination led him. Marston's idea was to go beyond linguistic conventions: he styled himself as a bold innovator in his use of language, viewing this as one way of overtaking his competitors and getting noticed. His revenge tragedy, known variously at the time as *Antonio's Revenge*, *The Second Part of Antonio and Mellida* and *Antonii vindictae*,[17] offers

a multi-faceted experience of language which was, depending on who was listening and assessing it, either highly innovative or an assault on the ear. One of the modern editors of his play, W. Reavley Gair, notes that 'Marston seems to have made it a particular mark of his style to use as many newly coined words and phrases (originating a very large proportion of these himself) as possible ... In *Antonio's Revenge* Marston may have been attempting to become the leading fashionable innovator in the speech habits of a socially prominent section of London society.'[18] As discussed above, he took care to keep all elements of his audience engaged, whether or not they understood Latin, and he would use both languages, English and Latin, in any way that could draw attention to himself.

Marston succeeded in making a name for himself and his rhetorical extravagance, partly thanks to the willingness of his fellow dramatists to parody him in their own plays. On the public stage, he appears thinly disguised under the name 'Crispinus' in Ben Jonson's *Poetaster*, an attempt at putting the wordsmith in his place by making him vomit up some of the vocabulary considered so objectionable. However, it was not just the professional dramatists who took pleasure in making fun of Marston's appetite for invention; his fellow university men deemed him a worthy target for their satire as well. *The Second Part of the Return from Parnassus* (1601–2), the third instalment in a trilogy of plays penned and performed by students of St John's, Cambridge, presents the self-important figure of Furor Poeticus ('Poetic Anger') whose fiery zeal for experimentation and confidence in his own 'liuing genius' brings him not success but ridicule and disillusionment. Ingenioso, suffering one of his extended speeches, asks him to pipe down: 'Nay prethee good Furor, doe not roare in rimes before thy time: thou hast a very terrible roaring muse, nothing but squibs and firewoorks. Quiet thy selfe

---

17 Martin Wiggins with Catherine Richardson, eds., *British Drama, 1533–1642: A Catalogue* (Oxford, 2011–) vol. 4, p. 267.
18 W. Reavley Gair, 'Introduction', to Marston, *Antonio's*, pp. 1–48; p. 21.

a while.'[19] It is tempting to see in the Cambridge lampooning of an Oxford graduate the old inter-university rivalry rearing its head. It also seems likely that the choice of 'Furor' for his pseudonym, coming so close to the date of *Antonio's Revenge*, is a dig at Marston's revenge tragedy in particular. *Furor* ('fury') is the Latin term not only for poetic inspiration but also for the wild, reckless kind of passion to which Seneca and his followers gave personified form: the Furies rise from the Underworld to incite their human agents to acts of revenge. Also of interest is the fact that these three plays – Marston's *Antonio's Revenge*, Jonson's *Poetaster* and the Cambridge play – all emerge within months of each other at the turn of the century, demonstrating that, whichever theatre company or venue dramatists were writing for, there was a keen interest in engaging with contemporary practitioners across the professional–amateur divide.[20]

IV

Antonio's Revenge reached print in 1602, and, in the following year, Jonson attempted to match him with his *Sejanus* on stage. Alongside Marston and Jonson, 1603 saw another revenge tragedian emerge from the woodwork, perhaps in response to their efforts. Matthew Gwinne was not a professional playwright; he had made his name in quite another arena, as a physician to aristocratic clients, including members of the royal family. After many years as an Oxford academic, he had come to London in 1597 to take up the post of Professor of Physic at Gresham College, the first person to occupy this prestigious role. What interest, then, did he have in revenge tragedy? He had written several plays at Oxford, one of which was a revenge tragedy of truly gigantic proportions. *Nero: Nova Tragædia* ('Nero, a New Tragedy') came in at more than 5,000 lines, an ambitious feat which threatened to outdo his competitors, at least in quantity. He took this play to a London publisher, Edward Blount, a name we now associate with Shakespeare, since he would go on to publish the First Folio in 1623; in 1603, however, Gwinne's *Nero* represented Blount's first foray into

drama, the first play that he ever published. As its title suggests, this is a history play, dramatizing the rise and fall of Rome's most infamous emperor. Composed in Latin, it is steeped in the conventions of Seneca's tragic style, in terms of both language and structure. Each of the first four acts dramatizes a conspiracy leading up to a murder, and the ghost of that victim then appears to introduce the next act. The chorus, consisting of Nemesis and the Furies, contributes to the effect of this patterning: Nemesis delivers the prologue and epilogue framing the play and supplies the chorus at the end of Act 4, whilst Tisiphone, Allecto and Megaera each take a chorus at the end of the first three acts. All four of them come together to deliver the final chorus at the end of Act 5, and, as J. W. Binns puts it, 'This gives the impression that the events of the play are being stage-managed by the Furies.'[21] The use of the Furies as characters who instigate and preside over schemes of revenge is an important feature of Senecan tragedy, as is the device of the chorus, and Gwinne's tour de force brings the two features together.

The *Nero* is an ambitious example of the tradition of neo-Latin tragedy at the universities, and Gwinne's decision to publish it was also rather daring. The academic establishment frowned on the publication of work (which ought, more properly, to be kept out of the commercial

---

[19] J. B. Leishman, ed., *The Second Part of the Return from Parnassus*, in *The Three Parnassus Plays (1598–1601)* (London, 1949), 3.4.1302, 1318–20.

[20] Scholarly consensus dates *Antonio's Revenge* to either 1600 or 1601, with Wiggins coming down on the side of early winter 1600 (Wiggins with Richardson, *Catalogue*, vol. 4, p. 267). It was entered into the Stationers' Register in October 1601 and printed in 1602. *Poetaster* was performed several times by 1602, the year that it was printed, and is dated by Wiggins to the autumn of 1601 (Wiggins with Richardson, *Catalogue*, vol. 4, p. 312). Leishman (*Parnassus*, pp. 24–6) summarizes the evidence for dating performances of *The Second Part of the Return from Parnassus* at St John's College, Cambridge, concluding that it was first performed in 1601 and revived in 1602.

[21] J. W. Binns, 'Seneca and neo-Latin Tragedy in England', in *Seneca*, ed. C. D. N. Costa (London, 1974), pp. 205–34; p. 221.

sphere), and the publication of a play was something worse than frivolous.[22] Evidently Gwinne considered it a worthy risk to his reputation, but it is not clear why he felt that 1603 was the right moment to resurrect a play from his Oxford days. Was he intrigued by the competition between Jonson and Marston and saw the vogue for revenge tragedy as an opportunity to get readers interested in his own creation? For the neo-Latin and English-language traditions of drama were not alienated from one another; nor were the people who wrote them. Gwinne and Marston had overlapped at Oxford and were both in London by 1597, the year that Gwinne took up his professorship at Gresham College. Marston's use of Latin, and his interest in selecting phrases from Seneca's *Thyestes* in particular, seems designed to entice men like Gwinne to engage with him, goading them to show whether they can do better:

> Invent some stratagem of vengeance
> Which, but to think on, may like lightning glide
> With horror through thy breast. Remember this:
> *Scelera non ulcisceris, nisi vincis.*
>
> (*Antonio's Revenge*, 3.1.48–51)

This Latin quotation, which means 'you do not avenge crimes unless you surpass them', is taken verbatim from Seneca's *Thyestes* (lines 195–6). It comes at a critical moment in Atreus' thinking: he has just announced his decision to 'dare some fierce, bloody outrage, such as my brother would wish his own', but now he must come up with dastardly deeds matching the extent of his ambitions. For it would not be enough simply to get back at Thyestes by doing something which equalled the original wrong; he must do something worse: 'You do not avenge crimes unless you surpass them' is the competitive revenge principle which drives Seneca's *Thyestes* and which Seneca passed down to generations of writers after him. Marston responds by placing the phrase in the mouth of Andrugio's ghost at the moment that he is instructing his son to punish Piero: it will not be enough simply to do something bad to Piero, it will have to be something worse than the original crime

(the murder of Andrugio). Seneca's Latin, 'scelera non ulcisceris, nisi vincis', spoken at such a moment, is a challenge to go one better.[23]

When Seneca's Atreus spoke this line, he had his own competitor in mind: Procne, who served her husband, Tereus, King of Thrace, a grisly dinner involving parts of their son. Atreus' revenge is inspired by and defined against Procne's revenge: he sees himself in her shadow, and can only feel that he has succeeded if he has gone one better than her. The Fury who appears at the beginning of the play sets up this scheme, demanding that Atreus commit 'the Thracian outrage' ('Thracium ... nefas': *Thyestes*, 56); that is, Atreus should emulate Procne and create his version of the cannibal banquet that took place in Thrace. The Fury qualifies her demand by adding that this time the outrage is to be achieved on a larger scale, 'with a greater number' of victims ('maiore numero': *Thyestes*, 57). Not content with Procne's example of the one son, Itys, killed and served up to his father, this revenge plot is to involve more bodies: Atreus has the opportunity to outdo Procne by virtue of the fact that his brother Thyestes has *three* sons who can be killed and cooked. When Atreus appears in person in Act 2, he gets to work on plotting against his brother, fulfilling, though unwittingly, the commands of the Fury, his hidden inspiration. Addressing Procne directly, in the vocative case, he identifies her as his muse: 'Thracian mother and sister, infuse me with your spirit, our cause is similar.'[24] Disappointed that following her

---

[22] See Elizabeth Sandis, 'University drama in print: curating your image and shaping your story', in *Early Modern Drama in the Universities: Institutions, Intertexts, Individuals* (Oxford, in press).

[23] It is on this note that Andrugio's ghost leaves the stage, the Latin line lingering in the air as his parting shot. Those familiar with Latin or Seneca, or both, therefore have a moment to take in the significance of the Thyestean challenge, before the new scene begins with the entrance of Antonio's mother.

[24] 'animum Daulis inspira parens / sororque; causa est similis', 275–6. Daulis is the name of Tereus' seat in Thrace and is used as an epithet for Procne, who is both a mother (to Itys, her victim) and a sister (to Philomela, Tereus' victim). Used in a context such as this, 'Daulian' and 'Thracian' are interchangeable.

lead is unoriginal, since the crime of killing and feeding a child's flesh to its father has already been appropriated ('occupatum', 274), Atreus declares that he must find a way to make his crime *greater* than that of the Thracian Queen ('*maius* hoc aliquid', 274 – my emphasis).

In responding to Seneca and to the revenge tragedians of his own time, Gwinne offers a wry and pointed echo of Atreus' language. Act 3, Scene 3, sees Paris the actor arrive at court to break some bad news, but he keeps the Emperor guessing as to what it might be. Nero's response is to ask: 'Surely a Thracian dinner is not being set at Rome? What is it?', to which Paris replies: 'A crime is being prepared, worse than the Thracian.'[25] Nero's question, 'It is not a Thracian feast, is it?', could be delivered with a hint of comedy, the audience enjoying the moment of a character wondering in which direction the plot is going to go. Gwinne has already set up Act 3, Scene 3, as a metatheatrical vignette, firstly by using the character of Paris the actor as Nero's interlocutor, and secondly by having Paris bemoan the fact they are discussing real events, not a play: 'It is a tragedy', he says, 'but I wish it were a play.'[26] Nero's question also hints at the idea of a stage set, suggested by his use of the verb 'struitur', which conveys the process of physically laying out the meal on the table: 'Surely the Thracian dinner is not being laid out at Rome?' Toying with the idea of recreating the cannibal banquet scene, now set in Nero's city, Gwinne has us wondering who is planning to take the role of Atreus, and who will be his Thyestes. Paris seems to be warning Nero that, if he is not careful, he will be the victim in this scenario, whilst his mother Agrippina will get to play Atreus.

A closer look at Paris' language shows us that Gwinne is not making a general sweeping gesture towards Seneca's *Thyestes* here; he has carefully and deliberately evoked specific moments in the play that are programmatic – that is, they lay down the principle upon which the Thyestean revenge plot is based. Paris declares: 'Scelus paratur Thracio maius' ('A crime is being prepared, greater than

the Thracian').[27] In translating 'maius' into English, we can also render it 'worse', as it is more idiomatic to speak of a worse crime than a bigger one. However, the key thing is the comparative element to this adjective, which announces that Gwinne has taken up the Thyestean challenge: 'maiore' said the Fury (*Thyestes*, 57) and 'maius' declared Atreus (*Thyestes*, 274). Whatever Gwinne does in his revenge tragedy, he has to show that his play offers something greater or bigger than that of his predecessors. Whether or not he was successful in this endeavour is still up for debate, but at over 5,000 lines of verse and with a cast featuring over 80 characters, Gwinne may have outdone his competitors on something.

For a well-paid, successful physician who had no intention of becoming a professional dramatist, publishing the *Nero* in 1603 was something of a vanity project, intended to enhance his reputation as a man of great learning. Gwinne would shortly be brought back to Oxford by his *alma mater*, St John's College, to produce entertainments for King James's visit to the university in August 1605. Two young dramatists who would have kept an eye on Gwinne's increasing fame (with a view to propagating their own) were Thomas Middleton and Philip Massinger, who may have encountered Gwinne by reputation while they were students at Oxford, or may have

---

[25] NERO : Odrysia Romæ mensa num struitur? quid est?
PARIS : Scelus paratur Thracio maius.
    (Matthew Gwinne, *Nero* (London, 1603), sig. G1v)

    The Odrysian Kingdom was a union of Thracian tribes, and we find 'Odrysian' and 'Thracian' being used interchangeably. Seneca, for example, refers to Tereus and Procne's place at Thrace as 'domus / Odrysia' at *Thyestes*, 272–3.

[26] 'Est tragica, at vt sit fabvla optandum': Gwinne, *Nero*, sig. G1v. The fact that Gwinne's play deals with historical events makes his treatment of a tyrant figure of particular interest. For the political significance of Gwinne's engagement with the *Thyestes*, see Emma Buckley, 'Matthew Gwinne's *Nero* (1603): Seneca, academic drama, and the politics of polity', *Canadian Review of Comparative Literature* 40 (2013), 16–33.

[27] Gwinne, *Nero*, sig. G1v.

seen copies of his plays when they came off the London press. Middleton was a student at The Queen's College until 1600 or 1601, while Massinger followed his father to Oxford to study at St Alban's Hall (now Merton College) from *c.* 1602–3. Both these scholars took up the Thyestean challenge to write their own revenge tragedies, though they each adopted different approaches.[28] Another Oxford scholar went on to stage his own revenge tragedy at Gwinne's old college in 1607: his work, the *Philomela*, is discussed further below.

Middleton adopts and twists Latin tags in the manner of Marston or Kyd, but, more specifically, he alters a quotation so that we see him entering a dialogue with Seneca and Gwinne, speaking their language. In Act 1, Scene 4, of *The Revenger's Tragedy*, Middleton constructs a scene of competitive mourning (a sad scene with a comical edge) between the Lord Antonio, who has just lost his wife, and Hippolito, who wants Antonio to know that he is suffering too:

> My lord, since you invite us to your sorrows,
> Let's truly taste 'em, that with equal comfort
> As to ourselves we may relieve your wrong.
> We have grief too, that yet walks without tongue:
> *Curae leves loquuntur, majores stupent.*
> (*The Revenger's Tragedy*, 1.4.19–23)[29]

This Latin expression, which we may translate as 'trifling worries are spoken about, greater ones are dumb', quotes line 607 from Seneca's *Phaedra* with one important change: whereas Seneca writes 'ingentes', Middleton writes 'maiores'.[30] This is a line regularly quoted by early modern writers as a maxim, and was easily checked by Middleton if he had wished to quote the Latin correctly. I suggest that this is not a casual error, and that Middleton has deliberately chosen to replace the positive adjective *ingens* ('huge') with the comparative adjective *maius* ('greater', 'bigger'). Like Gwinne, he has lighted upon this programmatic term, which makes such a bold statement in the *Thyestes*: Atreus' desire to think up 'something better' ('maius hoc aliquid': *Thyestes*, 274) is not just a character's but an author's desire to outdo his rivals.

This scene – Act 1, Scene 4 – like so much of Middleton's play, is built around tragic irony and black humour: Middleton adds several touches that strike a note of deliberate implausibility and comic excess. His doubling of the prayer-book motif, for example, ironizes the wronged woman's show of virtue by making it seem disingenuously staged and over the top: the husband in mourning finds his wife clutching not one prayer book but two, with pages neatly arranged to display the fact that she had been focusing on virtuous maxims. Hippolito's response, therefore, matches this desire for great show of doing the right thing: he wants Antonio to know that his wife was *so* virtuous that her husband is one among many who are stricken with grief at her loss. What better way of expressing strong passions and emotions than to turn to Seneca and let a Latin soundbite do the talking? The quotation from Seneca's *Phaedra* elevates Hippolito's speech to new heights, but then Middleton goes one further than Seneca: he changes 'huge' to 'bigger', asserting his play as a competitor in the game of one-upmanship. Writing *The Revenger's Tragedy* not long after Gwinne's *Nero* came out in print, Middleton takes up the Thyestean challenge with alacrity, going further than any previous author of revenge tragedy in his use of startling meta-theatre and razor-sharp black humour.

V

Gwinne's *Nero* came out in 1603; Middleton began writing *The Revenger's Tragedy* some time in 1604, 1605 or early 1606.[31] Soon afterwards, the

---

[28] Massinger's *The Roman Actor*, first performed in 1626, would be an interesting *comparandum* for Gwinne's *Nero*, not least because of the way in which both plays use the figure of a professional actor, Paris, as a tool to generate metatheatrical ironies.

[29] All quotations from *The Revenger's Tragedy* are taken from the following edition: Thomas Middleton, *The Revenger's Tragedy*, ed. MacDonald P. Jackson, in *Thomas Middleton: The Collected Works*, ed. Gary Taylor and John Lavagnino (Oxford, 2007), pp. 543–93.

[30] I have checked for manuscript variants in the transmission of Seneca and 'ingentes' appears consistently.

[31] See Wiggins with Richardson, eds., *Catalogue*, vol. 5, p. 333.

influence of both playwrights was brought to bear on the production of a new revenge tragedy, *Philomela*, at Gwinne's Oxford college. Gwinne had played a key role in getting drama established at St John's during the years when the college was financially unstable and not too keen on unnecessary expenditure. Alongside William Gager, who had come up to Oxford in the same year, Gwinne had fought to preserve and develop theatrical traditions in the college during the 1580s and 1590s.[32] By the turn of the century, when St John's was enjoying greater prosperity, its students were able to explore more ambitious dramatic endeavours. By 1607, they were planning a special (and conspicuously expensive) season of revels, capitalizing on the fact that the college authorities and alumni (whom they tapped several times for financial contributions) had recently been very pleased with the dramatic performances given by their own St John's students in front of King James. His visit to Oxford in August 1605 had been the occasion for bringing Gwinne back to the college to produce entertainments for the college students to act in. A professionally successful alumnus and passionate advocate of theatre, Gwinne may have inspired the students in their dramatic pursuits in the wake of the royal visit.

The result was an ambitious series of entertainments which ran from the end of November 1607 to the middle of February 1608, and which included a bold new revenge tragedy laced with Middletonian black humour. *Philomela* tells the story of the rape and mutilation of Philomela by her brother-in-law, King Tereus of Thrace, whose punishment is spearheaded by his wife, Queen Procne, Philomela's sister. The macabre revenge which Procne inflicts is 'the Thracian crime' identified by the Fury and then by Atreus as the inspiring exemplum he is to follow: Procne kills her son Itys, cooks him, and serves him to his father to eat. In this version of the story, the anonymous Oxford author has added extra crimes to the list of gruesome acts Tereus has committed: the character of Tereus' henchman Phalus, for example, who does not appear in any classical sources, has been added to the *dramatis personae* in order that Tereus can murder him. Phalus' conspicuous acts of loyalty to his master contribute to the portrayal of Tereus' vicious character.

Given the way in which Seneca highlights the story of Procne's revenge as the ultimate one to beat, the Oxford author's decision to choose this story for his own revenge tragedy is a bold move. Indeed, the play begins with an induction which dramatizes the choosing of the story at random from the pages in a book. This unusual ceremony is conducted by two figures: Fortuna, who holds the book, and the Christmas Prince, who is asked to read out the name he sees on the page: 'Tereus'. At this moment, the Christmas Prince figure is wearing a scholar's gown, signifying his identity as a member of the academic community at St John's College, but he now takes off the gown to mount the stage in his new role as tyrant Tereus, King of Thrace. This approach to the beginning of the *Philomela* sets the tone for what follows and encourages the audience to view the tragedy through a metatheatrical lens: whatever happens

---

[32] Gager's tragedies have received considerably more critical attention than other examples of the neo-Senecan tradition at the universities. In the 1990s, J. W. Binns' and Jozef Ijsewijn's surveys of early modern Latin literature had earmarked the Gagerian canon as an example of the kinds of treasures to be found by the neo-Latin explorer; this approach was intended to demonstrate the range on offer in the field and the benefits of further exploration, not to restrict attention to the texts which they had decided to feature: J. W. Binns, *Intellectual Culture in Elizabethan and Jacobean England: the Latin Writings of the Age* (Leeds, 1990); Jozef Ijsewijn, *Companion to Neo-Latin Studies*, 2nd edn, 2 vols. (Louven, 1990–8). However, two decades on and the field had not moved much further: Howard B. Norland's *Neoclassical Tragedy in Elizabethan England* (Newark, 2009) labelled the universities' contribution to the tradition in two chapters entitled 'Neo-Latin tragedy at Cambridge' (pp. 124–54) and 'Gager's neo-Latin tragedy at Oxford' (pp. 155–92). Gager's particular brand of Senecan tragedy at Christ Church, whilst engaging and significant, provides a more convenient than accurate representation of Oxford tragedy during this era, and I have sought to rebalance this a little in the present study.

to Tereus is happening to a St John's student in disguise. This will add an extra layer of black humour in the climactic banquet scene.

In the early modern period, as today, the most famous version of the story of Tereus appeared in the collection of stories known as Ovid's *Metamorphoses*, an epic-length work made up of a myriad of different, shape-shifting tales. The rape of Philomela and Procne's revenge against Tereus appears in Book VI, and it is likely that the book which Fortuna is holding is intended to represent (or may physically have been) a copy of Ovid's *Metamorphoses*. The Christmas Prince's selection of his story from the book is a powerful metatheatrical tableau which Shakespeare exploited in *Titus Andronicus*, as part of his sophisticated interweaving of two classical models, Ovid's *Metamorphoses* and Seneca's *Thyestes*. This is a natural pairing, for it reflects the fact that Seneca viewed his own work in relation to Ovid's, viewing the Augustan poet as a younger sibling eyes his elder brother.[33] The *Thyestes* is, as we have seen, structured around the desire to outdo what has gone before and impress by daring 'some fierce, bloody outrage, such as my brother would wish his own'. Seneca's creations are coloured by this desire to compete with a previous generation, and the early modern poets who emulate Seneca also emulate his competitive relationship to his predecessors. In many ways, the Renaissance response to Seneca is also a response to Ovid, and vice versa; as Robert Miola puts it, Ovid is 'erroneously considered at times a distinct alternative to Seneca. As sources in the Renaissance, Ovid and Seneca run routes parallel, identical, contiguous, and intersecting.'[34] In this scheme, the myth of Philomela functions as the symbolic nexus of these intersecting routes, and, as Patrick Cheney has pointed out, inspired a distinctively competitive response from Elizabethan poets such as Spenser and Marlowe.[35] In choosing this particular myth, then, as the subject for his tragedy, the author of *Philomela* at St John's College, Oxford, signals that he is positioning himself as the latest combatant to take on the tradition, hoping to prove his mettle in a complex intertextual battle that stretches back to Roman times.

Philomela successfully combines Ovidian inspiration with Senecan style: the story of Tereus, which occupies 250 lines of Book VI of the *Metamorphoses* now becomes a full-length neo-Senecan revenge tragedy of over 1,400 lines.[36] It is a sophisticated piece of writing which displays a confident mastery of Latin, but this in itself was not enough; to be competitive as a Jacobean revenge tragedy, it had to take the staging of the revenge plot to a new level. The author of the *Philomela* rose to this challenge by making clever use of his venue – St John's College dining hall – where ordinary meals were eaten daily. It now becomes the stage set for Act 5's grisly cannibal banquet. The Oxford author focuses our attention on the location and the everyday implements of eating by creating a preparatory scene, Act 5 Scene 3, in which the servants take over the action: 'Enter the maid and steward, together with other servants, to set the table.'[37] We watch students-turned-servants setting out the tableware for a symbolic meal that will turn everyday experience into a nightmarish caricature of itself. Dialogue between two of the servants heightens the tension as we contemplate what will be served up on the table: the maid depicts Procne spurring on the kitchen staff to cook her bloodcurdling meal faster, while the steward remarks on the pressure they are all under because there are such high expectations for this dinner ('Grandis expectatio', *Philomela*, 2837). The addition of this scene, with its

---

[33] Seneca's profound debt to Ovid is neatly summarized by R. J. Tarrant, who remarks that Ovid 'provided Seneca with models not only of diction and expression but also of characterization and thematic ideas': R. J. Tarrant, 'Senecan drama and its antecedents', *Harvard Studies in Classical Philology* 82 (1978), 259–60; p. 262.

[34] Robert Miola, *Shakespeare and Classical Tragedy: The Influence of Seneca* (Oxford, 1992), p. 4.

[35] See Patrick Cheney, 'Career rivalry, counter-nationhood, and Philomela in 'The passionate shepherd to his love', in *Marlowe's Counterfeit Profession: Ovid, Spenser, Counter-Nationhood* (Toronto, 1997), pp. 68–87.

[36] *P. Ovidi Nasonis: Metamorphoses*, ed. Richard J. Tarrant, Oxford Classical Texts (Oxford, 2004), 6.422–674.

[37] 'Ingrediuntur: Ancilla, et Anteambulo cum alijs famuljs vt mensam instruant': *The Tragedy of Philomela or Tereus & Progne*, in *The Christmas Prince*, ed. Frederick S. Boas and W. W. Greg (Oxford, 1922), pp. 56–102, 2834–5.

window onto the world of backstage preparations, is an effective innovation by the St John's dramatist; it allows the audience to savour the dramatic build-up to the grisly Thyestean feast in a way that is novel and finds no place in the author's Ovidian and Senecan sources. On one level, the audience is sitting under King Tereus' roof in the Thracian palace, living through the story as part of the theatrical construct; on another, they see in King Tereus the man who represents all of the St John's college men: their Christmas Prince in charge of college entertainments. He invited them to the dining hall for the play as part of his role, and all members of the audience are playing their roles as his guests. Better not try any snacks on the tables during the play, we might think; the boundary between the real and the theatrical is pleasingly blurred in this self-consciously institutionalized production.

We may compare the strategies of other early modern dramatists in staging their cannibalistic feast scenes. William Alabaster had upped the ante in the 1590s with his play *Roxana*, which expanded the Thyestean banquet by having the King and Queen *both* feed each other the flesh of loved ones, taking it in turns. In the Jacobean era, *The Bloody Banquet* outdoes its own title by offering us two banquets: the first feast, which forms part of the seduction of Prince Tymethes by the Queen, is repeated in a macabre second helping – this time Tymethes' body becomes the feast and the Queen is forced to eat him. Alabaster's Latin play comes to us from Trinity College, Cambridge, whilst *The Bloody Banquet* is written in English for the London stage, penned by Oxford alumnus Thomas Middleton, with additions from a collaborator, probably Dekker.[38]

In this brief study, I have endeavoured to open up the body of English revenge tragedy, to show that 'English' is not the same thing as 'English-language', and that we need to rethink our understanding of the genre as a monolingual culture. Writers such as Shakespeare, Marston and Middleton were writing in a bilingual culture where Latin dominated many areas of life, including the education they had received, at school or university, or both. Understanding what I have termed the 'Thyestean language' helps us to analyse Latin-language and English-language examples of revenge tragedy side by side, bringing us closer to the experience of the many sixteenth- and seventeenth-century readers or listeners who consumed literature and plays in both languages. If we keep in mind the university backgrounds (and, therefore, networks and cultural attitudes) of many early modern dramatists, and we focus not on either Latin or English, but on the competitive Thyestean language which is so influential in shaping revenge tragedy in the early modern period, we can hear the conversations which are taking place between authors, in different production centres and across the professional–amateur divide.

---

[38] It is difficult to date *The Bloody Banquet*. Wiggins limits the date of composition to between 1605 and 1613, with a best guess of 1610; see Wiggins with Richardson, eds., *Catalogue*, vol. 6, p. 91. For an in-depth discussion of the authorship of the play, see Gary Taylor, 'Thomas Middleton, Thomas Dekker, and *The Bloody Banquet*', *The Papers of the Bibliographical Society of America* 94 (2000), 197–233.

GOING TO SCHOOL WITH(OUT) SHAKESPEARE: CONVERSATIONS WITH EDWARD'S BOYS

HARRY R. McCARTHY AND PERRY MILLS

It sounds ridiculous because obviously we know we're all here for school and we do all these other things and there are so many different things going on, but my school experience has been going to school in and around shows. Edward's Boys is what my secondary school experience was.[1]

As well as being, in all likelihood, 'Shakespeare's School', King Edward VI School in Stratford-upon-Avon has another long-lasting connection to the plays of Shakespeare and his contemporaries.[2] For over a decade, 'K. E. S.' has been home to Edward's Boys, an all-boy acting troupe whose productions of plays by Francis Beaumont, Thomas Dekker and John Webster, John Ford, Ben Jonson, John Lyly, Christopher Marlowe, John Marston, Charles May, Thomas Middleton, Thomas Nashe and John Redford constitute the largest corpus of early modern drama in present-day performance. From their earliest experiments with Shakespearian cross-dressing in workshops led by Carol Chillington Rutter[3] to their full-scale productions which began in 2009,[4] Edward's Boys have attracted a great deal of scholarly attention. Specialists have hailed this company's work as 'transformative' to theatre-historical thinking,[5] 'recapturing what it must have been like to see the plays as they were intended to be performed'.[6] Edward's Boys, writes Callan Davies, 'bear the mark of a great early modern acting company: not only can they enliven seemingly impenetrable prose, maximise the multi-media possibilities of performance, take liberties with text and create fluidity and dynamism in clowning and comedy, but they can take and adapt those qualities as occasion, space and audience

require'.[7] Others have predicted that the company's work 'really will rewrite the academic theatre history books':[8] indeed, the first book-length study of the company was published in 2020.[9]

This article offers some of the 160 boys who have taken part in Edward's Boys the opportunity to 'speak back' to the critical work to which their productions have given rise. Framed by a conversation between Harry R. McCarthy and the company's director, Perry Mills, the article presents testimonials from Edward's Boys actors past and

---

[1] Ritvick Nagar, personal interview, 19 March 2020.

[2] King Edward VI School, Stratford-upon-Avon, is a state-funded selective ('grammar') school for boys aged 11–18 years with a co-educational Sixth Form. Girls were first admitted to the school in September 2013.

[3] The workshops are discussed in Carol Chillington Rutter, 'Playing with boys on Middleton's stage: and ours', in *The Oxford Handbook of Thomas Middleton*, ed. Gary Taylor and Trish Thomas Henley (Oxford, 2012), pp. 98–115.

[4] Full details of previous productions can be found on the company's website. See Edward's Boys, last modified 2020: http://edwardsboys.org.

[5] Andy Kesson, 'ABL 24. Perry Mills tells us about Edward's Boys, a company of schoolboys staging early modern drama', YouTube, uploaded by A Bit Lit, 27 April 2020: www.youtube.com/watch?v=AgmK2ZZOCIk.

[6] Leah Scragg, private correspondence, March 2009.

[7] Callan Davies, 'Review of Thomas Nashe's *Summer's Last Will and Testament* (directed by Perry Mills for Edward's Boys) at the Old Palace of John Whitgift School, 30 September 2017', *Shakespeare* 14.3 (2018), 259–61; p. 261.

[8] Emma Smith, private correspondence, June 2010.

[9] See Harry R. McCarthy, *Performing Early Modern Drama Beyond Shakespeare: Edward's Boys* (Cambridge, 2020).

present drawn from the company's website, private correspondence preserved in the school archive, and a number of extensive interviews carried out by McCarthy between 2018 and 2020. Taken together, the insights offered here paint a picture not only of how the company has developed and built on its successes, but also of what it means, for the boys, to go to school with(out) Shakespeare.

HARRY R. MCCARTHY – For a teacher, it must be rather special to hear boys saying, as Ritvick does [see epigraph], that the theatrical work you do with them shapes their entire school experience . . .

PERRY MILLS – And Ritvick is not alone in expressing that sentiment. Doing these plays is a large commitment of time if nothing else. Top of the league is taking part in thirteen productions, I believe. Yet for none of them is Edward's Boys their sole extra-curricular activity: they participate in sport, music, the Duke of Edinburgh award, and so on. But it would be foolish to deny that it has proved a significant and defining experience for many.

HRM – And it's an experience that's undeniably shaped by you. Before we hand over to the boys, could you describe your educational role in the company's activities?

PM – I always describe myself as 'an English teacher who does plays', although for the sake of accuracy I should declare that I am now Deputy Head with responsibility for pastoral care. Nothing is essentially different in the way I have worked with students on plays (and indeed in lessons) since the beginning of my career. This probably explains the common threads in what the students have said from the first Edward's Boys productions to the present.

I should also make it clear that it's my show. I cast it. Ultimately, I make the key decisions. However, the rehearsal process is profoundly collaborative, and as we approach production week I aim to withdraw as far as possible. I explicitly give the show over to them; they are responsible for running the performances, and that becomes even more evident once we go on tour. I am fully aware of the potential contradiction between 'my show' and 'profoundly collaborative'. I have a little paradoxical dictum: 'Do as

I say – Do what you want.' The games we play have complex rules, but they may become more clear as our conversation develops.

HRM – You're an English teacher; I'm an English academic. It probably makes sense, then, to begin with how the company approaches the text. Plays like John Redford's *Wit and Science* or Francis Beaumont's *The Woman Hater* are under-studied even by specialists, let alone grammar-school boys. Yet one of the most frequent comments made by audiences is how at ease the boys seem with the language. For Laurie Maguire, 'a hallmark of Edward's Boys is their clarity of verse speaking', which often prompts a uniform reaction of 'They understood every word they said and consequently so did I' among audiences.[10] When I was last working in the Edward's Boys Archive, I remember coming across some correspondence from Gregory Doran, the Royal Shakespeare Company's artistic director, which praised the boys' 'comprehension of difficult text, and the clarity of their diction which would put some of our own [RSC] actors to shame'.[11] High praise indeed!

PM – The entire process is focussed on an understanding of the text and the communication of that understanding as clearly as possible. The only way I know of achieving that is 'text-bashing'. We begin rehearsing in small groups, or even one to one, sitting around a table, speaking the text aloud, over and over again. Although I provide guidance, suggestions, there is a great deal of discussion. We question everything. At every stage we ask questions: 'Why does the character say or do that?' 'Why at that point?' 'Why in that way?' 'What does it mean – or what might it mean?' 'What possibilities are suggested for movement, "stage business"?' Punctuation may or may not be followed; editor's notes – if they exist – may be ignored. We look for 'triggers' or 'signposts' throughout. Alliteration, assonance, repetition, rhythm, rhyme and so on.

---

[10] Laurie Maguire, 'Company profile', Edward's Boys: http://edwardsboys.org/profile.

[11] Gregory Doran, private correspondence, March 2011.

As they explore the possibilities in the text by speaking it out loud, I listen very hard – I am an English teacher, as you say. 'Perhaps not like that . . . try another version'. We consider the full range of options available to the actor: pauses, emphases, volume, pitch, modulation, nuance, where to breathe. An appreciation of tone is crucial. I call it 'colouring' the language. This part of the rehearsal process takes time.

There is no pressure at this point to make final decisions but any decisions we might come to are agreed mutually. We work hard to ensure that, eventually, everyone understands what the text means – or what it might mean. As someone memorably put it in the early days, 'We get it under our fingernails – until it's ours.'

As all who have been a part of Edward's Boys will attest, work on a play starts with the text and never stops. . . . As school kids, these actors are perfectly prepared for this phase of the production, and a fairly traditional pupil–teacher dynamic is therefore more easily and productively achieved than may be the case with adult actors. This dynamic does not mean that the children aren't encouraged to attempt interpretation of the text for themselves and be creative ('playful') with it – this process is a collaborative affair and such endeavours are required. It is rather that there is, perhaps, a greater openness to becoming informed about what the text is saying via effective classroom techniques. In short, the lads are used to learning, so the learning for the play comes fairly quickly. Evidently, the actors use their 'transferable skills' acquired in the classroom of, well, learning, in the rehearsal room. In turn, the proficiency in handling play-texts, difficult ones at that, is developed in the rehearsal room and then transferred back into the classroom. It's something of an educational dream.[12]

The fact that we were working on 400-year-old text felt oddly irrelevant. We rigorously analysed every line, word, thought, emotion, mark of punctuation. At times, we briefly stopped to re-evaluate and experiment with our interpretation of the text, only to completely reset the very prism through which we had examined its meaning based on the mere transient flicker in the shade of sense within a word. For me, this phase of our work was critical and the most stimulating academically, a time where we plunged ourselves headfirst into the machinery of text. Only after this phase could I feel worthy of emotionally engaging with the scene and experiencing the language in

a richer sense. You gave us the tools not only to understand the words, but to *feel* every twist and turn in *sense* on the page, in its sound when read, and eventually in its channelling into physical movement.

When working with you, it felt as if each new idea was a genuine new discovery being made, a true development in the overall perspective of the text. They weren't stale bits of 400-year-old text to me. They were now living, breathing and organically evolving.[13]

HRM – You and the boys describe this work as very much a collaborative process, a site of mutual discovery rather than didactic instruction.

PM – Precisely. After one of our earliest performances, of Lyly's *Endymion* at Warwick University, a cast member's grandfather opined, 'Of course, they didn't know what they were saying; they were just parroting.' That comment made me very cross. Producing mindless automata mouthing empty phrases is not the point at all of the work we do.

There's knowing the lines and then there's something else, making them your own . . . As you know it better you're able to emphasize different and more things as you become more 'free'. It becomes ever more clear where the stresses need to be. The rhythms take you over. You pay more attention to each word.[14]

It's not just that you're there saying the lines – you're there, as an actor, understanding where you fit in to the whole picture: what is this play *about*? What are they *saying*? What are *you* saying? Are the words that you're saying *really* what you're saying? Often it's not, so then it's like, well, what *are* you saying? And that's the process – in the old days, in the Memorial Library [a room in the school where early rehearsals often take place], just sat [*sic*] there after school for a couple of hours every night, and I loved it, it's one of my favourite memories. It's bonding, but it's also intellectual nourishment, you know.[15]

A lot of boys offer a lot of opinions, and a rehearsal isn't like a typical school drama rehearsal where your drama teacher tells you what to do and you do it. Perry's

[12] Alex Mills, 'What has Edward's Boys ever done for us?', Edward's Boys: http://edwardsboys.org/old-boys/what-has-edwards-boys-ever-done-for-us.
[13] Nilay Sah, private correspondence, March 2020.
[14] Jack Hawkins, filmed interview with Perry Mills (privately owned DVD), 2015.
[15] Dan Wilkinson, personal interview, 11 June 2018.

very much a person who gives you the text and helps you understand the text, but after that he's very open to listening to what you have to say and your ideas.[16]

In terms of the group interaction with Mr Mills – it's an old habit for me to call him that – in some ways it's different from the dynamic you'd have with another teacher because he really gets students. He knows these plays like the back of his hand, and it's always a very fun environment. I think that one of the reasons he connects so well with us is that he was always open to our own input. During sessions in the Memorial Library, for example, you'd make a suggestion like, 'What if he does this?' And he wouldn't just say, 'That's an interesting idea.' He'd put the pen down, sit back, and say 'Now there's a thought', and make a note of it. It was very much a genuine connection and willingness to listen that made the boys respect him. Obviously, schoolboys have respect for the authority of their schoolmasters, but it's earned.[17]

HRM – What really emerges from the boys' and your descriptions of the work is a sense of ownership over the text. And that level of ownership becomes particularly crucial when it comes to physical staging, doesn't it?

PM – Once we have been through the entire text several times in short extracts, we get to the point where we can read the whole play aloud in chronological order: the 'radio play version'. At this point they are ready (desperate, gagging) to 'put it on its feet'. That stage of the process is usually remarkably swift. We blocked all five acts of *The Silent Woman* (2020) in a week – and that means a few rehearsals after school and a Sunday. They know their characters and how they fit into the whole story and their function in each scene so decisions about where to come on and off and where to move during a scene are, by that stage, pretty much obvious. At least to them. However, even when reading around the table, we are constantly imagining how to exploit the stage space to 'Tell the Story' – another of my little dicta. This facility also allows them to be confident enough to develop the 'blocking' as the production comes in to land. It also makes re-blocking when touring different venues comparatively straightforward.

The process of putting a play on its feet, once the text has been studied to a high enough standard, is rather a quick one. Firstly, every scene will be blocked, entrances and exits worked out to make sense with the text, then certain parts will require more intricate details and movement. Then moments of directorial genius that work on about twelve levels are thrown in throughout the play . . . simple as.[18]

The play just kind of happens, because the text is so ridiculously instructive . . . you know your character and everything you're involved with like the back of your hand, and it becomes a part of you and your brain and what you see.[19]

HRM – Hence their confidence and ease with frequently difficult texts . . .

PM – Absolutely. We are dealing here with competitive grammar-school boys who are ambitious to achieve. They are working in a company – and at a school – where being the best you can be is seen as exemplary. The sheer difficulty is part of the attraction. Challenging material + hard work = results which impress. By the time they take the stage Edward's Boys know what they're doing. Then they can 'fly'.

There is never any sense of the 'School Play', of 'the safe bet', of the 'dumbed-down' version. (Consequently, there is no sense of pupils being told how to do it properly by the teacher.)[20]

The resulting increased sensitivity to literary devices and dramatic form and, more importantly, their effects, is a skill that all the boys involved can take straight back into the classroom and subsequently into the university seminar-room. Although the specific skills have been more obviously and immediately useful in the route I have taken [studying for an English degree], they are invaluable assets no matter what path the boys take, since there is

---

[16] Henry Edwards, personal interview, 4 June 2018.
[17] Rory Gopsill, personal interview, 7 June 2018.
[18] Oliver Hayes, 'CAPITAL Centre – evaluation', 2008, Edward's Boys Archive, King Edward VI School, Stratford-upon-Avon, *A Chaste Maid in Cheapside* Folder 1.
[19] Wilkinson, interview.
[20] Tom Sharp, 'The spirit of Edward's Boys: "Just do it!"', Edward's Boys: http://edwardsboys.org/old-boys/the-spirit-of-edwards-boys-just-do-it.

a remarkable development of rhetorical skills and linguistic competence.[21]

Our rehearsals proved the most stimulating and exciting educational experience I can remember from my time at school. And now, a few years down the line and nowhere near a play, I can feel that and appreciate how important rehearsals were. Good rehearsals are an opportunity for shared discovery, thinking together in a way that we just don't do when reading alone. Ours were intellectual without being pompous and competitive; they involved sensitivity, empathy and a sense of humour.[22]

HRM – It's becoming more and more apparent just how collaborative Edward's Boys' theatremaking is. Of course, that's no great revelation given that these are plays designed to be performed by an ensemble. But would it be fair to say that teamwork has become as important as linguistic facility?

PM – It would be entirely fair. I'm reminded here of something Struan Leslie, who directs the movement sequences on our shows, wrote about the company: 'From his own private musings on what a production might be, Mills shares that in a forum, amongst the company and the players. They then kick the possibilities around, as a team might exploit the specific skills of a particular player – "football", as a metaphor, is very present in the room.

Theatre is a team game, and Edward's Boys is a team where a Cantona makes way for a Scholes and a Giggs makes way for . . . Similarly, there is no hierarchy. "The Boss" knows the objectives and has the respect of his team – much as Ferguson did. As the performance arrives, he ensures that each player knows his place and role, and supports and shares that with the whole team and what that might imply for each individual. "Boot boys", those with less to say, are essential too. They are no less important to the world of the play than the success of the team on the pitch is to having the correct boots and laces. The boys in those positions also know that there is much to be learned from simply being present, observing what is going on, and doing their jobs. . . . They are not doing it for the glory. They are doing it for the team – and perhaps "The Boss".'[23]

It's all about giving people roles – it's not prescriptive roles, but it's them feeling they can voluntarily have the confidence to say look, I'm gonna contribute to this scene. . . . I think being on tour is such a big part of the company, because, you know, if you go to the RSC, they've got teams specifically designed to get the lighting, to get the voice, to do all that work before. But for us, we physically have to go to a new place, build the set, experiment ourselves with the acoustics and things like that, on the day of the performance. And so everyone has to pull their weight, and the only way people pull their weight is by feeling responsible for each other.[24]

I probably shouldn't use 'the company' because it is 'a company', and it can kind of change and evolve. . . . So it's, 'can you fit into the idea of a company?' We have all these 'c' words: communication, commitment, that sort of thing. Teamwork. Understanding that there isn't one person in a company; it requires a really delicate balance of support and teamwork between each person, and that it's a kind of horizontal and vertical level of integration – between the different years as well, so, supporting people around you who are playing similar parts.[25]

If you want to get somewhere, you need the people around you. . . . This company wouldn't work if we all tried to make it as actors individually – it just wouldn't work. It's about working for each other, and that community thing is so important. It's taught me the value of other people within your own development.[26]

There are times in rugby as a forward where you might have to catch a really high ball, and that is a high-pressure environment where you have to have the team behind you, and that's definitely transferable.[27]

The raucous banter . . . kept us all going through tough times. The Edward's Boys in-jokes definitely created a sense of belonging which put everyone at ease, and got the best possible performance out of everyone involved. If these plays weren't fun to put together

21 Mills, 'What has Edward's?'
22 Harry Davies, 'Look back in gender', Edward's Boys: http://edwardsboys.org/look-back-in-gender.
23 Quoted from Struan Leslie, 'Edward's Boys', 2017, Edward's Boys Archive, A Trick to Catch the Old One, Box 1.
24 Nilay Sah, personal interview, 2 February 2020.
25 Adam Hardy, personal interview, 4 July 2018.
26 Joe Pocknell, personal interview, 4 July 2018.
27 Hardy, interview.

nobody would want to take part, and the end product wouldn't be something we can all be proud of.[28]

PM – One colleague described the atmosphere on the coach on the way back from one of our early performances as 'like the United team returning after an away win at Liverpool' . . .

HRM – And that's certainly what I've found when I've accompanied you on your tours. But I've also found a great deal of professionalism. You seem to hand a high degree of responsibility over to the boys themselves.

PM – That is true. The inculcation of a sense of responsibility inevitably means they have a greater stake in the production. Greater independence is evidence that they are learning to manage their own learning. And it involves everyone. I can recall John (our lighting wizard) onstage on his knees with a toothbrush immediately following a very successful show in the OBE Chapel in St Paul's Cathedral. He was removing traces of Kensington Gore from the inscriptions on the gravestones underfoot because he saw it needed doing.

The cast, the stage management and the musicians dispatch any necessary task with aplomb. 'Just do it!' is not a company maxim by chance. It is Mills's response to any question or problem that arises ('Sir, we haven't got this piece of set yet', 'Sir, we haven't rehearsed scene three enough', 'Sir, the lights aren't in the right place', etc.). Any problem is dealt with so swiftly that it ceases to be one. This attitude is exemplified by the director and displayed by the company: boys source their own costumes, practise lines and accents together, and calmly re-block scenes on tour, as a matter of course.

As a result, an attitude of ownership develops within the cast, and has been passed on through cohorts of boys.[29]

I remember putting in perhaps what's now an embarrassing amount of effort practising walking in heels up and down the school for Mistress Touchwood [in *A Chaste Maid in Cheapside*]. I found my mum's six-inch purple velvet stiletto heels . . . and I took them off to school with a blonde wig and a big old brown overcoat and fishnet tights, and after school, before the rehearsal started an hour later (because I couldn't walk in heels), I walked up and down the school corridors when everyone had gone in my school uniform and my big purple stiletto heels to make sure that I could walk in them before rehearsal. It's that

kind of stuff, that commitment, that I didn't even think was weird, but expected.[30]

PM – I considered it a significant moment when the boy playing Diana in *Galatea* (2014) first clicked his fingers and ushered his nymphs aside at the end of a scene to take them through notes. This aspect of our work has definitely developed over the years but it was there from the beginning. Oliver was in the Upper Sixth when he joined us on tour as an extra pair of hands with *Endymion* (2009). Each member of the cast was 12 years old. The London performance took place in the Inigo Jones Rehearsal Room 3 at Shakespeare's Globe. Oliver took notes for me during the run-through whilst I was otherwise engaged – meeting and greeting Globe staff and academics, checking acoustics, sorting sightlines, camera angles for the video camera – and then we vacated the space for the Read Not Dead actors to rehearse *Sappho and Phao*. In the bowels of the Globe we ate lunch, the boys got changed and applied their Emo make-up and then it was time for final notes. Oliver gave me his page of A4. I said, 'Why don't you give them yourself? They're your notes.' I listened. And heard my own 'voice'. Even my own lame jokes . . .

Between the initial run of *Galatea* and the revival for our performance at the Sam Wanamaker Playhouse, there was a six-week gap. Towards the end of that period George (then in Year 11) asked me if he could send me a few notes through. I readily agreed of course and received almost three typed pages of A4, in three sub-sections – 'To the Company', 'Specific Points' and 'General Points'. The first point was, 'A gap in a production schedule is a gift, and a rare opportunity to act upon hindsight realizations which are usually an irritation to actors . . .' Such maturity.

HRM – And this level of maturity must be expected from backstage personnel, too?

PM – From the whole company. The selection of Stage Manager is crucial. They need to possess the

[28] Dan Power, private correspondence, August 2016.
[29] Sharp, 'The spirit of Edward's Boys'.
[30] Edwards, interview.

right kind of effortless authority. Often it's a female Sixth Form student; there have been two others who were captains of the boys' 1st XV; sometimes a member of the cast with a less demanding role. It's important that the company turns to them at moments of crisis rather than to me. It's the same with the band, the lighting, the movement of stage blocks (the 'blockmeister').

The way in which Edward's Boys functions as a company is with the space and continuous effort of the boys to learn, grow and lead one another forward. That creates the company feel and is a careful and powerful feeling within the rehearsal room and onstage. It's what always amazed me about Edward's Boys. I had never (and still have never) been in a rehearsal room where the level of respect for each person in the room is as equal as imaginable, until I sat in that rehearsal and saw how the ideas and understanding was formed together and grew over the rest of the process.

This is only made possible by that forward motion, that never-ending rehearsal process that bleeds from one play to the next. The tools that you give them as a director and teacher, on how to feel confident in reading and performing these difficult texts, means they encourage one another and WANT to perform well, building from each of their personal and group performances to work harder, to give more. It's a craft and it takes time for the boys to learn it, expand it and express it for themselves.[31]

Perry, as director, may be in charge but it is a truly collaborative process, with the boys investing greatly in their work. And then, as the performance approaches, the director lets go, and control is given over to the actors, the kids, to 'us'. We run the show. There is no prompter, for example, and a student is Stage Manager. We manage the music, the scene changes, the special effects. We want to do ourselves justice, and we don't want to let anyone down. It is a liberating, exciting experience and this is a huge part of the reason the boys want to, and should be, involved. To be given such responsibility in a thrilling creative environment is a fantastic thing for a teenager. This responsibility feeds a desire for discipline (self-discipline – we all want to get it right), as the company learns how to behave off-stage as well as on-stage. The cumulative effect is the development of a highly positive sense of self, measured by an acknowledgment of what is owed to others and how fruitful and rewarding a team effort can be . . . In short, working on these witty, word-full texts, in the protected space of the rehearsal room, gives licence to play: joking and mocking, asking any question, exposing ourselves to intellectual and emotional honesty, developing camaraderie. [See Figure 8.][32]

PM – 'Play' is the operative word. Bear in mind that these boys never purport to be actors. They are players, not illusionists. They're playing at it, through:

1. Pretending, imaginative games.
2. Being playful: 'trying it out; and trying it on – in both senses!'
3. Recreation: relaxation; joking; humour; fun. Printed at the foot of the information form the boys fill in is this reminder from an Old Boy: '("And it's fun!" – Finlay Hatch, Sunday 27th September 2015)'.

When we're like six months not rehearsing a play – that's what happens in the corridors, you know, we rehearse whenever –

Yeah, we rehearse all the time, whether we're doing the play or not –

Oh! There it is – we're *always* rehearsing![33]

Overall, I think that the secret ingredient was the camaraderie and support which existed instantaneously.[34]

HM – It's no surprise that these friendships are discernible in rehearsals, but they are also clearly evident on stage. This is a far cry from clichéd notions of 'the birch', or of boy players frightened out of their wits by their masters. As Laurie Maguire reminds us, 'Despite all the Elizabethan anecdotes about beating buttocks, a text like Ascham's *Schoolmaster* displays the combination of affection and authority in a daily working relationship which transfers to an intimate and trusting theatrical relationship. This is not something one can rehearse. The unique house-style of Edward's Boys is thus born of their circumstances: a group of schoolboys studying and playing together, knowing each other and supporting each other, on and off stage. All the world's a school and all the men and women merely schoolboys.'[35]

31 Emma Benton, private correspondence, June 2020.
32 Mills, 'What has Edward's?'
33 Ewan Craig, Nilay Sah and Yiannis Vogiaridis, personal interview, 19 March 2020.
34 Jack Fielding, private correspondence, April 2008.
35 Maguire, 'Company profile'.

8 Backstage preparations for Edward's Boys' production of *Endymion* at Shakespeare's Globe (2009). Photo by Perry Mills, courtesy of Edward's Boys.

PM – Whenever television and radio have been in touch for interviews, this is one of the first topics they wish to explore. In the light of the Clifton case,[36] they want to ask about beatings and bullying. And of course I cannot give them the answers they seem to want. As I always say, the work we do has nothing to do with 'Original Practices'. I am not very interested in how they did it in 1592. We do it 'all-boy' and that is it. Our aim is simply to put on a good show for today's audience. However, for what it's worth, I have never understood how the original performers of these plays would have been able to give freely of their best, to be creative, if they had lived in a climate of fear. Particularly when it comes to these plays, so often transgressive and undermining of authority.

HRM – And would you say that the small-school environment of K. E. S. plays a part in this?

PM – Indeed. At K. E. S. one of the pastoral care systems we employ is Vertical Tutoring. A tutor oversees a group of perhaps 24 students who represent an age range of, say, 12–18 years. Mentoring is

inevitably central to this practice; tutors are encouraged actively to engage the support of older students and we devise specific activities which require mixing up the age groups. I truly believe that our best review ever came from the Headmaster when he called the company, 'The best vertical tutor group in the school' – and not just because he pays my wages . . .

I didn't feel uncomfortable working with people five years older than me. At K. E. S we have a vertical tutoring system, and this means that from Year 8, every morning and afternoon you register with people all through the years, and so I think that idea of mentoring, of being comfortable with people older than you, is kind of actually developed through the school, as well as the company.[37]

PM – In Edward's Boys I don't necessarily cast the best actors in the school. I couldn't if I wanted to because many of them are female! What I want are team players. A lot are sportsmen, as has been noted,

---

36 Mills is referring to the 'impressment' of Thomas Clifton, the son of a gentleman, into the Children of the Blackfriars in 1600. See Lucy Munro, *Children of the Queen's Revels: A Jacobean Theatre Repertory* (Cambridge, 2005), pp. 17–18.
37 Pascal Vogiaridis, personal interview, 4 July 2018.

but many of them are musicians – often both. They understand teams and mentoring. I must admit that the crucial importance of apprenticeship was initially a bit unexpected for me, but now is utterly central. We now focus on it explicitly and I exploit it relentlessly. We are all learning from each other. There isn't any formal mentoring; I don't pair boys up, but let me give you an example.

Unperfect Actors (2016) was a showcase of short extracts and songs from Shakespeare plays performed in 'Shakespeare's Schoolroom' to mark the 400th anniversary of his death. We celebrate that sort of thing in Stratford-upon-Avon. It gave a handful of the younger kids a lovely opportunity to 'step up' without the older lads nabbing the best parts. But it was different from our usual work. We threw it together in a few days, there was nothing new. It was, 'Find out what it means, learn the lines, don't bump into the furniture, do it.' And, given what it was intended to do, it worked really well. I'd done a similar thing twice before over the previous twenty years, with many of the same texts. Right at the beginning of Edward's Boys, we did the most recent version. However, in 2016 we were asked to perform the day before because some dreadful government minister was visiting town. As luck would have it, two of the previous cast, Alex and Oliver, were around. I invited them in that morning so they could take the next generation of Edward's Boys through their scenes. We'd blocked those scenes, of course; the kids knew their lines, but then Alex took the kids who were in the *Tempest* scene away, because he'd played Ariel years ago, and Oliver took the boys who were in the *Twelfth Night* scene away, because he'd played Viola. And they added a final polish.

HM – That transfer of knowledge is almost like kabuki, or Noh.

PM – It was passing it on. 'This is how you do it, boys.'

The concept of apprenticeship does really seem to be so prevalent in the company. I think this is the chief reason why the younger boys are becoming better and better performers. The older boys in the lead roles command such respect that the younger boys so clearly look up to

them and want to learn. This is not, however, something that only the boys can be praised for, because at the heart of it all is your direction and, having been through the process, I know that it's your trust in the boys that means they can trust each other.[38]

I personally enjoy that mentoring kind of thing. It's just really satisfying to see younger people improve on what they're doing because of your influence. I think it's kind of a nice way of almost paying back, because we were mentored when we were young, and again, everybody says it and it is so true.[39]

Looking up to all the boys above me, they were all incredibly impressive ... They were very smart, great leaders, great at organizing and instilling team spirit in everyone. They were really, really impressive people. It's a company, so everyone has different strengths.[40]

The most important thing of all is that these lessons were taught to [us] not by 'Sir' or 'Miss', but by our mates. By being in the company, we had been in the presence of boys far older, more mature and better than ourselves right from the start of our school lives. We could not have helped but learn something from them.[41]

One of the big things that always stuck with me was how all of the older guys could just speak 'early modern' so fluently – they could pick it up and read it and just speak it. I think you learn a lot from just listening to other people speak that, because it makes your ear more fluent in listening to it, so it aids you as a theatregoer but also as a performer, because you come across certain phrases and know how best to deliver the line in a certain context. It starts to give you an indicator of where you might be able to go with it, and I'm quite fortunate now in that I'm quite fluent reading and writing about early modern plays, and I think a lot of that is to do with watching them work, which is pretty amazing. Hopefully, in my last few years, the younger guys were learning from me as well. It's something that's very much handed down, a kind of acclimatization.[42]

Well, it's just something that we've learnt to do. I'm only doing what people have done before me and I'm sure what people have done before them. And as the older guys you've got a sort of responsibility to the

---

[38] Oliver Hayes, 'I'm just a jealous guy', Edward's Boys: http://edwardsboys.org/im-just-a-jealous-guy-westward-ho.
[39] Vogiaridis, interview. [40] Wilkinson, interview.
[41] Fin Hatch *et al.*, 'Exit, pursued by a bear . . . ', Edward's Boys: http://edwardsboys.org/old-boys/exit-pursued-by-a-bear.
[42] Edwards, interview.

younger ones who might not know as well, to sort of drum that into them. And I think people like that – people like being a part of it and being proactive, and feeling that they're really doing stuff.[43]

We used to discuss this, whether it's like a conveyor belt, but it's not so much that . . . The younger boys learn from the older boys, the older boys learn from the younger boys too . . . that's the way that it works. For a Year 7 to be there having a fun time and there to be some cool older boys having fun with you, it's like, 'Oh my God, I'm involved!' . . . You learn, and you get moulded into being able to do that. It's not easy, but then it becomes second nature.[44]

PM – I recall Sir Alex Ferguson, the highly successful manager of Manchester United, explaining the many advantages of working with young players. He listed such virtues as loyalty, longevity, consistency, challenge, desire, ambition – and the fact that they surprise you! I recognize all of that, but it's also true of the ex-members of the company, as you can see from some of these comments. They come to see the shows, they send messages of support to the company, they look back with nostalgia and are often bursting with pride. As one Old Boy, Dan, said, 'You only really get it when you've left.' They can often be of great practical use as well. After the St Paul's performance, one actor was distraught because a prop hadn't worked properly. I mouthed some platitudes, but two Old Boys had been in the audience so I explained to them how he was feeling and left it to them to talk him through it. Far more successful.

HRM – And how do you get new members used to all this?

PM – Again, it's carefully engineered. At the start of a production I hold 'The Big Meeting' where everyone involved is present. We make the new members of the company feel welcome and supported, but also aware of the tradition, of the expectations, of how we work. And why.

The idea of rehearsal and production as a 'Job o' Work' is one freely touted by both director and cast, and results in a company ethos not only 'professional' beyond its years but also lacking pretension.[45]

HRM – What you and the boys are describing here is clearly underpinned by trust, and that seems to work in all directions.

PM – Ah. Trust. THE most important word.

Trust is at the core of our work. As well as creating a cohesive company in the twentieth-first century, I suspect a similar approach was shared by the original boys' companies.[46]

Quite quickly you work out that it's a two-way street, and from then on there's very much a sense of you giving to the show and him helping you give back to the show. When you've got twenty-five boys all doing that, suddenly there's a whole wealth of knowledge and ideas from the 18-year-olds all the way down to the 11-year-olds, and they're all offering different inputs and insights.[47]

We all know that you're a brilliant director in terms of your vision for the plays and their theatrical potential, but I firmly believe that in addition to this, one aspect that makes our work particularly special is the fact that you seem to know exactly when to let the boys get on with it. This shows you trust them, and so the older boys trust you, and, as they take control, the younger boys trust them in their turn and they all learn. And this brings out the absolute best in every performer throughout the company every time.[48]

PM – It's one of the reasons why I don't watch the performances.

Mills's customary 'disappearance' during performances merely encourages and confirms this sense of ownership. I had always expected a director would watch the play we had worked on together so I was both surprised and disappointed when I first experienced his apparent indifference. Then I realized that, in effect, this was trust in action. We knew what we had to do. 'Just do it!'[49]

The philosophy of it is actually genius. On the night of the performance, it's not him [Mills], it's not his – he's not on stage, he can't do anything. It's ours. And it's so true. A week or so before, he'd kind of let go, and it was ours to do. On the night, you had to make sure that you were ready to go on stage at the point where you needed to go

---

43 Jack Hawkins, personal interview, 4 July 2018.
44 Wilkinson, interview.
45 Sharp, 'The spirit of Edward's Boys'.
46 Sharp, 'The spirit of Edward's Boys'.
47 Edwards, interview.   48 Hayes, 'Jealous guy'.
49 Sharp, 'The spirit of Edward's Boys'.

9 Senior members of Edward's Boys transporting costumes across the Thames during the tour of *When Paul's Boys Met Edward's Boys* (2018). Photo by Louisa Nightingale, courtesy of Edward's Boys.

on stage. There were no chaperones, no one telling us we had to be here or do anything – we were like adults, we had to go and listen, go on stage, nail our bit, and go off stage, listen again, go back on stage . . . Perry couldn't be there to manage, so there was no point him micromanaging the rehearsals.[50]

HRM – And assuming you haven't already disappeared when the coach leaves Stratford-upon-Avon, the dynamics of trust that you foster must be particularly beneficial when you go on tour . . .

PM – Everyone is aware that the performances and tour bring us even more closely together.

By this stage the production has been 'theirs' for some time. The very fact of collaborative physical activity encourages this: loading the coach; get-ins; warm-ups. And the challenges of new venues, mostly non-theatres, demand that we exploit the spaces to make something 'new'. Our aim is to treat it as an opportunity to improve the show. The act of re-creation by learning to do new things. [See Figure 9.]

From transporting a whole set and company from Stratford to London, and then entirely reconfiguring the whole play for a stage the size of a fish tank . . . was incredible. It was the perfect illustration of a well-oiled and orchestrated

machine . . . And a machine that was at harmony with its every movement and action of each and every component. . . . The way we were able to re-configure and re-block the entire show for the chapel was a testament to the sheer resilience of everyone in the company.[51]

PM – It sometimes surprises me what they are able to cope with. There was illness in the cast during the run of *A Trick to Catch the Old One* (2017). As another one succumbed, the rest kept doubling and trebling roles – and even nailed the accents!

The most challenging space I've ever worked in is the Priory Church of St John in Clerkenwell, where every word we uttered seemed to dissipate into an inaudible blur. It felt like a constant uphill struggle with the space indefatigably retaliating to any amendments we made in our delivery. But we persevered, listened, worked with each other and pulled through. That day I came to realize what the word company really meant.[52]

---

[50] Wilkinson, interview.
[51] Nilay Sah, private correspondence, June 2020.
[52] Sah, correspondence.

PM – Even our host at St John in Clerkenwell noticed that something was amiss and that the boys overcame it: 'When they began to rehearse in the morning my heart sank for them: the acoustics of the church, always such a success with musicians, were rendering their dialogue unintelligible. It all became a great booming wreckage of sound from which hardly a word could be salvaged – but to my delight and astonishment, after a hard afternoon's work, their evening performance was so crisp and crystal-clear that hardly a word was lost'.[53]

There are always challenges on tour and they always cope. The finest example, which highlights several strengths, was probably the Oxford performance of *A Chaste Maid in Cheapside*. For a number of reasons, we were under great pressure and my efforts to maintain calm and focus during our get-in and rehearsal were failing more than usual. So I walked out. I told them, 'You know what to do' and left. And they did.

In the two hours before we went on, we pulled ourselves together. In the tightly packed room of shivering bodies we went through, in whispers, virtually in silence, which entrance our props had to come on from:

'Promoter's basket – one or two?'
'One'.
'Crucifix – one or two?'
'Two'.
And it went on like this with a hypnotic effect. It was either 'One' or 'Two' because that was all we had. We did it though, we got the job done – a relatively simple task but it brought us together and made us focus on what needed to be achieved.[54]

PM – Of course I crept back in unnoticed after a few minutes and, unobserved, witnessed the older boys taking charge and leading the company in the direction it needed to go.

HM – Naturally. I'm struck by that sense of these performances and their tribulations 'bringing us together'. What the boys describe suggests that an education embedded in theatrical performance and touring runs deeper than an increased linguistic facility or a sense of teamwork – it's also an emotional education.

PM – Emotional, certainly. And psychological. It helps them gain an understanding of themselves and others. The powerful sense of trust allows everyone to be honest, candid, open. It partly accounts for the lack of awkwardness concerning gender impersonation. The boys always assert that it's just another role – they're not kings or soldiers either. Or adult males. During a Q&A with 350 French school and university students and their teachers in Montpellier, a young lad asked the whole cast, 'Are you gay?' The auditorium erupted. As order was restored, Jack said quietly, 'It doesn't matter. It's just a part. It's what we do.'

The guy in a dress thing, it's actually just really funny. It's a rite of passage, when you get to play a female role – I was always quite pissed off because I'd never been a prostitute, never put on a dress, until I played Diana in Year 11. You're actually just waiting for it to happen.[55]

PM – As one cast member's mother remarked, 'It seems to me that the boys (and not just the ones actually playing the female roles) were encouraged to explore deeply, various issues surrounding women. As young men – particularly in an all-boy school – this is a really important part of their education. What a great opportunity the theatre offers, both in rehearsal and on stage to explore and discover these things.'[56] They learn about a wide range of topics and themes – gender, sexuality, sex, violence, consent, exploitation, corruption and hypocrisy and . . . Need I go on?

HRM – That's quite the list. You might say that taking part in Edward's Boys amounts to no less than a way of being . . .

You become a completely different person doing Edward's Boys. Obviously, people always say 'Oh, it must help with your English', and stuff like that, and it does, but it's just completely – you learn the obvious things, you learn how to work in a team and stuff like that, but also you see so many different personalities, and you get to know them so well when they're under pressure, or when they're stressed.

[53] Quoted from Juliet Barclay, private correspondence, July 2019.
[54] Davies, 'Look back in gender'. [55] Wilkinson, interview.
[56] Maddy Lesser, private correspondence, April 2008.

Even things like when they've been told off or they've forgotten their lines or something – just being in that atmosphere adds so much to your own personality.[57]

One of the boys might come to me like, 'How do I do this line?', so it's quite practical to begin with, but there's also a sort of friendship level behind it that extends beyond the production to then something like, 'Can you help me think about this thing at school?', or 'I've got a problem with a girl', something like that. It's just sort of a friendship thing that has started within this company but that's what so beautiful about it. It's now, genuinely, not just about the company, and it's about developing these friendships which will continue beyond acting and beyond what's going on in the plays.[58]

PM – The boys learn how to behave offstage as well as onstage. They develop a highly positive sense of self, which is not the same as self-indulgence – and *not* arrogance! Certainly, public performance and acclaim are very exciting and gratifying after all that hard work, but learning how to acknowledge and deal with approbation is so important. Humility and a sense of perspective are expected, which is why I emphasize throughout that it's a 'Job o' Work'. Their manner is evident in the responses of our hosts on tour, who comment on 'the boys' charm and courtesy' and 'delightful personalities'.[59] It's always affirming when a stage manager at the RSC gets in touch to say that the boys 'were very professional and did an incredibly good job onstage'.[60] To be perfectly honest, this is why I carry on with Edward's Boys. Frankly, I have done enough plays over the years, but the evidence suggests that the company provides more than the chance to be in rarely performed plays.

I'm sure I'm not alone in this, when times in my personal life haven't been too easy in the past few years Edward's Boys has provided distraction, countless great friends, something meaningful to be a part of and most of all brilliant fun. The play wasn't half bad either.[61]

Honestly, it taught me the necessity of being laughed at every now and then – it really is good for the soul, I think, looking back; it was quite instrumental in making me personally take myself a lot less seriously, which was definitely important for me. Putting yourself out of your comfort zone, not only physically but also socially – you're doing things and showing interpretations of things that have potential to be ridiculed, have potential to go

wrong. Things like that taught me that if you're trying something new, to put it all on the line, otherwise it's not going to bear fruit. But also, on a social level, it taught me how to interact with people much better. The older boys do, to a certain degree, take some kind of pastoral role, again going back to the idea of rallying the troops, as it were, getting people focused in the last few days.[62]

Edward's Boys has given me so many formative opportunities and skills. Perseverance, willpower, the courage to stick at something when it's not going well. For that reason, I am forever grateful.[63]

It's a bit soppy but the plays have been the best thing I've done in my life so far. They've led me to great friendships, the full discovery of something I love, unique and special experiences, an appreciation of a truly amazing era of drama that'd be hard to get otherwise, abilities that I'm proud to have, as well as loads of other stuff. Most of all though, it's been so fun. When we're not doing a play I find myself looking forward to the next one, and when we are I desperately don't want the process to end. [See Figure 10.][64]

HRM – You and the boys have mentioned the psychological benefits, and at a time when teenage mental health is being discussed more widely than ever before, I think it's important to draw attention to that.

PM – I know that to be the case, partly from my own observations, but also from conversations with professionals. Our School Counsellor commented on the 'unique and tight sense of belonging and responsibility towards each other [which] allows for the exploration and discussion of subject areas that can enormously assist the development of a young person's emotional maturity and self-awareness . . . [and] can only exist in this safe and inclusive environment'.[65] A parent who is a Child

[57] Ritvick Nagar, personal interview, 2 February 2020.
[58] Pocknell, interview.
[59] Quoted from Barclay, correspondence.
[60] Quoted from Martha Mamo, private correspondence, March 2013.
[61] Anonymous, private correspondence, September 2017.
[62] Gopsill, interview.
[63] Tom Lewis, private correspondence, May 2020.
[64] Jack Hawkins, private correspondence, July 2019.
[65] Quoted from Steve Goodrem, private correspondence, May 2020.

10 A large squad of Edward's Boys (including ex-players) in 2013. Photo by Perry Mills, courtesy of Edward's Boys.

Psychologist asserted, 'Edward's Boys moulds respectful yet confident and uninhibited young men.... The lessons learned, in my opinion, will last the boys their entire lives.... They are given the opportunity to explore their own values, to consider and choose commitment, trust and freedom whilst developing a sense of responsibility and respect for themselves and each other.'[66]

HRM – With life-long lessons in mind, particularly those related to mental wellbeing, I think it's important to note the extraordinary times in which we're speaking. The lives of 2020's teenagers the world over will be marked indelibly by the COVID-19 pandemic, and Edward's Boys certainly weren't immune to this when your production of Jonson's *The Silent Woman, or Epicene* was cancelled days before the first

performance. I wonder if you could reflect on that experience, and how your and the boys' responses to the events were shaped by the strong company foundations on which Edward's Boys is built.

PM – For a few hours that was a difficult situation to negotiate. I could see that the chances of performing were receding but it had to be a company decision, and initially there was a range of different points of view. However, a couple of company meetings either side of a good-humoured run-through allowed everyone to accept the inevitable. And we managed to squeeze in a recording of extracts and a Q & A, which we developed into

---

[66] Quoted from Jayne Hawkins, private correspondence, July 2019.

a podcast.[67] It could be said that they showed the best of themselves through not performing. It wouldn't be true but it sounds good.

We keep talking about this as if we've lost something, but I think we've got to focus on what we've gained from it, rather than losing the performance, which is a loss, but we've got to focus on what we've gained throughout the whole process of rehearsals.[68]

Of course, it was devastating to have never performed the show to an audience. Yet, in retrospect, as the weeks passed and the scale of the Coronavirus crisis sunk in, I feel we were lucky in getting an audio version of some extracts recorded – the best outcome we could've got in such terrible times. Indeed, the fact that we never performed or went on tour underlined to me the most important reason why I do these plays. I do it for the process: the joy of feeling part of something special; the joy of sitting round a table with a couple of mates and having a right laugh; and the sheer joy of creating something unique and brilliant.[69]

I don't look back at all those hours with regret in light of what has developed since. It's about more than that. You'd call it 'company', that weird bond that makes us nod and smile knowingly at Year 8s in the corridor, like there's some kind of unspoken secret between us until the next play.[70]

In all the disappointment of not having the last kind of goal, in a way, amongst all that disappointment I think we also need to remember that we've had an absolute blast. Six months of great rehearsals, and such fun, and we've still built that company. We haven't got the shows which is such a shame, but also, we've had so much fun.[71]

Whether we've done one play or several, what we'll say is that there are no words to describe what we do. It's not just plays, is it? I mean, throughout the process of touring and of rehearsing, there's so much that goes into it that I know from this company I've made life-long friends. It's pretty special.... I can't even remember what the question was but I think it was something like 'how have we pulled together in these conditions?' Well, we were already together. Whether we did the performances or not doesn't really change a huge amount; we haven't suddenly been brought together in a time of tragedy. We were together, and we would have got through it had we done it, and we've got through it not doing it.[72]

HRM – So, performances or not, the company's a company. You can't sum up its long-lasting educational value better than that, can you?

PM – Not really. Except to repeat what a parent wrote in an email of thanks after *A Chaste Maid in Cheapside*: 'It's a wonderful way to learn!'[73]

---

[67] See 'The one that got away; or, the almost silent woman', Soundcloud: https://soundcloud.com/user-999191870/the-one-that-got-away-or-the-almost-silent-woman. Mills further reflects on the cancellation in 'The one that got away', Edward's Boys: http://edwardsboys.org/the-one-that-got-away.

[68] Will Groves, personal interview, 19 March 2020.

[69] Sah, correspondence. [70] Lewis, correspondence.

[71] Ewan Craig and Felix Kerrison-Adams, personal interview, 19 March 2020.

[72] Nagar, personal interview, 19 March 2020.

[73] Quoted from Joanne Wilkinson, private correspondence, April 2010.

INTIMACY AND SCHADENFREUDE IN REPORTS OF PROBLEMS IN EARLY MODERN PRODUCTIONS

CERI SULLIVAN

INTRODUCTION

Problems with putting on a play are a staple feature of drama at the turn of the seventeenth century, in both tragic and comic modes. Revenge tragedies, for example, use theatrical errors to correct moral errors, in productions like 'Soliman and Perseda' (in *The Spanish Tragedy*) and the 'The Masque of Juno' (in *Women Beware Women*). City comedies use problems on stage to comment on class, as when setting the script of 'The London Merchant' against the improvised plot of *The Knight of the Burning Pestle*. Literary critics tend to approach such moments in two ways, either relishing their metadrama or finding parallels with the main themes of the play. Only William West deals with early modern confusion in plays as a topic in its own right, arguing that plays of the 1580s and 1590s dramatized errors to prompt questions of epistemology and hermeneutics; he does not discuss real-life mistakes on stage.[1] Roger Savage looks at continental (especially Italian) playbook prefaces and production manuals which have advice implying a pragmatic understanding of what can go wrong. One such manual of 1630, for instance, suggests an event organizer ensures that actors, costumes and stage crew are in place well before the show starts, instruments tuned up, and ropes, winches, machines and lights checked.[2] However, no one has answered Hans-Thies Lehmann's parenthetical challenge – 'the real in theatre ... usually manifests itself only in mishaps ... (related in theatre anecdotes and jokes, the analysis of which would be tempting in this light)'.[3]

There are rich accounts of problems on the English stage, scattered over a variety of sources. Take the disastrous performance by students at St John's College, Oxford, of *Time's Complaint* (Christmas, 1607–8). The play's Prologue was:

most shamefully out, and having but halfe a verse to say, so that by the very sence the audience was able to prompt him in that which followed, yet hee could not goe forward, but after long stay and silence was compelled abruptly to leave the stage whereuppon beeing to play another part hee was so dasht, that hee did nothing well that night.

After him Good-wife Spiggot. comming forth before her time, was most miserably at a non Plus as made others so also whilst her selfe staulked in the middest like a great Harry-lion (as it pleased the audience to terme it) ether saying nothing at all or nothing to the purpose.

Meanwhile, the Drunken Man had done well in rehearsal, and 'was now so ambitious of his action that he needs would make his part much longer then it was, and stood so long upon it all that hee grew most tedious whereuppon it was well observed and said by one that ''twas pitty there should bee / In any pleasing thing satiety'. The

---

[1] William West, '"But this will be a mere confusion": real and represented confusions on the Elizabethan stage', *Theatre Journal* 60 (2008), 217–33.

[2] Roger Savage, 'Checklists for Philostrate', in *Court Festivals of the European Renaissance: Art, Politics, and Performance*, ed. J. R. Mulryne and Elizabeth Goldring (Aldershot, 2002), pp. 294–307.

[3] Hans-Thies Lehmann, *Postdramatic Theatre*, trans. Karen Jürs-Munby (London, 2006), p. 101.

show got only 'two or three cold plaudites' (improbably excused by its producers as being because 'wee onely proposed to our selves a shew but the toune expected a perfect and absolute play').[4] The account raises questions about stage fright, scene stealing, ironic help from an audience (which nonetheless stayed to the end) and why the students kept a record of the fiasco.

This article concentrates on such incident reports, usually about amateur or one-off productions in university, court, civic and domestic locations. Elizabethan and Jacobean culture was steeped in amateur drama. In Somerset between 1570 and 1630, for instance, lay people improvised performances in which they mock-christened a dog, held a mock-consistory court, celebrated a mock-eucharist, delivered a mock-sermon, impersonated local tradesmen, and put on plays mimicking the local gentry.[5] Boys at school practised role-playing, repeating classical orations ('As they learne these Dialogues, when they have construed and parsed, cause them to talke together; uttering every sentence pathetically one to another'), extemporizing around speeches, and acting plays.[6] Taking part in productions at the Inns of Court or universities was seen as good preparation for subsequent careers at court or in the church.[7] Those boys who went into trade might also expect to participate in royal, civic or corporate pageants, which were the most widely viewed of all shows in London (not excluding those in the theatres).[8] Moreover, even spectators expected to take a role: ad-libbing, heckling, moving about, clapping, hissing and so on (as schoolboys learned from Quintilian, listening responsively to a speaker was part of learning to speak oneself).[9]

Though there were – and are – many more amateur than professional productions, they are less studied. This is partly because they leave fewer records, but also partly because ideas about what constitutes a high-quality production tend to be aligned with theatre that is highly capitalized, and, hence, highly polished. However, the aesthetic developed by amateur theatricals is different, not lesser, as Claire Cochrane argues.[10] Michael

Dobson shows how success in these productions arises from focusing on local interests, sites and characters, and working with the way audience members and actors know each other off stage.[11] Such productions can afford to experiment with texts or staging that would not be more widely popular, especially since players may be volunteers,

---

[4] John R. Elliott, Jr, Alan H. Nelson, Alexandra F. Johnston and Diana Wyatt, eds., *Records of Early English Drama [REED] Oxford*, 2 vols. (London and Toronto, 2004), vol. 1, pp. 357–8.

[5] James Stokes and Robert J. Alexander, eds., *REED Somerset*, 2 vols. (Toronto, 1996), vol. 1, pp. 107–9, 118, 155, 263–4, 277–9, 363–4, 379, 399. See, likewise, Audrey W. Douglas and Peter Greenfield, eds., *REED Cumberland, Westmorland, and Gloucestershire* (Toronto, 1986), pp. 188–98; David George, ed., *REED Lancashire* (Toronto, 1991), pp. 26–7; Elizabeth Baldwin, Lawrence M. Clopper, and David Mills, eds., *REED Cheshire, including Chester*, 2 vols. (London and Toronto, 2007), vol. 2, p. 693; James Stokes, ed., *REED Lincolnshire*, 2 vols. (London and Toronto, 2009), vol. 1, pp. 269–304.

[6] John Brinsley, *Ludus literarius: or, the Grammar Schoole* (London, 1612), pp. 217ff.; Thomas Heywood, *An Apology for Actors* (London, 1612), sig. C3v; Frederick S. Boas, *University Drama in the Tudor Age* (Oxford, 1914), pp. 191–2, 349–51; Thomas Hubbard Vail Motter, *The School Drama in England* (London, 1929), pp. 13–26, 33–5, 60–5, 86–8, 91–5, 105–13, 137–53, 209–16.

[7] Alan Nelson, 'Emulating royalty: Cambridge, Oxford, and the Inns of Court', *Shakespeare Studies* 37 (2009), 67–76.

[8] See, for instance, the precepts issued to livery companies by London's Common Council over the royal visit to St Paul's in 1620: John Nichols, ed., *The Progresses, Processions, and Magnificent Festivities of King James the First, his Royal Consort, Family, and Court*, 4 vols. (London, 1828), vol. 4, p. 597. See also Tracey Hill, *Pageantry and Power: A Cultural History of the Early Modern Lord Mayor's Show, 1585–1639* (Manchester, 2011), pp. 129–30; Lawrence Manley, 'Of sites and rites', in *The Theatrical City: Culture, Theatre, and Politics in London, 1576–1649*, ed. David L. Smith, Richard Strier and David Bevington (Cambridge, 1995), pp. 33–54.

[9] Quintilian, *The Orator's Education*, trans. Donald A. Russell, 5 vols. (Cambridge, MA, 2001), 2.2.9–12.

[10] Claire Cochrane, 'The pervasiveness of the commonplace: the historian and amateur theatre', *Theatre Research International* 26 (2001), 233–42. See also Nicholas Ridout, *Stage Fright, Animals, and Other Theatrical Problems* (Cambridge, 2006), pp. 3–5.

[11] Michael Dobson, *Shakespeare and Amateur Performance: A Cultural History* (Cambridge, 2011), pp. 2–16.

equipment borrowed or hired rather than bought, and the staging space obtained free or at reduced cost.[12] Safety standards (and the framework to enforce them) are not those of the professional entertainment industry (especially today). Under such conditions, mishaps, mistakes and unscripted audience interruptions are normal, not exceptional, and not considered great failures. As the students behind *Time's Complaint* conclude, 'in these kinde of sports ... such is the daunger and trouble of them that something in the dooing will miscarry'.[13] The defence of university acting by an Oxford Latin playwright, William Gager, against an attack by the President of Corpus Christi College, John Rainolds, relies on failure. Unlike professional actors, students are only 'cumming on the Stage one in a yeere, or twoe yeere', and 'differ from them in the manner of ... playing' in three ways. Professionals stage their plays 'with excessyve charge; we thriftely, warely, and allmost beggerly'. Professionals act 'theire Playes in an other sorte than we doe, or can, or well knowe howe; ... so exquisytly, and carefully, that ... [our plays] may seeme, compared with them, eyther for skill, or diligence, rather *Recitare* [repeated] ... than *Agere* [acted]'. Professional acting could stir lust, but not so academic drama, 'wherin for owre penninge, we are base and meane as you see; and specialy for womanly behaviour, we weare so careless, that when one of owre actors shuld have made a *Conge* like a woman, he made a legg like a man'. Though professionals work for a large and heterogeneous audience, 'We contrarywise doe it to recreate owre selves, owre House, and the better parte of the *Universitye* ... ; to practyse owre owne style eyther in prose or verse; to be well acquaynted with *Seneca* or *Plautus*; honestly to embowlden owre yuthe; to trye their voyces, and confirme their memoryes ... [and] conforme them to convenient action'.[14] Gager defends amateur plays at university precisely because everyone knows they are meanly staged, poorly acted and only interesting to an in-group.

This article starts by considering three lines of research – on contemporary performance theory about mistakes, on schadenfreude's theatrical

modes, and on the genre of the theatrical anecdote – to think about humilitainment. It then brings together, for the first time, a selection of printed reports about things that went wrong, largely in amateur or one-off shows. Finally, it asks why these were reported, arguing that early modern theatrical anecdotes about errors relish incongruities arising between the real and the staged ideal, and celebrate the intimacy developed between audience and actors as they work around such interruptions.

WHY ENJOY WATCHING FAILURES ON STAGE?

Contemporary performance theory chiefly values failures on stage as moments which make clear that actions are both really happening and, at the same time, moments in a production. This creates, Lehmann considers, enjoyably unsettling points where the audience chooses whether to watch the event as reality or fiction.[15] Sara Jane Bailes and Nicholas Ridout agree such disturbance can be desired, allowing actors and audience to become co-present to each other, aside from the world of the play. It can also, however, be embarrassing if both parties want to be immersed in that world, so may elicit stage fright in the actors and surly uncooperation from the audience.[16] Some contemporary political theatre groups deliberately make mistakes to undermine dramatic realism, deeming this a capitalist fiction that falsely suggests that people are able to act in ways which produce neatly plotted conclusions.

---

[12] A. J. Hartley, 'Introduction', in *Shakespeare on the University Stage* (Cambridge, 2015), pp. 3–4.

[13] *Times Complaint*, in *The Christmas Prince*, ed. Frederick S. Boas and W. W. Greg (Oxford, 1922), pp. 102–32; p. 130.

[14] William Gager, 'Letter to Dr. John Rainolds of July 31, 1592', in *William Gager: The Complete Works*, ed. Dana F. Sutton, 4 vols. (New York, 1994), vol. 4, pp. 263, 271.

[15] Lehmann, *Theatre*, p. 101.

[16] Sarah Jane Bailes, *Performance Theatre and the Poetics of Failure: Forced Entertainment, Goat Island, Elevator Repair Service* (Abingdon, 2011); Ridout, *Problems*, pp. 5–15, 45–52, 70–81.

These groups either celebrate the tactics with which audience and actors cope with failure, or, alternatively, show indifference to the professional standards of the well-funded theatre. In doing so, they develop an 'expertise in performing the effects and affective behaviours of failed address', creating the sort of 'intimacy' between performers and spectators that Gager saw at student events.[17]

Slapstick is the mode most dependent on challenging the usual connotations of failure, encouraging its audience to enjoy mistakes. Louise Peacock suggests its humour comes from four sources, three of which are neutral or even benevolent. Spectators may laugh with amazement at the incongruity between what is expected and what actually happens (particularly if there has been a strong lead-up to establish a shared context and norms, then violated). They may laugh with relief if pent-up energy is released in an error (especially if made tense or uncomfortable beforehand at the control exerted to avoid it). Finally, they may laugh with admiration at the perverse skill of acting apparently real mistakes.[18]

But the fourth source of laughter mentioned by Peacock is less benign: schadenfreude, an enjoyment in another's mistakes when they make the watcher feel superior. Feeling oneself comparatively unappreciated may, says the psychologist Richard H. Smith, inspire effort to improve one's own rankings, or pleasure when another's position is lowered. The disadvantaged characteristically fantasize about such moments. Thus, for instance, Francis Bacon's discussion of envy talks of how it can 'fascinate, or bewitch' those who feel it, urging them to 'Imaginations, and Suggestions' when 'the Party envied is beheld in Glory, or Triumph'. Envy is felt most deeply by those whose rank is threatened by another's rise ('it is a like a deceipt of the Eye, that when others come on, they thinke themselves goe backe'), by those who cannot rise (so 'seeke to come at even hand, by Depressing an others Fortune'), and by those who 'taketh a kinde of plaie-pleasure, in looking upon the Fortunes of others'.[19]

Watching or hearing about higher-ranked people brought low tends to make up for a sense, in the observer, that official rankings are not always fair or correct. Schadenfreude is particularly likely to be felt where the elevated person is no more talented or diligent than the observer. Since taking pleasure in others' mistakes or pain is wrong and shameful, this feeling is often hidden. A downfall is spoken of as a form of extra-legal justice and perhaps put down to character flaws ('she had it coming to her').[20] Active hostility, however, is reserved for safe targets: laughing at mistakes by the powerless can make a spectator feel secure as well as superior. In a theatrical context, the genre of humilitainment (Smith cites reality television shows) has features to allow the expression of schadenfreude, as when a host or facilitator laughs at a participant, or those on the show are volunteers, or pressure brings out unattractive aspects in them.

The genre mostly used to report theatrical mistakes is the anecdote. Early modern schoolboys were taught to insert historical examples into their arguments, to give credibility and emotional power by tracing cause and effect in the link between character and outcomes in action.[21] Subsequently, though, the anecdote fell from use in historical analysis because of its interest in singularity: in subjective or bizarre viewpoints and coincidences. Yet such qualities have been recently revalued by historiographers and New Historicist literary critics. These note how Elizabethan and Jacobean histories habitually include entertaining anecdotes that turn out to aid a deeper analysis of structural theses.[22] The

[17] Bailes, *Performance Theatre*, pp. 3–12.
[18] Louise Peacock, *Slapstick and Comic Performance: Comedy and Pain* (Basingstoke, 2014), pp. 5–8, 62–80.
[19] Francis Bacon, 'Of envy', in *The Essayes or Counsels, Civill and Morall* (London, 1625), pp. 40–2.
[20] Richard H. Smith, *The Joy of Pain: Schadenfreude and the Dark Side of Human Nature* (New York, 2013); Richard H. Smith, ed., *Envy: Theory and Research* (New York, 2008).
[21] Quintilian, *The Orator's Education*, 5.11.1–39, 12.4.1–2.
[22] Richard Helgerson, 'Murder in Faversham: Holinshed's impertinent history', and Annabel Patterson, 'Foul, his wife, the Mayor, and Foul's mare: the power of anecdote in Tudor historiography', in *The Historical Imagination in Early Modern Britain: History, Rhetoric, and Fiction, 1500–1800*, ed. Donald R. Kelley and David Harris Sacks (Cambridge, 1997), pp. 133–58, 159–78.

anecdote's brevity, humour and association with rumour permit a more tactical or oblique questioning of official narratives, added as unofficial objects of proof.[23] In 1582, for instance, Stephen Gosson (playwright turned anti-theatrical polemicist) revived Xenophon's anecdote about how audience members of *Ariadne and Bacchus* hurried off to have sex after watching the play. Gosson's expressed intention was to deter people from going to the theatre, but the anecdote has, alternatively, been read as a sensational enticement to do so.[24]

Theatrical anecdotes are often formulated as miniature dramas, presenting characters in a dialogue that rapidly depicts a simple but memorable situation.[25] Paul Menzer's perceptive account of stories about Shakespearian productions from the Restoration onwards argues that they focus on gaps between what the actors are doing, what the script tells them to do, and what the audience think they are doing: on stage, 'actors live out literally prescriptive lives . . . [so] the theatre anecdote . . . [is] about breaking character or the fourth wall'.[26] The situation of a theatrical anecdote tends to be repeated with different actors in place at each reiteration (drunk on stage, dying on stage, and so on), spinning half-truths from contentious issues that a play has raised, then suppressed. For instance, anecdotes about unstable balconies in *Romeo and Juliet* stress-test romance against pragmatism, those about whether Yorick's prop skull is from a real human skeleton meditate on sincerity, and those about where Othello's blacking rubs off think about skin-deep equality.

These contemporary approaches to the experience or report of failure on the modern stage see it as an attack on official narratives, in recognizing the reality of other rankings, other conceptual structures. So what is at stake in the early modern anecdotes?

WHAT SORT OF THINGS WENT WRONG?

Issues typically arose in five areas: with the actors, the stage, the appliances (props, costumes and special effects), the text and event management.

Just getting enough healthy and willing bodies on stage, in the right place, at the right time, was the first hurdle for amateur productions (by contrast to professional companies, who could more easily fill sudden gaps). In 1609 at Christ Church College, Oxford, Thomas Goffe (the play's author and probable lead actor) sadly addressed to 'Voyce' 'An Eigie upon hoarsness occasioned by a sudden, and vehement could which tooke the representer of Amurath when he should have acted': 'without thee all is but vaine / All proves abortive, what hath cost / So many howers must be lost'.[27] When the chief actor in the St John's *Philomel* (1607–8) likewise became hoarse, the tragedy's author was primed to step in, merely because he 'Could say most of the verses'.[28] Sickness, the measles and a nasal 'polypus' put off a court masque planned for Christmas 1605, and so on.[29] But even healthy amateurs could not be relied on to show up. The show tournament in Stirling at Prince Henry's christening in 1594 went ahead without the Moors who were to fight the Turks, Amazons and Christians, 'by reason of the absence, or at the least, the uncertaine presence, of the three . . . Gentleman, who should have sustained these personages'.[30] A Puritan sub-tutor at Cambridge, for his 'parts and ingenuity' selected to act a woman in George Ruggle's *Ignoramus* before the King in 1615, refused to do so, not as being an evil in itself

---

[23] Malina Stefanovska, 'Exemplary or singular? The anecdote in historical narrative', and H. Deutsch, 'Oranges, anecdote, and the nature of things', *SubStance* 38 (2009),16–31.

[24] Stephen Gosson, *Playes Confuted in Fiue Actions* (London, 1582), sig. G5r; Xenophon, *Memorabilia, Oeconomicus, Symposium, Apology*, trans. E. C. Marchant and O. J. Todd, rev. Jeffrey Henderson (Cambridge, MA, 2013), p. 661.

[25] Peter Hay, ed., *Theatrical Anecdotes* (New York, 1987), Preface; Aoife Monks, 'Collecting ghosts: actors, anecdotes, and objects at the theatre', *Contemporary Theatre Review* 23 (2013), 146–52.

[26] Paul Menzer, *Anecdotal Shakespeare: A New Performance History* (London, 2015), p. 13.

[27] Elliott *et al.*, eds., *REED Oxford*, vol. 1, pp. 434, 436.

[28] Elliott *et al.*, eds., *REED Oxford*, vol. 1, p. 355.

[29] Ben Jonson, *The Works*, ed. C. H. Herford, Percy Simpson and Evelyn Mary Spearing Simpson, 11 vols. (Oxford, 1925–52), vol. 10, p. 446.

[30] William Fowler, *A True Reportarie of . . . The Baptisme of . . . Prince, Frederick Henry* (Edinburgh, 1594), sig. A4r.

but as having the appearance of evil; the Vice Chancellor was unable to argue, frown or laugh him out of his position.[31] At the 1607 St John's Christmas Day feast, the Reading waits had to be summoned to play 'because our owne Towne Musick had givenn us the slipp, as yei use to doe, at the time when wee have most need of them'.[32]

Any great skill in performing was a bonus. A drunk spectator at the Gloucester Boothall in 1602 may well have been right when he 'offered to present himself uppon the said stage, and sayd ... that he could play better then any of those stage players, and offered to goe uppon the same stage and to take one of the same players instrumentes out of their hands to have played uppon yt himself'.[33] The York waits would not be the only group with so terrible a musician that he made them a laughing stock (deaf, often drunk, and subject to fits when he played, he had to be pensioned off in 1596).[34] Most actors in the St John's *The Holy and the Working Days* (1607–8) 'were out both in there speeches and measures, having but thought of this devise some few hours before'.[35] Thomas Nashe refers to a university 'codshead, that in the Latine Tragedie of K. *Richard*, cride, *Ad vrbs, ad vrbs, ad vrbs* ['to the city'], when his whole Part was no more, but *Vrbs, vrbs, ad arma, ad arma* ['the city, to arms']'.[36] Not that such actors always handled their weapons well: the 'prince' in the St John's *Periander* (1607–8) gave his 'daughter' a flesh wound.[37]

Too much or too little energy was particularly deplored. Thomas Fuller relates how 'a company of little boyes were by their School-Master ... appointed to act the Play of *King Henry the Eighth*, and one who had no *presence* but (an *absence* rather) as of a *whyning voice, puiling spirit, Consumptionish body* was appointed to personate *K. Henry*' (the boy had influential parents). As a fellow actor said, '*if you speak not* HOH *with a better spirit your Parliament will not grant you a penny of Money*'.[38] At the masque of *Juno and Hymenaeus* (anon., Whitehall, 1605), Sir Thomas Germain had 'lead in his heels and sometimes forgot what he was doing'.[39] The converse problem also occurred, with well-known precedents: Thomas Heywood relates how Julius Caesar, acting the part of Hercules, so 'fashioned all

his active spirits' to the role that he killed his onstage opponent, and William Prynne how two pagan actors who hammed up a christening on stage were converted.[40]

Actors gathered, then came the blocking of action and audience, in spaces which could be inadequate, unfamiliar, distracting or downright dangerous. Weather, of course, was the principal problem for outdoor shows. 'A violent storme of rayne' is a common refrain, interrupting everything from the fireworks celebrating Henry's investiture as Prince of Wales in 1610 to Chester's production of 'Kinge Ebrauk with all his sonne' in 1589, when 'such rayne fell it was hindred much'.[41] The royal firework display by William Bettis in 1613 was praised for being 'contrived in such sort, that if the weather had bin rainy or windy, yet his dessignments should have beene accomplished'.[42] Carrying on without such precautions could be expensive: at York in 1585, one producer mourned

31 Samuel Clarke, *The Lives of Sundry Eminent Persons* (London, 1683), part 1, p. 156 [sig. X1v]; Emily D. Bryan, 'The government of performance: *Ignoramus* and the micropolitics of Tudor–Stuart relations', in *Early Modern Academic Drama*, ed. Jonathan Walker and Paul D. Streufert (Farnham, 2008), pp. 99–104.

32 Elliott *et al.*, eds., *REED Oxford*, vol. 1, p. 354.

33 Douglas and Greenfield, eds., *REED Cumberland, Westmorland, Gloucestershire*, p. 314.

34 Alexandra F. Johnston and Margaret Rogerson, eds., *REED York*, 2 vols. (Manchester, 1979), vol. 1, pp. 469–70.

35 Elliott *et al.*, eds., *REED Oxford*, vol. 1, p. 355.

36 Thomas Nashe, *Have With You to Saffron-Walden* (London, 1596), sig. B4r.

37 Elliott *et al.*, eds., *REED Oxford*, vol. 1, p. 380.

38 Thomas Fuller, *The History of the Worthies of England* (London, 1662), p. 66 [sig. Kk1v], incident undated but 'not many years since'.

39 *Dudley Carleton to John Chamberlain, 1603–1624: Jacobean Letters*, ed. Maurice Lee (New Brunswick, 1972), p. 67.

40 Heywood, *Apology*, sig. E3v; William Prynne, *Histrio-mastix: The Players Scourge* (London, 1633), pp. 118–19. Heywood was probably conflating stories about *Julius Caesar* and Nero: John Drakakis, '"Fashion it thus": *Julius Caesar* and the politics of theatrical representation', *Shakespeare Survey 44* (Cambridge, 2002), pp. 65–6.

41 Nichols, ed., *James*, vol. 2, p. 322; Baldwin *et al.*, eds., *REED Cheshire*, vol. 1, p. 156.

42 Nichols, ed., *James*, vol. 2, p. 534.

that 'for 5 visards wee borrowed, and with the rayne were rotte in peeces, I suppose at the leaste I shall aunswer 4s., and yet one of them was my owne'.[43] In 1605, the Merchant Taylors had to repeat their mayoral pageant after 'very wett and fowle weather' the first time, costing them repairs to the set, coal for fires to dry it, and new clothes for the child actors.[44]

Next to weather came complaints about poor audibility (more often than those about obstructed sightlines). This was a particular bugbear for the principal spectator, who might be expected to respond ad hoc. Elizabeth took direct action sometimes: at a 1564 Cambridge disputation, unable to hear three doctors speak 'by cause their voices weare smalle and not audible her majestic first sayde unto them *loquimini altius* ['speak up'] and when that would not helpe she lefte her seate and cam to the stage over their headdes' (perhaps inspiring awe rather than volume).[45] The children of Christ's Hospital, lined up to sing in the 1604 royal entry, could not be heard because they were 'all displaced by reason of the rudenesse of . . . a multitude', as was Divine Concord at the reception of James and Christian of Denmark into London in 1606.[46] Before James's visit to Oxford in 1605, there was a preparatory meeting at Christ Church College to decide where to seat the King so he could be seen. *Noblesse oblige*: the chair of estate was set in the middle of the room, 28 feet away from the stage, 'soe that there were manye longe speeches delivered, which neyther the Kinge nor anye neere him could well heare'.[47] Set, props and special effects tested producers, especially of one-off events. At the St John's *Ara Fortunae* (1607–8), the Fool sat down heavily without looking behind him, and smashed the Prince's staff. The hall tables (the stage) were repeatedly obscured by the Prince's 'courtiers' crossing them. At a second round of applause, 'ye Canopie which hunge over ye Altare of Fortune (as it had binne frighted with ye noise, or meante to signifie that 2 plaudites were as much as it deserved) suddenly fell downe; but it was cleanly supported by some of ye standers by till ye Company was voyded, yat none but our selves tooke notice of it'.[48] Thomas Campion's 1607 masque at Whitehall featured an engine beneath the stage that made three trees dip, split open to reveal masquers,

then vanish. Yet, a marginal note to the text complains, although the earlier technical rehearsal had gone well, 'either by the simplicity, negligence, or conspiracy of the painter, the passing away of the trees was somewhat hazarded'.[49] Alterations in plans also created problems. In 1611, the Goldsmiths planned a mayoral pageant with 'no extraordinarie shewes', until it suddenly became clear that the Queen would be present, forcing them to cobble together a new device only four days before the show.[50] Aldermen investigated 'abuses and badd workmanshipp' about the pageants part-made for the planned, then cancelled, 1626 royal entry into London.[51]

Some appliances were simply unsafe, especially those using flammable materials. At Warwick in 1572, the Queen viewed a mock battle over a canvas fort, that ended with a firework dragon roaring overhead to set the fort alight. One of the squibs fell on a nearby house, whose inhabitants barely escaped with their lives.[52] The Globe Theatre burned down in 1613, the fire started 'by negligent discharging of a peal of ordinance' during Shakespeare's *Henry VIII*, at the start of Cardinal Wolsey's masque. Since spectators were concentrating on this spectacular scene, they had ignored smoke rising from the Globe's thatch.[53] The second day of fireworks and mock battles planned to celebrate the

---

[43] Johnston and Rogerson, eds., *REED York*, vol. 1, p. 423.

[44] Hill, *Pageantry and Power*, p. 64.

[45] *The Progresses and Public Processions of Queen Elizabeth*, ed. Elizabeth Goldring, Faith Eales, Elizabeth Clarke and Jayne Elisabeth Archer, 5 vols. (Oxford, 2014–15), vol. 1, p. 411.

[46] Nichols, ed., *James*, vol. 1, p. 140; vol. 2, p. 87.

[47] Elliott *et al.*, eds., *REED Oxford*, vol. 1, p. 295.

[48] Elliott *et al.*, eds., *REED Oxford*, vol. 1, p. 347.

[49] Thomas Campion, *The Discription of a Maske . . . in Honour of the Lord Hayes and his Bride* (1607), in *Campion's Works*, ed. Percival Vivian (Oxford, 1909), p. 70.

[50] Hill, *Pageantry and Power*, p. 64.

[51] David M. Bergeron, *English Civic Pageantry, 1558–1642* (London, 1971), pp. 254–5.

[52] *Elizabeth*, ed. Goldring *et al.*, vol. 2, pp. 39–40.

[53] E. K. Chambers, *The Elizabethan Stage*, 4 vols. (Oxford, 1923), vol. 2, pp. 419–23. The Whitehall banqueting house fire of 1619 was said to be caused by a workman with a candle or glue pot, busied about scenery for Jonson's *Pleasure Reconciled to Virtue*: Nichols, ed., *James*, vol. 3, pp. 523–4.

1613 royal marriage was cancelled, partly because of royal boredom and partly because 'there were divers hurt in the former fight (as one lost both his eyes, another both his handes, another one hande, with divers others maimed and hurt)'.[54] People who sat on the stage were obviously vulnerable (as at the Red Bull in 1622, when a felt-maker's apprentice was injured in some way).[55] But being off stage was not necessarily safer when it came to arms. Sometime before 1616, an apparently unloaded rusty musket, borrowed from a local armourer, went off during a play and killed an audience member ('though ... [the actor's] part was Comical he therewith acted an unexpected Tragedy').[56] In 1587, the Admiral's Men:

having a devyse in ther playe to tye one of their fellowes to a poste and so to shoote him to deathe, having borrowed their Callyvers one of the players handes swerved his peece being charged with bullett missed the fellowe he aymed at and killed a chyld, and a woman great with chyld forthwith, and hurt an other man in the head very soore.[57]

Sadly for one 'George', who in 1583 tried to sneak free into a performance by the Queen's Men at the Red Lion in Norwich, the play required its characters to be armed. Three ran after him, and one, playing the Duke, struck at him fatally with a stage sword (albeit with its hilt).[58]

Some degree of risk might even be courted, to increase spectators' pleasure (at least, for those further away). Wild Men with water sprays and fireworks made room among the crowds for street shows, creating the thrilling possibility that slow-moving bystanders might be sprinkled or singed.[59] In 1584, bear baiting at Paris Garden was followed by a jig, interrupted when a large stage rose overhead was set alight by a rocket, to let fruit fall on the audience. 'Whilst the people were scrambling for the apples, some rockets were made to fall down upon them out of the rose, which caused a great fright but amused the spectators', said one.[60]

More usual than chaos or fatalities, though, were the anti-climaxes, especially when it came to animals. At Prince Henry's baptism in 1594, the plan by the show's author, William Fowler, to have a lion draw in the banquet was dropped, not merely because those closest might get nervous, but also

because the 'sight of the lights and torches might have commoved his tamenes'.[61] The opposite disappointment faced the royal party come to watch a wild beast fight at the Tower in 1609: 'the great Lyon [was] put forth, who gazed awhile, but never offred to assault or approch the Beare'; six dogs and a horse were added but they just fought each other, while the 'Lyon and Beare stared upon them'; the lion was then allowed back in his den ('which he endeavoured to have done long before') and other lions brought out, 'but they showed no more sport nor valour than the first, and every of them so soone as they espied the trap doores open, ran hastily into their dens'. Even the 'two young lustie Lyons', which started to 'march proudly towards the Beare', then fled.[62]

Timings were always a difficulty in the case of one-off and distributed productions, where run-throughs beforehand were difficult. During Munday's pageant of *Metropolis coronata: the Triumphes of Ancient Drapery* (1615), speeches by Robin Hood and his men had to be omitted because the previous episodes had over-run, 'our preparation requiring such decencie in order: yet much abused by neglect in marshalling, and hurried away with too imprudent hastinesse,

---

54 The Letters of John Chamberlain, ed. N. E. McClure, 2 vols. (Philadelphia, 1939), vol. 1, p. 423.

55 John Cordy Jeaffreson, ed., *Middlesex County Records*, 4 vols. (London, 1886–92), vol. 2, pp. 166, 175.

56 Fuller, *Worthies*, p. 223. See also *Elizabeth*, ed. Goldring *et al.*, vol. 1, p. 444; vol. 2, pp. 5–6.

57 Letters of Philip Gawdy of West Harling, Norfolk, and of London to Various Members of his Family, 1579–1616, ed. I. H. Jeayes (London, 1906), p. 23.

58 David Galloway, ed., *REED Norwich* (Toronto, 1984), pp. 73–4, 395.

59 Thomas Middleton, *The Collected Works*, ed. Gary Taylor and John Lavagnino (Oxford, 2007), pp. 978, 1268; Baldwin *et al.*, eds., *REED Cheshire*, vol. 1, p. 351; Philip Butterworth, *Theatre of Fire: Special Effects in Early English and Scottish Theatre* (London, 1998), pp. 21–5, 167–84; Hill, *Pageantry and Power*, pp. 130, 153–4, 185–6.

60 Chambers, *Elizabethan Stage*, vol. 2, p. 455.

61 Fowler, *Reportarie*, sig. C4r. On how even predictably behaved animals on stage disrupt the fictional world, being in it but not part of it, see Ridout, *Problems*, pp. 96–110.

62 Nichols, ed., *James*, vol. 2, p. 259.

albeit so advisedly set down in project that nothing but meere wilfulnesse can misplace them'. At least in the evening, 'as occasion best presenteth it selfe, when the heate of all other employments were calmly over-passt', the scene was played.[63] Some authors built in recovery spaces. When the King asked for an encore of the second dance of the nymphs in Jonson's *Masque of Beauty* (1608), they needed a pause for rest before obeying, 'which time, to give them respite, was inter-mitted with song' (either foreseen and kept in reserve, or moved on the occasion from another part of the production), as also happened after an hour of dan-cing by the masquers in *The Masque of Queens* (1609).[64]

There were problems with scripts. At Cambridge, Legge 'composed a *Tragedy* of the *Destruction of Jerusalem*, and having at last refined it to the *purity* of the *Publique Standard*, some *Plageary* filched it from him, just as it was to be acted'.[65] Perhaps for the same reason, promoters of a 1621 Chester extravaganza (featuring the nine worthy men, the nine worthy women, the five senses, language and the four sea-sons) wanted the city council 'to keepe this note in your owne handes lest it bee too Common in the mouthes of our advisaryes'.[66] In 1593, the Cambridge Vice Chancellor was asked to prepare a comedy for the court at Christmas, as plague had shut down the London theatres. He asked the Chancellor to inter-pose: he had no play to hand in English, and no time to translate one.[67] Most plays probably went the same way as Peter Heylyn dolefully noted of his own, in 1618 ('August 31. I began my Latin Comedie called Theomachia & finisht it September 14. It was never acted').[68] Thomas Watson, Master of St John's College, Cambridge, had a more professional reason for keeping his script from colleagues: he, 'to this day would never suffer, yet his *Absalon* to go abroad, and that onelie, because ... *Anapestus* is twise or thrise used in stede of *Iambus*. A smal faulte, and such one, as perchance would never be marked', in Roger Ascham's view.[69] When the King decided to dine with the Merchant Taylors in 1607, the headmaster of the Company's school got a heavy hint from court that an in-house script would not do.[70]

Advertised events fell through. In 1602, Richard Vennar of Lincoln's Inn announced a performance of his *England's Joy*, for one day only, in the Swan Theatre. Based on glorious episodes in English history, its plot promised hand-to-hand fights, the assumption into heaven of Elizabeth I, and gentry as actors. With a 2s entrance fee, money poured in, until Vennar disappeared with it.[71] In 1614, the entertainer William Fennor and the chapbook author John Taylor agreed to a public contest at the Fortune, Taylor impersonating characters in prose, Fennor replying in verse. On the day, though, Fennor did not turn up, and the audience would not accept Taylor's sketches alone (the Fortune actors had to step in with a show from their repertoire). Taylor charged Fennor with behaving just as Vennar had in 1602, and Fennor's reply recalled having been let down in the same way by the comedian William Kendall.[72] A similar trick was credited to George Peele in 1606, in his afterlife as the hero of jest books. He persuaded Bristol's Lord Mayor to fund a show about the Knights of Rhodes, the city's founda-tion, and some former mayors. Some travelling players rented him costumes, publicized the show, and acted as doorkeepers. Peele spoke the prologue and fireworks followed, while he made

[63] Anthony Munday, *Metropolis coronata: the Triumphes of Ancient Drapery* (London, 1615), sigs. B2r, B3r–v, C1r.

[64] Ben Jonson, *The Complete Masques*, ed. Stephen Orgel (New Haven, 1969), pp. 72, 140.

[65] Alan H. Nelson, ed., *REED Cambridge*, 2 vols. (Toronto, 1989), I.286.

[66] Baldwin et al., eds., *REED Cheshire*, 1.460–2.

[67] Nelson, ed., *REED Cambridge*, vol. 1, pp. 346–7. Linda Shenk argues that he objected to academics being used like professional entertainers, rather than hosts who staged a few shows for guests, in 'Gown before Crown: scholarly abjec-tion and academic entertainment under Queen Elizabeth I', in *Academic Drama*, ed. Walker and Streufert, pp. 19–20.

[68] Elliott et al., eds., *REED Oxford*, vol. 1, p. 426.

[69] Roger Ascham, *The Scholemaster* (London, 1570), fols. 57r–v; Boas, *University Drama*, pp. 62–3.

[70] Nichols, ed., *James*, 2.136.

[71] Chambers, *Elizabethan Stage*, vol. 3, pp. 500–3.

[72] All the Workes of John Taylor, the Water Poet (1630), pp. 159, 162; B. S. Capp, *The World of John Taylor, the Water-Poet, 1578–1653* (Oxford, 1994), pp. 14–15; Richard Preiss, 'John Taylor, William Fennor, and the "Trial of wit"', *Shakespeare Studies* 43 (2015), 50–78.

off with the takings.[73] Conversely, some productions went ahead despite a ban. Touring companies might put on shows, even when city authorities (alleging a fear of infection, a politically inappropriate time, and so on) paid them not to (a practice which F. S. Boas calls 'theatrical "Danegelt"').[74] In 1583, 1585 and 1590, for instance, Norwich paid 10s–26s apiece to travelling companies under the protection of Worcester, Essex and Beauchamp, only to find them playing in any case.[75]

Large audiences, especially if enthusiastic, could cause problems for amateur or touring shows, whose producers were either less experienced at, or had fewer facilities for, keeping numbers reasonable. Most volumes of the Records of Early English Drama have entries about repairs necessitated by 'the press of people at the play'.[76] The principal dilapidations were to benches and windows, though York's records in 1592 report a wider range of damages: 'the doores, lockes, keyes, wyndowes, bordes, benches & other buildinges of the Common Hall' were 'broken, shakne, Lowse & Ryven up' by those coming to see the plays.[77] At Gray's Inn (Christmas 1594), 'there came so great a number of worshipful Personages upon the Stage', resulting in such 'Throngs and Tumults', there was only space for dancing and a professional performance (though, admittedly, this was *The Comedy of Errors*). At Jonson's *Masque of Blackness* (1605), crowding was such that officials penned some women in the galleries to keep them away; even so, the banquet was overturned before being touched.[78] At *Periander*, packed spectators 'were Caried forth for dead', even though (as at *Ira fortunae* and *Philomathes*) their fellows were 'so favourable as to stand as Close and yeeld as-much backe as was possible', keeping 'very quiet and attentive'.[79] The expectation, fostered from schooldays on, that physical and verbal responses were part of the experience of a production, could overwhelm it. Spectators of comedies performed before Charles I at Cambridge in 1630 were accordingly banned from making 'rude or immodest exclamations ... any humming, hawking, whistling, hissing, or laughing ... or any stamping or knocking ... any clapping of hands ... untill the

Plaudite, at the end of the Comedye, excepte his Majestie, the Queene, and others of the best qualitie here do apparently beginne the same'.[80] Yet sometimes audiences regulated themselves, silencing interruptions or only briefly participating. When a few at *Ira fortunae* thought themselves satirized, and 'Laboured to raise an hissing ... [this] was soone smothered, and the whole Company in the end, gave us good applause'.[81] Heywood relates how a murderess in the audience of an English production of *Hamon*, touring to Amsterdam, was struck with guilt and made an 'out-cry, and loud shrike in a remote gallery'. Yet, after she was led away, 'The play, without further interruption, proceeded.'[82] Fuller (with a teasing parenthesis) tells how William Alabaster's *Roxana* (1592) was acted in Trinity College, Cambridge, 'so pathetically; that a Gentle-woman present thereat (Reader I had it from an Author whose credit it is sin with me to suspect) at the hearing of the last words thereof, sequar, sequar ['lead, lead'] so hideously pronounced, fell distracted and never after fully recovered her senses' – but she waited until the end of the play to do so![83] Gilbert Dugdale reports loyal additions to James's 1604 entry into London

---

[73] The trick had already appeared in jest books from 1532 and 1604: *The Life and Minor Works of George Peele*, ed. David Hamilton Horne (New Haven, 1952), p. 119.

[74] Boas, *University Drama*, p. 226.

[75] Galloway, ed., *REED Norwich*, pp. 65–6, 81, 96, 141.

[76] For example, M. C. Pilkinton, ed., *REED Bristol* (Toronto, 1997), pp. 112, 122; Elliott *et al.*, eds., *REED Oxford*, vol. 1, p. 177; Nelson, ed., *REED Cambridge*, 1.275, 285, 354, 361–2.

[77] Johnston and Rogerson, eds., *REED York*, vol. 1, p. 449.

[78] Lee, ed., *Carleton to Chamberlain*, p. 68.

[79] Elliott *et al.*, eds., *REED Oxford*, vol. 1, pp. 371, 379.

[80] Nichols, ed., *James*, vol. 3, p. 45. On the physicality of responses by playhouse audiences, see Andrew Gurr, *Playgoing in Shakespeare's London* [1987] (Cambridge, 2004), pp. 51–7.

[81] Boas and Greg, eds., *Prince*, p. 227.

[82] Heywood, *Apology*, sig. G2v; Ceri Sullivan, 'Armin, Shakespeare, and Heywood on dramatic empathy', *Notes and Queries* 62.4 (2015), 560–2.

[83] Nelson, ed., *REED Cambridge*, 1.339.

by an old man and an apprentice (the latter declaiming his own verses from the top of the Great Conduit), even though its organizers had cautiously 'apointed no such thing, but at several stays and appointed places': 'forward love is acceptable, and I would the King had heard them'.[84]

The converse, disengagement (especially in a significant spectator), could destabilize a show. The unexpectedly early departure by the English royal party from the Danish ships in 1606 brought forward a firework display, so its 'beautie . . . was not to be seene by reason of the brightnesse of the Sunne'.[85] In Cambridge in 1564, a version of Sophocles' *Ajax flagellifer* was cancelled because the Queen was tired. She made the same excuse before the second part of *Palamon and Arcite* in 1566 in Oxford (adding that she could make her courtiers turn up anyway, though the playwright, Richard Edwards, prudently declined to waste his material in this way).[86] Francis Beaumont's *The Marriage of the Thames and the Rhine* (1613) for Gray's Inn and the Inner Temple was put off for the same reason, though the masquers had already spectacularly arrived at court by barge, which was brilliantly lit and fired chambers as it came down the Thames. Implored by the show's sponsor, Sir Francis Bacon, not to bury it, the King replied that then they must bury him, he could last no longer. Although James permitted a repeat a few days later, students felt that 'the grace of theyre maske is quite gon, when theyre apparel hath ben already shewed and theyre devises vented . . . They are much discouraged.'[87]

Plays before the King at Oxford in 1605 (reported by Sir Thomas Bodley to be 'very clerkly penned, but not so well acted, and somwhat over tedious') were badly received. Attending a new version of *Ajax flagellifer*, 'the king was verye weary before he came to it, but much more wearied by that, and spake manye wordes of dislike'. He found *Alba* by Robert Burton and others (a four-hour stint) so boring he wanted to leave halfway through, and was only prevented by the pleas of the Oxford and Cambridge chancellors. At *Vertumnus*, by Matthew Gwinne, he fell asleep, then woke irritated to find he was still being performed at

(growling 'I marvell what they thinke mee to be').[88] According to Anthony à Wood, at Barten Holyday's *Technogamia, or The Marriage of the Arts* (Woodstock, 1621), James had to be 'persuaded by some of those that were near to him, to have patience till it was ended, least the young men should be discouraged, [and] sate down, tho' much against his will'.[89] A Cambridge satire on this came out in a popular jest book:

> When Christ-Church showed their mariage to the
> King
> Lest that their match should want an offering,
> The king himself did offer: what I pray?
> He offered twice or thrice to goe away.[90]

It was matched by one in an Oxford commonplace book, where the King leafs through the playbook:

> the leaves to number
> Who when hee seene
> Their lacke seaventeene
> In despayre hee fell in a slumber.[91]

These anecdotes could sting because James was known to thoroughly enjoy some amateur shows. For instance, in 1615 he made a return trip to Cambridge to see the six-hour-long satire on lawyers, *Ignoramus*, and he asked for two encores of the farewell song in a Merchant Taylors' show in 1607.[92]

---

[84] Thomas Dekker, Stephen Harrison, Ben Jonson and Thomas Middleton, *The Whole Royal and Magnificent Entertainment of King James Through the City of London, 15 March 1604*, ed. R. Malcolm Smuts, in Middleton, *Works*, pp. 219–79; p. 278. Nichols, ed., *James*, vol. 1, pp. 416–18.

[85] Nichols, ed., *James*, vol. 2, pp. 84, 89–90.

[86] *Elizabeth*, ed. Goldring *et al.*, vol. 1, pp. 432, 480. The 1566 cancellation might have been a diplomatic excuse, following a fatal accident the previous night, during the performance of Part One.

[87] Alan H. Nelson and John R. Elliott, eds., *REED Inns of Court*, 3 vols. (Cambridge, 2010), vol. 2, pp. 688–90.

[88] Elliott *et al.*, eds., *REED Oxford*, vol. 1, pp. 294, 298–9, 332.

[89] Gerald Eades Bentley, *The Jacobean and Caroline Stage*, 7 vols. (Oxford, 1956), vol. 4, p. 590.

[90] Archie Armstrong, *A Banquet of Jeasts* (1630), p. 43.

[91] Bentley, *Stage*, vol. 4, p. 594.

[92] Nichols, ed., *James*, vol. 2, p. 139.

WHY REPORT THESE PROBLEMS?

There are four pragmatic reasons – practical, providential, diplomatic and excusatory – why some disasters are recorded.

Court proceedings and incident reports by officials briefly note mishaps to deal with consequences or prevent future occurrences. For instance, Cambridge colleges record, with resignation, that they must replace glass broken by students who could not get in to see a play.[93] It was usual for amateur players from the universities and Inns to borrow or rent costumes of 'ancient princely attire', from the Office of the Robes in the Tower, noble patrons or professional theatre companies. Sometimes, these were either not returned, or sent back soiled. Officials briefly and sourly describe the problem and ask higher authorities to intervene.[94]

By contrast, providential histories gleefully point out a direct connection between staging, sinning and God smiting. When a carpenter worked on Sunday to put up a stage at St John's College, Oxford, then fell backward from it and broke his neck, he entered a collection of exemplary punishments on Sabbath-breakers.[95] Blasphemy was the target of another godly anthology:

there was acted a tragedie of the death and passion of Christ in shew, but indeed of themselves, for hee that plaied Christs part hanging upon the crosse was wounded to death by him that should have thrust his sword into a bladder full of blood tied to his side; who with his fall slew another that plaied one of the womens part that lamented under the crosse; his brother that was first slaine seeing this, slew the murderer, and was himselfe by order of iustice hanged therfore: so that this tragedie was concluded with four true, not counterfeit deaths, and that by the divine providence of God.

The same collection also recounted a medieval French court performance: six masquers 'attired like wild horses, covered with loose flax dangling down like haire: albedaubed with grease for the fitter hanging therof', were set alight when 'a spark of one of their torches fell into the greasie flax of his neighbor'. Four of the six died (the King himself was only saved because an onlooker used her robe as a fire blanket).[96]

Some reports come from a political need to assess shifts in attitudes and allegiances. When masques were put off in 1613 (*The Thames and the Rhine*) and 1624 (Jonson's *Neptune's Triumph*), Sir John Chamberlain tested out different explanations with various correspondents (the king's health or energy, diplomatic rivalry over precedence in seating, and so on): 'by what yll planet yt fell out I know not ... the reason wherof I cannot yet learne thoroughly ... the reason wherof some say ... but the most probable reason is ... '.[97] The notorious device of the visit of the Queen of Sheba to King Solomon (Theobalds, 1606), played before Kings James and Christian, was zestfully reported by Sir John Harington to 'Mr. Secretary Barlow': Sheba tripped up on the stairs up to the chair of estate so her tray of creamy sweetmeats went over Christian's face; he then tried to dance with her but fell down drunk; Hope was so tipsy that all she could utter were excuses before she joined Faith in vomiting in the lower hall; Victory had to be led off into the outer chamber to sleep off the alcohol, and Peace, incensed by not being able to get close to the two kings, hit the people blocking her way with her olive branch. Harington pointedly concluded that 'these strange pageantries ... do bring to my remembrance what passed of this sort in our Queens days; of which I was sometime an humble presenter and assistant: but I never did see such lack of good order, discretion, and sobriety, as I have now done'.[98] The

---

[93] Nelson, ed., *REED Cambridge*, 1.354.

[94] Nelson, ed., *REED Cambridge*, 1.355; Nelson and Elliott, eds., *REED Inns of Court*, vol. 1, pp. 165, 173, 2.716–17; Boas, *University Drama*, pp. 107, 194–5, 348–9.

[95] Henry Burton, *A Divine Tragedie Lately Acted ... Examples of Gods Judgements upon Sabbath-Breakers and Other Like Libertines* (London, 1642), p. 17.

[96] Jean de Chassanion and Thomas Beard, *The Theatre of Gods Judgements* (London, 1597), p. 192. See also pp. 373–4.

[97] Chamberlain, *Letters*, vol. 1, pp. 426, 428–9, 2.538–41.

[98] *The Letters and Epigrams of Sir John Harington*, ed. N. E. McClure (Philadelphia, 1930), pp. 118–21.

King's attitude to the liturgy, as well as the court's decadence, is hinted at in an anecdote reported by the providential historian Arthur Wilson. The Marquis of Buckingham tried to distract James from 1622's gloomy foreign news by pretending to christen a piglet (Buckingham stood godfather, his mother was dressed as midwife, and another courtier as bishop). 'The King hearing the *Ceremonies* of *Baptism* read, and the squeeking noise of that *Brute* he most abhorred, turned himself to see what *Pageant* it was', and was furious: '*away for shame*, what *Blasphemy is this*?'[99]

Some authors circulate reports to explain what went wrong (implying this was already being gossiped about, so could not be ignored) or to say what the best performance could have been (presenting a press pack for the ideal show, Tracey Hill argues).[100] Masques and city pageants are often reported in the present tense, making the contrast between the real and the planned production more obvious. Fowler describes a parade of exotic beasts (elephant, dragon, unicorn, and so on) for the second day of the Stirling celebrations, even though the workmen 'were employed in other businesse, who should have followed foorth that invention given them'.[101] In 1574, the city of Bristol's speech of welcome and dialogue between Wars and Peace before the Queen were prevented by 'an occasion unlooked for', but included in its official account.[102] When masquers presented an entertainment at Althorp in 1603 to the Queen and Prince Henry, 'by reason of the throng of the country that came in, their speaker could not be heard', and the same happened when they went out, but the producer printed the inaudible speeches anyway.[103] Jonson gives the whole text of a song in *Hymenaei* (1606) though only one verse was sung in performance (adding tartly that 'I have here set it down whole, and do heartily forgive their ignorance whom it chanceth not to please').[104] James's coronation entry into London was postponed and then altered, but printed versions contain the 'device' of the Genius of London 'that should have served at his Majesty's first access to the city'. Modifications on the day were to be expected: 'Reader, you must understand that a regard being had that his Majestie should not be wearied with tedious speeches, a great part of those

which are in this book set down were left unspoken.'[105]

Occasionally, such reports are self-congratulatory. During *The Thames and the Rhine*, the King's call for an encore from masquers 'attired in cases of gold and silver close to their bodie, faces, hands and feete . . . as if they had been solid Images of mettall' came too late, since 'one of the Statuaes by that time was undressed'.[106] The point of the anecdote is to emphasize royal enthusiasm, not mis-timing. Munday's 1609 Lord Mayor's pageant made riskily ambitious plans for 'a Whale with a Blackamore in his mouth with Musick and casting water out of his ffynnes, and fyre out of his mouth', 'A Mer mayd coming his tresses in a looking glass with lady Thamesis couched on his ffynes', and so on. However, Munday notes, the

time for preparation hath bene so short, as never was the like undertaken by any before . . . Besides the weake voyces of so many Children, which such shewes as this doe urgently require, for personating each devise, in a crowde of such noyse and uncivill turmoyle, are not any way able to be understood, neither their capacities to reach the full height of every intention, and in so short a limitation for study, practise, and instruction.

Accordingly, he praises his own ingenuity in providing two 'men of action and audible voices' to summarize the plot and lyrics for bystanders.[107] At Thomas Churchyard's device before Elizabeth (Surrey House, near Norwich, 1578), the earth was to have opened during orations by Nymphs

99 Arthur Wilson, *The History of Great Britain, Being the Life and Reign of King James the First* (London, 1653), p. 218.
100 Hill, *Pageantry and Power*, pp. 236–50.
101 Fowler, *Reportarie*, sig. B1v–2r.
102 *Elizabeth*, ed. Goldring *et al.*, vol. 2, p. 208.
103 Nichols, ed., *James*, vol. 1, pp. 184, 187.
104 Jonson, *Masques*, p. 90.
105 Dekker *et al.*, *Entertainment*, pp. 229, 231, 276.
106 Nelson and Elliott, eds., *REED Inns of Court*, vol. 2, p. 531.
107 [Anthony Munday], *Camp-bell, or the Ironmongers Faire Feild* (London, 1609), sig. B2v. The Ironmongers were also unhappy that the costumes were 'old and borrowed': *Pageants and Entertainments of Anthony Munday: A Critical Edition*, ed. David M. Bergeron (New York, 1985), pp. 31–2.

of the Water. The event was rained off, and Churchyard notes ruefully that 'it was a greater pastime to see us looke like drowned Rattes, than to have beheld the uttermost of the Shewes rehearsed. Thus you see, a Shew in the open fielde is always subject to the suddayne change of weather.' He repurposed both the speeches (given in full in the printed version) and what was left of the costumes into a simpler and shorter show, now to be spoken by Fairies of the Land (seven small boys in a thicket) 'because the time was short for learning'. His resilience in making-do is the point of his anecdote.[108] The same is the case for George Gascoigne's marriage masque for the Kenilworth entertainments in 1575. Perhaps too sensitive a topic, the actors were never asked by the Queen to perform it, though they were kept in costume two or three days. Leicester and Gascoigne regrouped by having the latter, dressed as Sylvanus, run beside the Queen's horse as she left, gasping out extempore speeches on Leicester's submission until she reined in her horse to listen.[109]

EARLY MODERN ANECDOTES OF HUMILITAINMENT?

Robert Weimann influentially argues that, though the period's professional theatre moved from medieval 'playing', with actors in dialogue with their audience, to a more naturalistic style of 'acting', which stayed within the world of the play, both modes still operated across the period, and even in the same play.[110] This also – and perhaps especially – holds true in anecdotes of problems in amateur and one-off performances. These emphasize a peer relationship between actors and their audience, regardless of how damaging this might be to the play. For instance, in 1602 Richard Carew reported an earlier miracle play in Cornwall in which local people appeared unrehearsed, an 'Ordinary' following behind them with the playbook to whisper their actions and lines to them. One 'actor' rebelled against being made into a puppet: he repeated everything the Ordinary said, from prompts ('Goe forth man and

shew thy selfe'), to directorial warnings ('Oh . . . you marre all the play'), and finally to 'flat rayling & cursing in the bitterest termes he could devise, which the Gentleman with a set gesture and countenance still soberly related'. The audience enjoyed how the convention was broken more than they would have twenty plays, Carew concludes.[111] Stories about errors seem particularly funny if attached to people one knows. The sardonic audience of *Time's Complaint* – prompting the Prologue, nicknaming Good-wife Spiggot, and producing Tarletonisms on the Drunken Man – were having a splendid time in reminding the student actors that they were performing to their peers, not their inferiors.

When there is a celebrity in the audience, then the show on stage is over before it starts. Literary critics point out how this sort of fracture is written into the court masque, when the ideal world of the text is momentarily forgotten in favour of recognizing the real presence of the masque's principal spectator, the monarch. Jonson's *Masque of Blackness* (1605), for instance, points out James to the rest of the company present: Britain is

Ruled by a sun that to this height doth grace it,
Whose beams shine day and night, and are of force
To blanch an Ethiop, and revive a corse.[112]

Sometimes this recognition is about humiliating the audience, so its embarrassment is the real show. At Clare Hall in *c.* 1600, Fuller relates, the Mayor

---

[108] *Elizabeth*, ed. Goldring *et al.*, vol. 2, pp. 738–9, 748; Matthew Woodcock, *Thomas Churchyard: Pen, Sword, and Ego* (Oxford, 2016), pp. 192–5.

[109] *Elizabeth*, ed. Goldring *et al.*, vol. 2, pp. 322, 325; Gillian Austen, *George Gascoigne* (Woodbridge, 2008), pp. 128–32.

[110] Robert Weimann, *Shakespeare and the Popular Tradition in the Theater: Studies in the Social Dimension of Dramatic Form and Function*, ed. Robert Schwartz (Baltimore, MD, 1978), pp. 208–24. See also Bridget Escolme, *Talking to the Audience: Shakespeare, Performance, Self* (Abingdon, 2005), pp. 6–11, 24–51.

[111] Clifford Davidson, Rosalind Conklin Hays, C. E. McGee, Sally L. Joyce and Evelyn S. Newlyn, eds., *REED Dorset and Cornwall* (Turnhout and Toronto, 1999), p. 537.

[112] Jonson, *Masques*, p. 56.

and aldermen who had been warmly invited to attend *Club Law* (anon.) found out too late that it was a satire on citizens. The students had already seated them, 'rivetted in with Schollars on all sides', and:

here did they behold themselves in their own best cloathes (which the Schollars had borrowed) so livelily personated, their habits, gestures, language, lieger-jests, and expressions, that it was hard to decide, which was the true Townsman, whether he that sat by, or he who acted on the Stage. Sit still they could not for chafing, go out they could not for crowding, but impatiently patient were fain to attend.[113]

There was a 'tradition, many earnestly engaging for the truth therof', that the Privy Council agreed to investigate the incident if the show was replayed before them with the same citizens in the audience (an offer that was not accepted). Though probably a fantasy by Fuller, the anecdote is revealing about expected actor–audience recognition.[114]

There are, then, both risks and opportunities for both sides in breaking or maintaining the surface of the play. During the Lady of the Lake show at Kenilworth, the Queen was to have been serenaded by one of Leicester's servants, Henry Goldingham, as Arion on a dolphin's back. Becoming hoarse, he 'teares of his Disguise, and sweares he was none of Arion not he, but eene honest Harry Goldingham; which blunt discoverie pleased the Queene better, then if it had gone thorough in the right way'.[115] A jest book relates how a university actor, supposed to be dead on stage, was 'forced to cough so loud that it was perceived by the generall auditory, at which many of them falling into a laughter, hee rising up excused it thus: you may see Gentlemen what it is to drinke in one's porridge, for they shall cough in their grave'.[116] In such cases, the willingness to abandon the official show remakes the event into a display of authenticity and familiarity with an in-group.

Hence, some actors were known for deliberately creating a hot dynamic between themselves and their audience, in which both parties risked losing face. When spectators interrupted the Queen's Man clown Richard Tarleton, he made 'sport at the least occasion given him' by responding with improvised rhymes. Hissed by students at a show in Christ Church around 1581, Tarleton came back with 'I am not in that golden land wheare Jason won the fleese / but I am in that hissing land wheare freshmen play the geese.'[117] Another time, when he walked on stage and an audience member pointed him out to a friend, Tarleton pointed two fingers back. The spectator thought he was being given the horn, and replied angrily, but 'This matter grew so, that the more he medled, the more it was for his disgrace; wherefore the standers by counselled him to depart', and he slunk out.[118] However, the risk in such humilitainment could run both ways, as Kendall, a fool in a play in Bristol in 1620, found out. An 'extempore' rhyme he added ('if thou a Brittane borne, it fitts thee to were ye horne') was taken personally by an apprentice present, called John Britain, and capped: 'A Brittans name I truly beare, I leave the Horne for thee to were / the horne becomes the saxons best, / I kisd thy wife, supose the rest.'[119]

Even inadvertent problems could give opportunities for performers or spectators to improvise entertaining ways of getting round them. When, during *Pleasure Reconciled to Virtue*, the dancers lagged after 'every sort of ballet and dance of every country whatsoever', James exploded with 'Why don't they dance? What did they make me come here for? Devil take you all, dance.' Buckingham was

---

[113] Nelson, ed., *REED Cambridge*, vol. 1, pp. 377–8.
[114] Christopher Marlow, *Performing Masculinity in English University Drama, 1598–1636* (Farnham, 2013), pp. 52–5.
[115] *Elizabeth*, ed. Goldring *et al.*, vol. 2, p. 308.
[116] Armstrong, *Jeasts*, p. 103.
[117] Elliott *et al.*, eds., *REED Oxford*, vol. 1, p. 173.
[118] Tarleton's Jests (London, 1613), sig. B2v. On 'Tarletonisms', see Gurr, *Playgoing*, pp. 150–8. Complete textual fidelity is a relatively recent aim; early modern actors improvised to keep a play more or less on track: Evelyn B. Tribble, *Cognition in the Globe: Attention and Memory in Shakespeare's Theatre* (Basingstoke, 2011), pp. 70ff.
[119] Pilkinton, ed., *REED Bristol*, p. 215.

widely praised for saving the occasion by springing forward with 'a score of lofty and very minute capers'.[120] As the chief actor of *Philomel* had a cold, the students provided an explanatory verse for a possible understudy, a 'Conceipte ... so-well liked of them all that heard of itt, that manye sayde that itt was pity itt was not put in practise, though there were noe need of itt'.[121]

The highest stakes came in productions before the monarch, in which, Mary Hill Cole argues, 'layered messages [were] exchanged between civic hosts and royal guest' about what each wanted from the other, and both co-operated to make the shows work. Subjects could chance raising sensitive topics because they did so within the safety of a ceremonial or theatrical discourse, where meanings could be disavowed by the speakers or ignored by the principal listener. Civic pageantry aimed to involve everyone, so crowd interruptions were frequent, making for risky openings but memorable moments. J. R. Mulryne and Helen Watanabe-O'Kelly consider that, in continental official festival records, problems appear as an 'ironic counterpoint to the claims of competence and authority embedded in performance'; thus, official reports mention them only briefly. However, British records are more expansive: 'when the ritual was challenged or warped, the interruption reinforced the power of the original ceremony as the participants headed back to their original script and roles'.[122]

Elizabeth was universally praised for her flexibility in repairing damage to a show's fabric. At her official entry into London in 1559, after crowds prevented her from seeing or hearing the pageant of York and Lancaster, she sent ahead to ask for quiet at the succeeding shows, and requested a brief of each so she could respond appropriately. This remedy turned into a potential problem when she asked someone to go ahead to collect the Bible she knew she was to get at the Little Conduit. Officials explained this would spoil the plan of lowering it to her there on a silk thread, with a devout speech (of course, she withdrew the request).[123] A bystander weeping she described as joyful; a commenter praised her 'gracious interpretation of a noble

courage, which wold turne the doutefull to the best'.[124] In 'fowle and rayny wether' at Worcester in 1575, Elizabeth donned rainwear to lend a 'very attentive ear' to speeches by boys. Departing from Elvetham in 1591, she listened to farewells by Nereus, Sylvanus, the Graces and the Hours; 'it was a most extreame rain and yet it pleased hir Majestie with great patience to behold and heare the whole action'.[125] A Savage Man (Gascoigne), emerging from the woods at Kenilworth, was supposed to be tamed by the sight of the Queen, and lay down his club: 'az this Savage for the more submission brake his tree a sunder, kest the top from him, it had allmost light upon her highness hors hed'. Elizabeth saved the day with an airy 'No hurt, no hurt', eliciting from the reporter of the accident, Robert Laneham, the relieved comments of 'See the benignitee of the Prins' and 'which woords I promis yoo we wear all glad too heeer, and took them too be the best part of the play'.[126] Realizing she had been distracted by a riotous bridale presented at the same time as the Coventry Hock Tuesday play at Kenilworth, the Queen asked for the show a second time, when she pointedly laughed heartily.

On most occasions both actors and spectators were committed to continuing a royally appointed show, as a sign that authority was unthreatened by incidental events. During the first night of *Palamon and Arcite*

---

[120] Allen B. Hinds, ed., *Calendar of State Papers Venetian, 1617–1619* (London, 1909), pp. 113–14.

[121] Boas, ed., *Prince*, p. 57.

[122] M. Hill Cole, *The Portable Queen: Elizabeth I and the Politics of Ceremony* (Amherst, 1999), pp. 97, 121, 128–31, 132; J. R. Mulryne, 'Introduction', and Helen Watanabe-O'Kelly, 'Early modern European festivals – politics and performance, event and record', in *Festivals*, ed. Mulryne and Goldring, pp. 10, 22–3.

[123] *Elizabeth*, ed. Goldring *et al.*, vol. 1, pp. 121–2, 127.

[124] *Elizabeth*, ed. Goldring *et al.*, vol. 1, p. 138.

[125] *Elizabeth*, ed. Goldring *et al.*, vol. 2, p. 344; vol. 3, p. 593.

[126] Robert Laneham, *A Letter ... of the Entertainment Untoo the Queenz Maiesty at Killingworth Castl in Warwik* (London, 1575), pp. 20–1; Nichols, ed., *Elizabeth*, vol. 2, p. 251. Gascoigne's own account omits this accident, though he referred to it in later productions, to remind the Queen who he was: Austen, *Gascoigne*, pp. 115–28.

in Christ Church College (1566), a crowd surge pushed over one of the stair walls leading to the hall, killing three and wounding five: 'The Quene understandinge theareof sente forthe presentlye Mr Vicechamberlayne & her owne surgions to helpe them. The actors notwithstanding so well performed their partes that the Quene laughed afterwardes hartelie.'[127] Only when Elizabeth felt she was being manoeuvred into a false position did she turn awkward. At Hinchingbrooke Priory in 1564, a group of students put on an anti-Catholic tableau that so incensed the Queen she departed abruptly with her torch-bearers, leaving the players in the dark.[128] This may also have been the case at court in 1559, when a company 'acted something so distasteful that they were commanded to leave off. And immediately the Mask came in, and dancing.'[129]

Were all these problems real? When things go wrong, there are metadramatic moments in which the real is welcomed into the fictional (or vice versa), and the relationship between actors and audience (whether regal or not) is valued above the integrity of the show. So authors even write in problems. *Periander* includes a carping audience member called Detraction. The play's most powerful spectators, not knowing he was an actor, ordered that he be noted and punished after the show, 'but as soone as it once appeared that hee was an actor their disdaine and anger turned to much pleasure and Content'.[130] The induction of Jonson's *Love Restored* (1612) likewise makes such problems part of the text, as Masquerado enters out of breath, explaining that, though the masquers are fully dressed and know the dances, and the poet stands ready to give a speech, the musician is missing and the boy who plays Cupid is 'so hoarse, your majesty cannot hear him half the breadth o' your chair'.[131]

Seemingly inadvertent interruptions are devised to show *sprezzatura* or gain support. During her 1592 visit to Oxford, the Queen sent twice to a disputant to end his speech as she intended to speak herself that evening, 'but he would not, or as some told her, could not put himself out of a set methodical speech for fear he should have marred all, or else confounded his memory'. The next day she delivered her speech, but interrupted herself to

call for a stool for the gouty Sir William Cecil. 'Then fell she to it again, as if there had been no interruption', said bystanders, suspecting this was a ploy to show her oratorial skills.[132] Sir James Hay's embassy to France in 1616 had a 'great Train of young Noblemen', who vied with each other to show 'the happiest fancy whose invention could express something novel'. At their entry into Paris, Hay shod his horse with silver shoes, tacked on so lightly that when he curvetted before eminent onlookers the shoes fell off and new silver ones were put on, amazing his watchers by such lavish expenditure.[133] The second (command) performance of *Ignoramus* in 1615 was interrupted by its own producers to gain the King's support against the irate legal profession the play satirized:

while this Comedy was acting before K. James in Cambridge, the inventors (to make the K. an actor in it) caused a post to come galloping into the Towne, & When he came upon the Stage, he commanded the Comedians to forbeare, for that My Lord Chiefe Justice Was enformed that they had made a knavish peice of worke to disgrace the Lawyers, & would haue them appeare befor him to answere it. The Actors gaue ouer as if they had not dared to proceed. Whereupon K. James rose out of his chaire, & beckened to them With his hand & saying – Goe on Goe on, I will heare you out.[134]

CONCLUSION

The greater number of productions in Shakespeare's plays go askew, from mishaps and ill-regulated

---

[127] *Elizabeth*, ed. Goldring *et al.*, vol. 1, p. 477. Similar fatal accidents due to crowding and poor building standards occurred at the Paris Bear Garden (1583) and at a puppet play in St John's Street, London (1599): Chambers, *Elizabethan Stage*, vol. 2, p. 462; Gurr, *Playgoing*, p. 257.

[128] *Elizabeth*, ed. Goldring *et al.*, vol. 1, pp. 432–3; Boas, *University Drama*, pp. 382–5.

[129] *Elizabeth*, ed. Goldring *et al.*, vol. 1, p. 169.

[130] Elliott *et al.*, eds., *REED Oxford*, vol. 1, p. 380.

[131] Jonson, *Masques*, pp. 186–7.

[132] Nichols, ed., *Elizabeth*, vol. 3, pp. 626–7.

[133] Nichols, ed., *James*, vol. 3, p. 184.

[134] C. E. McGee, 'Stuart kings and Cambridge University drama: two stories by William Whiteway', *Notes and Queries* 233 (1988), pp. 494–6.

audiences in amateur shows (like 'The Nine Worthies' in *Love's Labours Lost*) to deliberate undermining of professional performances (as in 'The Murder of Gonzago' in *Hamlet*). The resilient troupers of 'Pyramus and Thisbe' in *A Midsummer Night's Dream*, for instance, cope with an indisposed actor, poor stage lighting, a recalcitrant performing animal, scenery that does not move when it should, costume fastenings breaking, scene-stealing performances, stage fright, truncated rehearsal time, and hecklers in the audience. These failures create a web of contrasting interests: the real audience want the inset play to fail, so encourage those who create the problems. The inset play's audience want the inset play to succeed, so try to suppress those who interrupt it. The real actors want the inset play to fail, so the real production will succeed with the audience; the inset play's actors want the opposite.

West's explanation for these moments is that such confusion explores questions of what is possible to know for certain, without error. My justification for them is less noble: intimacy is created when the audience feels superiority to the actors. At least such intimacy is tempered by the sense that everyone present has been in a production themselves (whether as actors, stage crew or audience) which has gone wrong in some way. Perhaps, then, my readers might reflect on their own motives for skimming an article that promised to leave no turn unstoned![135]

---

[135] Diana Rigg, ed., *No Turn Unstoned: The Worst Ever Theatrical Reviews* (London, 1982). Thanks to Derek Dunne, and the editor and reader of *Survey*, for comments on my article.

THE TRUE TRAGEDY *AS A YORKIST PLAY?*
PROBLEMS IN TEXTUAL TRANSMISSION

RICHARD STACEY

There are many linguistic differences between the two variant texts (octavo and folio) of *Henry VI Part 3*. One feature which has been largely overlooked by critics is evidence of a fairly consistent pro-Yorkist bias in the octavo of 1595.[1] Richard of York's assertion that the throne is 'mine inheritance as the kingdome is' (sig. A3v) is modified in the folio to 'as the earldom was' (1.1.78), placing his claim as the next step on the ladder of ambition rather than the assertion of a *de jure* fact. On the field of Towton, in which Edward leads the Yorkists to their greatest triumph, Warwick declares that he will soon 'be crowned Englands lawfull king' (sig. C5 r); the folio line is 'England's royal king' (2.6.88), ambiguously suggesting that Edward will be royalized in an act of realpolitik. When an oath is sworn to effect a return to the Yorkist bloodline after Henry's death, the octavo text includes four lines not in the folio, in which Henry concedes that Richard is king 'by right and equitie' (sig. A4 v); in the folio, the line is transformed to a rare moment of defiance, with emphasis on the lineal strength of the Lancastrian line: 'Think'st thou that I will leave my kingly throne, / Wherein my grandsire and my father sat?' (1.1.124–5). This is a recurring feature of the political language included in the folio text, such as when Westmorland abandons Henry for being a 'faint-hearted and degenerate King' (1.1.185) who has abrogated the fealty of his pro-Lancastrian allies by refusing to defend the lawfulness of his own claim. When charting these subtle differences, we can see an interesting picture start to emerge: one in which the fundamental right of the Yorkist claim is asserted, whilst the

fact of Henry's own hereditary succession is downplayed, or even excised. The octavo is pro-Yorkist, the folio less so.[2]

It would be tempting to extract from this body of evidence a two-stage process of dramatic development, in which an 'early' pro-Yorkist position is cultivated in the context of the succession crisis, presumably to evoke the Plantagenet credentials of Elizabeth's great-grandfather, Edward IV. Plays on Yorkist themes were popular on the London stage throughout the 1590s. The most notable examples include *George a Greene*, anachronously set during the reign of Edward IV; the anonymous *The True Tragedie of Richard the Thirde* and Shakespeare's *Richard III*; Thomas Heywood's two-part comedy *Edward IV*; and the *Earl of Huntingdon* plays, whose

---

[1] Anon., *The true tragedie of Richard Duke of York* (London, 1595); and William Shakespeare, *Henry VI Part Three*, ed. Michael Hattaway (Cambridge, 1993). All act, scene and line references to the folio text will be cited from this edition, which is based on the 1623 copy; see Cox and Rasmussen, 'The texts of *The True Tragedy* and *3 Henry VI*', pp. 148–76. The two texts will be abbreviated to O and F for ease of reference.

[2] Several critics have explored the significance of the House of York to the dramatic representation of succession in Shakespearian dramaturgy. See Peter Lake, *How Shakespeare Put Politics on Stage: Power and Succession in the History Plays* (New Haven, 2016), pp. 108–44; David Womersley, *Divinity and State* (Oxford, 2010), pp. 237–60; and Howard Erskine-Hill, *Poetry and the Realm of Politics: Shakespeare to Dryden* (Oxford, 1996), pp. 46–69. For the identification of a Yorkist bias in editorial constructions of the deposition scene in *Richard II*, see Emma Smith, 'Richard II's Yorkist editors', *Shakespeare Survey 63* (Cambridge, 2010), 37–48.

titles allude to the prominent Yorkist heir Henry Hastings, 3rd Earl of Huntingdon, known for his role as Lord President of the Council of the North in York. *The True Tragedy* could easily slot into this contemporaneous theatrical milieu, given the divergences from the folio and the publication date of 1595. Such a view, however, is difficult to sustain when the linguistic and dramatic evidence is held up to scrutiny. Textual work by Randall Martin and, most recently, John Jowett has called the integrity of the octavo copy into serious question.[3] As opposed to a consistent and experimental early draft, as argued by Steven Urkowitz, the text which has come down to us is a mixture of memorial reconstruction and, most intriguingly, last-minute copy by an unidentified dramatist.[4] It is highly likely that the octavo and folio texts are versions of a lost collaborative play written by Marlowe, Shakespeare and a third hand, as revealed by stylometric analysis.[5] The octavo text may contain some traces of Shakespeare's writing in, say, the divisions which Gary Taylor and Rory Loughnane have identified as bearing textual markers indicative of the work of individual dramatists; but it is now untenable to posit that Shakespeare had a direct shaping influence on the written content of the octavo text as we have it, or the variations between both works.[6] Whatever is happening in *The True Tragedy* in relation to the pro-Yorkist evidence, we are able to detect Shakespeare's hand only derivatively, and cannot therefore use the material to provide us with a definitive insight into the authorial choices of our most famous playwright.

This is not to discount the effects generated for the readers of the octavo. A heightened focus on the Yorkist cause is certainly detectable at key moments throughout the text, prioritizing a *de jure* interpretation of political right, for example, or adding structural momentum to Edward's campaign for the throne. In order to account for these features, it is necessary to engage with the work of Martin and Jowett. Both scholars are in agreement that there is an original text underlying both versions of the play. But, whereas Martin approaches *The True Tragedy* as 'both a memorially reported text and as an early

version of *Henry VI Part 3*, almost certainly by Shakespeare', Jowett concludes, quite persuasively, that the octavo is a composite mixture of transmission and emendation, the two variants being the 'outcome of divergent development'.[7] Both theses overlap, but Jowett factors in the collaborative status of the original text. The Yorkist material provides an opportunity to bring these interpretative models into contact with each other. The shift away from a pro-Yorkist position to a more bipartisan view in the folio text may be indicative of a revisionary

---

3 For textual criticism on the variants between the octavo and folio texts, see John Jowett, 'The origins of *Richard, Duke of York*', in *Early Shakespeare, 1588–1594*, ed. Rory Loughnane and Andrew J. Power (Cambridge, 2020), pp. 235–60; Randall Martin, '*The True Tragedy of Richard Duke of York* and *3 Henry VI*: report and revision', *Review of English Studies* 53 (2002), 8–30; Steven Urkowitz, '"If I mistake in either text those foundations which I build upon": Peter Alexander's textual analysis of *Henry VI* Parts 2 and 3', *English Literary Renaissance* 18 (1988), 230–56; and Peter Alexander, *Shakespeare's Henry VI and Richard III* (Cambridge, 1927), pp. 89–91. For an article which doubts the presence of memorial recall in the octavo, see Heejin Kim, 'The memorial reconstruction theory and chronicles: the *Henry VI* plays', *Shakespeare* 15 (2019), 356–78.

4 Urkowitz, 'Mistake', p. 243. Jowett posits that the unidentified author is George Peele, based on the identification of several echoes of lines in his identified plays: Jowett, 'Origins', pp. 248–51.

5 For criticism outlining the argument for the presence of Marlovian authorship in the *Henry VI* plays, see John Burrows and Hugh Craig, 'The joker in the pack? Marlowe, Kyd, and the co-authorship of *Henry VI Part 3*', in *The New Oxford Shakespeare: Authorship Companion*, ed. Gary Taylor and Gabriel Egan (Oxford, 2017), pp. 194–217; John Burrows and Hugh Craig, 'A collaboration about a collaboration: the authorship of *King Henry VI, Part Three*', in *Collaborative Research in the Digital Humanities*, ed. Marilyn Deegan and Willard McCarty. (Farnham, 2011), pp. 27–65; Gabriel Egan, Mark Eisen, Santiago Segarra and Alejandro Ribeiro , 'Attributing the authorship of the *Henry VI* plays by word adjacency', *Shakespeare Quarterly* 67 (2016), 232–56; and John V. Nance and Gary Taylor , 'Imitation or collaboration? Marlowe and the early Shakespeare canon', *Shakespeare Survey* 68 (Cambridge, 2015), 32–47.

6 Gary Taylor and Rory Loughnane, 'The canon and chronology of Shakespeare's works', in *The New Oxford Shakespeare*, ed. Taylor and Egan, pp. 417–602; pp. 496–9.

7 Martin, 'Report', p. 10; Jowett, 'Origins', p. 236.

impulse, as suggested by Martin and other scholars, such as Urkowitz.[8] Yet, in light of Jowett's thesis, this would be a revision of the original collaborative playtext, rather than the text which comprises the octavo version. The Yorkist elements which remain are therefore a likely indication of the political content of this lost work – an example of what Jowett has termed 'remnanticity'.[9] From this perspective, it is possible to account for the Yorkist inflections and their subsequent modulation as a mixture of disrupted transmission in the octavo, and revision of some of the original or collaborative features in the folio, as this article will demonstrate.

REVISION, RECALL AND RECONSTRUCTION

The evidence for a clear divergence in the representation of Yorkist politics in the two versions of *Henry VI Part 3* is fairly substantial. I have compiled thirteen samples in O and F.[10] In all quotations, the metrical pattern of each line is carefully maintained, implying that a conscious process of word-selection is at work to preserve the scansion whilst subtly re-orienting the import of the sentence. Jowett's theory of the existence of a lost collaborative 'ur-text' behind the variants of *Henry VI Part 3* has helped to sever the pervasive critical assumption that a causal link exists between O and F, in which the former is superseded by the expanded playing script of the latter.[11] One could feasibly argue that it is O which exhibits the revision of multiple Yorkist cues which have been conserved in F, tailoring the play to dramatic trends which were in vogue in the commercial theatre of the 1590s. There is compelling evidence, however, to suggest this is unlikely to be the case. One of Jowett's most persuasive arguments for the derivative nature of O is the persistence of memorial or revisionary elements across the authorial boundaries identified by Gary Taylor and Rory Loughnane.[12] Marlowe's hand has been detected in Act 1, Scene 1; we can see that examples 1, 2 and 3 in the Appendix, which presumably retain

traces of Marlovian authorship, are modified to less pro-Yorkist sentiments in F, alongside other examples with a likely Shakespearian origin in O. If there is a revisionary impulse at work throughout F, then it consistently traverses the authorial boundaries in the lost original play. In the Appendix, there are samples from O taken from sections of the text which have been memorially reconstructed – such as nos. 9, 12 and 13 – alongside modified expressions from sources likely to be text-based in origin; again, phrases from both of these different textual sources in O are uniformly revised to less pro-Yorkist positions throughout the entirety of F.[13] For such an

---

8   Although Martin and Urkowitz differ over the extent of memorial interpolation in O, they are in agreement that various aesthetic choices can be detected which are the likely result of Shakespeare's hand. See Martin, 'Report', p. 25; Urkowitz, 'Mistake', pp. 255–6.

9   Jowett, 'Origins', p. 243.

10 In order to present the evidence in as clear a manner as possible, I have compiled an appendix of thirteen examples. The samples I have selected are not prescriptive by any means, and the reader may detect others (or, indeed, disagree with the pro-Yorkist readings I have perceived in the language). All of the examples preserve scansion, and all of them occur at roughly the same place in both texts.

11 Jowett, 'Origins', p. 236.

12 Jowett argues that the 'characterizing features' of O, such as the mixture of memorial recall with likely remnants due to preserved scansion, 'show no respect to the authorial division': Jowett, 'Origins', pp. 255–6.

13 In Act 2, Scene 6, from which example 9 is taken, there is evidence of phonetic reconstruction in the oddly spelled phrase 'inst inched thirst' (sig. C5r); this is modified to the correct word 'unstanched' (2.6.83) in F. In Act 3, Scene 3, from which examples 11 and 12 are taken, the number given for Warwick's years of service in O – 'thirtie and eight yeeres' – is corrected to 'thirty and six years' (3.3.96) in F, again suggesting imperfect recollection which is later amended. Interestingly, the word 'pettigree' (sig. D1v) is also corrected to the phonetically accurate 'pedigree' (3.3.94). In contrast, remnanticity can be detected in Act 1, Scene 1, via the extensive stage directions, which are unlikely to be the result of recall; this scene is also likely to have been written in its original form by Marlowe. We can see, therefore, that the Yorkist edits in F traverse a range of different authorial points of origin in O, strengthening the case for a later, more consistent process of textual and dramaturgical revision.

unstable copy to exhibit a consistent revisionist impulse in favour of the Yorkists, it would take a remarkable amount of co-operation from actors, compositors and other agents involved in the textual construction of O. It is, therefore, reasonable to identify F as the source of the more constant flow of revisionism we can see throughout the play.

Not all of the examples in O are likely to be remnants of the imperfectly preserved collaborative play; some are all but certain to be the result of theatrical interpolation via imperfect recall. Using EEBO as a test-case, it is possible to track the presence of individual words in proximity to each other in published early modern playing scripts.[14] If there are no 'hits', it is a possibility that the samples from either O or F are stand-alone constructions. When the differentiated words in each sample are searched in this way, we can see that ten word-clusters appear solely in F, whilst eight appear solely in O.[15] This measurement via EEBO suggests that there is scope for slightly more cross-pollination in O. If we look more closely at the word-clusters which do appear in other texts, we can see quite a lot of evidence of the insertion of lines from contemporaneous plays. In no. 12, the *de jure* phrase 'lawful heir' (sig. D1v), which is substituted in F by the more elective 'lawful chosen' (3.3.115), appears in a large number of different texts; these are *The Troublesome Reign of King John* (1591), *The Contention* (1600), *The True Tragedy of Richard III* (1594) and *Sir John Oldcastle* (1600).[16] Interestingly, the last two examples use the phrase in dramatic contexts which articulate the constitutional legality of the Yorkist claim. The first is spoken by the Duke of York in *The Contention* when asserting his right to sovereignty to Warwick; his declaration that he is 'lawfull heire vnto the kingdome' after reasoning that 'the issue of the elder should succeed before the issue of the yonger' is met with the cry 'Long liue Richard'. In *Sir John Oldcastle*, the phrase is used to delineate the transferred marital claim of the proto-Yorkist ancestor Richard, Earl of Cambridge, by his wife Anne, who is 'lawfull heyre to Roger Mortimer' and 'deriu'd from Lionell, / Third sonne vnto king Edward'. It appears that this example seen in O – functioning, in context, as a code-phrase for the perceived lawfulness of Yorkist kingship – may not actually be a remnant of the original collaboration; rather, it is likely to have been inserted into the play by actors who have recalled the phrase 'lawful heir' to capture the hereditary rhetoric spoken by members of the House of York on stage.

The use of EEBO reveals other instances of cross-pollination with other plays. In no. 13, the pro-Lancastrian substitution 'native right' (3.3.190), spoken by Warwick in F, does not appear anywhere else in the record. In O, the less committed phrase 'natiue home' (sig. D2v) occurs in *Massacre at Paris* (1594), *Battle of Alcazar* (1594) and *Fair Em* (1591).[17] In no. 7, the divergent but metrically exact phrases 'wilt thou yeelde thy crowne' (sig. B8v) and 'wilt thou kneel for grace' (2.2.81) appear in different plays. The former is similar to no. 12, and occurs

---

[14] In order to identify word-clusters in EEBO, I have used the 'advanced search' feature to set a date limit of 1588–1600 and narrow down the proximity of individual words to within three words of each other. All examples have been selected from dramatic publications. In some cases, the word-clusters appear in other genres and printed texts, but for the purposes of identifying possible examples of memorial interpolation by actors, I have chosen scripts which would have been spoken on stage.

[15] If we look at the Appendix, then we can see the following data: examples which are unique to O (1, 3, 4, 6, 8, 9, 10, 11); examples which are unique to F (1, 3, 4, 5, 6, 8, 9, 11, 12, 13); examples in O which appear elsewhere (2, 5, 7, 12, 13); and examples in F which appear elsewhere (2, 7, 10 – the latter two of which are in other Shakespearian texts).

[16] *The Troublesome Reign of King John* (London, 1591), sig. A4v; *The Contention* (London, 1600), sig. C4v; *The True Tragedy of Richard III* (London, 1594), sig. F2r–F2v; *Sir John Oldcastle* (1600), sig. D4v–E1r.

[17] Christopher Marlowe, *Massacre at Paris* (London, 1594), sig. B4v, sig. D3r; George Peele, *Battle of Alcazar* (London, 1594), sig. A3r; *Fair Em* (London, 1591), sig. B1r.

in *Tamburlaine* (1590), *Edward II* (1594), *The Contention* and *Blind Beggar of Alexandria* (1598).[18] The slightly different phrase 'yield the crown' is spoken by the Duke of York in *The Contention* to imply a degree of ownership of the royal jewels by demanding the return of property after theft. The phrase in F also appears in a play: *Titus Andronicus* (1594), co-authored by Shakespeare and Peele.[19] The number of possible sources for O, in tandem with the unstable copy of the text of *The Contention*, dilutes the chances that the variant phrase in F, rather than O, could be the result of interpolation. Rather, it reinforces the existence of a revisionist impulse in the expanded version of the play, in which an alternative phrase is sourced from an earlier moment in Shakespeare's dramatic corpus. Interestingly, the phrase 'kneel for grace' occurs in *Titus Andronicus* when the gathered Andronici are appealing to Saturninus for leniency; in this version of the scene, Edward seems more like an embryonic tyrant than a just ruler unlawfully held from his inheritance.

There are examples in which it is possible to surmise a pattern of revision at work in F. In no. 5, O's 'Englands royall king' (sig. B6r) is diluted to the less assertive 'England's royal throne' (2.1.193). The latter cluster is an example of sole usage, whilst the former appears in *The Contention*, again used as part of a Yorkist propaganda campaign to 'aduance the milke-white Rose'.[20] Conversely, no. 10 reveals a preference for this phrase in F, in which 'Englands lawfull king' (sig. C5r) becomes 'England's royal king' (2.6.88). Adjusting the dates on EEBO reveals that 'royal king' is used twice throughout the later play *Richard III* (1597), including in the well-known scene where Buckingham coerces the crowd to accept Richard as monarch.[21] Whereas the use of the phrase in O is a clear endorsement of hereditary right in a dramatic context of political debate, its cynical deployment in *Richard III* is associated with rhetorical deceit, tellingly in relation to Yorkist ambition. It is reasonable to surmise that the phrase in F is of a different import to its use in O, shifting the emphasis away from the word 'lawfull', and introducing a more transformative, and even coercive, dimension to Edward's newly acquired role. Taken together, such features offer several explanations for the divergences in O and F highlighted in the samples in the Appendix. In O, we see a fairly stable set of unique verbal clusters, mixed with instances of what is likely to be memorial interpolation; the examples of disrupted transmission from other plays tend to be imported from scenes which dramatize the lawfulness of the Yorkist claim. In F, however, we see slightly more unique verbal clusters, with transference occurring from plays which are written, or co-written, by Shakespeare. The textual evidence for what seems on first reading to be a heightened focus on Yorkist politics in the copy of *The True Tragedy* can be best explained as a mixture of remnanticity and recall.

One feature of O which could point towards memorial reconstruction is the significant compression in O of lines given to both Henry and Margaret in F. There are several indicators that some parts of these speeches may have been imperfectly recorded, as the two characters share quite a bit of stage time with Warwick and Clifford, whose lines are fairly stable in both versions of the play.[22] It is also true, however, that the roles and language of the Lancastrians are significantly expanded in F, in ways which are dramaturgically complex. In Act 2, Scene 5, F has 54 lines for Henry, whilst O has just 13; in Act 3, Scene 1, F gives him 47 lines, O 19. For Margaret, there are 50 lines in Act 5, Scene 4 in F, yet only 20 in O, alongside several cuts throughout Act 1, Scene

---

[18] Christopher Marlowe, *Tamburlaine* (London, 1590), sig. F1v; Christopher Marlowe, *Edward II* (London, 1594), sig. I3r; *Contention*, sig. A4v; George Chapman, *Blind Beggar of Alexandria* (London, 1598), sig. F1v.

[19] *Titus Andronicus* (London, 1594), sig. C2v.

[20] *Contention*, sig. C4v, sig. G4v.

[21] William Shakespeare, *Richard III* (London, 1597), sig. G4v, sig. H3r.

[22] Martin, 'Report', pp. 16–17.

1. The extra material in F could be a recovery of original dialogue in the collaborative source which was lost during the process of transmission. The body of work is so extensive, though, that some of the material could also be the result of revisionary interpolation in the scenes included in the original dramatic source. One way to investigate this possibility is to isolate extended metaphors which in O appear as garbled truncations, speeches given to other characters, or undeveloped cues in the last line of a speech. There are several examples in F which fit these criteria. The method is not foolproof, and cannot entirely discount the possibility that certain sections of the play – particularly ones involving the delicate and syntactically demanding construction of extended images – might not have been easy to construct without significant mangling. Taken in conjunction with what appears to be a consistent sanding of pro-Yorkist language throughout F, though, it is possible to detect a definite pattern, in which the broad endorsement of Edward's campaign in O is modified to a more bipartisan position.

In Act 2, Scene 5 in F, after losing the Battle of Towton, Henry enters the stage alone, wishing that he had been born a shepherd rather than a king. There are a few short sections of expanded dialogue in Henry's soliloquy which have no correlative in O, most notably lines 42–5 and 53–4, in which the shade of a 'hawthorn bush' (2.5.42) and a 'curious bed' (2.5.53) are fashioned as spaces of withdrawal. These sections mention the word 'treachery' and its cognate 'treason' (2.5.45, 54), reconceptualizing the Yorkist triumph as an act of political violence which is probably unlawful. In Act 4, Scene 6, when Henry has been restored by Warwick, the power-share with Clarence is expanded, with lines 38–42 and 49–52 having no clear equivalent in O. Henry's appeal 'Now join your hands and with your hand your hearts, / That no dissension hinder government' (4.6.39–40) is consolidated by Warwick's assurance that 'We'll yoke together, like a double shadow ... bearing weight of government' (4.6.49, 51). The phonetic echo of the word 'York' in 'yoke' instantiates

a vision of Lancastrian–Yorkist co-operation, couched in the discourse of participatory rule; as such, this scene makes Edward's entry into York look more like an act of aggression than the progress of a just political cause. We can see similar effects at work in the isolated images given to Margaret in F. In Act 5, Scene 4, lines 25–7 and 33–6 develop a complex tripartite metaphor of sea, sand and stone to castigate each of the Yorkist brothers in turn. Margaret's statement, 'That there's no hoped-for mercy with the brothers / More than with ruthless waves, with sands and rocks' (5.4.35–6), which does not appear in any sense in O, offers a warning which not only stresses the duplicitous nature of the dynasty as a whole, but anticipates the tyranny of Richard's rule when he eventually becomes king. Indeed, this shift to a more elongated narrative perspective could be one possible motive for revision, seeding the unlawful and often diabolical behaviour of the last Yorkist king throughout *Richard III*. Metaphoric spaces are opened up which add texture to the discourse of Lancastrian loss, stressing the unlawfulness of Yorkist behaviour, and providing a small glimpse of a conciliation in the context of interminable war.

There are specific discourses in O which are significantly more developed in F, most notably the representation of oath-taking.[23] An investigation of swearing in O and F reveals a number of changes, or interpolations, which maximize the role played by bonds in the political action of the play. The phrase 'Henries heires and your succession' (sig. B5 r), spoken by Warwick to Edward in reference to the Yorkists as adopted successors, is changed in F to 'henry's oath and your succession' (2.1.119); an expectation of royal status is turned to

---

[23] Oath Studies is a fairly emergent field in Shakespeare criticism. See John Kerrigan, *Shakespeare's Binding Language* (Oxford, 2016); Andrew Hadfield, *Lying in Early Modern English Culture: From the Oath of Supremacy to the Oath of Allegiance* (Oxford, 2017), particularly the discussion of Othello on pp. 286–310; and Lucy Munro, '"S'blood!": Hamlet's oaths and the editing of Shakespeare's plays', *Shakespeare Survey 70* (Cambridge, 2017),123–34.

a lawful pact, introducing a degree of fulfilled obligation – and its obverse, jeopardy – into the transference of rule. In Act 3, Scene 1, when Henry is held prisoner by two of his former subjects, the lines 'And therefore we charge you in Gods name & the kings / To go along with vs vnto the officers' (sig. C6r) are developed into a substantial rumination on obedience to a monarch who has not clearly abdicated. In F, the line is represented in the following way: 'And we his subjects, sworn in allegiance, / Will apprehend you as his enemy' (3.1.70–1). The word 'sworn' introduces lines 76–92, which are not included in O, and shift the focus of the scene to a complex argument for Henry's lawful right to rule. The Lancastrian hereditary descent is emphasized in the phrase 'My father and my grandfather were kings / And you were sworn true subjects unto me' (3.1.77–8), constructing anyone who shifts their allegiance to Edward as guilty of a 'lightness' of character, along with a 'sin' punishable by God (3.1.88–9). As these lines are not included in O, and develop another extended metaphor of a feather moving with the wind, complete with a cue for the actor to blow the prop on stage, we can see a more ambiguous approach to Henry's abdication. This is likely to be revisionist in nature due to the semantic shift in the line leading into an extended metaphor.[24]

Throughout the play, and in the chronicle sources, the Yorkists are defined by their willingness to break sacred oaths in the pursuit of power. Richard's masterclass in casuistry, when he assures his father that 'An oath is of no moment, being not took / Before a true and lawful magistrate' (1.2.22–3), associates perjury with Henry's unlawful kingship, eliding the act of swearing before God with the righteousness of the Yorkist cause. John Kerrigan has argued that the dramatic representation of oath-taking in the play is a 'realization of design' which allows the Yorkists to coalesce into a 'group formation' with a 'common objective'.[25] Although Kerrigan defines this cause as primarily one of 'revenge', the use of swearing to foment political grievances is also used to add political texture and causal weight to the transference of power from Lancaster to York, which is the

primary motor of the plot.[26] Some of the additions in F exploit the temporal properties of promissory swearing to complicate the structural patterns which will ultimately place Edward on the throne, not once but twice. In Act 1, Scene 1 – a likely Marlovian composition in its original form, as noted earlier – Henry's binding injunction to the Yorkists to 'honour me as thy king and Soueraigne' (sig. A5v) is followed in F by two inserted lines: 'And neither by treason nor hostility / To seek to put me down and reign thyself' (1.1.201–2). As this is exactly what happens later in the play, the additions stress the sacredness of the bond which will be broken, castigating the Yorkists as sinful usurpers. In Act 4, Scene 1, Edward's tentative discussion with Hastings and Montague, in which he suspects them of being 'hollow friends' (4.1.138), is reinforced with the inserted phrase, 'Give me assurance with some friendly vow, / That I may never have you in suspect' (4.1.140–1); the need for a pledge stresses Edward's uncertainty of his support-base whilst recalling his own repeated acts of betrayal earlier in the play. In Act 5, Scene 1, Clarence's return to the Yorkist faction is transformed from the rejection of the charge that he is a 'harsh vnnaturall' (sig. E2r) brother in O, to a public refutation of the 'holy oath' he swore to Henry: 'keep that oath were more impiety / Than Jephthah, when he sacrificed his daughter' (5.1.93–4). The reference to the previous pledge once again associates the Yorkist dynasty with repeated acts of perjury, reminding the audience that their path to power has been primarily facilitated through oath-breaking. As these interpolations simply do not occur in O, there is strong evidence of a sustained revisionary impulse in F. The heightened focus on promissory bonds encourages the audience to question the validity of the Yorkist cause, measuring the behaviour of

---

[24] Martin has detected evidence of revision in Act 3, Scene 1, observing that the modification of Henry's appearance 'in shew' to his mental state 'that's enough' is an example of 'F's reworking of O's less self-possessed and complex figure': Martin, 'Report', p. 28.

[25] Kerrigan, *Binding*, pp. 46, 44. [26] Kerrigan, *Binding*, p. 46.

Edward and his brothers against the terms of sacred bonds which are repeatedly severed. Again, O appears to be more pro-Yorkist than F.

There are further examples of interpolation which give rise to a consistent Yorkist aesthetic in the reading copy of the 1595 version of the play. One of the most well-known arguments for memorial recall is the inclusion in O of the name 'Lord Bonfield' (sig. D4r), which is amended to 'Lord Bonville' in F (4.1.57). As both Martin and Jowett point out, Bonville is likely to be a correction because it is the accurate name of the particular figure derived from the sources.[27] Conversely, Bonfield is a prominent character in the anonymous play *George a Greene*. One feature of *The True Tragedy* which helps to promote the conflict from a Yorkist perspective is a cluster of references to Wakefield; the word is spoken five times in O and just once in F, in a line which is the same in both versions.[28] The town of Wakefield is crucial in establishing a degree of empathy for the Yorkist family; it is where Rutland is murdered, and the Duke is executed after being taunted with a paper crown and a napkin stained with the blood of his youngest son. The anticipatory signifiers in O therefore establish this specific northern town as a space of tragic loss for the Yorkist family, and arguably one where sympathy of the audience is at its highest. The references, however, are all but certain to be interpolations from the text of *George a Greene*. The play is set largely in Wakefield and Bradford, and features a visit to Yorkshire by Edward IV; not surprisingly, the word 'Wakefield' is spoken seventeen times throughout the text.[29] The erroneous estimation of the Lancastrian forces as comprising 'thirtie thousand men' (sig. A7r) is modified in F to 'twenty thousand men' (1.2.50); in *George a Greene*, the army camped outside Wakefield is 'thirtie thousand men strong in power' (sig. A3v). The warning in O that the 'House of Lancaster, are marching towards *Wakefield*' (sig. A7r) establishes the threat to the town as explicitly dynastic in nature. In *George a Greene*, the Earl of Kendal promises Lord Bonfield that 'I will make thee Duke of Lancaster' (sig. A2v) if the siege of

Wakefield is a success. Mannering's injunction to the citizens of Wakefield to send Kendal 'such prouision as he wants' (sig. A3v) is echoed in the Duke of York's line, 'My selfe heere in *Sandall* castell will prouide / Both men and monie to furder our attempts' (O sig. A7r). Although Wakefield is a prominent location in *The True Tragedy*, as a scene of Lancastrian atrocity and child-murder, the cluster of references in O are unlikely to be a preservation of the original collaborative script. Rather, it appears as if the actors have mapped a moment onto the text from a scene in a play on similar themes, in which the pro-Yorkist city of Wakefield is besieged by a pro-Lancastrian antagonistic force.

One final example of disrupted transmission can be detected in the preservation of playing strategies. O includes substantial stage directions which do not appear in F, such as the Yorkists entering 'with white Roses in their hats' (sig. A2r). The significance of this particular prop is emphasized throughout the text. After Clarence reunites with his brothers, O includes the direction 'and then Clarence takes his red Rose out of his hat, and throwes it at *Warwike*' (sig. E2r), stressing the rejection of the Lancastrian cause

---

[27] Martin, 'Report', pp. 11–12; Jowett, 'Origins', pp. 240–2.
[28] Wakefield is mentioned in the following locations in O: sig. A7r; sig. A7v; sig. B4v.
[29] Anon., *A pleasant conceyted comedie of George a Greene, the pinner of Wakefield* (London, 1599), sigs. A3r; A3v; B1r; B2v; B3r; C3r; D3r; E1v; E2r; E3r; F1v. The dating of the two plays is complex. As *George a Greene* was first performed in 1593, a year after the first recorded staging of *The True Tragedy*, it would imply that Shakespeare's play is the earlier text. However, Martin Wiggins has dated *George a Greene* to 1591, a view corroborated in *Annals of English Drama* which identifies a date range of 1587–93 and settles on 1591. This would make the two plays so close in proximity as to be effectively indeterminate. For the purposes of this article, the question is somewhat moot as the octavo publication date of 1595 would render the recollection permissible, given the lapse of time. See Martin Wiggins and Catherine Richardson, eds., *British Drama 1533–1642: A Catalogue*, 10 vols. (Oxford, 2013), vol. 3, pp. 109, 119; Alfred Harbage, *Annals of English Drama, 975–1700*, 3rd edn, rev. Samuel Schoenbaum and Sylvia Stoler Wagonheim (New York, 1989).

through the heightened politicization of the rose prop on stage. Other moments seem to preserve the use of the prop in this way. In Act 2, Scene 2 – opening with the stage direction, 'Enter the house of Yorke', rather than F's listing of the relevant characters – Richard states, 'I cannot ioie till this white rose be dide, / Euen in the hart bloud of the house of *Lancaster*' (sig. B4r). The line is not included in F. The word 'this' in the syntax can be explained if Richard creates a metonymy of his own self for rhetorical effect; or, more likely, if the actor pointed to the prop of the white rose as he spoke the line, signalling his familial loyalty in the same manner as Clarence. The use of the deictic word 'this' to refer to action on stage occurs elsewhere in O. The Duke of York's line 'This is the But, and this abides your shot' (sig. B1r) is changed in F to 'I am your butt, and I abide your shot' (1.4.29); presumably, the actor recalled a gesture whereby York pointed to himself on stage, to emphasize his fraught role as a target of Lancastrian aggression. These traces all contribute to a distinct theatrical perspective in the 1595 edition. The examples are either the retention of textual features of the original collaboration, such as the extensive stage directions in Act 1, Scene 1; evidence of a playing style in the earliest performances, which tend to emphasize the Yorkist struggle and their demonstrable familial bond; or interpolations, which have reconstructed the dialogue in light of dramatic strategies from other plays on Yorkist themes, similar to the examples from EEBO in the Appendix discussed earlier. In all cases, it is likely that the original play was responsive to the interest of audiences in the dramatic story of the Yorkist family, who repeatedly committed familicide in their pursuit of a nominal hereditary claim. These features have been sanded down in F, or simply excised.

***

If we can detect the modification of Yorkist elements in F, then it is possible to speculate on why such a process was attempted. Part of the answer lies in the context of the succession crisis in the 1590s, which would help to date the possible revision of the play in F to this period. Scholars have drawn attention to the responsiveness of early modern drama to the political tensions occasioned by the expected death of Elizabeth. As Susan Doran and Paulina Kewes have suggested, the succession pamphlets debated and weighted the claims of the various contenders on the global stage.[30] The inherited claim of the House of York was a complex case. Catholic pamphleteers such as Robert Persons discounted the Lancastrian heritage of the descendants of Henry VIII, reminding his readers that the Tudor line was a cadet branch which derived from a legitimized bastard of John of Gaunt and Kathryn Swynford. Their only valid claim was via the House of York, which had been supplanted by the Lancastrians on the accession of Henry IV in 1399.[31] The great-grandchildren of Henry were thereby associated with the Yorkists, the most notable claimant being James VI of Scotland, who was personally identified as such by Persons.[32] The link was taken quite seriously by Elizabeth's council; in the margin of a missive concerning the marriage between Mary, Queen of Scots and Henry, Lord Darnley, there is a short sketch in William Cecil's hand outlining the dynastic link between Mary and Edward IV.[33]

---

[30] For criticism exploring the succession debate in relation to early modern literature, see Paulina Kewes and Susan Doran, eds., *Doubtful and Dangerous: The Question of Succession in Late Elizabethan England* (Manchester, 2014), and Lisa Hopkins, *Drama and the Succession to the Crown, 1561–1633* (Farnham, 2011). Paulina Kewes's new monograph on succession is sure to be a decisive intervention in the field: Paulina Kewes, *This Great Matter of Succession: England's Debate, 1553–1603* (Oxford, in press).

[31] Robert Persons cites an obscure figure named Heighington who argued that the Tudor claim was derived solely from Elizabeth of York, primarily due to the weakness of Henry VII's descent from the issue of Katherine Swynford, third wife to John of Gaunt: Robert Persons, *A conference about the next succession to the crowne of Ingland* (Antwerp, 1595), pp. 7–8.

[32] When Persons is outlining the Yorkist claim through Henry's wife, Elizabeth of York, he states 'I mean as well the line of Scotland': Persons, *Conference*, p. 8.

[33] PRO, State Papers (Dom.), XXXVII, 41, 15 August 1565.

At James's eventual accession in 1603, Elizabeth's funeral contained an elaborate parade of bannerols tracing her own genealogical claim from Lionel, Duke of Clarence, via Anne Mortimer to Edward IV. The banners implied to the gathered mourners, and the court more broadly, that the transference of power from Tudor to Stuart was legitimated by their shared Yorkist – and therefore Plantagenet – heritage.[34] If the original collaborative version of *Henry VI Part 3* was performed in this context, then its Yorkist affiliation was not merely commercial in nature but also political; it may have been possible for an audience member, or a reader of the 1595 octavo copy, to detect a dramatic case being made for a Scottish or indigenous claimant over a Spanish or Portuguese rival.[35] The multiple scenes set in Yorkshire, including Wakefield as well as Towton and York, may well have recalled the seat of Henry Hastings, 3rd Earl of Huntingdon, who presided over the Council of the North.[36] The northern locales may also have evoked James's own Yorkshire heritage through his father, Henry Stuart, Lord Darnley, who was raised in Temple Newsam near Leeds.[37] It may not have been a stretch to elide the cause of the hereditary Yorkist claimants in *The True Tragedy* with their lineal ancestors in the north, particularly the Scottish King across the border.

There are readings in this vein which can only be facilitated by the textual evidence unique to O. In the folio text, several recurring tropes are used to establish a parallel between Richard, Duke of York and Henry after their respective downfalls, one of which is the gesture of sitting down on a 'molehill' (1.4.67; 2.5.14). In O, the word 'molehill' is also used twice, but only in reference to the Duke of York; after the Battle of Wakefield, Margaret forces Richard to sit 'vpon this molehill here' in mockery of his 'high descent' (sig. B1v), and after his murder, a Messenger relates to the Yorkists that Margaret and Clifford 'set him on a molehill there, / And crownd the gratious Duke in high despite' (sig. B4r). The scene is derived from Holinshed in the first instance; the decision to sit Henry on a molehill,

however, is a Shakespearian invention.[38] Holinshed's own use, however, is likely to be influenced by a popular political movement centred on the figure of the Mouldwarp, a zoomorphic prophecy which argued that Henry VIII was the 'mold warpe / cursed of gods mouth / a caytyf / a coward' and was regularly rehearsed in the north of England during the Pilgrimage of Grace and, later, the Rising of the North.[39] The spatial metaphor of a king on a 'molehill' in Yorkshire could well have recalled the Mouldwarp narrative for a readership in the 1590s, particularly one attuned to outbursts of regional discontent in the northern counties. Its use in O solely in reference to Richard, Duke of York, which follows Holinshed more closely than

---

[34] The parade of Yorkist bannerols is included in the following two descriptions of Elizabeth's funeral: Henry Chettle, *Englands mourning garment worne heere by plaine shepheards, in memorie of their sacred mistresse, Elizabeth* (London, 1603), sig. F2v; and Richard Niccols, *Expicedium:. A funeral oration, vpon the death of the late deceased Princesse* (London, 1603), sig. C3v.

[35] For an account of the use of the Lancastrian heritage to fashion continental claims, see Thomas M. McCoog, SJ, 'A view from abroad: continental powers and the Succession', in *Doubtful and Dangerous*, ed. Kewes and Doran, pp. 257–75.

[36] 'Hastings, Henry, 3rd Earl of Huntingdon', by Claire Cross, *Dictionary of National Biography*: https://doi.org/10.1093/ref:odnb/12574 (published online 2004).

[37] 'Stewart, Henry, duke of Albany [Lord Darnley]', by Elaine Finnie Greig, *Dictionary of National Biography*: https://doi.org/10.1093/ref:odnb/26473.

[38] Holinshed states that Richard, Duke of York was 'in derision caused to stand vpon a molehill' after the Yorkist loss at Sandal. There is no corresponding use of the word 'molehill' in relation to Henry VI in either Holinshed or Hall, suggesting this is a Shakespearian invention: Raphael Holinshed, *The first and second volumes of Chronicles* (London, 1587), p. 659.

[39] Holinshed offers an account of the Mouldwarp prophecy derived from Hall, who references it in his own chronicle history. The Mouldwarp narrative appears in Latin in Geoffrey of Monmouth, although it is recreated in English by Ranulf Higden. See Holinshed, *Chronicles*, p. 520; Edward Hall, *The vnion of the two noble and illustre fameties of Lancastre [and] Yorke* (London, 1548), p. 20; and Ranulf Higden, *The Cronycles of Englonde* (London, 1528), p. 48.

F, could not repeat this particular stage action, or battlefield location, to establish a parallel between failed Yorkist and Lancastrian claimants. Rather, it would have suggested a more politically complex situation, whereby the Yorkist pretender is castigated as a mole-king by Lancastrian rivals who, through torture and child-killing, ironically enact the behaviour associated with the Mouldwarp themselves. As Richard, Duke of York is killed by the Lancastrians outside Wakefield, the scene in O would also have potentially evoked a long-standing tradition of anti-Lancastrian feeling in Yorkshire; for example, one insurgent in 1536 used the Mouldwarp Prophecy to describe Henry VIII as a 'red rose' who should have died 'in his mother's womb'.[40] Shakespeare was interested in associating the Mouldwarp narrative with hereditary politics, using it in *1 Henry IV* when Hotspur – or 'Hotspur of the North' (2.5.103) – states that he is angered by tales of 'the moldwarp and the ant, / Of the dreamer Merlin and his prophecies' (3.1.145–6) when helping to consolidate Mortimer's senior claim and rebel against the usurping Lancastrians.[41] The reading copy of O therefore provides the textual material to construct an interpretation which is more politically charged than is possible for the equivalent scene in F.

As the above features demonstrate, *Henry VI Part 3* is the result of an unusually complex process of transmission. The two versions of the play we are able to access today are bound together by their shared descent from a lost work. O is a hybrid text of remnanticity and memorial recall; F is a fairly consistent revision, in which Shakespeare expands his hand in a manner broadly similar to Ben Jonson in *Sejanus*, who revised an original playing script 'wherein a second Pen had good share', albeit Shakespeare preserved aspects of his collaborator's work.[42] When we measure particular lines against each other, we see a subtle and composite reading process at work, in which multiple origins of transmission, such as retainment, reconstruction and revision, each offer an interpretative critique of the original lost play. David McInnis and Matthew Steggle have

drawn attention to the methodological ingenuity required to excavate the playing conditions and dramatic content of early modern plays which have not survived.[43] Features such as memorial recall, when used in conjunction with stable fragments such as detailed stage directions, can show us how aspects of the play in production are likely to have been 'read' by the actors, in order to approximate the original work on the page. Conversely, a series of consistent alterations can allow us to reconstruct the tenor of the primary text via the pattern of dramatic and textual deviations which comprise a revisionary agenda. In the case of the representation of Yorkist politics, we can surmise with a fair degree of confidence that the collaborative play sided with the cause of Richard, Duke of York, and this bias was then subsequently revised to a more impartial position. More broadly, such a process of excavation can shed light on the reading practices used by textual agents when helping to assemble and re-construct composite texts.

---

40 Cited in Ethan H. Shagan, 'Rumours and popular politics in the reign of Henry VIII', in *The Politics of the Excluded, 1500–1850*, ed. Tim Harris (Basingstoke, 2001), pp. 30–66; p. 32.

41 These lines are likely to be influenced by the reference to the Mouldwarp in the poem on Owen Glendower in *Mirror for Magistrates*, when the alliance against Henry IV is being formed. See William Baldwin *et al.*, *A myrroure for magistrates* (London, 1559), p. 29.

42 Ben Jonson, *Sejanus his fall* (London, 1605), sig. A2r. For an excellent account of Shakespeare as a probable reviser of pre-existing plays, see Janet Clare, 'Shakespeare: revising and re-visioning', *Alicante Journal of English Studies* 25 (2012), 19–32.

43 The critical challenge posed by the investigation of lost plays is explored in David McInnis and Matthew Steggle, eds., *Lost Plays in Shakespeare's England* (Basingstoke, 2014). David McInnis develops the study of lost plays in his monograph *Shakespeare and Lost Plays: Reimagining Drama in Early Modern England* (Cambridge, 2021). The *Lost Plays Database* is an invaluable academic resource for the exploration of the culture and context surrounding early modern plays which have not survived: https://lost plays.folger.edu.

Appendix
Lines in *The True Tragedy* and *Henry VI Part 3* Which Appear to Show Either a Softening of a Pro-Yorkist Position or a Strengthening of Henry's Claim in F

1.
Edw.
O – Twas mine inheritance as the kingdome is (sig. A3v)
F – It was my inheritance, as the earldom was (1.1.78)

2.
Hen.
O – Thinkst thou that I will leave my kinglie seate (sig. A4v)
F – Thinkst thou that I will leave my kingly throne (1.1.124)

3.
Hen.
O – Let me but raigne in quiet whilst I live (sig. A5r)
F – Let me for this my lifetime reign as king (1.1.171)

4.
Rich.
O – Henry is none but doth usurpe your right (sig. A7r)
F – Henry had none but did usurp the place (1.2.25)

5.
War.
O – The next degree, is Englands royall king (sig. B6r)
F – The next degree is England's royal throne (2.1.193)

6.
Clif.
O – Didst give consent to disinherit him (sig. B6v)
F – Didst yield consent to disinherit him (2.2.24)

7.
Edw.
O – Now perjure Henrie wilt thou yeelde thy crowne (sig. B7v)
F – Now, perjured Henry, wilt thou kneel for grace (2.2.81)

8.
Rich.
O – to parlie thus with Englands lawfull heires? (sig. B8v)
F – To let thy tongue detect thy base-born heart? (2.2.143)

9.
Edw.
O – and we are grast with wreathes of victorie (sig. C4r)
F – And smooth the frowns of war with peaceful looks (2.6.32)

10.
War.
O – There to be crowned Englands lawfull king (sig. C5r)
F – There to be crowned England's royal king (2.6.88)

11.
Glou.
O – That from his loines no issue might succeed (sig. C8r)
F – that from his loins no hopeful branch may spring (3.2.126)

12.
Lew.
O – to linke with him, that is not lawful heir (sig. D1v)
F – To link with him that is not lawful chosen (3.3.115)

13.
War.
O – And thrust king Henry from his natiue home (sig. D2v)
F – Did I put Henry from his native right? (3.3.190)

HENRY VIII *AND HENRY IX: UNLIVED LIVES AND RE-WRITTEN HISTORIES*

LAURA JAYNE WRIGHT

In 1612, with the sudden death of Henry Frederick, King James I and VI's oldest son and heir, a potential future was cut short. Henry Frederick had been an icon of futurity, a 'champion of Protestant and national interests, promoted in the context of a neo-chivalric revival'.[1] As J. W. Williamson shows in his study of the prince's mythology, 'the quality of Protestant symbology as it applied to Prince Henry was unusually relentless'.[2] He was, to the Scots poets who eulogized his birth, a 'Hercules' who offered a future free from vice.[3] With his death, these hopes were ended. Henry Frederick, who fashioned himself as a far more militant figure than his father, could be mourned only for the battles he might have won.[4] In a letter to Lady Carleton, dated 19 December 1612, Isaac Wake describes Henry's armour being paraded before his mourners, 'every parcel whereof, to his very gauntlet & spurs was carried by men of quality'.[5] His funeral was punctuated by military music: 'Henry's obsequies, which buried him with the trappings of a Protestant warrior-king, were more reflective of what might have been than of what was.'[6] His death created a vacuum which could be filled by imagination, a space for speculative, alternative histories.

In Shakespeare and Fletcher's *Henry VIII, or All is True*, revived in the June of 1613, only six months after Henry Frederick's death, the death of heirs also represents not simply a lack of life, but an unlived potential life.[7] Reading *All is True* in the context of Henry Frederick's death serves to underscore the play's tense negotiation of history as at once repetitive and speculative. In this article, I consider the ways in which both *All is True* and the many elegiac

[1] Jennifer Woodward, *The Theatre of Death: The Ritual Management of Royal Funerals in Renaissance England, 1570–1625* (Woodbridge, 1997), p. 154.

[2] J. W. Williamson, *The Myth of the Conqueror: Prince Henry Stuart, a Study of 17th Century Personation* (New York, 1978), p. 1. See also James M. Sutton, 'Henry Frederick, Prince of Wales (1594–1612)', ODNB, 3 January 2008: https://ezproxy-prd.bodleian.ox.ac.uk:2362/view/10.1093/ref:odnb/9780198614128.001.0001/odnb-9780198614128-e-12961.

[3] Williamson, *Myth*, pp. 2–8.

[4] See James I, *The Peace-Maker, or Great Brittaines Blessing* (London, 1618), in which James shows 'the Idlenesse of a Quarrelling Reputation' (sig. A2r). For further discussion, see David R. Lawrence, *The Complete Soldier: Military Books and Military Culture in Early Stuart England, 1603–1645* (Leiden, 2009), pp. 105–26.

[5] Isaac Wake to Lady Carleton, 19 December 1612, The National Archives, SP 14/71, fol. 130r.

[6] Elizabeth Goldring, '"So iust a sorrowe so well expressed": Henry, Prince of Wales and the art of commemoration', in *Prince Henry Revived: Image and Exemplarity in Early Modern England*, ed. Timothy Wilks (London, 2007), pp. 280–300; p. 285. See also K. Dawn Grapes, *With Mornefull Musique: Funeral Elegies in Early Modern England* (Woodbridge, 2018), pp. 121–2, for a discussion of martial imagery in musical elegies for the Prince.

[7] Martin Wiggins proposes that the play was written in 1612 and revived in the summer of 1613: '*All is True* is more likely to date from earlier in 1612 rather than later. One possible counter-argument arises from the play's absence from the list of titles performed at court during the 1612–13 Revels season. However, this is not in itself evidence that it had not yet been written: it would have been tactless to offer a play about a royal Henry, with a climax showing the establishment of a Protestant succession, immediately after the death of Prince Henry. The play may even have been temporarily withdrawn from the repertory for that reason': Martin Wiggins with Catherine Richardson, eds., *British Drama, 1533–1642*, vol. 6: *1609–1616* (Oxford, 2016), p. 231.

responses to the death of Henry Frederick reveal that the process of imagining the future is ultimately caught in the past. Neurologists have shown that when we imagine what might happen next, we do so by looking backwards: 'the simulation of future episodes is thought to require a system that can flexibly recombine details from past events'.[8] Our lives become exemplars on which we model likely outcomes. This cognitive process is known as FMTT, Future-Oriented Mental Time Travel.[9] In this article, I show that a consciousness of FMTT's insistence on memory is integral to understanding constructions of the future in *All is True* and in responses to the loss of Henry Frederick. In FMTT, the neurotypical brain uses the past in a way that is, at once, conservative and permissive. It is permissive in that the thinker chooses, even unconsciously, memories from which to fashion an imagined future (a selective and episodic approach shared by *All is True*). It is conservative in that, whichever moments the thinker invests with significance, any conception of the future remains indebted to what has come before. Thoughts of tomorrow are, to borrow a line from Fitzgerald, 'boats against the current, borne back ceaselessly into the past'.[10]

All is True ends with a prophecy, but the play resists the idea that any prediction of the future can be given weight unless it pays close attention to the evidence of the past. Cranmer's prophecy, which ends *All is True*, imagines Elizabeth's future reign (and the reign of her heir, James I) without mention of her sister, the future Mary I, who has already been born.[11] This is, as Brian Walsh has put it, 'wishful thinking'.[12] In selecting from the past episodically, Cranmer slips, problematically, into FMTT – into mental time travel, rather than into divine or oracular prophecy. The two should be distinct: unlike FMTT, which offers evidence-based speculation, prophecy offers a seemingly fixed account of the future, based on divine or supernatural information and not on the evidence of the past. Yet Shakespeare rarely allows prophecy such undisputed authority over the future, especially when historical figures predict the future only with the vatic accuracy of

hindsight. An oracle is often simply a man whose conception of the future most closely aligns with the King's, as exposed in Richard III's description of Buckingham as 'my counsel's consistory / My oracle, my prophet … !' (*Richard III*, 2.2.12). In *Richard II* (1595), when the Bishop of Carlisle imagines Bolingbroke's reign, he offers, 'let me prophesy' (4.1.127). Carlisle projects the damage done onto 'future ages' (129), onto every 'child, child's children' (140). Cranmer too invokes 'Our children's children' (*All is True*, 5.4.54), but where Carlisle offers to 'prophesy', Cranmer does not. Although he begins with a claim of divine favour – 'For heaven now bids me' (5.4.15) – Cranmer goes on to insist: 'the words I utter / Let none think flattery' (5.4.15–16). To raise the possibility of flattery at all is to sweep aside any thought of inspired prophecy.

All is True does not allow the safety of a determined future promised by prophecy: the play's only explicit mention of prophecy is to deride the predictions of the monk Nicholas Hopkins.[13] Henry VIII deems Cranmer an 'oracle of comfort' (5.4.66), but audiences have heard this description once before. Wolsey describes Cranmer as a heretic who 'Hath crawled into the favour of the King, / And is

---

[8] Daniel L. Schacter, Donna Rose Addis and Randy L. Buckner, 'Remembering the past to imagine the future: the prospective brain', *Nature Reviews Neuroscience* 8 (2007), 659.

[9] For more on this terminology, see Kourken Michaelian, Stanley B. Klein and Karl K. Szpunar, eds., *Seeing the Future: Theoretical Perspectives on Future-Oriented Mental Time Travel* (Oxford, 2016).

[10] F. Scott Fitzgerald, *The Great Gatsby*, ed. Matthew J. Bruccoli (Cambridge, 1991), p. 141.

[11] For an alternative reading of this line and of prophecy in *All is True*, see Daniel L. Keegan, 'Performing prophecy: more life on the Shakespearean scene', *Shakespeare Quarterly* 62 (2011), 420–43.

[12] Brian Walsh, *Unsettled Toleration: Religious Difference on the Shakespearean Stage* (Oxford, 2016), p. 157.

[13] Nicholas Hopkins, a supporter and confidant of Buckingham, is said to have predicted that Buckingham would succeed Henry VIII and 'fed him every minute / With words of sovereignty' (1.2.150–1). See Raphael Holinshed, *The firste volume of the Chronicles of England, Scotlande, and Irelande* (London, 1577), p. 1514.

his oracle' (3.2.104–5). These are not oracular words: these are Cranmer's best guesses, easily (dis)proved by an audience of witnesses for whom Elizabeth's reign is now history. Those hearing that prophecy at the Globe in 1613, as Hester Lees-Jeffries puts it, 'hea[r] their own memories foretold, and perhaps rewritten in the process'.[14]

Althoug Lees-Jeffries uses 'rewritten' in the sense of revising, I want to consider a secondary meaning: that of 're-writing'. In this article, I will propose that allusion itself serves to replicate the cognitive process of FMTT. The insistent repetition and re-writing in *All is True* and in Henry Frederick's elegies mirrors FMTT's need to look backwards in order to look forwards.[15] Even the play's most obviously future-oriented moment of prophecy is dependent on allusion (just as Cranmer's speech seems a recycling of Carlisle's). In reading *All is True*, I therefore consider repeated imagery (such as the phoenix), as well as the influence of Samuel Rowley, Edmund Spenser and Virgil. I also propose that, in *All is True*, Shakespeare recycles motifs from *The Winter's Tale*, creating an echo chamber of grief between the plays. Finally, I will suggest that this desire to re-write lingers in contemporary responses to Henry Frederick and to Shakespeare. The past provides raw materials with which to construct what might happen next. Yet to fashion new material out of old is to make history an unescapable cycle, one which bears us backwards ceaselessly.

THE PHOENIX: RECYCLING EMBLEMS

The death of Henry Frederick was met with widespread displays of mourning, not only of his loss but of his lost potential. The Prince had lived under a cloud of promise and prophecy. In *A briefe view of the state of the Church of England* (1653), written for the education of Henry Frederick, John Harington claimed to have been inspired by the proverb, 'Henry the eighth pull'd down Monks and their Cells. / Henry the ninth should pull down Bishops, and their Bells.'[16] Henry Frederick is at once fashioned by memories of the past – here Henry VIII and the Reformation – and by an imagined future, a life as Henry IX that he did not in fact live. The sermon written by Henry Frederick's personal chaplain, Daniel Price, on the anniversary of his death, reveals a similar tension between these retrospective and predictive gazes: 'for in HIM, a *glimmering light* of the *Golden* times appeared, all *lines* of expectation met in this *Center*, all *spirits* of vertue, *scattered* into others were *extracted* into him'.[17] Henry is the lens through which the beams of a former golden age are refracted into light-lines of future expectations. Henry is also a lens through which literary allusions and commonplaces are refracted, in the fashioning of both his life and his death.

This repetitive fashioning is typical of literary responses to the death of the Prince. We see as much in Joshua Sylvester's collection of elegies, *Lachrimae lachrimarum* (1612), printed with an ink-stained black frontispiece, and skeletons in its margins. That ink, the text's own mourning clothes, is transferred to the fingertips, offering an insistent and material trace of grief.[18] Yet, despite its lingering ink,

---

[14] Hester Lees-Jeffries, *Shakespeare and Memory* (Oxford, 2013), p. 89. See also Gordon McMullan, who argues that, in *All is True*, 'the political prophecy is carefully updated, and is both legitimized and problematized by its incorporation into a history play, enabling the audience to verify the events which have already taken place and thus presume the accuracy of those which have not': William Shakespeare and John Fletcher, *King Henry VIII (All is True)*, ed. Gordon McMullan (London, 2000), 5.4.14–62 LN, pp. 438–9.

[15] Helen Cooper has compared romance's tropes or motifs with memes – 'a unit within literature that proves so useful, so infectious, that it begins to take on a life of its own': Helen Cooper, *The English Romance in Time: Transforming Motifs from Geoffrey of Monmouth to the Death of Shakespeare* (Oxford, 2004), p. 3.

[16] John Harington, *A briefe view of the state of the Church of England* (London, 1653), sig. A1r. See also Marcus K. Harmes, *Bishops and Power in Early Modern England* (London, 2013), p. 30.

[17] Daniel Price, *Prince Henry his First Anniversary* (Oxford, 1613), sig. A2v.

[18] Kim F. Hall has written of a binary between skin (presumed to be white) and black ink in the period: 'For example, Cleveland's "A Fair Nymph Scorning a Black Boy courting her" takes up, in order: smoke, night, eclipse, visors, checkers, ink, and mourning. . . . all are evoked either to surmount or reinforce the difference of black and white': Kim F. Hall, *Things of Darkness: Economies of Race and Gender in Early Modern England* (London, 1995), p. 119.

the primary loss depicted is a loss of futurity. In *Lachrimae lachrimarum*, Walter Quinn writes epitaphs in four languages, which are certain of what would have been Henry's success. In English, he is the 'hope of many Kingdoms'; in Latin, 'Patriae spes' ('the hope of the nation'); in French, 'la fleur de son age, Et de nostre esperance' ('the flower of our age and of our hope'); in Italian, 'Prencipi . . . delle nostre speranze' ('the Prince of our hopes'). For Sylvester, the death of the individual and the loss of a universal imagined future are elided in a poem which slips parenthetically between present mourning and future hope:

> . . . Prince's losse (our Expectations wrack)
> Our Places, Graces, Profits, Pensions lost,
> Our present Fortunes cast, our future crost) [sic].[19]

This sense of future, like the stray bracket printed here, is muddled by a retrospective use of the past. The 'present' fortune fails; the future falls into the past tense, suddenly 'crost'.

This is not the only moment at which Sylvester looks backwards as well as forwards. Sylvester draws associations between Henry Stuart and Edward VI, another Protestant royal who died young, and here called 'Henry's Pre-cedent'.[20] Edward's death led – if his sister Mary I's reign is tactfully forgotten – to the ascension of Elizabeth I. Henry's death might therefore also be refashioned as a necessary evil to allow for the rise of his siblings. Sylvester transplants Elizabeth Stuart into Henry's role: 'Loue shall render HER her Brother, / And make Her soon a happie Princes Mother.'[21] Elizabeth is both rendered her brother – made the new hope of the nation – and can render new 'brothers', new 'happie Princes', through child-birth. Her marriage offers fecundity and promise to neutralize the despair of Henry's death.[22]

Shakespeare and Fletcher's conclusion of the Henrician myth with Elizabeth I (and not Edward VI, as in Samuel Rowley's *When You See Me, You Know Me* (1605)) can be read alongside the wide-spread attempt to repurpose Elizabeth Stuart as the hope of the nation. Elizabeth I is also described as both heir and progenitor. Cranmer speaks of her regeneration in the manner of a phoenix: 'Her ashes new create another heir' (5.4.41). Fletcher, who is thought to have written this scene, uses

a commonplace image, employed, for instance, by Rowley in *When You See Me, You Know Me*. When Jane Seymour gives birth to her son, Edward VI, it is as 'One Phenix dying, giues another life.'[23] Emblematically, the phoenix stood for personal futurity but Elizabeth's own fame is not the purpose of the phoenix's regeneration.[24] In Cranmer's speech, the Book of Common Prayer (which the historical Cranmer revised) is inverted. Ash is a marker of death and of rebirth; the body is committed, 'asshes to asshes . . . in sure and certaine hope of resurreccion to eternall lyfe'.[25] Yet, for

[19] Joshua Sylvester, *Lachrimae lachrimarum, or The Distillation of Tears Shede for the Untymely Death of the Incomparable Prince Panaretus* (London, 1612), sig. C1r, C2r, D1r, D3r, B4r.

[20] Sylvester, *Lachrimae*, sig. B2r.

[21] Sylvester, *Lachrimae*, sig. B3r.

[22] Foakes proposed the performance of *All is True* might have been prepared by early 1613, in time for the marriage of Princess Elizabeth on 14 February: *King Henry VIII*, ed. R. A. Foakes (London, 1957), p. xxix.

[23] Samuel Rowley, *When You See Me, You Know Me* (London, 1605), sig. B3v (further references in parentheses in the text). See, amongst many others, a political connection between resurrection and phoenixes in: Henry Raymonde, *The Maiden Queene* (1607), STC2 20778; James Maxwell, *The Laudable Life and Deplorable Death, of our Late Peerlesse Prince Henry* (1612), STC2 17701; Robert Allyne, *Funerall Elegies Upon the Most Lamentable and Untimely Death of the Thrice Illustrious Prince Henry* (1613), STC2 384; and Robert Naile, *A Relation of the Royall Magnificent, and Sumptuous Entertainment, given to the High, and Mighty Princesse, Queen Anne* (1613), STC2 18347. Though such a connection could never have been intended, we also see the image in connection with the rebuilding of the Globe following the fire caused during a performance of *All is True*: 'And I haue seene the Globe burnt, and quickly made a Phoenix' – Henry Farley, *The complaint of Paules* (London, 1616), sig. A3r.

[24] The phoenix is used as an emblem in Henry Peacham's *Minerva Britanna* (1612). Here, the phoenix is associated with the 'coelebs' or bachelor, Robert Cecil, whose phoenix-life will burn to produce not a child, but immortal fame: Henry Peacham, *Minerua Britanna or A garden of heroical deuises furnished, and adorned with emblemes and impresa's of sundry natures, newly devised, moralized, and published* (London, 1612), sig. E1r.

[25] *The booke of the common prayer and administracion of the sacramentes, and other rites and ceremonies of the church* (London, 1549), sig. T6v.

Cranmer, ash promises a political, not spiritual, regeneration. The Virgin Queen must turn to dust in order to give due space to a Stuart king.

The potentiality of the phoenix as symbol of succession is also played out in Jacobean mourning verse. Just as FMTT requires the need to look backwards to look ahead, mourning literature for royal children must weight its expression of grief against a need to look to the living heir. In his *Obsequies*, elegies written in 1612, George Wither gives both Prince Henry and his father King James a shared pair of metaphors: 'Thy Father both a Sunne, and *Phoenix* is, / Prince *Henry* was a Sunne and *Phoenix* too.' The cycle of history continues: each heir is both son and phoenix, taking their place in history. The sonnet itself is addressed to Henry's younger brother, Charles, who 'now dost thou to be a *Phoenix* trye'.[26] Charles is not, however, given the final words of praise: Wither's *Obsequies* stage a dialogue between the ghost of Prince Henry and the figure of Great Britain, keeping Henry's memory alive, even while ceding space to Charles. In his second anniversary sermon, Price also looks forwards and backwards, addressing Charles as the new hope of the nation and wishing 'vnto him the doubled spirit of his now blessed and immortall brother'.[27] In 'doubled', Price both suggests that Charles will be twice the prince his brother was and hints at the double-vision of history: Charles's reign runs parallel to Henry's imagined life.

Lee Bliss has argued that the final scene of *All is True* serves to 'explode the play's framework to create a world where humanity's endless, profitless cycle of rise and fall can be translated into the more miraculous image of the death and rebirth of "the maiden phoenix"'.[28] This is to give too much hope to the phoenix, which does not offer any miraculous regeneration, but rather a repetition or re-writing of the same 'profitless cycle' that has come before. The continual 're-writing' of this literary topos not only by Shakespeare and Fletcher but across verse written for both Elizabeth I and Prince Henry Stuart creates an uncanny echo from one royal death to another, until each seems not distinct loss, but merely an inevitable link in a long chain. Audiences too are caught in a cycle of constant allusion, of playwrights remembering phrases and images from their own reading and employing those ideas in their creation of something new.

ALLUSIVE HISTORY

The phoenix emblem is just one 're-written' image through which the process of reading looks insistently backwards. There is something inherently paradoxical about imagining the future by turning backwards to older texts, yet the future-oriented mental time travel in both the elegies for the death of Prince Henry and the christening of Elizabeth I in *All is True* take their place in a classical tradition of predictions. Although it has not yet been acknowledged, the representation of Prince Henry's imagined future owes much to propaganda in both the *Eclogues* and the *Aeneid*, which was deeply familiar to political writers of the seventeenth century.[29] Here, Virgil writes of the broken promise of the Augustan age, an age marred, as James I/VI's was, by the sudden loss of Augustus' supposed heir, Marcellus. The epic's great patriarch, Anchises, predicts the death of Marcellus uncountable generations before it occurred, offering a model of 'present-prophecy' which promises the death of the teenager that was, in 23 BC, a present reality:

O son, thy peoples huge lamented losse séeke not to knowe.
The destinies shall this child, onto the world, no more but showe, . . .

---

[26] George Wither, *Prince Henries Obsequies or Mournefull Elegies Vpon His Death: Vvith a Supposed Inter-locution Betweene the Ghost of Prince Henrie and Great Brittaine* (London, 1612), sig. B2r.

[27] Daniel Price, *Prince Henry His Second Anniversary* (Oxford, 1614), sig. F2v.

[28] Lee Bliss, 'The Wheel of Fortune and the maiden phoenix of Shakespeare's "King Henry the Eighth"', *ELH: A Journal of English Literary History* 42 (1975), 1–25; p. 23.

[29] John H. Betts proposed at least an indirect use of Virgil's *Georgics* in *Henry V*: John H. Betts, 'Classical allusions in Shakespeare's *Henry V* with special reference to Virgil', *Greece and Rome* 15 (1968), 147–63.

What wailings loude of men in stretes, in féeldes, what
mourning cries
In mighty campe of *Mars*, at this mans death in *Rome* shall
rise?[30]

Marcellus and Prince Henry, heirs apparent, were
both praised for martial acts not yet performed,
both mourned in the subjunctive for futures not
achieved. Henry's association with Marcellus was
itself in turn recycled, even well into the next
century. In *The Life of Henry, Prince of Wales*
(1760), the historian Thomas Birch compares
Henry with Marcellus and then, in turn, offers
Henry as a model for the future George III, who
must live through 'the revival of his example'.
Birch's work offers three perspectives on the life
of Henry Frederick: 'The character of the illustrious Prince, who is the subject of these memoirs;
the vast expectations conceived of him in his own
time, equal to those formed of Marcellus and
Germanicus by the Roman people; and the universal admiration of him transmitted to the present
age by the concurrent testimony of all the writers of
the last'.[31] In an insistence that the future is shaped
by the evidence of the past, Birch urges Prince
George in turn to model his own actions on
Henry's. This reflexive use of the past maps with
ease onto FMTT, which sees memory as 'a tool
used by the prospective brain to generate simula-
tions of possible future events'.[32] There is a cycle of
self-fashioning: each ruler attempts to follow the
precedent of past rulers. As Birch would put it, the
present age is dependent on the 'testimony' of past
writers, both early modern and classical: to look
ahead is to look backwards.

Beyond Anchises' 'present-prophecy', there is
another Virgilian echo in Cranmer's speech. Virgil's
fourth Eclogue, commonly known as the Messianic
Ode, is written in praise of a child. Virgil left the child
unnamed, 'spur[ring] the curiosity of his readers and
commentators', including Constantine and
Augustine, who both read the child as Christ.[33]
Virgil's prophecy was a familiar allusion in the political poetry of early modern England, having been
adapted by Spenser in *The Shepheardes Calender*
(1579), in his own fourth eclogue, 'Aprill', written

in praise of Queen Elizabeth. Like Cranmer, Spenser
imagines the life of the Queen and projects his mind
forward into the future, and, ultimately, to her inevitable death:

> She shalbe a grace,
> To fyll the fourth place,
> And reigne with the rest in heaven.[34]

> Would I had known no more. But she must die –
> She must, the saints must have her – yet a virgin,
> A most unspotted lily shall she pass
> To th' ground, and all the world shall mourn her.
> *(All is True, 5.4.59–62)*

In Spenser, as in *All is True*, the pagan Messianic
Ode must be adapted: classical graces become
saints, and the praise is not for a boy, but
a woman who will precede a boy. Spenser transforms the impossibly fertile land of Virgil's eclogue,
where oak trees pour with honey, into the red and
white roses of Lancaster and York.[35] In *All is True*,
the golden age offers new crops again: corn and
vines.[36] Cranmer promises that 'In her days, every
man shall eat in safety / Under his own vine what

---

[30] *The whole xii. bookes of the Æneidos of Virgill* (STC (2nd edn)
24801), trans. Thomas Phaer and Thomas Tyne (London,
1573), sig. S2r. Sheldon Brammall makes the case that 'The
complete translation of the *Aeneid* by Thomas Phaer and
Thomas Twyne has every reason to be considered the central
English Renaissance *Aeneid*. Other translations in the period
include Stanyhurst's (1582), Harington's (1604) and Wroth's
(1620)': Sheldon Brammall, *The English Aeneid: Translations of
Virgil, 1555–1646* (Edinburgh, 2015), p. 19.

[31] Thomas Birch, *The Life of Henry, Prince of Wales* (London,
1760), sig. A3v, A5r.

[32] Daniel L. Schacter, Donna Rose Addis and Randy L. Buckner,
'Remembering the past to imagine the future: the prospective
brain', *Nature Reviews Neuroscience* 8 (2007), 657–61; p. 660.

[33] Sabine MacCormack, *The Shadows of Poetry: Vergil in the
Mind of Augustine* (Berkeley, 1998), p. 23.

[34] Edmund Spenser, *The Shepheardes Calender* (London, 1579), sig.
D1v.

[35] Spenser, *Calender*, sig. D3r.

[36] '[M]olli paulatim flauescet campus arista / incultisque rubens
pendebit sentibus uua / et durae quercus sudabunt roscida
mella' ('slowly will the plains yellow with the waving corn,
on wild brambles the purple grape will hang, and the stub-
born oak distil dewy honey'): Eclogue IV.28–30, in *P. Vergili
Maronis: Opera*, ed. R. A. B. Mynors (Oxford, 1969).

he plants' (5.4.33–4). McMullan notes that this Old Testament verse (Micah 4.4) is used in Daniel Price's *Lamentations for the Death of the Late Illustrious Prince Henry*, and argues that such verses were also 'repeatedly associated with James I'.[37] Even the imagery used to describe Elizabeth in *All is True* is prescient of a Stuart future. The verses associated with James I are pulled backwards, onto Elizabeth. No monarch is unique in the imagery applied to them.

Cranmer's prophecy is not the only moment at which *All is True* proves slippery in its appropriation of both classical and Elizabethan tropes. The ritual Spenser imagines for Elizabeth finds an uncanny echo in the lengthy stage direction which accompanies the angelic visitation of Katherine of Aragon. In 'Aprill', the Muses bring 'Bay braunches, which they doe beare, / All for *Elisa* in her hand to weare?', the Graces 'dauncen deffly' around her, and the Nymph Cloris crowns Elizabeth with olive garlands.[38] In *All is True*, Katherine dreams of 'six personages clad in white robes, wearing on their heads garlands of bays, and golden visors on their faces. They carry branches of bays or palm in their hands. They first congé unto Katherine, then dance; and, at certain changes, the first two hold a spare garland over her head' (4.2.82, s.d.). Katherine, the Catholic Queen, not Elizabeth the Protestant Princess, is given this divine blessing. The vision, with its resonance of Spenser, himself an ardently Protestant poet, offers divine support, even if only in Katherine's wishful thinking, 'whilst I sit meditating / On that celestial harmony I go to' (4.2.79–80). This lengthy dance of golden-masked spirits precedes Cranmer's prophecy. His certainty that Elizabeth will rest amongst the saints sounds hollow in its wake.

Formally, this repetition of images has its own cyclical effect. The phoenix, the political-messianic prophecy, the pastoral and agrarian bliss, the garlands of bay, used for Henry Stuart, and used for Elizabeth, and used for the dying Katherine of Aragon, have the effect of semantic satiation.[39] This collection of images, from the phoenix and its ashes to a Virgilian 'hope of the nation' topos, articulates hopes for the role of future heirs, if not

its reality. Cumulatively, unbroken ranks of Elizabethan and Stuart writers, all turning to the same commonplaces, create a sense of similitude: this is 'the concurrent testimony of all the writers of the last [age]', as Birch would put it. Recycling these images creates a sense of inevitability. Princes are simply sequels waiting to be written, children who serve as understudies for their fathers.

'REMEMBER MINE'

The repetitive imagery of *All is True* is further complicated by the theatrical legacy that Shakespeare and Fletcher inherited. Rowley's *When You See Me, You Know Me*, a play about the life of Henry VIII, had been performed in 1606, and had foregrounded Edward VI as the heir to the Tudor throne. Its performance by the Prince of Wales's Company strengthened the text's already evident connections between the Protestant princes, Edward Tudor and Henry Stuart (Rowley's Henry VIII imagines the child of Jane Seymour will be 'a ninth Henrie to the English Crowne': B1r).[40] Yet *When You See Me* is not the only play about princehood and prophecy

---

37 McMullan, ed., *Henry VIII*, 5.4, nn. 33–5. McMullan examples include: Thomas Adams, in *The Gallant's Burden*, who 'suggests that "[o]ur feare of warre is lesse then theirs [because] Wee sitte vnder our owne Figge-trees, and eate the fruites of our owne Vineyards" (D2r)'; and Daniel Price, who in *Lamentations*, 'addresses Prince Henry's courtiers, who "liued vnder the Branches of our *Princely Cedar* . . . : you onely returne to your owne *Families* to drinke of your owne *Vines*, and to eate vnder your owne *Figge-trees*" (E3r)'. McMullan also notes that Fletcher parodies the lines in *Beggars' Bush*.
38 Spenser, *Calender*, sig. D1r–v.
39 To this list might also be added the image of the 'ruined city', as discussed in Adrian Streete, 'Elegy, prophecy, and politics: literary responses to the death of Prince Henry Stuart, 1612–1614', *Renaissance Studies* 31 (2017), 87–106.
40 Mark H. Lawhorn proposes that the play was written with its royal patron in mind: Mark H. Lawhorn, 'Taking pains for the Prince: age, patronage, and penal surrogacy, in Samuel Rowley's *When You See Me, You Know Me*', in *The Premodern Teenager: Youth in Society 1150–1650*, ed. Konrad Eisenbichler (Toronto, 2002), pp. 131–50; p. 132. See also Mark Rankin , 'Henry VIII, Shakespeare, and the Jacobean royal court', *Studies in English Literature, 1500–1900* 51 (2011), 349–66.

which *All is True* recalls. *All is True*'s repetition is further compounded by its echoing of the death of Mamillius in *The Winter's Tale* (1611), revived at court for the Christmas season of 1612 and so, like *All is True*, performed amidst national grief for the loss of Henry Stuart.[41] In both Rowley's *When You See Me* and in *Winter's Tale*, the connection between prophecy and the loss (or risk of loss) of royal lineage that is played out at the end of *All is True* is also evident.

When Shakespeare and Fletcher's Henry VIII speaks of his miscarried, stillborn or dead male children, he speaks not of individual losses – there are no numbers or names here – but of lost potential. For Henry, children either represent the past – 'a judgement on me' (2.4.191) for his own ill deeds – or the future, as a promise of his legacy.[42] In *When You See Me, You Know Me*, Henry VIII is compelled to choose between the life of his wife (Jane Seymour) or the foetus she is carrying (the future Edward VI). Like the Henry represented in *All is True*, Rowley's Henry also considers the loss of a foetus to be divinely ordained, although here he assumes the loss to represent divine favour, not punishment. Rowley's Henry speculates that:

Perhaps [God] did mould forth a Sonne for me,
And seeing (that sees all) in his creation,
To be some impotent and coward spirit,
Vnlike the figure of his Royall Father:
. . . Ile thanke the Heavens for taking such a Sonne.

(B2v)

This is not a Henry wracked with guilt, terrified of divine punishment; this is a king secure in the knowledge that, if he were to father a weak child, God would intervene. However, the child lives, and is a son, and so Henry must, yet again, change tone. History is shifting, moment by moment.

A final prophetic role is given to Jane's father, who, like Cranmer, imagines the life of an heir. Seymour offers hope of a 'gallant Prince' (B3r), and Henry commands, 'Be thou a Prophet *Seymer* in thy words' (B3v). Like Cranmer, these men predict and shape their legacy, interpreting God's will in self-serving exegeses. Henry VIII was, moments earlier, far less confident in his hopes of a gallant

prince. Seymour is no more plausible an oracle than Cranmer, but his words suit Henry's desires. Shakespeare and Fletcher's Henry also accepts Cranmer's oracle with ease – and, indeed, he forces the play towards a sharp conclusion before the promised future can be subject to any debate. Henry attempts to end the play with a simple summation:

> This day, no man think
> He's business at his house, for all shall stay –
> This little one shall make it holiday.

(5.4.74–6)

Henry tries to bring the play to a close, but he is refused the last word; the epilogue lingers, a postscript which unravels his neat couplet by sowing doubts. This narrative does not co-operate with those who try to shape it from within: history will not be so easily re-written.

This is not the only moment at which Henry's idea of the future does not fit neatly onto what audiences know of the past. The palpable absence of Anne Boleyn at the christening serves only to remind us that, within months, another of Henry's wives will die. Henry also writes Mary out of his history play, with the claim that 'Never before / This happy child, [Elizabeth] did I get anything' (5.4.64–5). This linguistic sleight of hand runs through the play. Elizabeth is always a 'child', a term which in its neutrality avoids reference to Henry's desired male heir. Katherine alone describes a child of Henry's as a 'daughter' (4.2.133). Katherine resists her husband's history when she insists she has 'been blessed / With many children by you' (2.4.34–5).[43] Although *All is True* turns the historical Katherine of Aragon's

---

[41] Wiggins with Richardson, *1609–1616*, p. 118.

[42] Olga L. Valbuena, *Subjects to the King's Divorce: Equivocation, Infidelity, and Resistance in Early Modern England* (Indiana, 2003), pp. 10–11.

[43] I'd like to thank the cast of Creation Theatre's *Henry VIII, or All is True* (2020), and especially Funlola Olufunwa (Queen Katherine) and Rhodri Lewis (King Henry) with whom I had several productive conversations about Katherine and Henry's differing descriptions of their lost children during our rehearsals. Their performances can be viewed at www.youtube.com/watch?v=BFMh1jzzB9w.

speech nearly verbatim into verse, the play's Katherine does not add the qualifier found in records of her trial: 'by me ye have had divers children, although it had pleased God to call them out of this world, which hath been no default in me'.[44] This is no phoenix-view of history: there is no easy sense that one heir replaces another. Katherine resists futurity in order to keep the present memory of her stillborn children alive.

In this trial scene – the trial itself marking a moment in which the evidence of the past is retrospectively analysed – *All is True* echoes *The Winter's Tale*. At Hermione's trial, Leontes ignores the oracular evidence he is given and disowns his daughter. Where Cranmer's oracular speech offers life, the oracle of *The Winter's Tale* brings death. Its words have not long been reported before Mamillius dies. Henry and Leontes (and Rowley's own Henry VIII) are, however, alike in their reaction to prophecy, using oracles to confirm what they already believed. On hearing the oracle, Leontes breaks up his court. On hearing Cranmer's speech, Henry ends the christening (and, with it, the play) at once, allowing no opportunity for debate. Henry becomes a negative image of Leontes, at once an echo and a foil. At the end of *Winter's Tale*, Leontes wishes to look backwards, to have answers as to what has been 'Performed in this wide gap of time since first / We were disseuered' (5.3.155–6). Henry VIII, however, does not look backwards. Slipping into FMTT at the end of the play, Henry thinks of the future, but not by imagining the life of his daughter. Henry can only conceive of a future if he is part of the narrative: he imagines himself in heaven (as so many in *All is True* do) but not at last at peace.[45] Henry imagines watching his own legacy play out:

> This oracle of comfort has so pleased me
> That when I am in heaven I shall desire
> To see what this child does, and praise my maker.
>
> (5.4.66–8)

Henry fashions himself as the audience of the future, watching history play out, as we do when we watch *All is True*. He will see Elizabeth but he will also (the audience assumes) see the reigns of Mary and Edward, proving Cranmer's oracle

tainted by lies of omission. More than this, he will exist beyond the play's conclusion. Henry cannot imagine a future which does not remember him. *All is True* does not allow for a future which is not dependent on and trapped by the past.

BLANK PAGES, GHOST IMAGES

Henry VIII's imagined future makes space for his own legacy but leaves none for the pieces of history that do not suit his narrative. The ending of *All is True* is marked by the absence of Mary I and Edward VI. Though the role of Edward VI is left blank, his absence leaves a mark, not unlike ink stains left behind by *Lachrimae lachrimarum*. More ghostly still is Mary, an unstaged 'ghost character' who has no place in Henry VIII's desired history.[46] The absence of expected history creates a space for imaginative response. Here, I follow Chloe Porter in reading 'incompleteness as a functional part of cultural production in sixteenth- and seventeenth-century England', and Emma Smith in her articulation of the 'sheer and permissive gapiness' of Shakespeare's drama.[47] The play gives space for a split vision of history, for a historical narrative flanked by 'permissive' alternative narratives. These alternative narratives are, as I will show, only complicated by the play's absence of bodies and prevalence of books. Jeffrey Todd Knight has written of 'ghost images' in early printed books, an 'almost imperceptible darkening of the paper' as

---

44 George Cavendish, 'The life and death of Cardinal Wolsey', in *Two Early Tudor Lives: The Life and Death of Cardinal Wolsey*, ed. Richard S. Sylvester and Davis P. Harding (New Haven, 1962), pp. 1–194; p. 84.

45 See Buckingham who prays, 'lift my soul to heaven' (2.1.79); Wolsey, whose 'hopes in heaven do dwell' (3.2.460); and Katherine, who meditates on 'that celestial harmony I go to' (4.2.80).

46 For more on Shakespeare's ghost characters, see Kristian Smidt, 'Shakespeare's absent characters', *English Studies* 61 (1980), 397–407.

47 Chloe Porter, *Making and Unmaking in Early Modern English Drama: Spectators, Aesthetics and Incompletion* (Manchester, 2013), p. 99; Emma Smith, *This is Shakespeare* (London, 2019), p. 2.

ink is transferred from one page to another while both are drying, one on top of another, in the printing house.[48] We might think back to Price's description of Prince Charles, living under the ghostly image of Henry Frederick. We might also think of Constance's imaginative mourning in *King John*: 'Grief fills the room up of my absent child' (3.4.93). Shakespeare's histories are full of ghost images, each page covered with the suggestion of another story.

In both *All is True* and *Winter's Tale*, the loss of the imagined future of a child is marked not by the staging of death, but by a show of absence, a blank space. Mamillius dies off stage and Katherine's children either die before the play's action, or, like Mary, are never brought on stage. A corpse is a stage property which fractures past and future: between the life that was and the loss that will be made real, once the body itself is gone. It is, Sophie Duncan has argued, a disruptive prop 'both because the actor-as-corpse is not "dead" and because the man-made corpse was never alive'.[49] This liminality plays out in records of Henry Frederick's funeral, at which death was made insistently present when an effigy of the prince was paraded along the route.[50] The effigy offered the public one last look at a body suspended between past and future, life and death. To stage the death of a child without staging a body is therefore to evade even this disruption of time: there is no definite before and after. By denying his audience a corpse, Shakespeare denies death its presence, and its existence in the present. Audiences are left with a ghost image, an absence which begs them to imagine the alternative reality of the off-stage world.

Instead of bodies, we are offered books as records of what has come before. Mamillius is plausibly Leontes's son because his nose is 'a copy out of mine' (1.2.124); Perdita is called 'the whole matter / And copy of the father' (2.3.99–100). The heir is a copy, a textual replica of their father's narrative. Prince Henry too was conceptualized as a text almost immediately after his death. We see as much in Drummond's mourning verse for Prince Henry: 'So *Heavens* faire face to the unborne which reedes, A Booke had beene of thy illustrious deedes.'[51] Wither's *Obsequies* (Elegy 5) similarly

describe Henry as a prince 'Who was himself a booke for Kings to pore on: /And might have been thy Basilikon Doron'.[52] Here, James I's tract, written to model princely behaviour for his son, and published in 1599, is only an idealized text. In time, Henry might have become a *Basilikon Doron*, a model text; but his life did not live out the potential imagined in print.[53] Princes lived lives that would be treated as lessons. This 'living history' is captured in Cranmer's description of Elizabeth: she will be a 'pattern to all princes living' (5.4.22), her descendants 'shall read [her] perfect ways of honour' (5.4.37). This model of a text as demanding constant and renewed engagement is typical of Shakespeare's histories, where epilogues leave narrative threads decidedly untied, or promise another instalment, a new 'copy'.[54]

Books are not a metaphor for stability or resolution. Juliet Fleming reminds us that 'early modern readers cut as they read, and read by cutting'.[55]

---

[48] Jeffrey Todd Knight, 'Invisible ink: a note on ghost images in early printed books', *Textual Cultures: Texts, Contexts, Interpretations* 5 (2010), 53–62; p. 55.

[49] Sophie Duncan, *Shakespeares's Props: Memory and Cognition* (New York and Oxford, 2019), p. 172.

[50] Woodward, *Theatre of Death*, pp. 148–65.

[51] William Drummond, 'Teares on the death of Moeliades' in *Poems* (London, 1616), sig. K2v.

[52] Wither, *Obsequies*, sig. B1r.

[53] Michael Ullyot has described the role of *Basilikon Doron* in shaping the popular perception of Prince Henry: 'Henry became an object not only of his father's pedagogical influence but of his subjects' rhetoric and imaginations – of unsolicited advice that drew inspiration from his father's own counsel': Michael Ullyot, 'James's reception and Henry's receptivity: reading Basilikon Doron after 1603', in *Prince Henry Revived*, ed. Wilks, pp. 65–84; p. 66.

[54] *1 Henry IV*, for instance, ends with victory over Hotspur, but with a promise of further battles to come: 'And since this business so fair is done, / Let us not leave till all our own be won' (5.5.44–5). *2 Henry IV* promises a sequel: 'our humble author will continue the story with Sir John in it, and make you merry with fair Catherine of France' (Epilogue, 25–7). The conquests seen in *Henry V* are undone by the final Chorus: 'they lost France and made his England bleed' (Epilogue, 12).

[55] Juliet Fleming, 'The Renaissance collage: signcutting and signsewing', *Journal of Medieval and Early Modern Studies* 45 (2015), 443–56; p. 446.

11   *The Family of Henry VIII, c.* 1545, RCIN 405796, Royal Collection Trust / © Her Majesty Queen Elizabeth II 2020.

Collage is at once a new creation formed out of fragments of the old: collage is also a model for a new reading of history. This view of history is not particular to *All is True*. A sixteenth-century painting, previously attributed to Hans Holbein the Younger, offers an impossible collage of history (see Figure 11). It shows Henry's third wife, Jane Seymour, standing beside her young son, Edward, despite the fact that Seymour died shortly after giving birth to him. With Henry's daughters, Princess Mary (left) and Princess Elizabeth (right), also present, we see pieces of history, cut up and stuck together.

All is True offers just such an imagined collage of Henry VIII's life – one not marked as this painting is, by the presence of too many children, but by the absence of them. Its audiences, like viewers of the painting, are encouraged to hold all possibilities to be true at once. At the end of *All is True*, Time's face is Janus-like, at once looking backwards and forwards, to the past and to the future, as it does so often in Shakespeare's late plays.[56] This is Shakespeare thinking, as Kiernan Ryan has put it, 'in the future perfect tense, as the way it *will have been*'.[57] The cognitive process of future thought is itself a collage, an impossible collection of past images.

To think in the future perfect tense is to create work that cannot ever be fully resolved. *All is True*

demands the imaginative participation of its audience to craft a resolution, depending on their own recollection of history. If we are required to read historical fiction actively, cutting as we read, then audiences and adaptors of *All is True* (and *Winter's Tale*) have not shirked their responsibilities. The reception of these plays, alongside the history of Henry Frederick, reveals a lingering fascination with alternative histories. In 1628, for instance, George Villiers, Duke of Buckingham, funded a revival of *All is True* only to walk out at the execution of his namesake. Villiers's publicity stunt performatively reinterprets history, offering himself as the ghost image of another Buckingham

---

[56]   Writing of *The Tempest*, Bernard Harris describes 'the dependence of the present upon the past and the posited freedom of future actions': Bernard Harris, '"What's past is prologue": "Cymbeline" and "Henry VIII"', in *Later Shakespeare*, ed. John Russell Brown and Bernard Harris (London, 1966), pp. 203–34; p. 203. Marjorie Garber writes on the 'logic of retrospective anticipation' in '"What's past is prologue": temporality and prophecy in the history plays', in *Renaissance Genres: Essays on Theory, History, and Interpretation*, ed. B. K. Lewalski (Cambridge, MA, 1986), pp. 301–31.

[57]   Kiernan Ryan, '"Here's fine revolution": Shakespeare's philosophy of the future', *Essays in Criticism* 63 (2013), 105–27; p. 111. See also Harry Berger on the future perfect in *Richard II* in *Imaginary Audition: Shakespeare on Stage and Page* (Berkeley, 1989), pp. 104–37.

and allowing the play to progress no further than Buckingham's death. Yet Cogswell and Lake cite a contemporary report of the incident which suggests Villiers should have waited until 'the fall of Cardinal Wolsey, who was a more lively type of himself'.[58] History becomes a material that can be torn and refashioned to suit one's own perspective.

Historians, too, create alternate narratives. While Henry VIII's lost heirs have met with some of these speculations – including in Suzannah Lipscomb's alt-history essay, 'What if Henry VIII's son by Katherine of Aragon survived?' – few princes have been so frequently subject to imaginative re-writings as Henry Frederick.[59] In his historical biography, Roy Strong examined the Prince he styled Henry IX: even the text's title, *Henry, Prince of Wales, and England's Lost Renaissance*, presumes an imagined renaissance which was cut short.[60] An exhibition at the National Portrait Gallery in 2012, 'The Lost Prince: The Life & Death of Henry Stuart', is equally telling in its framing of Henry Frederick's life. 'In a historical guessing game', Sandy Nairne notes, 'if Henry had lived, his younger brother Charles would not have taken to the throne.'[61] Sarah Fraser's 2017 biography was titled *The Prince Who Would Be King: The Life and Death of Henry Stuart*.[62] A documentary directed by George Cathro in 2017 similarly followed the life of 'The Best King We Never Had'.[63] Novelist Philippa Gregory also adds to this alt-history: 'Henry's death is one of the many "what ifs" of history – if he had survived to become Henry IX of England, would the country still have followed the path to civil war?'[64] Henry Frederick's death has become a turning point in our understanding of the past. Like his contemporaries, writers today are still tempted to reflect on Henry's potential, and not on the realities of his short life.

This selective and speculative view of history is typical of the way a neurotypical brain is programmed to think about the past and future. This speculation is evident in rewritings of *The Winter's Tale* in novel form (*All is True* has had no such adaptation, although Tudor historical fiction abounds). Jeanette Winterson's *The Gap of Time:*

The Winter's Tale Retold (2015) begins by summarizing Shakespeare's 'original' before offering a 'cover version', in acknowledgement that her adaptation both mirrors and changes Shakespeare.[65] Adaptation itself becomes a kind of mourning, a need to keep the original alive by remembering it. This retrospection can be found both within a contemporary use of Shakespeare, and in our contemporary view of Shakespeare.

The popular imagination also attributes to Shakespeare an inability to move forward following the death of his own son that seems drawn from the plots of his own late plays. In 2018, the title 'All is True' was repurposed by Ben Elton for a film featuring an ageing Shakespeare accepting the death of his own son, Hamnet, even as Hamnet's twin sister Judith must live in her brother's ghostly shadow.[66] Elton has called this the '"reverse Hamlet" of a son haunting his father', but to make this point he need not have looked beyond *All is True*.[67] While the play does not stage a ghost

[58] Anonymous newsletter, 9 August 1628, BL MS Harl. 383, fol. 65r, in Thomas Cogswell and Peter Lake, 'Buckingham does the Globe: Henry VIII and the politics of popularity in the 1620s', *Shakespeare Quarterly* 60 (2009), 252–78; p. 278.

[59] Suzannah Lipscomb, 'The glorious reign of King Henry IX', Unherd, 9 September 2020): https://unherd.com/2020/09/what-if-henry-viiis-son-by-katherine-of-aragon-survived.

[60] Roy Strong, *Henry, Prince of Wales and England's Lost Renaissance* (London, 1986).

[61] Sandy Nairne, 'Director's foreword' in Catharine MacLeod, *The Lost Prince: The Life and Death of Henry Stuart* (London, 2012), p. 6.

[62] Susan Fraser, *The Prince Who Would Be King: The Life and Death of Henry Stuart* (London, 2017).

[63] 'The Best King We Never Had', dir. George Cathro (BBC 2, 30 November 2017). This proposal was also raised by Steven Brocklehurst in an article published on the day of broadcast – 'How Henry Stuart became the king who never was' (*BBC Scotland News*, 30 November 2017): www.bbc.co.uk/news/uk-scotland-42082710.

[64] Philippa Gregory, 'Death of Prince Henry Frederick', 6 November 2018: www.philippagregory.com/news/death-of-prince-henry-frederick.

[65] Jeanette Winterson, *The Gap of Time: The Winter's Tale Retold* (London, 2015), pp. xi–xvii.

[66] *All is True*, dir. Kenneth Branagh (Sony Pictures, 2018).

[67] Interview with Ben Elton: www.sonyclassics.com/allistrue.

in physical form, it offers Henry VIII as an endlessly haunted father. This haunted father is the Shakespeare offered in Maggie O'Farrell's *Hamnet*, which casts Shakespeare as Old Hamlet's Ghost in the play written in memory of his son. *Hamlet* becomes an act of mourning Hamnet, who, in this ghostly re-writing, remains 'both dead and alive': fiction, like FMTT, allows for all realities to exist at once.[68] Allusion keeps texts both alive and dead, as images and quotations remain caught in stasis between their past and present uses. The more we reanimate the plots and imagery of *Winter's Tale* and *All is True*, the more power we give to their continual haunting, to their repetitions, to their uncanny collage of images we have seen before.

'I FEEL NOW / THE FUTURE IN THE INSTANT' (*MACBETH*, 1.5.57)

The association of memory and repetition with ideas of haunting plays out across Shakespeare's work. The future becomes an uncanny shadow of the past: even in Macbeth's famous 'Tomorrow, and tomorrow, and tomorrow' (5.5.18), there is a sickening sense that Macbeth cannot escape even this articulation of the future. Queen Margaret's grim insistence on the pointlessness of war is captured in the slow and sickening repetition of her memories:

> I had an Edward, till a Richard killed him;
> I had a husband, till a Richard killed him.
> Thou hadst an Edward, till a Richard killed him;
> Thou hadst a Richard, till a Richard killed him.
>
> (*Richard III*, 4.4.40–3)

Again, and again, one man is replaced with another. There is a horror of repetition, a fear that what has come before will play out again. In *All is True*, Wolsey captures this relentless cycle in the play's most uncanny image: the living statue. The play's second scene sees Henry VIII and Wolsey in an extended dispute over taxation. Henry looks backwards, insisting on the value of history to shape the present and future: 'Things done without example, in their issue / Are to be feared' (1.2.91–2). But Wolsey thinks only of

futurity: the 'chronicles of [his] doing' (1.2.75) will be 'ignorant tongues' (73) and he therefore must act without thought of what the future will fashion as his history. To be concerned with the future is, counter-intuitively, to be held in stasis:

> If we shall stand still,
> In fear our motion will be mocked or carped at,
> We should take root here where we sit,
> Or sit state-statues only.
>
> (1.2.86–9)

Wolsey's lines offer a difficult blurring of times: a future 'if' and a future 'fear' might lead those in the present to 'take root', and act as living markers of the past, 'statues'. In 'motion', there is a linguistic hint of puppet shows or motions – to live in the present is to offer cheap entertainment that might easily be mocked.[69] But a motionless puppet is a lifeless simulacrum – not unlike the effigy of Henry Frederick, paraded along his funeral route to offer an uncanny semblance of life.[70] Like a statue, a puppet or effigy is a mere model of human life, reverting to the wood from which it was fashioned as it takes root. To live as a statue seems impossible (although *The Winter's Tale* might prove otherwise) but it is the fate of those who fear their future chroniclers. To evade the judgement of history is to remain trapped in the present.

The capacity to shape the narrative of history is particularly associated with Wolsey, who renders his word into law with a God-like speech act: 'As he cried "Thus let be", to as much end / As give a crutch to th' dead' (1.171–2). Of course, Wolsey himself is a reanimated memory: a history play is, by definition, a crutch given to the dead, with all the inherent impossibility and contradiction

---

[68] Maggie O'Farrell, *Hamnet* (London, 2020), p. 366.

[69] Although motions are generally understood to be puppet shows, Scott Cutler Shershow suggests the motions are not quite puppets but 'flat cutout figures that the heat of the candle moved' or 'shadow figures': Scott Cutler Shershow, *Puppets and Popular Culture* (Ithaca, 1995), p. 107. This reading offers an interesting contrast between the fixed stone statue and the moving shadow suggested by motions.

[70] Woodward, *Theatre of Death*, p. 163.

implied in that phrase. The audience of *All is True* are explicitly called upon to reanimate the dead through their own wishful thinking:

> Think ye see
> The very persons of our noble story
> As they were living
>
> (Prologue, 25–7)

As Henry Wotton wrote in a letter describing the fire at the Globe in 1613, sparked by a cannon shot during *All is True*, these are simply 'principal pieces' of history.[71] This is history that has been selectively remembered, not history as it was. As such, the debate which *All is True* tempts over Henry's heirs – unmentioned Edward, idealized Elizabeth or absent Mary – is rendered pointless. Tudor history is made petty, the machinations of every player serving only to stage-manage the arrival of James I. Katherine or Anne, Wolsey or Cranmer, Elizabeth or Edward: internal logic fails, binaries collapse, and when the epilogue speaks of 'The merciful construction of good women, / For such a one we showed 'em' (10–11), the desire to interpret history in simple terms is exposed as naïve. Between Katherine, who ends her life blessed by angels, or Anne, who gives birth to the future Virgin Queen, who is the one good woman? Or should audiences, like Cranmer, be thinking ahead, to imagine the good woman that Elizabeth I will become?

The kind of creative response to history found in Shakespeare and Fletcher's play is justified by Philip Sidney, who claims in his *An Apologie for Poetry* (1595) that 'the Historian is bound to recite, that may the Poet (if he list) with his imitation make his owne'.[72] The possibilities of poetic licence, blurring the already frayed edges of history and fiction, is not limited to those who write history: reading the past actively, mining the memory of history for information, offers what Clement Edmondes called, in his commentary on Caesar's *De bello gallico* (1600), 'history and speculatiue learning'.[73] History can be selectively re-written: the equivocations of *All is True* are not a lack of coherence but a deliberate negotiation of history's ambivalence.

Historical drama depends on speculative possibilities. But if history is unstable, our capacity to imagine the future through knowledge of the past is compromised. We are looking into a distorted mirror: the future is a false reflection of the past. The prologue of *All is True* makes this distortion evident: this will be 'our chosen truth' (18), which is no truth at all. *All is True* is a history play determined to keep alive the possibility of other histories. I began this article by demonstrating two distinct ways of thinking about the future: the memory-driven and evidence-based speculation of FMTT, and the divine and insistently forward-looking accounts of prophecy. To this binary I would add two distinct models of writing history. In the first, truth is refracted through a lens, with '*all lines of expectation ... scattered*' – it suggests possibility, alt-history. In the second, history is borne backwards, working cyclically and recycling past events, like the phoenix which is reborn from its own ash. In its recycling of tropes, in its echoes of Virgil, Spenser, Rowley, and even of Shakespeare's own *Winter's Tale*, *All is True* is made up of pieces of past texts. Read in the aftermath of Henry Frederick's death and the recycled imagery of his own elegies, the play's insistence on repetition is only underscored.

Between its collage of past texts and its future imaginings, the two conceptions of history offered by *All is True* cannot cohere. Yet, as the play suggests, pieces can be chosen from the historical whole and all interpreters will be happy: those seeking the glorification of Elizabeth, those waiting for Edward, and those desiring redemption for

---

[71] 'July 2 1613', in *The Life and Letters of Sir Henry Wotton*, ed. Logan Pearsall Smith (Oxford, 1907), vol. 2, p. 32.

[72] Philip Sidney, *An Apologie for Poetry* (London, 1595), sig. E2v.

[73] Clement Edmondes, *Observations vpon the fiue first bookes of Cæsars commentaries setting fourth the practise of the art military in the time of the Roman Empire* (London, 1600), sig. A1r. See also Sasha Roberts, 'Reading in early modern England: contexts and problems', *Critical Survey* 12 (2000), 1–16; and Stephen B. Dobranski, *Readers and Authorship in Early Modern England* (Cambridge, 2005).

Katherine and her daughter Mary. The epilogue, which laments ''Tis ten to one this play shall never please / All that are here' (1–2) reminds us that each audience member will offer their own reading. We can even choose the play's title: *Henry VIII* or *All is True*. The encompassing, concessive 'All is True',

held against the concretely historical 'Henry VIII', allows for both speculation and reality. The hairline fracture between those titles offers an imaginative space in which, in our own mental time travel at least, all lives can be lived fruitfully, and all futures idealized, although not ever realized.

'AND HIS WORKS IN A GLASS CASE': THE BARD IN THE GARDEN AND THE LEGACY OF THE SHAKESPEARE LADIES CLUB

GENEVIEVE KIRK

On 6 October 1754, the travel diarist Richard Pococke visited St Giles House in Wimborne St Giles, Dorset, and recorded his observations of the manor and its surrounding grounds:

The Gardens are very beautifully laid out, in a serpentine river, pieces of water, Lawns, & c: & very gracefully adorn'd with wood. One first comes to an Island in which there is a Castle, then near the water is a Gateway, with a tower on each side, & passing between two waters, there is a fine Cascade from the one to the other, a thatch'd house, a round pavilion on a Mount, Shake Spears house, in which is a small statue of him, & his works in a Glass case; & in all the houses & seats are books in hanging Glass cases.[1]

This easily overlooked passage within a somewhat obscure volume describes what may very well be the first private shrine to Shakespeare, an indication of the long-departed playwright's elevated status in this particular household.

The household in question was that of the 4th Earl of Shaftesbury and his wife, the Countess, Susanna Ashley-Cooper, foundress and leader of the Shakespeare Ladies Club. This group of women, in the late 1730s and through the turn of the decade, was responsible for petitioning and persuading London theatre managers to stage Shakespeare's plays more frequently and revive many of his dramatic works that had not been performed since the Restoration. Now that the theatre was a commercial venture, no longer sustained by royal patronage, it was common for influential aristocratic persons to request (or 'bespeak') performances of particular plays.[2] Shakespearian plays advertised as being staged 'At the Desire . . . ' or 'At

the particular Desire of several Ladies of Quality' are considered a strong empirical indication of the Shakespeare Ladies Club's influence.[3] Scholars have demonstrated a correlation between appearances of this 'bespeaking phrase' in performance advertisements and a spike in the percentage of Shakespearian plays in London theatres' repertories, showing that the Club's campaign was indeed successful.[4] Eliza Haywood would write in *The Female Spectator* that the Ladies' initiative 'deserves the highest Encomiums, and will be attended with an adequate Reward; since, in preserving the Fame of the dead Bard, they add a Brightness to their own, which will shine to late Posterity'.[5]

---

[1] Quoted in John Dixon Hunt and John Willis, *The Genius of the Place: The English Landscape Garden, 1620–1820* (Cambridge, MA, 1988), p. 265. See also Richard Pococke, *The Travels through England of Dr. Richard Pococke, Successively Bishop of Meath and of Ossory, during 1750, 1751, and Later Years*, 2 vols. (London, 1889), vol. 2, pp. 137–8, and The Earl of Shaftesbury and Tim Knox, *The Rebirth of an English Country House: St Giles House* (New York, 2018), p. 219.

[2] Felicity Nussbaum, *Rival Queens: Actresses, Performance, and the Eighteenth-Century British Theater* (Philadelphia, 2014), pp. 140–1. See also Arthur H. Scouten, ed., *The London Stage: 1660–1800, Part 3: 1729–1747*, 2 vols. (Carbondale, 1961), vol. 2, p. clxx.

[3] This was noted first in Emmett L. Avery, 'The Shakespeare Ladies Club', *Shakespeare Quarterly* 7 (1956), 153–8; p. 154.

[4] See especially Fiona Ritchie, *Women and Shakespeare in the Eighteenth Century* (Cambridge, 2017), pp. 144–5.

[5] Eliza Haywood, *The Female Spectator*, 4 vols. (London, 1745), vol. 1, p. 323. Quoted in Ritchie, *Women*, p. 146, and Katherine West Scheil, '"Rouz'd by a woman's pen": the Shakespeare Ladies' Club and reading habits of early modern women', *Critical Survey* 12.2 (2000), 106–27; p. 108.

The Shakespeare Ladies Club also played a major role in garnering public support and funds to raise the monument to Shakespeare in Westminster Abbey's Poets' Corner. This memorial was erected in 1741, an event that formally and publicly enshrined the Bard as Britain's national poet. In that same year, nearly one in four theatrical performances in London was of a Shakespearian play, likely due to the dual effects of the Ladies' campaign and the public hype surrounding the unveiling of the monument.[6] David Garrick, who would further deify Shakespeare over the course of his career (and build his own private garden temple in Shakespeare's honour), made his official stage debut as Richard III that autumn.[7] Garrick would not soon forget that he likely owed the success of his career and his reputation as Shakespeare's emissary to the revival instigated by the Ladies Club, and in fact directly addressed (or, rather, eulogized) them in his speech delivered at the Stratford Jubilee in 1769, three decades after the Club's campaign and many years since the deaths of its members: '*It was You Ladies* that restor'd Shakespeare to the Stage, you form'd yourselves into a Society to protect his Fame, & Erected a Monument to his and your own honor in Westminster Abbey. *He has been always supported* in his universal Dominion by his fair Admirers, & his throne has been best Establish'd in their Smiles & Tears.'[8]

Though brief, Pococke's description of Shakespeare's House (also referred to as Shakespeare's 'Cell' or 'Seat' in documents in the Shaftesbury Archives) on the grounds of St Giles House invites further analysis and contextualization in light of other examples of Shakespearian iconography that emerged during this time period, and illuminates some hitherto unexplored aspects of the Shakespeare Ladies Club's campaign. The statue of Shakespeare at St Giles was an early prototype of the Westminster Abbey monument, presumably a gift from the sculptor Peter Scheemakers to Lady Shaftesbury.[9] As the private counterpart of the Westminster Abbey monument to Shakespeare – which itself was, as Michael Dobson has pointed out, 'essentially a continuation of the statuary project initiated by Cobham's Temple of British Worthies' at Stowe[10] – Shakespeare's House likewise stood as

a testament to the rise of Bardolatry during this era and reinforced Shakespeare's reputation as emblematic of the Patriot Whig ideal. Moreover, the veneration of Shakespeare's 'works in a glass case' indicates the Countess's fondness not only for Shakespeare as a figure, but specifically her reverence for his collected works and appreciation for the volumes that preserve the words of 'one of her Ladyship's most favourite Authors'.[11] Shakespeare's House, then, is a site where politics, Bardolatry and literary Shakespeare intersect, a three-faceted pursuit mirrored in the Shakespeare Ladies Club's campaign from 1736 to 1741. This article situates the Shakespeare Ladies Club with two seemingly separate but concurrent developments that had a significant impact on Shakespeare's reception during this period: the Patriot Whig opposition to Robert Walpole, and the emerging culture of widespread readership that increased demand for unaltered Shakespeare productions on the stage. I contend that the Shakespeare Ladies Club not only co-existed with these movements, but actively participated in and in some ways accelerated them. In the following pages, I will explore the implications of this new information and show how it enhances our understanding of Shakespeare's rise to prominence in the early eighteenth century.

---

[6] Jonathan Bate, *Shakespearean Constitutions: Politics, Theatre, Criticism, 1730–1830* (Oxford, 1989), p. 25, and Michael Dobson, *The Making of the National Poet: Shakespeare, Adaptation and Authorship, 1660–1769* (Oxford, 1992), p. 161.

[7] Avery, 'Shakespeare', p. 158; and Ritchie, *Women*, p. 146.

[8] The draft of this speech appears in the manuscript 'Journal of David Garrick's journey to France and Italy, begun at Paris, September 21, 1763', held at the Folger Shakespeare Library (W.a.156). It includes a poem entitled 'Address to the Ladies' that praises women and Shakespeare's female characters. Also partially quoted in Dobson, *Making*, p. 148; Scheil, 'Rouz'd', p. 108; and Fiona Ritchie, 'The influence of the female audience on the Shakespeare revival of 1736–1738: the case of the Shakespeare Ladies Club', in *Shakespeare and the Eighteenth Century*, ed. Peter Sabor and Paul Yachnin (Aldershot, 2008), pp. 57–69; p. 67.

[9] Shaftesbury and Knox, *Rebirth*, p. 219.

[10] Dobson, *Making*, p. 138.

[11] Thomas Cooke, 'The dedication', in *A Demonstration of the Will of God by the Light of Nature* (London, 1742), pp. iii–vi; p. v.

There exists already a small body of scholarship investigating the activities and impact of the Shakespeare Ladies Club; numerous other works mention the Club in passing, as either a noteworthy component of a broader argument or merely a fascinating yet underappreciated detail of eighteenth-century theatre history. Emmett L. Avery offered the first modern scholarly analysis of the Club in a 1956 *Shakespeare Quarterly* article. His evaluation of the Club's activities and impact was significant: everyone who has since written on the Shakespeare Ladies Club cites him. In the same journal issue, Arthur H. Scouten mentions the Club as a factor in his argument that David Garrick could not have been the sole or principal cause for Shakespeare's astounding elevation in the eighteenth century.[12] Research on the Shakespeare Ladies Club then appears to have remained largely dormant until Michael Dobson's landmark monograph on eighteenth-century Shakespeare, *The Making of the National Poet*, revitalized interest. He acknowledged, as Avery and Scouten had, the Club's role in reviving Shakespeare in the London theatres, ostensibly as an alternative to more low-brow foreign entertainments such as pantomime and Italian opera, but further emphasized the Ladies' involvement with the Westminster Abbey monument project as evidence of their nationalistic agenda.[13]

Dobson also uncovered some of the members' identities and showed how they as individuals, particularly Susanna Ashley-Cooper, were already 'busy in artistic circles at the time of the Ladies' Club'.[14] Though it is difficult to ascertain who may have been an official member or merely a supporter of the Club's objectives, other women possibly involved with the Shakespeare Ladies include Mary Churchill, Duchess of Montagu, unambiguously named as a member in the poem 'An Ode to her Grace the Dutchess of Montague, and the Rest of the Illustrious Ladies of Shakespear's Club',[15] and Mary Cowper (a cousin of the poet William Cowper), whose poem 'On the Revival of Shakespear's Plays by the Ladies in 1738' indicates that she may have been a member – at the very least, she was 'a fervent supporter of the Club and its aims'.[16] In 1739 (when fundraising efforts for the Poets' Corner project were

under way), the writer Elizabeth Boyd penned the never-performed play *Don Sancho, or The Students Whim*, which aligned her with the Club by featuring a scene in which the goddess Minerva resurrects Shakespeare in the form of a monument,[17] and Eliza Haywood's commendation of the Ladies in *The Female Spectator* suggests the possibility of a connection. These discoveries have opened the way to increasing our understanding of the Club and its intentions by researching these women and their accomplishments as individuals.

In her article '"Rouz'd by a woman's pen": the Shakespeare Ladies' Club and reading habits of early modern women', Katherine West Scheil recognizes the Club's significance as a distinctly female consortium, and therefore a platform 'for women's participation in the intellectual and cultural life of eighteenth-century London' through their campaign in the theatres. Significantly, Scheil comments that the Shakespeare Ladies Club was 'one of the first female groups to combine public service with literary taste', and even speculates about which edition of Shakespeare's works they might have read, a detail the present study will scrutinize in depth.[18] Most recently, Fiona Ritchie has published several articles and book chapters on the Shakespeare Ladies Club that have done much to increase our knowledge and understanding of the Club and its activities. She not only examines the data suggesting that the increasing representation of Shakespeare in London theatre repertories was due to the Club's influence, but also closely analyses the significance

---

[12] Arthur H. Scouten, 'The increase in popularity of Shakespeare's plays in the eighteenth century: a caveat for interpretors of stage history', *Shakespeare Quarterly* 7.2 (1956), 189–202.
[13] For Dobson's full analysis of the Shakespeare Ladies Club and its activities, see Dobson, *Making*, pp. 146–64.
[14] Dobson, *Making*, p. 149. [15] Nussbaum, *Rival*, p. 143.
[16] Ritchie, 'Influence', p. 59. This poem is reproduced in full in Dobson, *Making*, pp. 150–1.
[17] See Dobson, *Making*, pp. 151–2; Scheil, 'Rouz'd', pp. 119–21; Ritchie, 'Influence', p. 59; and Suzannah Fleming, 'David Garrick: his garden at Hampton and the "Cult of Shakespeare"', *The London Gardener* 8 (2002), 51–71; p. 57.
[18] Scheil, 'Rouz'd', pp. 106, 117.

of specific plays they requested – particularly the all-but-forgotten history plays as evidence of the Ladies' nationalistic intentions.[19]

Suzannah Fleming mentions the structure dedicated to Shakespeare on the St Giles House estate in a 2003 article published in the *London Gardener*, though this detail seems not to have reached the attention of Shakespeare scholars. She traces the evolution of Bardolatry evident at Garrick's temple to Shakespeare at his home in Hampton, demonstrating that Garrick 'inherited the legacy of Bardworship from previous generations of *devotees*' and astutely noting that it was Susanna Ashley-Cooper, not Garrick, who was 'the first to build a garden temple solely devoted to Shakespeare'.[20] In a subsequent volume of that journal, Fleming offers perspective on the Patriot Whig iconography at Vauxhall Gardens and contends that the 4th Earl and Countess of Shaftesbury would have been 'undoubtedly influential' in its development, given their instrumental involvement with the Patriot opposition movement throughout the 1730s and beyond.[21]

Christine Gerrard gives a full-length study of the Patriot Whig opposition to Robert Walpole, exploring in great detail how the movement became an extra-parliamentary artistic battleground evident in the art, poetry, literature, drama and architecture of the era.[22] This enterprise was generally characterized by 'a strong sense of *cultural* patriotism: an acute anxiety about Britain's role and future as a model of artistic achievement';[23] the Patriots' optimistic anticipation of the future reign of Frederick, Prince of Wales; and, particularly relevant to the present study, a romanticized nostalgia for the Elizabethan era. This was, in part, a rebuke to Walpole's reluctance to go to war with Spain – 'an issue frequently associated with the Ladies' Club's campaign'[24] – as the Patriots proclaimed Elizabeth to be 'the Armada heroine using English sea power to humble Catholic Spain'.[25] As one of Elizabeth's 'most famous literary sons',[26] Shakespeare, too, was elevated and propagandized by the Patriot opposition campaign.

Richard Temple, 1st Viscount Cobham, who had long felt that Walpole's governance had forsaken Whig principles, officially opposed Walpole over the excise crisis in 1733, resigned from politics and became the leader of the Patriot Whig faction;[27] Walpole retaliated by stripping Lord Cobham of his colonelcy. Cobham had been developing the landscape gardens (designed by William Kent) at his home at Stowe House, and by 1735 the latest addition, the Temple of British Worthies, was completed. Here, he installed Shakespeare as one of sixteen busts sculpted by Peter Scheemakers and Michael Rysbrack in an assemblage of 'exemplary Britons . . . chosen to constitute a gallery of the great national achievements, both political and intellectual, which the current regime was supposedly betraying'.[28] Shakespeare appears among the 'men of contemplation', in the company of the likes of John Milton, Francis Bacon and John Locke. The 'men (and one woman) of action' included navel heroes Walter Raleigh and Francis Drake and, of course, Queen Elizabeth.[29]

Similar statuary would be installed by 1750 in the Rotunda built in Prince Frederick's honour at the Vauxhall Pleasure Gardens. Once again, a bust of Shakespeare was displayed alongside those of fifteen other British cultural heroes, including Milton, Dryden and Locke. They encircled the room, each situated in front of a window over which hovered the crest of Frederick, and 'in the centre, on a plinth, was a full-length figure of Apollo – the god of the arts',[30] evidently intended to represent future 'Patriot King' Frederick

---

[19] See Ritchie, *Women*, pp. 149–56 for this analysis.

[20] Fleming, 'David', p. 54

[21] Suzannah Fleming, 'Frederick as Apollo at Vauxhall: a "Patriot" project?' *The London Gardener* 13 (2007), 46–66.

[22] Christine Gerrard, *The Patriot Opposition to Walpole: Politics, Poetry, and National Myth, 1725–1742* (Oxford, 1994).

[23] Gerrard, *Patriot*, pp. 48–9. [24] Dobson, *Making*, p. 149.

[25] Gerrard, *Patriot*, p. 154. [26] Gerrard, *Patriot*, p. 106.

[27] Dobson, *Making*, pp. 135–6. [28] Dobson, *Making*, p. 136.

[29] Robinson, quoted in Francesca Orestano, 'Bust story: Pope at Stowe, or the politics and myths of landscape gardening', *Studies in the Literary Imagination* 38.1 (2005), 39–61; p. 39. See the full article for a more extensive account of the Stowe landscape gardens' political iconography.

[30] Fleming, 'Frederick', p. 50.

himself. Thus, as Gregory Nosan has articulated, Vauxhall was unequivocally exhibited as a 'site of patriotism, public spiritedness, and national cultural renewal'.[31] The presence of Shakespeare's image contributed to this agenda.

There is a tremendous body of evidence suggesting that the Earl and Countess of Shaftesbury were active participants in the Patriot Whig cultural opposition movement. Both were from prominent Whig families (the 4th Earl's great-grandfather was one of the party's founders) and politically active through their artistic associations and patronage. Particularly worth noting is their support for John Gay's *Polly* (the sequel to his immensely successful *The Beggar's Opera*), the staging of which Walpole prohibited. This earned them immortalization as the '*married Pair*' Florio and Clara, who show '*A single Concord in a Double Name*' – that is, Ashley-Cooper – in the poem *The Female Faction: or, the Gay Subscribers*.[32] Samuel Madden's 1729 Patriot drama *Themistocles, the Lover of his Country* was dedicated to Prince Frederick and published thanks to the Shaftesburys' private patronage. They also patronized Henry Fielding – whose political satires were an extraordinary nuisance to Walpole, prompting him to censor new plays widely with the Licensing Act of 1737 – and may have collaborated with him on the Patriot periodical *Common Sense; or the Englishman's Journal*.[33] The Shaftesburys were also patrons and friends of George Frideric Handel and possibly encouraged Prince Frederick's patronage of the composer. Correspondence between the Shaftesburys and their cousins the Harrises indicate that, in June 1741, the Countess purchased a 'busto of Hendal' sculpted by Louis François Roubiliac and 'dispos'd of it in a place of highest eminence in my room'.[34] Roubiliac had carved the statue of Handel installed at Vauxhall in 1738, which strongly suggests a connection there as well.[35] The Shaftesburys also evidently persuaded Handel to favour English oratorios over Italian opera, a theme echoed in the Shakespeare Ladies Club's campaign by its apparent preference for British drama over foreign opera and pantomime.[36]

It is worth mentioning, too, that in 1732, the 4th Earl of Shaftesbury published the fifth edition of the influential treatise *Characteristicks of Men,* *Manners, Opinions, Times*, written by his father, the 3rd Earl. *Characteristicks* was 'a collective series of philosophical tracts representing a striking cultural manifesto for the emerging Whig society of the eighteenth century',[37] and this new edition included the previously unpublished 'Letter Concerning the Art, or Science of Design'. In this document, the philosopher Earl reflects on what he has 'observ'd of the rising Genius of our Nation' and declares that 'the Figure we are like to make abroad, and the Increase of Knowledg, Industry and Sense at home, will render *united* BRITAIN the principal Seat of Arts'.[38] Fleming has remarked elsewhere that this 'was part of the Earl's famous call for a "national taste", invisaged [*sic*] to owe little to European influences'.[39] The Shakespeare Ladies

---

[31] Gregory Nosan, 'Pavilions, power, and patriotism: garden architecture at Vauxhall', in *Bourgeois and Aristocratic Cultural Encounters in Garden Art, 1550–1850*, ed. Michel Conan (Washington DC, 2002), pp. 101–21; p. 118.

[32] *The Female Faction: or, the Gay Subscribers* (London, 1729), p. 7. See also Dobson, *Making*, p. 149, and Fleming, 'David', p. 61.

[33] Fleming, 'Frederick', pp. 58, 62. The strict censorship imposed by the Licensing Act, which designated Drury Lane and Covent Garden as the only patent theatres and required new plays to be approved by the Lord Chamberlain, in practice meant that, at the height of the Shakespeare Ladies Club's campaign, new plays were harder to bring to the stage, but Shakespeare's already approved antiquated plays enjoyed an additional advantage.

[34] Donald Burrows and Rosemary Dunhill, *Music and Theatre in Handel's World: The Family Papers of James Harris, 1732–1780* (Oxford, 2002), p. 115.

[35] Fleming, 'Frederick', p. 50.

[36] More details regarding the Shaftesburys' Patriot activities and associations can be found in Fleming, 'Frederick', p. 62, and Dobson, *Making*, p. 149. For more on the Shaftesburys' relationship with Handel, see also Shaftesbury and Knox, *Rebirth*, p. 215, and, generally, Burrows and Dunhill, *Music*.

[37] Fleming, 'Frederick', p. 57.

[38] Anthony Ashley-Cooper, Earl of Shaftesbury, *Characteristicks of Men, Manners, Opinions, Times. The Fifth Edition, Corrected. With the Addition of a Letter Concerning Design*, 3 vols. (London, 1732), vol. 3, p. 398.

[39] Suzannah Fleming, *The Garden and Landscape of St Giles's House, Wimborne St Giles, Dorset*, 3 vols. (Report for English Heritage (now Historic England) in co-operation with the Shaftesbury Estate, 2007, revised and updated 2011), vol. 1 pt 2, p. 172.

Club's fervour for promoting Shakespeare as a homegrown genius may have been a response to this rallying cry of its leader's late father-in-law. It stands to reason, then, given Susanna Ashley-Cooper's Whig heritage and steadfast participation in the Patriot opposition movement, that she formed the Shakespeare Ladies Club as an opposition organization, convened to champion Shakespeare not just as one of an array of British Worthies, but as the most worthy of the lot.

As is generally recognized, the committee assembled to organize the raising of the Westminster Abbey monument to Shakespeare likewise 'held impeccable Patriot credentials'.[40] Led by Lord Burlington (Lady Shaftesbury's second cousin), who had, like Cobham, defected from Walpole over the Excise Bill, the committee also included Benjamin Martyn, author of the opposition drama *Timoleon* and a close friend of the 4th Earl. Lord Shaftesbury was one of the Trustees for Establishing the Colony of Georgia in America, and Martyn served as secretary to this group beginning in 1732; this was apparently the origin of their association. The Earl had commissioned Martyn to research and write a biography of his great-grandfather, the 1st Earl of Shaftesbury, to redeem his reputation (and concurrently elevate old Whig values), which had been tainted by his political failings during the Exclusion Crisis, imprisonment in the Tower of London and subsequent self-imposed exile.[41] Martyn composed the prologue delivered at the 28 April 1738 performance of *Julius Caesar* at Drury Lane theatre, the first of two benefits 'Towards raising a Fund for Erecting a Monument to the Memory of Shakespear',[42] while the Honourable James Noel (the Countess's brother) prepared the epilogue. Both speeches unambiguously designate the public-spirited effort to erect the monument an 'anti-Walpole demonstration', as Shakespeare – as he was also portrayed at Stowe, a fact underscored by the committee's commissioning of Kent and Scheemakers to design and sculpt the statue – is regarded as 'both a foe to tyranny and a genuinely national hero, above the reach of bribery or invidious patronage'.[43]

Nosan has perceived the Abbey monument to Shakespeare to be the result of 'the collective efforts of both Opposition political circles and the Shakespeare Ladies' Club'.[44] What is missed here (and, indeed, what seems to have been overlooked by all scholars, excepting Fleming) is that the Shakespeare Ladies Club, as a group of passionate activists in the campaign for a Britain-centric cultural renewal, was in fact an arm of the Patriot opposition movement. This component is crucial to understanding the Club and ought not to be ignored in any future scholarship on its role in propelling Shakespeare's cultural elevation in the eighteenth century. In both the national pantheon and the theatre, the Ladies promoted Shakespeare as a venerable native Briton who, to echo the philosopher Earl's vision, 'pleases his Audience, and often gains their Ear, without a single Bribe from Luxury or Vice'.[45] They also ostensibly adopted the crucial covert nature typical of Patriot opposition activity, given Walpole's proclivity for retaliation. This likely helps to explain the scarcity of records pertaining to the Club's aims and activities and the scant references to its members' identities, which has long been a point of frustration for scholars. It seems telling, too, that contemporary evidence of the Shakespeare Ladies Club's activity dwindles after 1741. Thanks to the Ladies' efforts, the unveiling of the monument in Westminster Abbey completed Shakespeare's apotheosis in Britain's cultural consciousness, and he now dominated the theatre repertory, so the Club had fulfilled its mission in that respect. Additionally, Walpole was crippled by that year's general election results, and he officially fell from power in

---

[40] Dobson, *Making*, p. 138.

[41] For a comprehensive account of Martyn's undertaking, see J. R. Milton, 'Benjamin Martyn, the Shaftesbury family, and the reputation of the first Earl of Shaftesbury', *The Historical Journal* 51 (2008), 315–35.

[42] Scouten, ed., *London*, p. 716.

[43] Dobson, *Making*, p. 138. Both speeches are printed in Peter Bayle *et al.*, *A General Dictionary, Historical and Critical*, 10 vols. (London, 1734–41), vol. 9, p. 189, and quoted and analysed in Dobson, *Making*, pp. 138–9.

[44] Nosan, 'Pavilions', p. 115.

[45] Shaftesbury, *Characteristicks*, vol. 1, p. 275.

February 1742.[46] Perhaps this is why, in the following year, opposition poet Thomas Cooke at last felt at liberty to identify publicly the Countess of Shaftesbury as the leader of the Shakespeare Ladies Club.[47]

Not long after securing Shakespeare's prominence in London's theatres and seeing the Abbey monument unveiled, Lady Shaftesbury turned her attention to raising the private monument to Shakespeare at her home in Dorset. St Giles House accounting records indicate that, on 16 July 1742, 'Shells for Shakespear's Cell' were purchased for £1 8s 6d, and, four months later, on 19 November 1742, 'an entry was made relating to a payment of £6 5s 5d: "Paid George Osboldstone & men as per Bill working about Shakespear's Cell"'.[48] Dedicating space to deify Shakespeare in the heart of a landscaped garden perpetuates the trend initiated at Stowe of glorifying Britain's history to amplify the Patriot ideal, though at St Giles House (as in Poets' Corner), Shakespeare is the singularly incomparable British Worthy. Evidence suggests that the Patriot message at St Giles likely extended beyond this one structure and may indeed have been, as at Stowe, the theme of the entire landscape. In examining the St Giles House records, Fleming has observed that 'the works to the grounds essentially came to a halt in 1751',[49] the year of Prince Frederick's untimely death, which quashed all hope for the future reign of the beloved 'Patriot King'. Additionally, an 1886 biography of the 7th Earl of Shaftesbury notes the presence of a 'summer-house' on the estate 'in which are deposited the memorials of the poet Thomson, who was a great friend of the fourth Earl'.[50] James Thomson was a prolific opposition writer whose own Westminster Abbey monument is right beside Shakespeare's.

But what especially distinguishes Shakespeare's House from other Patriotic and Bardolic iconography of the era is the presence of Shakespeare's 'works in a glass case'. While Stowe, the Abbey monument and Vauxhall honoured the ideals Shakespeare represented, Lady Shaftesbury further paid homage to his corpus of written works as a key feature of this memorial. Indeed, the books

are given as much weight in Pococke's description as the 'small statue of him' and are evidently as central to the shrine's message as the playwright's image. This invites us to explore how the Shakespeare Ladies Club's campaign might have been analogously text-centric. While existing scholarship has recognized the Ladies' role in the Shakespeare revival of the 1730s, comparatively little has been written on the literary aspect of the Club. Since the Shakespeare Ladies Club was formed at the height of a Shakespeare publishing boom and burgeoning editorial tradition (a fact Scheil has emphasized already), its members were no doubt reading Shakespeare's plays as well as frequenting the theatre. So how might this significant overlap – encountering Shakespeare on both page and stage – have had an impact on the Club's campaign and goals?

James Harriman-Smith has aptly observed that 'These two spheres, page and stage, are too easily distinguished and kept separate when we write about the literature of the theatre.' He contends that this severance originated with Shakespeare's eighteenth-century editors who were obliged to 'confront ... the inability of each medium to mirror the experience of the other'.[51] I agree with his

---

[46] Gerrard, *Patriot*, p. 44.

[47] Thomas Cooke, *An Epistle to The Right Honourable the Countess of Shaftesbury, with A Prologue and Epilogue on Shakespeare and His Writings* (London, 1743), pp. 3–5. Fleming remarks on the timing of this poem's publication in relation to Walpole's resignation in Fleming, *Garden*, vol. 1 pt 1, p. 86. See also Dobson, *Making*, 148–9.

[48] Fleming, *Garden*, p. 258. From the St Giles House accounts book for 1732–57, ref. E/A/78 in the St Giles archives. Fleming conducted much archival research at St Giles for her report on the estate's history for Historic England. I am grateful to her for making this information available to me for the present study.

[49] Fleming, *Garden*, p. 269.

[50] John W. Kirton, *True Nobility; or, the Golden Deeds of an Earnest Life* (London, 1886), p. 28. Also mentioned in Fleming, *Garden*, p. 194.

[51] James Harriman-Smith, 'The anti-performance prejudice of Shakespeare's eighteenth-century editors', *Restoration and Eighteenth-Century Theatre Research* 29.2 (2014), 47–61; p. 47. Harriman-Smith cites Harry Berger, *Imaginary Audition: Shakespeare on Stage and Page* (Berkeley, 1989), pp. 139–40.

diagnosis and suggest the following reason for the need to unify the two: in any study of the theatre history of this period, page and stage ought not to be severed because, as Julie Stone Peters has recognized, 'theatrical and play-reading publics were more or less made up of the same individuals, and play-going and play-buying were in a symbiotic relationship'.[52] At the time the Shakespeare Ladies Club first assembled, page and stage were effectively operating independently of one another. While the theatres staged versions of Shakespeare's plays liberally altered by contemporary playwrights to conform to the taste of the times, Jacob Tonson's editors strove to canonize Shakespeare and establish an authoritative text. This division was not seen as peculiar at the time, and, while Jean I. Marsden has shown that it would take until the end of the century for theatrical alteration to fall completely out of favour,[53] what has yet to be recognized is that the genesis of the trend towards favouring Shakespearian textual purity in performance occurred not only during, but possibly even partially in consequence of, the Shakespeare Ladies Club's campaign, and, I would argue, likely stemmed from the Ladies' reading habits. Consequently, the page began to be regarded as having authority over the stage.[54]

An oft-mentioned but hitherto unexamined detail about the Shakespeare Ladies Club is that, during its campaign, unaltered productions of Shakespeare's plays came to outnumber altered productions for the first time since before the Restoration, a detail first mentioned in modern scholarship by Scouten in 1956. But, intriguingly, it appears that Victorian writer and editor Dr John Doran may have been the first scholar to recognize the Ladies' role in the revival of more textually pure Shakespearian performances. In a lecture delivered at the Royal Institution on 13 February 1874 entitled 'On the opponents of Shakespeare', Doran condemned 'the long line of Shakespearian "improvers" who caused inextricable confusion by mixing up and mutilating his plays' until 'there was formed an association of "Shakespeare ladies"' who 'enabled the managers once more to play the works of the great poet on the stage with the original text'. Unfortunately, the only surviving traces of this lecture are an article printed in the *Standard* recounting the meeting, and a summary recorded in the Royal Institute's *Proceedings*, so we cannot presently know what evidence Doran used as the basis of his claim.[55] In any case, Scouten similarly observed that the Ladies 'raised by subscription enough funds to underwrite the staging at Covent Garden of Shakespeare's plays from a good text', and, by the end of the decade during which the Club was most active, 'there were eleven good versions in the repertory, together with eight adaptations, one of which (Betterton's *2 Henry IV*) was continued at Drury Lane while Covent Garden played the original'.[56]

Other scholars have since echoed Scouten's claim regarding the Club's apparent preference for unaltered Shakespeare but have, in some cases, expressed varying degrees of scepticism. Ritchie, for instance, writes that 'Scouten assumes that the Club promoted the revival of Shakespeare's original works in place of performance of the adaptations, but my analysis does not suggest that this is in fact the case.'[57] Indeed, before proceeding with my own analysis, it must be acknowledged that not every Shakespearian performance endorsed by the Ladies of Quality was unaltered; their requests included several alterations, such as Nahum Tate's *King Lear*, Thomas Betterton's

---

[52] Julie Stone Peters, *Theatre of the Book, 1480–1880: Print, Text, and Performance in Europe* (Oxford, 2000), p. 242. See also Jean-Christophe Mayer, *Shakespeare's Early Readers: A Cultural History from 1590 to 1800* (Cambridge, 2018), p. 110.

[53] Jean I. Marsden, *The Re-Imagined Text: Shakespeare, Adaptation, & Eighteenth-Century Literary Theory* (Lexington, 1995). See also Mayer, *Shakespeare's*, p. 126.

[54] For a nuanced overview of Shakespearian alteration in print and on stage, see Jenny Davidson, 'Shakespeare adaptation', in *Shakespeare in the Eighteenth Century*, ed. Fiona Ritchie and Peter Sabor (Cambridge, 2014), pp. 185–203.

[55] 'Dr. Doran on Shakespeare', *The Standard*, 16 February 1874, p. 6; and 'On the opponents of Shakespeare', in *Notices of the Proceedings at the Meetings of the Members of the Royal Institution of Great Britain, with Abstracts of the Discourses Delivered at the Evening Meetings* (London, 1875), vol. 7, pp. 218–19.

[56] Scouten, 'Increase', p. 198.

[57] Ritchie, *Women*, p. 216, n. 5.

II Henry IV, James Miller's *The Universal Passion* (an alteration of *Much Ado About Nothing*) and George Lillo's *Marina* (an altered version of *Pericles*). Considering this, Scheil has likewise inferred that the Ladies must have had 'little concern for authenticity or originality in their advocacy of Shakespeare'.[58] I would argue, however, that this conclusion is worth reconsidering.

While we have no immutable evidence that the Shakespeare Ladies Club personally and directly advocated for textually pure productions to the theatre managers, we must recognize that this phenomenon of unaltered productions beginning to eclipse the alterations is repeatedly correlated with the Club's campaign, and analyse it accordingly. Certainly, we can say that the publication of scholarly print editions of Shakespeare's works and increased readership contributed to the public's knowledge of what constituted unaltered Shakespeare, so while the Ladies could not have been single-handedly responsible for this initial shift towards more purist preferences in performance, we can surmise that their own reading habits contributed to this wider cultural development. Combined with their social standing and influence, which allowed them to shape the public's taste upon which theatre managers depended, this enabled the Shakespeare Ladies Club to play a role in initiating the conviction that performance must defer to Shakespeare's text.

It may be relevant, too, that Ritchie has raised a valid challenge to the Shakespeare Ladies Club's contemporary (and enduring) reputation for banishing pantomime to make way for Shakespeare.[59] For all of the various newspapers' and prologues' commendations of the Ladies, whose 'Example has already prevail'd upon the Town to neglect and despise Harlequin and his Harlot Colombine, for Shakespear and his lawful Spouse Common Sense',[60] Ritchie's examination of the afterpieces accompanying performances of Shakespearian plays requested by the Ladies of Quality reveals that they apparently 'had no objection to the pairing of Shakespeare and pantomime and their championing of Shakespeare did not move Harlequin off the stage'.[61] We might reasonably surmise that the Shakespeare Ladies Club likewise tolerated alteration to an extent, despite its preferences. As vital agents in the first concentrated effort to have more Shakespearian plays staged in their unaltered states, the Ladies could hardly have been expected to eradicate a 75-year-old tradition of alteration overnight; rather, their campaign marks the beginning of incremental change towards revering the text in performance. It is telling, too, that the alterations requested by the Club were consistently advertised as such. To list just a few examples, *King Lear and his Three Daughters* is flagged as 'Alter'd from Shakespear, by N. Tate, Esq.'; *The Tempest* is 'Alter'd from Shakespear by Sir W. Davenant and Mr Dryden'; *The Universal Passion* is presented as 'Founded on Shakespear's Much Ado About Nothing'.[62] This explicit identification of productions as altered further indicates the growing awareness of the distinction between theatrical alterations and Shakespeare's original.

At this juncture, it is helpful to pause and review how Shakespeare's plays came to be widely altered and examine the attitudes towards alteration that would have been prevalent at the time of the Ladies Club. Notwithstanding the minor cuts and adjustments the theatre of Shakespeare's day would have made to his scripts, we can say that the widespread practice of major alteration originated during the Restoration. Because there were no new plays readily available upon the reopening of the theatres in 1660, old plays dating from before the civil wars were staged instead, allowing Shakespeare to be, in a way, rescued during the Restoration, when his works might otherwise have slipped irretrievably into 'the quicksands of obscurity'.[63] Of course, the Restoration theatre was

[58] Scheil, 'Rouz'd', p. 125, n. 28.

[59] See Fiona Ritchie, 'The impact of the Shakespeare Ladies Club on John Rich's repertory in the 1737–1738 theatrical season: Shakespeare versus pantomime?' in *'The Stage's Glory': John Rich, 1692–1761*, ed. Berta Joncus and Jeremy Barlow (Newark, 2011), pp. 287–92.

[60] Quoted in Avery, 'Shakespeare', p. 155.

[61] Ritchie, 'Impact', pp. 208–9.

[62] Scouten, ed., *London*, pp. 629, 637, 650.

[63] Gary Taylor, *Reinventing Shakespeare: A Cultural History, from the Restoration to the Present* (Oxford, 1989), p. 12. For more detail on Restoration Shakespeare, see pp. 7–51.

not the theatre of Shakespeare's time, and playwrights accordingly updated his plays for the new era – adding and expanding female roles for actresses, making use of newly developed technology, and altering certain plays to avoid stirring up memories of recent political upheaval.[64] Additionally, Shakespeare's language was considered outmoded by the 1660s, and modernizing it was perceived to be an act of benevolence, rather than tampering with a sacred text as subsequent generations have judged it.[65] Thus, the Restoration and the ensuing decades initiated the trend – which persists to this day in one way or another, though not usually through substantially altering the plot and text – of modifying Shakespeare's works to suit the contemporary climate.[66]

Altered Shakespearian productions surpassed the unaltered ones by the 1690s,[67] so, by the early eighteenth century, alteration was commonplace and conventional. In fact, Tiffany Stern has observed that contemporary playwrights altering Shakespeare now rarely went to the source but, rather, used existing Restoration alterations as their starting point, further updating Shakespeare for the new era.[68] Restoration and eighteenth-century alterations went beyond the customary reduction of lines and other minor adjustments made to the scripts and instead involved significant plot deviations, as well as substantial changes to the text. Additionally, Shakespeare's name may or may not have been attached to ephemeral material (such as playbills and newspaper advertisements) announcing the performance.[69] In contrast, 'Unaltered' productions re-emerging in the eighteenth century remained largely faithful to Shakespeare's late sixteenth- and early seventeenth-century texts, though they likely still involved some innocuous cutting of lines and would have incorporated an afterpiece along with 'the addition of the kind of dances, music, and scenic effects that were a standard feature of all professional dramatic productions in London' during this era.[70] Furthermore, the unaltered plays were consistently advertised as having been written by Shakespeare.

Prior to the release of Nicholas Rowe's first edition of Shakespeare's collected dramatic works in 1709, alterations were prevalent in printed playbooks as well as the theatre: 78 per cent of playbook editions published between the Restoration and Rowe's edition were alterations, versus 22 per cent unaltered.[71] These editions frequently featured on the title page what Don-John Dugas calls a 'performance link': some kind of 'formulaic, theatrical-tie-in sales phrase (for example, "As it is now Acted at His Highness the Duke of York's Theatre," and "As it was Acted at the Theatre-Royal, by His Majesty's Servants")'.[72] This seems to indicate that acquiring the performance text, presumably to re-live the theatrical experience, was the priority.[73] Robert D. Hume has likewise noted that 'Probably only a textual purist – rare birds in those times – would have worried about how much of the [printed] text was actually Shakespeare's.' For instance, the title page of a copy of *1 Henry IV* published in 1700 says, 'Revived, with Alterations. Written Originally by Mr. Shakespear'. However, Hume remarks that

---

[64] Taylor, *Reinventing*, pp. 23–4. See, especially, Emma Depledge's analysis of the impact of the Exclusion Crisis on Shakespearian adaptation in Emma Depledge, *Shakespeare's Rise to Cultural Prominence: Politics, Print and Alteration, 1642–1700* (Cambridge, 2018). See also Dobson, *Making*, pp. 63–4.

[65] Taylor, *Reinventing*, p. 47.

[66] See also David Scott Kastan, *Shakespeare and the Book* (Cambridge, 2004), pp. 84–90.

[67] Taylor, *Reinventing*, p. 20.

[68] Tiffany Stern, 'Shakespeare in drama', in *Shakespeare*, ed. Ritchie and Sabor, pp. 141–57; pp. 141–2.

[69] Robert D. Hume explains that the average post-Restoration / early eighteenth-century playgoer likely would not have known or cared about the identity of a play's author (let alone concerned themselves over fealty to the nameless author's original text) but, rather, frequented the theatre to be entertained by spectacle and favourite popular actors. See Robert D. Hume, 'Before the Bard: "Shakespeare" in early eighteenth-century London', *ELH* 64.1 (1997), 41–75; pp. 43–6.

[70] Don-John Dugas, *Marketing the Bard: Shakespeare in Performance and Print, 1660–1740* (Columbia, 2006), p. 11. See also Taylor, *Reinventing*, pp. 56–9, and Robert Shaughnessy, 'Shakespeare and the London stage', in *Shakespeare*, ed. Ritchie and Sabor, pp. 161–84; p. 165.

[71] Dugas, *Marketing*, p. 87. See also Hume, 'Before', pp. 51–2.

[72] Dugas, *Marketing*, pp. 88–9.

[73] See also Mayer, *Shakespeare's*, pp. 112–13.

the playtext itself is not, in fact, an alteration, but a 'surprisingly pure text, slightly cut'. He explains, '"Alter'd" implies horrors to us, but probably signified "improved and helpfully corrected" to the early eighteenth-century buyer of quartos ... Clearly John Deeve (the publisher) thought that both "Shakespear" and "Alterations" would have positive connotations for potential purchasers.'[74] This again confirms that the alteration of Shakespeare's text, even in print, as on the stage, was not yet regarded as unusual or unacceptable to the average early eighteenth-century reading playgoer, an attitude that would begin to change as Shakespeare's first editors strove to determine and establish Shakespeare's ever-elusive authoritative text, which would go on to be consumed by reading playgoers.

In his monograph *Marketing the Bard*, Dugas explores how the relationship between print and performance reversed during the early decades of the eighteenth century. That is, 'theatrical revivals of some of Shakespeare's plays (many of them significantly altered to meet the taste of the times) in the late seventeenth century began to fuel an interest in publishing his plays',[75] until the theatre began to take its cues from the world of print in the wake of the publication of Tonson's collected editions of Shakespeare's works edited by Nicholas Rowe, Alexander Pope and Lewis Theobald, and especially following the 1734–5 price war between Tonson and Robert Walker, who challenged Tonson's exclusive rights to publish Shakespeare. Dugas argues that 'This flooding of the reading market with inexpensive editions of all the plays sparked interest among play-reading theatregoers in reviving Shakespeare's more obscure comedies and romances (many of which had not been performed in more than a hundred years) as well as in Shakespeare as a figure.'[76] The single editions produced during the price war also contain evidence that the practice of printing altered Shakespearian playtexts was on the wane. In a series of advertisements included with his single-play editions, Tonson slammed Walker for publishing non-canonical plays and theatrical alterations:

Whereas one *R. Walker* has proposed to pirate all *Shakespear*'s Plays, but through Ignorance of what Plays are *Shakespear*'s, did in several Advertisments propose to print *Oedipus King of Thebes*, as one of *Shakespear*'s Plays; and has since printed *Tate*'s *King Lear* instead of *Shakespear*'s, and in that and *Hamlet* has omitted almost one half of the Genuine Editions printed by J. *Tonson* and Proprietors. The World will therefore judge how likely they are to have a compleat Collection of *Shakespear*'s Plays from the said *R. Walker*.[77]

While the theatres were slower to reject Shakespearian alteration than the printing houses, evidence shows that the accepting or apathetic attitude towards altering Shakespeare for the stage was beginning to wane by the mid-1730s, right around the time of the formation of the Shakespeare Ladies Club. In the 'Occasional Prompter' section of the *Daily Journal* issue published on 29 December 1736, an anonymous writer expresses delight that:

A NOBLE Attempt to revive the Stage, by a Club of Women of the First Quality and Fashion is now going forward: Would the Men of Fashion form a Club to extirpate Entertainments, the *Shakespear Club* (for so the Ladies have dignified themselves) would find a noble Association there; and a Union of both, in all Probability, might restore the Stage, and make the

---

74 Hume, 'Before', p. 53. 75 Dugas, *Marketing*, p. ix.
76 Dugas, *Marketing*, p. ix. See also Anthony Brano, 'The 1734–5 price wars, *Antony and Cleopatra* and the theatrical imagination', in *Canonising Shakespeare: Stationers and the Book Trade, 1640–1740*, ed. Emma Depledge and Peter Kirwan (Cambridge, 2017), pp. 63–78; p. 69; and Scouten, 'Increase', pp. 197–8.
77 Jacob Tonson, 'Advertisement', in *The Works of Shakespeare*, 8 vols. (London, 1734–5), vol. 3, p. 72 (single editions bound together in eight volumes held at the University of Victoria's Special Collections, PR2752 T65 1734). Jonathan Bate remarks, 'The jibe at Walker for printing Tate's *King Lear* instead of Shakespeare's is especially interesting in view of that fact that these editions were to be sold at the theatres: Tonson clearly expects the discerning gentleman to want to *see* Tate's version but *read* Shakespeare's. The massive discrepancy between the text as spoken on the stage and as sold in the foyer is testimony to the extraordinary multiplicity of Shakespeare's identities in the eighteenth century' (Bate, *Constitutions*, p. 24).

Profession of an Actor as valuable in publick Opinion as it is really in itself.

On the same page, a letter complains about the preponderance of pantomime on the stage and then mentions 'The other Night we had *Macbeth* (I had like to have said *Shakespear's Macbeth*, but I beg his Pardon, for he would scarce know it as it is now acted)',[78] indicating that some playgoers were beginning to recognize – and disapprove of – the disparity between Shakespeare's text and the versions produced on stage.

Especially derided were Colley Cibber's attempts to stage his alteration of *King John*, an endeavour he ultimately abandoned.[79] In his 1737 play-within-a-play entitled *The Historical Register for the Year 1736*, Henry Fielding mocked the Poet Laureate for 'having the audacity to alter a play that had not been performed in more than 130 years and that has never been considered one of Shakespeare's more inspired efforts'.[80] In Act 3, as Fielding's characters cast roles for Cibber's adaptation, one character, Medley, remarks, 'as *Shakespear* is already good enough for People of Taste; he must be alter'd to the Palates of those who have none'.[81] At the play's conclusion, Medley addresses the audience and includes a tribute to the Shakespeare Ladies Club, saying, 'you, Ladies, whether you be *Shakespear's* Ladies, or *Beaumont* and *Fletcher's* Ladies, I hope you will make Allowances for a Rehearsal'.[82] The 4 March 1737 issue of the *Daily Advertiser* included a letter from the ghost of Shakespeare 'from Elisium, to the Fair Supporters of Wit and Sense, the Ladies of Great Britain', whom he praises for being 'so earnest to prop the sinking State of Wit and Sense, that they form'd themselves into a Society, and reviv'd the Memory of the forsaken Shakespear'.[83] This letter appears to have been partially intended as an advertisement for that evening's performance of *The Life and Death of King John*, '*As originally written by Shakespear. Supervised, Read over, Revised, and Unalter'd*' at the New Haymarket Theatre. The letter goes on to say, 'My Shade, this present Evening, intends to visit you at the New Theatre in the Hay-Market . . . to pay you my Devoirs, and

to introduce my own Play of King John on that Stage'. Shakespeare's ghost further expresses an intention 'to confront that Bard of Corinth' – that is, Colley Cibber – 'who I hear has been very free with me'.[84] It is worth noting that this 'unalter'd' production featured 'a New Prologue . . . concluding with an Address to the Ladies of the Shakespear's Club'.[85] To my knowledge, the text of this address does not survive; nevertheless, this indicates that *King John* was possibly staged in its unaltered state in consideration of the Shakespeare Ladies Club's preferences. It is uncertain whether this shifting attitude towards more purist preferences was in fact initiated by the Shakespeare Ladies Club, or whether the formation of the Club was an additional expression of it; regardless, the Ladies' campaign, by all appearances, would increase the momentum of the public's growing inclination towards reverence for Shakespeare's unaltered text in performance. Cibber's woes stemming from his alteration of *King John* demonstrate that the public consensus was, as Dugas explains, that 'even minor Shakespeare plays "deserved" to be presented in their original states . . . And the only way that theatergoers could have conceived of what constituted the "original state" of a play that had not been performed in more than a hundred years was through texts.'[86]

In a letter to her cousin Elizabeth Harris dated 13 March 1753, Susanna Ashley-Cooper lamented, 'I have been at none of the new plays that have been lately exhibited, but have read them all.'[87] This document confirms that play-reading was

[78] 'The Occasional Prompter. Number X.', *The Daily Journal*, 29 December 1736.
[79] Avery, 'Shakespeare', p. 154.   [80] Dugas, *Marketing*, p. 181.
[81] Henry Fielding, *The Historical Register for the Year 1736* (London, 1737), pp. 1–33; p. 27.
[82] Fielding, *Register*, p. 33.
[83] Quoted in Avery, 'Shakespeare', pp. 155–6.
[84] Quoted in Emmett L. Avery, 'Fielding's last season with the Haymarket Theatre', *Modern Philology* 36.3 (1939), 283–92; p. 287.
[85] Quoted in Avery, 'Shakespeare', p. 155.
[86] Dugas, *Marketing*, p. 182.
[87] Burrows and Dunhill, *Music*, p. 287.

indeed a lifelong pastime for the Countess of Shaftesbury, who died in 1758. Compelling evidence that the Shakespeare Ladies Club's ambitions originated through reading lies in an examination of the plays bespoken by the Ladies of Quality. For instance, the advertisement for Covent Garden's 6 February 1738 staging of *Richard II* (at the Ladies' desire) noted that it had been 'Not Acted these Forty Years'. Likewise, the 16 February 1738 and 13 March 1738 performances of *II Henry IV* and *I Henry VI*, respectively, were both advertised as 'Not Acted these Fifty Years. At the Desire of several Ladies of Quality. Written by Shakespear'.[88] The advertisement for the former additionally stressed that 'The above Play of King Henry IV is the Genuine Play of Shakespear, and not that alter'd by Mr Betterton, and so frequently acted at the other Theatre', indicating that openly staging unaltered Shakespeare might have even offered Covent Garden a competitive edge over Drury Lane. As Taylor has reinforced, 'Since these women were encouraging the performance of plays that had not been produced in decades, their knowledge of them could have come only from reading.'[89]

Dugas rightly underscores the role of the Shakespeare Ladies Club in the theatrical revival of this decade and is correct to emphasize the Club's readership as a driving factor in its campaign; however, he assumes that the Ladies likely read the cheap single editions produced during the price war. Considering Pococke's description of the 'works in a glass case' (which does not evoke images of stacks of single-play leaflets) and the following additional evidence, I am more inclined to agree with Scheil, who has noted the challenge of determining which edition the Ladies read but supposes it was likely a Tonson collected edition of Shakespeare's works with editorial intervention, such as Pope's or Theobald's.[90] Though the price war certainly increased the accessibility of Shakespeare texts and emphasized the value of unaltered Shakespeare (the significance of which ought not to be underestimated and no doubt contributed to the enduring success of the Club's campaign), Dugas and others have also conceded that 'The real beneficiaries of the

Tonson–Walker price war were the less-affluent readers of Shakespeare' who could not have afforded a Tonson edition.[91] The wealthy, aristocratic Ladies of Quality, however, were of the 'elite book-buying market',[92] for whom a Tonson collection would have been a status symbol to display in their libraries, as well as a 'handsome, convenient, and modern' reading edition.[93] Additionally, both Tonson and Walker included apocryphal Shakespearian plays among their printed single editions. None of these plays was performed during this revival nor requested by the Ladies; the connection therefore is unconvincing.[94]

In commissioning his collected editions, Tonson, Dugas explains, 'abandoned the traditional formats in which Shakespeare's plays had always been published, and ... replaced them with what has become the dominant form for a collected dramatic works in English literature: an octavo edition ... prepared by a prominent expert and featuring a biography, a critical introduction, and textual intervention'.[95] In 1710, the year after Tonson acquired his monopoly on publishing Shakespeare by purchasing the rights to the Fourth Folio, a new Copyright Act was passed which 'contained a clause limiting the duration of copyright, to twenty-one years for works already in print at the date of enactments, and to fourteen

---

[88] Scouten, ed., *London*, pp. 701, 703, 707.

[89] Taylor, *Reinventing*, p. 93. This conclusion is echoed in Scheil, 'Rouz'd', pp. 114–15.

[90] Scheil, 'Rouz'd', p. 117.

[91] Dugas, *Marketing*, p. 228. Rowe's edition cost 30s; Pope's, a 'staggeringly expensive' £6 6s (Dugas, *Marketing*, 195); Theobald's, 42s. See Edmund G. C. King, 'Discovering Shakespeare's personal style: editing and connoisseurship in the eighteenth century', in *Canonising*, ed. Depledge and Kirwan, pp. 130–42; p. 134.

[92] King, 'Discovering', p. 134. [93] Dugas, *Marketing*, p. xi.

[94] These included *The London Prodigal, Thomas Lord Cromwell, Sir John Oldcastle, The Puritan, A Yorkshire Tragedy* and *Locrine*. Notably, Theobald's edition 'returned the canon of Shakespeare's plays to thirty-six after some sixty years of a forty-three play canon' (Peter Kirwan, 'Consolidating the Shakespeare canon, 1640–1740', in *Canonising*, ed. Depledge and Kirwan, pp. 81–8; p. 86).

[95] Dugas, *Marketing*, p. 73.

years for books newly printed, if the author was still living'.[96] Thus, Tonson devised a loophole operating on the assumption that he could theoretically maintain his exclusive hold on the rights to publish Shakespeare by producing a new edition derived from the latest Tonson Shakespeare edition before the fourteen years expired.[97] This arrangement led to the succession of early eighteenth-century Shakespeare editors. By the time the Shakespeare Ladies Club formed in the mid-1730s, three editions had been published: Nicholas Rowe's, Alexander Pope's and Lewis Theobald's, each attempting to expose and correct the flaws in the previous edition, thus to supersede its predecessor. The early editors understood the challenges posed by the absence of extant manuscripts in Shakespeare's hand. They noticed the range of textual differences across various playbooks, including the folios compiled after Shakespeare's death as well as the quartos dating from Shakespeare's lifetime, whose printing, in theory, he could have supervised.[98] The consensus was that 'there were so many errors that even the First Folio was ... unable to reproduce Shakespeare's original intentions. Rather, this ideal text was now buried, and had to be retrieved.'[99] Each editor would have his own approach to doing so.

Taylor acknowledges that Pope, in his role as editor, 'had looked at more old editions than anyone else before him; but he had not looked at them all or noticed or used all that was in them'. Pope was hostile towards the surviving folios and quartos, determining that 'all the early texts of Shakespeare reeked of corruption' and 'could be saved only by wholesale adaptation'.[100] Not wholly unlike the playwrights of the day, Pope attempted to update Shakespeare to suit eighteenth-century aesthetic standards by regularizing the metre, removing 'a number of "suspected passages" as "excessively bad", either without notice, or "degrading" them to the foot of the page', and censoring Shakespeare's 'bander, quibble, and vulgarity'.[101] He considered his method, which amounted to little more than capricious alteration, to be a redemptive process and believed himself to be posthumously elevating Shakespeare out of the unfortunate circumstances

of his time and audience. Perplexingly, the main source of textual corruption Pope identified was Shakespeare's associations with actors, theatres and performance, and a significant component of his editorial practice was to excise Shakespeare's pristine, 'original' text from the damaging influence of the theatre.[102] For Pope,

the theatrical provenance of the plays was ... a decided liability. The source texts for the earlier editions were likely ... to have been cobbled together from 'the *Prompter's Book*, or *Piece-meal Parts* written out for the use of the actors', text which 'had lain ... in the playhouse, and had from time to time been cut, or added to, arbitrarily'. Where speeches were, in Pope's view, assigned to the wrong character, this was probably because 'a governing Player, to have the mouthing of some favourite speech himself, would snatch it from the unworthy lips of an Underling'.[103]

Pope's edition, so overtly contemptuous towards the theatre and the early surviving printed texts of Shakespeare, could hardly have been the inspiration behind the first movement towards favouring unaltered Shakespeare in performance.

An alternative approach to editing Shakespeare's text was offered almost immediately. Published in 1726, the year after the release of Pope's edition,

---

[96] Marcus Walsh, 'Editing and publishing Shakespeare', in *Shakespeare*, ed. Ritchie and Sabor, pp. 21–40; p. 22. Sandra Clark has remarked that this Copyright Act influenced 'the development of the concept of the author as owner of his works, and the status of Shakespeare changed accordingly' (Sandra Clark, *Shakespeare Made Fit: Restoration Adaptations of Shakespeare* (London, 1997), p. xliii).

[97] Dugas, *Marketing*, p. 191.

[98] Andrew Murphy, 'The birth of the editor', in *A Concise Companion to Shakespeare and the Text*, ed. Andrew Murphy (Oxford, 2007), pp. 91–108; p. 94.

[99] Harriman-Smith, 'Anti-performance', p. 49.

[100] Taylor, *Reinventing*, pp. 85–6. [101] Walsh, 'Editing', p. 25.

[102] For more on Pope's editorial approach, see J. Gavin Paul, 'Performance as "punctuation": editing Shakespeare in the eighteenth century', *The Review of English Studies* 61 (2010), 390–413; pp. 398–406; Stephen Orgel, 'The authentic Shakespeare', *Representations* 21 (1988), 1–25; pp. 12–13; and Harriman-Smith, 'Anti-performance', pp. 49–51.

[103] Murphy, 'Birth', p. 95.

Theobald's scholarly critique of Pope's methods was mercilessly entitled *Shakespeare Restored: or, a Specimen of the Many Errors, as Well Committed, as Unamended, by Mr. Pope in His Late Edition of This Poet. Designed Not Only to Correct the Said Edition, but to Restore the True Reading of Shakespeare in All the Editions Ever Yet Publish'd*. In this volume, Theobald asserted that 'whenever a Gentleman and a Scholar turns Editor of any Book, he at the same Time commences Critick upon his Author'. He proposed that Shakespeare should receive similar editorial treatment to the classic writers: that all of the extant editions ought to be collated, and 'wherever [the editor] finds the Reading suspected, manifestly corrupted, deficient in Sense, and unintelligible, he ought to exert every Power and Faculty of the Mind to supply such a Defect, to give Light and restore Sense to the Passage, and, by a reasonable Emendation, to make that satisfactory and consistent with the Context'.[104]

Theobald 'conducted a close interrogation of a number of cruces from *Hamlet*' in the bulk of *Shakespeare Restored*, and included an appendix that demonstrated his professed approach on select cruces in other Shakespearian plays.[105] Emma Depledge and Peter Kirwan have remarked that *Shakespeare Restored* 'was not dissimilar to ... the New Bibliography in its belief that the role of the editor was to capture and preserve what the author originally wrote',[106] as opposed to updating Shakespeare for contemporary tastes as Pope had attempted and as was customary in the theatre.

Tonson soon offered Theobald the opportunity to apply the scholarly talent he exhibited in *Shakespeare Restored* to the rest of Shakespeare's dramatic works as his next editor. Pope's edition had not sold well, Tonson's copyright claim on Shakespeare's works was close to expiring, and he stood to benefit from some free publicity owing to the public feud between Pope and Theobald.[107] Theobald's edition of the works of Shakespeare was released in January 1734, despite the 1733 imprint,[108] making his the most recent scholarly edition published prior to the establishment of the Shakespeare Ladies Club. His edition earned him his reputation as 'the prime mover in a drive for

printed authenticity',[109] as he professed in his preface his 'Hopes of restoring to the Publick their greatest poet in his Original Purity: after having so long lain in a Condition that was a Disgrace to common Sense.'[110] Theobald promised that Shakespeare's 'genuine Text is religiously adher'd to, and the numerous Faults and Blemishes, purely his own, are left as they were found. Nothing is alter'd, but what by the clearest Reasoning can be proved a Corruption of the true Text; and the Alteration, a real Restoration of the genuine Reading.'[111] Given that we have established significant overlap between eighteenth-century readers and theatre attendees, and considering that 'Theobald's edition was particularly popular with the reading public',[112] it seems likely that reading playgoers absorbed the inherent value of Shakespeare's unaltered text professed by Theobald – an attitude that apparently spread to performance by the end of the decade.

[104] Lewis Theobald, *Shakespeare Restored* (London, 1726), p. v.
[105] Walsh, 'Editing', p. 26.
[106] Emma Depledge and Peter Kirwan, 'Editing Shakespeare, 1640–1740', in *Canonising*, ed. Depledge and Kirwan, pp. 145–52; p. 150. See also Jack Lynch, 'Criticism of Shakespeare', in *Shakespeare*, ed. Ritchie and Sabor, pp. 46–7.
[107] Perceiving *Shakespeare Restored* to be an extended personal insult, Pope retaliated by ridiculing Theobald in his 1728 mock-epic poem *The Dunciad*. However, Pope also 'tacitly accepted many of Theobald's charges, incorporating more than a hundred of Theobald's readings into the second edition of his Shakespeare, though he never publicly acknowledged the corrections' (Lynch, 'Criticism', p. 46). Additionally, like Pope and Rowe before him, due to the same copyright laws driving the continual reissue of Shakespeare's edited works, Theobald's starting point had to be 'from the latest Tonson-owned offering', which was, rather ironically in his case, Pope's second edition of 1728. Even so, he 'included Pope's editions, along with Rowe's, among the "Editions of no authority" in his table of editions collated' (Kastan, *Shakespeare*, p. 100).
[108] Dugas, *Marketing*, p. 196.
[109] Brean Hammond, 'Shakespeare discoveries and forgeries', in *Shakespeare*, ed. Ritchie and Sabor, pp. 78–98.
[110] Lewis Theobald, *The Works of Shakespeare: In Seven Volumes: Collated with the Oldest Copies, and Corrected, with Notes, Explanatory, and Critical*, vol. 1 (London, 1733), p. xxxix.
[111] Theobald, *Works*, p. xl. [112] Scheil, 'Rouz'd', p. 117.

It is important to recall, too, the reverence shown towards Shakespeare's written works at the Countess of Shaftesbury's garden memorial to the Bard – an extraordinary affirmation of the almost prophetic remark Theobald made in *Shakespeare Restored*: 'there is scarce a Poet, that our *English* Tongue boasts of, who is more the Subject of the Ladies Reading'.[113] Building upon Scheil's speculations about which edition the Shakespeare Ladies Club's members might have read, I have since discovered that Theobald's edition appears in catalogue records of the library at St Giles House. An inventory of the 4th Earl's assets and possessions taken shortly after his death lists 'Shakespear (Theobalds) 7 vols.' among the books held at the estate.[114] (Notably, Pope's edition does not appear in this inventory, nor do any single editions produced by Tonson or Walker.) This is compelling evidence that the edition Lady Shaftesbury displayed in a glass case in Shakespeare's House was almost certainly Theobald's. It therefore seems probable that, in addition to exerting its considerable influence to promote native British drama, elevate Shakespeare's status and reform public taste through its theatrical campaign, the Shakespeare Ladies Club may have advocated for the same reverence for Shakespeare's text professed by Theobald and reflected in Shakespeare's House at St Giles.

Ritchie's analysis of the Shakespeare Ladies Club's campaign suggests that, after successfully persuading Charles Fleetwood, manager of Drury Lane theatre, to stage more Shakespeare, the Ladies were optimistic that they might likewise be positively received by John Rich at Covent Garden. She remarks, 'Rich was identified as the person responsible for the development of pantomime on the English stage: an article in *Lloyd's Evening Post* . . . lauded him as the "Father of Pantomimes" and he was famous for dancing the lead role in many of these entertainments.'[115] Considering this, Ritchie regards the Club's triumph in 'the more difficult challenge at Covent Garden', where Shakespeare's proportion of the repertory increased from 16 per cent in the 1736–7 season to 29 per cent in 1737–8, as an even greater indication

of the Ladies' success.[116] Perhaps so. My own analysis of John Rich's role in this Shakespeare revival, however, paints a more complex picture than previous scholarship, and even some aspects of his contemporary reputation, might suggest.

Lewis Theobald had dedicated *Shakespeare Restored* to John Rich (who went on to be listed as one of the subscribers to Theobald's edition), writing, 'It may seem a little particular that, when I am attempting to restore SHAKESPEARE, I should address that Work to One, who has gone a great Way towards shutting him out of Doors; that is, towards banishing him the Benefit of the Stage, and confining us to read him in the Closet.'[117] So far, this dedication appears to be consistent with contemporary criticism of the 'Father of Pantomimes'. However, Theobald goes on to absolve Rich of the allegation somewhat, saying, 'it is not You, indeed, but that Affection, with which *Entertainments* of a *different Species* are pursued, has done this; and therefore I would fain transfer the Fault from You to the Town'.[118] Theobald was employed by Rich, writing libretti, a few successful pantomimes, the infamous *Double Falshood* (allegedly based on Shakespeare's lost play *Cardenio*) and even an altered version of Shakespeare's *Richard II*.[119] This

---

[113] Theobald, *Shakespeare*, p. vi.

[114] *A Catalogue of Books at the Seat of the Earl of Shaftesbury at St. Giles's, Dorset* (1772), p. 33. Held at the National Archives, Kew: C 109/308.

[115] Ritchie, *Women*, p. 146. See also Avery, 'Shakespeare', p. 156.

[116] Ritchie, *Women*, p. 145.

[117] Theobald, *Shakespeare*, sig. A2r.

[118] Theobald, *Shakespeare*, sig. A2r–v.

[119] Dugas, *Marketing*, pp. 196–7. Kastan has shrewdly noted how Theobald's sentimental alteration of *Richard II* is a testament to the eighteenth century's 'schizophrenic relation to Shakespeare – always admiring, but, in one mode, presumptuously altering his plays for success on the stage, while, in another, determinedly seeking the authentic text in the succession of scholarly editions' (Kastan, *Shakespeare*, p. 93). While Theobald's authorship of stage adaptations may have tarnished his reputation somewhat among modern critics, it hardly invalidates the impact his edition of Shakespeare's works must have had on the contemporary reading–playgoing public.

criticism of the taste of the town may in fact have reflected a mutual understanding between Rich and Theobald: in the printed text of Theobald's wildly successful 1727 pantomime *The Rape of Proserpine*, Rich included an apologetic dedication lamenting the commercial necessity of pantomimes but proclaiming, 'whenever the Publick Taste shall be disposed to return to the works of the *Drama*, no one shall rejoice more sincerely than my self'.[120]

Additionally, the monument to Shakespeare in Poets' Corner – that enduring legacy of the Shakespeare Ladies Club – was originally Rich's idea. In 1726, the same year *Shakespeare Restored* was published, Rich had been granted permission by the Westminster Abbey Dean and Chapter to build a memorial to Shakespeare, though it is unclear why the project stalled for so many years.[121] Theobald's dedication verifies this, going on to declare:

I am justified in this Address by another Consideration, which is, That however you may have been a Sinner against SHAKESPEARE, you are not an impenitent one. And as King *Henry* IV. erected a Chapel to expiate the Injuries which he had done to his Predecessor, King *Richard*; so, the Town at least say, you intend to appease the *Manes* of our POET by erecting a MONUMENT to him. Go on in that pious, that reputable Intention; and, while the Taste of the Publick demands it of you, continue to sacrifice fresh *Pantomimes* to his Memory; when their Palates alter, convince them that You are provided to entertain them with an Elegance suitable to their Expectations.[122]

Finally, it ought not to be ignored that Rich had attempted to revive Shakespeare in the late 1710s and early 1720s during his tenure as manager of the theatre at Lincoln's Inn Fields. Scouten writes that Rich staged '16 different Shakespearean dramas . . . on 66 nights in a season of 164 performances, truly an amazing record', but reveals that, upon examining Rich's financial records, a full third of those performances generated a deficit.[123] It stands to reason, then, that Rich resorted to staging pantomimes in the interest of business. However, when the Shakespeare Ladies Club approached Rich to stage more Shakespeare – its track record at Drury Lane already having indicated the shift in the public's taste he had long hoped for – while promising

a subscription of funds to alleviate any of Rich's lingering fiscal concerns about reviving Shakespeare at his theatre again and professing a desire to fundraise and secure public support for the long-dormant Abbey monument project, I assume that John Rich, the so-called 'Father of Pantomimes', would have been elated to oblige. Championing Shakespeare at Covent Garden theatre may not have been such an insurmountable challenge for the Ladies after all.

Theobald composed a prologue to be recited at Covent Garden's 10 April 1739 performance of *Hamlet* – the second benefit performance for the Abbey monument – just as James Noel and Benjamin Martyn had for the production of *Julius Caesar* the previous year, so it seems probable that the Shakespeare Ladies Club's foundress may have invited him to contribute the piece. Significantly, Theobald's prologue concludes with a direct address to the Ladies. He thanks them for their activism on Shakespeare's behalf and makes a point to implore them and those they inspire to 'frequent Visit' Shakespeare in the theatre as well as Poets' Corner:

For the dead Bard, receive our thanks and praise;
　And make us Sharers in the Tomb you raise.
Ye Fair, who have distinguished Favours shewn,
　And made this Poet's Patronage your own;
Urge those, whose gen'rous Hearts confess your Sway,
　To follow, where your Virtues point the Way:
Then think, this Pile his honour'd Bones contains,
　And frequent Visit – here – the lov'd Remains.[124]

This is a poignant entreaty 'for the cause of live drama'[125] from the editor who laboured to restore

---

[120] John Rich, 'Dedication', in Lewis Theobald, *The Rape of Proserpine* (London, 1727), pp. iii–vii; p. vi. See also Matthew J. Kinservik, 'John Rich, theatrical regulation, and the dilemma of the commercial stage', in '*The Stage's Glory*', ed. Joncus and Barlow, pp. 75–82; pp. 77–8.

[121] Morris R. Brownell, *Alexander Pope & the Arts of Georgian England* (Oxford, 1978), p. 354. See also 'William Shakespeare': www.westminster-abbey.org.

[122] Theobald, *Shakespeare*, sig. A3r.

[123] Scouten, ed., *London*, pp. cxlix–cl.

[124] Lewis Theobald, 'Prologue', *London Daily Post and General Advertiser*, 12 April 1739. See also Dobson, *Making*, p. 160.

[125] Dobson, *Making*, p. 160.

Shakespeare's words on the page and whose resulting edition was now apparently instigating a corresponding restoration on the stage. Significantly, as Dobson has observed, the Westminster Abbey monument unequivocally venerates a 'strictly literary Shakespeare'. As he describes it, 'Certainly there is nothing about the statue to suggest that it commemorates a mere working playwright … Shakespeare, meditating gravely in what appears to be a library, leans with one elbow on a lectern topped with a pile of immense leather-bound books – presumably his own works.'[126] Indeed, it is Shakespeare's corpus of written works, which comparatively recently had been derided as archaic and unfit for the present age without substantial modification, that is now revered: his genius is inherent in his words, and the page is authoritative and permanent, worthy of commemoration.

Though it would yet take many years for theatrical alteration to fall completely out of fashion, the Shakespeare Ladies Club's campaign coincides with the first shift in that direction. Marsden has identified the end of the eighteenth century as the point when the writing of new alterations would cease completely and 'the taboo, which we feel today, against tampering with Shakespeare's works is irrevocably established'. In the more immediate aftermath of the Club's campaign, she explains that:

Shakespeare's text was no longer being substantively rewritten; instead, playwrights made their changes by simply cutting out portions of the original plays and retaining the Shakespearean language of the parts which remained, or by changing older adaptations, restoring large sections of original Shakespearean dialogue to the stage … While alterations that involved little meddling with language were tolerated, changing Shakespeare's word was not … In contrast to earlier periods, playwrights treated Shakespeare's language as a 'given,' a set of words that could be chopped or pieced out, but not subverted.[127]

Garrick immediately comes to mind as the apparent exception to this, considering that he wrote, produced and performed in alterations of possibly as many as twenty-two Shakespearian plays

throughout his career. We should note, however, that he often did so apologetically, calling his never-published alteration of *Hamlet*, for example, 'the most imprudent thing I ever did in all my life'.[128] Moreover, some critics have perceived Garrick's alterations to show 'a close study by the adapter, a great respect for the original texts, and the restoring of much of Shakespeare's poetry that had not been heard in the century',[129] confirming that phasing out alteration in the eighteenth century was a gradual process. Garrick also faced varying degrees of criticism for altering Shakespeare. While some commentators imagined Shakespeare's ghost bestowing its blessing upon Garrick to 'Freely correct my Page: / I wrote to please a rude unpolish'd age',[130] others countered the sentiment, insisting, 'Were *Shakespear's* Ghost to rise, wou'd he not frown Indignation, on this pilfering Pedlar in Poetry who thus shamefully mangles, mutilates, and emasculates his Plays?'[131] Though, clearly, alteration was not universally vilified by the time Garrick inherited the designation of Shakespeare's primary promoter from the Shakespeare Ladies Club, this evidence nevertheless indicates that there was pervasive knowledge of Shakespeare's identity, his works and any disparities between his text and performance – a far cry from his relatively anonymous status at the turn of the century.

Thus, while Lewis Theobald's methods and emendations may not be considered flawless by our modern editorial standards, he nevertheless precipitated the widespread, enduring penchant for printed authenticity in his editorial approach,

---

[126] Dobson, *Making*, p. 160.
[127] Marsden, *Re-Imagined*, p. 152.
[128] David Garrick, *The Private Correspondence of David Garrick*, ed. James Boaden, 2 vols. (Cambridge, 2013), vol. 2, p. 126. Also referenced in *The Plays of David Garrick*, ed. Harry William Pedicord and Frederick Louis Bergmann, 7 vols. (Carbondale, 1981), vol. 3, p. xvi.
[129] *Garrick*, ed. Pedicord and Bergmann, p. xvi.
[130] *An Asylum for Fugitives*, 2 vols. (London, 1776), vol. 1, p. 158. Quoted in Stern, 'Shakespeare', p. 155.
[131] Theophilus Cibber, *To David Garrick, Esq. with Dissertations on Theatrical Subjects* (London, 1759), p. 36. See also Marsden, *Re-Imagined*, p. 121.

professed objectives, and conviction that the editor ought to be the author's textual servant. Theobald's edition materialized his 'Hopes of restoring to the Publick their greatest Poet in his Original Purity' on the page; in the hands of a group of influential, literate women who served as a bridge between the theatres and the reading public, and therefore between literary and theatrical Shakespeare, it impelled a movement inspired by those same principles to restore likewise unaltered Shakespeare to the stage. Thomas Cooke's 1743 poem *An Epistle to the Right Honourable the Countess of Shaftesbury, with A Prologue and Epilogue on Shakespeare and his Writings* identifies Susanna Ashley-Cooper as the Shakespeare Ladies Club's leader and lauds her as the 'Fair Patroness of long departed Worth / . . . whose Spirit wak'd a drowsy Age / To pay a due Regard to *Shakespeare*'s Page'.[132] The closing lines of this ode interestingly anticipate Sir Thomas Hanmer's forthcoming 1744 edition of Shakespeare's works.[133] With the words 'May that great Work, O! *Hanmer*, crown thy Days; / And may'st thou well deserve our *Shaftesb'ry*'s Praise',[134] Cooke hopes that Hanmer will secure the Countess's approval as the reigning authority on 'Shakespeare's page'. Theobald, it would seem, already had.

Many scholars have remarked that Shakespeare's elevation to the forefront of Britain's cultural consciousness – to national poet status – in the early eighteenth century was never preordained. Rather, it was the result of a confluence of key events and movements and the concentrated effort of a handful of individuals, including the women of the Shakespeare Ladies Club, advocating on Shakespeare's behalf. I have sought to increase our understanding of the Shakespeare Ladies Club by exploring its involvement with the Patriot opposition movement, which predominantly inspired its promotion of Shakespeare as a figure, and additionally situating the Club as an influential organization within a broad culture of increasing readership. I contend that by reading Lewis Theobald's edition of Shakespeare's works, the Ladies came to revere Shakespeare's original text and exercised their influence accordingly – both with the reading and playgoing public and in theatrical circles – to begin the long and arduous process of shifting away from the widespread practices of alteration.

While Shakespeare's House no longer stands on the grounds of the St Giles estate, and the small statue of the Bard and the Countess's copy of Theobald's seven-volume octavo edition of Shakespeare's works have also vanished over the centuries, thanks to a seemingly inconsequential description in an eighteenth-century travel diary, we know they were once there. And, given who these artefacts belonged to, we can explore their wider implications for the Shakespeare Ladies Club's role in shaping our enduring cultural perception of the Bard – and establishing that we must all 'pay a due regard to Shakespeare's page'.

---

132 Cooke, *Epistle*, p. 3.

133 Far from being a formidable scholarly accomplishment, Hanmer's edition rather serves a kind of 'commemorative function', incorporating illustrations by Francis Hayman (whose paintings of scenes from Shakespearian plays adorned the walls of the Prince's Pavilion at Vauxhall) and an engraving of Shakespeare's Westminster Abbey monument. In his preface, Hanmer indicates that he was inspired – directly or indirectly – by the Shakespeare Ladies Club, writing, 'as a fresh acknowledgement hath lately been paid to his merit . . . by erecting his statue at a public expense; so it is desired that this new Edition of his works . . . may be looked upon as another small monument designed and dedicated to his honour' (see Nosan, 'Pavilions', pp. 117–18).

134 Cooke, *Epistle*, p. 4.

HAMLET *AND JOHN AUSTEN'S DEVIL WITH A (DIS)PLEASING SHAPE*

LUISA MOORE

INTRODUCTION

The Ghost's depiction in recent film and stage productions of *Hamlet* ranges from paternal and benevolent to potentially demonic. In Branagh's 1996 film, it (Brian Blessed) whispers to Hamlet from among the trees in an ominous wood, before descending out of nowhere and grasping him by the throat. It continues to whisper with a harsh intensity, but its voice conveys little change in emotion and its expression is fixed. Its eyes are a shining pale blue, evoking the supernatural; it is easy to think that this Ghost might be demonic. In contrast, Doran's Ghost (Patrick Stewart) speaks and acts like a living person, alternating between distress, outrage and indignation, physically expressive and pacing about energetically. At one point it clutches Hamlet in a fervent embrace – after temporarily assaulting him. Doran's performance was consistent between stage production and its accompanying film released the following year.[1]

But this has not always been the case: until the mid twentieth century, the Ghost, as represented on stage and in visual art, had little of this demonic ambiguity, but tended to resemble a cold distant father,[2] perhaps due to Victorian (and earlier) patriarchal assumptions that typically coded such an austere *paterfamilias* as 'masculine' and admirable.[3] I suggest that John Austen in his 1922 illustrated edition of *Hamlet* offered a revision of this Victorian tradition, anticipating (some) modern performances.[4] His reading of the scene builds upon and extends the unorthodox depictions of Hamlet encountering

[1] Patrick J. Cook observes of Almereyda's filmic *Hamlet* (2000) that 'The ghost [Sam Shepard] makes physical contact with his son [Ethan Hawke] in a way that conveys both menace and affection ... When the ghost places his left hand on Hamlet's chest, Hamlet glances down at it, as confused as we are about whether his visitor wishes him good or ill': Patrick J. Cook, *Cinematic Hamlet: The Films of Olivier, Branagh and Almereyda* (Ohio, 2012), p. 179.

[2] In *Hamlet's Absent Father* (2015), Avi Ehrlich notes that 'King Hamlet was absent on the day his son was born. His ghost is also absent for most of the play ... Imposing and imposed upon, terrifying yet pitiable, he is an ambiguous figure who both comes to renew his son's sense of purpose, and, ultimately, to crush him': Avi Ehrlich, *Hamlet's Absent Father* (Princeton, 2015), p. 51.

[3] John Tosh points to the existence of four types of fathers in Victorian England: distant, tyrannical, intimate and absent (John Tosh, *A Man's Place: Masculinity and the Middle-Class Home in Victorian England* (New Haven and London, 1999), p. 95). Intimate fathers had to remain wary of appearing 'effeminized' in the eyes of those around them or being seen to usurp the culturally assigned roles of their wives (p. 95). As Barbara K. Greenleaf observes, 'Not for nothing was the patriarchal Victorian father called "the Governor"': Barbara K. Greenleaf, *Children Through the Ages: A History of Childhood* (New York, 1978), p. 79. Natalie McKnight remarks in respect of Dickens's *Bleak House* that 'In the figure of Sir Leicester Dedlock, and his broader social deadlock in relation to the rest of a national infrastructure, Dickens encrypts the absent fathers of an entire nation': Natalie McKnight, *Fathers in Victorian Fiction* (Cambridge, 2011), p. 145.

[4] Austen's slim and elegant edition of *Hamlet* was published as an expensive issue *de luxe*, printed on hand-made paper (a copy can be found in the Cambridge University Library Rare Books Room and the Folger Shakespeare Library). Its text was that of the popular Globe Edition (*The Works of William Shakespeare*, ed. William George Clark and William Aldis Wright (London, 1864)). Just sixty copies were made, only fifty of which were for sale, numbered and signed by the artist. Its expense and rarity suggest that the edition was meant not for the mass market of the cheap Globe Edition, but for a sophisticated intellectual's private consideration – someone likely to be capable of appreciating the complexity of meaning in Austen's drawings.

12 Robert Thew, engraving after a painting by Henry Fuseli, *Hamlet, Horatio, Marcellus and the Ghost* (London, 1796). Held in the
Folger Shakespeare Library.

the Ghost by Henry Fuseli, John Gilbert and
Henry C. Selous.

Inevitably, Austen's influences will have been
theatrical as well as textual; however, we have
little (or no direct) evidence for his theatre-
going.[5] In any case, his *reading* of the plays, or
analysis of them as poetic texts, forms the core of
this investigation. The text appears to have been
more of an informing factor in Austen's illustrations than the theatre: he seems to have been
fascinated by the hermeneutical potential of the
illustrator's art.[6]

Fuseli produced three images of Hamlet and
the Ghost, one of which was put on display as
part of the late eighteenth-century Boydell
Gallery venture (see Figure 12), while Gilbert's
(Figure 13) and Selous's (Figure 14) illustrations
were widely available in popular editions of
collected Shakespeare. These works were well
known among London's middle class, suggesting

5 Because of their close acquaintance, Dorothy Richardson is the
best (and, incidentally, only) source we have for uncovering what
kind of theatre (and which performances) Austen attended. She
observes that, before returning to Kent and while still living in
London, 'he devoted the scant leisure he allowed himself to
amateur theatricals': Dorothy Miller Richardson, *John Austen
and the Inseparables* (London, 1930), p. 20. Based on this remark,
he may not actually have seen any of the critically reviewed, more
professionally acted *Hamlet*s. However, Austen moved in educated, middle-class circles where the theatre would have been
discussed, and probably would have seen performance reviews
and the exhibited artworks which it inspired: he is thus likely to
have been influenced by major performances of Shakespeare, if
only indirectly.

6 The examination of illustrated editions of Shakespeare has been
largely confined to nineteenth-century examples (such as by
Stuart Sillars, one of the most prolific and influential writers on
the topic – see his 'Shakespeare in colour: illustrated editions,
1908–14', *The Yearbook of English Studies* 45 (2015), 216–38, and
The Illustrated Shakespeare, 1709–1875 (Cambridge, 2008), among
other works), excepting Stephen Orgel's chapter 'Shakespeare
illustrated', in *The Cambridge Companion to Shakespeare and Popular
Culture*, ed. Robert Shaughnessy (Cambridge, 2007), pp. 84–5.
However, the latter does not venture into discussion of the 1920s,

13 John Gilbert, illustration of Hamlet encountering the Ghost, *The Works of Shakespeare, The Illustrations by John Gilbert, Engraved by the Dalziel Brothers*, vol. 3, ed. Howard Staunton (London, 1867).

that Austen would have seen them. However, despite the similarities they share with Austen's illustrations, his exceed them, offering a radical new reading of Hamlet's relationship with the Ghost, and, by extension, the nature of their suggested interiorities. Evoking the trope of the *femme fatale*, he portrays the Ghost as feminized and demonic, anticipating G. Wilson Knight's

leaving Austen's designs outside its investigatory scope. While Orgel claims of the Cranach Press *Hamlet* (1927) that 'There is no illustrated Shakespeare in which the images are so thoroughly integrated with the typography, and in which text, book, and performance are conceived so completely as a whole', and this edition 'reconceives the book of the play as a performance' (Orgel, 'Shakespeare illustrated', p. 89), he omits Austen's edition of *Hamlet* (1922) from this assessment, despite its apparent congruence with this description.

14 Henry C. Selous, illustration of Hamlet encountering the Ghost, *The Plays of William Shakespeare, Illustrated by H.C. Selous*, ed. Charles Clarke and Mary Cowden (London, Paris and Melbourne, 1864–8).

insistence on the Ghost's diabolism in 1930.[7] Departing from nineteenth-century depictions, these combined readings comprise a unique aspect of Austen's vision.

I will treat the following of Austen's *Hamlet* images as case studies. These include those on page 37 ('Hamlet Encounters the Ghost'; Figure 15); page 8 ('Seated Hamlet'; Figure 20); page 5 (the 'Dramatis Personae' ('DP') illustration; Figure 21); page 9

---

7 George Wilson Knight, 'The embassy of death: an essay on Hamlet', in *The Wheel of Fire*, ed. H. Milford (Oxford, 1930).

('The Ghost and the Guardsmen'; Figure 22); and page 42 ('Hamlet Leaves the Ghost'; Figure 23).

Austen shares with Fuseli a radical reinterpretation of the Ghost through visual imagery. As I will show, while their interpretations differ in that Fuseli amplifies the Ghost's powerful masculine physicality and sublime presence, whereas Austen depicts a far more sinister and even decrepit spirit, these images also feature some telling similarities, suggesting that Austen was inspired by his Romantic predecessor. Austen's more sinister reading of the Ghost's influence on Hamlet's mind is revealed in four main ways: first, through its lack of armour and feminized appearance; second, through the eerily static impression which the figures convey; third, through the Ghost's gesture which, when paired with Hamlet's, communicates symbolic and abstract meanings, implying a shared agenda and its diabolical intent; and last, through the Ghost's disturbing Janus-face, hinting at covert intentions. While Austen's Ghost as shown in the 'The Ghost and the Guardsmen' image (the preface to 1.1; Figure 22) differs from that on page 37 ('Hamlet Encounters the Ghost'; Figure 15) in that the Ghost is stately in appearance, it still conveys an aura of otherworldly, even seductive, danger.

Despite the differences in Austen's and Fuseli's artistic styles, chronology and intended audiences, a comparison of their works is illuminating. Fuseli painted in a Romantic, though somewhat idiosyncratic, style. His works were impressionistic, with soft lines and a strong use of shadow, and yet classical, with monumental figures. In contrast, Austen's illustrations are reminiscent of Beardsley's, with a monochromatic palate, hard lines, an art nouveau aesthetic, and stark, highly unrealistic figures. Fuseli painted his *Hamlet* images for the gallery, while Austen illustrated his limited-edition *Hamlet* for the select few readers who could afford it. The generational divide between the artists is likewise significant, resulting in broad differences in the cultural contexts and reception of their work; Fuseli began illustrating and painting in the late eighteenth century – fuelled by a Romantic enthusiasm for what Keats called Shakespeare's 'fierce dispute / Betwixt damnation and impassion'd clay' – and Austen in the more cynical, world-weary wake of World War I. One last factor influencing their works' reception was that Fuseli was one of the most famous painters of his generation while Austen was far less known and far less influential. These distinctions make their shared agenda in creating unconventional Ghosts all the more noteworthy.

Like Austen, Fuseli was influenced by his imagination, appearing to have been informed more by his own (readerly) critical insights than contemporary performances. As Alan Young observes of one of Fuseli's 'Hamlet and the Ghost' drawings: 'like most of Fuseli's Shakespeare works, this is far from being a reproduction of what he might have seen in the theatre'.[8] Similarly, Sillars notes that the artist 'went and saw [Shakespearian plays] in London'; however, 'he wrote no extended critical statement on the theatre as an interpretive medium … Fuseli's main visual source was the close imaginative reading of the texts themselves'.[9] Highlighting his artistic achievement, Sillars adds that Fuseli's 'work [demonstrates] a deep knowledge of Shakespeare's texts … produc[ing] an innovative and forceful critical reading of the plays'.[10]

---

[8] Alan Young, *Hamlet and the Visual Arts, 1709–1900* (Newark, 2002), p. 159.

[9] Stuart Sillars, *Painting Shakespeare: The Artist as Critic, 1720–1820* (Cambridge and New York, 2006), p. 100.

[10] Sillars, *Painting Shakespeare*, p. 98. Similarly, Michael Benton and Sally Butcher explain of Fuseli's *Lady Macbeth Seizing the Daggers* (1812) that 'such illustration is far removed from being a decorative response; it is an interpretive act of critical insight' (Michael Benton and Sally Butcher, 'Painting Shakespeare', *The Journal of Aesthetic Education* 32.3 (Autumn 1998), 53–66, esp. p. 61). One of Fuseli's early biographers, John Knowles, observed that 'few men recollected more of the text, or understood better the works of Chaucer, Shakespeare [etc.]' (John Knowles, *The Life and Writings of Henry Fuseli*, vol. 2 (London, 1831), p. 358). Fuseli himself noted (during one of his lectures on painting) that 'by this radiant recollection of associated ideas, the spontaneous ebullitions of nature, selected by observation, treasured by memory, classed by sensibility and judgement, Shakespeare became the supreme master of passions and the ruler of our hearts' (quoted in Eudo C. Mason, *The Mind of Henry Fuseli: Selections from his Writings with an Introductory Study* (London, 1951), p. 343).

FIRST AND SECOND ENCOUNTERS: EARLY VISUAL TRADITIONS

But how are we to understand the Ghost, with its disturbing ambiguity? We may dismiss, to begin with, theories that (like Banquo's) the Ghost is to be interpreted as a projection of Hamlet's unconscious: Shakespeare goes to great lengths to provide three independent witnesses to its autonomous existence, one of them a card-carrying sceptic. Despite the fact that scholars like Brett E. Murphy attempt to confine the Ghost to a single source – in Murphy's case, Lewes Lavater's *Of Ghosts and Spirits Walking by Night* (1572),[11] the Ghost in *Hamlet* is a kind of palimpsest, drawing upon conflicting early modern traditions about revenants. Of course, the churches had their official positions: for Catholic theologians, something claiming to be a ghost might conceivably be a soul on temporary release from Purgatory, but for Protestants, for whom Purgatory was merely a Popish fiction, it was bound to be a devil. J. Dover Wilson claims that 'the Ghost *is* Catholic: he comes from Purgatory', but he overlooks the ambiguity not only of the 'sulphurous' flames of its 'prison-house' but also of the damnable nature of its mission, seeking not intercessory prayers but revenge.[12]

Yet people heard about ghosts long before they encountered theology: think of Mamillius, Hermione's little son, and his 'winter's tale' that begins 'There was a man ... dwelt by a churchyard' (*The Winter's Tale*, 2.1.29–31).[13] As Catherine Belsey observes, 'there were other influences at work that were not so firmly under the control of orthodoxy, whether Catholic or Protestant'.[14] She pinpoints moments in the plays which point to Shakespeare's awareness of the oral transmission of ghost stories: 'Macbeth's terrified reaction to Banquo's ghost "would well become," his wife scathingly insists, "A woman's story at a winter's fire, / Authoris'd by her grandam" (*Macbeth,* 3.4.63–65).'

One obvious point of origin for the Ghost is the Senecan plot device through which the shade of a murder victim discloses his murder and seeks justice, like the ghost of Don Andrea in *The Spanish Tragedy*. Such 'informant' ghosts tend towards dignity and *gravitas* rather than supernatural horror. Shakespeare's ghost, however, whose 'canonized bones, hearsèd in death, / Have burst their cerements' (1.4.28–9), reminds us a little of the more physical and terrifying avenger-ghost of folklore, as mentioned by the Duke in *Measure for Measure*: 'Should she kneel down in mercy of this fact, / Her brother's ghost his pavèd bed would break, / And take her hence in horror' (5.1.432–4).

As I will argue, Austen's Ghost captures the play's fundamental ambivalence regarding its nature. Horatio, as an orthodox Protestant from Wittenburg, initially takes the Ghost for a devil pretending to be Old Hamlet, demanding of it 'What [*not 'who'*] art thou that usurp'st ... / ... the majesty of bury'd Denmark?' (1.1.44; 46). Hamlet, on the other hand, seems to entertain the Catholic idea that it might be a soul on temporary release from Purgatory to solicit prayers to shorten its stay, as there are no other grounds upon which, in early modern thought, it could be considered an honest Ghost. However, the play problematizes this perception of the Ghost, as the spirit sacrilegiously calls for revenge. Just as the Ghost's portrayal suggests contrasting strains of the supernatural, the play espouses conflicting moral, ethical and religious traditions: Senecan stoicism, the Norse revenge code, Catholicism and reformed Protestantism. Hamlet is unsure whether to follow the Senecan, but deeply anti-Christian, path of suicide, or to pursue vengeance unhesitatingly, like his literary predecessor

---

[11] Brett E. Murphy, 'Sulphurous and tormenting flames: understanding the Ghost in Hamlet', *Shakespeare in Southern Africa* 26 (2014), 117–22.

[12] J. Dover Wilson, *What Happens in Hamlet* (Cambridge, 1951), p. 70.

[13] All references to Shakespeare's plays are from *William Shakespeare: The Complete Works*, ed. Stanley Wells and Gary Taylor (Oxford, 1986).

[14] Catherine Belsey, 'Shakespeare's sad tale for winter: *Hamlet* and the tradition of fireside ghost stories', *Shakespeare Quarterly* 61 (2012), 3. She also argues along these lines in *Why Shakespeare?* (Basingstoke, 2007), and 'Beyond reason: Hamlet and early modern stage ghosts', in *Gothic Renaissance: A Reassessment*, ed. Elizabeth Bronfen and Beate Neumeier (Manchester, 2014).

Amleth. He doesn't properly follow any of these frameworks: the play refuses to decide between them.

While Austen intuits *Hamlet*'s darker Ghost, nineteenth-century critics largely viewed the Ghost as a benign father figure, preferring to overlook clues in the text suggesting otherwise. Their Ghost is solemn, justified and dignified. A. C. Bradley, the spokesperson for nineteenth-century critical opinion on Shakespeare, gives us a typically Victorian view of the old King's ghost, 'the messenger of divine justice', as 'so majestical a phantom' with its 'measured and solemn utterance' and its 'air of impersonal abstraction'.[15] Consider, for example, his benign reading of the Ghost's wishes for Gertrude. Bradley sees its intervention in the closet scene as coming to her rescue. Since 'Hamlet has already attained the object of stirring shame and contrition in his mother's breast', his continued admonition of her 'is agonising his mother to no purpose', especially since 'the Ghost, when it gave him his charge, had expressly warned him to spare her; and here again the dead husband shows the same tender regard for his weak, unfaithful wife'.[16] But Shakespeare's text contains clues that, for a reader less committed to a compliantly patriarchal reading, point to a darker interpretation.

If we look at the Ghost's 'warn[ing . . .] to spare her', we find something more ambivalent. Its request to avenge murder ('If thou hast nature in thee, bear it not') is immediately followed by an utterly irrelevant (to the crime of murder) invitation for Hamlet to imagine his detested uncle and his mother thrashing about in 'a couch for luxury and damnèd incest':

> O, horrible! O, horrible! most horrible!
> If thou hast nature in thee, bear it not.
> Let not the royal bed of Denmark be
> A couch for luxury and damnèd incest.
> But, howsomever thou pursuest this act,
> Taint not thy mind, nor let thy soul contrive
> Against thy mother aught. Leave her to heaven.
>
> (1.5.80–6)

Worse, having deliberately 'tainted' Hamlet's mind with this image, it disingenuously counsels him to forget it, and not to entertain ideas of revenging himself upon his mother. It is true that, at the moment of the Ghost's intervention, the Prince has succeeded in evoking 'shame and contrition in his mother's breast', but, like Claudius in the preceding scene, the Ghost knows that these are not enough — that the sacrament of penance requires restitution and absolution, and that, without these, contrition is of no avail. Bradley thinks it is 'obvious' that the Ghost's intention, in not appearing to Gertrude, is to 'spare' her. But if its aim is to damn her, then appearing only to the Prince is a way of granting her the escape she wants: Hamlet's accusations have merely been 'ecstasy', or temporary madness. It diabolically foils her possible salvation.

The increasingly eerie depiction of the Ghost during the eighteenth and nineteenth centuries, shifting from solid, armoured, active figures in the late eighteenth century,[17] to often transparent and/or impassive ones in the nineteenth,[18] probably stems from the Victorians' interest in spiritualism and their cultural obsession with the Gothic and macabre. The ghost novella with its interest in the Todorovian *fantastique*, such as Henry James's *Turn of the Screw* (1898), appeared towards the end of the Victorian period. Pepper's Ghost, a visual trick used on stage and during seances, whereby a mirror was

---

[15] A. C. Bradley, *Shakespearean Tragedy: Lectures on Hamlet, Othello, King Lear, Macbeth* (Basingstoke, 1904), p. 174.

[16] Bradley, *Shakespearean Tragedy*, pp. 138–9.

[17] Fuseli's paintings as described in this chapter are a case in point. Charles Grignion's 1773 engraving of the closet scene after Francis Hayman's painting (located in the Garrick Club), found in Charles Jennen's edition of *Hamlet*, is another example. Its armour is clearly defined and its movements human: it strides forward, one hand extended and upturned, and the other holding a long cylindrical shape (possibly a truncheon) away from its body.

[18] For example, in the wood engraving signed 'A. H.', published by *The Graphic* in 1874, the Ghost (Tom Mead) is physically insubstantial, shyly looking back at Hamlet (Irving). Meanwhile, in a photographic reproduction of an illustration (by Hawes Craven) of Forbes-Robertson's 1897 production, showing the closet scene, the Ghost is physically impassive and less visible than the living characters, while standing close to the tapestry as if having just emerged from it.

used to create ghostly projections, accounted for the interest in transparency. Gilbert, Selous and Meadows – whose widely disseminated illustrated editions show notable imaginative engagement with the texts – all produced transparent-looking Ghosts.[19] Gilbert's Ghost of 1867, from *The Works of Shakespeare*, is increasingly insubstantial from the waist downwards, such that it doesn't visibly touch the ground. It appears to be levitating. Selous's Ghost (from the Clarkes's *The Plays of William Shakespeare* (c. 1864–8)) is entirely transparent, while Meadows's, as shown in 1.1 and included in *The Works of Shakspere* (1846), is an ambiguous-looking, airy phantasm. Gilbert's and Selous's Ghosts, despite their supernatural transparency, remain dignified, physically powerful and masculine-looking in appearance, adhering to the Victorian perception of the Ghost as patriarchal and benevolent.

In Austen's 'Hamlet Encounters the Ghost' drawing (Figure 15),[20] Hamlet is standing before the spirit against a backdrop of stars; the latter faces away from us, recalling its reluctance in the play to speak with anyone but the Prince. A strip of fabric encircling Hamlet's right knee anticipates his 'Ungarter'd' stockings (2.1.81) when feigning the antic disposition he promises after the Ghost's departure in 1.5. This illustration portrays one of two scenes in the play: either the scene when Hamlet, accompanied, first sees the apparition (1.4), or the scene when he subsequently enters alone with it (1.5). However, suggesting that only Hamlet and the Ghost are present, the edition places the illustration immediately opposite the text containing the spirit's private conversation with Hamlet. The full-page size of the image points to the significance of this moment in the play.

Both scenes were popular choices for visual artistic depiction from the late eighteenth century onwards. In depictions of either scene, the Ghost's pointing gesture is a common visual motif, signalling its desire that Hamlet follow it – the trope seemingly draws on the popular notion that spirits of the dead point mutely at significant objects to communicate messages to those they visit. In Fuseli's first two paintings of the Prince

and Ghost, the spirit prompts Hamlet to follow it, although his companions try to prevent him (Figure 17). Featuring the same 'pointing' motif (although depicting Scene 5) is a wood engraving of 1814 by John Thompson after a design by John,[21] and an engraving by Hollis after a painting by Reid (first names unknown) depicting Macready as Hamlet (Figure 16).[22] Both show Hamlet alone with the Ghost on the battlements, responding to its gesture.

Austen's Ghost is also pointing. It is much closer to the foreground than Hamlet and consequently a much larger figure. It dominates the composition, lending greater emphasis to its ominous gesture. This in turn reinforces the impression, conveyed by its pointing hand, that the spirit is eerily commanding, recalling the trope in ghost stories whereby spectres make demands of those they haunt. This Ghost's signal hints at an additional significance rather than simply directing Hamlet to follow it, appearing silently to name the object of its vengeance.

While the suspended height of Austen's Ghost evokes traditional depictions of 1.5, the physical distance between the characters does not, opening up a space for alternative readings of their relationship. For example, their proximity, especially in conjunction with Hamlet's hiding of his face, communicates an increased impression of threat. In traditional portrayals, the Ghost is often physically elevated over Hamlet and at a distance; Thompson's engraving is a case in point. According to Young, the 'visual effect' of the Ghost's distant removal is 'expressive of the psychology of Hamlet's yearning to be reunited with his father'.[23] Early nineteenth-century English theatre also tended to situate the

---

[19] *The Works of Shakspere, Revised from the best Authorities, With a Memoir, and Essay on his Genius*, vol. 2, ed. Barry Cornwall, illustrated by Kenny Meadows (London, 1846).

[20] Invented title.

[21] This is found in *The Dramatic Works of William Shakespeare*, published in Chiswick in 1814 and held in the Folger Shakespeare Library. There is a quotation underneath: 'Whither wilt thou lead me? Speak, I'll go no further.'

[22] John Tallis published this engraving in 1849.

[23] Young, *Hamlet and the Visual Arts*, p. 167.

15 John Austen, 'Hamlet Encounters the Ghost'. Held in the Folger Shakespeare Library.

spirit at a remove in an effort to produce this impression,[24] as in the case of Macready's *Hamlet* production at the Haymarket in 1849, in which the Ghost (John Stuart) stood at the top of a 'flight of steps', having 'ascended from the ramparts'.[25] This implied emotional attachment remained a prominent trend in productions, with Charles Kean 'sinking slowly to his knees – as over-awed by the solemn presence – addresses [the Ghost] with touching and affectionate adjuration'.[26] This continued into the twentieth century. In Burton's 1964 *Hamlet*, Gielgud adopted a 'tender tone', having realized that the Ghost was 'a helpless pitiful thing'.[27] In 1963, George Grizzard, in Tyrone Guthrie's directed play, conveyed 'a real love and reverence' for the Ghost (Ken Ruta).[28]

[24] Young, *Hamlet and the Visual Arts*, p. 167.
[25] Quoted in Marvin Rosenberg, *The Masks of Hamlet* (Cranbury and New Jersey, 1992), p. 313.
[26] William Moelwyn Merchant, *Shakespeare and the Artist* (Oxford, 1959), p. 111.
[27] Rosamund Gilder, *John Gielgud's Hamlet: A Record of Performance* (Oxford, 1937), p. 111.
[28] Alfred Rossi, *Minneapolis Rehearsals: Tyrone Guthrie Directs Hamlet* (Berkeley, 1970), p. 15.

16 (?) Hollis, engraving of Act 1.5 depicting William Charles Macready as Hamlet, after a painting by (?) Reid (London, 1849). Held in the Folger Shakespeare Library.

In Austen's illustration, the Ghost is still higher in the picture plane (than Hamlet). However, in contrast to most nineteenth-century depictions, it seems uncomfortably close to him; there is little reason to think that the Prince covets its attention. Coupled with the diminution of Hamlet's figure relative to the Ghost, this emphasizes his vulnerability and mortal insignificance. Gilbert's illustration (Figure 13) produces a similar effect, suggesting a broadly similar interpretation, but he

17 Henry Fuseli, 'The Ghost and Hamlet', 1780–5. Zürich, Kunsthaus Zürich.

forgoes creating an impression of the Prince's traditional emotional yearning. Instead, his Hamlet hunkers down, recoiling from the Ghost which seems to tower over him, a hair's-breadth away. However, Austen alters this 'looming' trope, as his Ghost is eerily suspended in space rather than situated on the ground. Consequently, despite standing, Hamlet is level with the Ghost's knees. In contrast, Gilbert's Ghost, although its lower body gradually fades into nothingness from the waist down, still appears to be standing since its head is a realistic height from the ground.

Gilbert, Fuseli and Austen share an emphasis on supernatural terror, also suggesting either the influence of the first two on the latter or a shared imaginative sensibility. Austen's Ghost sinisterly hides its face from the viewer (Austen's original initiative), while Hamlet shields his face protectively as if threatened. In Gilbert's image, he buries his face in the crook of his arm. This furthers an atmosphere of unease and emphasizes the Ghost's disturbing, preternatural origins. Austen's, Gilbert's and Fuseli's third (*c.* 1785;

Figure 18) images of Hamlet interacting with the Ghost position the figures similarly and use comparable lighting effects, creating an atmosphere of tension and unease.[29]

Fuseli drew on stereotypical portrayals of the spirit's intrusion in Scene 4 for the purpose of depicting its arrival during the closet scene (3.4). In both Austen's and Fuseli's portrayals, the Ghost is positioned to the right, monopolizing the foreground and towering over Hamlet, dominating the vertical space in the illustration. Gilbert arranges

---

[29] Hapgood remarks that, 'From the first, "special effects" have been lavished on the appearances and disappearances of the Ghost. In Shakespeare's time, a trapdoor may well have been used for his descent into the "cellarage"'; 'Various spectral lighting devices have been employed . . . in modern productions all is often dark and obscure' (Robert Hapgood, *Hamlet* (Cambridge, 1999), p. 101). In Burton's *Hamlet*, the Ghost was 'a great black shadow which suddenly took shape above the stage' (John Gielgud, *Acting Shakespeare* (New York, 1992), p. 41). In Branagh's film, the Ghost literally 'swoops down' on the guards (Hapgood, *Hamlet*, p. 101), tearing its sword from its scabbard as if prepared to attack.

the figures similarly, although Hamlet is slightly closer to the foreground than the spirit. Reeling back in shock, the prince in these images resists the apparition (although in Fuseli's painting, this is because Hamlet simultaneously strives to protect the Queen; Fuseli's image portrays the moment when the Ghost appears in the Queen's private chambers and the Prince speaks to it, much to Gertrude's alarm, as she cannot see it). The space around the characters is darkly lit and claustrophobic, contributing to an impression of Hamlet's vulnerability and terror. This suggests that his relationship with the Ghost is powered by fear, and that he is threatened with supernatural possession or lunacy (as Horatio had warned).

Since the eighteenth century, artists and stage directors have routinely portrayed Hamlet holding a sword defensively upon first encountering the Ghost and when in doubtful pursuit. Hollis's and Thompson's engravings are cases in point. However, Fuseli, Selous, Gilbert and Austen eschew this motif, perhaps to imply that a weapon is ineffectual against an intangible spirit ('For it is, as the air, invulnerable, / And our vain blows malicious mockery' (1.1.126–7). In Fuseli's first depiction of the scene, Hamlet is without a sword (Figure 12); in the second, he wears an undrawn sword at his waist (Figure 17); while in the third, there is merely a glint of silver at his hip (Figure 18). In the first image, Hamlet's classical proportions counteract an impression of vulnerability which the sword's absence might imply; in the second, his athletic build and desperate attempt to reach the Ghost achieve a similar effect. It is only in the third image that Hamlet seems helpless, recoiling from the Ghost with an expression of horror absent in the preceding works. Fuseli's final painting places increased emphasis on the supernatural horror of the Ghost and the danger it represents. Hamlet's alarm is likewise evident in Austen's illustration. Paired with the sword's absence, this makes him appear more vulnerable than in Fuseli's series, and thus more susceptible to the Ghost's potentially malevolent influence.

Austen's Ghost is less 'masculine' and more unnerving than its traditional counterparts. Late eighteenth- and nineteenth-century depictions of the Ghost in 1.4 and 1.5 show it wearing armour. In some cases, its armour is partially or completely covered by drapery. Mead's Ghost pulls a large cloak around itself protectively but remains a masculine figure with prominent beard and broad shoulders – suggesting, in conjunction with its 'beaver', that it is in armour. Gilbert's and Selous's Ghosts are similarly attired. The Ghost's war helmet remains visually prominent, despite its drapery. By contrast, Austen's Ghost, 'in his habit as he lived' and not wearing armour (3.4.126), is endowed with an aura of seductive danger, lessening its masculinity while exaggerating its eeriness.

The unsettling, supernatural appearance of Austen's Ghost, exaggerated by its ethereal aspect, contributes to an impression of Hamlet's vulnerability, due to being faced with powerful, supernatural forces. The tendency to portray the spirit in military attire in performances, regardless of implicit stage directions, has continued up until the present, most likely because directors prefer to reflect Horatio's description of it as 'Armed at all points exactly, cap-à-pe' (1.2.200). However, Austen's Ghost is an exception, dressed in a way which anticipates its depiction in 3.4. Although it is not transparent, it is so physically insubstantial as to seem in danger of being swallowed up by the tasselled shawl and white, loose flowing robes that it wears, reminiscent of a nightdress. Save for a sheathed sword, its attire bears no trace of the military garb Horatio mentions. Along with refined hands and long, slender fingers, this Ghost appears unusually fragile; its fingers – absent of an armoured gauntlet – and shawl with its abundant, attractive patterning, render its appearance stereotypically feminine.

The Ghost's attire also elicits stereotypical nineteenth-century depictions of spirits. These tend to be vulnerable-looking, ethereal creatures. The more feminine they appear, the more they seem preternaturally dangerous. Accentuating their otherworldliness, these are portrayed in white, flowing, shroud-like garments, as if newly risen from the grave; Gilbert's and Selous's Ghosts are attired thus, although their garments hang over armour.

Also contributing to an impression of the supernatural, the drapery of Austen's Ghost hangs in the air where we might expect to see feet. Combined with its levitation and physical frailty, this renders it shadowy and unsettling. In contrast, the physical solidity, classical forms and armour of Fuseli's figures emphasize their humanity,[30] evoking Old Hamlet's life on the battlefield rather than his disintegration in a tomb. Armoured and physically broad, Gilbert's and Selous's Ghosts (Figures 13 and 14) are equally commanding.

Despite their similarities (see below), Austen's Ghost provides a striking contrast with Fuseli's decisively 'masculine' version. Fuseli's first two Ghosts grasp a 'truncheon', while all three have a bulky, armoured body, underscoring their implied virility. Fuseli describes his second Ghost (*Hamlet, Horatio, Marcellus and the Ghost* (1785–90); Figure 12)[31] as 'strik[ing] with majestic dignity, and look[ing] like a king'.[32] Not just strong physicality but anger has traditionally been regarded as a masculine trait. A commentator remarked of the Boydell painting that 'The superhuman height of the figure, the frown fierce and ominous, like that which the living king wore, when "in an angry parle / He smote the sledder Polack on the ice"; the compelling motion of the truncheon which it seems impossible to resist, all are admirable.'[33]

Fuseli's third Ghost (Figure 18) has an even greater body mass than its forebears, its solidity and height underscoring its masculine potency. According to Young, its 'long cloak that drags upon the ground ... emphasise[s its] forward momentum', contributing to an impression of physical power.[34] Fuseli's Ghosts are more physically impressive than their eighteenth- and nineteenth-century counterparts, visibly embodying the power implied by the spirit's description: its 'warlike form' (1.1.50), its 'stately' march (1.2.202) and its feats in 'combat' – both when Old Hamlet 'smote the sledded Polacks on the ice' and when he 'Did slay [Old] Fortinbras' (1.1.89). In the play, the Ghost's potency is such that it symbolically emasculates the guards: 'Within his truncheon's length' they are 'distilled / Almost to jelly with the act of fear' (1.2.204–5).

However, despite the 'masculinity' conveyed by Fuseli's third Ghost, it shares some feminized traits with Austen's. It conveys a more sinister air than its heroic forebears. The Ghost's masculinity is partially deemphasized in favour of its supernatural potency and the scene's intense psychological horror. In the artist's two initial drawings of the Ghost, it holds a truncheon, while the plates of its armour are clearly defined through lighting effects, evoking the muscularity of Michelangelo's figures. These additions are absent in the third image.[35] Unarmed and wearing 'a long cloak that drags upon the ground behind [it]',[36] this Ghost partly resembles Austen's 'feminine' one. The latter bears no trace of the 'majestic dignity' Fuseli attributed to his second Ghost, dressed in a tapestry or shawl and carrying a sheathed sword rather than a 'truncheon', a weapon feminine by comparison, particularly when passively resting in its scabbard.[37] Perhaps also accounting for the sword Austen's Ghost carries, Horatio describes it as 'Armed at point' (1.2.200), evoking a sword. Arguably, the most clearly feminine trait of this Ghost is its hand, with its long, gracile, bejewelled fingers, echoed in Hamlet's equally feminine hands.

---

[30] Allan Cunningham describes Fuseli's visit to the Sistine Chapel as partly having inspired him to paint classical figures in the style of Michelangelo (Allan Cunningham, 'Pictorial illustration of Shakespeare', *Quarterly Review* 142 (July and October 1876), 457–79; pp. 460-1). Similarly, Sillars also refers to classicism and Renaissance painting as his influences (Sillars, *Painting Shakespeare*, p. 102).

[31] Which he submitted to the Boydell Gallery exhibition.

[32] Henry Fuseli, 'Catalogues of pictures in the Shakespeare Gallery', *Analytical Review* (May 1789), 112.

[33] Cunningham, 'Pictorial illustrations of Shakespeare', pp. 461-2.

[34] Young, *Hamlet and the Visual Arts*, p. 161.

[35] As art historians have repeatedly observed, Fuseli was inspired by the immense power of Michelangelo's figures, and sought to instil the same grandeur in his own. For example, Sillars notes that the artist was 'hugely influenced by artists of the Renaissance, especially Michelangelo ... he also found their heroic universality in the writings of Homer and Shakespeare' (Sillars, *Painting Shakespeare*, p. 99).

[36] Young, *Hamlet and the Visual Arts*, p. 161.

[37] 'Vagina' is the Latin for 'sheath' or 'scabbard'.

18 Henry Fuseli, *Gertrude, Hamlet and the Ghost of Hamlet's Father*, c. 1785. Oil on canvas. Fondazione Magnani Rocca, Mamiano di Traversetolo.

The spirit's hand is juxtaposed with Hamlet's as it only lengthens two fingers and a thumb; its smallest finger is barely visible. The Ghost's fingers are adorned with large rings, recalling '[Old Hamlet's] signet' (5.2.49), which the Prince uses to seal a letter to the English King, fatally condemning Rosencrantz and Guildernstern. The rings foreshadow this event; the Ghost's imperative sets in motion these characters' demise and the fall of the court. Paired with the decorative pattern of its shawl, the spirit's jewellery also denotes its royal office when alive. Austen's Ghost is truly a 'precurse of fear'd events' (1.1.124).

The Ghost's exaggerated but sinister femininity partly derives from the Victorian fascination with the predatory female character, as exhibited in Gothic novels and ghost stories. This fascination reflected deeper masculine anxieties regarding female sexuality as something predatory and vampiric, capable of draining men of their vitality. This in turn accounted for the increasing interest in vampirism and the *femme fatale* during this period. The vampire novel *Carmilla* (1872) was the first of its kind – the vampire is a woman.

The Ghost's femininity seems due in part to the increasing social and artistic interest in androgyny around the *fin de siècle*. This in turn reflected the emergence of feminism (as we know it) as a social and political movement in this era, and increasing interest in the experiences of women and divergent expressions of femininity. Shearer West observes that 'the androgyne or human with the qualities of both man and woman, was a crucial image in late nineteenth-century art. It stood as metaphor for the confusion stimulated by the "battle of the sexes"', caused by the growing legal autonomy of women and the movement for female suffrage. It was an 'oblique icon for homosexual love, and a symptom of a larger crisis in the construction of male identity at the turn of the century'.[38] West explains that, 'if men became more "manly" and women more "womanly", the progress of society was assured; if men became more like women and women more like men, they were both[, according to prevalent patriarchal assumptions,] experiencing an atavistic regression to a state of primitive homogeneity or hermaphroditism'.[39]

Androgyny effectively represented femininity invested with 'masculine' power, or masculinity 'weakened'; this was concerning to many because it confused the gender binary and, like female sexuality, threatened established patriarchal social structures. Consequently, androgyny was often perceived or cast in a disturbing and even sinister light. It appears that Austen was influenced by the increasingly unstable gender norms of the *fin de siècle*, norms which anticipated the androgynous, empowered, 'flapper' woman.

THE GREAT OUTDOORS: HAMLET AND THE GHOST

While the backdrop in Austen's illustration is an outdoors space as found in traditional depictions of Scenes 4 and 5 (described below), it is unusually minimalist. However, what little is there is deeply symbolic, alluding to Hamlet's vulnerability and the Ghost's disturbing supernatural agency. Portrayals of the Ghost and Hamlet's first encounter generally evoke the castle's exterior in the form of battlements, drawbridge or an external gate,[40] recalling that the Ghost appears on 'the platform where [the guardsmen] watch' (1.2.213). In some instances, the sea constitutes the background,[41] in reference to Horatio's concern that the Ghost will trick Hamlet 'towards the flood' or 'the dreadful summit of the cliff / That beetles o'er his base into the sea' (1.4.50–2).

Austen's image, however, lacks a fortress or sea. Instead, the backdrop is comparatively stark, pitch-black and punctuated by either falling snow or stars – the latter would be suggestive of their night-time encounter. Further, if interpreted as stars, these white specks suggest impending destiny, made ominous by the Ghost, particularly as they are shown in apparently intricately patterned but inscrutable arrangements. Save for these natural elements, the surroundings appear devastatingly empty. While an absence of visible terrain, coupled with falling snow, evokes a blizzard (a sublime phenomenon) – recalling Hamlet's observation on the battlements that 'The air bites shrewdly' and Horatio's retort, 'It is a nipping and an eager air' (1.4.1–2) – this also points to Hamlet's overwhelming emotion and consequent blindness to his surroundings. Further, this vacuum underscores the intensity of focus between the characters, accentuating Hamlet's vulnerability and isolation and foreshadowing its continuation throughout the play. It also suggests that the Ghost drives nature into hiding by 'Making night hideous' (1.4.35).

Through this spaciousness and wild, natural environment, Austen's drawing evokes the sublimity of some traditional depictions. This contributes to an impression of the Ghost's overwhelming supernatural influence and its threatening impact on Hamlet's implied psyche. In cases where the sea

---

[38] Shearer West, *Fin de Siècle* (London, 1993), p. 71.

[39] West, *Fin de Siècle*, p. 69.

[40] Young, *Hamlet and the Visual Arts*, p. 150.

[41] Young, *Hamlet and the Visual Arts*, p. 151. In Benjamin Wilson's painting *William Powell as Hamlet encountering the Ghost* (1768–9), a sea is visible in the background; the same image also features the drawbridge and/or gate motif. The latter stemmed from theatrical productions (Young, *Hamlet and the Visual Arts*, p. 150).

dominates the background, the Ghost and Hamlet, and possible company, are often dwarfed by it, mirroring the psychological tumult the character(s) are experiencing.[42] Related to this, Young notes that nature in these images sometimes evokes the Romantic Sublime,[43] citing Fuseli's Boydell painting as an example: the 'wild and raging sea [. . .] is suggestive of immense elemental forces';[44] arguably, the billowing clouds and starkly emanating moonlight in Gilbert's drawing have a similar effect – again, suggesting a shared aesthetic sensibility.

As in Fuseli's Boydell painting, Austen conveys the division between the spirit and mortal worlds. However, unlike Fuseli, he insinuates that Hamlet is lured into the realm of the supernatural. Fuseli's image, as Young observes, clearly distinguishes these realms by situating the human characters in front of a castle wall, and the Ghost in front of unobstructed sky.[45] The spirit's supernatural potency is also suggested by its implied physical power and pale aura. Gilbert's illustration is comparable, as it depicts Hamlet crouching with his head beneath the battlements while the Ghost looms, its body forming a part of the sky imagery. In Austen's drawing, the stars or snowflakes extend all the way down the picture plane, suspending the figures together in space; furthering this impression, the Ghost levitates, eliciting a disturbing otherworldly power. Here, there is little evidence of the mortal realm. Hamlet is its sole representative. This reinforces the impression that Hamlet becomes a part of the Ghost's disturbing universe, and perhaps complicit in its dark affairs.

Austen's, Gilbert's and Fuseli's third (post-Boydell) image share a similar composition and a portrait format, producing a sense of verticality which indirectly furthers an impression of Hamlet's vulnerability and intimidation. This is because the Ghost looms over Hamlet, overwhelming his more diminutive figure. The resemblance between these images also suggests that Austen is influenced by these works. In Austen's drawing, vertical lines dominate the attire of both figures and thus dominate the image. This accentuates the Ghost's levitation, and creates the impression that Hamlet is

drifting upward to meet it in space, leaving the safety of the mortal realm behind him. Also contributing to this vertical sweep, the spirit's head approaches the upper border. Rendering it larger in scale than Hamlet, it occupies the frontal picture plane while Hamlet is relegated to the back; consequently, the image is dominated by the vertical lines of its attire. In Gilbert's image, the vertical lines in the spirit's drapery likewise seem to lengthen the composition, and to similar effect. In Fuseli's painting, the Ghost's enormous physical stature exaggerates the illustration's verticality. All three Ghosts dominate the picture plane, towering over the Prince. What is distinctive about Austen's vision, however, is that the Ghost is, as mentioned, significantly higher in the picture plane than in either of these examples. While this contributes to an impression of Austen's Ghost posing as a secretly demonic angel, it also implies that the danger of this Ghost lies more in its supernatural – rather than masculine – qualities.

MORE THAN FATHER AND SON

Austen draws on Fuseli's unorthodox portrayals of Hamlet and the Ghost, although demonstrating his unique interpretive emphasis, which departs from these in some significant respects, such as by portraying the Ghost as a more eerily 'feminine' figure. During the eighteenth and early nineteenth centuries, Hamlet was often shown in one of three physical attitudes: pointing at the Ghost, usually in alarm; extending his upturned palm in a gesture of

---

[42] An example of this 'dwarfing by nature' is found in the 'The Platform by the Sea at Elsinore', an 1887 photogravure (produced by the Gebbie Company after a contemporary oil painting) (Folger Shakespeare Library, art file S528h1. no 105). Olivier realizes emotional turbulence through nature imagery in his film version of *Hamlet* (1948); Grigori Kozintsev draws on the same in his 1964 film.

[43] Young, *Hamlet and the Visual Arts*, p. 158.

[44] Young, *Hamlet and the Visual Arts*, p. 158. Similarly, Sillars observes of Fuseli's style that is contains 'a romantic sense of the sublime, in which vastness of spirit is all' (Sillars, *Painting Shakespeare*, p. 99).

[45] Young, *Hamlet and the Visual Arts*, p. 158.

19 Mezzotint portrait of David Garrick (1754) by James McArdell, after a painting (now lost) by Benjamin Wilson; it depicts Hamlet encountering the Ghost. Held in the Folger Shakespeare Library.

pleading enquiry; or turning it outwards in an attempt to ward off the spirit. For example, a wood engraving of 1874 signed 'A. H.', showing Henry Irving as Hamlet and Tom Mead as the Ghost, is a case in point:[46] Hamlet wears a determined expression while directing an index finger at the Ghost, suggesting fearless agency. In Thompson's engraving, Hamlet is shown pursuing the Ghost at the beginning of 1.5, one elbow bent and corresponding palm turned outward questioningly, denoting supplication and a desire to help his father.[47] A mezzotint portrait (1754) of David Garrick by James McArdell, after a painting (now lost) by Benjamin Wilson (Figure 19), portrays the actor instinctively trying to resist the Ghost, with hands raised. Although we cannot see the Ghost, this implies that it is terrifying to behold, evoking the trope of the demonic 'folk' ghost. Similarly,

Gilbert's illustration (Figure 13) shows Hamlet weakly attempting to repel the Ghost with one hand, his face buried in the nook of his arm.

Austen's depiction of Hamlet draws on some of these motifs, but with subtle changes. Rather than hiding his face in his arm as in Gilbert's drawing, one hand shields his face as if blinded; instead of pointing at the Ghost as in the A. H. engraving, the other hand points skyward. Two of Fuseli's images seem to anticipate this unusual posture. His pre-Boydell illustration (Figure 17) portrays Hamlet's right arm stretching vertically over his head, while the artist's post-Boydell image (Figure 18) depicts him with his right hand cast across his temples, as if blinded by the sight of the Ghost. However, despite these similarities, Austen's drawing is more than an homage to his eighteenth-century predecessor, as Hamlet's body language, in conjunction with the Ghost's, communicates symbolic and abstract meanings.

Gesturing towards the same vacancy, Hamlet's right hand and the spirit's left draw two invisibly converging lines. This intersection in empty space suggests the meeting of their purposes, the prince complying with the Ghost's implied demand. This suggests that they are equally aggrieved by Gertrude's behaviour. Unable to touch Hamlet, the Ghost can only facilitate implied contact through gesturing; also reinforcing the impression of its being ethereal/insubstantial, Hamlet's arm is visible through the Ghost's robes. The communication of their hands in space also implies that the stars are ominously aligned, foreshadowing the bleak consequences of their meeting.

Austen's Hamlet and Ghost resemble one another in that both shield their faces. However, the effect is contrasting: the former is cast sympathetically, while the spirit appears diabolical. The Ghost's gesture – extending the first three digits of

---

[46] Published by *The Graphic* (14 November 1874), this was based on a production by Irving at the Lyceum theatre in the same year. It is held in the Folger Shakespeare Library.

[47] The significance of this gesture may also have something to do with the formal gestural vocabularies at play in nineteenth-century stage performances.

its hand – would be interpretable as oathtaking if it were its right hand ('as God is my witness'). With the left hand, however, this represents a diabolic parody. Hamlet seems blinded by the Ghost's supernatural, pale radiance, clad principally in white underneath its shawl. His protective gesture also implies that he is horrified by its tidings, particularly as his eyes are fixed on the Ghost's sword; the prospect of murderous revenge alarms him. Hamlet may also physically reel because he is overwhelmed by the spirit's hideousness. A forehead is visible where we should instead see the back of its head, implying that its frontal aspect, facing the prince, is equally disturbing. Its ulterior face and obscured body indicate that it hides something demonic from the viewer: namely, its malevolent intentions. Further, a Janus face – one in front, one behind – symbolizes knowledge of the past and of the future: Austen's Ghost knows what is to come.

Bernard Paris has pointed to the similarities between the Ghost and Hamlet in the play. The two share a language, especially when condemning Gertrude's 'incestuous' desire for Claudius. The critic observes that 'both speeches stress the nobility of King Hamlet, the sexual depravity of Gertrude, and the inferiority of Claudius to his brother. There is in both a sense of outrage that this faithful, loving husband, this radiant angel, this Hyperion, has been betrayed by his wife and replaced in her affections by the bestial Claudius.'[48] When Hamlet enters Ophelia's closet, he resembles an apparition, 'Pale', almost 'As if he had been loosed out of hell / To speak of horrors' (2.1.81; 83–4). Early in Austen's edition, in the 'Seated Hamlet' illustration (Figure 20), his appearance resembles the Ghost's, suggesting not only kinship but a shared purpose. Gazing shrewdly from black-rimmed eyes and clad in white, Hamlet looks like the spirit both in the 'DP' image (Figure 21) from where it glares between the curtains, and in the ensuing image prefacing 1.1 ('The Ghost and the Guardsmen'; Figure 22). Likewise, the Ghost and Hamlet as shown in the 'DP' illustration also look alike, both in pose and appearance. This resemblance suggests that Hamlet may even physically subsume the Ghost after hearing its command, abandoning

his own interests in order to pursue its vendetta ('thy commandment'). Notably, the Ghost in the 'DP' image resembles the spirit in A. H.'s engraving of Henry Irving (1874), both seeming to clutch themselves defensively.

In Austen's illustrations, Hamlet and the apparition also share a similar pose, suggesting a shared implied interiority. Both are vertical (although the Ghost levitates) with legs pressed together. Their bodies convey a sense of stasis rather than forward momentum, evoking stagnation and – especially when compared with Fuseli's physically impressive Hamlet and Ghost images – impotence. The latter convey an impression of sudden action and power. In the pre-Boydell image, Hamlet's legs lunge in a v shape while he leans backwards; the Ghost's legs mirror his, but its chest remains authoritatively erect. In the Boydell painting, Hamlet surges forward as if desperate to pursue the Ghost, his torso twisting towards it – again, the Ghost's posture mirrors his, only its chest faces away in the direction in which it points. In the post-Boydell image, Hamlet lunges protectively sideways in front of his mother while the Ghost takes an intimidatingly minimal forward step, recalling its 'solemn march' in the play (1.2.201). This last image shows the greatest disparity in the postures of Hamlet and the Ghost, perhaps implying that he has lost intellectual sympathy with the spirit when the closet scene unfolds – for which he is reprimanded. In short, the implied momentum and thus masculine power of Fuseli's figures starkly contrasts with Austen's, frozen where they stand. This underscores the eeriness of the Ghost and the supernatural dimension from which it issues, suggesting that Hamlet is in grave danger.

AUSTEN'S GHOST: A SAINTLY DEMON

As briefly discussed, critics have long since questioned the Ghost's intentions, referring to Hamlet's internal query: 'The spirit that I have seen / May be

---

[48] Bernard J. Paris, *Character as a Subversive Force in Shakespeare: The History and Roman Plays* (Rutherford, 1991), p. 39.

20 John Austen, 'Seated Hamlet'. Held in the Folger Shakespeare Library.

the devil, and the devil hath power / T' assume a pleasing shape' (2.2.600–2). Harold Jenkins notes that Hamlet's tone in addressing the Ghost under the stage recalls the disrespectful manner in which the stage Vice traditionally spoke to the devil; he also observes that 'old mole', etc., evokes the below-ground activities of devils. Benjamin Robert Haydon described Fuseli's Boydell Ghost in terms which invoke a similar reading of the spirit:

round its visored head was a halo of light that looked sulphureous, and made one feel as if one actually smelt hell, burning, cindery and suffocating … the ghost looked at Hamlet, with eyes that glared like the light of the eyes of a lion, which is savagely growling over his bloody food. But still it was … not the ghost of Shakespeare. There was nothing in it to touch human sympathies combined with the infernal; there was nothing at all of his 'sable silvered beard', or his countenance more 'in sorrow than in anger'; it was a fierce demonical,

335

21 John Austen, the 'DP' illustration. Held in the Folger Shakespeare Library.

22 John Austen, 'The Ghost and the Guardsmen'. Held in the Folger Shakespeare Library.

armed fiend reeking from hell, who had not yet expiated 'the crimes done in his days of nature', to 'qualify him for heaven'.[49]

49 Quoted in Ruthven Todd, 'The reputation and prejudices of Henry Fuseli', in *Tracks in the Snow: Studies in English Science and Art* (London, 1946), pp. 75-6.

However, it can be argued that Fuseli's Ghost is not so diabolical as the critic imagined, and that the demonic malevolence of Austen's Ghost exceeds that of Fuseli's. One way in which it does this is through its (symbolic) physical convergence with the halo-like moon behind it. As I will explain, Austen seems subtly to adapt this motif, as found in Fuseli's Boydell painting, portraying the Ghost ironically as both diabolic and yet saint-like. Gilbert's illustration also loosely adopts this motif, as, perfectly round and shining brightly, the Ghost's helmet resembles the moon and is adjacent to it – this circular motif is repeated in the arched frame. This suggests that Gilbert's incorporation of this symbolic aesthetic may also have influenced Austen.

Since the mid eighteenth century, there has been a tradition of portraying moonlight in representations of 1.4 and 1.5. A full moon denoted a late-night setting and provided means by which to illuminate the figures dramatically.[50] Austen and Fuseli manipulate this motif in similar ways, using a moon to suggest that the Ghost wears a nimbus. In Fuseli's painting, a moon is suspended in the sky directly behind the head of the Ghost. This endows it with a 'halo' as well as a 'powerful supernatural aura'.[51] Made to seem divine, the Ghost's commanding appearance evokes Hamlet's description of him as 'Hyperion' (1.2.140; 3.4.55). Similarly, a nimbus-like disc surrounds the head of Austen's Ghost, denoting the moon behind; however, in pale drapery and without the same muscularity, this Ghost is more reminiscent of a saint than a god.

Although Fuseli and Austen both treat the moon as a nimbus, their representation of it differs significantly. In Fuseli's image, the nimbus is an actual moon; this is suggested by its being situated in the background behind the Ghost. In Austen's, placed directly between the Ghost and the foreground (an illogical position for an actual moon), it seems merely to symbolize one. By implying that the Ghost wears a literal nimbus, Austen places probably ironic emphasis on its saintliness. The disc's empty night-time interior seems sinister when compared with the starry surrounds, a foreboding absence of starlight perhaps signifying the Ghost's

arrival. If, instead, interpreted as an ominously eclipsed moon, it contrasts with the full moon in Fuseli's painting. Either reading casts Austen's Ghost in a more disturbing light than Fuseli's. An eclipsed moon surrounded by stars recalls Horatio's sober description of the visual 'precurse' of Caesar's downfall:

> As stars with trains of fire and dews of blood,
> Disasters in the sun; and the moist star,
> Upon whose influence Neptune's empire stands,
> Was sick almost to doomsday with eclipse.
>
> (1.1.10–13)[52]

Incorporating this 'eclipse[d]' 'moist star' into the Ghost's appearance, Austen's illustration implies that the Ghost's visitation presages 'disasters'. Likewise, on pages 42/Figure 21 and 113/Figure 22, the disc's vast, shining magnitude recalls Horatio's bleak reference to 'Disasters in the sun'.

Despite its ostensibly saint-like aspect, Austen's Ghost is sinister. It seems more diabolical than Fuseli's, which is physically powerful in aspect. The latter's overwhelming physicality recalls the saints occupying the ceiling of the Sistine Chapel, rendering it almost sublime – a manifestation of divine power.[53] In contrast, Austen's Ghost appears decrepit and far from "admirable." Because of its nimbus, physical suspension in space, and loose, flowing robes, this Ghost resembles an angel, suggesting an ironic allusion to the

---

[50] Young, *Hamlet and the Visual Arts*, p. 152. The first instance of this was in an engraving by Gerard Van de Gucht (1740) after a design by Hubert Gravelot, portraying Hamlet's encounter with the Ghost in Scene 4 (held in the Folger Shakespeare Library).

[51] Todd, 'The reputation and prejudices of Henry Fuseli', p. 75; Young, *Hamlet and the Visual Arts*, p. 156.

[52] *Antony and Cleopatra* includes a similar sentiment to that expressed by Horatio: 'our terrene moon / Is now eclips'd and it portends alone / The fall of Antony!' (3.13.156-8).

[53] In his Lecture IV (1805), Fuseli claimed that the 'artist' and 'poet' should seek to evoke 'that magic which places on the same basis of existence, and amalgamates the mythic or superhuman, and the human parts of the *Ilias*, of *Paradise Lost*, and of the Sistine Chapel, that enraptures, agitates, and whirls us along as readers or spectators' (Knowles, *The Life and Writings of Henry Fuseli*, pp. 199-200).

23 John Austen, 'Hamlet Leaves the Ghost'. Held in the Folger Shakespeare Library.

24 John Austen, 'Hamlet Drags Polonius' Corpse'. Held in the Folger Shakespeare Library.

angelic delivery of holy tidings. In the play, the spirit is ambiguously interpretable, seeming more like a fallen angel. It explicitly compares itself to an angel – 'So lust, though to a radiant angel linked, / Will sate itself in a celestial bed, / And prey on garbage' (1.5.55–7) – yet, as discussed, tells the Prince to exact vengeance despite God's injunction to the contrary. Hamlet knows that its claim to issue from purgatory may be a fiction. Reflecting this anxiety, Austen's Ghost seems more demonic than authentic, partly on account of its Janus-face.

If we return to one of the earliest images of Austen's Ghost, we observe that the illustration introducing 1.1, 'The Ghost and the Guardsmen' (Figure 22), portrays the Ghost as only potentially treacherous, reflecting Hamlet's ambivalence. Rather than eerie, it is 'stately', as in Bradley's description above, and has 'assume[d] a pleasing shape', as if 'Abus[ing Hamlet] to damn [him]' (2.2.598–9). The emphasis on the Ghost's face in this image may be due to Horatio's and the guards' description of it, although there is no sign of its armour, nor the 'beaver' which it wears up (1.2.129; 200). Depicted with a human aspect, it narrowly observes ('fixe[s its] eyes upon') the guardsmen, who reel backwards in shock (recalling their 'oppress'd and fear-surprised eyes') (231; 203). Its expression seems intent and somewhat mocking; its forehead is furrowed, and the underside of its moustache curves upwards at the corners, suggestive of a sardonic smile. It wears a 'sable silvered ... beard' (241; 239); however, its 'countenance' expresses neither 'sorrow' nor 'anger' (229–30) – its sideways glance makes it appear sly and conspiratorial. As in the 'Hamlet Encounters the Ghost' image, there is nothing in its expression to 'touch human sympathies'. Its eyes are large and effeminately lashed; in combination with his watchful expression, this creates an impression of seductive danger, hinting at the feminine and the diabolic. Austen again emphasizes the Ghost's dangerous femininity.

Partly accounting for the difference between this and the Ghost's appearance in Scene 5, Horatio vacillates between a noble description

of the Ghost as Hamlet's father – 'a figure like your father / ... / Goes slow and stately by them; thrice he walk'd' (1.2.199; 202) – and as a (dehumanized) lowly spirit: 'at the sound it shrunk in haste away' (219). Hamlet's descriptions of the Ghost are similarly contrasting, calling it 'My father's spirit' (1.2.254) but also an 'old mole' (1.5.164). His abrupt switch between filial reverence and jocular familiarity seems to depend on the Ghost's presence or absence. When it is present, exerting its diabolic glamour, Hamlet abandons his doubts ('Thou com'st in such a questionable shape / That I will speak to thee. I'll call thee Hamlet, / King, father, royal Dane' (1.4.24–6); when it cannot be seen, his doubts return ('this fellow in the cellarage' (1.5.153)). Skulking in aspect, the Ghost pictured in the 'Hamlet Encounters the Ghost' illustration recalls its being called an 'old mole', while here ('The Ghost and the Guardsmen'), the Ghost's appearance evokes the respected patriarch, 'King, father, royal Dane'. By depicting the Ghost as alternately benevolent and malign, Austen underscores the characters' perception of its disturbing ambiguity, demonstrating a detailed readerly understanding.

Night-time's appearance in this image contrasts with Hamlet's and Horatio's descriptions of it during the Ghost's visitations, ostensibly contributing to an impression of the Ghost's being sincere rather than demonic. The former claims that the apparition 'hideously' distorts night's aspect; similarly, Horatio describes the moon as being 'sick ... with eclipse'. However, despite the 'hideous[ness]' we might expect either of Austen's Ghost or of its surrounds, and despite its crafty expression, it has ordinary, human features, while the pale, billowing clouds are far from dark and ominous. While the bleached atmosphere may represent the breaking dawn, the spirit shows no sign of uneasiness or a desire to 'shr[i]nk in haste away'. The lighting in the scene is evenly balanced throughout the image, suggesting that the moon is featured for its symbolism rather than its evocative lighting effects.

However, notwithstanding the spirit's wily expression, the illustration highlights the Ghost's uncanniness in other ways, portraying it with the same dimensions as the moon. Similarly, like a moon, the spirit seems to issue from a thick stratum of cirrus ('horse-tail') clouds, its right shoulder almost indistinguishable from the sky cover. The moon is full, albeit partially obscured by the Ghost. Because spirit and moon are of equal size, the moon seems to be in danger of being 'eclipsed' entirely. This illustration introduces the scene in which the speech about the eclipse is delivered, implying a clear connection between image and text. By underscoring the Ghost's foreboding materialization (which Horatio compares to an eclipse, the 'precurse of fear'd events'), the image anticipates the play's tragic outcome. The physical juxtaposition of moon and spirit also recalls Hamlet's anxious description of the Ghost 'Making night hideous'. Hamlet speaks as if the spirit were a malign planet 'visit[ing]' its neighbouring moon, casting both in equally significant, otherworldly terms.[54] The spirit's huge looming face, threating to eclipse the moon, evokes the terror which it instils in the characters.

One very distinctive interpretive choice of Austen's is to include the Ghost in the court scene (I.2 – the 'DP' image; Figure 21), clarifying its agenda. The stage in this illustration may represent Hamlet's mind, where the image of his murdered father is constantly present. It is shown skulking in the background, shielding its face. This suggests that it bears angry witness to the marriage, prompting it to approach the Prince. The image implies that it is Gertrude's remarriage and supposed sexual betrayal – rather than the spirit's own murder – that spurs it to action.[55] In the 'DP' and the 'Hamlet Encounters the Ghost' illustrations, the spirit disguises its face with its cloak; in contrast, in the illustration introducing I.I, it lowers it to reveal its features, including its 'beard . . . sable silver'd', recalling its decision to appear before the guardsmen and communicate its message to the Prince. All of this loosely suggests that the Ghost is genuine. Austen prompts the reader to entertain two contrasting possibilities of its real nature: that it is either the 'devil' or an 'honest Ghost'.

CONCLUSION

For the attentive reader, *Hamlet* provides suggestions that the Ghost is more ambivalent and more insidious than eighteenth- and nineteenth-century critics, reading the play through a simplifying patriarchal lens, were inclined to believe. In his illustrated edition of *Hamlet*, John Austen makes this ambiguity explicit. This article has explored his illustrations of Hamlet and the Ghost in terms of their representation of the former's agency, and charted the ways in which the artist's images differ from, but also draw on, traditional (nineteenth-century) depictions. It has compared Fuseli's and Austen's – and to a lesser degree, Gilbert's and Selous's – demonic Ghosts, particularly with respect to their use of masculinity or effeminacy as a means of communicating supernatural potency. I have endeavoured to demonstrate that Austen's imaginative and symbolic depictions reflect his insight into the possibilities of Shakespeare's text that Romantic and Victorian readings had obscured. His inclusion of the Ghost affects how we view Hamlet. Implying that the Ghost largely determines the play's outcome, the artist's imagery renders the Prince sympathetically. *Hamlet* is treated as a human tragedy.

This article has sought to demonstrate, through a detailed examination of Austen's *Hamlet*, that illustrated editions can provide intricate, thought-provoking readings of a complex text which merit intellectual debate. Austen's images encourage the viewer to question both their assumptions regarding the moral status of the Ghost, and their habits of reading though a simplifying patriarchal lens – expecting a benevolent Ghost. These illustrations ask the viewer to actively participate in investigating

---

[54] The *OED* 3a(a) gives one meaning of 'to visit' as: 'To inflict hurt, harm, or punishment' ('visit, v., 3a(a)': OED Online). This could be considered to be the Ghost's role in the play.

[55] In early modern culture, a widow who remarried was felt to be adulterous towards her dead husband (see Peter L. Groves and Geoff Hiller, *Character Books of the English Renaissance* (Asheville, NC, 2008), p. 32).

Hamlet's omissions, inconsistencies and ambiguity. I have shown that Austen highlights the critical value of interpreting artistic renderings of Shakespeare's characters as a form of literary critique. The recent republication of Austen's *Hamlet* by Dover Publications in 2010 signals a renewed appreciation for illustrated editions of Shakespeare. Holding appeal for a twenty-first-century sensibility, his edition highlights the importance of revisiting early illustrated editions of Shakespeare, for the creative and sometimes subversive interpretations found there.

SHAKESPEARE, #METOO AND HIS NEW CONTEMPORARIES

PAMELA ROYSTON MACFIE

In 2017, the American Shakespeare Center (ASC) launched an initiative to engage new plays in conversation with Shakespeare's. Proposed by Jim Warren (ASC co-Founder, with Ralph Alan Cohen) and implemented by Ethan McSweeny (named Artistic Director in 2018), 'Shakespeare's New Contemporaries' promises to debut thirty-eight new plays – one for each of Shakespeare's thirty-eight – over the next few decades. To date, three 'New Contemporaries' have been performed in repertory, with the works that inspired them. In February 2019, during the ASC's Actors' Renaissance Season, Amy E. Witting's *Anne Page Hates Fun* debuted beside *The Merry Wives of Windsor*; in May 2019, during the 'Hand of Time' Tour Homecoming, Mary Elizabeth Hamilton's *16 Winters, or The Bear's Tale* played in repertory with *The Winter's Tale*; in May 2020, in the face of the coronavirus pandemic, Emma Whipday's *Defamation of Cicely Lee* debuted as a live-stream reading in consort with a streamed performance of *Cymbeline* offered under the title of *Imogen*.

Unlike the Oregon Shakespeare Festival's 'Play On' project, which commissioned 'translations' of Shakespeare's plays to endow their language with a present charge, the 'New Contemporaries' have been identified through a competition. The ASC invites playwrights to submit new (or previously unproduced) works that engage a Shakespeare play the company will perform in the upcoming year; a panel of theatre practitioners and scholars judges the submissions anonymously; McSweeny and ASC Literary Manager Anne G. Morgan name

the winning playwright, award them a $25,000 prize, and bring them to Staunton, Virginia, when their work is in rehearsal and, again, when it debuts at the ASC's Blackfriars Playhouse: the world's only re-creation of Shakespeare's indoor theatre. Notably, each 'New Contemporary' must work with those early modern theatrical practices that define all ASC productions: universal lighting, minimal sets, doubling within a small cast, the inclusion of audience members on the stage, and the actors' performance of all music and sound effects in real time.

Attending the series's first three pairings to gauge how the 'New Contemporaries' might turn a fresh lens on Shakespeare, I discovered the new plays darkened their doubles in genre and tone. Far from retelling Shakespeare's plays, these works surrender their audiences to energies Shakespeare either banishes or redeems; often they develop what merely glimmers at his margins, making a story out of something that had been nearly invisible. Against *Merry Wives*'s spirited comedy, in which women collaborate to scourge a predator, Witting's *Anne Page* unfolds a bittersweet elegy whose main character keeps secret her molestation at a teacher's hands. Hamilton's *16 Winters*, creating a dystopian Bohemia consumed by tedium, denies *The Winter's Tale*'s miracles. A similar tension defines *Imogen* and *Cicely Lee*. Where Shakespeare unfolds a conversion-story blessed by a god, Whipday concentrates on a traumatized woman who realizes no god will redress her woes; Cicely's hope resides solely in the pledge of an itinerant writer (who has been a forger) to tell the story of her rape until it is finally believed. Without exception, the new plays sustained a melancholy their foils had defused. Doing so, they invited us to reconsider the full sweep of details in Shakespeare's works, to engage the things that depend on silence and muse upon the untold story.

Each 'New Contemporary' also addressed a particular set of present ills: the inequities that prevent abused women from finding an audience that will adjudicate their suffering. Performed against the #MeToo movement, the Kavanaugh hearings, and the Weinstein and Epstein arrests, the plays exposed how frequently male predation inhabits the familiar. In each, at least one woman struggles to escape victimization by a man she knows well. Witting's Anne Page cannot speak of her molestation by her high school English teacher. Hamilton's postmodern Hermione considers becoming an adulteress to fulfil her husband's naming her a whore. Cicely Lee (her story set in 1611) commissions a writer to tell the story of her rape because she knows her word cannot stand against that of a lord. Confronting male trespass and urging their audiences, often through direct address, to decry its privilege, these works complicated my sense of the plays they engaged. I began to wonder whether *The Merry Wives*, *The Winter's Tale* and *Cymbeline* ask us, at least implicitly, to consider the cost of those energies by which Mistresses Ford and Page foil Falstaff's seductions, Paulina restores her slandered Queen, and Imogen triumphs over misogyny.

My perception that *Merry Wives* and *Anne Page* engage the debts women incur in negotiating male threat resonated with reactions issued by the plays' shared audience. My back-to-back attendance of the plays coincided with a Virginia community college's weekend visit to the ASC; members of its drama club energized the house at both performances. Ten danced in front of the stage during *Merry Wives*'s pre-show music, which rocked Jimi Hendrix's 'Red House' and Carl Carlton's 'Bad Mama Jama'. Eight occupied gallant stools, where they formed an on-stage chorus; these students were unafraid to react openly, even boisterously, to the play. One young woman on a gallant stool

groaned in disgusted protest when John Harrell's greasy Sir John Falstaff splayed himself across her lap; her friends cheered when she capsized him to the floor.

Harrell's Falstaff (like the production at large) effected a strange mixture of the comic and the forbidding. When he ambled on stage fitted with an inflated prosthesis, a tall man became a thing of grotesque hybridity. Gangling legs supported a swelling stomach and chest that spelled diseased distortion; in profile, Harrell seemed a pregnant hermaphrodite. This transformation was not invented by a costume designer. *Merry Wives* opened the Actors' Renaissance Season, in which the ASC's players direct, choreograph and costume themselves, rehearsing a play in days (not weeks). Though the actors primarily wore period dress, a woman clearly familiar with the company's costume stores asked at the interval, 'Did Falstaff's buckled balloon-belly come from *A Christmas Carol?*' Her husband's 'you've got it' reminded me that the knight embodies both holiday humour and a death's head.

This Falstaff teetered on the verge of expiration. His belly-led swagger left him breathless; his cramming of his bulk into a laundry tub swaddled him in stink; his attempt to rub his bottom across the woman balanced on the stool left him scrambling on the floor. Throughout, his sexual bravado seemed designed to deny his incapacity. Sprawled in the tavern, where he boasts, and mincing about household chambers, where he double-talks women, Harrell's 'mountain of mummy' (3.5.16–17) was impossibly animated; alone, he sank in sad-faced exhaustion. The extremes almost suggested the knight is harmless; his confidence seemed mere bluster, his depletion fully real.

In 1.3, Falstaff was comically childlike. Strutting before the audience as he prepared identical love letters for Mrs Ford and Page, he fingered a large paper heart, folded it crisply, and tore it in two. The letters became mangled school-day valentines. Gleeful at his economy, Harrell waggled his missives before the students on stage; they hissed him on his way. When Mrs Ford and Page (Abbi Hawk and Meg Rodgers) reunited the heart's severed halves, they also fluttered their handiwork. Nodding right and left from centre stage, the spot previously commanded by Falstaff, they elicited genial applause.

At every turn, the audience validated these merry wives. A couple seated on stage actually toasted them when, canny to Falstaff's eavesdropping from the discovery space, the wives laid a trap for him and shared their own split of champagne. Mistress Page's commentary on Falstaff's mass-produced love notes prompted murmurs of assent from every woman in my row: 'I warrant he has a thousand of these letters, writ with blank space for different names ... He will print them, out of doubt – for he cares not what he puts into the press, when he would put us two' (2.1.70–6). The murmurs seemed to say, 'we know this man and his trophy hunt'. When the wives packed Falstaff into a metal washtub (a bruising substitute for the traditional basket) so he may elude discovery, they patted the tub, directing attention to its dimensions, and we laughed in wonder that Falstaff could be so reduced. When they heaped it with soiled linen and directed their servants to dispatch it to the river, where its contents might be beaten and bleached, we laughed in recognition that Falstaff is one with filth. A blues rendition of J. Geils's 'Love Stinks' in the immediately succeeding interval confirmed this pungent truth.

Intervals at the ASC swirl with music, dance and drinking. The audience lines up at the bar cart located on one side of the stage. The actors carry on stage bass, drums, accordion and fiddle, and croon songs that resonate with the play. The house fills with conversation. I asked two students occupying gallant stools if they knew they had become part of the performance; they answered 'yes'. One hazarded that Falstaff 'just has to be mocked'; another said, 'it takes a village'. When Falstaff returned after the interval, the students showed him no sympathy. Extracting a fish from his vest and tossing it off stage, he demanded, 'Have I lived to be carried in a basket?' (3.5.4); his question was answered by a meow.

In Act 5, the ASC's spectacular masque confirmed how deftly Falstaff is reduced by the women he would ruin. Though he enters Windsor Park praying to 'the hot-blooded gods' for a 'hot back' and successful 'rut time' (5.5.2, 11, 13), the heat he experiences results from burning tapers wielded by Masters Ford and Page, newly received in their wives' confidence, and the pinching fingers of fairies and hobgoblins played by the townspeople of Windsor. The ASC emphasized that Mistresses Page and Ford preside in the end not merely over Falstaff, but also over their jealous husbands, whose separate plans to take revenge on Falstaff dwindle before their wives' agency. The wives' feminist triumph was augmented by Mistress Quickly. Played with high-pitched gusto by a rotund, kerchiefed Rick Blunt, the hostess thrilled to the cry she issues as Fairy Queen, 'Pinch him, and burn him, and turn him about' (5.5.100), and a circus of noise and motion churned over the stage. One 'fairy' bleated in Falstaff's ear; one beat a drum; some paddled him; others spun him like a top. In the house, people stamped the floor as if to say, 'Brava, Mrs Ford and Page! Brava, Mistress Quickly! Bravo, the town that puts down the man who would ruin a woman!'

Merry Wives presents, of course, a second plot concerned with female resourcefulness: that of Anne Page (played by the tiny but powerful Shunté Lofton), who is wooed by a multitude of suitors. As her father advances Abraham Slender, whom K. P. Powell actually made shrink in Anne's modest presence, Mistress Page promotes the French Doctor Caius, played by Calder Shilling as a prancing, tittering fool. Anne commandeers the chaos of Falstaff's humiliation to elope with Fenton (Chris Johnston), her spendthrift paramour. Entering the masque's hurly burly, Anne pinched Falstaff with lightning efficiency, seized Fenton's right hand, raised it in triumph, and danced him from the fray. As Fenton, wide-eyed and open-mouthed, capered off stage behind her, the production seemed again to underscore the nimble joy of female resolve. Such celebration does not endure. When Anne later stands before her parents, she cannot persuade them to accept her marriage; in this matter, a man enjoys the final word, an entitlement Johnston signalled to the audience with a slick, knowing wink as, talking of contracts and surety, he bent the Pages to his will.

Sitting in the theatre the next night, I considered Witting's title: *Anne Page Hates Fun*. Did it suggest the rewards of female solidarity in Shakespeare's comedy have their limits? Mrs Page, who tries to manipulate the fairy scene so Doctor Caius might capture Anne, discloses how little she knows her daughter. Anne has told her she had rather be buried alive, 'set quick i' th' earth' (3.4.86), than marry the physician. The gulf between mother and daughter seemed at odds with recent interpretations of the wives' feminist achievements. If Mrs Page had been less devoted to scourging Falstaff, might she have counselled Anne in negotiating courtship? Does Anne fulfil desire in marrying Fenton? Lofton's romp off stage suggested so, but Fenton's assertion that her 'father's wealth / Was [his] first motive' (3.4.13–14) in marrying her is not easily forgotten. What does Anne Page really want?

Witting recasts *Merry Wives* to answer this question. Set in twenty-first-century New Windsor, Connecticut, *Anne Page Hates Fun* elevates Shakespeare's marriage plot and places its resolution fully in Anne's hands. Shakespeare's Anne is a commodity traded on the marriage market; effusively described by men, she speaks a mere handful of lines. Witting's Anne is a 30-something teacher who easily puts down her mother's pestering insistence that only married women know fulfilment; her voice is generous yet authoritative, attributes realized in Meg Rodgers's appealing performance. This Anne Page offers mature counsel to two other women: Courtney (Abbi Hawk), her best friend, who is dying of cancer; and Aaliyah Essam (Shunté Lofton), her Muslim exchange student, who aspires to be independent of an arranged marriage. Witting's Anne is, however, less fully self-determined than we might wish. Her dedication to being single, like her no-nonsense demeanour, was forged by trauma. Anne was molested by her high school English teacher, an ugly truth disclosed in a series of flashbacks.

Witting's recasting of Shakespeare's enflamed Lothario emphasized how danger may inhabit the familiar. In the place of Falstaff, whose vaunting marks him for disgrace, Witting offers a more insidious predator. Vernon Kunze, Anne's English teacher, is no sweating grotesque, but a coolly polished intellectual. Played by the handsome Calder Shilling, he is seemingly gentle, elegantly soft-spoken and deftly manipulative. A flashback to his harassment of his student fixed the audience's gaze with a strange, hypnotic languor: Shilling padded behind Anne and breathed upon her neck; Rodgers made herself small, hunching her shoulders together. All the while, Kunze talks of Anne's essay and the grade she wants to appeal. The essay is on *Merry Wives*. The school teaches this play every year, a tradition 16-year-old Anne resists: 'the whole play is stupid; they are trying to sell off her virginity and she has no say'. Kunze dismisses her words: 'the play is not about Anne Page'. Anne replies, 'That is the problem.'

Anne (like Witting and the ASC) is determined we discover that Shakespeare speaks to our moment; this is her goal when she teaches the play that her community prizes. Aaliyah embraces the challenge. Noting that a male character asserts vitality in declaring 'we are the sons of women' (2.3.45), she asks of Shakespeare's play and her father's culture, 'if men come from women's wombs, how can they be dismissive of women?' Aaliyah parallels Shakespeare's Anne in facing a marriage arranged by parental edict. Unlike her double, however, she is a fully developed character who speaks eloquently about her father's insistence on custom, confessing, 'I don't believe in becoming the property of a man, and I don't even know if I like men. What if I like women, and what would papa say to that?'

Lofton's Aaliyah enjoyed an immediate rapport with the audience. Alone on stage, she opened the play musing, 'I'm seventeen today, and I miss my mother's cake', then observed that New Windsor believed its charm compensated for its lack of diversity; the audience laughed softly in self-recognition. When she mounted on the village green a one-woman demonstration against marriage, she brandished a hand-lettered sign above her hijab ('DOWN WITH MARRIAGE') and two young women on gallant stools raised their fists in solidarity. Countering Courtney's romantic reflection that a blue jay might be a spirit watching over the village, she stated as a matter of fact, 'Blue jays are mean'; we laughed in agreement. Aaliyah is honest and mercurial. In quick-turned soliloquies, she misses her mother, decries her father's expectations, and wonders whether her teacher is sad because she has never married. As her character plumbed these feelings, Lofton, at the apron of the stage, folded us into her passion and wonder. Our hush was palpable.

Witting gives us a threshold play. Aaliyah stands at the verge of adulthood; Courtney waits at that of death. The community honours Courtney's desire that her final months be a celebration of living, not dying. Death, however, is everywhere in New Windsor. A friend of Courtney and Anne, Charley Garvey (Chris Johnston), lost his parents when he was 17; the audience receives this news in a flashback shocking in its intensity. The uncle who became Charley's guardian has cancer. When Charley, a struggling writer, comes home to tend his uncle, Anne too stands at a limen. Tugged into the world of memory, she measures her openness before her victimization against her reserve afterwards. Charley's confession of his disappointments, like Courtney's frankness regarding her terminal diagnosis, challenges Anne's reticence.

Playing Anne, Rodgers offered a performance opposite to her buoyancy as Mistress Page; it was impossible not to notice the difference, which highlighted Witting's transformation of her source. Shakespeare's Mistress Page shares with her best friend an irrepressible confidence that their words can expose Falstaff's guile. Witting's Anne cannot speak of the taint she believes she carries. She performs an unchanging pantomime that keeps her best friends at a distance. As Courtney numbers her days, Anne's opportunities to explain herself decline. Still, she does not share her story. Rodgers's studied poise cast Anne as both a survivor and a silenced victim. To declare what

happened to her would be to confess what she believes was her part in the transgression.

Two things break the mask Anne wears. When she remembers for the second time what happened in Kunze's classroom, a grim abstraction passed over Rodgers's face. Shilling's Kunze, floating through the house, ascended the stage like an apparition. The audience flickered uneasily; one person moaned. I watched Rodgers's mouth quiver, then close in a frown. Kunze insinuates he took Anne's smile, 'a smile you would think sweet', as an invitation to erotic play. As Anne remained suspended in this memory, I felt a voyeuristic shame; the scene seemed uncomfortably elongated. Kunze has dismissed the school choir before Anne arrives to practise her graduation solo; he insists she has nothing to fear; he describes her beautiful voice and caresses her. Then, the energy shifted. Kunze passed into the discovery space and Charley entered, interrupting Anne's concentration. The words tumbled out: 'Charlie, I stayed in New Windsor because Mr Kunze would harass me at school. I didn't know how to talk about it and I'm still trying to sort that out. I don't want to talk about it Charley. Not now.' Rodgers's sudden confession freed both her character and the audience.

The close of Witting's play variously reprised Shakespeare's. Two friends (Anne and Charley) orchestrate a masque that involves an entire community: a pageant that crowns Courtney, in her final weeks of life, as New Windsor's Queen. A young woman slips the noose of parental expectation though she, unlike her Shakespearian double, manages to persuade her parents to grant her freedom: Aaliyah announces she will matriculate at Harvard. Anne realizes what she wants: she marries Charlie Garvey.

This final flourish did not sit easily with all women in the audience. The marriage, which tightened the play's sentimental links with Thornton Wilder's *Our Town*, invited a nostalgia that belied the play's inventiveness. Anne's marriage will differ from that of her parents (Charley will do the cooking; Anne will keep her surname), but its function as resolution seemed too pat. If

Shakespeare seals his play with a marriage, why can't Witting? The answer inheres in how we imagine these marriages. Shakespeare permits a question to shadow Anne's future with Fenton. We cannot know whether he has abandoned prodigality or whether Anne's monies will finance new excess. Witting creates a saccharine impression that denies any uncertainties the couple might face. I wished I could find the student who had said of *Merry Wives*, 'it takes a village'. How would she characterize *Anne Page*'s completion in marriage? Though New Windsor's citizens promise to support this union, they never condemn the predator who abused his student. The community remains in the dark. In this detail, the play disappointed. Can we exorcise trauma if it remains sequestered? Could Witting's Anne ever say '#MeToo'?

These questions stayed with me as I anticipated attending *The Winter's Tale*, which dramatizes how swiftly a marriage may be destroyed. Requiring quick adjustments of perspective, this play confirms how life and love change on a syllable. The ASC forecast the play's vertiginous instability with pre-show music that reeled from Amy Winehouse's 'Love is a Losing Game' to Muddy Waters's 'Jealous Hearted Man', Farruko's 'Obsessionado' and Shakey Graves's 'Dearly Departed'. Although four audience members danced before the actor-musicians, the songs boded sorrow. As 'Dearly Departed' wailed, 'Ooooh well, / You and I both know that the house is haunted. / Yeah, you and I both know that the ghost is of me', its lyrics anticipated at least two things: Hermione's son will whisper a 'winter's tale' that may 'fright' her with 'sprites' (2.1.29); Leontes will be haunted by jealousy and grief.

As Ronald Román-Meléndez, who played Leontes, belted out Jack White's 'Love Interruption', an uneasy tension held the house. This song catalogues desires so destructive they cancel all reason. Eyes closed, Román-Meléndez howled, 'I want love to / Split my mouth wide open and / Cover up my ears / And never let me hear a sound'; he charged 'love / to murder [his] own mother', ordered it 'to / Change [his] friends to enemies' and begged it to 'leave [him] dying on the ground'. His petitions chilled the audience.

The dancers took their seats; pre-show chatter died away. When the play opened from this heart-break song (the ASC having cut Archidamus and Camillo's conversation), Román-Meléndez became a whip-coiled Leontes and White's lyrics ghosted the air.

When this Leontes swept to the corner to survey the conversation that he orders Hermione to hold with Polixenes, his strides shook the stage. With jutting chin, he watched his wife, then fixed the audience with a stare that dared us to see with his eyes. At Hermione's pronunciation of the word 'verily', he sneered to the heavens. Polixenes swears 'verily' he cannot stay in Sicilia; Hermione, swearing he must remain, maintains 'a lady's "verily" 's / As potent as a lord's' (1.2.51–2) and wins the argument. Is a woman's 'verily' really so potent? Not in the trial that sentences Hermione for adultery. Not in Anita Hill's claims in 1991. Not in the Kavanaugh hearings. Different levels of authority, Shakespeare knew, are accorded to male and female oaths of truth.

Establishing the production's use of wordless spectacle, the continuing action brought three tableaux into view. Stage-right, Hermione (Ally Farzetta) raised her face to Polixenes (Kenn Hopkins, Jr), drew his hand to her pregnant belly, and fluttered in laughter. In the opposite corner, Román-Meléndez fisted his hands, flashed them open, and counted with an index finger the seconds Hermione smiled with his friend; seconds seemed minutes. Directly before the audience, Constance Swain's Mamillius stretched out on his stomach, propped himself on his elbows, and opened a cat's cradle. Pedalling the air with upturned feet, the child seemed carefree, though something forbidding inhered in his manipulation of the skein of string. Fingering complexity, he seemed a juvenile Fate. Later, in an effective addition to Shakespeare's text, Mamillius's ghost, webbed string in hand, haunted the stage as if he would divine his father's sorrow.

Román-Meléndez's Leontes badgered Mamillius in Act 1 with inhuman fervour. Spitting out manic repetitions of the word 'play' (and aligning it with theatrical illusion and erotic sport), his Leontes swiftly forgot he was speaking to his child. Advancing upon the audience, he pointed at one, then another man seated with a woman. The first shook his head at the implication all women play the whore; the second batted away the accusation with his right hand. Román-Meléndez swivelled, cocked his head and challenged a man whose gallery seat set him in full view. When this man sniggered, the audience groaned. We would not endorse such misogyny.

Nowhere was our antipathy to Leontes sharper than in the scene arranging Hermione's trial. When he declared, 'as she hath / Been publicly accused, so shall she have / A just and open trial' (2.3.203–5), someone near the stage barked out 'right'. Leontes matched eyes with his interlocutor and the house tightened in silence. Later, I asked Román-Meléndez about playing a character an audience must revile. What, for instance, about the patron who had jeered 'right'? 'That was nothing', he replied:

A week or so ago, a man seated in the back of the house actually argued with me. I said, 'so shall she have / A just and open trial', and he asked, 'What are you talking about?' I stared him down as if to say 'you won't mock me, I am the King' and spoke my next line, 'While she lives'. He harrumphed and repeated, 'What are you talking about?' This man had the audience's attention every bit as much as I did. I was forced to repeat 'While she lives' before saying 'My heart will be a burthen to me' (2.3.205–6).

Román-Meléndez had made the audience Leontes's court: if we remained silent, we were complicit in his tyranny; if we spoke against him, our protest dissipated. The play's impetus, like our culture's, affords scant space for listening to, much less endorsing, a woman's story.

When I pushed Román-Meléndez on Leontes's abusive misogyny, he insisted we can't dismiss Leontes as a monster: 'Shakespeare doesn't write a lead character as one-dimensional. The characters we are supposed to hate are never one thing; they ask us to believe in the human capacity to love and forgive in spite of everything.' Regarding his interpretation of Leontes, he offered:

I wasn't interested in playing a man who is just insane. Who wants to watch a guy lose his mind for three acts? I was interested in making the audience believe Leontes is capable of redemption. If we can understand why he doubts Hermione's honesty, we don't absolve him of abusing her; we do, however, see him as complicated: the victim on the one hand of insecurity, on the other of an overactive imagination.

Román-Meléndez asked me to consider a friendship 'where one male is always a little better, a little more impressive, a little more accomplished than the other'. I recalled how Hopkins's imposing Polixenes had towered over Román-Meléndez's Leontes and how Farzetta's beautiful Hermione had flirted with everyone in her orbit. Leontes had seemed physically diminished, his chin cropped to his chest, his shoulders bunched to his heart, when he watched Hermione stand on tiptoe, raise her head to Polixenes, and laugh. In an instant, his Leontes changed.

Hermione's trial shamed the audience. Clad in a dirty, grey shift, Hermione – her face pale, her eyes ringed with shadow – mounted the stage as a scaffold. Though her step faltered, she spoke with determination. At one point, raising her rope-bound hands in petition, she extended her right index finger to emphasize the word 'love'. Leontes responded with whipcord anger and her face crumpled in defeat. The house was silent. What had happened to audience protest? Is it impossible to contest a dominant male's assertion of truth where a woman's victimization is at issue?

Perhaps any *Winter's Tale* privileges Leontes's inner story over Hermione's. We witness his turn from jealous obsession to penitential guilt; Hermione, who slips from view early in the action, barely speaks when she is finally restored. The focus falls upon Leontes's transformation. Román-Meléndez's Leontes entered Act 5 as a self-scourged, rough-clad penitent. Kneeling, he placed a metal prayer bowl on the stage floor and traced its rim with his index finger; a sad sound belled the air. Paulina entered, lifted the bowl from him, bowed, and touched it with a small baton; at her crystalline chime, the curtains to the discovery space opened and the statue glided into view.

Leontes did not merely collapse, face-down, before the seeming effigy; extending his arms at right angles from his body, he made the sign of the cross on the floor.

This long, still moment characterized the final scene's suspension between human and otherworldly mystery. In it, time seemed to collapse. With the brocaded ruby gown Hermione had worn in Act 1, the statue called back her original splendour. With its folded hands and downturned gaze, it evoked the Virgin at the Annunciation. Someone behind me whispered, 'she is a manuscript illumination'. Farzetta's performance was numinous. As she floated from the platform, she seemed lighter than flesh and bone; standing before Leontes, she bowed her head as if in prayer. Her movements' simplicity contrasted with the dancing spontaneity she had embodied in Act 1. When she asked the gods to pour grace on Perdita, she slowly raised her hands and I remembered the last time she had extended them in petition: the moment in her trial when she had failed to summon Leontes's love.

As to whether Hermione's statue actually comes alive or Paulina stage-manages an illusion, the ASC pursued the latter solution, which made female wisdom the agent of change. Striking the prayer bowl, Annabelle Rollison's Paulina appeared as a maestro before an orchestra, her authority (together with Hermione's) confirming two additions director Kevin Rich made earlier to Shakespeare's text. Hermione, gowned in spectral white, had moved across the balcony immediately after the trial scene; from its elevated perspective, she watched the storm-tossed mariners convey her infant daughter to a desolate shore and declared, with prophetic fury, they will be punished for enacting Leontes's will. Shakespeare ascribes such words to Hermione only indirectly (when Antigonus reports to the sailors what Hermione had told him in a dream); the ASC endowed Hermione (whom the audience believes to be dead) with the will to speak beyond the grave. A similar empowerment of Paulina occurred when she appeared on the balcony, as the interval yielded to Act 4, as Time and Fate. Peering at the audience through spectacles riding her nose, Rollison clacked together two four-foot knitting needles and counted out sixteen years, then unfurled a woollen shroud to the stage-floor; settling the cloth and waving her hand over it, she smiled as if its lineation spelled what was yet to come.

As this *Winter's Tale* closed, I wondered about so many things: its status as a ghost story that remains haunted by memory; its implicit condemnation of a society that silences a righteous woman; its half-promise, as Román-Meléndez, returning to Jack White's lyrics, closed the performance singing 'How long can love disrupt, corrupt, or interrupt me anymore'. Most of all, I wondered about Paulina's and Hermione's self-determination during Leontes's sixteen-year penance. I did not have to wonder long. Paulina and Hermione's journey would take centre stage in *16 Winters, or The Bear's Tale*.

Hamilton's 'New Contemporary' opens with two women in modern dress – Pauly (played, like Paulina, by Rollison) and Her (played, like Hermione, by Farzetta) – lurching on stage. Introduced by Topher Embrey's sonorous Bear (who, chorus-like, counts the years throughout the play), Pauly carried Her piggyback into a hut, let three suitcases clatter to the floor, and, huffing a bit, restored her friend to her own two legs. Her squealed, 'Did you see his face?' and pronounced, with mock gravity, '"She's dead."' Pauly forced her voice to a bass register and intoned, '"I killed her."' The women's purpose became clear when Her trilled, 'I would've never thought of *that*. "She died of shock." Is that even a thing?' The women are re-enacting the moment when Pauly felled Leo by telling him Her is dead.

Parodying Shakespeare's presentation of Hermione's reported death, which had summoned pathos the night before, Hamilton's characters wheedled from the house a laughter that was not entirely sympathetic. As they revelled in their own histrionics, Rollison and Farzetta's characters remained aloof from the actual audience before them. When I asked a colleague what she had made of the women's opening antics, she observed,

'It was awfully stagey; they seemed like exhibition-ists before a mirror.' I put the same question to a young woman on a gallant stool, who replied, 'Well, Hermione is no longer on any kind of pedestal. Still, she seems more or less helpless; it's all up to Pauly.'

Little of Rollison's Paulina endured in Pauly. Obsessed with controlling the situation she has devised, Pauly's tension closely resembled that of Román-Meléndez's Leontes. In the opening of the ASC's *Winter's Tale*, he had riveted his gaze upon Farzetta's Hermione; in the opening of *16 Winters*, Pauly fixed hers upon Farzetta's Her. Her, like Hermione, is initially oblivious to how she is sur-veilled; in her case, however, a nearly adolescent self-concern cancels attention to the friend who has saved her from prison. In Hamilton's opening scene, Her shrugs off an embrace in which Pauly takes comfort, sniffs in the direction of a woodstove, asks what it is, and wonders whether a person can actually eat and sleep in the same room. Pauly's description of tiny-house intimacy cannot hold her preening friend's attention. As the audience laughed, Her looked wistfully beyond the hut; her yearning drew from Pauly a stark warning: 'you can't go outside; you will be jailed if you are discovered'. Her's reply, 'so, I'm to be imprisoned here . . . or there', seemed sharply prescient. Pauly, an apparent student of the Stockholm syndrome, has initiated a waiting game in which she imagines material deprivations will compel mutuality between captive and captor. Rollison shared that Pauly underwent several iterations in rehearsal. Initially, she was saintly (as her foil is typically played in Shakespeare); by opening night, she was 'every bit as bad as all the men in the play, every bit as possessive, underhanded, and corrupt'.

Pauly's selfish motives are matched by Leo's. Standing before Her's grave, he does not pray for her soul. He whines, 'What am I going to do?' and mutters 'nothing', recalling yet flattening Leontes's meditations on 'nothing' the night before. At this word, Mamillius's ghost (Constance Swain) enters from the stage trap, plants himself beside his father, and tugs at his sleeve; he goes unnoticed until he explodes, 'What a load of self-indulgent crap'.

Though Leo's tyrannical behaviour has sundered his son's life, he does not ask his forgiveness; he demands his otherworldly counsel. The ghost puts him in place: 'you think you get a *guide ghost*, after everything you did?' Part pre-teen angst and part moral absolutism, Swain's wise-cracking revenant compelled attention, his fateful authority (like that of Mamillius the night before) symbolized by the cat's cradle he held in his hand.

The ghost receives from his father persistent retribution and abuse; in this, he assumed the place of Hermione in the opening of Shakespeare's play. When the wraith sidles to Leo and offers a 'tale for winter' – 'an obsessive maniac kills his wife' – Leo drives him into the discovery space and slams its doors upon him. The ghost quickly commandeers the balcony (recalling Hermione's and Paulina's *Winter's Tale* appear-ances thereon); there, high above his father, he scoffs as Leo bleats, 'I'm feeling a lot right now.' Upon Leo's exit, the ghost knowingly observes, 'some people turn to the arts when they're feeling a lot'. His words forecast Leo's appropriation of the balcony to perform a discordant song Román-Meléndez had written for his character: 'I had a dream the castle was infested / With tiny little women / Who were also insects.' Punctuated by a squawk forced from a manhandled guitar, the song closed by keening 'They crawled all over the walls, and into my bed / And into my ears, / And into my head.' As Leontes, Román-Meléndez had inhabited a character wild in fury and repentance; as Leo, he became a punk-rock poseur.

If Hamilton's characters, with the ghost's excep-tion, seemed lesser versions of their Shakespearian doubles, her Bohemia seemed equally flattened. A seaside artist colony, this second setting featured no seasonal festival; there, it was always winter. Its inhabitants lounged on Turkish pillows, smoked marijuana and wondered, in their lassitude, what they could find to eat. Though their conversations decried monogamy as 'a construct of patriarchy' and disowned 'the nomenclature of the father', something dystopian haunted the air. Calling women 'slippery', Shep and Flory reproduced Leo's (and Leontes's) misogynist slurs; mocking

P (Perdita's double) when she rebukes their mansplaining, the men vie to possess her. When verbal machismo turns to wrestling, P is tossed to the floor, her person nearly crushed before she manages to crawl away. Beside the fracas, a girl named Spring snaps photos for an Instagram post and grumbles jealously.

When I asked others what they thought of this Bohemia, one friend complained, 'God, we were there a long time.' Another said she felt 'dropped into a Beckett play, where there's nothing but endless waiting and finally nothing to wait for'. Rollison, who attempted to correct these impressions, maintained that the Bohemians' dialogue resembled Chekhov's, not Beckett's: 'the talk about nothing is actually about very deep things'. I wasn't sure. Hamilton, it seemed to me, exposes her Bohemians' resourcefulness to be limited, their desires vain and their hospitality superficial. When Her wanders into their camp and tells of her abusive marriage, she receives one stoned response: 'I dig old people.'

Though Her ventures from the hut's confines several times, she experiences neither freedom nor epiphany in the forest. When her path crosses with that of Pol (Polixenes's double), she invites the King to imagine what it would be like to commit the sin of which they have been accused, and arranges for a tryst when Pauly will be hunting. Waiting for Pol to arrive, Her practises pursing her lips and jiggling her breasts so they fall from her shirt; for a second time, she appeared like an exhibitionist before a mirror. When Pol arrives, Her's game of bait and switch recalls how she has toyed with Pauly by climbing into her lap, covering her with kisses, and then jumping away. The present game is interrupted when Pauly, a brace of rabbits in triumphant hand, returns to the hut early. Barking in fury, Pauly pulls Pol from Her's bed, claws him, and chases him about the stage. The snarling fight draws from Her neither hope nor distress; she watches impassively, her greatest care devoted to combing her dishevelled hair. Her's indifference suggested something more than narcissism; earlier, she had confessed she does not miss conjugal intimacy: 'When I think of him lying down on top of me heavy with booze and desire the only thing I feel is a vague nausea. As if tiny little fingers were creeping down my throat and pulling out my stomach like thread.' These words, echoing Leo's song of 'tiny little insects', evinced the loathing beneath Her's need to frustrate others' desires.

At the play's close, Her and Leo meet in their wanderings and share their stories. They speak eagerly and fully, but listen with something less than care. Her glanced about the stage as Leo confessed his faults; Leo tented his fingers (reminding the audience of Leontes's flashing hands the night before) as Her catalogued her suffering. Neither recognized the other. When Leo fell silent and Her wistfully declared, 'I used to think it would really be something to have someone to talk to', her intent seemed uncertain. Does she measure the silence of her marriage against the fullness of her present conversation with a seeming stranger, or does she consign to the past the belief that words can save us? Leo and Her exit after this observation: he into the shrouded discovery space, she through the audience. *16 Winters* cannot reunite these characters; their story's resolution belongs to Shakespeare. It does, however, invite us to recognize how miraculous their rapprochement in *The Winter's Tale* surely is.

In spring 2020, the Blackfriars was shuttered as a result of the pandemic, and production of the third 'New Contemporary' was suspended; the company was not, however, idle. It made available through a streaming venture called BLKFRSTV several performances of *Imogen* filmed in its playhouse, and offered in May, in real time, a 'Zoom' reading of Whipday's *The Defamation of Cicely Lee*. Presenting women ruined by false accusation, these plays sustained the cry raised by the earlier 'New Contemporary' pairings: why is a woman contested ground? How long must we tell the story of a woman's rape or defilement before that story is believed?

Cicely Lee, mourning a woman's violation and her struggle to make others understand what she has endured, issued the cry more acutely than *Anne*

Page and *16 Winters*, in part because it locked its audience within Cicely's narrative. Where Witting keeps Anne's molestation at her play's margins and Hamilton subsumes Her's story within other characters' misadventures, Whipday focused wholly on Cicely's plight. Doing so, she challenged her audience, again and again, to consider how closely Cicely's plight haunts our present moment.

Whipday opened her play with speakers who separately pronounce what they know of Cicely's ravishment by William Heron (Chris Bellinger), the gentleman who has seduced her after she left his employment. Sara (Madeline Calais), who has laughed with Cicely all her life, wonders why Cicely 'did not rebuke him'; Reverend Wintersgill (Kenn Hopkins, Jr) proclaims 'I hereby depose you on charges of adultery'; Cicely (played by the sympathetic Mia Wurgaft) swears, 'My name is Cicely Lee. I tell you the charges against me are false', then remembers, speaking to herself alone, 'I heard the lock click shut.' This ominous preface gives way to the first scene of Cicely's story, which unfolds in the maidservants' chamber she shares with Sara. Giggling, the friends fuss over who will be crowned Queen of the May at the next day's festival; when sleep comes, their master, William Heron, pads to their bed and gazes, open-mouthed, at their beauty. At the May dance, Cicely must deflect not merely Heron's leer, but also his hands, which press her body as the music thrums. When Cicely weds Sara's brother, the farmer James Lee, she gives thanks, in sombre soliloquy, not that she has found love, but that she will never lie in bed again, watch her door open, and not know who would enter. Later, Cicely opens her home's door to Heron and he rapes her. Her account of this crime is mocked as a lie; the church court sentences her, together with Heron, for adultery and she is ordered to stand, all night, next to the man who has defiled her, on blocks within the village square. When darkness falls, Heron leaves a bag of coins on his pedestal and moves away; Cicely, praying to Diana, mourns her shame until dawn.

Whipday never swerves from Cicely's plight; she confronts the audience with its violence before the action begins and accentuates, from start to finish, its possessive charge by having each of her characters, including Cicely, revisit and retell its scandal. Standing apart from the others' noise in Whipday's prologue, a mysterious figure we learn is the writer Daniel Sterrie is magnetized by Cicely's story. He promises, over the villagers' cacophony, to write it for her, and she insists he must tell it whole, not piecemeal. Initially, a flustered Sterrie (played earnestly by Andrew Tung) struggles to keep time with Cicely's revelations; by the end, having written her tale and his own as well, he prays that the gods may grant Cicely the courage to walk in freedom with him and provides a forged marriage document permitting them to travel as man and wife.

The sense that Cicely's story offers no escape until this final turn deepened in the play's repetition of whole passages from *Cymbeline* and *The Rape of Lucrece*. The citations, often drawing commentary from the characters who issue them, cast Cicely as an archetypal victim. When Heron invades Cicely and Sara's chamber to spy upon them as they sleep, he celebrates himself as a 'smooth tongued Iachimo', cites as if they are a fetish the words Shakespeare's character utters as he creeps upon Imogen, then disparages Iachimo's predation as 'a poor business, this hiding in trunks'. Heron's point is clear: his spoils, if not his rhetoric, will top Iachimo's. Tarquin's rape of Lucrece, remembered in the long passage Heron repeats from *Cymbeline* 2.2, variously haunts the audience's perception of Cicely, who laments as she struggles to make sense of her rape, 'when I opened the door, I was lost', then swiftly notes that Lucrece did the same and 'did then kill herself'. The effect of these allusions was twofold: spreading backward, they reminded the audience how narrowly Shakespeare's play averts rape; oscillating in the present moment, they reinforced the truth of Sterrie's final words: 'there will always be Iachimos'.

In the Zoom interval, Whipday shared what had inspired her play's creation. She had been teaching *Cymbeline* when the call for the third 'New Contemporary' went out and had also been reading the 1581 testimony of Cicely Lee of Edgefield, a married woman brought before the Archdeacon of Norwich on charges she had committed adultery with a gentleman she had served as a maidservant before she had married. Whipday asked herself what a real woman's words could bring to a play that explores, in dialogue with Shakespeare: (1) how gender and class hierarchies govern vocal authority; and (2) how a writer's words might redeem prior meanings.

Throughout, Whipday engaged her audience with words' power. Workshopping the play in January, she calibrated which characters would address the audience and emphasized the significance of the elite characters speaking verse and the non-elite prose. Verse in the play, she noted, should spark surprise, especially when it unfolds lines already written by Shakespeare. Whipday's previous work at the Blackfriars (where *Shakespeare's Sister* debuted in 2017) helped her to imagine how she would use the stage's several levels. Had *Cicely Lee* been produced, Daniel Sterrie would have remained on stage, seated on a gallant stool unless he was speaking, from start to finish. At those moments when, rising to his feet, Sterrie would insist he must publish Cicely's story, truth-telling would have appeared, both practically and symbolically, to rise from witness; the audience, of which Sterrie would have been a part, would have been challenged to embrace his example.

Cicely Lee's virtual delivery muted the participation Whipday had hoped to inspire; still, if viewers enabled Zoom's chat function during the reading, a stream of reactions tumbled down their screens' right margins. One comment identified a dark allusion. When Cicely declared, 'I might as well pluck out my tongue for all the good it hath done me', someone typed out 'Philomela'. Cicely, of course, is a Philomela with a difference: her conviction that her words count as nothing makes it unnecessary for her Tereus to eviscerate her tongue. Emojis of sorrow popped onto my screen, then disappeared; strange marginalia that failed, like the character they mourned, to sustain a plea.

Cicely's self-identification as Philomela sent me back to the ASC's *Imogen*, which, though I had

seen it performed in early February on my university campus, I had watched again several days before *Cicely Lee*'s Zoom reading. Where Whipday drew attention throughout her play to the power of texts, *Imogen* excised several details through which Shakespeare emphasizes the same. Director Vanessa Morosco dropped the soothsayer from the play's performance, as well as Posthumus's reading from a prophetic book while he is jailed. She also cut the lines in which Iachimo identifies what Imogen had been reading as she fell asleep: Ovid's story of Philomela's rape. Shakespeare's detail threatens that Ovid's words may move from the page; that Iachimo, noting how Imogen has turned down the leaf 'Where Philomel gave up' (2.2.46), may perform what Ovid has scripted.

In the place of such threat, the ASC played the scene for laughs. Alexis Baigue's Iachimo secured entrance to Imogen's chamber through delivery in a Fed-Ex box (rather than a trunk), sawed the container open from within, and lowered himself to the stage in an awkward scramble of arms and legs. The audience chortled at the saw's strident scissoring of the cardboard, which made Imogen stir in her sleep, then howled at Baigue's inelegant emergence from the box's uncomfortable confines. On all fours, this Iachimo scuttled crablike to Imogen's bed, stretched with some difficulty to a standing position, and smacked his face at her beauty. His movements hijacked the scene's forbidding charge. In Morosco's hands, the threat Iachimo bears Imogen was only slightly differentiated from that embodied in Topher Embrey's belly-proud Cloten, who in the next scene roars about the stage motioning for applause at his seamy innuendoes that music may 'finger' and 'tongue' (2.3.13–14) a woman. Cloten's attempt to soften Imogen through song is often played for laughs (Tom Hiddleston's 2007 Cheek by Jowl boy-band performance of 'Hark, hark, the lark' comes to mind); Iachimo's performance is less frequently reprised as folly.

Concentrating upon *Cymbeline*'s melodramatic potential, *Imogen* included a mere handful of quiet scenes. One came into being when Guiderius and Arviragus take Imogen for dead. As they wrapped her in a grey-gold winding sheet, they knelt beside her, and sang 'Fear no more the heat o' th' sun'; pale blossoms sifted onto her impossibly small body. This elegiac scene invited its audience to mourn fragility. When Imogen, upon waking, wondered at a petal that fell from her brow, the invitation opened anew. Later, Imogen beat a drum at the side of the stage while Iachimo and Posthumus engaged in a slow-motion combat that seemed a grinding dream; her percussion seemed funereal. Shifting the production's tempo, these moments signalled that time was running out, that inflated displays of violence and desire must give way to resolve, a surrender achieved in the quiet order of *Imogen*'s final scene.

Madeline Calais's winning Imogen presided over this scene with an aplomb that contrasted her character's unfocused energies in the first half of the play. In her initial conversation with Posthumus, Imogen, swaying on tiptoe before her beloved, seemed unequal to love's demands. This impression deepened when, disguising herself as a man, she adopted a swagger that made her trip. In the final scene, standing at the centre of the stage, she was steady on her feet. Posthumus, who enters through the house, must rise to her level. Morosco's blocking of this scene authenticated the company's re-titling of Shakespeare's play as Imogen's story.

In spite of the final scene's achievement, I felt *Imogen* staged male toxicity more fully than female resilience. Iachimo and Posthumus's verbal contest over Posthumus's claim that Imogen is chaste happened in a game of beer-pong that crossed the audience's eyes. Guiderius and Arviragus tumbled Cloten's severed head in a game of brutish one-upmanship. Jupiter's oracular speech, turned into a rap song written by Michael Morét (who played the god), noised a machismo at odds with the play's imminent close. Considered in relationship to *Cicely Lee*, *Imogen* had invited laughter at behaviour that should evoke shame. In this way, the production had missed the mark, though I arrived at this conclusion only after *Cicely Lee* stood against *Imogen*'s high camp. *Imogen* kept at arm's length the energies that threaten tragedy, a distancing signalled in the pre-show's closing song: Tupak's 'Keep Ya Head Up', in which the male actors had rapped, 'why we take from our women / Why we rape our women, do we hate our women'. Responding to this song, the audience sang only its refrain: 'Ooh, child, things are gonna get easier.'

Cicely Lee, even more urgently than the other 'New Contemporaries', reprises tensions oscillating within its Shakespearian foil and invites us to consider how those tensions gather impetus (and may be defused) in being retold; all three 'New Contemporaries' demonstrate that Shakespeare speaks to concerns that demand attention in our moment. Opening seams within their companion plays, these works create for those plays a new audience; they also model new forms of engagement with Shakespeare and performance. Witting, Hamilton and Whipday coax truth from stories of abuse and predation that Shakespeare has not fully told; doing so, like Daniel Sterrie, they bear out the necessity to tell the full story until, one day, it is finally heard.

'WHILE MEMORY HOLDS A SEAT IN THIS DISTRACTED GLOBE': A LOOK BACK AT THE ARDEN SHAKESPEARE THIRD SERIES (1995–2020)

JENNIFER YOUNG[1]

The Arden Shakespeare third series began publication in 1995 with editions of *Antony and Cleopatra, Henry V* and *Titus Andronicus*. Thanks to the sustained commitment of a generation of scholars and other professionals, it was completed with the publication of *Measure for Measure* in 2020. Over those twenty-five years, the series navigated mergers and restructuring in the publishing industry, persisting through four changes in publishing house with the support of multiple publishing editors.[2] It realized the vision of four General Editors who set more ambitious parameters and supported more variety in editorial practices than any of their predecessors. The efforts of fifty volume editors produced forty-four new editions that also added four new plays to the series and editions dedicated to the Sonnets and the Poems. These editions addressed some of the most significant changes to Shakespeare studies in this century and, in the process, helped to define editorial practice and shape the modern scholarly series. Now complete, Arden 3 stands as a book of memory and of aspiration, a record of our progress as a field and a profession, and a reminder of how much further we have to go.

This review of the Arden Shakespeare third series examines significant moments of its development and publication in order to highlight its contributions to scholarly editing and the study of Shakespeare over its tenure. It considers how the series and its editors responded to major shifts in Shakespeare studies concerning issues of performance, critical theory, textual agency and authorship. It also recognizes important firsts and innovations introduced in the third series, including efforts to diversify scholarly editing by recruiting Arden's first class of women editors. The third series is by no means perfect, but, as we will see, it takes notable first steps on a number of issues. This review also acknowledges the people behind the practice. In January 2020, I attended 'The End Crowns All', an event hosted by Bloomsbury to celebrate the completion of the third series. The evening featured a discussion with three of the series General Editors: Richard Proudfoot, Ann Thompson and H. R. Woudhuysen. After seeing the audience riveted to stories of the day-to-day work of editing, I realized that this retrospective would not be complete without insights from those who edited the series. Many Arden 3 editors

---

[1] I wish to thank the General Editors and the many volume editors who graciously shared their time and knowledge with me during this project, especially Ann Thompson, Richard Proudfoot, Suzanne Gossett and Valerie Wayne, who also offered valuable feedback on this article. Many thanks also to Margaret Bartley whose support made this article possible.

[2] Arden was originally launched by Methuen in 1899. In 1996, Thomson International transferred the series to Thomas Nelson, who in turn transferred it to Thomson Learning (later Cengage); it was finally acquired by Bloomsbury in 2008 (Ann Thompson, 'Arden completed', paper for Shakespeare Association of America Conference, 2019). See also Richard Wray, 'Bloomsbury buys Arden Shakespeare', *The Guardian*, 6 January 2009.

generously shared their experiences (so many and so generous, there was not enough space to include them all).[3] As a result, this article is a narrative of texts and of people, not with any intention of being comprehensive, but with the wish that it serve as a starting point for further study of the editorial and scholarly practices used in this distinctive series, and of the contributions of the agents who made it possible.

'WHAT'S PAST IS PROLOGUE': ARDEN 2 TO ARDEN 3

Comparing volumes across the Arden Shakespeare, the third series stands apart from its predecessors. The cover art for Arden 2's paperback editions evolved through a series of traditional looks from eighteenth-century illustrations to the nature-inspired art of the Brotherhood of Ruralists. In contrast, the concept for the Arden 3 covers was commissioned by the General Editors at an early stage of planning to ensure a unified look over the course of the series.[4] These modern, misty collages gesture, some more obscurely than others, towards the darker drama of the plays. This is most striking in the comedies: the twins sharing an eye on the cover of *Twelfth Night* and the sober face almost overtaken by the forest of Arden on the cover of *As You Like It*.

Such cosmetic changes, however, understate a re-envisioning of the third series by its initial General Editors: Richard Proudfoot, Ann Thompson and David Scott Kastan. 'I wanted it to be a new series not just an update', Thompson recalled, '... and we wanted to maintain Arden's position as the first choice of scholarly edition'.[5] Key to this objective was eliminating the practice whereby some Arden 2 editions used the edited text, notes and commentary of their predecessors as a basis for their new editions. As was becoming the practice in other modern series, Arden 3 editors would 'begin with the earliest printed texts and not be influenced by their predecessors' work'.[6] This approach required that 'the variety of textual sources be appraised in relation to individual histories, not a single imposed model'.[7]

Described by Proudfoot as an 'essential' element of editing Shakespeare, each play would be unified by the Arden editorial guidelines, but also individual in its response to the issues and conditions of its text(s).[8] This bespoke approach gave editors the chance to develop and use a range of editorial techniques.

Editors of the third series were also tasked with making their work accessible to a wider readership. The General Editors' Preface identifies 'scholars, students, actors and "the great variety of readers"' as the series target audience, an ambitious goal for a series promising the comprehensive approach of the Arden Shakespeare. In order to compete with the many editions of Shakespeare on the market, most modern series now focus on a particular niche market, with editions geared to students (New Cambridge, Norton) or to performers and performance (Penguin). *The New Oxford Shakespeare* produces *The Complete Works* for classroom use while publishing increasingly technical debates of authorship in companion texts for researchers. Every approach requires compromises: a focus on performance and stage history means less space for critical theory; introductions focused on the complexities of textual transmission leave less room for global performance and burgeoning fields of theory.

In its mission to remain 'the first choice of scholarly edition', the third series expanded its introductions to cover more diverse topics, including sections on performance history and emerging areas of critical theory, such as gender and race studies.

The needs and interests of a broader readership also prompted changes in tone and in how information was presented. Introductions that in Arden 2 began with a review of early textual history, in Arden 3 begin with an essay-style 'hook' meant to engage non-specialist readers. The adjustment is perhaps most visible in commentary notes. In Arden 2, it is not unusual to encounter a note that

---

[3] Editors responded to short surveys, cited throughout as General Editor Response (GER) and Volume Editor Response (VER).
[4] Richard Proudfoot, GER. [5] Ann Thompson, GER.
[6] Thompson, GER. [7] Proudfoot, GER. [8] Proudfoot, GER.

could look a bit like calculus to the uninitiated: '41–3. *double business . . . both neglect*] Bound is usually interpreted as the adj. from M.E. *boun* < O.N. *búinn* (*OED* bound *ppl. a.*[1])'.[9] 'Aiming for a wider readership including for example, people who had not studied Latin or Greek', Arden 3 editors are aware that they may not be speaking exclusively to other seasoned scholars.[10] In a necessary response to changes in modern education, Latin and other non-English languages are now translated, allusions to classical and religious texts and rhetorical figures are explained. The overall result is clear, for example, when comparing how Claudius's reference to the 'primal eldest curse' in *Hamlet* is presented in Harold Jenkins's seminal Arden 2 edition and in Ann Thompson and Neil Taylor's Arden 3 edition:

Arden 2: 'Genesis iv. 11–12. This reference to Cain is ironically anticipated at I.ii.105 and echoed at V. i.75–6.'

Arden 3: 'The first murder in Judeo-Christian tradition is Cain's killing of his brother Abel; see Genesis, 4.11–12, and 1.2.105 and n.'[11]

Both note the biblical allusion, but in citing the Bible chapter and verse first, the Arden 2 note presumes familiarity with texts of Western Christianity and the story of Cain and Abel. It is a note for a well-versed reader who is already familiar with the story's significance to this moment in the play, and who will largely refer to Jenkins's notes for supplemental information like the cross-references to lines in 1.2 and 5.1. The Arden 3 note offers similar information, but first contextualizes 'primal eldest curse' in the religious tradition, enabling the reader to deduce why Claudius references this story. The notes in Thompson and Taylor's edition remain a place for advanced readers to find supplemental insights, but they are first a place to gain knowledge and guidance for developing an informed reading. As such, the subsequent references to Genesis and the 'first corpse' at 1.2.105, now positioned at the end of the Arden 3 note, are no longer obscure references but opportunities for further discovery.

With this wider readership in mind, the General Editors also aimed to demystify the editorial process. 'We wanted to make our editorial practices more transparent', Ann Thompson explained 'by . . . for example, introducing a sample passage with a discussion of the editor's interventions'.[12] Thus, readers of the third series benefit from concise introductions to a variety of editorial practices and issues. For example, Lois Potter uses pages from the 1634 quarto of *The Two Noble Kinsmen* to explain how an editor decides when and how much of a text to edit.[13] In *Pericles*, Suzanne Gossett demonstrates the broader impact of editorial choice by removing a phrase from 1.2 of *Pericles* and then tracking the changes to scansion and character interpretation that result.[14] These tutorials are also a place for some delightfully nerdy details, such as how Hamlet's first soliloquy in Q2 'uses thirty-five commas, a couple of semicolons, one question mark and one full stop; [and] F's almost identical soliloquy uses . . . twenty-six commas, two semicolons, nine colons, a pair of brackets, four question marks, two exclamation marks and ten full stops'.[15]

Peter Holland's 'A note on the text' from his edition of *Coriolanus* exemplifies the potential of this feature. 'In the hope that readers . . . might crack the code' and 'enjoy following the process of creating a modern Shakespeare edition', Holland connects the editorial conventions used in commentary notes directly to reader experience.[16] His candid discussion of editorial intervention in stage directions is an important lesson in critical reading that, delivered in just one paragraph, also provides

---

[9] *Hamlet*, ed. Harold Jenkins, Arden Shakespeare 2nd ser. (London, 1982), p. 314, nn. 41–3.

[10] Thompson, GER.

[11] Jenkins, ed., *Hamlet*, p. 314, n. 37; *Hamlet*, rev. edn, ed. Ann Thompson and Neil Taylor, Arden Shakespeare 3rd ser. (London, 2016), p. 359, n. 37.

[12] Thompson, GER.

[13] *The Two Noble Kinsmen*, rev. edn, ed. Lois Potter, Arden Shakespeare 3rd ser. (London, 2015), pp. 124–9.

[14] *Pericles*, ed. Suzanne Gossett, Arden Shakespeare 3rd ser. (London, 2004), pp. 43–4.

[15] Thompson and Taylor, eds., *Hamlet*, p. 552.

[16] *Coriolanus*, ed. Peter Holland, Arden Shakespeare 3rd ser. (London, 2013), pp. xxiv–xxv.

an example of this 'rarely appreciate[d]' element of editing in a form ideal for class discussion.[17] Another strength of these sections is when editors disclose the limits of editorial practice. Holland's observation that 'modernizing is a difficult process and a complex art' gives readers insight into the balancing of procedure, skill and subjectivity that is modern editing.[18] Suzanne Gossett's observation that 'it is not always possible to distinguish interpretative from textual problems' in *Pericles* presents ambiguity not as a failure of reading or editorial practice but as a condition of the early modern playtext.[19]

With editing and bibliography taught less frequently in classrooms, sections such as these offer vital instruction that students need to attempt their first collation or editing assignment, making these sample passages one of the hidden gems of the third series. Sadly, their presence is inconsistent across the series. They are highlighted in sections like 'editorial procedures' or 'editing and interpretation' in some editions, but are relegated to the appendix or simply absorbed into broader textual discussions in others. This was a missed opportunity to use the expertise of a generation of editors to transform textual editing from an exclusive mystery of the academe into a set of skills appreciated by all readers. I hope to see more such moments of deliberate editing pedagogy in future series as it is a vital part of Shakespeare studies and of training the next generations of critical thinkers.

The General Editors' ambitious agenda set expectations high for Arden 3, and striking a balance between comprehensive scholarship and the needs of a wider readership would remain a challenge throughout the series. Reviewers looking for scholarly editions would mistake elements aimed at student readers as unnecessary, while some were frustrated when new research areas replaced topics required by first-time readers.[20] In spite of the expectations of readers and the marketing campaigns of publishing houses, no edition or series can be everything to everyone. Arden 3's efforts to bring newer readers into the advanced scholarly discourses that are central to its identity is a compelling approach that, because it is a *via media*, will always leave some

dissatisfied, but I believe any work that makes the study of Shakespeare more accessible and welcoming to new scholars is worth the effort.

A SCHOLARLY COMMUNITY

Arden editors are very individual when it comes to describing their practice. For some, the appeal lies in unravelling the analytical complexity of textual variation. For others, editing is a chance to revel in language 'line-by-line, word-for-word, to observe at close quarters how the play works to express feelings and generate its own rhetorical music'.[21] Some highlight the chance to refine their skills further at this level and the opportunity to participate in this tradition of Shakespeare scholarship as their motivation. However, as David Scott Kastan observed, 'No form of scholarly work more obviously reveals itself less as an individual labour and more as a collective activity than an edition of a Shakespeare play.'[22] The 'collective activity' Kastan mentions is revealed in the extended network of expertise that made Arden 3 possible.

The series's aspirations for high-quality scholarship and editorial practice originated with its General Editors. Richard Proudfoot, who first read Shakespeare in his family's copy of the original Arden series, led the series as one of the foremost textual scholars and editors in the field.[23] Ann Thompson, one of the first wave of Shakespeare feminist scholars and editors to shatter the glass ceiling and advocate for the benefits of feminist editing, was also central to the early development of the series. They were joined by David Scott

---

[17] Holland, ed., *Coriolanus*, p. xxvii.
[18] Holland, ed., *Coriolanus*, p. xxiii.
[19] Gossett, ed., *Pericles*, p. 43.
[20] See, for instance, Brian Vickers, 'The Two Noble Kinsmen', *The Review of English Studies* 50 (1999), 79–84, and Leah Scragg, 'Review of *King Lear* by William Shakespeare and R. A. Foakes', *The Review of English Studies*, 49 (1998), 510–12.
[21] René Weis, VER.
[22] *King Henry IV Part 1*, ed. David Scott Kastan, Arden Shakespeare 3rd ser. (London, 2002), p. xv.
[23] Proudfoot, email, 14 August 2020.

Kastan, whose synthesis of literature and book history inspired scholars to reconsider the relationship between Shakespeare, his plays, and agents of the book trade; and finally by H. R. Woudhuysen, whose expertise in poetics and manuscript circulation changed discussions of textual transmission and reception. George Walton Williams, described by René Weis as 'to editing what Bobby Fischer was to chess', accepted the honorary title of Associate General Editor and assisted editors of the Histories and early plays.[24] The General Editors were described by their grateful volume editors as: inscrutable critics, wells of knowledge, correctors, guides, mentors, teachers, collaborators, morale officers and friends.

The General Editors were, above all, a source of rigorous critical feedback. Their relentless attention to detail was unanimously welcomed by editors, who expressed gratitude for Thompson's 'penetrating questions and comments' and Proudfoot's 'thoroughness and eye for detail'.[25] Richard Proudfoot's lengthy and detailed notes were received with pleasure and deep appreciation, and even kept as cherished items. A good copy, as Peter Holland observed, would be returned with 'warm praise for how good it was and only ten pages of single-spaced suggestions'.[26] Underlying such generosity was a commitment to elevating the work of others. Thompson and Proudfoot graciously recount how they 'enjoy working with volume editors' and 'working out how best to realise their aims for their editions'.[27] Much of this work was done behind the scenes, so some editors made a point of crediting their General Editor in commentary notes. Peter Holland, for example, retained the '(RP)' alongside many of Proudfoot's suggestions 'so that readers can see a great textual scholar at work'.[28] The General Editors also knew when to step back. Proudfoot's reminder that 'this is your edition' was a vivid memory from Suzanne Gossett's experience editing *Pericles*.[29] As we will see, encouraging editors to pursue innovative editorial policies was a hallmark of their approach.

General editors and volume editors are only the most visible collaborators. A range of other professionals helped to maintain the quality of Arden 3. The series persisted through multiple publishing houses with the support of a series of dedicated publishing editors. Jane Armstrong, Jessica Hodge and, most recently, Margaret Bartley, who saw the edition to its conclusion, were regularly thanked by editors for their support and for even applying a bit of motivational pressure when required. Copy-editors were also vital contributors. Tasked with the job of 'editing the editor', Jane Armstrong, Jessica Hodge, Hannah Hyam, Alison Kelly and others were praised as 'heroic' for their 'exemplary' copy-editing, 'efficiency and critical acumen' and 'unflagging devotion to clarity, order and accuracy'.[30]

Support stretched beyond those working under the Arden label. While editing *Richard III*, James Siemon remarked how 'old friends rose to the occasion, and new friends appeared wherever I went'.[31] Help was found in the support of co-editors, a multitude of librarians from around the world and a global department of academic colleagues who shared ideas at seminars, at conferences and in chance meetings in reading rooms. There are stories of exceptional generosity: works-in-progress shared by so many scholars it is impossible to name them all, and a single question about pronunciation answered with a full recording of *Romeo and Juliet* read in Original Pronunciation by David Crystal.[32] Add to this the many 'Arden families' who lived with the highs and lows of the process alongside their editors and the completion of the third series becomes the story of all textual productions: a network of diverse agents collectively contributing tremendous amounts of visible and invisible labour.

---

24 Weis, VER.
25 *Macbeth*, ed. Sandra Clark and Pamela Mason, Arden Shakespeare 3rd ser. (London, 2015), p. xvii; *Double Falsehood*, ed. Brean Hammond, Arden Shakespeare 3rd ser. (London, 2010), p. xvii.
26 Holland, ed., *Coriolanus*, p. xxi.
27 Thompson, GER; Proudfoot, GER.
28 Holland, ed., *Coriolanus*, p. xxi.
29 Gossett, interview, 28 July 2020.
30 *Richard III*, ed. James R. Siemon, Arden Shakespeare 3rd ser. (London, 2009), p. xvii; Potter, ed., *The Two Noble Kinsmen*, p. xviii; *As You Like It*, ed. Juliet Dusinberre, Arden Shakespeare 3rd ser. (London, 2006), p. xviii.
31 Siemon, ed., *Richard III*, p. xvi. 32 Weis, VER.

RESPONDING TO CHANGE

When asked about the biggest challenges of producing Arden 3, Proudfoot and Thompson both mentioned creating a series that effectively engaged with the unprecedented amount of research published since the release of the last Arden 2 edition in 1982. The following sections consider the series response to several of these changes: performance history, multi-text editing, collaboration and authorship, and diversity of critical theory through the inclusion of the first group of women editors. Examining how editors engaged with these issues in their respective plays while negotiating the traditional parameters of editorial practice in an Arden Shakespeare, reveals the tension between innovation and discipline as a key element of the successes and struggles of Arden 3's response to this dynamic time in Shakespeare studies.

PERFORMANCE HISTORY

Performance history was undergoing significant change and growth as new understandings of historical theatre spaces and stagecraft combined with unprecedented access to global productions. As Ann Thompson observed, the third series accordingly expanded its focus: 'there had to be more attention to the plays in performance ... film and television versions and all kinds of adaptations' and 'the focus here needed to be international: a scattering of references to productions by the Royal Shakespeare Company would not be sufficient'.[33] Whereas stage histories were an optional component of Arden 2, comprehensive performance histories would be a required feature of Arden 3.[34] Promising 'full' introductions that would not only educate students in each play's 'performance contexts' but support the development of future productions, the third series emphasized the plays as 'texts for performance'.[35] This enhanced connection between editors and performance is reflected in the numerous theatre practitioners thanked by Arden editors for their valuable advice and contributions to their editions. Those acknowledged range from actors and directors from well-known institutions such as the Royal Shakespeare

Company, Shakespeare's Globe and the Oregon Shakespeare Festival to a student production of *Edward III* in Toronto.[36]

Editors developed a variety of techniques for engaging readers with 'the conditions and possibilities' of Shakespeare in performance.[37] In his edition of *The Comedy of Errors*, Kent Cartwright skips the traditional stage chronology, beginning instead with short case-studies on 'stage houses' and offstage voices that ground readers in the basics of early modern stage practices. Dissatisfied with how performance histories were typically 'cloistered away in a chronological account in the intro', Peter Holland provided readers of *Coriolanus* with commentary notes rich in details of individual performance choices, allowing readers to walk in the footsteps of great actors and major productions as they constructed their own interpretations.[38] I found both of these approaches more functional and enjoyable than reading traditional performance overviews, and hope that such practices will become standard in more editions interested in being texts for professional and classroom performance.

Performance histories now often take pride of place at the beginning of Arden 3 introductions, usurping the role of the textual narratives that began most volumes of Arden 2. This change is not always embraced by reviewers and readers. Moreover, the promise of a 'full' performance history for each play is a bit uneven across the series. However, the decision to devote the expertise and rigour of the Arden Shakespeare to performance has produced some valuable results. The third series, for example, has produced some of the most comprehensive stage histories of Shakespeare's plays, and in the cases of *Edward III*, *Double Falsehood*, *Sir Thomas More* and *The Two Noble Kinsmen*, the first such

---

33 Thompson, GER.
34 Thank you to Ann Thompson for bringing this to my attention.
35 Third series back cover.
36 *Edward III*, ed. Richard Proudfoot and Nicola Bennett, Arden Shakespeare 3rd ser. (London, 2017), p. xvii.
37 General Editors' Preface. 38 Peter Holland, VER.

studies of performance for these plays ever published in a scholarly series.

Aiming to be a reliable source for performance history also comes with the challenge of keeping up with the continuous launching of new productions, a situation at odds with the slow pace of producing a scholarly edition. A number of editions including *Much Ado* and *Hamlet* have accounted for this by publishing revised editions that aim to keep the performance histories, if not up to date, at least sufficiently current to remain viable for classroom use. These editions now smartly give particular attention to recorded performances that will be widely accessible to students.

Arden 3 stage histories record an expanding scholarly understanding of 'performance', incorporating a range of styles and media into their narratives, from early staging practices to adaptations including opera and ballet; however, North American and European productions continue to dominate these narratives. The rising interest in global Shakespeares is an opportunity for future editors to engage a wider readership with a broader range of Shakespeare performance in their editions. The potential for fascinating research through such exposure is realized in Sukanta Chaudhuri's edition of *A Midsummer Night's Dream* (2017). The first non-North-American/ Anglo-European Arden editor, Chaudhuri's participation is an important first step towards creating a truly global roster of Arden editors. In his edition, Chaudhuri gives extended attention to the play's production history beyond North America and Europe, including a staging in Australia that explored colonial and Aboriginal connections, anti-Apartheid era productions with mixed-race casting in South Africa, multilingual productions in India, and a Japanese production set in a Buddhist stone garden that brought together Western elements with sumo wrestling and Japanese Noh play. By offering performances that dramatically challenge and reshape conventional impressions of the intergroup dynamics of the play, Chaudhuri's examples give readers a valuable glimpse into the rich world of global Shakespeare that is not only refreshing but also vital to maintaining the relevance of Shakespeare's works to a modern, global audience, and to securing the Arden Shakespeare's place in a wider theatrical world.

'WHAT IS YOUR TEXT?' REVISION AND MULTI-TEXT EDITING

Harold Jenkins's suggestion that 'every variant imposes upon [the editor] the inescapable responsibility of choice' was probably never more relevant than for editors of multi-text plays in the third series.[39] Recent changes to scholarly understandings of early modern playwriting would have significant consequences for editorial practice in Arden 3. In particular, the idea that playwrights, including Shakespeare, revised their plays as part of theatrical production re-presented multiple texts of the same play as distinct stages of the creative process, making each version a valuable textual artefact in its own right. The most visible example of this revisionist theory in practice was The Oxford Shakespeare's publication of both the Quarto and Folio texts of *King Lear* in their *Complete Works* in 1986. Supported by the controversial collection *The Division of the Kingdoms*, the Oxford editors grounded their two-text theory in narratives of authorial intention. The 1608 Quarto and 1623 Folio *Lear*s, they proposed, denoted two distinct conceptions of the play: the Quarto representing *Lear* 'as Shakespeare first conceived it', and the Folio as a later revision 'that represented changes from performance' or 'Shakespeare's own dissatisfaction with what he had first written'.[40] Whether one accepted the author-centred argument for the two-text *Lear* or not, most scholars agreed that the integrity of variant texts needed additional consideration. In editorial practice, this included 'abandoning the notion . . . that by comparing texts we can arrive at a single, authentic original'.[41] Thus, an argument for revision or for

---

[39] Jenkins, ed., *Hamlet*, p. 76.
[40] *William Shakespeare: The Complete Works*, ed. Stanley Wells and Gary Taylor (Oxford, 1986), pp. 909, 1153.
[41] Stephen Orgel, 'What is an editor?' *Shakespeare Studies* 24 (1996), 23–30; p. 23.

preserving the unique qualities of each text also became a challenge to the traditional practice of conflating multiple versions of a play into a single edited text. However, the impracticalities of editing, publishing and teaching multiple edited texts of a single play made a complete change to variant-text editions unlikely. Thus, the 'inescapable responsibility of choice' Jenkins had warned of now included balancing the integrity of multiple authorized texts with the practical limitations of a modern scholarly series.

Third series editions of *Othello* edited by E. A. J. Honigmann, *King Lear* edited by R. A. Foakes and *Hamlet* edited by Ann Thompson and Neil Taylor demonstrate a range of approaches to this dilemma. On first encounter, E. A. J. Honigmann's edition of *Othello* looks like a standard conflated text that, like most modern editions at the time, used the First Folio text as its copy. Within this traditional format, however, Honigmann used revision theory to challenge the restrictive binary of good/bad texts. 'We are not entitled to assume that, when Q and F disagree, one or the other must be corrupt', he argued. Instead, in the case of variant readings, editors should consider that 'Shakespeare could have written both.'[42] Focusing on the extensive collection of Shakespearian variants to choose from in the 1623 Folio and 1622 Quarto, the job of the editor was then to accept this 'authorial instability' and choose the 'better text' for their edition.[43] The concept of 'better' in this instance equals the most correct variant by rules of metre, punctuation, etc., suggesting a false alignment of early modern playtexts with modern standards of correctness. However, Honigmann's thinking proposed a useful adjustment to conflation practice. Rather than 'slavishly' following F except in cases where its readings were problematic, Honigmann argued that editors 'should lean towards whichever text seems better at lineation when we consider lineation, whichever seems better at punctuation when we consider punctuation, and so on'.[44] Avoiding revision theory's preference for multiple edited versions while keeping focus on the substantive qualities of

each text, Honigmann rationalizes using a variety of elements from the two texts in his edition: stage directions from Q and F, punctuation and profanity from Q, verse lineation from F except in instances when it was better in Q.

To scholars for whom editing was a determinate act of textual construction, the idea of 'lean[ing]' towards texts must have felt akin to rejecting one of the most fundamental of Jenkins's editorial choices. Far from a resistance to editing, however, Honigmann's approach actually advocated choice on potentially every variant, making his edition, as Virginia Mason Vaughan suggests: 'the most thoroughly conflated version ever published'.[45] In addition to reconfiguring conflation to accommodate the optimal evidence from multiple texts, Honigmann's 'full-texts' approach had implications for thinking about agency in early modern playtexts. In identifying examples of 'better' variants for his conflation, Honigmann demonstrated that, within their general instability, playtexts also recorded agents' varying proficiencies. Now, not only were quartos neither strictly good nor bad, the contributions of the agents who produced them were similarly variable throughout a text. Moreover, this focus on the 'better' parts of texts, as opposed to the most Shakespearian parts, authorized 'perhaps hundreds − of F variants that are scribal or compositorial substitutions' in Honigmann's edition.[46] Drawing attention to the beneficial contributions of non-authorial agents in these texts, Honigmann avoided narratives in which Shakespearian intention lay behind every substantive variant, offering in its place a more diverse narrative of playtext revision.

---

[42] *Othello*, rev. edn, ed. E. A. J. Honigmann, Arden Shakespeare 3rd ser. (London, 2016), p. 365. For Honigmann's comprehensive discussion of the texts and his theory, see *The Texts of Othello and Shakespeare Revision* (London, 1996).
[43] Honigmann, ed. *Othello*, p. 365.
[44] Honigmann, ed., *Othello*, pp. 365–6.
[45] Virginia Mason Vaughan, 'The Arden Shakespeare *Othello*. Edited by E.A.J. Honigmann', *Shakespeare Quarterly* 51 (2000), 478–80; p. 478.
[46] Honigmann, ed., *Othello*, p. 366.

Ann Thompson and Neil Taylor's *Hamlet* (2006, revised 2016) on the other hand, combined revision theory and multi-text editing to refine our knowledge of playwright practice. Thompson and Taylor argued that, since the Q1 (1603), Q2 (1604–5) and F texts were not only all published either during or shortly after Shakespeare's lifetime but also sufficiently different to be considered 'remarkably distinct entities', each text 'ha[d] a case to be considered authentic'.[47] Arden 3 would therefore include three texts of *Hamlet*: a fully annotated edition of the Q2 and an additional volume with edited Q1 and F texts. Thompson and Taylor decided on a 'conservative' approach to editing, emending only when the copy was so unintelligible it obstructed reader access.[48] In this way, the editors avoided letting what Speed Hill described as 'the underlying idealism of authorial intention' govern their editorial practice.[49] Instead, Thompson and Taylor let the character of each version with its varying moments of confusion and clarity stand as a historical record of the play in that moment of transmission. Presenting the imperfections in each version, Thompson and Taylor's edition challenged textual narratives in which revision implied continuous aesthetic improvement to a play. This approach also questioned perceptions that Shakespeare's own revisions always improved a text, undermining theories that markers of so-called 'improvement' were necessarily a means to determining the order in which versions were produced.

With its interest in revision and the textual instability it revealed in both the early modern and the modern edited text, the Arden 3 *Hamlet* was lauded by some as 'attuned to the relativism, pluralism, and skepticism of our time'.[50] Others viewed the three texts as the product of an unfortunate trend of unediting, reflecting a practice 'more in line with copy editing ... than scholarly editing'.[51] Notably, scholars who saw editing as text creation or who admired editions like Jenkins's Arden 2 *Hamlet* for their pursuit of 'certainties ... and conclusions' were generally critical of the edition, using phrases such as 'refuse to repair' and 'versioning' to condemn what they saw as a rejection of the editor's duty to produce

a definitive text.[52] In spite of the divergent opinions, Thompson and Taylor's *Hamlet* affirmed the fundamental premise of revision: that plays existing in multiple versions have valuable literary and historical stories to tell in their own right. They also created a landmark edition that will stand as the definitive collection of *Hamlet* for years to come.

Positioned between Honigmann's conflation of *Othello* and the three-text *Hamlet* in terms of editorial intervention is R. A. Foakes's *King Lear* (1997). Foakes accepted that both Q and F texts contained useful variants, but because he believed that 'none of the differences between Q and F radically affects the plot of the play, or its general structure', he was less convinced by the narrative of authorial intention that justified Oxford's two-play conclusion.[53] He instead decided that, rather than two different plays, 'we have two versions of the same play'.[54] Translating his position into editorial practice, Foakes followed D. F. McKenzie's idea that the dramatic text 'may be conceived of as always potential': the idea being that, if the text is inherently unstable, there is no one correct *Lear*, only a concept that contains recognizable elements of the play.[55] In this light, the question was no longer which text of *Lear* to edit, but 'how best to make available to readers the *play* of *King Lear*'.[56] In order to feature the conceptual 'play' rather than the various texts in which it originated, Foakes

47 Thompson and Taylor, eds., *Hamlet*, pp. 94, 92.

48 Thompson and Taylor, eds., *Hamlet*, p. 541.

49 Speed Hill, 'Where we are and how we got here: editing after post-structuralism', *Shakespeare Studies* 24 (1996), 38–46; p. 41.

50 MacDonald P. Jackson, 'The Arden Shakespeare *Hamlet*, and The Arden Shakespeare *Hamlet*: the texts of 1603 and 1632', *Shakespeare Quarterly* 58 (2007), 388–91; p. 389.

51 William Proctor Williams, 'William Shakespeare, *Hamlet*, Hamlet the Texts of 1603 and 1623', *Notes and Queries* 59 (2012), 263–6; p. 264.

52 Jackson, '*Hamlet*', p. 390; Williams, '*Hamlet*', p. 264.

53 *King Lear*, ed. R. A. Foakes, Arden Shakespeare 3rd ser. (London, 1997), pp. 118–19.

54 Foakes, ed., *Lear*, p. 119.

55 D. F. McKenzie, *Bibliography and the Sociology of Texts* (Cambridge, 1999), p. 37.

56 Foakes, ed., *Lear*, p. 119 (emphasis mine).

devised an editorial apparatus in which substantive textual variants from both F and Q would appear in the body of the text marked off by superscript Fs and Qs. The 'jigsaw-puzzle effect' produced by this technique was questioned by reviewers who were sceptical that the superscripts actually enabled the reader 'to grasp the differences between Quarto and Folio versions'.[57] However, Foakes's goal for this edition was not to solidify distinctions between Q and F, but 'to make available the text(s) in a form that enable[d] readers to understand the relation between them and to appreciate the problems caused by textual differences'.[58] In other words, the superscript additions were meant to blur the boundaries of the single text so as to remind readers that both Q and F were always present in *Lear*. Whether they wished to consider the variants or not, anyone who has read the edition would be hard-pressed to deny that their eye is inevitably drawn to the superscripts; they make it impossible to ignore how the play known as *King Lear* is comprised of choices.

By highlighting the 'relation' between texts as well as their differences, Foakes invites readers into the textual challenges of *King Lear* but does not offer answers. Rather, he leaves them with the same 'inexhaustible possibilities for shaping and interpreting' faced by scholars and editors of the play.[59] Looking back at Foakes's edition from a present where we are more conditioned to expect cultural experiences in books, theatre and television to leave us off balance or uncertain of the conclusion, we are now perhaps better prepared to appreciate the dissonance produced by Foakes's edition. The disruption caused by having the variants inside the text and the experience of trying to make choices between them while reading destabilizes the reader, preventing them from constructing a distinct impression of either the Q or F texts. 'Highlighting problems' was Foakes's goal, and the inability to track one 'version' while trying to follow the 'play' of *Lear* is a readerly experience of his textual theory. As an attempt to translate the fragmented textual agency of a playtext into experience, Foakes's *King Lear* was perhaps ahead of its time. It may be, as digital editions continue to

push the capabilities of reader experience, that future editors will reconsider its efforts. For now, one of its greatest contributions may be the reminder of how much we as modern readers are still conditioned to expect 'definitive' texts.

In trying to integrate revision theory into the practical and textual considerations of modern scholarly editing, the editors above show there is still much room for creativity and interpretation. While each edition incorporated the theory's fundamental interest in attending more closely to variant texts, they largely avoided narratives of authorial intention and aesthetic achievement in favour of the collective agency of play production. In hindsight, this choice has helped the editions to retain their relevance for the duration of the series. The editors had considerable freedom to develop these editorial techniques, and this is not the only instance where innovative moments of scholarly practice can be traced back to the General Editors' belief that editing should follow the text. In the case of editing these multi-text plays, it produced provocative responses to one of the most heated debates of modern Shakespearian scholarship.

'WHAT IS YOUR TEXT?' NEW PLAYS, COLLABORATION AND AUTHORSHIP

Revision was not the only opportunity for editors of Arden 3 to integrate scholarship creatively into editorial technique. The idea that 'dramatists collaborated in various ways and degrees' had become a widely accepted feature of playhouse practice, shifting perceptions of early modern authorship from Romantic ideas of isolated genius to writers co-operating in a shared process.[60] The idea that, as part of this community, Shakespeare also participated in collaborative writing likewise changed

---

[57] Scragg, '*Lear*', p. 512. [58] Foakes, *Lear*, p. 4.
[59] Foakes, *Lear*, p. 4.
[60] Grace Ioppolo, *Dramatists and Their Manuscripts in the Age of Shakespeare, Jonson, Middleton and Heywood: Authorship, Authority and the Playhouse* (London, 2006), p. 1.

impressions of his co-authorship from 'an unfortunate aberration . . . likely to produce inferior art' to an opportunity to learn more about the character of his writing.[61] Across the series, editors of plays such as *Pericles* and *Henry VIII* included detailed narratives of collaborative writing in their editions. The change was most notable in the case of *Titus Andronicus* (1995). In another instance where editions must fight to keep pace with scholarship, Jonathan Bate originally argued for Shakespeare's single authorship of the play, but later released a revised edition (2018) in which he acknowledged that new evidence confirmed *Titus* as a work co-authored by Shakespeare and George Peele. To build on the interest in Shakespeare's collaborations, the series also brought in plays in which 'a scholarly consensus exists for regarding portions . . . as being the work of Shakespeare'.[62] The addition of *The Two Noble Kinsmen* (1997), for example, confirmed the series position that all plays with significant evidence of Shakespeare's co-authorship should be considered within the canon, regardless of their inclusion in the First Folio. The General Editors extended this thinking by commissioning editions of *Edward III*, *Double Falsehood* and *Sir Thomas More*: three plays historically associated with Shakespeare but previously considered too peripheral to be included in the series.

Richard Proudfoot and Nicola Bennett's edition of *Edward III* (2017) examined the play's authorship and, in particular, Shakespeare's participation in its writing by highlighting the broader interconnectedness of artists, creative trends and sources in the play's collaborative practice. Identifying 'verbal connection[s]' in metre and phrasing between *Edward III*, other surviving plays from commercial theatres at the time, and other plays from Shakespeare's canon, the editors concluded that 'the language of *Edward III* is firmly located in the norms of professional playwriting between 1587 and 1595'.[63] Additional similarities between the play and Shakespeare's canon 'demonstrate[d] his intimacy with and depth of knowledge of the play', affirming a Shakespearian connection.[64] In addition, where most attribution studies distinguished co-authorship by acts and scenes, Proudfoot and

Bennett offered evidence of 'division of authorship within scenes', a finding that challenged how 'conclusive lines of demarcation between sharply defined areas of the text' were used by such studies.[65] Co-authorship in Proudfoot and Bennett's model became a variable practice, more human than algorithm, with Shakespeare the starting point for a more complex portrait of shared writing.

Where revisionist theory could prompt pessimistic accusations of non-editing, theories of collaborative authorship produced a belief that even the most challenging textual puzzles could be solved with rigorous scrutiny of the text. Brean Hammond's edition of *Double Falsehood* or *The Distressed Lovers*, Lewis Theobald's eighteenth-century play best known as the only surviving text that may bear any relation to Shakespeare's lost play *Cardenio*, is perhaps the best example of this optimism in Arden 3. A 'radical adaptation of a Shakespeare–Fletcher collaboration probably already subjected to a layer of adaptive revision in the Restoration period', *Double Falsehood* would stretch collaboration across centuries, testing scholarly editing's capacity to reveal even remote traces of authorial agency.[66] The edition was the inspiration of Proudfoot, whose earlier work on the Shakespeare apocrypha convinced him that Theobald's play required a scholarly edition with a modern, annotated text.[67] The prospect of recovering even a glimpse of *Cardenio* raised expectations for the edition. Reviewers anticipated how 'it should be able to put us in the position of being able to identify genuine Shakespeare and genuine Fletcher'.[68] However, Hammond was aware that 'the main challenge . . . was to produce an edition capable of

[61] *King Henry VIII*, ed. Gordon McMullan, Arden Shakespeare 3rd ser. (London, 2000), p. 181.
[62] Proudfoot, email, 14 August 2020.
[63] Proudfoot and Bennett, eds., *Edward III*, p. 50.
[64] Proudfoot and Bennett, eds., *Edward III*, p. 51.
[65] Proudfoot and Bennett, eds., *Edward III*, pp. 62, 49.
[66] Hammond, ed., *Double Falsehood*, p. 159.
[67] Proudfoot, email, 28 August 2020.
[68] Bernard Richards, 'Now I am in Arden: *Double Falsehood, or The Distressed Lovers*', *Essays in Criticism* 61 (2011), 79–88; pp. 80–1.

persuading the scholarly community that *DF* deserved at least a marginal place in the Shakespeare canon'.[69] Careful to note that, without the lost manuscript, it was only possible to 'reinforc(e) the accumulating consensus that the lost play has a continuing presence' in Theobald's text, Hammond combined a base of stylometric analysis not previously seen in an Arden edition with textual analysis to confirm that there was 'some relationship between the lost play performed in 1613 and the play printed in 1728'.[70]

Beyond affirming the Shakespearian connections to Theobald's play, Hammond's edition should be noted for its skilful editing. Annotating an eighteenth-century text so that it also provided access to 'the range and scale of Shakespearean and Fletcherian allusion' required Hammond to attend to two plays in two very different eras of theatre.[71] The scope of this challenge is visible where reviewers who admired the edition as 'magisterial' still could not resist citing instances where Hammond annotates with a medieval or early modern interpretation when they believed the Restoration or Augustan reading was more relevant (and vice versa).[72]

By publishing a play in which Shakespeare's contributions are not only fragmented but hidden under layers of time and the agency of other authors, Arden 3 sent a clear message that if scholars were going to claim to accept and investigate early modern collaboration in relation to Shakespeare, then the entire range of such interventions should be included in the canon for study. Not everyone supported this position. Some reviewers found *Double Falsehood*'s presence in the series 'tendentious', while others saw the publication as not only the end of the series, but also a serious threat to the literary status of Shakespeare himself.[73] Including *Double Falsehood* in a Shakespeare series does create openings for biased interpretations. For instance, the title page of the edition lists Shakespeare before Fletcher in spite of the evidence for Shakespeare's agency being 'much scantier'.[74] *Double Falsehood* remains the most controversial edition of Arden 3 and is in some ways still looking for its audience. However, its General Editor Proudfoot was satisfied that the edition 'brought the play, and its enigma,

back into focus as a Shakespearean topic', suggesting that an edition that generates more discussion than conclusion can still be considered a success.[75]

The benefits of Arden 3's approach to collaboration, however, are most fully realized in the edition of *Sir Thomas More* (2011) edited by John Jowett. The reader confronts the intensely collaborative environment of Jowett's *More* from the title page: an extensive list of all its textual agents, including Jowett as editor. A key moment in this memorable paratext is the appearance of Shakespeare's name at the very bottom, situating the author of the series in an unusual minor role. An inevitable shortcoming of the two-dimensional printed page, the title page's single-column layout gives the false impression that the collaboration depicted is linear in progression. It also privileges the primary authors, in this case Anthony Munday and Henry Chettle, even though Jowett convincingly argues that the revisor (traditionally known as Hand C) is the central figure in this textual production. Such misconceptions, however, are quickly clarified in Jowett's meticulous analysis. Noting how '*More* lacks fixity and completion, whilst bearing more witness to process than one could possibly expect of a single document', Jowett's edition focused not on reproducing a finished text but on presenting the continuous process of its development.[76] Special attention was given to the agency of the revisor, whom Jowett credits with 'bringing [the manuscript] into a state as near completion as it was to reach'.[77] At times updating authorial contributions while leaving

[69] Brean Hammond, VER.
[70] Hammond, ed., *Double Falsehood*, pp. 3, 8.
[71] Hammond, ed., *Double Falsehood*, p. 148.
[72] Richards, 'Double', p. 88.
[73] Robert Folkenflik, '"Shakespeare": the Arden double falsehood', *Huntington Library Quarterly* 75 (2012), 131–43; p. 133. See, for instance, Ron Rosenbaum, 'The double falsehood of *Double Falsehood*', *Slate* (May 2010).
[74] Hammond, ed., *Double Falsehood*, p. 160.
[75] Proudfoot, email, 28 August 2020.
[76] *Sir Thomas More*, ed. John Jowett, Arden Shakespeare 3rd ser. (London, 2011), p. 129.
[77] Jowett, ed. *More*, p. 128.

other elements unfinished for writers to complete, the revisor is revealed as the hub of the project, grounding *More* in a narrative of circulation that affirmed the 'incomplete' and the 'varied' as regular conditions of play production.

Rightly praised as 'textually perfect', the edition achieves two equally challenging and potentially opposing outcomes.[78] First, although there is hardly space to do it justice here, the detailed yet disciplined interventions of Jowett's editorial apparatus are exceptional. For anyone who daydreamed about poring over the manuscript but lacked the credentials to study it in person, Jowett's system provided an unprecedented account of the shifting collaborations and varied textual interventions that make the manuscript so fascinating. Second, for all the evidence it conveys, the editorial interventions sustain a surprisingly light touch that keeps the play accessible to the general reader. Readers new to the textual features of *More* were further supported by a Reader's Guide that introduced the different collaborative relationships through discussion of the various markings used in the edited text. This informative, concisely written section, combined with Jowett's remarkable editorial apparatus, will remain an example for new textual scholars and editors for years to come.

In its study of collaboration, Jowett's edition highlights the inherent link between agent collaboration and textual instability. Art is messy, but Jowett's edition proves that editing can go some way towards representing the variable process of playtext production contained in even the most complex manuscripts. In terms of Shakespeare's portrait as a collaborator, *More* is also an important edition in the series for the unique image it offers of Shakespeare as a minor collaborator, a necessary part of replacing the literary icon's dominance in cultural and scholarly discourses with the more accessible efforts of the writer.

With their collective focus on the relationships inherent in the play-making process, Arden 3's editions of *Edward III*, *Double Falsehood* and *Sir Thomas More* complicate the range and character of known collaborative interactions between textual agents. As a result, they also extend the definition of collaboration beyond co-authorship to include a variety of agents involved in play production. Their collective contributions also convincingly argue that if we truly value Shakespeare's work, we should attend to all of his artistic contributions with similar scholarly rigour. The varied approach to collaboration in these editions is supported by the innovative editorial practices developed to accommodate these complex textual narratives. On this point, Jowett credits the 'intellectual generosity' of the General Editors, who encouraged volume editors to pursue solutions that elevated the unique features of their texts and advanced the knowledge of Arden readers.[79] Their efforts fostered some of the most challenging and innovative editorial projects in the history of the series.

LOOK TO THE LADY — WOMEN EDITORS AND EDITING IN ARDEN 3

With the exception of *As You Like It* edited by Agnes Latham (1975), the most likely place to find evidence of women's editorial intervention in the Arden 2 series was in an editor's preface. Combining statements of editorial rationale with personal acknowledgements, the prefaces are an accidental record of women's hidden contributions to the editing of Shakespeare at a time when, as Valerie Wayne puts it, 'few endeavours in the humanities [had] been so consistently exercised by men to the exclusion of women'.[80] The prefaces note the intellectual contributions of women such as the wife of J. M. Nosworthy, who 'shed light on many of [*Cymbeline's*] dark places' for her husband.[81] They

---

[78] Eric Rasmussen, 'The year's contribution to Shakespeare studies: editions and textual studies', *Shakespeare Survey 65* (Cambridge, 2012), 524.

[79] John Jowett, VER.

[80] Valerie Wayne, 'Remaking the texts: women editors of Shakespeare, past and present', in *Women Making Shakespeare: Text, Reception, Performance* (London, 2014), 57–67; p. 57.

[81] *Cymbeline*, ed. J. M. Nosworthy, Arden Shakespeare 2nd ser. (London, 2004), p. ix.

also document the editorial work of women such as Mrs P. A. Burnett, whose edition of Thomas Lodge's *Rosalynde* became a valuable resource for Latham's *As You Like It*. Mrs F. M. H. Bone not only shared her notes on *King John* with E. A. J. Honigmann, but 'generously allowed [him] to print some of her discoveries for the first time'.[82] The prefaces also record the expertise of Una Ellis-Fermor, who served as Arden's first female General Editor from 1946 to 1958. Nosworthy described her as 'the wisest of *Cymbeline* scholars', and Kenneth Muir praised her efforts as 'all that a General Editor should be'.[83]

The examples above remind us that, for the majority of its tenure, the Arden Shakespeare, by following the broader practices of Shakespeare scholarship and editing at the time, was the employ of (White) men only. For scholars trained over the twenty-five years of Arden 3, who have benefitted from the work of women as instructors, Ph.D. supervisors and scholarly role models, it is surprising to realize that women's contributions to the Arden Shakespeare only became a prominent fixture in the third series, and that this was far from inevitable. The fourteen women who edited plays and poems for Arden 3 were part of a significant first wave of women editors and feminist textual scholars of Shakespeare and early modern drama. They asserted their ideas amidst suggestions that 'women may read Shakespeare, but men edit him', and navigated resistance ranging from 'mindless misogyny' to outright 'hostility to women editing Shakespeare at all'.[84] They wielded the knowledge and authority of precedent-changing editors amidst requests to make tea and take the minutes of meetings. As with any new endeavour, successes and shortfalls were part of the process, but their collective efforts made a significant contribution to the broad appeal of Arden 3 and a lasting contribution towards more diversity in the editing of Shakespeare.

By the time work began on Arden 3, feminist textual scholars were already arguing for the benefits of a feminist approach to scholarly editing. Ann Thompson's assertion that 'feminist theory challenges patriarchal ideology and questions how "ideas" themselves are produced, assessed and distributed in our society' aligned feminist criticism

with scholarly editing's interest in deconstructing processes of production, interpretation and dissemination.[85] At the same time, Suzanne Gossett argued that the feminist editor 'can do a great deal to affect what we think we know about the literature(s) of our tradition(s)'.[86] While an 'awareness of gender issues' was becoming more widely viewed as a way to enrich editorial practice and enhance editions, integrating this approach into the Arden, which had achieved much success on a foundation of traditional scholarly practice, would require doing things differently.[87] A significant move in this direction was commissioning Ann Thompson as a General Editor. General editors, as Valerie Wayne notes, are pivotal 'first readers of an edition', and now a woman would be 'in the best possible position to encourage or redirect an editor's perceptions and can also recruit others'.[88] To this end, one of Thompson's most important contributions was to advocate for a more diverse group of editors for Arden 3, including more opportunities for women. In order to maintain the high standards of scholarship expected of the Arden Shakespeare, General Editors traditionally recruited scholars with previous experience editing Shakespeare, either for Arden or for another series.[89] Because, up to this point, established Shakespeare editors were generally all men, the system offered few opportunities for women – or, indeed, any other newer scholars – to qualify. The General Editors responded by broadening the criteria, reaching out to scholars such as Potter and Gossett who already had reputations for

[82] *King John*, ed. E. A. J. Honigmann, Arden Shakespeare 2nd ser. (London, 2006), p. vii.
[83] Nosworthy, ed., *Cymbeline*, p. x; *Macbeth*, ed. Kenneth Muir (London, 2006), p. x.
[84] Gary Taylor, 'Textual and sexual criticism: a crux in *The Comedy of Errors*', *Renaissance Drama* 19 (1988), 195–225; p. 195; Thompson, VER.
[85] Ann Thompson, 'Feminist theory and the editing of Shakespeare: *The Taming of the Shrew* revisited', in *The Margins of the Text* (Ann Arbor, 1997), p. 84.
[86] Suzanne Gossett, 'Why should a woman edit a man?' *Text* 9 (1996), 111–18; p. 115.
[87] Thompson, 'Feminist theory', p. 84.
[88] Wayne, 'Remaking', p. 63. [89] Thompson, GER.

editing early modern texts. They also sought scholars with less editorial experience, but who had made significant contributions to feminist Shakespeare criticism and textual scholarship. Bringing in new Arden editors, men or women, could be a risky proposition: at the minimum, it required extra work as the General Editors guided new editors through the process, but taking this chance helped the Arden to move towards becoming a series that represents more closely the scholarly field.

Assigning plays to this first class of Arden women editors was of particular significance. Earlier series followed a gendered tradition in which men overwhelmingly edited the 'masculine' tragedies and histories, while women would edit the comedies and romances. In the first Arden series, Grace Trenery editing *Much Ado About Nothing* (1924), and in the second series Latham editing *As You Like It*, followed this trend. Preparing to edit *Cymbeline* for the third series, Ann Thompson was also set to follow this precedent. However, on becoming 'aware of how few women edited Shakespeare and how almost none had edited tragedies or more textually challenging plays', Thompson shifted her focus ... '[and] more or less talked myself into editing *Hamlet*'.[90] The tradition was disrupted further as Lois Potter created the first edition of *The Two Noble Kinsmen* in an Arden series, Suzanne Gossett edited the textually complex *Pericles*, Gretchen Minton co-edited *Timon of Athens*, and Sandra Clark and Pamela Mason took on *Macbeth*. On balance, Arden 3 includes women editors across the canon: alongside the three tragedies, three women edited comedies (*As You Like It*, *Shrew*, *Much Ado*), five edited late plays / romances (*All's Well*, *Cymbeline*, *Two Noble Kinsmen*, *Tempest*, *Pericles*) and Katherine Duncan-Jones edited volumes of the Poems and the Sonnets. However, Nicola Bennett's contribution to *Edward III* is the only example of a woman editing an English history play. We will have to look to Arden 4 to see, hopefully, the results of women editing the lines of Queen Margaret, Joan La Pucelle, Prince Hal and Richard III.

It hardly needs stating that editing is a demanding task that becomes more challenging due to the

scrutiny editions will face as a part of the Arden Shakespeare. Women editors were also forging new paths as they made their way through this challenging process. Even an experienced textual editor such as Valerie Wayne noted how 'very few women editors preceded me on [*Cymbeline*], especially of full scholarly editions'.[91] No doubt many of these editors were well aware of their unique position and, along with it, the importance of securing through their success the place of women editors in future Arden series. In the end, the contributions of the women editors of Arden 3 are enlightening, informative and, in light of their position as first role models, inspiring. Commentary such as Clark and Mason's annotations for Lady Macbeth's 'Come you spirits | That tend on mortal thoughts' speech (1.5.40–54) offers the important new perspectives that Gossett and Thompson promised. Where Arden 2 offers no note for 'unsex me', Clark and Mason ground their commentary in an emerging feminist tradition that engaged head on with the powerful, organic reality of Lady Macbeth's 'biological femininity'.[92] Where the Arden 2 paraphrase of 'take my milk for gall' is a perfunctory 'Nourish yourselves with my milk which ... has turned to gall', Arden 3 offers scholarship that engages with both the erotic and biological implications of breastfeeding.[93] By approaching Lady Macbeth as a woman who used the forms of power immediately available to her, Clark and Mason demonstrate the insights to be gained from including more cultural information and diverse perspectives in their edition. This phenomenon is repeated across the series as issues that were previously given little to no attention in earlier series – such as sisterhood / female friendship, virginity (as a state and a commodity), marriage, gender fluidity and misogyny – are given serious consideration in Arden 3.

Commissioning women editors does not necessarily ensure a feminist editor or feminist editing.[94]

---

[90] Thompson, VER. [91] Valerie Wayne, VER.
[92] Clark and Mason, eds., *Macbeth*, p. 157, n. 43.
[93] Muir, ed., *Macbeth*, p. 30.
[94] A point emphasized by both Thompson and Gossett in their VERs.

Nevertheless, more prominent contributions by women in Arden 3 and an increased consideration of feminist elements and the presence of female characters in the series draws attention to other opportunities for more balanced representation. For example, while the majority of Arden 3 character lists reflect the relative importance of characters regardless of gender, the series decision to draw on extant lists from the First Folio produces the occasional list where all male characters appear before female characters, placing roles like Miranda and Desdemona after nameless mariners and gentlemen.[95] Attention to historical texts is an important feature of Arden 3's editorial practice, but the silent privileging of textual history over representation has the potential to reinforce historical gender hierarchies unintentionally, especially when encountered by newer readers who are probably unaware of how such editorial decisions can influence their interpretations.

The contributions of women editors to Arden 3 have shaped every facet of the series, setting an important precedent for further efforts to diversify the field of Shakespeare editing. A downside to this current series of changes is that they may be easily missed by the general reader. Recent feminist book history stresses the importance of 'writing [women's] labour back into our histories', not only as a way to combat women's continued marginalization but also as a means of alerting us to the progress yet to be made.[96] Silently assimilating changes into the general practice of a series can erase their impact as markers of progress for anyone not familiar with earlier editions, lulling us into a sense that bias is a non-issue when there is still more to be done to diversify Shakespeare studies and editorial practice.

An additional example of the inclusive work that will hopefully continue to inform the Arden Shakespeare's critical practice is Ayanna Thompson's new introduction to Honigmann's edition of Othello, published in 2016. Appearing nearly twenty years after the first edition, Thompson's introduction was a welcome and long overdue update that brought the edition into line with contemporary literary critical discourse

and classroom discussions. Clear in her intention that she 'did not want there to be a doubt that the play engages with race in complex ways, and the tools we use to analyse race must be as complex', Thompson brought a needed introduction to the methodology and application of critical race studies to the edition and the series.[97] Setting a necessary example for future scholarly editions, Thompson's approach is driven by a call for readers and audiences to recognize how the stories we bring to plays like Othello 'will impact the way the play will be understood and performed'.[98] Encouraging readers 'to be sceptical of adhering to one frame or one story', Thompson highlights how questioning what we 'know' creates space for new and potentially unsettling perspectives. Most important, in preparing the way for readers to step out of their comfort zone, Thompson actively encourages reading with empathy: 'to imagine if, when and how different readers and audience members were affected by these histories, contexts and performances'.[99]

New perspectives not only change our readings, they also teach us to consider and learn from the experiences of others. Thompson's introduction combines history, critical race theory and performance history to examine Shakespeare's Othello through stories of inequality that are so necessary to our present as a global society and to our future as a scholarly field. Equally important, Ayanna Thompson's presence as the first Black woman editor for Arden is a significant moment of representation that will inspire more students of Shakespeare, particularly women of colour and other marginalized groups, to see themselves as the next generation of editors, an essential step for

[95] The list for Much Ado, drawn from Rowe's 1709 edition, classifies characters by rank and gender, listing Beatrice below Leonato, his brother Antonio and Hero, and above Margaret, Ursula and a nameless 'Boy' of the household.
[96] Kate Ozment, 'Rationale for feminist bibliography', Textual Cultures 13.1 (2020), 149–78; p.172.
[97] Ayanna Thompson, VER.
[98] Thompson, 'Introduction', p. 2.
[99] Thompson 'Introduction', p. 5.

further diversity in Arden and in Shakespeare studies.

CONCLUSION: 'WHAT'S PAST IS PROLOGUE' (AGAIN)

The life expectancy of an Arden Shakespeare edition is about twenty years, not even the span of time it took to publish the entire third series. Perhaps for this reason, editors envision modest legacies for their editions, hoping they will be dependable and spark further discussion. We cannot predict which editions will still stand as cornerstones of scholarship and editorial practice twenty years from now, but the third series offers a valuable record of where we have been as a field and a potential glimpse of where we might, and in some instances should, go.

The third series charts a generation of scholars using Shakespeare to engage with the more varied topics and wider readership that are modern Shakespeare studies. As the field continues to evolve, it will be vital that the Arden continues to bring new perspectives into the discourse. The third series made notable strides in this area by expanding its editorial roster, but there is still more work to be done to make the series truly represent the global field.

While early modern contexts still loom large in Arden 3 editions, Shakespeare is now also a means for reflecting on the challenges and opportunities of our own time, and viable editions need to provide readers with access to these current discussions. Arden 3 responded to these changes, expanding its content to engage with major areas of new scholarship. The publication of revised editions with updated introductions was another welcome innovation, but it reveals the difficulty of keeping a scholarly edition relevant even for the time it takes to plan and produce its replacement. So long as the hard-copy textbook dominates classrooms and libraries, remaining comprehensive and up to date will remain a challenge for future series.

Navigating increasingly complex ideas of authorship and textual production, the series also tested the resilience of scholarly editing. In perhaps the most traditional area of academic practice, the third series demonstrated editing's capacity to continually renegotiate the relationship between text, knowledge and reader. Changes in scholarly thinking and technology will continue to demand editors rethink their approaches, but editorial practices developed in the third series established a precedent for innovation and discipline while producing texts that engaged readers with the most exciting advances of early modern textual studies.

The successes of Arden 3 were the result of an extended commitment from all involved to pursue new paths of scholarship and to confront editorial challenges, none of which could have been achieved without that most valuable resource – time. Editors across the series acknowledged how sabbaticals and fellowships provided needed time to complete their editions. With competition for such awards reaching unprecedented levels and sabbaticals not guaranteed at many institutions, not to mention the scores of precariously employed scholars with no institutional research support, the time necessary to complete an edition is becoming increasingly difficult, if not impossible, for many academics to secure. It prompts the question of how the next generation of Arden editors will manage, particularly in light of the urgent need for further diversity in scholarly editing. If we are truly to expand the image of the Shakespeare editor, researchers from a variety of backgrounds must be provided with equal access to the time and resources required to produce an Arden Shakespeare edition. Since general editors and scholarly series cannot rely on traditional lines of support from foundations and institutions to do the work of expanding access, they will have to look elsewhere, perhaps closer to home or to resources not yet tapped to identify and support these new editors. Such schemes are aspirational, but the efforts of those involved in Arden 3 have taught us to aim for more, and that is a lesson worth embracing.

SHAKESPEARE PERFORMANCES
IN ENGLAND, 2020

LOIS POTTER, *Shakespeare Productions in London,*
or, Much Review About Nothing

Two productions of *Romeo and Juliet* (at the Globe and Regent's Park) had been scheduled for summer 2020. When these are finally put on, I predict an audible audience reaction to the words of the usually unnoticed Friar John:

> The searchers of the town,
> Suspecting that we both were in a house
> Where the infectious pestilence did dwell,
> Sealed up the doors and would not let us forth.

Moments like this, when the experience of the characters coincides with the experience of the audience (usually in references to weather conditions or, as here, recent events), are those in which we are most aware that we are involved with 'live theatre'. For almost the whole of 2020, this experience was taken away, or, rather, replaced by a completely different digital experience. By the time you read this, theatre will probably have been brought back to life, but I wonder whether its community will be the same. This review will be an attempt to give some shape to the small and random series of productions that I saw before lockdown, some of which deserve, and will get, much more discussion than others.

THE TAMING OF THE SHREW AND
WOMEN BEWARE WOMEN AT THE SAM
WANAMAKER PLAYHOUSE

In its 2020 issue, *Cahiers Elisabéthains* focused on the various experiences of Shakespeare in the early months of lockdown.[1] Reviewers (disclosure:

I was one) frequently commented on the difference in their level of engagement when they watched a play alone in their room, and I shall return later to this issue. But they also noted the one unquestionable advantage of digital theatre: none of its seats has restricted views.[2] Of course, the computer's view *is* restricted, especially in livestream, but we don't usually notice the limitation of our viewpoint because we assume that, as in film, there is an intention behind it. And if we occasionally become aware that we are not being allowed to look at what we most want to see, this is still preferable to not being able to see much of the stage at all. It's particularly annoying when a new theatre, which should be able to provide good visibility for everyone, deliberately chooses to make some seats so bad that spectators will be

---

[1] 'Shakespeare Under Global Lockdown', *Cahiers Elisabéthains*, ed. Peter J. Smith, Janice Valis-Russell and Daniel Yabut, 103 (2020), 1–95; ' Introduction': https://doi-org.ezpupv.biu-montpellier.fr/10.1177/0184767820946173; Reviews: https://doi-org.ezpupv.biu-montpellier.fr/10.1177/0184767820946175.

[2] For Neil Allen, who had watched the RSC *Tempest* from a very poor theatre seat and missed many of its spectacular effects, the digital experience of the same production was, of course, an improvement, but one that he still felt was only a 'supplement' to live performance: review of *The Tempest*, directed by Gregory Doran for the Royal Shakespeare Company, the Royal Shakespeare Theatre, Stratford-upon-Avon, UK, 8 November 2016 – 21 January 2017; filmed for Live from Stratford-upon-Avon (screen director: Dewi Humphreys), released in 2017. Viewed in Stratford-upon-Avon, 12 November 2016, side stalls (restricted viewing). Accessed via Digital Theatre Plus in Shropshire, UK, 16 April 2020: *Cahiers Elisabéthains*, pp. 1–4.

willing to pay higher prices for better ones; some set designers and directors also seem to conspire to make important moments invisible to a substantial part of their audience.

The Sam Wanamaker Playhouse is, of course, a special case, since it is a recreation of a generic seventeenth-century indoor theatre and it is clear from Pepys's *Diary* that the pleasure of seventeenth-century spectators, like ours, was often spoiled when they were unable to see properly. This was (and still is) mainly because of the shape of the theatre. Pepys does, however, mention the strain of looking down from the gallery through the light of the chandeliers, something that recent renovations have tried to diminish. The indoor playhouses normally gave afternoon performances and relied on light from the windows, using torches and candles to signify that it was night or to provide extra visibility. Artistic lighting effects seem to have been reserved for masques. Wanamaker productions, however, draw on our assumption that candlelight is romantic. They often involve a kind of candle choreography that is really a new art form. The cast have to learn how to use lanterns as personal spotlights, while trying not to set their hair on fire from the torches round the sides of the stage. No one seems to be sure whether there really was an early modern category of play called 'the Nocturnal', but this theatre has either invented or recreated it. Plunging the audience into complete darkness, penetrated only by eerie noises (as in the 2018 *Macbeth*), is unquestionably effective, and plays have been written to take advantage of this possibility. Anders Lustgarden's *The Secret Theatre*, a play about Walsingham's secret service, with its eavesdroppers and informers, seemed to me a genuine 'nocturnal', making excellent use of figures suddenly emerging out of almost total darkness. Since the theatre acoustics are excellent and actors often seem to be chosen for their distinctive voices, the experience of performance can often involve a rather welcome focus on the words.

In other contexts, however, such as plays that are not meant to be spooky, the Wanamaker is problematic. When actors perform by candlelight against a dark background, those with dark skins become almost invisible, a fact that has led some to describe the space as racist. Not surprisingly, some directors

have decided to forgo the candlelight altogether, though this does not solve the problem of the difficult sightlines. I have sometimes needed to see a production twice in order to know what happened at crucial moments. When Blanche McIntyre directed *Bartholomew Fair* in August 2019, she turned on the electric lights and reconfigured the theatre space, thus bringing the play to life in vivid colour. Reviewers still complained about not being able to follow the plot, but they would have had even more difficulty if, amid all the play-acting and disguises, they had been straining to see who was who.

The two productions that I saw in the Wanamaker in early 2020 were obviously trying to use this beautiful but difficult space to the best advantage. For *The Taming of the Shrew*, the designer, Liam Bunster, changed the configuration of the seating so that the actors could climb from a centrally placed platform all the way to the upper gallery. The action took place all over the theatre, with a great deal of vertical movement, a fact that probably allowed most of the audience, for once, actually to see what was going on. Unfortunately, not much was. The production had been a communal effort and the cast had conscientiously tried (as the programme explained) to strip every preconceived idea from the play. This process, like Peer Gynt's peeling off the layers of his onion, had revealed absolutely nothing at the centre. The size of the acting area that had been opened up resulted only in allowing the actors to be located as far as possible from those with whom they were supposed to be interacting. Many people (not me) have problems with this play. The production tried to remove some of these by emphasizing everyone's status as actors rather than as characters, so that no one could be identified with any of the views expressed in it. As far as I could make out from the programme, however, the apparently numerous ideas that had been floating around in rehearsal were too distant from anything in the text to be conveyed without rewriting.

Amy Hodge's production of *Women Beware Women*, appropriately enough for this example of Jacobean *theatre noir*, reverted to candlelight and the usual pit and galleries seating, but also tried to use as much of the theatre space as possible, as when the

Ward ran round the lower gallery, glimpsed and heard through the windows behind the audience, before he finally appeared. This is a play in which a number of important moments need to be visible to the audience, particularly the simultaneous staging of the women's chess game on one level and the rape/seduction of Bianca (equated with the white pawn) on another. Middleton seems to have envisaged this as taking place 'above' (the upper stage level, invisible to everyone in the side galleries). Placing the Duke and Bianca in the pit made for somewhat better visibility, with the actors finally moving up onto the stage to become part of the ongoing game (the chess pieces, played by actors, were apparently being operated by remote control). At the deliberately ambiguous line, 'All things draw to an end', Bianca collapsed on the floor and everyone else disappeared, while we heard from off stage the singing of 'Never were finer snares for women's honesties'. Here and elsewhere, setting some of the quasi-choric passages to music was an interesting way of dealing with the different levels of realism.

Many of Middleton's non-dramatic works are religious pamphlets and he could probably count on his audience to see his characters' moral blindness as both funny and horrific. But, if this seriousness is largely lost in the modern theatre, it can also be argued, as Amy Hodge does in the programme, that this very fact makes the play enormously relevant. Costumes were very modern and the set was meant to give a vague suggestion of the Trump Tower, though this was probably obvious only to those who had read the programme. Some events, like the fight between Leantio and Hippolito, lost much of their point in this setting, but Hodge's treatment of the final wedding masque in which all the characters kill each other, often considered unstageable, was surprisingly effective, though I felt that, having brought the Ward on stage in his devil costume, she could have made more of it as a comment on the situation. She omitted the episode (always difficult to make clear) in which the poisoned goblets are accidentally switched. Instead, the Cardinal sat on stage, with the fatal glass tantalizingly nearby, while the Duke, seated in

the pit with Bianca, kept puzzling over the discrepancy between the mayhem in the masque and the synopsis in his programme. When he finally came up onto a stage full of corpses, he naturally decided that he needed a drink, grabbed the Cardinal's still untouched glass, and downed its poisoned contents.

Appropriately, women outnumbered men in the cast: the actors of the Ward and Sordido were both female, as were Guardiano and the Cardinal, who doubled as the Mother. They played the male roles as male, and there was no focus on gender ambiguity.

A MIDSUMMER NIGHT'S DREAM AND MUCH ADO ABOUT NOTHING AT WILTON'S MUSIC HALL

The ways in which they provided more parts for women were the most interesting aspect of the two visiting productions at Wilton's Music Hall. The Watermill's *A Midsummer Night's Dream*, directed by Paul Hart, cast a woman (Victoria Blunt) in the crucial comic role of Bottom, as also happened at the Globe in 2018; both performances were very successful and it was good to see them disproving the notion that women can't be funny. Of course, it helps that Bottom is a brilliantly written role. The *Dream*'s basic jokes about the vanity of amateur actors and plays that go wrong have dated less than most Shakespearian humour, and Bottom's common sense defeats any attempt to patronize him. Like a number of recent productions of the comedies, this one developed the play's musical possibilities and was generally very audience-friendly, without being particularly memorable.

It was clear that *Much Ado* (directed by Elizabeth Freestone) was trying to build an interpretation from the regendering of a number of the characters, though it was not always clear exactly what that interpretation was. Leonato's wife, mentioned in the opening stage direction but then forgotten, was very much present here, cleverly created by combining lines from Antonio and Ursula (whose name she took, since Innogen, her name in the Quarto, is now so strongly associated with *Cymbeline*). She had a teasing conversation with her husband during the masked ball, took part with Hero in the deception of Beatrice, and was horrified as well as furious at Leonato's denunciation of his daughter in the wedding scene. Rather surprisingly, they seemed reconciled on their next appearance, where she was now speaking Leonato's lines while he was comforting her in his brother Antonio's words. She even joined him, rather absurdly, in challenging Don Pedro and Claudio to fight. Another major gender change – casting Dogberry and Verges as two young women (played as women) – succeeded only in making their scenes even less funny than usual. This was not necessarily their fault: Dogberry's humour, unlike most of Bottom's, depends on verbal rather than physical gags.

It was clear that the production had a lot of ideas about the gender relationships in the play (the men were costumed as superheroes in the masquerade scene and it was never clear how far Benedick had really broken away from the group), but, short of actually writing in extra dialogue, there was no way of conveying them. The problem was most obvious in the depiction of Don John, who was female and spoken of both as female and as Don John. This unstable and unhappy teenager may have been intended as someone transitioning from one gender to another, though, given the current sensitivity on this subject, the production was obviously afraid to push the idea to its potentially offensive conclusion. Although she reappeared at the end, the absence of text kept her from being further integrated into the action. Again, as often happens, Hero attempted to suggest that she wasn't just a sweet and docile creature: after her final unveiling, 'Another Hero!' and her 'Nothing surer' seemed intended to show that her experiences had changed her – but, like 'Ursula' and Don John, she had no lines to take this idea any further.

ALL'S WELL THAT ENDS WELL AND THE TEMPEST AT THE JERMYN STREET THEATRE

As I write, my pre-lockdown life sounds like a quaint piece of social history that needs to be recorded for posterity. Yes, I really used to leave home and travel, sometimes quite long distances, to see life-sized actors in three dimensions; I had to decide for myself where to look. I even used to mill around in close proximity to other people and talk about the play.

The last time I did all that was on 13 March 2020, just a week before lockdown. It was the press night for The Tempest at the little Jermyn Street Theatre. Since Michael Pennington was playing Prospero, the evening had sold out, but a number of spectators had heeded government warnings and turned in their tickets. Plenty of other people had been willing to buy them at the door, so it was a crowded house, something for which the director, Tom Littler, thanked us at the beginning. I now realize that this would have been the perfect time and place to catch the coronavirus and I hope that the rest of the audience were as lucky as I was in escaping it. The basement premises are so small that you reach the loos by walking across the stage, and the first and second halves of every play are elegantly prefaced by a sonorous announcement, or a lighted sign, declaring that 'The toilets are now closed.' The play had in fact been intended to go on for a short season at a medium-sized venue, the Theatre Royal in Bath, but this of course didn't happen. As I write, the production is announced as reopening at the same time next year, so this review may end up being a preview.

My sense of what Littler and Pennington were doing in The Tempest benefitted from my having also seen, in the same theatre, his 2019 production of All's Well That Ends Well. This was in itself a tour de force, with only six actors, two of whom (Stefan Bednarczyk and Ceri-Lyn Cissone) were sometimes occupied in playing the piano between scenes. In particular, Miranda Foster played all three of the women who help Helena (Hannah Morrish) in the play: the Queen of France (regendered from the sick King of the original), the Countess of Rousillion, and the Widow in Florence. A number of characters inevitably disappeared, the most important of them the clown Lavatch, who is unlikely to be much missed by anyone.

The play as we know it ran parallel to scenes in which Helena, apparently locked in her bedroom and refusing to answer the knock on the door, is going through boxes of old mementos and listening to records and tapes. It was a curious echo of the opening of *Hamlet* at the Barbican in 2015, where the hero, playing David Bowie records and mourning his father, finally answered a knock on the door that turned out to be Horatio. As if a tape recorder had been rewound, we heard the opening lines of the play twice: the Countess's 'In delivering my son from me, I bury a second husband' and Bertram's reply that leaving her was like mourning the death of his father. The three deaths mentioned in the first scene – those of the Count and of Helena's father, along with the symbolic death of Bertram's departure – merge in Helena's mind, just as the bed, a place for dreams, becomes a sickbed where we first see the French Queen, and also the location where we watch Helena taking the place of Diana after Bertram has been blindfolded. The doubling of the actors becomes part of Helena's attempt to understand her own story, whose improbability is explained by the suggestion that it is a (cathartic?) fantasy on Helena's part. Another dreamlike parallel was the blindfolding of both Bertram (Gavin Fowler) and Parolles (Robert Mountford), but the comic scenes were allowed to be funny rather than forced into an interpretation.

Though I know from reviews that Helena was listening to Fleetwood Mac, a choice that apparently carries great significance, the recordings that really struck me were the sounds of gunfire, the voice singing the words of *Ecclesiastes* about 'a time to be born and a time to die', and a fragment of a funeral service. Helena had been afraid that Bertram would die in the war, and in retrospect the words spoken by Helena at the very beginning ('The web of our life is a mingled yarn, good and ill together') sounded like his epitaph. After the supposed final scene, Helena is back again in her bedroom, alone, and she finally answers the door. The Countess enters, sits on the bed beside her, and puts the family ring on her finger. The woman who has always said that Helena was like a daughter to her now joins her in shared grief – and perhaps forgiveness, since, on this reading, Helena's insistence on marrying Bertram did in fact lead directly to his death.

The idea that the action of *The Tempest* is happening in Prospero's head has been around for a long time – for instance, in Declan Donnelan's productions for Cheek by Jowl (1988–9, 2011). Even further back, in Michael Bogdanov's production at the Phoenix Theatre in Leicester (1974), the play began and ended with an elderly man in a café in some warm country of exile, sipping his absinthe and dreaming of a revenge that would never come. Littler's production was much more sympathetic to Prospero, but also suggested that he, like Helena, was struggling with ways of telling a difficult story.

Though the programme suggested that Prospero's island was inspired by Gauguin's Tahiti, the background of his study looked as if someone had taken the shelves from Holbein's *The Ambassadors*, with their sophisticated Renaissance lute and astrolabe, and turned their straight lines into waves. Realistically, they might be warped and unusable as a result of so many years on the island, or they might be the distorted images in Prospero's memory. Against a background of sea noises, we first see him holding a small boat and speaking, in different voices, the play's opening lines. Then, though he continues to mouth the words, other voices take over. Michael Pennington had said that he had wanted to play a Chekhovian Prospero, and his gentle, poetic performance emphasized old age and the sense of proximity to death. With the rest of the cast, he played out the conclusion of a story that had begun not 'twelve years since', as Prospero says in the text, but, as Pennington said, 'almost two score'. Miranda (Kirsty Bushell), then, had lived on the island for nearly forty years, and was an independent, energetic woman, apparently used to talking to her father like an equal. Ferdinand (nearly Miranda's age; one did not wonder why the heir to the throne of Naples was still unmarried) arrived on the island in pyjamas. Perhaps the storm had happened at night; perhaps he too was in a dream. The only young character was the 'delicate' Ariel (Whitney Kehinde), for whom that adjective was more appropriate than I have ever known it. Perhaps an idealized memory of Miranda as a child, she delighted in mimicking and teasing the castaways on the island, as when, while Ferdinand was carrying his logs to one side of the stage, she kept returning them to the cave from which he had taken them. The Harpy was voiced by Prospero and Ariel, but Miranda got to speak, with them, some of the words of the wedding masque.

The doubling was both significant and efficient. The bandages creating a mask round Caliban's head made it easy for Tam Williams to double as Ferdinand, who, as is often pointed out, plays a similar role when he is Prospero's prisoner, sentenced to carrying logs. The parallel was emphasized, since, as Cindy Marcolina pointed out in *Broadway World*, one scene ends with Stephano unbinding Caliban's hands, while in the next one Miranda unbinds Ferdinand's wrists. Doubling Antonio and Sebastian with Stephano and Trinculo also emphasized the extent to which both pairs are jokers. Asked about his conscience, Antonio pretended to search his pockets as he replied, 'Ay, sir, where's that?' Usually, the two cynical courtiers amuse no one but themselves, and Trinculo sometimes muttered 'Joke's over' at the end of a remark that had failed to elicit a response. In the final scene, where the entire cast has to appear on stage, the doubling problem was solved as Ferdinand disappeared back into the cave and Prospero dismissed the two villains from the stage (and the play) with 'Let us not burden our remembrance with / A heaviness that's gone.' It reminded me of Carol Ann Duffy's line about how, in the safety of 'Mrs. Tilscher's Class', the Moors murderers 'faded, / Like the faint, uneasy smudge of a mistake'.

As with Littler's *All's Well*, then, much of what seems unbelievable in the story makes sense when it is seen as a product of the central character's memory and imagination. Although I have often been annoyed by the assumption that the only way to make a fantastic story work for an audience is to suggest that it is all some kind of hallucination, these two productions haunted me for some time. Perhaps this was simply because many of the production choices offered what I felt was a puzzle I needed to solve.

CONCLUSION

Whether because of the influence of the Globe, because outdoor theatres encourage a more casual atmosphere, or because social media have created an appetite for interactive experiences, many theatres in recent years have exploited the liveness of live theatre, making audience involvement, and a sense of community, their main object. Yet I realize in retrospect that in my pre-lockdown experience of Shakespeare my sense of the liveness of live theatre was due less to the actors than to the rest of the audience. Perhaps because of the smallness of the theatre spaces, we were usually aware of the interiority of the actors and I don't find myself remembering moments where they invited a specific response (even Trinculo's 'Joke's over' seemed directed to the others on stage rather than to us). On the other hand, I was often aware of the reactions of other people.

The special nature of the live theatre experience is one of the points frequently made by the *Cahiers Elisabéthains* reviewers, particularly when they were comparing a recorded performance with their experience of the same production in the theatre. Emily R. Lathrop, who had been impressed by Lucy Bailey's *Titus Andronicus* at the Globe in 2014, found it equally impressive on the screen, but noted that it now was less visceral, but also less funny, more like 'a horror film'. She was also aware of 'a disconnect with the audience', particularly when there was laughter.[3] Curiously, I can recall having the same sense of 'disconnect' when I saw the production in the theatre – like her, as a groundling – and was upset by two teenagers near me who were giggling at the sight of the raped and mutilated Lavinia. In the light of her review, I now think that these spectators' 'live' experience of the play was similar to the one she describes

---

[3] Emily R. Lathrop, review of *Titus Andronicus*, directed by Lucy Bailey for Shakespeare's Globe, London, UK, 24 April – 14 July 2014; filmed for Globe on Screen (screen director: Ian Russell), 2014. Viewed in London, 22 April 2014, the yard. Accessed via Globe Player in Washington, DC, USA, 12 May 2020: *Cahiers Elisabéthains*, pp. 44–6.

having on screen: they were watching the play as they would watch a horror film, where the whole point is to laugh in order to show their friends how cool they are. Some reviewers of *Women Beware Women* also objected to audience laughter at what they considered inappropriate points. Like *Titus*, this is a play about awful events but with a strongly comic element. Laughter is perhaps the hardest aspect of performance response to interpret. Is it directed by, or at, a play, or a production? Does it imply (as is often thought with regard to Iago) complicity with a character? It seems to me that it can divide an audience as well as unite it.

The attempts at socially distanced 'live' theatre in the later stages of the pandemic were the opposite of communal experiences, with the audience being told, as Lovewit tells Face in *The Alchemist*, 'Breathe less, and farther off.' By contrast, digital Shakespeare sometimes managed to recreate the sense of community, but with a significant difference. Digital performances, even if they had once been livestreams, now belonged to the past, but their producers encouraged spectators to think of them as happening in the present, to make special cocktails for the occasion (recipes provided), to form 'watch parties' and to text or tweet their reactions to friends. A number of the *Cahiers* reviewers describe the pleasure they found in conducting, as Lathrop said, 'a running commentary via text during the production'. Similarly, Eoin Price found that the commentaries of his friends (many of which he quotes) became inseparable from his experience of watching the Thomas Ostermeier production of *Hamlet*.[4] Both reviewers comment on being able to 'pause' the performance, as one cannot in the theatre; Price, who sometimes had technical difficulties that slowed down his viewing, was not bothered by finding that other viewers were commenting on moments that he hadn't yet seen. Admittedly, the production itself had been deliberately disjunctive in its treatment of the text; he concluded that the experience of live-texting had 'recreated some of the cacophonous chaos that the camera obscured'.

The experience of sharing their reactions with friends was clearly as important for these viewers as their experience of the production. As with social media in general, connectivity with like-minded people was replacing the attempted community of strangers at a live performance. This was theatre as the Restoration and eighteenth century knew it. It's clear that would-be critics were not supposed to behave like Sparkish in *The Country Wife*, who explains that 'the reason why we are so often louder than the players, is, because we think we speak more wit, and so become the poet's rivals in his audience'. And yet even respectable people engaged in the practice, as is clear from Fanny Burney's *Evelina*, in which the heroine regrets being so embarrassed by the bawdiness of *Love for Love* that she is unable to join in the witty conversation of her companions. In the privacy of your own living room, there is nothing to prevent you from commenting as much as you like. Yet Cécile Decaix, watching the Cheek by Jowl *Winter's Tale* on-screen in France, was so absorbed that, 'at times, I could not get my eyes off the screen to read a tweet, much less tap one out'.[5] Similarly, eighteenth-century audiences, amid all their distractions, were still able to find themselves in tears while watching Garrick as *King Lear*. Perhaps one century's emotional flexibility is another's multitasking.

---

[4] Eoin Price, review of *Hamlet*, translated by Marius von Mayenburg, directed by Thomas Ostermeier for the Schaubühne am Lehniner Platz, Berlin, Germany, in co-production with the Festival d'Athènes and the Festival d'Avignon, Cour d'honneur du Palais des Papes, Avignon, France, first performed in 2008; filmed for Arte ZDF and the Compagnie des Indes (screen director: Erich Schneider), 2008. Accessed via the Schaubühne website in Swansea, Wales, UK, 1 April 2020: *Cahiers Elisabéthains*, pp. 76–8.

[5] *The Winter's Tale*, directed by Declan Donnellan for Cheek by Jowl, The Barbican, London, UK, 5–22 April 2017; filmed for The Barbican (screen director: Ross MacGibbon), 19 April 2017. Accessed via YouTube in Montfaucon, France, 21 April 2020: *Cahiers Elisabéthains*, pp. 10–12.

Paul Prescott concluded the last survey of Shakespeare productions outside London with mention of his favourite production of 2019, a *Hamlet* in Tórshavn in the Faroe Islands. His injunction to remember that there is 'a world elsewhere' feels ever more timely in a year that has seen the UK government neglecting (or forgetting) Northern Ireland as it negotiates trade deals, and whose devolved policies on COVID-19 restrictions have made border crossings within mainland Britain an unusually fraught process. In inheriting this column – with its remit to cover productions in England outside London – the question of borders that separate Theatr Clwyd from Liverpool Everyman (my two local theatres growing up) or Watford Palace from the Globe (at what point is one outside London?) feels part and parcel of an England that too often forgets it is not, in John of Gaunt's words, 'bound in with the triumphant sea'.

Such borders seem ever more arbitrary as I write this in October 2020, at a point when I haven't left Beeston, Nottinghamshire in some seven months, and when the last time I stepped foot inside a theatre was in March to see the wonderful *Night of the Living Dead – Remix* by the theatre company imitating the dog, a production in which a group of people shuttered themselves into a house in order to socially distance themselves from the infection plaguing their country. I've watched a lot of theatre since that point, all of it on a screen, much of it from other countries and often from years – if not decades – ago. And where new Shakespeare performance has been created – especially by innovative companies such as Creation, The Show Must Go Online, The Shakespeare Ensemble and others – regional and national borders have mattered less than bandwidth and time zone, allowing international collaborators to develop performances aligned with no single point on a map.

The trade-off of enjoying such a wealth of archival and new online Shakespeare has been the long list of cancelled entries in my diary. Sheffield Theatres got as far as opening its *Coriolanus* on 6 March 2020, but the theatre closed its doors before I could get to it. Productions of *The Comedy of Errors*, *The Winter's Tale* and *Pericles* at the RSC have been postponed until 2021; productions aimed at young people of *The Merchant of Venice* (Nottingham Playhouse) and *Romeo and Juliet* (Birmingham Rep) will probably now not happen; and a projected touring production of *The Merchant of Venice* starring Tracy-Ann Oberman as Shylock has disappeared from schedules. Shakespeare's Rose Theatre, which in 2019 had expanded to include a venue at Blenheim Castle as well as in York, and which formed such a significant part of my predecessor's coverage, didn't even survive to the start of the pandemic, citing economic concerns caused by Brexit as it ceased to operate.

Where in-person Shakespeare has survived, it has often been in the form of curated selections of excerpts and readings, such as the games and family events performed by members of the RSC's summer ensemble in the Dell in Stratford-upon-Avon in small groups to socially distanced spectators, or in amateur/semi-professional outdoor performances of full productions. Before the pandemic cancelled them, too, many regional audiences were able to enjoy the RSC's touring trilogy of *As You Like It*, *Measure for Measure* and *The Taming of the Shrew*, and *King John* in Stratford-upon-Avon (all reviewed by Paul Prescott in *Shakespeare Survey 73*). For this volume, though, I confine myself to the two full-scale productions I was able to see in person, both looking askance at a 'poor *England* / Almost afraid to know itself' before the theatres they were in closed their doors.

MACBETH, MACBETH

At the end of 2019, the Royal Exchange in Manchester hosted a production that dramaturg Bridget Escolme claimed in her programme note to be the first major professional production of *Macbeth* to cast a woman in the title role in a mixed-sex production (there have been other instances of this worldwide, but most often in fringe or heavily compressed productions). This was by far the most notable decision in Christopher Haydon's confident take on the play, which followed the standard pattern in UK *Macbeth*s in recent years for contemporary settings, military aesthetics and a gruesome excoriation of violence in wartime.

Lucy Ellinson played Macbeth as a butch lesbian with shorn hair, combat trousers and boots, and military vest and jacket, a choice that placed conscious emphasis on the language of masculinity and virility throughout the play. Paired with Ony Uhiara as Lady Macbeth, the two women's alliance was designed to take on a world suffused by an inherent misogyny that ensured David Hartley's non-combatant, politely spoken Malcolm was promoted above the blood-steeped Macbeth (it was worth noting that Duncan was also a woman, played by Alexandra Mathie, suggesting that Duncan had also herself relied on patriarchal values to sustain her position). Macbeth herself expected on no special treatment or exceptionalism, insisting that she be treated according to the same expectations and subjected to the same dangers as the men she fought alongside. But the values of masculinity were also a source of anxiety and conflict. 'I dare do all that may become a man', she spat at Lady Macbeth, who retaliated with 'When you durst do it, *then* you were a man.' The masculinity of this woman was her currency in this world, and Lady Macbeth's challenge to that masculinity undermined Macbeth's fundamental value in ways that drove her subsequent actions.

Macbeth, in many ways, was defined by her pursuit of an ultimately destructive masculine ideal; it was no accident that, to evoke the witches' apparitions, she downed their potion and became the vessel for the apparitions herself, a performance of her own strength and agency. She was paired from the start with Theo Ogundipe's Banquo, who towered over her and who, especially in his athletic sparring with Fleance, played by Ayanda (Yandass) Ndlovu, embodied the freedom and virility that Macbeth insisted on for herself. The conflict between the two interestingly resulted in a murder that attacked Banquo's freedom of movement first, the murderers distracting him with a 'Men at Work' roadblock and stoving in his legs with heavy mallets. The subsequent confrontation between Macbeth and Banquo destabilized their previously held identities amid a chaotic fancy-dress party with games of musical chairs, dancing and cake. While Macbeth wore a dress for the only time in the production, Banquo turned out to be the person wearing an over-size bear costume, their choices of costume heightening the impression of Banquo's potential to overpower Macbeth physically; in a lovely coup, Macbeth chased the bear under a table and out the other side, and triumphantly pulled off the bear's head only to reveal that a different actor was now in the costume. Banquo then subsequently erupted through the centre of the table, looming over his enemy and leaving Macbeth in a state of hysteria; she put a tablecloth over her head and made *Scooby-Doo*-style 'woo' noises at other guests, leaving Lady Macbeth to take over the task of shutting down the party with some dignity.

As was partly the case with the Liverpool Everyman's *Othello* of the previous year, which similarly played both Desdemona and Othello as women, the production placed rather more emphasis on gendered behaviour than on queerness. In Macbeth's descent into hysteria and Lady Macbeth's embarrassment, the production veered interestingly, if briefly, into gendered images of mental fragility, Lady Macbeth briskly ushering the party guests away from what she treated as an indecorous spectacle, an image that would haunt her own reappearance in the sleepwalking scene. But the distance between the Macbeths at this point also seemed part and parcel of a standoffishness that existed between them. It was welcome to see two women have their relationship represented as normal within the world of the play, especially during the banquet scene, when Macbeth's choice to wear a dress seemed like a gesture of confidence in her own self-representation now she was Queen. But Uhiara and Ellinson seemed to have surprisingly little stage time together, and their physical intimacy was restricted to the occasional peck on the lips, making this a rather more chaste production of *Macbeth* than is often seen in more heteronormative castings. Lady Macbeth herself seemed incidental to the action, crowded out by the busy-ness of a production with more ideas than it was able to integrate fully.

The witches were the most inconsistent of the production's elements, often at the centrepiece of evocative images, but with no clear tone or purpose. The witches began the production as victims of war, as soldiers shot dead in a helicopter raid evoked by ropework and a pounding sound design that filled the theatre with explosions and distant conflict. There seemed to be an implication that the witches were working in concert to lure fresh victims to them – two of them were killed in machine gun fire and then, as a medic attended to them, another soldier slid down a rope, killed the medic and resurrected the original two bodies to become the witches. Such a potentially serious reading of war's victims and evils was undermined by a playful sarcasm elsewhere in the production, as they invited audience members to complete their more famous lines for them and tortured a plant in the audience for eating popcorn too loudly; they also undermined their own lines, offering child-like commentary on their own pronouncements with drawls of 'Ooooh'. And with the witches simply disappearing after Macbeth's second visit, there was no attempt to close the loop or consolidate their relationship to the cycle of violence. The seven-pointed star that sat at the centre of the in-the-round stage, made up of a grille covering water that boiled as the witches' cauldron, ensured that a supernatural symbol formed the foundation for everything that happened, but this symbol had no clear reference other than unto itself.

Yet if the production was inconsistent in its ideas, its ideas were at least often riveting. At the schools' matinee I attended, the extraordinary monologue of the Porter was met with complete silence, yet offered a beautifully re-imagined local update by Chris Thorpe that integrated Morrissey quotations and local references into its excoriation of property developers and Manchester business-men. The Porter, played by Rachel Denning, emerged initially as a stage manager in response to an electrical short, and this momentary interruption to the play's diegesis – while not having any obvious impact on the rest of the production – gave the performance a welcome specificity. And in a brutal scene at Macduff's home, Ross and Lady Macduff were forced to kneel and watch as a murderer plunged a knife into Lady Macduff's crying baby, silencing it abruptly. In theory, if not always in practice, the production's hard work on modes of implicating its local audience through the jokes of the Porter and witches fed into the production's insistence, at its most traumatic moments, on our complicity in watching acts of extreme violence.

The production finally, and oddly, kept its most significant act of violence off stage. Macbeth and Macduff's final fight was a slow affair, with Macduff even stopping to tie his shoelace at one point (it was unclear, from the one performance I saw, whether this was the character showing disdain for his opponent or an actor's due diligence in relation to health and safety). In the final reckoning, Macbeth was more than a match for Macduff, outclassing him throughout their fight and roaring with pointed emphasis 'Damned be *him* that first cries hold, enough!' But Macduff eventually turned and fled the stage, pursued by a Macbeth crying 'I will not yield' – and then, the next we saw, Macduff returned victorious. The final image of Macbeth, then, was of a woman triumphant on male-determined terms over another man, and the production refused to show that woman being beaten by a man; leaving the final revelation of her defeat dispiritingly anticlimactic.

A few months later, Derby Theatre and Queen's Theatre Hornchurch produced a *Macbeth* that enjoyed at least part of its national tour just before lockdown began. Douglas Rintoul's production was most notable for its stunning lighting design. On the deep Derby Theatre stage, Daniella Beattie divided the play's environment into a brightly lit downstage and a pitch-black upstage, the dividing line so sharp that actors disappeared and appeared in the blink of an eye from the void. As opposed to the playfulness of the Manchester production, the attention paid here to stage effects allowed this production to commit to a more serious version of the supernatural, with the potential to be frightening and uncanny; and by staging battles via enormous back-lit silhouettes projected onto slatted white curtains that descended from the gods, the production managed to evoke the scale of the wars.

The simple but effective design supported a production that was similarly simple but effective. Bucking trends in modern *Macbeth*s, the production was period-set, with witches who cackled around a cauldron; an unapologetically villainous and scheming Lady Macbeth; and a Macbeth who smiled with relish at the idea of his future crown. The witches were given motivation through an opening series of lightning flashes that showed a young boy flying a kite, then an image of battle, then the boy dead and his mother screaming; that woman took to revenge with her two companions. While the production was far less formally inventive than that of the Royal Exchange, its choices aimed for clarity of motivation and consequence, roundly condemning corruption while insisting on the personal cost facing those who fight it.

The politics of the Scottish court came across with unusual focus, Macbeth's power and influence (manifest in the lurking figure of Seyton) insisting on the need for the thanes to bond in solidarity. Angus and Lennox muttered together, raising their voices to make sure protestations of loyalty could be heard by Seyton, before confiding their true intentions to one another. Ross and Macduff bonded through embraces and constant touching. Both Angus and Ross had clear trajectories – Ross travelling straight from the scene of Lady Macduff's murder to his meeting in England with Macduff and Malcolm, while Angus greeted Macbeth after his final encounter with the witches

and then went directly to his plotting with Lennox. The necessity for the thanes to protect themselves through duplicity offered pointed commentary on Macbeth's own need to 'look like the innocent flower, / But be the serpent under't', while also showing the difficulty faced by those trying to consolidate resistance when faced by a violent and oppressive state.

This oppressive state was peopled by society's victims. The Old Man was presented as a homeless beggar, pronouncing how things used to be before accepting a coin from Ross; the two murderers, meanwhile, were abject, sitting on a bench slumped and looking down as Macbeth marched up and down in front of them, calling them dogs. The Doctor was terrified, desperate to get away from Macbeth as quickly as possible while reporting on Lady Macbeth's mental state, and doing everything he could to put as light a spin on it as possible. And even those closer to power were anxious in their positions, especially when put in the position of delivering bad news. David Nellist's quiet, dignified Ross hesitated painfully over his delivery of the news of Lady Macduff's death; Daniel Kendrick's brutish Seyton did the same when telling Macbeth about Lady Macbeth's death, his stumbling over the delivery showing his awareness of how this would affect his King. The attention given to the supporting roles worked to decentre the leads a little and emphasize the role played by all of Scotland in turning the tide of events, both giving a clear sense of the consequences of Macbeth's reign and showing the Scots (pointedly, only the Scots; the Siwards were cut) slowly allying under oppressive conditions to take back their own country.

While these smaller personal moments suggested an instinct towards characterization in psychological terms for the minor characters, the Macbeths themselves pulled the other way, becoming emblematic and even at times ironic. Paul Tinto's Macbeth made extensive use of the forestage, coming forward to deliver his closing couplets as if summing up the scene with a moral. His reaction to Banquo's Ghost was initially one of panic, swiping desperately at the empty air with a knife, but at the end of the scene he staggered out weary and laughing, finding an ironic detachment in the experience – an impression replicated when receiving the news of Lady Macbeth's death with a simple nod and a monologue of resigned bitterness. He laughed confidently and conspiratorially with Seyton as he awaited the English troops, and greeted Macduff's final approach with laconic indifference, at least at first. Macbeth's confidence emerged partly as a result of the apparitions' prophecies – delivered effectively as back-lit silhouettes who represented the shapes of the apparitions while the witches screamed their words into Macbeth's face – and partly from the natural confidence of the soldier who has never lost a battle. Lady Macbeth's proactive role was essential here, too; she was industrious both in encouraging Macbeth to murder and in castigating him whenever he hesitated. As such, her surprise when she found herself dismissed by Macbeth once crowned suggested that she had helped to create a monster she was now unable to control.

The production struggled in its closing moments to find an effective image on which to end. The production's finest visual moments had used lighting to evoke scale, especially during Lady Macbeth's sleepwalking as a single candle threw a long shadow up and along the theatre's wall. By contrast, the production's closing images of Fleance standing with a crown and a sword, and Macbeth's head swinging from a hook, felt prosaic and out of keeping with the production's aesthetic. But far more powerful was the conclusion of Macbeth and Macduff's final fight. Bethan Clark's fight direction created a multifaceted combat full of surprisingly detailed defensive gestures as the two men grabbed one another's blades, and then climbed up the banqueting table; Macduff then kicked Macbeth behind the curtains that bisected the stage and, in silhouette, drove his sword through Macbeth's head. But when Macduff returned to the stage, he got up on the table to present Malcolm with Macbeth's head, then wearily got down, his tired descent an indictment of what he had gone through rather than a celebration of the victory. Malcolm, for his part, shook vocally as he dubbed the Scottish nobles earls, and quickly left the stage rather than taking time to celebrate his new position. The anti-climactic ending refused a sense of victory, instead portraying the overthrow of a tyrant as an exhausting, painful task.

Macbeth's ongoing popularity as a vehicle for exploring political dissent and tyrannical leaders in the era of Trump, Putin *et al.* remains undiminished, and while neither of these two productions offered a specific critique of contemporary strongmen, both looked for political purpose. The Royal Exchange's indictment of performative masculinity sought to diagnose the problem, attributing Macbeth's rise to a culture of desensitization and senseless violence; and the Derby/Hornchurch production offered a solution in its depiction of the work of solidarity and resistance, however hard that work may be. One only hopes that *Macbeth* will, at some point in our near future, feel less relevant to our current political climate.

PROFESSIONAL SHAKESPEARE PRODUCTIONS IN THE BRITISH ISLES, JANUARY–DECEMBER

2019

JAMES SHAW

Most of the productions listed are by professional companies, but some amateur productions are included. The information is taken from *Touchstone* (www.touchstone.bham.ac.uk), a Shakespeare resource maintained by the Shakespeare Institute Library. *Touchstone* includes a monthly list of current and forthcoming UK Shakespeare productions from listings information. The websites provided for theatre companies were accurate at the time of going to press.

ALL'S WELL THAT ENDS WELL

Heady Conduct Theatre Company. Minack Theatre, Penzance, 3–7 June.
https://headyconduct.com

Jermyn Street Theatre and Guildford Shakespeare Company. St Nicolas' Church, Guilford, 12 October–2 November; Jermyn Street Theatre, London, 6–30 November.
www.jermynstreettheatre.co.uk
Director: Tom Littler

Guildford Shakespeare Company's first London transfer. Cast of six.

ANTONY AND CLEOPATRA

National Theatre. Olivier Theatre, London, 11 September 2018–19 January.
www.nationaltheatre.org.uk
Director: Simon Godwin
Cleopatra: Sophie Okonedo
Antony: Ralph Fiennes

Theatre 41 and York Shakespeare Project. John Cooper Studio at 41 Monkgate, York, 28 October–2 November.
www.41monkgate.co.uk
Director: Leo Doulton
Year 19 of the York Shakespeare Project's twenty-year mission to perform all thirty-seven plays.

AS YOU LIKE IT

Royal Shakespeare Company. Royal Shakespeare Theatre, Stratford-upon-Avon, 14 February–31 August and UK tour to 1 April 2020.
www.rsc.org.uk
Director: Kimberley Sykes
Rosalind: Lucy Phelps

Cream Faced Loons Theatre Company. Hulme Garden Centre, Manchester, 8–14 April.
www.creamfacedloons.co.uk

The Play on Theatre Company. Cockpit Theatre, London, 7 and 10 May.
Director: Shayde Sinclair

Rain or Shine Theatre Company. Wolvesey Gardens, Winchester, 2 June and UK tour to 30 August.
www.rainorshine.co.uk

Bard in the Botanics. Botanic Gardens, Glasgow, 26 June–13 July.
www.bardinthebotanics.co.uk
Director: Gordon Barr

Cambridge Shakespeare Festival. King's College Gardens, Cambridge, 29 July–17 August.
www.cambridgeshakespeare.com

Shakespeare's Globe Theatre, London, 7 August–21 September.
www.shakespearesglobe.com

PROFESSIONAL SHAKESPEARE PRODUCTIONS

Adaptation

Queen's Theatre Hornchurch and the National Theatre. Queen's Theatre, Hornchurch, 24–27 August.
www.queens-theatre.co.uk
Director: David Rintoul
Adaptation: Shaina Taub
Musical adaptation including a cast of over 100 community performers. Second show in the National Theatre Public Acts scheme, following *Pericles* in 2018.

THE COMEDY OF ERRORS

Shakespeare's Globe Touring Ensemble. Globe Theatre, London, 6 May and UK tour to 24 August.
www.shakespearesglobe.com
Director: Brendan O'Hea
Touring with *Pericles* and *Twelfth Night*.

Downpour Theatre. Stroud Shakespeare Festival, 1–2 June and tour to 14 July.
www.downpourtheatrecompany.co.uk
Director: Andrew Cullyer

Petersfield Shakespeare Festival. Bedales School, Steep, Petersfield, 17–22 July.
https://petersfieldshakespearefestival.co.uk
Director: Becky Hope-Palmer

Archway Theatre Company. Archway Theatre, Horley, 20–31 August.
www.archwaytheatre.com
Director: Gary Andrews

Folksy Theatre. Brighton Open Air Theatre (B.O.A.T.), 31 August; and UK tour.
www.folksytheatre.co.uk

HAMLET

Leeds Playhouse. The Pop-Up Theatre, Leeds, 4–30 March.
https://leedsplayhouse.org.uk
Hamlet: Tessa Parr
Director: Amy Leach
Hamlet played as a woman.

Girl Gang Manchester Theatre Company. Hope Mill Theatre, Manchester, 2–11 May.
Director: Kayleigh Hawkins
All-female production.

Iris Theatre. St Paul's Church, London, 25 June–27 July.
https://iristheatre.com
Hamlet: Jenet Le Lacheur
Director: Daniel Winder
Promenade production.

Lunchbox Theatrical Productions. Shakespeare's Rose Theatre, York, 25 June–31 August.
Director: Damian Cruden

Cambridge Shakespeare Festival. King's College Gardens, Cambridge, 8–27 July.
www.cambridgeshakespeare.com

Bard in the Botanics. Botanic Gardens, Glasgow, 18 July–3 August.
www.bardinthebotanics.co.uk
Director: Gordon Barr
Hamlet: Nicole Cooper

Petersfield Shakespeare Festival. Bedales School, Steep, Petersfield, 24–28 July.
https://petersfieldshakespearefestival.co.uk
Director: Jake Smith
A cast of ten repeatedly switch roles.

Adaptation

Ophelia Rewound
The Cellar Theatre, Sheffield, 2–5 May; People's Theatre, Camden, 24–25 August.
www.cellartheatre.co.uk
Solo show blending autobiography and Ophelia's attempted suicide.

Outrageous Fortune – Hamlet: As Told by Gertrude
Greenwich Theatre, London, 30 May
Performer: Debs Newbold

Shit-Faced Shakespeare – Hamlet
Leicester Square Theatre, London, 19 June–14 September.

Rosencrantz and Guildenstern Are Plebs
Alma Tavern Theatre, Bristol, 3–4 July.
Loose adaptation of Stoppard's play.

Noir Hamlet
Yasplz LLC Theatre Company. TheSpace @ Venue45 (Venue 45), 12–17 August.
Playwright: John Minigan
Film noir version set in 1940s Los Angeles.

Ophelia Is Also Dead
Sightline Productions. TheSpaceTriplex – Studio, 12–17 August.
Ophelia reflects on her life and times.

To Be or Not to Be? Purgatory Is the Question
Falling Stars Theatre Company. Paradise in the Vault, Edinburgh, 12–17 August.
http://fallingstarstheatre.co.uk
Hamlet, Old Hamlet and Ophelia meet in purgatory.

HENRY IV, PART I

Henry IV Part 1 or Hotspur
Shakespeare's Globe. Globe Theatre, London, 23 April–11 October.
www.shakespearesglobe.com
Directors: Sarah Bedi and Federay Holmes
Hal: Sarah Amankwah
Hotspur: Michelle Terry

Cambridge Shakespeare Festival. Robinson College Gardens, Cambridge, 8–27 July.
www.cambridgeshakespeare.com

HENRY IV, PART 2

Henry IV Part 2 or Falstaff
Shakespeare's Globe. Globe Theatre, London, 30 April–11 October.
www.shakespearesglobe.com
Director: Sarah Bedi and Federay Holmes
Hal: Sarah Amankwah
Falstaff: Helen Schlesinger

Cambridge Shakespeare Festival. Robinson College Gardens, Cambridge, 29 July–17 August.
www.cambridgeshakespeare.com

HENRY V

Henry V or Harry England
Shakespeare's Globe. Globe Theatre, London, 30 April–11 October.
www.shakespearesglobe.com
Director: Sarah Bedi and Federay Holmes
Henry V: Sarah Amankwah

Built by Barn Theatre. Barn Theatre, Cirencester, United Kingdom, 22 May–22 June.
https://barntheatre.org.uk
Director: Hal Chambers

Fluellen Theatre Company. Grand Theatre Arts Wing, Swansea, 12–13 June and tour to 19 July.
www.fluellentheatre.co.uk

Here to There Productions. Ludlow Castle, Ludlow, 24–28 June.
https://heretothereproductions.com

Bard in the Botanics. Kibble Palace Glasshouse, Glasgow, 27 June–13 July.
www.bardinthebotanics.co.uk
Director: Jennifer Dick

Lunchbox Theatrical Productions. Shakespeare's Rose Theatre, York, 28 June–31 August.
Director: Gemma Fairlie
Henry V: Maggie Bain

Grosvenor Park Open Air Theatre, Chester, 26 July–25 August.
Director: Julie Thomas

Adaptation

Into the Breach
Alma Tavern Theatre, Bristol, 19 September.
Playwright: Mark Carey
During the World War II, a village drama club performs *Henry V*.

HENRY VI

Shakespeare's Globe. Sam Wanamaker Playhouse, London, 21 November–26 January 2020.
www.shakespearesglobe.com
Director: Sean Holmes and Ilinca Radulian
Henry VI: Jonathan Broadbent
A conflation of Parts 2 and 3.

JULIUS CAESAR

Stamford Shakespeare Company. Rutland Open Air Theatre, Tolethorpe Hall, Stamford, Lincolnshire, 12 June–4 August.
http://stamfordshakespeare.co.uk

Cotswold Players. Cotswold Playhouse, Stroud, 10–12 and 16–19 October.
www.cotswoldplayhouse.co.uk
Gender-blind casting.

PROFESSIONAL SHAKESPEARE PRODUCTIONS

Adaptation

Julius 'Call Me Caesar' Caesar
Gilded Balloon Patter Hoose, Edinburgh, 1–25 August.
Festival Fringe.
Director: Russell Bolam
Playwright: Owen McCafferty
Re-imagined as storytelling in an Irish pub.

KING JOHN

Royal Shakespeare Company. Swan Theatre, Stratford-upon-Avon, 19 September–21 March 2020.
www.rsc.org.uk
Director: Eleanor Rhode
King John: Rosie Sheehy

KING LEAR

Yard Players. Brockley Jack Studio Theatre, London, 19–30 March.
www.yardplayers.com
Director: James Eley
Ada (Edmund): Evangeline Beaven

Tread the Boards Theatre Company. The Attic Theatre at Cox's Yard, Stratford-upon-Avon, 28 March–21 April.
www.theattictheatre.co.uk

Stockwell Playhouse, London, 12–18 August.

Adaptation

Jack Lear
Hull Truck Theatre. Northern Stage, Newcastle upon Tyne, 12–16 February.
www.northernstage.co.uk
Director: Barrie Rutter
Adaptation without Gloucester, Edmund and Edgar subplot.

A Bunch of Amateurs
Bingley Little Theatre, Bingley, 27 May–1 June.
www.bingleylittletheatre.co.uk
An ageing Hollywood star plays Lear with a local amateur dramatics company.

Songs of Lear
Song of the Goat Theatre Company. Shakespeare's Globe, London, 6 July.

http://piesnkozla.pl/en
A blend of music, dance, and song.

Trump Lear
Project Y Theatre, Richard Jordan Productions. Pleasance Courtyard, Edinburgh, 1–27 August.
Political satire.

Oddbodies Theatre Company. Alderney Island Hall, Alderney, 20 September and UK tour to 28 November.
Director: John Mowat
Adaptor and performer: Paul Morel
Retelling from the perspective of the Fool.

LOVE'S LABOUR'S LOST

Masque Theatre. Abington Park Museum, Northampton, 25 July–3 August.
http://masquetheatre.co.uk
Director: Beverley Webster

MACBETH

Shakespeare's Globe. Sam Wanamaker Playhouse, London, 7 November 2018–2 February.
www.shakespearesglobe.com
Director: Robert Hastie

National Theatre. New Theatre, Oxford, 8–12 January and tour to 23 March.
www.nationaltheatre.org.uk
Director: Rufus Norris

Shakespeare Up Close Theatre Company. Orange Tree Theatre, London, 9–20 February.
Director: Nathan Powell
Abridged version for younger audiences, with a cast of six.

Watermill Theatre Company. Watermill Theatre, Newbury, 28 February–30 March.
www.watermill.org.uk
Director: Paul Hart

Daniel Taylor Productions. Epstein Theatre, Liverpool, 7–16 March.
Director: Daniel Taylor

Royal Shakespeare Company. Royal Shakespeare Theatre, Stratford-upon-Avon, 13 March–18 September; Barbican, London, 23 October 2018–18 January; and UK tour.
www.rsc.org.uk
Director: Polly Findlay

Proteus Theatre Company. Haymarket, Basingstoke, 15 March; Jackson's Lane, London, 21–22 March.
www.proteustheatre.com
Director: Mary Swan

This Is My Theatre. Guildhall, Chichester, 5 May and on tour through 2020.
www.thisismytheatre.com
Director: Sarah Slator

Three Inch Fools. Eastbury Manor House, Barking, 24 May and UK tour to July.
www.threeinchfools.com
Cast of five.

Lunchbox Theatrical Productions. Shakespeare's Rose Theatre, Blenheim Palace, Woodstock, 8 July–7 September.

Antic Disposition. Temple Church, London, 20 August–7 September.
www.anticdisposition.co.uk
Director: Ben Horslen and John Risebero

South Devon Players. The Barnfield Theatre, Exeter, 7 September and tour to 14 October.
www.southdevonplayers.com

Royal Exchange Theatre. The Theatre, Manchester, 13 September–19 October.
www.royalexchange.co.uk
Director: Christopher Haydon
Macbeth: Lucy Ellinson
Lady Macbeth / Porter: Rachel Denning

Arrows and Traps Theatre Company. New Wimbledon Theatre, London, 17 September–5 October.
www.arrowsandtraps.com
Director: Ros McGregor

Chichester Festival Theatre. Festival Theatre, Chichester, West Sussex, 21 September–26 October.
www.cft.org.uk
Director: Paul Miller
Macbeth: John Simm
Lady Macbeth: Dervla Kirwan

Downpour Theatre. Mission Theatre, Bath, 18–19 October and tour to 2 November.
www.downpourtheatrecompany.co.uk
Director: Andrew Cullyer

The Shakespeare Project. Salomons Estate, Royal Tunbridge Wells, 5–24 November.

www.theshakespeareproject.co.uk
Inaugural production for The Shakespeare Project.

Adaptation

The Paper Cinema. Traverse Theatre, Edinburgh, 7 February; Birmingham Repertory Theatre, 15 March.
http://thepapercinema.com
Audio-visual performance with paper cut-outs without dialogue.

The Factory Theatre Company. Theatr Clwyd, Mold, 8–9 April and local tour to 13 April.
www.factorytheatre.co.uk

Cho-in Theatre Company (Korea). C venues, Main Theatre, Edinburgh, 1–26 August.
Solo performance with Korean puppets, music and dance.

Opera

English Touring Opera Company. Hackney Empire Theatre, London, 9 March and tour to 24 May.
http://englishtouringopera.org.uk
Composer: Giuseppe Verdi

Duchy Opera Company. Minack Theatre, Penzance, 8–12 July.
Composer: Giuseppe Verdi

MEASURE FOR MEASURE

Guildford Shakespeare Company. Holy Trinity Church, Guildford, 4–23 February.
www.guildford-shakespeare-company.co.uk
Director: Charlotte Conquest
The first half presented an abridged version. Post-interval, a shorter version was performed with six roles gender-reversed.

Royal Shakespeare Company. Royal Shakespeare Theatre, Stratford-upon-Avon, 28 June–29 August and on tour to March 2020.
www.rsc.org.uk
Director: Gregory Doran

Forge Theatre. Bolton Little Theatre, Bolton, 9–16 November.
www.boltonlittletheatre.co.uk
Abridged version.

PROFESSIONAL SHAKESPEARE PRODUCTIONS

THE MERCHANT OF VENICE

First Encounters with Shakespeare: The Merchant of Venice
Royal Shakespeare Company. Swan Theatre, Stratford-upon-Avon, 30 September–5 October and tour to 16 November.
www.rsc.org.uk
Director: Robin Belfield
Abridged version for younger audiences.

Adaptation

Shylock
Ropetackle Arts Centre, Shoreham-by-Sea and tour to 18 May.
Playwright: Gareth Armstrong
Performer: Rhodri Miles
From the perspective of Tubal.

Gratiano
Grist to the Mill Theatre Company. Everyman Theatre, Cheltenham, 8–10 October; Yvonne Arnaud Theatre, Guildford, 28 November.
Playwright: Ross Ericson
Sequel from Gratiano's perspective.

THE MERRY WIVES OF WINDSOR

Royal Shakespeare Company. The Barbican, London, 7 December 2018–5 January.
www.rsc.org.uk
Director: Fiona Laird
Falstaff: David Troughton

Shakespeare's Globe. Globe Theatre, London, 23 May–12 October.
www.shakespearesglobe.com
Director: Elle While

Guildford Shakespeare Company. Stoke Park Railway, Guildford, 13–27 July.
Director: Caroline Devlin

A MIDSUMMER NIGHT'S DREAM

Shakespeare at the Tobacco Factory. Tobacco Factory Theatres, Bristol, 20 February–6 April.
www.tobaccofactorytheatres.com
Director: Mike Tweddle

Terra Nova Productions. Queen's Hall, Newtownards, Belfast, 2–5 May.
www.terranovaproductions.net
Director: Andrea Montgomery
Included eighty community performers aged between 6 and 82.

Lord Chamberlain's Men. Brighton Festival, St Nicholas Rest Garden, Brighton, 23–25 May and tour to 1 September.
www.tlcm.co.uk
All-male cast.

Bridge Theatre. Bridge Theatre, London, 3 June–31 August. Broadcast to cinemas as part of National Theatre Live, 27–29 October.
https://bridgetheatre.co.uk
Director: Nicholas Hytner
Bottom: Hammed Animashaun
Titania and Oberon's lines reversed.

Oddsocks. Brighton Open Air Theatre, Brighton, 6–8 June and tour to 17 August.
www.oddsocks.co.uk

Quantum Theatre Company. Trinity Theatre, Tunbridge Wells, 6 June and tour to 28 August.
www.quantumtheatre.co.uk

Shakespeare in the Squares. Leinster Square, London, 19 June, and at garden squares throughout London to 11 July.
www.shakespeareinthesquares.co.uk
Director: Tatty Hennessy

Chapterhouse Theatre Company. Ballykeeffe Amphitheatre, Ballykeeffe, 21 June and on tour to 1 September.
www.chapterhouse.org

Open Air Theatre. Regent's Park, London, 28 June–27 July.
https://openairtheatre.com
Director: Dominic Hill

Shakespeare's Globe. Globe Theatre, London, 28 June–13 October.
www.shakespearesglobe.com
Director: Sean Holmes
Bottom: Jocelyn Jee Esien

Sun and Moon Theatre. Cardinham Woods, Bodmin, 6 July and tour to 4 August.

https://sunandmoontheatreuk.com
Director: Melissa Barrett and David Johnson

Bowler Crab Productions. Manor Barn, Bexhill, 7 July
and tour to 2 August.
www.bowler-crab.com

Cambridge Shakespeare Festival. St John's College
Gardens, Cambridge, 8–27 July.
www.cambridgeshakespeare.com

Rough Cast Theatre. UK tour 8–27 July.
www.roughcast.co.uk
Director: Mark Burridge

Lunchbox Theatrical Productions. Shakespeare's Rose
Theatre, Blenheim Palace, Woodstock, 8 July–2
September.

Shakespeare from Russian. The Dell, Stratford-upon-
Avon, 25 July.
Part of the Royal Shakespeare Company's open-air Dell
performances.

RIFT. Alexandra Palace, London, 3–28 September.
www.r-ft.co.uk
Director: Felix Mortimer and Joshua Nawras

The Watermill Ensemble. Northern Stage, Newcastle
upon Tyne, 11–14 September and touring to 7 March.
www.watermill.org.uk
Directed by Paul Hart
Resident Shakespeare company of Watermill
Theatre.

Adaptation

Flute Theatre. Minerva Theatre, Chichester,
16–26 January.
www.flutetheatre.co.uk
Director: Kelly Hunter
Participatory performance for children aged 10+ on the
autism spectrum.

Shit-faced Shakespeare. Epsom Playhouse, Epsom,
1 October and tour to 29 November.
www.shit-facedshakespeare.com

A Mini Summer Night's Dream – Shakespeare Unlocked
Watermill Ensemble Company. The Watermill Theatre,
Newbury, 4–8 November.
Director: Robert Kirby
Abridged version with cast of three.

MUCH ADO ABOUT NOTHING

Northern Broadsides and New Vic co-production.
New Vic, Newcastle-under-Lyme, 8 February–
2 March; Dukes, Lancaster, 5–9 March; and tour to
25 May.
www.northern-broadsides.co.uk
Final production of outgoing artistic director Conrad
Nelson.

Tread the Boards Theatre Company. The Attic Theatre
at Cox's Yard, Stratford-upon-Avon, 4–28 April.
www.theattictheatre.co.uk

The HandleBards. Copper Beech Cafe @ JAGS
Sports Club, Dulwich, 18 May and tour to
11 September.
www.handlebards.com

Three Inch Fools. Eastbury Manor House, Barking,
24 May and UK tour to July.
www.threeinchfools.com
Cast of five.

The Festival Players. Ickleton Village Hall, Ickleton,
1 June and tour to 26 August.
http://thefestivalplayers.co.uk
All-male cast.

The Groundlings Theatre Company. Stonham Barns,
Stowmarket, 5 July and tour to 2 August.
https://groundlings.co.uk

Cambridge Shakespeare Festival. St John's College
Gardens, Cambridge, 29 July–17 August.
www.cambridgeshakespeare.com

Norwich Players. The Maddermarket, Norwich,
20–28 September.

Shakespeare at the Tobacco Factory. Tobacco
Factory Theatres, Bristol, 16 October–9 November;
and at Wilton's Music Hall, London, 12–23
November.
http://stf-theatre.org.uk
Director: Elizabeth Freestone

OTHELLO

The Phil Willmott Company. Union Theatre, London,
13 March–6 April.
https://philwillmott.org
Director: Phil Willmott

The Play on Theatre Company. Cockpit Theatre, London, 8–9 May.
Director: Danäe Cambrook
An all-female production.

Adaptation

Othello Remixed
Intermission Theatre Company. Omnibus Theatre, London, 5 June–14 July.
Director: Darren Raymond
Set in the London boxing circuit.

Ainu Othello
Shakespeare Company of Japan and Pirikap. Tara Arts, London, 7–10 August.
Director: Kazumi Shimodate and Debo Akibe
Exploring tensions between Japanese society and the Ainu ethnic minority.

Love Deadline (Desdemona): Love Is Like the Moon
United Solo Theatre Festival. Studio Theatre, New York, 29 September 2018; Studio Theatre, York, 14–15 May; Rose Playhouse, London, 21–23 May and on tour.
Performer and adaptor: Ji Young Choi
Solo piece.

Pantaloons Theatre Company. Bacon Theatre, Cheltenham, 2 October and tour to 24 November.
https://thepantaloons.co.uk;

Becoming Othello: A Black Girl's Journey
New Heritage Theatre Group and Shakespeare Birthplace Trust. The Shakespeare Centre, Stratford-upon-Avon, 9 October; Helen Martin Studio, University of Warwick, 16 October and tour.
www.becomingothello.global
Director and performer: Debra Ann Byrd
Recollections about playing the role of Othello.

Opera

R'Otello – The Rugby Opera
Bridewell Theatre, London, 4, 6–7 September.
Otello leads Samoa to the Rugby World Cup Final, including arias from a selection of well-known operas.

Otello
Royal Opera House, London, 9–22 December.
www.roh.org.uk
Composer: Giuseppe Verdi

PERICLES

Shakespeare's Globe Touring Ensemble. Globe Theatre, London, 5 May and UK tour to 21 August.
www.shakespearesglobe.com
Director: Brendan O'Hea
Touring with *Comedy of Errors* and *Twelfth Night*.

RICHARD II

Almeida Theatre, London, 10 December 2018–2 February.
https://almeida.co.uk
Director: Joe Hill-Gibbins
Richard II: Simon Russell Beale
100-minute version with cast of eight.

Shakespeare's Globe. Sam Wanamaker Playhouse, London, 22 February–21 April.
www.shakespearesglobe.com
Director: Adjoa Andoh and Lynette Linton
Richard II: Adjoa Andoh

Anərkē Shakespeare. The Rose Playhouse, London, 13–18 August.
Actor-led company without a director.

Puppet King Richard II
Pocket Epics Theatre Company. PQA Venues @Riddle's Court, Edinburgh, 2–14 August. Festival Fringe.
Puppet version.

RICHARD III

Headlong Theatre. Alexandra Palace, Bristol Old Vic, Royal and Derngate, and Oxford Playhouse production. Bristol Old Vic Theatre, Bristol, 1–9 March and tour to 25 May.
https://headlong.co.uk
Director: John Haidar

Lunchbox Theatre Productions. Shakespeare's Rose Theatre, Blenheim Palace, Woodstock, 8 July–7 September.

Bard in the Botanics. Kibble Palace Glasshouse, Glasgow, 19 July–3 August.
www.bardinthebotanics.co.uk
Director: Jennifer Dick

Cast of four.

Shakespeare's Globe. Sam Wanamaker Playhouse, London, 21 November–26 January 2020.
www.shakespearesglobe.com
Director: Sean Holmes and Ilinca Radulian
Richard III: Sophie Russell

Adaptation

The Travesty of Richard III
The Culture Conspiracy. The Green Room, Dorking, 11 October.
Abridged comic version with cast of two.

ROMEO AND JULIET

Royal Shakespeare Company. Barbican Theatre, London, 2 November 2018–19 January and tour. Broadcast live to cinemas worldwide, 18 July.
www.rsc.org.uk
Director: Erica Whyman
Mercutio: Charlotte Josephine
Friar Laurence: Andrew French

Forest Forge Theatre Company. Ringwood, 16–19 January.
www.forestforgetheatre.co.uk

National Production Company. Grand Theatre, Lancaster, 20 March.

This Is My Theatre. St Wilfrid's Chapel, Church Norton, West Sussex, 31 May and tour to 29 June.
www.thisismytheatre.com
Director: Sarah Slator

Attic Door Productions. Lancaster Castle, Lancaster, 5–22 June.
www.atticdoorproductions.co.uk

Heartbreak Productions. Jephson Gardens, Leamington Spa, 5–6 June and tour to 28 August.
www.heartbreakproductions.co.uk

Archway Theatre Company. Archway Theatre, Horley, 4–6 July.
www.archwaytheatre.com

The Groundlings Theatre Company. Stonham Barns, Stowmarket, 4 July and tour to 1 August.
https://groundlings.ticketsolve.com

Lunchbox Theatrical Productions. Shakespeare's Rose Theatre, Blenheim Palace, Woodstock, 8 July–7 September.

Moving Stories Theatre Company. Minack Theatre, Penzance, 22–26 July.
www.movingstories.org.uk

Red Rose Chain Theatre Company. Jimmy's Farm, Suffolk, 31 July–25 August.
https://redrosechain.com

Action to the World Theatre Company. Stockwell Playhouse, London, 3–14 September.
www.stockwellph.com

Bedouin Shakespeare Company. Silvano Toti Globe, Rome, 8–13 October; Harold Pinter Theatre, 21 October.
www.bedouinshakespeare.com
Director: Chris Pickles

Adaptation

Juliet and Romeo
Lost Dog Theatre Company. Aberystwyth Arts Centre, Aberystwyth, 23 January and tour to 31 March.
https://lostdogdance.co.uk
Dance sequel with Romeo and Juliet in their 40s.

Romeo and Juliet: Mad Blood Stirring
China Plate Theatre. Contender Charlie at the Albany Theatre, London, 1–8 February and on tour.
www.chinaplatetheatre.com
Director: Paul Warwick and Ben Walden
For younger audiences.

Oh, Romeo
Guildbury's Theatre Company. Electric Theatre, Guildford, 20–23 March.
www.guildburys.com
Playwright: Ephraim Kishon
A sequel thirty years on with a bickering Romeo and Juliet.

West Side Story
Royal Exchange Theatre, Manchester, 6 April–25 May.
Director: Sarah Frankcom
Choreography: Aletta Collins

Curious Pheasant Theatre Company. Hanger Farm Arts Centre, Southampton, 18 May and tour to 11 July.

www.curiouspheasanttheatre.co.uk
All-male production with attraction between rival rugby teams.

Maverick Theatre Company. Assembly George Square, Edinburgh, 1–24 August. Festival Fringe.
www.mavericktheatrecompany.com
Director: Nick Hennegan

R'n'J: The Untold Story of Shakespeare's Roz and Jules
Stolen Cactus Theatre Company. Gilded Balloon, Edinburgh, 1–26 August. Festival Fringe.
Rosaline and Juliet have an adventure.

& Juliet
Opera House, Manchester, 10–12 September; Shaftesbury Theatre, London, 2 November– .
Director: Luke Sheppard
Book: David West Read
Jukebox musical.

West Side Story
Curve Theatre, Leicester, 23 November–11 January 2020.

Ballet

Moscow City Ballet. Palace Theatre, Manchester, 17 January; Kings Theatre, Portsmouth and Southsea, 8–9 February.
Royal Opera House, London, 26 March–11 June.
www.roh.org.uk

Romeo + Juliet
New Adventures Company. Curve Theatre, Leicester, 13–18 May and tour to 12 October.
https://new-adventures.net
Choreography: Matthew Bourne

Ballet Cymru. The Riverfront, Newport, 30–31 May and tour to 4 December.
http://welshballet.co.uk

New Adventures. Sadler's Wells, London, 7–31 August and tour to 12 October.
https://new-adventures.net
Director: Matthew Bourne

Radio & Juliet / Faun / McGregor+Mugler
MuzArts and PMB Presentations. London Coliseum, 7–8 December.
Choreography: Edward Clug
World premiere set to the music of Radiohead.

Opera

I Capuleti e i Montecchi
Over the Pond Productions. Arcola Theatre, London, 2–4 September.
Composer: Vincenzo Bellini

THE TAMING OF THE SHREW

Sherman Theatre Company. Sherman Theatre, Cardiff, 28 February–16 March.
www.shermantheatre.co.uk
Director: Michael Fentiman
Reverse gender production.

Royal Shakespeare Company. Royal Shakespeare Theatre, Stratford-upon-Avon, 8 March and on tour.
www.rsc.org.uk
Director: Justin Audibert
Petruchia: Claire Price
Reverse gender production.

Adaptation

Kiss Me Kate
Sheffield Theatre Productions. The Crucible Theatre, Sheffield, 7 December 2018–12 January.
www.sheffieldtheatres.co.uk

Shit-Faced Shakespeare. Leicester Square Theatre, London, 17 April–1 June.

Kiss Me Kate
Watermill Theatre Company. Watermill Theatre, Newbury, 25 July–21 September.
www.watermill.org.uk

THE TEMPEST

Lazarus Theatre Company. Greenwich Theatre, London, 5–16 February.
Director: Ricky Dukes
Gender reversal for Prospero/Miranda.

The HandleBards. The Fleece Inn, Bretforton, 24 April and tour to 11 September.
www.handlebards.com
Cast of four.

Lunchbox Theatrical Productions. Shakespeare's Rose Theatre, York, 26 May–1 September.
Director: Philip Franks

Illyria Theatre Company. Gyllyngdune Gardens, Falmouth, 21 June and tour to 8 September.
www.illyria.co.uk
Cast of five.

Creation Theatre. Osney Mead, Oxford, 19 July–15 August. Adapted and restaged with Big Telly (www.big-telly.com) for online performances on Zoom, 11 April–10 May 2020.
www.creationtheatre.co.uk
Director: Zoe Seaton

Cambridge Shakespeare Festival. Trinity College Gardens, Cambridge, 29 July–17 August.
www.cambridgeshakespeare.com

Adaptation

Return to the Forbidden Planet
BOS Musical Theatre Group. Blackfriars Arts Centre, Boston, 5–13 April.

Caliban's Codex
Fetch Theatre. Sweet Novotel – Novotel 1, Edinburgh, 12–25 August.
Playwright: John Knowles
Solo performer. Sequel with Caliban in control of Prospero's books.

TIMON OF ATHENS

Royal Shakespeare Company. Swan Theatre, Stratford-upon-Avon, 7 December 2018–22 February.
www.rsc.org.uk
Director: Simon Godwin
Lady Timon: Kathryn Hunter
Apemantus: Nia Gwynne

Canterbury Shakespeare Festival. Canterbury Christ Church University, 19 July–11 August.
Director: Caitlin Fox

TWELFTH NIGHT

Southwark Playhouse, London, 17 January–9 February.
Cast of six, relocated to a music festival.

OVO. Maltings Arts Theatre, St Albans, 4–13 April; Rose Playhouse, London, 23 April–5 May.

www.ovotheatre.org.uk
Director: Adam Nichols

Shakespeare's Globe Touring Ensemble. Globe Theatre, London, 4 May and tour to 24 August.
www.shakespearesglobe.com
Director: Brendan O'Hea
Viola: Eric Sirakian
Touring with *Comedy of Errors* and *Pericles*.

Ad Hoc Players. Brentwood Theatre, Brentwood, 6–8 June.
https://adhocplayer.co.uk

Stamford Shakespeare Company. Rutland Open Air Theatre, Tolethorpe Hall, Stamford, Lincolnshire, 12 June–4 August.
http://stamfordshakespeare.co.uk

Guildford Shakespeare Company. Guildford Castle Gardens, Guildford, 13–29 June.
www.guildford-shakespeare-company.co.uk
Director: Charlotte Conquest

Bridge House Productions. Bridge House Theatre, London, 17 June–14 July.
Director: Guy Retallack
Cast of five.

Lunchbox Theatrical Productions. Shakespeare's Rose Theatre, York, 27 June–1 September.
Director: Joyce Branagh

Grosvenor Park Open Air Theatre, Chester, 5 July–24 August.
www.grosvenorparkopenairtheatre.co.uk

Arcola Theatre Academy. Arcola Theatre, London, 4 August.
www.arcolatheatre.com
Director: Bec Martin-Williams

Iris Theatre. The Scoop at More London, London, 7 August–1 September.
http://iristheatre.com
Director: Rae McKen
A 90-minute adaptation.

New Wimbledon Theatre, London, 12–16 November. Tread the Boards Theatre Company. The Attic Theatre (Cox's Yard), Stratford-upon-Avon, 21 November–1 December.

PROFESSIONAL SHAKESPEARE PRODUCTIONS

Adaptation

Flute Theatre. Craiova International Shakespeare Festival, Romania, 25 April 2018; at the Minerva Theatre, Chichester, 15–26 January.
www.flutetheatre.co.uk
Director: Kelly Hunter
Participatory performance for children aged 10+ on the autism spectrum.

2Elfth Night

Keane & Doyle. Paradise in Augustines, Edinburgh, 12–17 August. Festival Fringe.
www.adriandeane.com
Director: Samantha Rasler
Cast of two.

Toby Belch (Is Unwell)

Sidney Kean Theatre Company. Sweet Grassmarket – Grassmarket 4, Edinburgh, 12–25 August.
Playwright: John Knowles
Performer: Sidney Kean
Toby reflects on his life and times.

THE TWO NOBLE KINSMEN

Adaptation

The Jailer's Daughter

The UnDisposables Theatre Company. The Space, London, 20–24 August.
Playwright: Esther Joy Mackay
Billed as a blend of Shakespeare, *Love Island* and *Black Mirror*.

THE WINTER'S TALE

The National Theatre. Dorfman Theatre, London, 6–21 February.
www.nationaltheatre.org.uk
Director: Ruth Mary Johnson
Abridged version for younger audiences.

Changeling Theatre. UK tour June–August.
http://changeling-theatre.com
Director: Robert Forknall

Cambridge Shakespeare Festival. Downing College Gardens, Cambridge, 8–27 July.
www.cambridgeshakespeare.com

Adaptation

A Winter's Tale

Helikon Theatre Company. OSO Arts Centre, London, 19–23 March.
www.helikontheatrecompany.com
Helikon's inaugural production, with modernized language.

POEMS AND APOCRYPHA

Lucrece

The Shakespeare Edit Theatre Company. TheSpace @ Niddry St – Upper Theatre, Edinburgh, 12–24 August.
www.theshakespearedit.com
Dramatic adaptation.

MISCELLANEOUS (IN ALPHABETICAL ORDER)

(The Absurdity & Failure of) Life after Shakespeare

The Carlton Theatre Group. The Colourhouse Theatre, London, 6–10 August.
www.colourhousetheatre.co.uk
Director: Jake Mills

Billy Shakes – Wonderboy!

Wrongsemble. Theatre Royal, York, 28 July–24 August.
www.wrongsemble.com
Director: Elvi Piper
A show covering Shakespeare's childhood. For younger audiences.

Clowns, Lovers, Women in Pants and Shakespeare

Theatre OCU. Greenside @ Nicolson Square – Lime Studio, Edinburgh, 5–10 August.
Comic exploration of humour in Shakespeare.

Come Dine with Mr Shakespeare

Roo Theatre Company. North Bridge – Perth Theatre, Edinburgh, 20–24 August.
Reality TV cooking show with four contestants: Orsino, Cordelia, Petruchio and Lady Macbeth.

A Comedy of Edric's!
New Vic Theatre, Newcastle-under-Lyme, 19–31 August.
Playwright: David Graham
William Shakespeare visits Edric's inn.

Death by Shakespeare
The HurlyBurly Players. Niddry St – Upper Theatre, Edinburgh, 5–9 August.
A selection of death scenes.

Fifty Shades of Shakespeare
The HurlyBurly Players. Niddry St – Upper Theatre, Edinburgh, 5–9 August.
A selection of love scenes.

House Party on Henley Street
Compass Presents for the Shakespeare Birthplace Trust. Will's Kitchen and Shakespeare's Birthplace, Stratford-upon-Avon, 1–2 November.

Ian McKellen on Stage: With Tolkien, Shakespeare, Others, and You
Ian McKellen and Ambassador Theatre Group Productions. The Space, London, 25–26 January; and UK and international tour.
www.ianonstage.co.uk
Director: Sean Mathias
Career retrospective including selections from Shakespeare.

Kemp's Jig
Blue Fire Theatre Company. TheSpace on the Mile, Edinburgh, 2–17 August.

www.bluefiretheatre.co.uk
Comic retelling of Kemp's jig from London to Norwich.

Last Life: A Shakespeare Play
The Box Collective and Piece of Yourself Theatre Company. Greenside, Mint Studio, Edinburgh, 2–17 August.
Movement-based piece: a man and woman, trapped in a circle of salt, face the wounds of their past.

ShakeItUp: The Improvised Shakespeare Show
The Hen and Chickens Theatre Bar, London, 11 November and 5 December.
A new play created from audience suggestions.

Shakespeare in Love
Theatre Royal Bath and Eleanor Lloyd Productions. Theatre Royal, Newcastle upon Tyne, 25 February–2 March.
Director: Phillip Breen
Adaptation of 1998 film.

Where We Belong
Shakespeare's Globe. Sam Wanamaker Playhouse, London, 17 June.
Playwright: Madeline Sayet

Will, or Eight Lost Years of William Shakespeare's Life
Will & Co Theatre Company. Royal Terrace – Jade Studio, Edinburgh, 12–24 August.
www.willandco.co.uk
Dramatization of the lost years.

THE YEAR'S CONTRIBUTIONS TO SHAKESPEARE STUDIES

1. CRITICAL STUDIES

REVIEWED BY JANE KINGSLEY-SMITH

In a year of political turbulence, racial injustice and a devastating global pandemic that made not only democratic freedom but life itself feel more precious and precarious – bringing us closer to the lived experience of Shakespeare himself – critical works on Shakespeare and early modern drama have taken on new and more urgent meanings. This has sometimes been quite deliberate, with critics including James Shapiro and Jeffrey R. Wilson examining the relevance of Shakespearian tragedy to the state of American politics, but it has also extended the resonance of works with a more tangential relationship to 2020's multiple catastrophes.

Pascale Aebischer's *Shakespeare, Spectatorship and the Technologies of Performance* sets itself a number of ambitious tasks, not the least of which is to address the question of how effective/affective viewing Shakespeare productions at a distance can be 'in the context of the Covid pandemic in which so much of our experience of watching Shakespeare is digital'. At the simplest level, it is an account of how British mainstream theatre engaged with technology – including video feeds, motion capture, social media and live streaming – between 2009 with the first NT Live broadcasts and 2016 with the celebration of Shakespeare's quatercentenary. But it is also an impassioned defence of these technologies in the face of anxiety about the loss of co-presence between spectators and actors, and the 'liveness' of performance, and the concomitant potential damage to response-ability/responsibility. Aebischer concludes that, in fact, audiences can be engaged more deeply – in emotional, intellectual and ethical ways – through the use of these technologies, which intensify what was already built into the early modern play. For example, the camera can reproduce ethical perspectives on the action that would originally have been generated by playing on the platea in the early modern theatre. The use of social media to gain feedback from online fan communities replicates the 'analogue feedback loop that had connected audiences to companies . . . and had determined the success, failure or revision of a play'.

Whilst the book is divided into three distinct sections – performance technologies in the Jacobean theatre; digital technologies in productions by the National Theatre and the RSC; and live broadcasts – these sections are woven together by Aebischer in a remarkably seamless fashion through a number of shared preoccupations. One of the most compelling is the discovery space – or, more specifically, the 'obscene dynamics of the discovery space'. In the chapter on Marlowe's *Edward II*, directed by Joe Hill-Gibbins at the National Theatre (2013), for example, Aebischer describes the central building on stage, into which the actors disappeared, whilst their actions were conveyed to the audience through two large screens on either side which relayed live video feed. When this showed pornographic images of Edward and Gaveston, at a party from which the audience was excluded, it created the voyeurism which would be condemned later in relation to Edward II's murder. The actor's presence on the platea was here enhanced and intensified by the use of technology which 'implicated [the audience] ever more uncomfortably, in the disciplining of the King's unruly body, indicting them for their failure to take an ethico-politically responsible/response-able stance and resist the gravitational pull of the production's obscene provocation of homophobia'.

As much as the book is concerned with where things happen on stage, it is equally concerned with how one's perspective alters depending on where one sits. Aebischer explores the different sightlines available to spectators at the Sam Wanamaker Playhouse, specifically in relation to Dominic Dromgoole's production of *The Changeling* (2015), where those in the pit and lower galleries had a significantly different view of the action from those in the upper galleries. This was particularly the case in relation to the dumbshow which staged Beatrice-Joanna's sexual transaction with De Flores. From the perspective in the pit, Aebischer notes, this looked like a cynical and consensual settling of accounts between the two, but one's perspective from the upper gallery revealed 'the obscene rape at the heart of the play'. Sightlines are again crucial to Aebischer's discussion of the RSC's *Hamlet*, directed by Simon Godwin (2016), generated this time not by the architecture of the theatre but by the camera angles and framing which reshaped the production as a live broadcast. Here, Aebischer offers a detailed account of the way in which Camera 4 becomes a character in the action, specifically that of Old Hamlet: crane shots create 'an uncanny awareness of supernatural presence and the ghost's obscene viewpoint peering in from humanly impossible vantage points above and beyond the margins of the stage'. In fact, this is almost a cliché of filmed *Hamlet*s – it was a feature of both the Kenneth Branagh and Olivier films,

and is thus perhaps less original than Aebischer suggests here. Nevertheless, it reinforces her argument that technology can deepen the emotional and ethical engagement of the audience.

This is not to say that technology always works in the way that Aebischer believes it should, and part of the book's achievement is its exposure of the blindspots in specific productions and technologies. In the case of Cheek by Jowl's *Measure for Measure*, for example, directed in the theatre by Declan Donnellan but reconceived for the cinema by Thomas Bowles (2015), the broadcast edit intensified the production's 'provocative sidelining of Isabella's ethical force' through the camera's repeated exclusion of her from the frame. More troubling is 'technology's bias in favour of a lighter skintone', as evident in the filming of Godwin's *Hamlet*, in which Hamlet was played by Paapa Essiedu in an almost exclusively BAME cast. Aebischer explores how 'many present-day HD video cameras, including those used in this broadcast, do not incorporate the dual skin colour circuit feature that was developed in the 1990s to ensure that both darker and lighter skin tones would be sharply defined within a single video camera shot'. In the case of the Godwin *Hamlet*, the lack of definition produced by the camera was compounded by a stage design which allowed darker skin tones to recede into the background. Aebischer shows an invigorating attention to the 'backstage' processes not only of putting on a play but of publishing an academic book. Here, she discusses the problem of finding stills which were deemed of sufficient quality, and the case she put to her publishers that 'failing to include the images would perpetuate the elision of darker-skinned performers from the visual record'.

If technology does not always challenge the gender and racial inequalities that arguably still pertain in mainstream British theatre, Aebischer's spectacular book is a powerful argument in favour of its potential. Video, social media, live streaming: these are 'tools that help us excavate and reactivate performance's intense experiences of fleeting and absolute co-presence and co-creation for new generations of "plugged-in" audiences'. I'm not sure that I would want to sit next to Aebischer in the theatre or cinema – a 'sanctimonious' member of the audience who asks her to turn off her phone gets short shrift – but I would definitely want to see the performance through her eyes.

Another book which examines the visual frames placed around Shakespeare and how they determine meaning is Sally Barnden's *Still Shakespeare and the Photography of Performance*. The slightly awkward title tells us something about the book's range and scope. It begins with photography as a record of Shakespearian performance; 'still' Shakespeare recalls Barbara Hodgdon's image of the photograph's 'violent stilling' of stage action. But it also raises the question of whether or not those iconic Shakespearian images which photography allows to escape their theatrical context – the subject of the book's second part – are 'still' Shakespeare. A better title might have been simply 'Shakespeare and Photography', for it is to the strange affinities between these two entities that Barnden repeatedly, brilliantly, returns. Throughout the book, we encounter moments when the ways in which Western culture has thought about photography and about Shakespeare are oddly similar – for example, Shakespeare's ability to offer 'universal truths about human mortality' and 'the photograph's supposed affinity with death'. Shakespearian subject matter elevates the new art form of photography, whilst photography democratizes Shakespeare and extends its cultural authority beyond the stage.

The book begins with RSC productions of *A Midsummer Night's Dream* between 1954 and 1977, to explore the ways in which, as Thomas Postlewait put it, 'photographs may provide unreliable testimony because both their final cause or aim (publicity shot) and their formal cause (aesthetic principles of portrait) subvert their documentary potential'. Barnden demonstrates how, in the early years, photographs are taken in a studio, with the photographer's own blocking, and stylized to reflect a Hollywood aesthetic. By the 1970s, there is a greater emphasis on recording live stage action, although the photograph's authenticity is often undermined by its having been taken during rehearsal. Bringing us into the present, Barnden discusses the binary of performance as 'liveness' versus photography as a remnant or dead thing, which was also challenged by Aebischer. Here, Barnden interjects an awareness of how the photograph is often required to create an impression of 'liveness', impelled by institutional pressure to make Shakespeare as vital as possible, whilst 'live' performance in the theatre often relies upon a photographic archive of past productions. This alertness to paradox is one of the chief pleasures of the book.

Chapter 2 moves back to the invention of photography in the nineteenth century, which created the expectation that the past might now be preserved accurately by 'the pencil of nature'. This had some interesting implications for Shakespeare on stage, particularly the history plays. Charles Kean's 1857 production of *Richard II* was praised for its reproduction of the costume and pageantry of fourteenth-century England: 'Mr Kean may be said to have *photographed the past*, not, indeed, by the rays of the sun, but by the enduring light of antiquarian research.' One of the circularities that emerges here is that, although to be 'photographic' suggests an accurate record of the past, photography also contributes to a larger sense of historical crisis through its ability to isolate a particular moment from the sequence of time. Barnden offers some compelling analysis of the photographs Martin Laroche took of Kean's production and their indebtedness to painting, as a means to confirm what is already known about the past, even as the production's antiquarian style of Shakespeare looked very modern.

The second half of the book explores how iconic images of Shakespeare have been popularized through photography, so that they have become increasingly dislocated from Shakespearian performance or from Shakespeare's works. John Everett Millais's painting of the drowning *Ophelia* (1851), for example, encouraged the recycling of Ophelia as a visual trope for the mad, tragic, love-sick woman, and Barnden extends this tradition into the twenty-first century with analysis of photographs by Toshiko Okanoue, Tom Hunter and Gregory Crewdon, who variously challenge the objectification of the female body, and 'the aesthetic pleasure derived from Ophelia's distress'. In another chapter, Barnden argues that the image of Hamlet holding Yorick's skull came to supplant the more popular illustration of Hamlet and the Ghost in the early nineteenth century, at around the same time as the invention of photography, because the former was easier to light and fitted the preference for one actor-idol standing alone. This image continues to shape modern performances, which 'stutter to a halt in the graveyard because the image of Hamlet and the skull is subject to a compositional imperative older than the play itself'. Some of the most interesting work in the Yorick chapter explores how the photograph's essential stillness and morbidity, as 'the corpse of an experience' in Eduardo Cadava's phrase, resonates with the much older *memento mori* tradition.

Whilst the book's structure produces a sense of dislocation – one is required to move from the mid-twentieth-century photography of performance back to the invention of photography in the nineteenth century – and there is an inevitable repetition of key ideas and concepts when one reads the book through, rather than dipping into discrete 'case studies', *Still Shakespeare and the Photography of Performance* is written with an intellectual acuity, depth of research and a delight in paradox that makes its ideas at least as arresting as the images it explores.

One of the theories that informs Barnden's work is Marvin Carlson's 'ghosting' – the way in which theatre is haunted by the memory of past performance. This also underpins the more literal hauntings that are explored by the collection of essays *Shakespeare and the Supernatural*, edited by Victoria Bladen and Yan Brailowsky. This book offers a remarkable breadth of work on the supernatural, with topics ranging from demonic puns in the cellarage scene of *Hamlet* to the use of motion capture to represent Ariel on stage, from alchemical allusions in *Tempest* songs to the supernatural reinvention of Ophelia in Japanese popular culture. It is a little disappointing that the Introduction does not do more to explain why the book needed to be written now or to demonstrate how it challenges or re-directs current work in this area. The rationale of the performance-based chapters is explicitly stated – exploring 'the ways in which the discursive field of the supernatural has been appropriated for a range of contemporary agendas and interpretations' – but what we should come away with from the literary critical / historical-facing essays is less clear. That said, the five sections – 'Embodying the Supernatural', 'Haunted Spaces', 'Supernatural Utterance and Haunted Texts', 'Magic, Music and Gender' and 'Contemporary Transformations' – aptly demonstrate and contribute to the scope of the Shakespearian supernatural.

Victoria Bladen's essay, 'Shakespeare's political spectres', for example, deploys some effective close reading to argue that the ghosts in *Hamlet*, *Macbeth*, *Julius Caesar* and *Richard III* are produced by, and symbolize, violent and disrupted successions, externalizing the disjunction between the King's two bodies. By emphasizing the spectatorial as well as the judgemental role of the ghosts, she argues, Shakespeare encourages early modern audiences to take up a similar judging position on their own, specifically monarchical, system. Bladen's thesis pays off particularly in her analysis of *Hamlet*, where the lines 'The body is with the King, but the King is not with / The body' gain new resonance, and Old and Young Hamlet are shown to share a similar political and corporeal insubstantiality. Also striking is Bladen's argument that *Macbeth* includes a spectre that we never see, that the regicide unleashes 'an uncanny presence that seems to join the Macbeths and come between them', and that this is potentially the source for their confusion in 2.2, when Macbeth hears a disembodied voice cry 'Macbeth shall sleep no more', like a revenging ghost.

One of the most immediate questions about the supernatural in performance is how much to realize it – for example, whether or not to embody Macbeth's dagger. Florence March's essay, 'Performing the Shakespearean supernatural at Avignon: a challenge to the festival', which covers fifteen productions from 1947 to 2016, reveals how frequently decisions about the supernatural are revised in the course of a production, often in response to audience feedback. March also offers some valuable broader perspective on the essential relationship between theatre and the supernatural, with the latter 'question[ing] the very notion of performance, sitting on the dividing line between the visible and the invisible, the audible and the inaudible'. Both share a structural reliance on doubling, so that theatre produces meaning through a dialectic between the real and the illusory, whilst the supernatural is defined as a world other to the natural one. Doubling will be a recurrent motif in the Avignon festival, through costume choices and set design, but it is also a theme taken up elsewhere in the collection. Yukari Yoshihara's essay on Ophelia, for example, begins with a discussion of how the supernatural elements of *Hamlet* offered a kind of entry-point for Asian – and specifically Japanese – engagement with Shakespeare at the end of the nineteenth century. Ophelia may not be a supernatural character in the play, but she was doubled with the ghosts of women who drowned for love in Japanese culture, a trope David Kalat identifies as 'dead wet girls'. Yoshihara traces the further influence of Millais's painting, in a fashion that supports and extends Barnden's work discussed above, citing the example of *The Ring 2* (2005), directed by Hideo Nakata, in which the protagonist looks at a reproduction of Millais's painting which has been annotated with the phrase 'Vessels of Death'. If Barnden's photographs criticize the patriarchal and misogynist assumptions behind this comment, Japanese pop culture gets Ophelia out of the river/bath-tub to enact a violent revenge.

That a challenge to, and rewriting of, a 'patriarchal' supernatural could already be seen in the seventeenth-century theatre is one of the intriguing discoveries of Lucy Munro's *Shakespeare in the Theatre: The King's Men*, where she argues that *The Winter's Tale*, and its redistribution of magical power to Paulina, is a reaction against the patriarchal magicians of *The Merry Devil of Edmonton* and *The Tempest*. Munro's book appears under the aegis of Arden's *Shakespeare in the Theatre* series, which has so far focused on modern directors/companies, such as Yukio Ninagawa, Mark Rylance at the

Globe, and Cheek by Jowl. If it has taken some time to go back to the beginning, with the King's Men, it was worth the wait. Munro's meticulous archival research has allowed her to piece together an often conjectural but fascinating account of the King's Men from their inception at the behest of King James I in 1603 to their demise in 1642. One of the stated aims of the *Shakespeare in the Theatre* series is to 'de-centre Shakespeare from within Shakespeare studies, pointing to the range of people, artistic practices and cultural phenomena that combine to make meaning in the theatre'. Munro's book is certainly not the place to come for any tired clichés about Shakespeare writing *Macbeth* for James I. Rather, it focuses on the story of the King's Men as a dynamic repertoire of plays, continually re-imagined by new configurations of player and playhouse. To this extent, it is as much a reception history as it is the biography of a theatre company.

The book is made up of five thematic chapters, interspersed with 'interludes' which focus on the court seasons of the King's Men: 1604–5, 1612–13, 1619–20, 1633–4 and 1636–7. These allow for a chronological backbone which reveals emergent trends – for example, the rise of John Fletcher and the fashion for tragicomedy, and the privileging of a court audience. The thematic chapters focus on the interaction between Shakespeare's and other King's Men plays, both at their inception and subsequently through performance in the same seasons, with shared casts. Among the intriguing thematic relationships that Munro finds in contiguous plays are the staging of racial difference in *Othello* and *The Alchemist*; 'trafficking' of women and actors in *Pericles*, *The Custom of the Country* and *The Princess*; and the use of the Globe as a venue for political drama in the form of *Richard II*, *Henry VIII* and *A Game at Chess*.

The opening chapter, 'The art and faculty of playing: the King's Men and their roles', establishes the premises for these later readings. Munro draws on a variety of evidence about casting to provide information about the composition of the King's Men at various points, and to shed light on the performance styles and specialisms of particular actors. By reading everything potentially played by the actor Thomas Pollard, for example, Munro concludes that he specialized in 'rapid shifts from one emotional state to another and the representation of decayed or debauched glamour'. It is as much Munro's delicious turn of phrase as the detail she excavates from her reading that brings to life these long-forgotten players. Her 'characterization' of actors also has some intriguing possibilities for different refractions of key roles. For example, if it is true that, among the boy players, Richard Sharpe had a speciality in performing vulnerability and mental suffering, whilst John Thompson's women were usually 'charismatic and imperious', then their performance of the roles of the Duchess of Malfi and Julia might have created 'two contrasting versions of femininity'. One of the most compelling discoveries of the book is the creative conflict between pairs of actors, whether that was between an old guard and the up-and-coming young actors, or between rival boy players with different strengths, and, in a rare concession to authorial intention, Munro argues that this was something that playwrights might actively exploit. In her discussion of the repertory relationship between *Othello* and *The Alchemist*, Munro observes that 'Shakespeare and Jonson enjoy the queasy energy that is provoked when the implicit competition between performers is thematized within the structures of tragedy and comedy respectively.' The book's discussion of the subsequent casting of *Othello* is highly suggestive. Joseph Taylor may have 'replaced' Richard Burbage, but he preferred to play Iago rather than Othello. This may have been an effect of the King's Men's access to the indoor Blackfriars theatre. In a role that required blackface, Taylor's features would be harder to see by candlelight (Munro refers here to a recent workshop at the Globe which suggests the indoor lighting did discriminate between the dull blackface and the lustrous white paint of the boy actor). Taylor may have decided that Othello was no longer the role for the leading man and chosen Iago, thereby initiating a critical shift in the power relations between those characters that still pertains in the theatre today. In this respect, Munro

makes good her claim that the role of the King's Men 'in shaping the earliest Shakespearean performance traditions has been underestimated'.

The book's attention to theatrical spaces is also intriguingly revisionist. Munro finds no evidence that outdoor theatres 'went into decline' after the Blackfriars became accessible, based partly on their appeal for audiences and for actors as described in an account of 1615. Moreover, the Globe is revealed to have attained a special function at a time when it might have seemed most superfluous. During the summer months, when the law courts were closed and many affluent spectators had left London, Munro argues that 'the King's Men used political and topical plays as a way of drawing audiences to the Globe'. Whilst the so-called 'Vacation play' is mentioned in the 1630s, Munro shifts this phenomenon earlier in the Globe's history to at least the 1610s, in a chapter that compellingly articulates a line of political (often censured) plays, performed by the King's Men at the Globe. This enables her to adjust some assumptions about the Duke of Buckingham's supposed sponsorship of a performance of *Henry VIII* there in 1628. *Contra* critics who have argued that the Globe was 'an unlikely venue ... for a duke, an earl, and a foreign envoy', Munro's attention to the King's Men's political repertoire from as early as *Richard II* suggests that it was no such thing. Not only the associations of particular roles, then, but the timing of performances in a particular theatre affect the reception and interpretation of King's Men plays. In this respect, Munro's book more than fulfils its ambition to demonstrate how the King's Men 'exercised a generative and transformative influence on Shakespeare's plays'. Early modern theatrical culture also looks different in this light.

The effect of shifting plays between theatrical venues is also of interest to Andrew Bozio, who sees it as contributing to the 'heightened lability in the way that early modern drama imagines the nature of place'. His book *Thinking Through Place on the Early Modern English Stage* proposes an approach he calls 'ecological thinking ... a model of cognition in which an environment – defined as the physical, social and cultural surroundings of an individual creature – functions as both the object and the medium of thought'. Drawing on the work of James J. Gibson, Bozio explores how the 'affordances' of an environment – which include other people, objects and various cultural features – both enable and constrain certain kinds of thinking and behaviour. The early modern period is more sensitive to 'ecological thinking', Bozio argues, because of the redefinitions of place and space that were emerging, in a pre-Cartesian moment defined by 'the impossibility of separating thought from its foundation in embodiment and environment'.

Having established a working definition of 'ecological thinking' and positioned it historically, Bozio identifies three examples of such thinking: the architectural mnemonic – exemplified by a building or a street being used to prompt memories; the art of chorography, which insists on the historical and physical details of place, as opposed to the symbolism of cartography; and early modern drama, which works as a 'cognitive technology, shaping and scaffolding the way that playgoers thought through their surroundings'. The book then offers extended discussions of ecological thinking in Marston's *The Malcontent*, Marlowe's *Dido, Queen of Carthage* and *Tamburlaine*, Shakespeare's *King Lear*, Beaumont's *The Knight of the Burning Pestle* and Jonson's *Bartholomew Fair*. There are perhaps two strands which emerge as particularly persuasive across these plays. The first is what Bozio terms 'the difficult work of getting into place'. After only a few examples, it becomes striking how often characters on the stage ask where they are, or, more tellingly, 'what place is this?', and the frequency with which a loss of place is identified with a threat to identity and/or sanity. This is obviously central to the experience of Gloucester and Lear in *King Lear*, and Bozio offers a gripping account of how sensory perception shapes the experience of place, and the tragic consequences when it starts to falter. Gloucester's line, 'I see it feelingly', encapsulates the range of senses that are required to generate place, and emphasizes the importance of touch. At the same time, Edgar's insistence that his father's sensory experience betrays him – that the land rises sharply and the sea roars beneath it – leads to a disorientation that deepens Gloucester's despair.

For Lear too, an insensitivity to his environment and then an inability to read it are signs of mental disturbance. Bozio (following Flahiff) suggests that editors have unconsciously revealed their own discomfort with the storm's 'ability to dissolve all points of orientation', in the convention of giving the location of the scene as 'A Heath'. This stage direction originates from Nahum Tate's 1681 adaptation of the play, rather than the early texts of *Lear*.

Another illuminating aspect of Bozio's study is the lamination of location through attention to its theatrical venue. In Jonson's *Bartholomew Fair*, for example, the place of the fair is created by the play's fiction, the spatial memories of London spectators, and the physical features of the Hope Theatre. The play begins with the Stage-keeper complaining that what is represented on stage is nothing like Smithfield. Drawing upon an influential essay by Holly Dugan on the smellscape that was common to both Smithfield and the Hope, Bozio explores the extent to which location is here an assemblage of sensations rather than a spatial region. Moreover, the Scrivener's description of Smithfield as dirty, when the ground had recently been paved, encourages an audience to juxtapose their memories of the original market with what it is now, creating a kind of chorographic depth to the dramatic representation. Bozio also writes persuasively of the performativity of place, and how the imagined movements of two characters, Zeal-of-the-Land Busy and Bartholomew Cokes, both constitute and alter the shape of the fair. Edward S. Casey's comment about place, cited here, is particularly resonant: 'Rather than being one definite sort of thing ... a given place takes on the qualities of its occupants, reflecting these qualities in its own constitution and description and expressing them in its occurrence as an event: places not only *are*, they *happen*.' As Bozio's work demonstrates, this is a phenomenon not limited to the dramatic experience but reflective of ways of thinking outside it.

Where Bozio's book arguably falters is in its distribution of alternative theoretical perspectives across the chapters. These are intended to extend and nuance the notion of 'ecological thinking' but work, rather, to dissolve its outlines. One glaring example is the chapter on *The Knight of the Burning Pestle* in which Bozio explains that 'to theorize the way that normative power shapes and suffuses an environment, I turn to disability studies, specifically the claim that disability is less an inherent feature of a particular body than the result of a mismatch between a person and their surroundings'. This is intriguing, but very little of it actually gets into the analysis of the play, and it seems curious to bring disability studies in now when they have played no role in the preceding chapter on *King Lear*. Where Bozio is subtle in his interrogation of terms like 'place' and 'space', he is much less sensitive about the word 'madness', which surely requires more investigation. There are also some broader claims which the analysis of the plays does not seem to fulfil. If 'place itself functions as the expression or materialization of a structure of belief', which beliefs specifically are being challenged in these plays? If 'Halberstam's conception of failure allows us to reconceive disorientation as a generative form of displacement, in which the inability to grasp the normative demands of a particular location challenges both the hegemony of those demands and their apparent naturalness', what, apart from the conventions of theatre, is being revealed here and how is it generative? In some places, the implications of Bozio's theory remain still to be teased out.

Another scholar concerned with early modern conceptions of place is Stephanie Elsky. Her book *Custom, Common Law, and the Constitution of English Renaissance Literature* imagines the communal spaces defined by English common law and the kinds of debate that this 'common' language generates. Elsky's restlessly probing style, in which a statement often turns back on itself, and she frequently pauses to nuance or adjust an assertion, well serves the ambiguities she finds at the heart of her subject.

Central to the meaning of 'custom' is its legal basis in 'common law'. The Introduction offers an accessible and illuminating explanation of the features of the 'common law', which 'governed the ownership, possession, transfer and inheritance of that most important category of property: land'. Unlike civil law, common law had no foundational texts but was pieced together from the learning of the Inns of Courts, from plea rolls, yearbooks and law reports. More profoundly, it was instantiated through 'general custom' or the 'custom of the realm'. Whilst the common law, and its derivative 'custom', thereby had an intriguing relationship to various kinds of textuality, it also presumed a certain relationship to time, being traced back to 1189, 1066 or even further to 'time immemorial'. Elsky writes fascinatingly about the 'common learning' which was practised at the Inns of Courts, a body of knowledge, communicated orally, which was 'indifferent to origins that would divide up the past, or even to distinguishing between moments at all. Instead, common learning suggests a process of accumulation that does not draw attention to the past as past, and in this way imagines it on a continuous plane with the present.'

Elsky follows and extends the work of historians such as Alan Cromartie and Janelle Greenberg to argue for common law's (and, by extension, custom's) political clout in the sixteenth century: 'While common law itself provided no totalizing, definitive statement on monarchical authority, it was put to different political uses by different people, even as its meaning remained complex, multivalent, and contested.' In the chapters that follow, Elsky amply demonstrates this complexity through discussions of Thomas More's *Utopia*, Gabriel Harvey and Edmund Spenser's Letters and Spenser's *A View of the Present State of Ireland*, Sir Philip Sidney's *Old Arcadia*, Isabella Whitney's *A Sweet Nosgay*, and Shakespeare and co.'s *The Book of Sir Thomas More* and *Hamlet*.

To take one of the most obviously political uses of custom, in the chapter on *Sir Thomas More* and *Hamlet*, Elsky explores the external and internal censorship that leads to insurrections being kept off the stage. Whilst modern readers will usually identify rebellion with novelty, Elsky reminds us that this was not how Tudor rebellions usually framed themselves, emphasizing their violence as 'attempts to restore ancient customs rather than institute new, more equitable practices'. In *Sir*

Thomas More, More's arguments to dissuade the rebels from rioting partly succeed by casting their actions as 'innovation' – i.e., against custom. However, Elsky argues that this approach is in turn problematized when the rebel, Lincoln, is given the last word, or rather the last prophecy, allowing him to re-enfold the revolt within custom. As Elsky remarks: 'the very form of the proverb itself was strongly associated with custom because of the two's shared unwritten status, lack of a point of origin, and dependence upon communal consent for their rhetorical value'. In the debate over the relationship between insurrection and custom, a critical distance is created which enables audiences to perceive how the discourse of rebellion is being manipulated by the monarch and his representatives. *Hamlet* is a play acutely concerned with 'custom', at the same time as it deploys a remarkably desacralizing, anti-monarchical language. Elsky notes that the rebels' calls for Laertes to become king are taken as an example of 'Antiquity forgot, custom not known', thereby implicitly condemning the rebellion. At the same time, Elsky notes the ironization of this condemnation, when the chief defender of the monarch's divine right in the play is Claudius, and when it is an infringement against custom – the hugger-mugger burial of Polonius – that has partly prompted the rebellion. In this way, Elsky amply demonstrates the flexibility of custom as a discourse to layer meaning, both to evade censors and to generate multiple points of view.

The overlap between custom and the linguistic commonplace is another strong thread through the chapters of the book. Elsky argues that More's turn to proverbs or commonplaces in *Utopia* is politicized when they are used to counterpoint the debate about enclosures and the shrinking of England's common land. Another attack on private property, this time from the perspective of women's authorship and access to the canon, is discovered in Isabella Whitney's *A Sweet Nosgay*. Here, Elsky argues that the accessibility of legal works on common law, including historical chronicles, enabled even someone outside the privileged world of male authorship to appropriate the idea of

custom for their own purposes. Whitney's commonplace book consists of extracts from Hugh Plat's *Floures of Philosophie* (1572), in which the compiler repeatedly used proprietary images and pronouns to demonstrate his ownership of what was commonplace, entitling his opening poem 'The Description of my Garden'. Elsky demonstrates Whitney's resistance to this language through the repeated phrase 'Plat his plot': 'Whitney's repeated references to his supposed ownership of a common literary inheritance lays bare the wrongheaded nature of this conception of the commonplace, and her subtle mocking of Plat's work as property undermines for the reader any sense that it should be accepted as such.'

Elsky's attention to the language of custom in these literary texts demonstrates its inherent politicization, and illuminates what was at stake for these writers in calling upon its authority. More ambitiously, on a macro level, Elsky argues that this attention to custom has implications for our sense of periodization. Her discussion of common law as encouraging a set of shared, consensual practices extending across 'time immemorial' certainly problematizes any sense that the English Renaissance should be defined through its new 'historical consciousness', as opposed to the 'diachronic innocence' of the medieval period. The book should therefore be of interest to historians of both 'periods', as well as to students of their literature.

Another work that is critically and historically attuned to the limits of monarchical power in early modern England is Peter Lake's *Hamlet's Choice: Religion and Resistance in Shakespeare's Revenge Tragedies*. This offers a remarkably detailed, almost scene-by-scene, reading of *Titus Andronicus* and *Hamlet* in relation to its central concern: the late Elizabethan conflation of private revenge and public resistance or 'justice'. As Lake explains, revenge was a familiar aspect of European politics and statecraft. The threat of assassination against political rulers (successfully realized, in the case of William of Orange and the Duke of Guise) meant that 'at various times, in various places, and on both sides of the confessional divide, contemporaries felt a pressing need to cast or recast allegedly private acts of revenge – undertaken it was said by deranged, malcontent or fanatical individuals or factions – as inherently legitimate acts of resistance, that is to say as "public acts of justice"'. Lake also reminds us that, from 1584, signers of the Bond of Association, passed by the Queen's Privy Council, had 'introduced the notion of revenge into the very centre of the politics of the regime'. Anyone who signed it had ostensibly agreed to seek revenge not only on the Queen's murderer but on anyone who might gain from her death. This was specifically aimed against English Catholics and their figure-head Mary Stuart, and one of the great strengths of Lake's book is the visceral way in which he renders the Catholic struggle against Elizabethan persecution as immediately relevant to his two chosen plays. He brings together some of the finest close reading on *Titus* and *Hamlet*, but views it from a broader perspective. He does not allegorize the plays, but these issues emerge more vibrantly and at a deeper structural level than they have before.

In *Titus Andronicus*, for example, the 'ruinous monastery' in which Aaron is discovered, and his aspersions against Lucius' 'popish tricks' have long suggested that there is something elegiacally Roman Catholic about the pagan Roman setting of the tragedy. To this acknowledgement, Lake brings a host of other details. There is the brilliant observation of John Klause that the martyrological language that describes Lavinia seems to echo Robert Southwell's *An Epistle of Comfort to Those Restrained in Durance for the Catholic Faith* (1587), in terms of branches lopped and conduits spouting. There is also the Clown who attempts to petition Saturninus, but is immediately put to death, recalling the fate of the Catholic petitioner Richard Shelley, who died in prison at the command of Elizabeth I. Earlier in the play, Lake draws a compelling analogy between the Titus who is willing to be loyal to his enemy, Tamora, and the Catholics who were initially loyal to Elizabeth. Just as Titus' sons fall victim to Aaron's Machiavellian scheme, so English Catholics would often

complain that they suffered 'on trumped up charges of disloyalty and treason' to justify their persecution. Ultimately, Lake pulls back from arguing that the play favours the proto-Catholicism of the Andronici and justifies it at the end. Lucius, who restores political order, is named for the mythical King who had brought Christianity to Britain: 'Put succinctly, we are being told that a pious paganism is better than atheism, and that Christianity is better than both.'

Lake's discussion of *Hamlet* sees Shakespeare repeating some of the same formulae, but with a deeper engagement in the controversies attendant on the English Reformation – specifically, the questions of divine providence and predestination. Again, Lake deploys some of the most illuminating criticism of the last few decades, with his argument indebted to Stephen Greenblatt and Margreta de Grazia in particular, but also drawing upon smaller, local readings. Particularly resonant here, for example, is his citation of Alison Chapman's argument that at least some of Ophelia's mad songs – she 'chanted snatches of old lauds' – are suggestive of Catholic praises to God. This speaks to the larger elegiac tone of the play, in which dead fathers are synonymous with a lost religion. More pressingly, Lake argues that Hamlet's infamous delay as a revenger is no such thing when viewed in the context of his spiritual journey, both as a sinner confronting his own sins, and as a divine agent, forcing Claudius and his mother to confront their vices. Lake's reading of Hamlet's response to the murder of Polonius is key here: 'For this same lord / I do repent, but heaven hath pleased it so / To punish me with this, and this with me, / That I must be their scourge and minister' (3.4.170–4). Lake is also fascinating on the differences between Q1 and Q2 *Hamlet* in terms of the character's spiritual condition. In Q1, Claudius's failure at prayer leads him to conclude that 'my words fly up, my sins remain below. / No king on earth is safe if God his foe', which, Lake argues, 'emphasizes the objective distance between God and the reprobate, centring God's enmity towards them on the basis of their sin'. In Q2, however, it is Claudius's thoughts that remain below, 'Words without thoughts never to heaven go', which 'emphasizes his incapacity truly to repent as the distinguishing characteristic, perhaps even the cause, of Claudius' reprobate state'. Hamlet looks more like a member of the elect in Q1, where he commends his soul to heaven, and less so in Q2 when he concludes that 'The rest is silence.'

There are some gaps in Lake's reading, and some details that have escaped inclusion in the final edit. He refers frequently to 'murder pamphlets' as a source for the generic conventions which both plays engage with, but does not name any of these specifically or quote from them, which feels like a missed opportunity. The most pressing question at the end of his discussion of *Hamlet* is whether or not the play is endorsing the view of predestination that it seems to imply. Lake does not rush to judge: '*Hamlet* can certainly be read and experienced not only as an intensely providentialist, but also an intensely predestinarian play. But it is by no means clear that it contains an unproblematically Calvinist account of that doctrine.' He goes on to make the connection with anti-Calvinist, proto-Arminian ideas which Shakespeare might have heard at the time, not least from the lips of Lancelot Andrewes, who was preaching something like this in Holborn, next door to where Shakespeare was living. However, I would have liked Lake's thoughts on John E. Curran's brilliant and disturbing take on the play in *Hamlet, Protestantism and the Mourning of Contingency* (2013), which is omitted here. Nevertheless, Lake writes throughout with admirable clarity. One could not fail to have one's understanding of these plays enriched by his attention to the psychological – and often very physical – suffering attendant on being a Catholic at this time.

Lake's perception of the similarity between *Titus* and *Hamlet* is initially surprising, but, the more one reads, the more one becomes aware that the differences that we have erected between the two plays are partly the effects of chronological prejudice. This is a perception usefully and importantly developed by *Early Shakespeare, 1588–1594*, ed. Rory Loughnane and Andrew J. Power. The follow-up to their collection *Late Shakespeare, 1608–1613* (2012), this book also acts as a companion to the

New Oxford Shakespeare, ed. Gary Taylor, John Jowett, Terri Bourus and Gabriel Egan (2017), consolidating and extending the discoveries of this ground-breaking edition, and packaged in a volume less likely to break your bookshelf.

The reshaping of the canon through various new digital technologies continues here apace. In his essay 'Shakespeare's early verse style', Macdonald P. Jackson reviews reactions to the *New Oxford Shakespeare* and argues that its 'most contentious claim is that the anonymously published domestic tragedy, *Arden of Faversham* (1592), can be added to early Shakespeare's co-authored plays'. Jackson sets about extending the argument of the *NOS* by demonstrating the stylistic overlap between passages in *Arden*, *Venus and Adonis* and *Titus Andronicus*. Something similar happens with *The Taming of the Shrew*. In the *NOS* essay, 'The canon and chronology of Shakespeare's works', Taylor and Loughnane had questioned the authorship of *The Shrew*, arguing that it was extremely likely that it was the work of Shakespeare with one or more authors: 'However, as our own work goes to press there is no peer-reviewed consensus about this re-emergent hypothesis. More research from multiple angles, and more debate, is needed.' *Early Shakespeare* supplies this deficit with an essay by John V. Nance, who argues that Shakespeare did not write Scene 3, and that Marlowe most likely did, thereby extending the inroads that Marlowe continues to make into early 'Shakespeare'.

One of *Early Shakespeare*'s main achievements is to embed *Arden of Faversham* and *Edward III* into the body of works we call 'Shakespeare'. *Arden* is probably the star of the volume. It emerges as the earliest Shakespearian tragedy, which is also a domestic tragedy, and it overlaps intriguingly with *Macbeth*, *The Merry Wives of Windsor* and *Henry VIII*. For Laurie Maguire, *Arden* demonstrates that Shakespeare was engaged with Chaucer – here, specifically, 'The Franklin's tale' – at the beginning as well as the end of his career, but she also confronts head on the problem of writing about a collaborative play. The use of Franklin as a character to explore the limits between narrative and drama offers 'an illuminating view of the thematically integrated way the collaborators worked together in planning this play'. Terri

Bourus writes thrillingly about the practical staging issues that emerge from and shape *Arden*. She demonstrates the respite built into its structure for the actor playing Alice – an unusually large part for a boy actor – and suggests that this might have been an early role for Richard Burbage. This argument constitutes a lengthy rejoinder to Martin Wiggins's suggestion that *Arden of Faversham* might have been written by an amateur playwright. Although contested here, Wiggins's extraordinary work with Catherine Richardson on *British Drama 1533–1642: A Catalogue* is referred to throughout *Early Shakespeare* in a way which finally accords this work its rightful significance.

More generally, it is worth asking how the discoveries and contextualizations of individual essays impact on the larger notion of 'early' Shakespeare. For a start, he looks earlier, with the plays pushing further back into the 1580s. The canon also appears more incomplete – given how many plays from the 1580s have been lost, it is likely that something of Shakespeare's has vanished too. Moreover, the quality of early Shakespeare looks different, as the essays interrogate the usual clichés about early work as 'opportunities not yet seized, craft not yet mastered, the first steps, or something that has not fully come into being ... writing that is undeveloped, undistinguished, and inauthentic'. This is partly replaced by a perception of young Shakespeare as an ambitious writer, willing to try his hand at a variety of genres and producing work that is often sensational and controversial. Against the charge that the early Shakespeare is 'too rhetorical', Goran Stanivukovic argues for the creative energy behind his use of rhetoric; the extent to which he operates within a marketplace of words, competing with his collaborators to produce the ornament and bombast that audiences looked for; and the increasing self-consciousness about rhetoric of the later 'early' plays, such as *Love's Labour's Lost*, which become 'exercises in self-scrutiny'. The addition of new plays into the canon does not necessarily dilute the sense of Shakespeare as an author, but brings into greater clarity features of his early work that we might not have noticed before. In *Arden of Faversham*, *Titus Andronicus* and

Edward III, Shakespeare contributes lengthy speeches for Alice, Tamora and the Countess, suggesting that part of his perceived value as a young playwright was his ability to write women's parts.

The last word in *Early Shakespeare* goes to Gary Taylor, who uses it to urge scholars to rely less on anecdotal evidence – their recall of a particular phrase that recurs between texts as a means of establishing indebtedness and/or chronology – and more on the computational analysis that produces reliable data. This shades into a more politically engaged defence of empiricism:

a conviction that some things actually did happen in the past, and other things did not, and that a properly conducted investigation can often establish that some things probably did happen, and other things are extremely unlikely to have happened ... I suspect that almost every reader of this book is horrified by the rejection of science, fact and truth in the new American fascism.

It is no surprise that a number of Shakespeare critics in 2020 have felt it necessary to use their platform to inveigh against post-truth and the erosion of the humanities in the West.

James Shapiro's *Shakespeare in a Divided America* probes the reasons why England's cultural hero should have retained his hold on the American imagination long after British political control had been cast off. Rather than attempt an expansive, chronological account, Shapiro wisely creates a series of case histories, demonstrating how, at particular historical moments, Americans have turned to Shakespeare to debate issues such as Miscegenation, Assassination, Immigration, Marriage and Same-Sex Love. Each chapter has a Dickensian vitality and eye for detail, with a cast of extraordinary characters whose individual voices come through clearly in the original documents that Shapiro quotes. The images in the book are often remarkable and speak volumes. But whilst there is much that is new and startling in each chapter, perhaps most revelatory is the emergence of Shakespeare as a figure perpetually on the side of the devil in the American imagination.

Othello, unsurprisingly, looms large. In the chapter on Miscegenation, Shapiro explores the conflict experienced by former president and famed abolitionist John Quincy Adams, in the 1830s. A fateful encounter with the actress Fanny Kemble at a dinner party drew from Adams his 'real' feelings about relationships between Black and White, although his disgust at the physical affection between Desdemona and Othello seems to be as much about the threat of the White woman's desires as it is about those of the Black man. Shapiro demonstrates how Shakespeare 'licensed Adams to say what he otherwise was too inhibited or careful to say'.

In the chapter on 'Assassination', Shapiro explores how John Wilkes Booth performed the part of Brutus at the Winter Garden in New York a few months before his assassination of the president, and quoted from *Julius Caesar* in the letter he left behind to justify his actions. His victim, Abraham Lincoln, found no lighter reading in Shakespeare: his favourite speeches were from political leaders tortured by their own guilt, including Claudius and Macbeth. Shapiro notes how the eulogy for murdered Duncan was repeatedly applied to Lincoln after his death, even as Lincoln saw himself more clearly as Macbeth. Whilst this misidentification might have been personally (if posthumously) irksome, it was damaging in a cultural sense, Shapiro argues, because it allowed everyone to ignore the ideological motivation for Lincoln's murder: 'For a divided America, the universal currency of Shakespeare's words offered a collective catharsis … permitting a blood-soaked nation to defer confronting once again what Booth declared had driven him to act: the conviction that America was "formed for the white not for the black man"'.

The consequences of reading Shakespeare in American history seem often to have been either the authorization of abhorrent beliefs or obfuscation. Nevertheless, Shapiro celebrates Shakespeare's value as the canary in the mine, sounding the alarm where divisions in American culture call for action. In the final chapter of his depressing and wonderful book, Shapiro raises his own alarm. He confronts the possibility that Shakespeare's function as a shared language

for America to confront its deepest fears – the articulation of its id – may be coming to an end. He sees the violent reactions and calls for censorship provoked by Oskar Eustis's production of *Julius Caesar* in 2017 at the Delacorte Theater as evidence that a right-wing portion of American society is no longer interested in the multiplicity of perspectives and the value of debate central to Shakespeare's play, and that the ambivalence so essential to Shakespeare might be losing its appeal: 'There has always been a tug of war over Shakespeare in America; what happened at the Delacorte suggests that this rope is now frayed. When one side no longer sees value in staging his plays … things can unravel quickly'.

Jeffrey R. Wilson's study, which also gives a chapter to the Delacorte production, shares Shapiro's dismay at the devaluing of Shakespeare in American culture, with the concomitant damage to political debate and nuanced thinking. However, for Wilson, whose gaze is firmly fixed on recent American politics, the enemy has a name. In the first few pages of *Shakespeare and Trump*, Wilson observes that 'Whining, lying, cheating, and being an asshole are now demonstrable paths to success in America.' But whilst it is as impassioned as this statement suggests, Wilson's book is also intellectually curious, deeply humanist and a blisteringly good read.

William Shakespeare, the provincial sixteenth-century playwright, and Donald Trump, the billionaire Leader of the Free World, may not ostensibly have much to say to each other. Trump's quotation of *Romeo and Juliet* in his book *How to Get Rich* suggests he has never read the play. Shapiro notes, in a devastating sideswipe, that he 'may be the first American president to express no interest in Shakespeare'. Nevertheless, as Wilson notes, a sense that 'something about Trump calls for Shakespeare' has been a consistent part of responses to the US president since his election in 2016. This collision manifests itself in different ways. In Chapter 1, Wilson explores what the Shakespeare adaptations co-written by Steve Bannon, Trump's chief political strategist, reveal about Bannon's, and therefore Trump's, ideology. Chapter 2 looks at explicit references to Shakespeare in responses to the presidential election in 2016. Here, Wilson distinguishes between 'citational opportunism' – a phrase coined by Scott Newstok and Harry Berger, Jr to mean superficial analogies, often a quotation or character taken out of context – and what he calls 'Public Shakespeare', wherein knowledge of Shakespeare's writing, in all its ethical and political complexity, is used to inform an analysis of the present. Chapter 3 examines a moment when Shakespeare and Trump seemed to represent the same anti-inclusive values: when students at the University of Pennsylvania tore down an image of Shakespeare and replaced it with one of the Black, lesbian poet Audre Lorde. Chapter 4 examines the intersection between *Richard III*, the Netflix series *House of Cards* and Trump's first 100 days in office. The final chapter looks at the performance of *Julius Caesar* at Shakespeare in the Park in the summer of 2017, which nightly saw the assassination of Caesar/Trump, and which led to the withdrawal of corporate sponsorship, protesters storming the stage, and even death threats against the director and his family.

Whereas Shapiro analyses figures in history who have cited or fashioned themselves through Shakespeare, Wilson urges Trump's critics to make use of Shakespeare to understand how things have turned out this way and what is likely to happen next. Throughout the book, Wilson argues that Shakespeare's comic villains, particularly Richard III, can offer insights into the psychology of the president and explain his rise to power. Here, Wilson acknowledges the prescience of another 'Public Shakespearean', Stephen Greenblatt, who developed this analogy in a piece for the *New York Times*, published a month before the election. Greenblatt implied that Richard III and Trump were '"haunted by self-loathing", finding "refuge in a feeling of entitlement, blustering overconfidence, misogyny and a merciless penchant for bullying" with a "weird, obsessive determination to reach a goal that look[s] impossibly far off, a position for which he ha[s] no reasonable expectation, no proper qualification and absolutely no aptitude"'. To explain how such a person might achieve their goal, Wilson turns to the Vice figure in early modern drama, whose amoral approach to

life, including a penchant for outrageous lies, offers a kind of thrilling escapism for his audience. One is left with the uncanny sense that, if Shakespeare did not predict a specific American president, he did understand how people might vote such a person into office.

How this Vice/president might remain in office is also explained by Wilson through a brilliant analysis of the different kinds of complicity evident in both *Richard III* and *House of Cards*. Wilson divides complicity into three categories. There is 'the *conscienceless complicity* of the henchmen and -women without scruples who help a diabolical villain execute his plots; *conscientious complicity*, where people want to resist villainy but are afraid to speak out; and *unconscious complicity*, in which audiences are hypnotized into support for a villain whose comic vitality eclipses his obvious immorality'. Key Republican figures emerge from this discussion as poorly as Buckingham and Claire Underwood, but the uneasy sensation that we are all complicit lingers throughout the book.

Finally, Wilson explores the violent fantasies that such a villain/tyrant might produce, through Eustis's production of *Julius Caesar*. Gregg Henry played 'an orangish, vulgar, blustery, coarse-voiced, pussy-grabbing Julius Caesar with a blond coif, expensive suits, unbuttoned overcoat and too-long red tie'. Through an extended interview with Eustis, Wilson explores the perceived affinity between these characters; the Delacorte Theater's intentions in pushing the analogy; and the larger questions that the production inspired. For example, if other presidents had been assassinated in the guise of Julius Caesar on stage (e.g. Obama and Clinton) without much objection, why was this assassination so troubling? And if it was because Trump appears more tyrannical than his predecessors, wherein does his tyranny lie? When does theatrical performance become an incitement to violence, and what place should art have in the republic? Where Shapiro focuses on the dialectical nature of the play, Wilson is more concerned with its tragic affect. For him, this production was an example of tragedy working as it was supposed to: '[it] acknowledged the fantasies of radical political violence that many on the Left had been harboring, but it also refused to let them fester in silence behind closed doors . . . The Public Theater's *Julius Caesar* led audiences and commentators not to imitate the harmful act it represented, but to purge themselves of passions that are harmful to society.' Wilson's deeply thoughtful analysis of what went wrong in the responses to this piece of art, informed by discussions of Plato and Aristotle, is humanist in the best sense of that word, and takes the book beyond a political polemic into something more broadly philosophical. But there is no denying that *Shakespeare and Trump* is driven by an earnest desire to understand what happened in the 2016 election, and by a profound belief in the usefulness of Shakespeare to answer this question. One persistent argument is that Shakespearian tragedy can tell us how this will all end, and even that 'The echo of Shakespearean tragedy in Trump forces us to take seriously the possibility that this is the beginning of the end of America.' In the wake of Joe Biden's victory, Wilson's readers may not wish to follow him to this bleak conclusion. But there is abundant stimulus here for anyone, whatever their politics, to consider the value and the responsibility of the humanities at a time when they are losing influence across the Western world.

WORKS REVIEWED

Aebischer, Pascale, *Shakespeare, Spectatorship and the Technologies of Performance* (Cambridge, 2020)

Barnden, Sally, *Still Shakespeare and the Photography of Performance* (Cambridge, 2019)

Bladen, Victoria, and Yan Brailowsky, eds., *Shakespeare and the Supernatural* (Manchester, 2020)

Bozio, Andrew, *Thinking Through Place on the Early Modern English Stage* (Oxford, 2020)

Elsky, Stephanie, *Custom, Common Law, and the Constitution of English Renaissance Literature* (Oxford, 2020)

Lake, Peter, *Hamlet's Choice: Religion and Resistance in Shakespeare's Revenge Tragedies* (New Haven, 2020)

Loughnane, Rory, and Andrew J. Power, eds., *Early Shakespeare, 1588–1594* (Cambridge, 2020)

Munro, Lucy, *Shakespeare in the Theatre: The King's Men* (London, 2020)

Shapiro, James S., *Shakespeare in a Divided America* (London, 2020)

Wilson, Jeffrey R., *Shakespeare and Trump* (Philadelphia, 2020)

2. EDITIONS AND TEXTUAL STUDIES
reviewed by EMMA DEPLEDGE[1]

The years 2019–20 saw the publication of editions and monographs that offer new insight into the afterlives of Shakespeare's plays and poems, and their reception and circulation, especially in continental Europe. The final edition in the Arden Third Series was released, as was an Arden Early Modern German Shakespeare edition containing two re-translations of early modern German versions into English, as well as an updated New Cambridge *King Lear* and an edition of the *First Quarto of The Merry Wives of Windsor*. It was also a very exciting year for textual studies, with a new generation of scholars returning to the work of New Bibliographers with renewed energy and new methodologies, and an open-access database reshaping our knowledge of and access to extant copies of the Shakespeare folios and pre-1700 quartos.

EDITIONS

The third series of the Arden Shakespeare is now complete, as demonstrated by the full shelves of paperback copies bringing colour to Zoom backgrounds the world over in 2020. A variant noted by those opting to buy the complete set was that some copies of the *Sonnets* lacked the characteristic black stripe found on the upper spine of all other editions within the series. Corrected copies, complete with spine stripes, were then sent out, with Arden putting the variant down to a 'warehouse glitch'. Whatever the reason for the variant covers, they were a welcome reminder of the early print history of the *Sonnets* which, as Erin A. McCarthy's new study (discussed below) demonstrates, sometimes were and sometimes were not presented in a material form that resembled editions of the individual plays and narrative poems already on the market.

The final entry in the third series of the Arden Shakespeare was *Measure for Measure*, with A. R. Braunmiller editing the text, Robert N. Watson contributing the Introduction and index,

and Richard Proudfoot providing 'extensive assistance' (xviii). The Introduction returns to the issue of the play's genre, its status as a 'problem' play, and its position in the likely chronology of Shakespeare's oeuvre. The question of collaborative authorship is handled both in the Introduction and in Appendix I. The Introduction states that 'the 1623 text of *Measure for Measure* may well include changes made by Thomas Middleton, probably late in 1621' (117), before specifying why the editors believe there is good reason to attribute 1.2.1–18, in particular, to him. Sections of the Introduction are also dedicated to the play's sources, to individual characters and to topics such as 'Morality', 'Sexuality, law and marriage' and 'Catholicism, Protestantism and Puritanism'. A particularly strong section is dedicated to the play's handling of 'substitution', of its 'insistent indifference about the unique personhood of bodies in either sex or death' (16), in which Watson combines close textual analysis with performance analysis and discussion of the practice of doubling in productions from 1992 to 2019.

The framing of certain topics in the Introduction is, however, disquieting. For example, Watson is keen to present *Measure for Measure* as a play that portrays 'many levels of consent [each occurring] in a different matrix of forces' (30), but some of the examples of 'consent' he provides would more accurately (not to mention responsibly) be defined as rape and sexual violation. He writes of 'women who consent to sexual intercourse . . . under legal extortion . . . or who are at least under pressure to consent, whether under the influence of alcohol (Elbow's wife) or under a more benign form of obligation' (30). In fact, so many different things are discussed under the heading 'consent', from 'a couple's wholly voluntary consent' to 'consent to the body's death' (30), that the word is in danger of

[1] I wish to thank Honor Jackson for precious help and assistance with this review.

losing all meaning and of obscuring the play's treatment of sexual coercion.

Later in the same section, Watson laments that 'commentary on consent in *Measure for Measure* has mostly focused on Isabella's reluctance to consent to sexuality' – I assume he means Isabella's wish to remain celibate as one might consent to sex, but it is problematic to suggest that one *consents to sexuality*. Watson adds that 'such an emphasis is intensified by a feminist era in the academy, and an era also when many institutions are struggling with definitions of women's consent during sexual harassment or sexual assault by more socially or physically powerful men' (30). He fears that the emphasis on Isabella has caused critics to overlook 'the way the play encourages its audiences to consider men's consent as well' (30), but scholars such as Pascale Aebischer – whose 2008 *Shakespeare Bulletin* article, 'Silence, rape and politics in *Measure for Measure*: close readings in theatre history' is not cited in the edition – have in fact offered sensitive analysis of the play's treatment of both male (in the bed-trick) and female rape.

The text, which is based on F1, as one would expect – F1 being the earliest surviving textual witness for *Measure for Measure* – is conservative but clear and contains a wealth of explanatory notes. Braunmiller records readings from William Davenant's adaptation of *Measure for Measure* and *Much Ado* into *The Law Against Lovers* (first published in Davenant's *Works* of 1673), which is only briefly touched on in the Introduction, as well as significant textual variants introduced in later reprints of the Folio and in editions beginning with Nicholas Rowe's *Works* (1709), but amends little, even retaining F1's arrangement of Claudio's (verse) lines to Escalus as prose (4.4.13–15). The collation line of the text pages is slim, with most textual notes handled in the appendices, as is often the case with Arden editions.

The 'Note on the text', presented in Appendix I (and attributed to Richard Proudfoot), carefully explains the different theories regarding Folio compositors, including reference to Pervez Rizivi's 2016 challenge to Charlton Hinman's *The Printing and Proof-Reading of the First Folio of*

Shakespeare (1963). Proudfoot offers detailed discussion of the ways in which the printers' casting off of copy may have impacted the text, with careful consideration given to moments in the text where contractions appear to have been used to counter a lack of space, or else where short verse lines have been split in order to fill empty spaces when typesetting. There are also helpful sections on the role, idiosyncratic practices and influence of Ralph Crane, the professional scrivener behind the manuscript from which *Measure for Measure* was set, and on the impact that the 1606 Act to Restrain Abuses of Players may have had on the text of the play.

This edition does not, however, follow John Jowett's decision (here described as 'bold': 373), in the Oxford Middleton, to restore references that would have been deemed too profane for safe inclusion in the wake of the Act. It is therefore curious to read in the Introduction the opinion that 'several times the word "heaven" fits neither the metre nor the sense as well as "God," which was therefore probably the original word' (121), or that 'Angelo's "Heaven in my mouth"' (2.4.4) – the reading offered in the text of this edition – 'seems more like an advertisement for candy than a lament for failed transubstantiation or insincere prayer' (121). The present text's choice of 'coin heaven's image' is also dismissed in the Introduction as 'a similarly nonsensical substitution' without further discussion of the reasons why it has been retained (121). In sum, this edition of a text with debated authorship is in itself a mixed bag. It offers lucid accounts of the play's textual and performance history and provides a clear and reader-friendly text, but it is debatable whether the different editors shared the conservative principles applied to the text of *Measure for Measure*. Regretfully, the Arden third series is thus rounded off with more of a fizzle than a bang.

The Arden series was supplemented this year by English translations of early German versions of *Hamlet* and *Romeo and Juliet*: *Der Bestrafte Brudermord / Fratricide Punished* and *Romio und Julieta* respectively, edited by Lukas Erne and Kareen Seidler. The two-play volume, which will be followed next year by a second volume containing translated editions of *Tito Andronico* (*Titus Andronicus*) and *Kunst über alle Künste, ein bös Weib gut zu machen* (*The Taming of the Shrew*), makes the plays available in annotated English translations for the first time. The plays – which fall somewhere between adaptations and translations, but which (as Erne and Seidler argue persuasively) remain sufficiently close to their source texts for them to be considered versions of Shakespeare's plays – are thought to be the products of collaboration and exchange between itinerant English players performing in central Europe (from the 1580s), the local actors with whom they performed, and the performance practices of later German acting troupes.

The plays may be considered witnesses to early performances of *Hamlet* and *Romeo and Juliet*, as they represent versions of the plays taken to continental Europe in the late sixteenth and early seventeenth centuries which were adapted and translated to cater for German-speaking audiences. Unfortunately, the surviving textual witnesses for these plays do not date from the Renaissance period. However, as the editors demonstrate in their Introduction, it is nonetheless possible to distinguish between the plays in their current state, and the versions (probably) performed by the English itinerant players at the start of the seventeenth century. No manuscript has survived for *Brudermord*. The earliest extant text is that published in Heinrich August Ottocar Reichard's 1781 journal *Otta Potrida*, which is based on a lost manuscript from 1710. Erne and Seidler offer detailed analysis of how and why the text may have been adapted in the 1660s. For example, we are informed that the added prologue and the character of Prinzipal Carl likely date from Carl Andreas Paulsen's company and their late seventeenth-century productions of the play, whereas other passages, such as those unique to Q1 *Hamlet*, reflect *Brudermord*'s earliest state. *Romio und Julieta* survives in the form of an extant manuscript, held at the Austrian National Library in Vienna, that originates from the court theatre of Česky Krumlov in *c.* 1688, where the play was performed by a company

known as Eggenberg's Comedians. Again, the editors' analysis and detailed knowledge of continental European theatre traditions and history leaves readers of the Introduction with a clear idea of the additions made for later productions and the version of the play performed in Germany at the start of the seventeenth century.

The German Shakespeare plays have been known to the scholarly community for some time – *Der Bestrafte Brudermord* in particular – but until now they have remained largely inaccessible to Anglophone readers. These are not bilingual editions with the English and German on facing pages, but instead fully edited and annotated English translations of the plays. The commentary alerts readers to echoes and departures from Shakespeare's early texts, and a series of appendices then alert us to more detailed, localized correspondences between the German plays and Q1, Q2 and F1 *Hamlet* and *Romeo and Juliet*. Appendix 1, on *Brudermord* and *Hamlet*, details 'thirty-three instances that are found in *BB* and Q2/F, but not in Q1'; 'three instances that are found in *BB* and Q2, but not in Q1 or F'; and 'seventeen instances that are only found in Q1 and *BB*, but not in Q2/F'. Appendix 2, on *Romio und Julieta*, presents 'thirty-five instances that are found in *RUJ* and Q2, but not in Q1'; and 'six instances that are found in Q1 and *RUJ*, but not in Q2'. In the case of *Brudermord*, we are told that the Folio text of *Hamlet* rarely features in the collation because 'the differences between Q2 and F have little bearing on *Brudermord*' (52); regarding *Romio und Julieta*, similarities with the Folio are said to be restricted to coincidental agreements between stage directions or the omission of the prologue. The editors are thus able to draw important conclusions about the relationship between the German plays and the early quartos of *Hamlet* and *Romeo and Juliet*: 'it is clear that *Brudermord* was not Shakespeare's source'; this is not a German translation of the infamous Ur-*Hamlet*; and the presence of Q1-only and Q2-only passages in *Brudermord* likely points to an 'early acting version' (59–60). *Romio und Julieta*, the editors demonstrate, is based on

Q2, with very close correlation in a number of passages. Thus, the edition makes early foreign-language versions of Shakespeare's plays available to a wider readership, whilst making important contributions to ongoing debates about the status of the early texts of *Romeo and Juliet* and *Hamlet*.

The two plays make for fascinating and entertaining reading, and they merit consideration in their own right, but they will also be valuable to anyone with an interest in *Hamlet* and *Romeo and Juliet*, the reception and alteration of Shakespeare's plays and characters, and the relationship between English and continental European theatre traditions more generally. The text of *Hamlet* is much streamlined in *Brudermord*: the soliloquies and philosophy replaced by new scenes of action, farce and slapstick comedy. Ophelia, no longer grieving for her father and Hamlet's absence, is instead sexually aroused and hot in pursuit of Phantasmo (loosely based on Osric who, incidentally, is in on the fencing plot against Hamlet); the Queen's monologue on Ophelia's death, with its deferral of homicidal agency onto branches and Ophelia's clothes, is likewise rendered less tragic through replacement with a straightforward statement that Ophelia 'has taken her life' by throwing herself off a 'high mountain' (5.6.4–5). As the editors state, this is *Hamlet* 'with the foot on the accelerator'; it is short (*c.* 1,200 lines) and fast-paced and, as such, it is not hard to see how it would have facilitated both comprehension for a non-Anglophone audience and performance by a small troupe of actors (18).

A key example of *Brudermord*'s use of physical theatre to traverse language barriers is the replacement of letters (or Q1's scene between the Queen and Horatio) with a new scene in which Hamlet tricks his would-be-assassins – Rosencrantz and Guildenstern have been replaced by two characters referred to variously as 'bandits' and 'servants' – into shooting each other. Audiences/readers are thus prepared for the later reported action (as in Q2 and F, Hamlet tells Horatio about his journey to England) by a very physical display of how Hamlet cheated death not through the intervention of pirates, but instead by begging the opportunity to deliver a final prayer, spreading 'out his hands', yelling 'shoot', and then falling 'forward between the two' bandits so that they accidentally 'shoot each other' (4.1.53). *Brudermord*, as this example suggests, is in places farcical and very amusing, but it should not, the editors insist, be taken as a mere parody of *Hamlet*. To see either German play as such would be to accord Shakespeare's texts a measure of importance and fame that they had yet to acquire. Shakespeare's *Hamlet* was the source of *Brudermord* (and not vice versa, as was once suspected) and this German version helped *Hamlet* to achieve popularity in continental Europe.

Romio and Julieta, presented here in a new edition after a hiatus of over 150 years, largely follows Shakespeare's texts, but reorders scenes and takes 'longer to reach the topic of Juliet's marriage', before moving 'swiftly towards the final catastrophe' (67). Major changes to the characters of *Romeo and Juliet* include the augmentation of Paris's role and the addition of a new character known as Pickleherring, a stock comic figure in the German stage tradition, who helps to add to the humour of the piece (like the changed role of Phantasmo/Osric in *Brudermord*), whilst also delivering asides and bawdy commentary, particularly at moments of heightened tension or pathos. Examples include his allusion to Romeo kissing Rosalina 'where her spine ends' (1.4.51) and Tipald(Tybalt)'s death, which is swiftly followed by Pickleherring's description of the dead body as a drunkard that lies 'bleeding like a pig' (4.2.85–6). I can see how this new character would have added to the play's appeal, with his direct addresses creating 'a special relationship with the spectators' (75), but I am less convinced by the editors' argument that 'Pickleherring's foolery . . . results in a *complex* blend of the serious and the comic in which neither cancels the other out' (emphasis mine: 77–8). To my mind, his lines do tend to undermine the serious scenes in which he appears.

The strength of the Introduction, which treats the two plays individually, is its illuminating examples of ways in which the action found in the German texts can help modern scholars to solve ambiguities in the Shakespearian texts, particularly at the level of implied stage directions (for example, Romeo and Juliet's kisses on first meeting). The German play again shows a concern for performance in that Julieta's (supposed) death remains off stage, with the Nurse and Pickleherring withdrawing to observe her before voicing their sorrow on stage. As Erne and Seidler note, this eliminates a problem that has often troubled modern directors in that it removes the need to conceal or remove Juliet's (supposedly dead) body at the end of the scene. Scholars of early modern drama will further appreciate Erne and Seidler's discussion of the presence and reception of other early modern English plays in continental Europe, with Shakespeare's *The Merchant of Venice*, *A Midsummer Night's Dream*, *King Lear*, *Julius Caesar*, *Othello*, *The Comedy of Errors* and *Richard III* joined by Christopher Marlowe's *Dr Faustus*, Thomas Dekker's *Old Fortunatus*, Thomas Kyd's *The Spanish Tragedy*, James Shirley's *The Maid's Revenge,* and others.

The translated texts are easy to read, they flow naturally without forcing the texts to sound more like Shakespeare's texts than they really do, and Erne, Seidler and Anthony Mortimer – who is credited with assisting them – are in particular to be congratulated for the skilful rendering of German verse passages into English. (Those keen to consult an edited version of the German originals can do so via an open-access platform hosted by the University of Geneva.) The decision to translate the plays into modern British English – as opposed to early modern – was wise as the alternative would have risked readings of the texts as pastiches of Shakespeare, or of Shakespearian English more generally. The translation into an English that is neither archaic, nor 'aggressively modern', instead supports the editors' appeal for readers to put in the effort of 'historical imagination' and accept that these plays were not conceived as parodies of their Shakespeare source texts (52, 114). In sum, the printed volume is an Arden edition through and through and the plays' presentation in the Arden house style provides *Brudermord* and *Romio und Julieta* with a platform for further serious scholarly enquiry, whilst the quality of the

translations and the appeal of the playtexts promise to establish them as firm favourites in the extended Shakespeare canon.

The updated New Cambridge critical edition of *The Tragedy of King Lear* likewise provides sensitive analysis of the afterlife of the play in a brand-new Introduction, written by Lois Potter. Potter provides a plot summary, entitled 'experiencing the play', and sections on conventional topics, such as contexts, sources and the play's genre, as well as more novel approaches to the play, like *Lear's* relationship to ecocriticism, changing audience expectations for – and actors' handling of – the main characters, the politics of casting, and '*Lear* in Europe before 1900'. In the latter, Potter analyses the 1778 adaptation by the German actor Friedrich Schröder, and Jean-François Ducis's influential *Léar*, famous for being the first Shakespeare play acted at the Comédie-Française (19). Potter also discusses responses to performances by Ira Aldridge when he played 'Lear in whiteface on the European continent and in provincial English theatres between 1858 and his death in 1867' (19); the performances delivered by female Lears, from Marianne Hoppe in Frankfurt (1990) to Glenda Jackson in New York (2019); and more recent adaptations of *Lear*, from Gordon Bottomley's *King Lear's Wife* and Edward Bond's *Lear*, of 1920 and 1970 respectively, to Edward St Aubyn's *Dunbar* (2017), written for the Hogarth Press's Shakespeare retellings series, and Preti Taneja's magisterial 2017 novel *We That Are Young*. The section on 'Global *Lears*' is mostly dedicated to Asian and Russian productions. *The Shadow King*, 'a free adaptation performed by a company of black Australians in a mixture of English and Kriol', is also mentioned (44), but Potter does not provide sustained engagement with many of the listed productions. There is, nonetheless, plenty in this Introduction to inspire new work on *Lear*, and it is understandable that the payoff for the rich range of topics covered is that the subsections tend to be short, with some subjects given only light coverage.

J. L. Halio's Folio-based text, along with his notes, and his masterful textual introduction –

essential reading for students of textual scholarship – have been retained, though the latter has been slightly abbreviated, and it is now prefaced by a short piece by Brian Gibbons that clearly aims to make the edition accessible to a much wider audience. Gibbons offers a brief account of the journey of an early modern play from foul papers, through casting off, to typesetting, and he does a good job of simplifying matters for non-experts. An illustration to demonstrate his discussion of printing in formes would have been helpful, and the piece contains some unacknowledged generalizations, but that is only to be expected with simplification. In sum, it remains a very accomplished edition, with Quarto-only passages printed in an appendix, and a number of passages from the Quarto and Folio texts offered for comparison on facing pages after the Introduction. Potter's Introduction brings the edition and the play into the twenty-first century, and Gibbons's preface to Halio's 'Textual analysis' helps to translate an edition ideal for graduate students and scholars of the play into an edition that will also appeal to readers approaching textual criticism for the first time.

In the latest addition to the New Cambridge Shakespeare's series of stand-alone editions of the early quarto texts of Shakespeare's plays, David Lindley argues that the first Quarto of *The Merry Wives of Windsor* 'was intended as a reading text, rather than as a theatrical script', and he accordingly provides a text that is 'as "readable" as possible' (29). For Lindley, the Quarto, which differs radically from the Folio version of the play, 'undoubtedly derives from theatrical performance', but does not reflect an abbreviated version prepared by Shakespeare's company; instead, he argues for a case of 'disruptive textual transmission', borrowing Jowett's helpful phrase, and believes that note-takers (perhaps with the help of 'an editor or actors' memories') likely provided the manuscript printed in 1602 by Thomas Creede for the bookseller Arthur Johnson. The Introduction to the edition makes reference to two recent performances of the Quarto: an impromptu reading at the University of Leeds, and a 2018 stage production by Ohio State University's Lord Denny's Players, directed by

Sarah Neville, the editor of the Folio text of *Merry Wives* for the *New Oxford Shakespeare* (2016). Lindley acknowledges that the latter performance in particular convinced him that 'the Q text could indeed function successfully in the theatre' (19). However, he maintains that 'a narrative creakiness' remains and that this 'renders the proposition that the Quarto text we now have is straightforwardly a company playhouse script less certain' (19).

It is true that we cannot offer incontrovertible proof for the issues of the play's dating, for whether the shorter Quarto or the Folio derives from the earliest version of the text, or for the relationship between this play and Shakespeare's other Falstaff plays, and nobody can accuse Lindley of pushing his own agenda at the expense of clear presentation of the facts (and a lack thereof). Concerning the much-debated issue of *Merry Wives*' relationship to the *Henry IV* plays and *Henry V*, Lindley offers the view that '*Merry Wives* is neither sequel nor prequel, and its composition was not predicated on the kinds of narrative consistency and continuity that have come to be our conventional expectations in novelistic or filmic series', adding that, as a comedy, *Merry Wives* 'stands generically apart from the history plays, and though it is entirely plausible to date its origin to roughly the same time, any attempt to place it more precisely in a historical sequence on grounds of narrative consistency is bound to fail' (5). He dates the first composition of the play to *c.* 1600 – thus rejecting the oft-touted theory that the play was written for the Garter Feast of 1597 – and is persuaded that the Folio's version of the last scene 'was probably part of a later revision of the play, possibly prepared for court performance', but adds that 'how thorough a revision that might have been of the play as a whole is a matter for conjecture' (7). It is thus an introduction that provides a helpful overview of the various issues at stake when editing *Merry Wives* without threatening to obfuscate matters with dogmatism.

Lindley is most forthright in his discussion of the play's problematic mixing of prose and verse. The typography often suggests verse where the metre makes it clear that what we actually have is prose – 'there are many lines which are printed with an initial upper-case letter and do not extend to the right-hand margin, but transparently are not verse of any kind' (13) – but there are also pages in which prose is accurately set as prose (Lindley gives Sig. E2v as an example: 14). Rather than see the discrepancies as the result of scribes failing to distinguish prose and verse during dictation, or stationers' attempts to use the appearance of verse to appeal to consumers, Lindley suggests that they may be due to 'decisions made in casting off the copy' (14). His second proposition, which is supported by Creede's use of larger than usual type is that, rather than attempt to save money on paper, as one might expect, Johnson and Creede were trying to make the play – which runs to only 1,624 lines – appear longer so that consumers felt they were getting more for their money. The Quarto's full title, 'A Most pleasant and excellent conceited Comedie, of Syr *Iohn Falstaffe*, and the merrie Wiues of *Windsor*. Entermixed with sundrie variable and pleasing humors, of Syr *Hugh* the Welch Knight, Iustice *Shallow*, and his wise Cousin M. *Slender*. With the swaggering vaine of Auncient *Pistoll*, and Corporall *Nym*', promises more than is actually contained in the playtext, particularly concerning the role of Shallow – a point Lindley himself makes earlier in the Introduction (2) – and this detail further supports his theory that Johnson and Creede were padding the text to make their product appear more substantial.

Although he largely rejects the suggestions of memorial reconstruction involving an actor / the actor playing the Host, Lindley does find that the substantive differences between the Quarto and Folio texts may be explained, at least in part, by the theory that the Quarto was produced by a notetaker within the audience. The shorthand argument, he reflects, 'draws strength from its apparent ability *in principle* to account for the mixed nature of the text' (emphasis mine: 24). The Quarto contains scenes – such as Scene 5 – that 'pose a real challenge to any theory of notetaking' (27) and, Lindley further acknowledges, there are a variety of explanations that one might put

forward for the presence of homophones (e.g. Q's 'Hugh and cry' and F's 'hue and cry', 16.50) and what appears to be evidence of mishearings (e.g. Q's 'bullies taile' and F's 'bully stale', 7.15). He nonetheless sees the shorthand theory as a possible explanation for the abbreviation of Mistress Quickly's speeches and the overall close resemblance between Q Scene 6 and 2.2 of F – especially in the opening exchange between Pistol and Falstaff (24) – and between Q Scene 13 and 4.2 of F.

Spelling has been modernized throughout, as per Cambridge conventions. Lindley is sometimes more and sometimes less interventionalist than Helen Ostovich, whose editions are collated in the present volume. For example, he often refrains from emending possible turned letters where the Quarto text makes sense as is (thus retaining 'yon' rather than opting for 'you', 1.67–9), and he chose not to modernize or impose consistency on Q's efforts to convey Sir Hugh Evans's Welsh and Dr Caius's French accents. He does, though, opt for ''tis' over Q1's 'it tis' and Q2's 'it is' in Sir Hugh's first speech of '[scene 2]', where meaning is in no way impeded by Q1's text and where, as Ostovich rightly argues, we may again have an example of idiolect (this time a stammer) being conveyed. I appreciate Lindley's decision not to overly amend Caius's speeches, though I do find plausible Ostovich's suggestion that 'Bully-moy, mon rapier' might be read as a corruption of 'baille-moi' (from *bailer*, 'to give'), but I would have appreciated further discussion of his choices regarding the French he retains. For example, unlike Ostovich – who amends to 'ma rapière', in line with modern (and early modern) French usage – he retains Q1's 'mon rapier' but does so without explaining why. Is it because he finds the choice of article irrelevant as either ('mon'/'ma') is enough to convey French to an early modern English audience? Or does he see it as an example of Shakespeare / the hypothetical notetakers making a mistake? It is a missed opportunity, given his otherwise compelling analysis of Q1's handling of Caius's speeches.

On the whole, the text is clearly presented and annotated. It has not been collated fully against F –

a wise choice given the large number of substantive differences between the two versions – but Lindley nonetheless offers detailed notes under passages where there is close proximity between the texts; he here records localised variants. He also collates the Folio when it 'casts light on some kind of textual problem or option in Q' (29), and substantial textual criticism is offered in the notes on these occasions. These analyses are one of the real strengths of the edition, especially when discussing choices regarding Caius's English (though, as noted above, I do not always agree), and where Lindley uses etymology and definitions to defend and uphold Q1 readings that previous editors may have rejected. In sum, this is a very competent edition that is to be applauded for its clear presentation of the text and for its lucid explanation of theories about Quarto and Folio variants, and the kinds of cruxes that need to be addressed when staging or editing *The Merry Wives of Windsor*.

TEXTUAL STUDIES

The importance of dialogue analysis for Shakespeare editions and textual studies is demonstrated in Oliver Morgan's *Turn-Taking in Shakespeare*, an intelligent study that encourages us to return to Shakespeare's plays with 'a heightened sensitivity to dramatic dialogue' (259), by which he means an awareness not of oratory and rhetoric so much as of conversations and their typographical layout within the plays. Shakespeare, Morgan argues, scripts more than the words characters speak as he also represents 'an ongoing negotiation between them about whose turn it is to speak' (10). Drawing on, critiquing and adapting linguistic analysis to offer a 'literary critical point of view' (23), Morgan redefines dramatic speeches as 'turn[s] at talk' and encourages us to approach them, not as 'a series of rhetorical set-pieces – lengthy, poetic, persuasive, a treasure-trove for auditioning actors and aspiring anthologists' – but instead as dialogue (3). His aim is to provide us with new terminology with which to discuss how turn-taking operates in Shakespeare's plays and I imagine most readers will indeed feel 'more alert to the interactional shape of

[Shakespeare's] writing and better able to describe it' after reading Morgan's two-part book (259).

Each part of the book is made up of an initial chapter outlining the theoretical framework on which Morgan builds in the three short chapters that follow. The first part, entitled 'Sequence', focuses on groups of characters engaged in dialogue (what he terms 'conversational sequence'); the order in which they speak (the sense in which he uses the word 'sequence'); the ways in which they negotiate turns at speaking; and exactly what is at stake when a character speaks out of turn. Chapter 1 draws on examples as varied as Geoffrey Chaucer's *Canterbury Tales*, Jane Austen's *Pride and Prejudice* and *King Lear*, and the work of conversation analysts Harvey Sacks, Emanuel Schegloff and Gail Jefferson, to introduce what Morgan calls the 'speak-when-you're-spoken-to assumption' (38). If we assume that it is normative for a speaker to speak when spoken to, 'as the default solution to the speaker sequencing problem', then examples where speakers fail to respect this rule in Shakespeare's plays can prove meaningful. Chapter 2 considers 'Figures of dialogue'; Chapter 3, concerned with apostrophizing in history plays and their sources, offers fascinating discussion of Edward Capell's use of dashes and other punctuation marks in his 1768 edition of Shakespeare's plays; and Chapter 4 is dedicated to 'Asides', which he sees as 'speeches which are not, or not quite, turns at talk' (106).

The second part, entitled 'Timing', consists of chapters interested in the ways in which individual speakers know when it is and is not their turn to speak, and in the important role punctuation plays in our understanding of Shakespearian dialogue. Morgan here considers ways in which syntax, punctuation and metre can be used 'to suggest abandoned, interrupted, or overlapping speech' (17), topics which are also central to Claire M. L. Bourne's *Typographies of Performance* (discussed below), and it is a shame that the timing of these two studies did not allow them to engage with each other's work.

Morgan's central thesis is demonstrated through examples such as the Queen's intervention when the King is appealing for Hamlet not to return to Wittenberg. The Queen has not been spoken to, but she nonetheless speaks before Hamlet has had chance to reply and the failure to recognize the rule of speaking-when-spoken-to enables her to 'relieve Hamlet of the obligation to reply to Claudius' whilst also anticipating an impertinent response and preventing either man from losing face: Hamlet gets to answer (and 'obey') his mother and not his 'uncle-father', and the King gets what he requested in that Hamlet agrees to stay in Denmark. Morgan compares the Queen to 'a barman stepping between two drunks in a pub', but I would instead think that this characterizes her as precisely what she is: a mother intervening in a (potentially) confrontational exchange between her son and his stepfather. Morgan also gives examples of what he terms 'blanking', blanking without ignoring, and apostrophe, which is defined as 'a turning away of the voice from one addressee to the other' as ways in which speakers engaged in a conversation can avoid 'lapsing into duologue' (47).

The importance of dialogue analysis for editing and textual criticism is again demonstrated through Morgan's discussion of the 'Abhorred slave' speech in *The Tempest*, a speech once reassigned from Miranda to Prospero in editions of the play, and one that is at times still reassigned in performances of the play (Chapter 2). Morgan explores the ways in which characters of the play interact with each other and, more importantly, with Prospero, reasoning that the decision of Lewis Theobald – the first editor to reassign the speech in 1733 – may spring less from concerns over the propriety of a 15-year-old girl delivering such a speech, and more from the play and its 'patterns of interaction and habits of speech' (73).

In his discussion of the scene in which Cleopatra manages to delay Antony's delivery of the news that he must return to Rome, Morgan defends Cleopatra from an editorial tradition that he feels has been 'unjust' in its handling of her interjections. He claims that 'Cleopatra's ability to hold the floor has more to do with skill than brutality. Rather than ignore the rules of conversation, she exploits

them'; through analysis of metre and syntax, he offers a persuasive case for instead seeing Antony as 'reluctant to go on because he knows how Cleopatra is likely to react', adding that 'it is this reluctance that gives her the opportunity to speak' before providing illuminating discussion of Cleopatra's figures of dialogue (228). He elsewhere argues that 'there are ways of understanding consistency of character that do not rest on unexamined impressions of psychological credibility', but instead on 'figures of dialogue that can be identified in the text with as much confidence as alliteration, chiasmus, or feminine rhyme' (73). One of the most exciting suggestions made by this study is that dialogue analysis has the potential to open up new readings of Shakespeare's female characters as more verbally assertive than is often thought.

Charles Dickens crops up more often than necessary, and some of the chapters take a while to get going, but Morgan's analysis of Shakespeare's plays and characters is a joy to read. He ends his book with a tentative offer to pay 'the same kind of attention to a wider range of material' in order to offer analysis of the 'development of dramatic dialogue across the period and to draw comparisons between the turn-taking styles of different playwrights' (259), and my own reply would be 'yes, please' as a study that does for turn-taking what Bourne's study (discussed below) has done for typography would be a very welcome addition to scholarship. In welcoming such a study, I do not wish to detract from the achievements of *Turn-Taking in Shakespeare*; on the contrary, this is a field-reshaping monograph that promises to encourage new thinking and rich discussions about Shakespeare's handling of dialogue. Morgan's study has much to teach us about the structure and presentation of dramatic dialogue, and I look forward to seeing the impact it has on future editions of Shakespeare's plays.

New attention is given to Shakespeare's *The Comedy of Errors* in Chapter 5 of Alice Leonard's *Error in Shakespeare, Shakespeare in Error*. The book's other chapters focus on error and figurative language, error and the 'mother tongue', and 'Error and the nation', but in the final chapter, Leonard suggests that 'the editorial tradition has played an equal, if not more crucial part than the theatre, the educational institution or the film industry, in determining what Shakespeare means to us today' (8). 'Error and the text' focuses on printing errors concerning the two sets of twins in *The Comedy of Errors*. Leonard analyses both ambiguous speech prefaces and stage directions in the Folio text, as well as early readerly interventions documented in material copies, in order to suggest that what have often been perceived as textual errors in need of correction instead convey 'the easy exchangeability of the twins' whose 'distinguishing features disappear under each further textual error' (180). Indeed, readers, like audience members, are challenged to try to make sense of the ambiguities introduced by both the dramatic plot and the printed text. She concludes that the printed text 'returns the genre to farce in the constant maintenance of the confusion of the twins' (180). Thus, the textual and the dramatic, print and performance, intersect in ways previously overlooked, particularly by editors from Nicholas Rowe onwards, who have tended towards emendation over textual preservation. Audience and readerly confusion, Leonard contends, are something that the play actively encourages. *Error in Shakespeare, Shakespeare in Error* thus makes an important contribution to the field by arguing for the need to push back against an editorial tradition that seeks to canonize Shakespeare through standardization and the eradication of 'errors' that never needed correction.

I turn now to two terrific new texts that focus on the material forms in which Shakespeare's poems and plays – and those of a wealth of other early modern writers – circulated. Building on recent work by Adam G. Hooks (*Selling Shakespeare: Biography, Bibliography, and the Book Trade*) and the chapters collected in *Shakespeare's Stationers* and *Canonising Shakespeare*, Bourne's *Typographies of Performance in Early Modern England* and Erin A. McCarthy's *Doubtful Readers: Print, Poetry, and the Reading Public in Early Modern England* highlight the important role stationers have played in shaping literary history and the posthumous fortunes of specific authors and texts.

Bourne argues that typography, by which she means 'the arrangement and appearance of printed

matter on the page' (as opposed to the more limited definition of typography as type design), was mobilized by stationers 'to make the extra-lexical effects of performance – from the most basic (like textually articulating a change in speaker) to the more complex (like registering on the page the meaningful kinesis of bodies on stage) – intelligible on the page' (2). McCarthy highlights the vital role publishers played 'in translating poems from their original social contexts into the broader print market' (2), arguing that stationers consistently strove 'to identify and accommodate new readers of verse that had previously been restricted to particular social networks' (1). Both monographs thus take a formalist view of literature that takes seriously the 'expressive possibilities' of material books (*Doubtful Readers*, 2) and encourage us to rethink the relationship between the different media – performance, print, manuscript, oral – in which early modern drama and poetry circulated.

Like Bourne, whose monograph includes discussion of playbooks by a wide range of canonical and lesser-known dramatists, from Richard Pynson's collection of Terrance's comedies in 1495–7 through to the early eighteenth century, McCarthy focuses not simply on Shakespeare, but also on a wealth of other early modern poets to 1660, including John Donne and Aemilia Lanyer. Recognizing that 'print did not change poetry in a single way', she offers a series of case studies that focus on the editorial practices, material presentation and structure of poetry collections, whilst providing sensitive readings of the poems they contain to demonstrate how 'material instantiations create meaning' (2).

Bourne's monograph, which is the most richly illustrated academic text I have ever seen, is structured around typical, but often overlooked, elements found in early modern plays. The first chapter deals with dramatic pilcrows – paragraph markers first used in the scribal tradition, as evidenced in medieval manuscripts – and the ways in which they helped to make dialogue legible; the second explores action, which is translated, she argues, through the use of dashes and asterisks in particular. Chapter 3 focuses on the use and demarcation of scene divisions; Chapter 4 concentrates on plot, with woodcuts, engravings and other illustrations seen as 'indicative of a publishing strategy aimed at adapting into print the new kind of suspenseful, plot-driven plays that seventeenth-century commentators regularly identified with Beaumont and Fletcher's dramaturgy' (186), and as ways of conveying 'the ingenuity and effects of their formal structures' in ways that would remain visible on the printed page (228). The final chapter is dedicated to scene changes, the ways in which noting fictional places in playbooks became more prevalent in response to both the renewed interest in neoclassical decorum after 1660 and the introduction of movable scenery on the Restoration stage. A part entitled 'Coda' concludes the study through attention to Edward Capell's use of glyphs in his 1768 edition of Shakespeare. Through analysis of these features, which she claims stationers exploited in order to mediate performance or theatricality, Bourne's monograph offers illuminating ways of rethinking the relationship between print and performance.

Bourne's study also aims to revise histories of printed drama. She does so by surveying the typographical make-up of printed plays over a 200-year period, drawing on approximately 1,900 editions of plays printed in England. In a breath-taking commitment to bibliographical research, she consulted at least one copy of every edition published from the late fifteenth century to the 1660s, and at least one copy of every first edition of plays printed between 1660 and 1709. In doing so, Bourne surpasses D. F. McKenzie's influential study, 'Typography and meaning: the case of William Congreve' (1981), in which he used the example of Congreve's collaboration with the publisher Jacob Tonson (to produce the early eighteenth-century edition of Congreve's *Works*) to make broader points about the book as 'an expressive means', stating that 'the material forms of books, the non-verbal elements of the typographical notations within them, the very disposition of space itself, have an expressive function in conveying meaning' ('Typography and meaning', 82). McKenzie's narrow focus led him to see novelty in how Tonson used typography to offer readers 'a

theatrical experience in book form' ('Typography and meaning', 83). The wider scope of Bourne's study enables her to observe subtle changes in typography over more than 200 years of theatre and print history.

By starting in the late fifteenth century, Bourne is able to demonstrate the 'design acumen' of early playbook printers, such as John Rastell, Wynkyn de Worde, Richard Pynson and others. She offers a corrective to the 'false sense' that Tonson in the early eighteenth century 'inaugurated a set of consistent typographic principles for printed plays that marked a vast improvement in legibility and intelligibility over the relative messiness of earlier editions' (18). Indeed, one of *Typographies of Performance*'s greatest contributions is Bourne's astute analysis of short-lived or isolated experiments with playbook design. As she rightly argues, both temporary and more permanent developments in page design help to 'expose which aspects of modern theatricality were thought to need a way of signifying on the page' (6), and it is only by taking a long view of the so-called 'early modern' period that scholars can hope to draw reliable distinctions between fleeting experiments with *mise-en-page* and layouts that can be considered conventional for playbooks printed at a given moment.

She challenges the assumption that early playbooks, with what may now strike us as unconventional use of typography, disrupt readings that engage simultaneously with text and performance. Instead, Bourne suggests that this typography was specifically designed to allow the early modern reader access to drama's dual media. However, she does not wish to imply that page design recorded real past performances, nor that it necessarily provided 'scores for future performances', but rather that it materializes the promises stationers made – usually on the title pages to playbooks – to give consumers the play as it was performed at a particular venue. In other words, 'the book is a viable version of what audiences might have seen and heard on a London stage' (10). She demonstrates how, by recognizing the ways in which drama was fashioned as a distinct print genre, we can learn to 'cultivate new (old) ways of seeing and understanding these books' textual designs' (3). Put differently, modern readers can potentially learn to respond to typographical features in the way that stationers hoped early moderns would. Her study also promises rich insight into the concerted efforts stationers across the period made to experiment with, and help to bring about, what we now recognize as conventional dramatic *mise-en-page*.

Studies of early modern drama and poetry frequently impose arbitrary cut-off dates, such as 1600, 1640 or 1660, but this is not the case here. Indeed, *Typographies of Performance*, like *Doubtful Readers*, provides a blueprint for the kind of discoveries that await scholars willing to think beyond traditional period boundaries. I was disappointed not to see Bourne interact with Judith Milhous and Robert D. Hume's *The Publication of Plays in London, 1660–1800: Playwrights, Publishers and the Market* (2015), Don-John Dugas's *Marketing the Bard: Shakespeare in Performance and Print, 1660–1740*, and some other key studies on the trade in playbooks during the Restoration and early eighteenth century. However, her handling of the many twists and turns of recent (and historical) scholarly debates about the earlier early modern book trade is impeccable, and I do appreciate that there is a limit to how much scholarship one can hope to cite in any monograph, let alone one that includes analysis of thousands of playbooks.

McCarthy's study is also full of compelling analysis that draws on the methodologies of book history and bibliography. The case study offered in Chapter 2 is of most relevance to this review as she here reads the material features of the 1609 edition of Shakespeare's *Sonnets* and William Jaggard's *The Passionate Pilgrim* (1599) in the context of other English sonnet sequences then in vogue. She urges us to read Jaggard's publication not as a printed miscellany, but instead as a sonnet sequence in its own right. The argument is particularly thought-provoking as she goes on to suggest that the reason why Thomas Thorpe's 1609 collection of Shakespeare's *Sonnets* did not reach a second edition is because it was 'stymied by the success of *The Passionate Pilgrim*' – reprinted in 1599 and

1612 – in which Jaggard had offered a product that seemed both more 'sequence-like' and more Shakespearian than the book of *Shake-speares Sonnets* (58). Modern scholars may protest that *The Passionate Pilgrim* bore Shakespeare's name on the title page but contained only a handful of poems now thought to have been by Shakespeare. No matter, McCarthy insists, as the collection's authorship 'was mostly unquestioned until 1780' and was 'for early modern readers, a real and significant part of Shakespeare's poetic reputation' (60).

Thus, the argument goes, if Shakespeare's *Sonnets* did not sell well enough to justify a second edition, then this is not due to a lack of demand for Shakespeare, nor to a loss of interest in sonnet collections, or even to Jaggard having hampered the market for authentic Shakespeare poems, as some scholars have claimed. Instead, it was the result of Thorpe's failure to match Jaggard's efforts to align his publication bibliographically 'with a genre for which there was continued demand', or with editions of Shakespeare's oeuvre already circulating in the London book trade (57–8). By the time Thorpe's *Shake-speares Sonnets* was released in 1609, McCarthy argues, 'as far as most early modern readers knew, [the book market] already included a book of Shakespeare's sonnets' (58).

McCarthy traces not just the poetic form and content, but also – importantly – the bibliographical history of the English sonnet tradition. She notes that scholars have long recognized the 'powerful authorial paradigm established in the editions of *Astrophel and Stella* authorized by the Countess of Pembroke' and the volume's significance as a 'landmark in poetry's emergence as an English literary genre', but she claims that the effect of *Astrophel and Stella* will have been less apparent to early modern readers (62). They, McCarthy claims, will have been more influenced by the bibliographical precedent established by Samuel Daniel's *Delia*, and further bolstered by Constable's *Diana*. In his *Delia*, which 'featured one poem per page between decorative borders for the first time in printed English collections' (71), Daniel, she claims, introduced 'a set of recognizable typographical conventions for printing English sonnet sequences' (60), and it is these material features that made the *Passionate Pilgrim* legible and appealing in ways that the 1609 *Sonnets* was not (76).

The *Passionate Pilgrim* entered a market in which demand for both Shakespeare and sonnet sequences was high (77). Jaggard marketed his collection as a sonnet sequence by including twelve- or fourteen-line poems 'flanked by ornamental borders', thereby linking their *mise-en-page* to that of Daniel's collection. All but the final three leaves have blank versos and the fact that Jaggard retained this feature, along with the second title page identifying the content as falling within the genre of sonnets, lead McCarthy to claim that 'the book's appearance thus seems to have been an integral part of Jaggard's strategy' (80). It is further argued that Jaggard's choice of format – octavo – and size may have encouraged consumers to purchase it alongside other Shakespeare poetry books, particularly his bestsellers *Venus and Adonis* and *Lucrece*, so that they could be bound as *Sammelbände*. McCarthy convincingly supports this claim by pointing to the fact that three of the five surviving copies of *The Passionate Pilgrim* are bound with 'at least one of Shakespeare's narrative poems' (81). She also suggests that frequent reference in the texts collected in *The Passionate Pilgrim* to Venus and Adonis (the characters), like the inclusion of poems from *Love's Labours Lost*, may have attracted early modern readers looking for more Shakespeare.

McCarthy's talent for bibliographic analysis is on show throughout, but she also provides sumptuous literary analysis, particularly when she explores the impact the ordering of Shakespeare's sonnets in *The Passionate Pilgrim* (it opens with what is now known as 138, followed by 144), and textual variants between the poems' appearance here and in the 1609 collection, have on the way in which we read them. This chapter is so rich that one feels it could have formed the basis of an entire monograph. I regret that Table 2.1, containing 'Sonnet sequences published individually, 1580–1640' – a wonderful resource that will be of great use to anyone studying or teaching English sonnet

sequences – and which surely reflects a sustained period of research, was not utilized more. A breath-taking amount of data has been collected, surveyed and analysed by both Bourne and McCarthy, and readers will be grateful for the lucid ways in which complex material is handled in both studies.

Shortly after reading McCarthy's account of the ways in which Shakespeare's sonnets and other poems appeared in print accompanied by sonnets from within the plays, I received a copy of Stanley Wells and Paul Edmondson's *All the Sonnets of Shakespeare*. Like Jaggard in *The Passionate Pilgrim*, the editors and publishers (Cambridge) have been generous with paper, allowing one page per sonnet, though they have not left versos blank. It is a gorgeous material book, complete with lilac end papers and a gold-ribbon bookmark, that presents all of Shakespeare's sonnets in the (conjectured) chronological order in which they are thought to have appeared. By 'sonnets', the title refers not simply to those of the 1609 volume, but also to the numerous other examples of Shakespeare's use of the sonnet form, be it in the creation of prologues and epilogues, or else as key sequences within the main body of the plays. Each poem is summarized through paraphrase, and essential context is provided by Edmondson and Wells, who situate Shakespeare's use of the genre and his use of paired poems in the context of Sir Philip Sidney and Robert Greene's work and Shakespeare's career as a whole. They also offer a lucid overview of the publication history of Shakespeare's sonnets and the ways in which they were shaped by the work of editors and collectors in manuscript and print, from the early editions of Thorpe and John Benson (1640) through those of Bernard Lintott (1711), George Steevens (1766) and Edmond Malone (1778), many of which were designed as appendages to collected editions of the plays.

The online Shakespeare Census, a magisterial new resource for Shakespeare and textual studies, went from strength to strength in 2019–20. Building on the work of Henrietta C. Bartlett (1873–1963), one of the most tenacious and talented bibliographers in the history of Shakespeare studies, Adam Hooks and Zachary Lesser set themselves the challenge of recording not just the current location of all extant copies of all pre-1700 Shakespeare editions, but also physical descriptions of the size, binding, marks of ownership and provenance, annotations, damage and other distinguishing features found in each material copy. From 1913 to 1916, Bartlett worked alongside A. W. Pollard to co-edit the first *Census of Shakespeare's Plays in Quarto, 1574–1709*, a project commissioned by the Elizabethan Club of Yale. Bartlett, whose extensive correspondence with private collectors, scholars and libraries around the world is now housed at the Beinecke Library, went on to produce an updated and expanded version of the Census on her own in 1939. The new Census, which is open access, may not consider editions published after 1700, but it is nonetheless more comprehensive in scope than the censuses of 1916 and 1939, and the distinctions Hooks and Lesser make between different editions, variant issues, and checked versus potential 'ghost copies' make it a more reliable source for Shakespeare and textual studies than the *English Short Title Catalogue* hosted by the British Library website.

Hooks and Lesser use early modern attributions, as opposed to the attribution practices of modern scholarship, to determine what constitutes a Shakespeare play or poetry book. At the time of going to press, the Census included 1,863 copies of the plays and poems, and the creators were in the process of integrating data on all four folios, having taken over from the Shakespeare Folios Project led by Cyrus Mulready. Poems and plays, quartos and other formats are already included, and the addition of data on the Shakespeare folios will make this the most comprehensive database of Shakespeare books of all time.

Some of the most exciting features of the Census are the clarification it provides concerning ghost copies, which are copies listed in the ESTC's Holdings Details, or in library catalogues, that do not exist; verified links to digital facsimiles of not just the correct edition, state and issue of a given text, but the specific copy described in the Census (this currently applies to 622 of the listed copies); information concerning the other books with which

Shakespeare texts are currently bound; and a search function that includes 'keywords', 'provenance name' and 'specific features', meaning that users can gain valuable insights into the number of Shakespeare books linked to a specific name, 'with a known woman owner', including marginalia, or else bound in an early *Sammelbände*. The resource has yet to be exploited to its full potential and it will be a vital source of evidence for future editors, bibliographers, libraries and general readers. The kinds of new research it will allow for are staggering.

The Census is also a fantastic example of scholarly collaboration, with Hooks and Lesser receiving precious assistance from researchers and library staff the world over. Entries in the Census have been given a unique identifier (SC#) for ease of citation, and these are cross-referenced with the numbers Bartlett used in 1939 and 1916, ESTC numbers and, where relevant, whether they are included in *The Database of Early English Playbooks*, another invaluable resource Lesser co-edited with Alan Farmer. Work on the Census has already led to the discovery of a number of previously unknown copies, including a fifth quarto of *Hamlet* (1637), complete with a 1664 performance record, at Herzog August Library, Wolfenbüttel (see SC#89.3 and Erne's forthcoming *Notes and Queries* article), and a copy of *Pericles* (1611) listing its original owner and price in the Zurich Central Library (see SC#55 and more forthcoming work from Erne). Those wishing to assist in the project can consult a list of copies yet to be verified and the downloadable list of known ghost copies will provide welcome relief to anyone who has ever trogged to a far-flung library only to find that what the library actually contains is not a material copy but merely microfilm or access to Early English Books Online.

It is wonderful to have so many related monographs arrive at once and my only regret is that the timing of Bourne's, Leonard's, McCarthy's and Morgan's studies meant that they were not able to engage with each other's ideas and arguments. Faith Acker's *First Readers of Shakespeare's Sonnets, 1590–1790* and *Bel-vedére or the Garden of the Muses: An Early Modern Printed Commonplace Book*, edited by Lukas Erne and Devani Singh, did not arrive in time for inclusion in this year's review, but I look forward to discussing them next year. Another monograph to look forward to is Zachary Lesser's *Ghosts, Holes, Rips and Scrapes: Shakespeare in 1619, Bibliography in the Longue Durée*, which promises to reshape our thinking about one of the most famous case studies in the history of Shakespeare bibliography: the so-called 'Pavier Quartos' of 1619. The field is not only alive and well but thriving, and I am excited to follow the conversations and debates inspired by the publication of the excellent monographs discussed in this review.

WORKS REVIEWED

Bourne, Claire M. L., *Typographies of Performance in Early Modern England* (Oxford, 2020)

Braunmiller, A. R., and Robert Watson, eds., *Measure for Measure*, The Arden Shakespeare (London, 2020)

Edmondson, Paul, and Stanley Wells, eds., *All the Sonnets of Shakespeare* (Cambridge, 2020)

Erne, Lukas, and Kareen Seidler, eds., *Hamlet and Romeo and Juliet: Der Bestrafte Brudermord and Romio und Julieta in Translation*. Early Modern German Shakespeare 1, The Arden Shakespeare (London, 2020)

Halio, Jay, ed., *The Tragedy of King Lear*, 3rd edn, with new introduction by Lois Potter, New Cambridge Shakespeare (Cambridge, 2020)

Hooks, Adam G., and Zachary Lesser, eds., Shakespeare Census (2018): www.shakespearecensus.org

Leonard, Alice, *Error in Shakespeare, Shakespeare in Error* (London, 2020)

Lindley, David, ed., *The First Quarto of The Merry Wives of Windsor*, The New Cambridge Shakespeare Early Quartos (Cambridge, 2020)

McCarthy, Erin A., *Doubtful Readers: Print, Poetry, and the Reading Public in Early Modern England* (Oxford, 2020)

Morgan, Oliver, *Turn-taking in Shakespeare* (Oxford, 2019)

ABSTRACTS OF ARTICLES
IN *SHAKESPEARE SURVEY 74*

GINA BLOOM, NICHOLAS TOOTHMAN AND EVAN BUSWELL

Playful Pedagogy and Social Justice: Digital Embodiment in the Shakespeare Classroom

Too often in Shakespeare classrooms, physical, game-based learning ('playful pedagogy') overlooks race, gender and other embodied differences. Through a case study of *Play the Knave*, a mixed-reality Shakespeare game created by the authors, this article argues that social justice concerns can be addressed more effectively when playful pedagogy is digitally remediated.

CHRISTIE CARSON

Digital Resources, Teaching Online and Evolving International Pedagogic Practice

This article provides an overview of writing on the topic of Shakespeare pedagogy over two decades, examining the way that a shift towards the study of performance and the use of digital resources has made what was formerly a quite narrowly defined Anglo-American debate into a truly global discussion.

RUI CARVALHO HOMEM

Forging a Republic of Letters: Shakespeare, Politics and a New University in Early Twentieth-Century Portugal

This article addresses the role played by Shakespeare in an intriguing educational endeavour of the early twentieth century. In the framework of Portugal's 'First Republic' and a then-new university, Shakespeare refracted the tensions between royalists and republicans, conservatives and innovators, through a period of intense social and political change.

SHEILA T. CAVANAGH

'In India': Shakespeare and Prison in Kolkata and Mysore

Indian practitioners Alokananda Roy (in Kolkata) and Hulugappa Kattimani (in Mysore) each run significant arts initiatives involving Shakespeare with incarcerated people in their regions. This article discusses their syncretic practices, which incorporate studio arts, martial arts, yoga, music and dance into their public productions of Shakespeare and other writers.

427

ALEXA ALICE JOUBIN AND LISA S. STARKS

Teaching Shakespeare in a Time of Hate

Drawing on Emmanuel Levinas's theory that the human being is constituted in, through, by and for the Other, this article offers innovative approaches to teaching Shakespeare in ethics-first pedagogical theories and praxis. Special attention is given to issues of race and gender, and the exigencies of remote learning in the era of the COVID-19 pandemic.

GENEVIEVE KIRK

'And His Works in a Glass Case': The Bard in the Garden and the Legacy of the Shakespeare Ladies Club

This article considers a contemporary description of a garden temple on the Shaftesbury estate as the first ever dedicated to Shakespeare exclusively. This evidence connected to the eighteenth-century Shakespeare Ladies Club suggests the group's involvement with the Patriot Whig opposition movement and its corresponding role in promoting unaltered Shakespeare in performance.

PAMELA ROYSTON MACFIE

Shakespeare, #MeToo and his New Contemporaries

This article evaluates the first pairings in the American Shakespeare Center's initiative, 'Shakespeare's New Contemporaries', which will debut at their Blackfriars Playhouse thirty-eight new plays (one for each of Shakespeare's). With the Shakespeare plays, they engage in dialogue and, through repertory performance, the 'New Contemporaries' address female victimization and resolve.

HARRY R. MCCARTHY AND PERRY MILLS

Going to School with(out) Shakespeare: Conversations with Edward's Boys

This article presents conversations with members of Edward's Boys, the all-boy theatre troupe based in Stratford-upon-Avon, reflecting on performance-based explorations of early modern drama, the company's educational aims and values, their collaborative rehearsal processes, and the social ties that lie at the core of Edward's Boys' work.

LUISA MOORE

***Hamlet* and John Austen's Devil with a (Dis)pleasing Shape**

John Austen's illustrated edition of *Hamlet* (1922) depicts a dark Prince with a problematic, ambiguous relationship to the Ghost. The imagery interrogates Hamlet's agency, offering conflicting readings which render the interpretation on offer almost unique. Austen shares with his Romantic predecessor Henry Fuseli the decision to reinterpret the Ghost radically.

SHARON O'DAIR AND TIMOTHY FRANCISCO

Whither Goest Thou, Public Shakespearian?

What is Public Shakespeare? What will it become? We describe three placements within the field to generate answers: first, within a fifty-year effort to politicize and democratize our work; second, within debate about methodology, about what counts as intellectual work; and third, within deteriorating economic conditions for higher education.

SARAH OLIVE

Using Performance to Strengthen the Higher Education Sector: Shakespeare in Twenty-First-Century Vietnam
This article uses Ho Chi Minh City Open University's production of *Romeo and Juliet* to explore 'what Shakespeare is' in twenty-first-century Vietnam, from the creative industries to higher education. It suggests that the perceived benefits of university students' performances could ameliorate weaknesses identified in the Vietnamese higher education system.

KEVIN A. QUARMBY

PPE for Shakespeareans: Pandemic, Performance and Education
Shakespeare and performance pedagogy changed with COVID-19's arrival. Live performances ceased, theatres closed and pre-recorded Shakespeare dominated. Actors either accepted dangerous work or experimented unsuccessfully with technology. San Francisco Shakespeare Festival, however, developed 'live' Zoom performances, their safe employment practices offering alternative models for student engagement in the post-pandemic world.

MADHUMITA SAHA

Shakespeare in Nineteenth-Century Bengal: An Imperative of 'New Learning'
This article seeks to interrogate how Shakespeare's position in the curriculum altered the dynamics of nineteenth-century intellectual and political history in Bengal; and how it also stimulated a growing appetite for the ideas of humanism and rationality, which in turn shaped modernity in the rapidly changing milieu of nineteenth-century Bengal.

ESTHER B. SCHUPAK

Teaching Shakespeare with Performance Pedagogy in an Online Environment
This article explores methods of teaching Shakespeare with performance pedagogy, re-imagined for the online environment. Beginning with a brief overview of performance and active learning as they have been developed for physical classrooms, a range of methods is discussed, including actual performance, improvisation, language play and acting preparation work.

JILLIAN SNYDER

Counterpublic Shakespeares in the American Education Marketplace
This article examines how student editions of *Macbeth* from two American religious publishers refract Shakespeare's works through their own confessional prisms. These editions challenge those like the Folger's, and demonstrate how

proliferating counterpublics vie for market shares in a fracturing educational landscape.

EMILY SOON

Cultural Inclusivity and Student Shakespeare Performances in Late-Colonial Singapore, 1950–1959
How did students in colonial schools engage with Shakespeare? How can Shakespeare education facilitate the emergence of a new national culture? This article explores these questions by analysing student performances in 1950s Singapore, then a British colony preparing for self-govern-ance, with a multicultural population drawn from diverse parts of Asia.

RICHARD STACEY

***The True Tragedy* as a Yorkist Play? Problems in Textual Transmission**
This article identifies a Yorkist bias throughout *The True Tragedy*. Although it is tempting to interpret this as evidence that the play is an early draft of *Henry VI Part 3*, such traces are likely to be either remnants of the lost collaborative play behind both texts, or due to imperfect memorial recall by actors.

CERI SULLIVAN

Intimacy and Schadenfreude in Reports of Problems in Early Modern Productions
More often than not, things go wrong in amateur and one-off shows, as the Records of Early English Drama richly demon-strate. Contemporary performance theory about mistakes, ideas about schadenfreude's theatrical modes, and the genre of the theatrical anecdote all suggest how such humilitainment binds actors and audience together.

JEFFREY R. WILSON

Shakespeare for Cops
This article discusses the 'Shakespeare for Cops' programme, arguing that it can help scholars and citizens to understand how crime and justice work in Shakespeare's plays, and lead to better policing.

NIGEL WOOD

Taking *Love's Labour's Lost* Seriously
Love's Labour's Lost has proven a difficult play to interpret as anything other than an escapist comedy, yet its preoccupation with rhetoric and the responsible use of words should be regarded rather more seriously, as an exploration of just what the reign of Mercury might entail after the songs of Apollo.

LAURA JAYNE WRIGHT

***Henry VIII* and Henry IX: Unlived Lives and Re-written Histories**
The future imagined in Shakespeare and Fletcher's *Henry VIII* depends on past memories (a perspective that cognitive theory terms 'FMTT': future-oriented mental time travel). Through

insistent allusions to Virgil, Spenser and Rowley, and funeral elegies for Henry Stuart, *Henry VIII* remains caught in backward-facing repetitions even while offering alt-histories and speculative futures.

JENNIFER YOUNG

'While Memory Holds a Seat in this Distracted Globe': A Look Back at the Arden Shakespeare Third Series (1995–2020)
A review of the Arden Shakespeare Third Series focusing on the series response to significant moments in scholarship including in performance history, revision and multi-text editing, authorship and collaboration. It also examines the impact of the first group of women editors on the series.

INDEX

NOTE: locators in italics denote illustrations.

INDEX

INDEX

INDEX

INDEX

INDEX

INDEX

INDEX